ORACLE8 HOW-TO

THE DEFINITIVE ORACLE8 PROBLEM-SOLVER

Edward Honour, Paul Dalberth, Ari Kaplan, Atul Mehta

D1294836

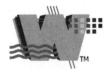

Waite Group Press™
A Division of
Macmillan Computer Publishing
Corte Madera, CA

PUBLISHER: Mitchell Waite
ASSOCIATE PUBLISHER: Charles Drucker
EXECUTIVE EDITOR: Susan Walton
ACQUISITIONS EDITOR: Stephanie Wall
PROJECT DEVELOPMENT EDITOR: Andrea Rosenberg
CONTENT EDITOR: Russ Jacobs
TECHNICAL EDITORS: Amy Sticksel, Robert Muller
PROJECT EDITOR: Maureen A. McDaniel
COPY EDITORS: Michael Brumitt, San Dee Phillips
MANAGING EDITOR: Jodi Jensen
INDEXING MANAGER: Johnna L. VanHoose
EDITORIAL ASSISTANTS: Carmela Carvajal, Carol Ackerman, Rhonda Tinch-Mize, Karen Williams
SOFTWARE SPECIALIST: Dan Scherf
DIRECTOR OF MARKETING: Kelli S. Spencer
BRAND DIRECTOR: Greg Wiegand
BRAND ASSOCIATE: Kim Spilker
MARKETING COORDINATOR: Linda B. Beckwith
PRODUCTION MANAGER: Cecile Kaufman
PRODUCTION TEAM SUPERVISOR: Brad Chinn
COVER DESIGNER: Karen Johnston
BOOK DESIGNER: Kathy Matanich
PRODUCTION: Mike Henry, Linda Knose, Tim Osborn, Staci Somers, Mark Walchle

Printed in the United States of America
98 99 • 10 9 8 7 6 5 4 3 2 1

Library of Congress Cataloging-in-Publication Data Number: 97-40533
International Standard Book Number: 1-57169-123-5

DEDICATION

To my wife, Barbara, and my parents, Salvatore and Joan.
– Paul Dalberth

To Raoul Wallenberg wherever you are, and to my family.
– Ari Kaplan

To my loving parents and the Supreme Lord.
– Atul Mehta

Edward Honour has worked with Oracle products since 1989 and has participated in the design and development of several large-scale client/server applications for a variety of industries. Edward is the author of *Oracle How-To*, the previous edition of this book.

Paul Dalberth specializes in the discriminating application of technology to problems confronting a variety of industries particularly those in the pharmaceutical and financial sectors. His ten years of information technology experience include database administration, database design, and applications development. He currently serves as Associate Director of Database Administration and Clinical Data Management at Family Health International in Research Triangle Park, North Carolina. He can be reached via email at **pdalberth@fhi.org**.

Ari Kaplan is an independent computer consultant specializing in Oracle product design, development and management. He currently serves as the lead Oracle database consultant for 3Com, the world's largest modem company. Prior to becoming a consultant in 1994, Ari worked for Oracle Corporation. As a lifelong baseball enthusiast, Ari has turned his passion into a year-round endeavor. Since 1992, he has worked as a consultant for the Montreal Expos baseball club, where he has developed and managed their scouting department's software systems. Ari has appeared on NBC's Today Show and CNN and is a frequent guest speaker on Oracle in the United States and abroad. He lives in Chicago and can be reached through email at **akaplan@interaccess.com** or through his Web site of Oracle tips at **http://homepage.interaccess.com/~akaplan**.

Atul Mehta is a software engineer with a forte in database design. A savvy PL/SQL developer, he is also proficient in a wide variety of programming languages like C, JavaScript, Java, Perl, and Informix 4GL. Atul is a senior software consultant with Sesame Software, a leading technical consulting firm, specializing in Intranet application development using Oracle WebServer. He is currently helping Keystone Communications in creating an order entry system to schedule their daily broadcast business for domestic and international services, and manage cost containment analysis as well as revenue generation. In the past, other clients included MCI, MBNA, OfficeMax, Frontier Technologies Corporation, and NEC.

TABLE OF CONTENTS

CONTENTS

ACKNOWLEDGMENTS

Paul Dalberth: Thanks to Frank Wellnitz and other members of senior management at Family Health International who allowed me time to pursue this undertaking. Special thanks to my colleague and friend Dave Kinney who found a spare workstation to grace my desk at home and so eased the potential for marital discord arising from competition for computer resources. Thanks also to my project editor at Waite Group Press, Andrea Rosenberg, who was there when I needed her but still managed to grant me as much creative room as I wanted. Most heartfelt gratitude to my wife, Barbara, who never told me I was spending too much time with "that Oracle stuff" even when the monitor glowed past midnight.

Ari Kaplan: Most thanks go to my family and Rachel Greene, the best public relations pro in Chicago, hands-down. Thanks to Thomas and Dolores Everhart, along with Caltech's Summer Undergraduate Research Fellowship program. Additional thanks to Aaron Lipman and Zion B'Ayin™, David Max, Keith Langer, Rich and Carrie Brody, Meir Kahane, Mark Hodes (yes I wrote this book), Jim Bertsch, and Tyrone Kimp. I would like to acknowledge co-authors Paul Dalberth and Atul Mehta, along with Andrea Rosenberg, Stephanie Wall, Amy Sticksel, and Russ Jacobs at Waite Group Press for their great skills in keeping the book on track. Special thanks go to Edward Honour, the author of the original *Oracle How-To* book, for setting the groundwork for this second edition.

Atul Mehta: First and foremost to my parents for their encouragement and support to go live out my dreams. I take this opportunity to express my gratitude to Rick Banister, also my best friend, who made me realize that I could do well as a technical writer. Finally, a thank-you to all the co-authors and the editorial team at Waite for making it all possible.

INTRODUCTION

Oracle is the most prevalent Relational Database Management System (RDBMS) in the world. Information technology professionals will find Oracle serving the database needs of the enterprise in manufacturing, financial, pharmaceutical, and telecommunications environments all over the globe. The Oracle database runs on every major machine and under every prominent operating system available. Versions of Oracle exist for platforms from modestly equipped portable computers up to powerful database servers accommodating thousands of concurrent users. Oracle databases act as on-line transaction processing engines, decision support systems, data warehouses, and repositories for web-enabled applications. The prevalence and flexibility of Oracle have given rise to groups of information technology professionals—database administrators, application programmers, and database designers—whose skill sets are tailored to leveraging an investment in the Oracle database.

No information technology professional looks forward to frantic migration efforts or to discarding legacy applications. The very strength of Oracle's installed base can make capitalizing on the promise of new technology difficult. One such technology is object orientation. Object oriented databases are certainly not new; industry-wide acceptance of object databases, however, has not been forthcoming. Oracle8, the next major release Oracle, promises transparent support of legacy applications *and* object oriented extensions. This long-awaited product will generate a considerable amount of questions among Oracle information technology professionals. The answers to these questions are at the heart of this book.

The first edition of *Oracle How-To* posed and answered myriad real-world questions confronting anyone who worked with Oracle7. The idea behind this work was simple and appealing to any Oracle practitioners who explained, "I understand what a database does, I know my way around computers in general, and I'm tired of looking through thousands of pages of documentation only to wind up deciphering railroad diagrams. Just show me how to get my Oracle work done." *Oracle8 How-To* extends this popular and easy-to-read format to Oracle8 in 17 chapters full of what anyone who wants to understand Oracle8 needs to know. This second edition includes six completely new chapters and a significant number of new additions to topics covered in the first edition.

NEW CHAPTER! **Chapter 1, "Selected Database Instance Installation Topics,"** describes the process of creating a new Oracle instance, establishing communication with it using Oracle utility programs such as SQL*Plus, Server Manager, and SQL Worksheet. This chapter also addresses what a DBA needs to do to configure a new instance for production use.

Chapter 2, "SQL*Plus," will show you how to improve your productivity with the tool that provides the most direct access to an Oracle database instance.

Chapter 3, "Database Users," begins with the simple operation of adding user accounts and subsequently introduces database administration tasks like determining who is connected to the database and how to disconnect user sessions. The How-To's in this chapter provide a suite of helpful reports about user access privileges, defaults, and profiles.

Chapter 4, "Tables," covers creation and management of this most elementary database structure. This series of How-To's also introduces new Oracle8 topics including index-only and partitioned tables.

NEW CHAPTER! **Chapter 5, "Indexes,"** focuses on index creation and management tasks like detecting and rebuilding unbalanced indexes. New Oracle8 functionality explained in this chapter includes partitioned and bit-mapped indexes.

NEW CHAPTER! **Chapter 6, "Constraints,"** will be particularly helpful to database designers. This chapter deals with referential integrity and column constraints and includes a How-To summarizing a new Oracle8 construct: deferred constraints.

Chapter 7, "Views," explains creation, management, and use of database views, including updatable join views and object views.

Chapter 8, "Security," defines system and object privileges and how to grant them. The important topic of reporting on the current security configuration of the database has special prominence here. This chapter also explains the new password management features of Oracle8.

NEW CHAPTER! **Chapter 9, "Space Management,"** is a compilation of the basic information every DBA needs at hand to manage the physical side of an Oracle8 database. Performance tuning, covered in Chapter 15, might be more intriguing, but for those who want to make sure their database is available when it should be, this is where to look.

Chapter 10, "PL/SQL," covers the important procedural extensions of the Oracle8 server. PL/SQL blocks creation, error handling, and stored procedure management are only some of the topics covered in this series of How-To's.

NEW CHAPTER! **Chapter 11, "Querying Data,"** is devoted entirely to the important topic of getting data into and out of Oracle8 databases using PL/SQL.

Chapter 12, "Built-In Packages," explains how to use some of the useful PL/SQL procedures that ship with Oracle8. Dynamic SQL and the DBMS_LOB package, new in Oracle8, are two of the topics discussed here.

Chapter 13, "Triggers," builds on the previous two chapters by explaining use of PL/SQL to encapsulate business rule information within database objects.

Chapter 14, "**SQL Statement Tuning,**" shows how and where to start improving the performance of your database. The EXPLAIN PLAN, AUTOTRACE, AND SQL*Trace methods of SQL statement analysis all appear in this chapter's How-To's. Tuning strategies covered here include optimizer hints and star query optimization.

Chapter 15, "**Database Tuning,**" provides a survey of must-know techniques for any IT professional, particularly DBAs, who want to get the most performance out of an Oracle investment. Application of the techniques in this chapter could improve the performance of all of your Oracle applications.

NEW CHAPTER! **Chapter 16, "Create an Object Relational Database,"** is an in-depth introduction to the object-oriented extensions of Oracle8 including object types, object tables, and nested tables. Oracle professionals need not abandon familiar relational constructs to make use of Oracle8 object extensions; this chapter shows you how.

Chapter 17, "**Oracle Web Application Server,**" profiles creation and management of Internet and intranet applications within the Oracle WebServer development environment.

Who Will This Book Help?

The information in this book will benefit anyone who works with, or is planning to work with, Oracle8, particularly database administrators and application developers. Much of the material applies to earlier versions of Oracle as well. The authors assume familiarity with basic principles of database technology and programming, but the complexity of covered topics ranges from the very straightforward to the very complex. The format lends itself to direct answers to specific questions, but much of the material will contribute to a general knowledge applicable to questions not explicitly included in this book. Regardless of topic complexity, the emphasis is on a practical, problem-solving approach supplemented wherever possible with specific examples of the techniques and the programming code that will get the job done.

Using the Sample Scripts

All of the sample scripts used within the book are available on the World Wide Web at **http://www.mcp.com/info**. To download the scripts, put the ISBN number in the Search field and click the Search button. Windows 95/NT users should download the Windows executable to a temporary directory. Once you've downloaded the file to your hard drive, double-click it to run the installer. UNIX users should download either the SOURCE.TAR.Z or SOURCE.TAR.GZ file. Once either of the files is downloaded, uncompress or unzip the file and then `untar` it. When working with a particular chapter, readers may wish to copy all of that chapter's scripts into the SQL*Plus working directory. The default location of this directory under Windows NT is \ORANT\BIN. Alternatively, run the scripts by providing the script's full path name to the SQL*Plus START command. The INSTALL.SQL script from Chapter 1 creates the WAITE user account used throughout the book as the book's working account. Any account with the DBA role, however, will suffice.

CHAPTER 1

SELECTED DATABASE INSTANCE INSTALLATION TOPICS

1

SELECTED DATABASE INSTANCE INSTALLATION TOPICS

How do I...

3

After a DBA installs Oracle8, the Oracle installer can configure and start a trial database instance. This instance is suitable for test use only because the installer has not optimally configured database structures such as the control files, the rollback segments, and the redo log groups. Modifications to the archive mode, product user profiles, and the checkpoint process are also useful in some environments. A DBA can also manually create a new Oracle instance without using the Oracle installer. The How-To's in this chapter explain the process of instance creation and methods for minimally configuring Oracle8 to support SQL*Plus and Server Manager connections. The remainder of the chapter focuses on some of the steps necessary to transform the default configuration of a typical trial instance to a working database capable of supporting production work.

1.1 Create a New Oracle Instance Without Using the Installer

The trial database instance is useful for testing and initial orientation to Oracle8, but it is likely that the demands of production applications will eventually justify an additional instance or instances. This How-To includes instructions that enable you to create a new Oracle instance using the Instance Manager and Server Manager utilities.

1.2 Create Windows NT and Oracle Client Services for the New Instance

After you create a new Oracle instance, there is still some configuration work to do before Server Manager, SQL*Plus, or Enterprise Manager can communicate with it. This How-To explains configuring NT and Oracle services to enable these tools to access the database.

1.3 Use the Password File to Authenticate Database Administrators

If you have followed the steps in the previous How-To's, the database is running and the SQL*Plus, Server Manager, and Enterprise Manager tools can communicate with it. You need not confine database administrator duties to the SYS or SYSTEM accounts, nor does Oracle require continued use of the connect internal command to connect to the instance via Server Manager. This How-To describes generation and use of the password file to assign database administration privileges and authenticate users who hold them.

1.4 Multiplex Control Files

Oracle Corporation recommends that copies of the control file reside on multiple disks. The database doesn't run without a current control file, and this practice, called *multiplexing*, protects the control file from disk failure. This How-To illustrates the steps to multiplex the control files and build an extra margin of safety into an Oracle database.

1.5 Create a New Control File

Many Oracle parameters, such as the shared pool size, are based solely on the parameter file. Oracle requires a new control file, however, before it can recognize changes to some features of the database configuration such as database name or the maximum number of data files. This How-To explains the process of rebuilding the control file to change this latter type of database parameter.

1.6 Create New Tablespaces

Under Windows NT, the only Oracle tablespace that the installer will create is the system tablespace where the data dictionary tables and views will reside. Most Oracle instances contain additional tablespaces. The exact architecture depends on the business needs that the databases address, but it is likely that some specific tablespaces will enhance database performance. This How-To is a guide for adding additional tablespaces and provides some guidance about which new tablespaces to create.

1.7 Change the Rollback Segment Configuration

Rollback segments provide database clients with the capability to reverse uncommitted changes. They also provide read consistency in the multiuser Oracle environment. The configuration and default number of rollback segments will probably not be optimal for installer-generated instances. This How-To presents instructions for querying and enhancing the rollback segment configuration for an Oracle instance.

1.8 Create and Mirror Redo Log Groups

Oracle8 keeps track of all changes made to a database in redo log files. These files are important in recovery, and Oracle8 can maintain multiple copies of them in a multiplexed architecture. Learn how to create additional redo log groups and members in this How-To.

1.9 Enable Archive Log Mode

This How-To focuses on how to preserve redo logs so that changes made since the last backup are recoverable. Using Oracle8's archive capability is one way to guarantee up-to-the-minute transaction recovery.

1.10 Start the Checkpoint Process

Without the checkpoint process, the LGWR background process handles all the I/O associated with a database checkpoint. The CKPT (checkpoint) process can aid LGWR (log writer) during checkpoints by writing the file headers of the physical database files. If your database is composed of many data files, the CKPT process might expedite checkpointing in Oracle8. This How-To explains starting, stopping, and determining the status of the CKPT process.

1.11 Enable Product User Profiles

Product user profiles provide an easy way to prevent selected users from executing selected commands from the SQL*Plus environment. Even if an Oracle installation makes no use of these profiles, enabling them eliminates an annoying message at SQL*Plus invocation. This How-To describes how to enable and use product user profiles.

COMPLEXITY

ADVANCED

1.1 How do I...
Create a new Oracle instance without using the installer?

Problem

I have already installed the Oracle server but don't want to use the Oracle installer's trial database. I want to create a new Oracle instance from scratch.

Technique

The Oracle Instance Manager automates some of the tasks required to set up a new Oracle database instance. The starting point of the process is a new parameter initialization file. When this is available, the Instance Manager will create a new instance and run the scripts that build the data dictionary.

Steps

Create a new parameter initialization file with any ASCII editor. Start the Oracle Instance Manager and create the new Oracle instance, specifying the locations of the new parameter file and the other parts of the physical database layer as necessary. After instance creation, allow Enterprise Manager and SQL*Plus sessions to access the new instance by using network configuration manager to set up a new service. You will create an instance called O8HT to illustrate this process.

1. Create a new copy of the parameter initialization file. Under Windows NT, the Oracle8 installer placed a sample parameter initialization file in the \ORANT\DATABASE subdirectory and named it INIT<DATABASE SID>.ORA. Alternatively, the sample parameter initialization file in Listing 1.1 will suffice as a starting point. If you let the installer create a trial database instance, you can safely take the default for all the parameters except db_name and control_files; you can modify the other parameters later based on database performance history. The initialization parameter file in Listing 1.1 specifies multiplexed control files named

CTL1O8HT.ORA and CTL2O8HT.ORA (learn more about multiplexing, or mirroring, control files in How-To 1.4). Lines beginning with the # symbol in Listing 1.1 are commented out; Oracle8 ignores them during instance startup.

Listing 1.1 A sample parameter initialization file

```
db_name = o8ht
db_files = 1024
control_files = (C:\ORANT\DATABASE\ctl1o8ht.ora,
C:\ORANT\DATABASE\mirror\ctl2o8ht.ora)

db_file_multiblock_read_count =  8          # INITIAL
# db_file_multiblock_read_count = 8            # SMALL
# db_file_multiblock_read_count = 16           # MEDIUM
# db_file_multiblock_read_count = 32           # LARGE

db_block_buffers =  200                     # INITIAL
# db_block_buffers = 200                       # SMALL
# db_block_buffers = 550                       # MEDIUM
# db_block_buffers = 3200                      # LARGE

# shared_pool_size =  6500000                # INITIAL
shared_pool_size = 3500000                    # SMALL
# shared_pool_size = 6000000                   # MEDIUM
# shared_pool_size = 9000000                   # LARGE

log_checkpoint_interval = 10000

processes =  50                             # INITIAL
# processes = 50                               # SMALL
# processes = 100                              # MEDIUM
# processes = 200                              # LARGE

dml_locks =  100                            # INITIAL
# dml_locks = 100                              # SMALL
# dml_locks = 200                              # MEDIUM
# dml_locks = 500                              # LARGE

log_buffer =  8192                          # INITIAL
# log_buffer = 8192                            # SMALL
# log_buffer = 32768                           # MEDIUM
# log_buffer = 163840                          # LARGE

sequence_cache_entries =  10                # INITIAL
# sequence_cache_entries = 10                  # SMALL
# sequence_cache_entries = 30                  # MEDIUM
# sequence_cache_entries = 100                 # LARGE

sequence_cache_hash_buckets =  10           # INITIAL
# sequence_cache_hash_buckets = 10             # SMALL
# sequence_cache_hash_buckets = 23             # MEDIUM
# sequence_cache_hash_buckets = 89             # LARGE

# audit_trail = true                        # if you want auditing
```

continued on next page

continued from previous page

```
# timed_statistics = true            # if you want timed statistics
max_dump_file_size = 10240           # limit trace file size to 5 Meg each

# log_archive_start = true           # if you want automatic archiving

# define directories to store trace and alert files
background_dump_dest=%RDBMS80%\trace
user_dump_dest=%RDBMS80%\trace

db_block_size = 2048

snapshot_refresh_processes = 1

remote_login_passwordfile = shared

compatible = 8.0.0.0.0
```

2. Click the NT Instance Manager v8.0 icon in the Oracle for Windows NT program group.

NOTE

If the NT Instance Manager does not appear on the Start menu, you can invoke it by double-clicking ·the executable file ORADIM80.EXE from Windows Explorer. The default location of this program is the \ORANT\BIN subdirectory.

Click the New button and in the dialog box that appears, type in the name and location of the initialization file you created in step 1 in the Parameter Initialization Filename field. Type in the system identifier (a name of your choice up to four characters long) in the SID field. If you want the new instance to start as soon as it is created, check the Services and Instance check boxes in the Startup After Creation section of the New Instance dialog box. If you want the instance to start automatically whenever the host computer boots, check Automatic in the Instance Startup Mode section of the New Instance dialog box. These options are indicated in Figure 1.1.

3. Click the Advanced button and specify the same name in the Database Name field as you did for the DB_NAME parameter in the parameter initialization file. Specify the redo log file names and the names of the data files in the appropriate fields. You can specify more than one of each of these file types by separating the filenames with commas. It is easy to add more data files or redo log files later, so there is no need to agonize over these decisions now. Take particular care with the values of

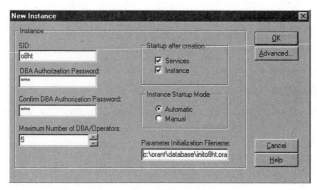

Figure 1.1 Instance Manager's New Instance
dialog box.

MAXDATAFILES, MAXLOGFILES, and MAXLOGMEMBERS, though.
Changing these values later requires a control file rebuild, an intricate
process. An example of the advanced parameters screen appears in Figure 1.2.

4. Click the OK button to create the Oracle instance.

5. Instance Manager presents a dialog box reporting that it has created a
password file for the database and that password file use depends on the
value of the initialization parameter REMOTE_LOGIN_PASWORDFILE.
Click OK. How-To 1.3 covers password file administration in depth.

6. The Create Instance Information dialog box asks whether you want to run
the CATALOG.SQL and CATPROC.SQL SCRIPTS. These scripts configure

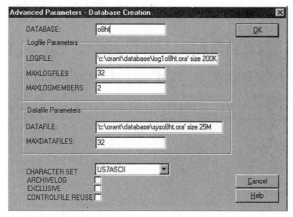

Figure 1.2 The Oracle Instance Manager
advanced parameters screen.

the data dictionary views and procedural options. You can choose to run the scripts now, or you can wait and run them outside this instance creation procedure by using the CREATE.SQL file in C:\ORANT\BIN.

How It Works

Instance Manager writes a script to create the database that will contain, by default, two redo log files and one system file. The installer also writes a CREATE.SQL file that connects to the newly created instance and runs the CATALOG.SQL and CATPROC.SQL scripts to create the data dictionary views and enable the procedural option, respectively.

Comments

Instance Manager is also useful if you need to delete an instance. It will remove the NT service and the password file created for the instance; the DBA need only remove the remaining physical files to complete instance removal. If you did choose to run the CATPROC.SQL and CATALOG.SQL scripts during the installation procedure or if you ran the CREATE.SQL script without modifying it, the new instance will be shut down at the completion of these steps. See How To 1.2 to learn how to connect to the new instance from Enterprise Manager, SQL*Plus, or Server Manager.

Instance Manager does not provide a forum to build a complicated database architecture. It is best used to configure a minimally functional database. The only details worth deliberating at any length, when using Instance Manager to build a new Oracle instance, are those that are difficult to change later, as specified in Step 3.

COMPLEXITY
INTERMEDIATE

1.2 How do I...
Create Windows NT and Oracle client services for the new instance?

Problem

I have created a new Oracle instance under Microsoft Windows NT, but I get an ORA-12547 or ORA-12545 error when I try to connect to it from Server Manager or SQL*Plus, respectively. How do I configure the instance so I can use these tools?

Technique

Under Windows NT, all Oracle8 database instances have a corresponding Windows NT service. A Windows NT service is an executable process. Any and all user connections to an Oracle8 instance require a running NT service specific to the instance. The Oracle8 Instance Manager creates this service during instance creation (see How-To 1.1 for an explanation of the Oracle8 Instance Manager). You can change the characteristics of the NT service from the Windows NT Control Panel, regardless of the options you specified during instance creation. Use the Windows NT Control Panel to start and configure the NT service associated with any Oracle instance. Use the Oracle Network Configuration Wizard to create an Oracle client service for SQL*Plus to use to connect to the instance.

Steps

1. Select the Control Panel menu option from the Settings section of the Windows NT Start menu. Enter the NT Service Manager by double-clicking Services. The Windows NT Service Manager, shown in Figure 1.3, will appear.

2. Click once on the Oracle service corresponding to the instance you want to access. If the status of the service is Stopped, click the Start button to start the service.

3. If the Startup column for the service indicates Manual and you want the service to start every time the computer starts, double-click the line describing the service or single-click the Startup button. Now click the radio button to the left of the word Automatic.

4. Click OK and Close to exit the NT services manager.

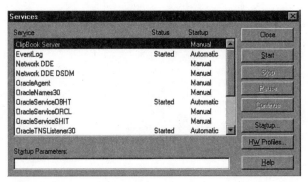

Figure 1.3 The Windows NT Services screen.

5. Select the Programs menu from the Windows NT Start menu, select the Oracle for Windows NT menu, and then select the Oracle Network Configuration Wizard.

6. Click once on the Create New Service button, and supply the database SID and a service name of your choosing in the appropriate fields. Click once on the Next button. You will avoid confusion later if you configure the service so that the values of the database SID and the service name are identical. The Create New Service screen appears in Figure 1.4.

7. Select the protocol the client will use to communicate with the server and specify any protocol specific information required in the following dialog box. If you specified Bequeath (for a local database), no additional information is necessary.

How It Works

Steps 1 through 3 start the NT service associated with the Oracle instance and instruct Windows NT to start the service whenever the server starts up, so that the Server Manager interface will be available for the associated database instance. Steps 5 through 7 make an entry in the TNSNAMES.ORA file specifying the

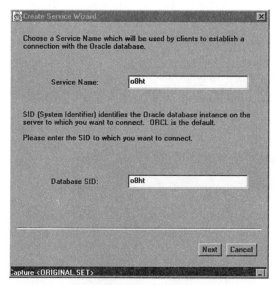

Figure 1.4 The Create New Service screen of the Oracle8 Network Configuration Wizard.

connection information necessary for communication via the SQL*Plus and Enterprise Manager interfaces. The Network Configuration Wizard protects users and DBAs from the esoteric syntax of the TNSNAMES.ORA file.

Comments

At some sites, it might be useful to start the NT service corresponding to the database instance even if the instance itself does not start every time the machine starts up. Otherwise, starting the instance will necessitate an extra step to start the associated NT service. The NT Instance Manager enables DBAs to modify the startup mode of the database and the associated NT service together. It does not, however, enable you to specify one startup mode for the instance and a different mode for the NT service.

COMPLEXITY
ADVANCED

1.3 How do I...
Use the password file to authenticate database administrators?

Problem

I created a database using the instructions in How-To 1.1. I want some other users to use Server Manager or Enterprise Manager with database administrator privileges. How do I create and maintain a password file?

Technique

Examine the value of initialization parameter REMOTE_LOGIN_ PASSWORDFILE and modify it, if necessary, so that it has the value SHARED. Query the V$PWFILE_USERS dynamic performance view to ascertain the current configuration of the password file. Grant the SYSOPER and SYSDBA privileges to the appropriate users and connect to the database using the AS SYSOPER or AS SYSDBA clause of the **connect** command.

Steps

1. Use the Server Manager `show parameter` command to determine the value of the initialization parameter REMOTE_LOGIN_PASSWORDFILE. In this case, the value is SHARED. The possible values and their meanings follow. The results of the `show parameter` command appear in Figure 1.5.

```
SQL> describe dba_tablespaces
 Name                            Null?    Type
 ------------------------------- -------- ----
 TABLESPACE_NAME                 NOT NULL VARCHAR2(30)
 INITIAL_EXTENT                           NUMBER
 NEXT_EXTENT                              NUMBER
 MIN_EXTENTS                     NOT NULL NUMBER
 MAX_EXTENTS                     NOT NULL NUMBER
 PCT_INCREASE                    NOT NULL NUMBER
 MIN_EXTLEN                               NUMBER
 STATUS                                   VARCHAR2(9)
 CONTENTS                                 VARCHAR2(9)
 LOGGING                                  VARCHAR2(9)

SQL> describe dba_data_files
 Name                            Null?    Type
 ------------------------------- -------- ----
 FILE_NAME                                VARCHAR2(513)
 FILE_ID                         NOT NULL NUMBER
 TABLESPACE_NAME                 NOT NULL VARCHAR2(30)
 BYTES                                    NUMBER
 BLOCKS                          NOT NULL NUMBER
 STATUS                                   VARCHAR2(9)
 RELATIVE_FNO                             NUMBER
 AUTOEXTENSIBLE                           VARCHAR2(3)
 MAXBYTES                                 NUMBER
 MAXBLOCKS                                NUMBER
 INCREMENT_BY                             NUMBER
```

Figure 1.5 Determining the value of REMOTE_LOGIN_PASSWORDFILE in Server Manager.

✔ NONE: The Oracle8 server ignores the password file; the operating system is responsible for database administrator authentication.

✔ SHARED: The Oracle8 server uses the password file but only the users SYS and INTERNAL can appear within the password file as users with administration privileges. More than one database can use this password file.

✔ EXCLUSIVE: The Oracle8 server uses the password file, and you can add users other than SYS and INTERNAL to the file. These users can connect as themselves to Server Manager and Enterprise Manager and still have administrator privileges. Only one database can use this password file.

2. Use any editor to change the value of REMOTE_LOGIN_PASSWORDFILE to EXCLUSIVE.

3. Shut down the database and restart it. Repeat Step 1 to verify that the value of REMOTE_LOGIN_PASSWORDFILE is now EXCLUSIVE.

4. Query the view V$PWFILE_USERS to determine which users currently appear in the password file. In Figure 1.6, this view indicates that only SYS and INTERNAL can currently connect with administrator privileges.

5. Use the **grant** command in Server Manager to grant SYSOPER or SYSDBA privileges to users that need to connect to the database as administrators. Table 1.1 describes the SYSOPER and SYSDBA privileges; Figure 1.7

```
SQL> start c:\data\chapters\chp1_1.sql
SQL>
SQL> SELECT ts.tablespace_name, df.file_name, df.bytes, ts.status
  2  FROM dba_tablespaces ts, dba_data_files df
  3  WHERE ts.tablespace_name = df.tablespace_name;

TABLESPACE_NAME       FILE_NAME                                  BYTES STATUS
--------------------  --------------------------------- ---------- ---------
SYSTEM                C:\ORANT\DATABASE\SYSO8HT.ORA   26214400 ONLINE

SQL>
SQL> set echo off
SQL> |
```

Figure 1.6 The structure and contents of the
V$PWFILE_USERS dynamic performance table in
Enterprise Manager's SQL Worksheet.

```
SQL> start c:\data\chapters\chp1_2.sql
SQL> spool create_tablespaces.log
SQL>
SQL> CREATE TABLESPACE users
  2       DATAFILE 'c:\orant\database\users.dat' SIZE 5M
  3       DEFAULT STORAGE (INITIAL 20K NEXT 20K
  4                        MINEXTENTS 1 MAXEXTENTS 999
  5                        PCTINCREASE 0)
  6       ONLINE;

Tablespace created.

SQL>
SQL> CREATE TABLESPACE temp
  2       DATAFILE 'c:\orant\database\temp.dat' SIZE 5M
  3       DEFAULT STORAGE (INITIAL 20K NEXT 20K
  4                        MINEXTENTS 1 MAXEXTENTS 999
  5                        PCTINCREASE 0)
  6       ONLINE;

Tablespace created.

SQL>
SQL> CREATE TABLESPACE rbs
  2       DATAFILE 'c:\orant\database\rbs.dat' SIZE 5M
  3       DEFAULT STORAGE (INITIAL 20K NEXT 20K
  4                        MINEXTENTS 1 MAXEXTENTS 999
  5
```

Figure 1.7 Granting SYSOPER and SYSDBA to
the WAITE account and verifying the operation in Server Manager.

illustrates grant statements that will assign these privileges to the WAITE
user account.

Table 1.1 Operations enabled via the SYSOPER and SYSDBA privileges

PRIVILEGE	OPERATION
SYSOPER	STARTUP, SHUTDOWN, ALTER DATABASE OPEN/MOUNT, ALTER DATABASE BACKUP, ARCHIVE LOG, RECOVER, RESTRICTED SESSION
SYSDBA	All system privileges with accompanying ADMIN option, all privileges from the SYSOPER role, point-in-time-based recovery, CREATE DATABASE

```
SQL> start c:\data\chapters\chp1_1.sql
SQL>
SQL> SELECT ts.tablespace_name, df.file_name, df.bytes, ts.status
  2  FROM dba_tablespaces ts, dba_data_files df
  3  WHERE ts.tablespace_name = df.tablespace_name;

TABLESPACE_NAME        FILE_NAME                          BYTES STATUS
--------------------   ---------------------------   ----------- ---------
RBS                    C:\ORANT\DATABASE\RBS.DAT        5242880 ONLINE
SYSTEM                 C:\ORANT\DATABASE\SYSO8HT.ORA   26214400 ONLINE
TEMP                   C:\ORANT\DATABASE\TEMP.DAT       5242880 ONLINE
USERS                  C:\ORANT\DATABASE\USERS.DAT      5242880 ONLINE

SQL>
SQL> set echo off
SQL>
```

Figure 1.8 Logging in as a database administrator, querying the data dictionary, and shutting down the database in Server Manager.

6. In Server Manager, connect to Oracle8 as WAITE and use the **as sysoper** clause. Figure 1.8 shows the syntax of the **connect** command, illustrates how the SYSOPER privilege does not grant access to the Oracle data dictionary, and finally demonstrates that the WAITE user can now shut down the database.

Comments

If the Oracle Instance Manager created the database under Microsoft Windows NT, it automatically created a password file in the default location \ORANT\ DATABASE with default name PWDSID.ORA. If you neglect to alter the value of initialization parameter REMOTE_LOGIN_PASSWORDFILE to EXCLUSIVE, you will receive an ORA-01994 error when you try to grant SYSOPER or SYSDBA to a user account.

COMPLEXITY
BEGINNING

1.4 How do I...
Multiplex control files?

Problem

I used Oracle Instance Manager to create a new instance, but I did not mirror, or multiplex, the control file so that it simultaneously resides on two or more disks. This will help protect the control file from a single disk failure. How do I change my Oracle configuration so that Oracle will maintain two copies of the control file on more than one disk?

Technique

Shut down the database, use operating system commands to make a copy of the existing control file, and modify the parameter initialization file so that it specifies two or more control files in the CONTROL_FILES parameter.

Steps

1. Use Server Manager or Enterprise Manager to shut down the database.

2. Use operating system utilities such as the Windows NT Explorer, the UNIX **cp** command, or the OpenVMS **copy** command to copy the single control file to another location, preferably on a different disk.

3. Modify the parameter file, usually called INITSID.ORA, so that the parameter CONTROL_FILES reflects the locations of all the control files you want Oracle to maintain.

```
control_files = C:\ORANT\DATABASE\ctl1o8ht.ora,
D:\ORANT\DATABASE\ctl2o8ht.ora
```

4. Start, mount, and open the database using server or the Oracle Instance Manager module in Enterprise Manager. An ORA-00205 error at this point indicates that the CONTROL_FILES parameter in the parameter file is incorrectly specified and Oracle cannot find one or more of the control files.

How It Works

Oracle will automatically maintain as many copies of the control file as the DBA lists in the CONTROL_FILES parameter of the parameter file.

Comments

It is easier to specify multiplexed control files during instance creation by specifying all the control file locations in the parameter initialization file. This way, when the NT Instance Manager creates the instance, the control file will be multiplexed from its inception.

COMPLEXITY
INTERMEDIATE

1.5 How do I...
Create a new control file?

Problem

I have an existing Oracle instance for which I want to modify one or more of the permanent database settings, such as the database name or the maximum number of redo log files. How do I create a new control file so that I can change the value of one or more of these permanent parameters?

Technique

Use the `alter database` command to generate a script summarizing the current state of the control file. Modify the script to reflect the desired changes to the permanent database parameters. Run the modified script to create a new control file.

Steps

1. Use Server Manager or Enterprise Manager to disconnect all user sessions. An easy, if unfriendly, way to do this is to shut down the database in Immediate mode after warning currently connected users.

2. Restart the database in Restricted mode by issuing the `startup restrict` command from Server Manager.

3. Enter the following `alter database` command.

```
alter database backup controlfile to trace;
```

This command creates a script that will generate a new control file. Under Windows NT, the script resides in a trace file that in turn resides in the subdirectory pointed to by initialization parameter USER_DUMP_DEST. The name of the trace file under Windows NT is of the form ORA*xxxxx*.TRC where *xxxxx* is a five-digit number equal to the Windows NT thread ID. If you are not using Windows NT, review your operating-system–specific documentation to ascertain the location of this trace file.

4. Open the trace file using any ASCII editor and modify the values of the permanent database parameters in the `create controlfile` command to the desired new values. Save this modified `create controlfile` command to another file. An example of a script containing a `create controlfile` command appears in Listing 1.2. In this case, the command will change the MAXDATAFILES parameter from the default value of 32 to a new value of 100.

Listing 1.2 The `create controlfile` **statement**

```
CREATE CONTROLFILE REUSE DATABASE "O8HT" NORESETLOGS NOARCHIVELOG
    MAXLOGFILES 32
    MAXLOGMEMBERS 2
    MAXDATAFILES 100
```

```
    MAXINSTANCES 1
    MAXLOGHISTORY 449
LOGFILE
  GROUP 1 'C:\ORANT\DATABASE\LOG1O8HT.ORA'  SIZE 200K,
  GROUP 2 'C:\ORANT\DATABASE\LOG2O8HT.ORA'  SIZE 200K
DATAFILE
  'C:\ORANT\DATABASE\SYSO8HT.ORA';
```

5. Use Server Manager to shut down the database, and then start the instance again but don't mount it.

6. Execute the script saved in Step 4 to create a new control file (or control files, if the instance uses a multiplexed control file).

7. Open the database by issuing the `alter database open` command from Server Manager.

How It Works

Steps 1 and 2 disconnect all users from the database and open the database in Restricted mode so that only users with restricted session privilege (presumably, database administrators only) can connect to the instance. This will prevent any database changes that can invalidate the control file script you created in Step 1. Steps 3 and 4 generate a script to create a new version of the control file with new values for some or all of the permanent database parameters. After the script is run in Step 6 and the database is opened in Step 7, the new database parameters are in effect.

Comments

It is difficult and tedious to manually generate `create controlfile` statements. It is also potentially hazardous because mistakes in this command can result in corrupted data files. If possible, it is a good idea to regularly run the statements in Steps 1 through 3, even if it is not immediately necessary to create a new control file. Some sites run these statements as part of scheduled jobs or database shutdown scripts. The resulting `create controlfile` script summarizes all the physical files comprising the database and can be useful during a database recovery effort.

This is the simplest example of creating a new control file, particularly because the Oracle8 instance in question is not running in Archive Log mode. If your database is in Archive Log mode, review your documentation, especially with regard to the `resetlogs` option of the `create controlfile` command.

In general, use extreme caution when rebuilding the control files for a production instance.

COMPLEXITY
BEGINNING

1.6 How do I...
Create new tablespaces?

Problem

I have created a new Oracle instance and want to prepare it for user account creation. What tablespaces should I add for a minimally sufficient production instance, and how do I add them?

Technique

To determine the tablespaces and data files that currently comprise the instance, query the data dictionary views DBA_TABLESPACES and DBA_DATA_FILES. The structures of these views appear in Figure 1.9.

The Oracle server will enable you to open a database for production work and add users, even if the only tablespace in the instance is SYSTEM. Unfortunately, this architecture is likely to introduce fragmentation in the SYSTEM tablespace. This situation is certain to adversely effect database

```
SQL> describe v$rollstat
 Name                               Null?    Type
 ---------------------------------- -------- ----
 USN                                         NUMBER
 EXTENTS                                     NUMBER
 RSSIZE                                      NUMBER
 WRITES                                      NUMBER
 XACTS                                       NUMBER
 GETS                                        NUMBER
 WAITS                                       NUMBER
 OPTSIZE                                     NUMBER
 HWMSIZE                                     NUMBER
 SHRINKS                                     NUMBER
 WRAPS                                       NUMBER
 EXTENDS                                     NUMBER
 AVESHRINK                                   NUMBER
 AVEACTIVE                                   NUMBER
 STATUS                                      VARCHAR2(15)
 CUREXT                                      NUMBER
 CURBLK                                      NUMBER

SQL> describe v$rollname
 Name                               Null?    Type
 ---------------------------------- -------- ----
 USN                                         NUMBER
 NAME                               NOT NULL VARCHAR2(30)

SQL> |
```

Figure 1.9 The DBA_TABLESPACES and DBA_DATA_FILES data dictionary views.

performance. A good rule of thumb is to add three additional tablespaces prior to adding user accounts:

✔ A tablespace (suggested name: TEMP) to contain temporary segments, such as those produced by a sort or an index creation

✔ A tablespace (suggested name: USERS) to act as the default tablespace for all users

✔ A tablespace (suggested name: RBS) to contain rollback segments

Use the CREATE TABLESPACE statement to create new tablespaces and data files.

Steps

1. Run SQL*Plus and connect as the SYSTEM user account. The script called CHP1_1.SQL queries the DBA_TABLESPACES and DBA_DATA_FILES data dictionary views to summarize the current tablespaces in the instance. The results of this script appear in Figure 1.10.

2. Run the script named CHP1_2.SQL to create the USERS, TEMP, and RBS tablespaces. This script and its results appear in Figure 1.11.

```
SQL> describe dba_rollback_segs
 Name                                  Null?      Type
 ------------------------------------- ---------- ----
 SEGMENT_NAME                          NOT NULL   VARCHAR2(30)
 OWNER                                            VARCHAR2(6)
 TABLESPACE_NAME                       NOT NULL   VARCHAR2(30)
 SEGMENT_ID                            NOT NULL   NUMBER
 FILE_ID                               NOT NULL   NUMBER
 BLOCK_ID                              NOT NULL   NUMBER
 INITIAL_EXTENT                                   NUMBER
 NEXT_EXTENT                                      NUMBER
 MIN_EXTENTS                           NOT NULL   NUMBER
 MAX_EXTENTS                           NOT NULL   NUMBER
 PCT_INCREASE                          NOT NULL   NUMBER
 STATUS                                           VARCHAR2(16)
 INSTANCE_NUM                                     VARCHAR2(40)
 RELATIVE_FNO                          NOT NULL   NUMBER

SQL> |
```

Figure 1.10 The results of CHP1_1.SQL in SQL*Plus.

```
  3  FROM dba_rollback_segs rs, v$rollstat vs, v$rollname vn
  4  WHERE rs.segment_name = vn.name and
  5        vn.usn = vs.usn;

SEGMENT_NAME TABLESPACE INITIAL_EXTENT NEXT_EXTENT MIN_EXTENTS OPTSIZE STATUS
------------ ---------- -------------- ----------- ----------- ------- ------
SYSTEM       SYSTEM          51200        51200          2             ONLINE

SQL>
```

Figure 1.11 The results of CHP1_2.SQL in SQL*Plus.

```
SQL> start chp1_4
SQL> create rollback segment rbs1
  2      tablespace rbs
  3      storage (initial    25K
  4               next       25K
  5               minextents 19
  6               maxextents 121
  7               optimal    500K
  8              )
  9  ;

Rollback segment created.

SQL>
SQL> alter rollback segment rbs1 online;

Rollback segment altered.

SQL> |
```

Figure 1.12 The results of
CHP1_1.SQL in SQL*Plus
after a CREATE TABLESPACE
operation.

3. Run the CHP1_1.SQL script again to verify that the new tablespaces exist,
reside in the intended location, and are online. Figure 1.12 shows that the
CHP1_2.SQL script successfully created three new tablespaces.

How It Works

The script in Step 1 creates a report of the current tablespaces and data files that
comprise the database. Step 2 creates three tablespaces commonly found in
Oracle instances, and Step 3 verifies the correct operation of the script in Step 2.

Comments

Don't attempt the reverse operation, dropping tablespaces and data files, at the
operating system level without using the DROP TABLESPACE command first.
Failure to use this Server Manager command prior to physically dropping a data
file will cause Oracle to report that it cannot find a data file when you attempt to
open the database. This error indicates a conflict between the physical structure
of the database and the structure reflected in the control file.

After completion of this How-To, connect to Oracle as SYSTEM or as any user
with DBA privilege, and run the INSTALL.SQL script to create the WAITE
account. This CREATE USER script names the TEMP and USER tablespaces
created in Step 2 as the temporary and default tablespaces, respectively, for the
WAITE account.

```
SQL> start install
SQL>
SQL> create user waite identified by waite
```

```
   2   temporary tablespace temp
   3   default tablespace users;

User created.

SQL>
SQL> grant dba to waite;

Grant succeeded.
```

COMPLEXITY
INTERMEDIATE

1.7   How do I...
Examine and change the rollback segment configuration?

Problem

I want to review the number, size, and location of the rollback segments for my new Oracle instance. Historical database performance information is not available yet, but I want to alter my database to include a serviceable rollback segment configuration.

Technique

Rollback segments summarize the state of the database prior to any currently uncommitted transactions. They provide read-consistent views of the database and the capability to undo or rollback uncommitted database inserts, updates, or deletes. To view the current rollback segment configuration, query the DBA_ROLLBACK_SEGS data dictionary view and the V$ROLLSTAT and V$ROLLNAME dynamic performance tables. Figures 1.13 and 1.14 describe these views. Create and size rollback segments using the **create rollback segment** statement.

```
SEGMENT_NAME  TABLESPACE  INITIAL_EXTENT  NEXT_EXTENT  MIN_EXTENTS  OPTSIZE  STATUS
------------  ----------  --------------  -----------  -----------  -------  ------
SYSTEM        SYSTEM               51200        51200            2            ONLINE
RBS1          RBS                  26624        26624           19   512000  ONLINE

SQL>
SQL> set echo off
SQL> |
```

Figure 1.13 The V$ROLLSTAT and V$ROLLNAME dynamic performance tables.

```
C:\>set oracle_sid=o8ht

C:\>svrmgr30

Oracle Server Manager Release 3.0.2.0.1 - Beta

Copyright (c) Oracle Corporation 1994, 1995. All rights reserved.

Oracle8 Server Release 8.0.2.0.2 - Beta
With the distributed, heterogeneous, replication, objects
and parallel query options
PL/SQL Release 3.0.2.0.2 - Beta

SVRMGR> connect internal
Password:
Connected.
SVRMGR> show parameter remote_login
NAME                                   TYPE      VALUE
-----------------------------------    ------    -------------------
remote_login_passwordfile              string    SHARED
SVRMGR>
```

Figure 1.14 The DBA_ROLLBACK_SEGS data dictionary view.

Steps

1. Run SQL*Plus and connect as the WAITE user account. Use the START command to load and execute the CHP1_3.SQL script.

The results of the script in Figure 1.15 show that one rollback segment exists and it resides in the system tablespace.

```
SQL> start chp1_3
SQL>
SQL> SELECT segment_name, tablespace_name, initial_extent,
  2          next_extent, min_extents, optsize, rs.status
  3  FROM dba_rollback_segs rs, v$rollstat vs, v$rollname vn
  4  WHERE rs.segment_name = vn.name and
  5          vn.usn = vs.usn;
```

2. Use the START command to load and execute the CHP1_4.SQL script, as shown in Figure 1.16.

```
SQLWKS> describe v$pwfile_users
Column Name                            Null?     Type
-----------------------------------    --------  ----
USERNAME                                         VARCHAR2 (30)
SYSDBA                                           VARCHAR2 (5)
SYSOPER                                          VARCHAR2 (5)
SQLWKS> select * from v$pwfile_users
     2>
USERNAME                               SYSDB SYSOP
-----------------------------------    ----- -----
INTERNAL                               TRUE  TRUE
SYS                                    TRUE  TRUE
2 rows selected.
```

Figure 1.15 The results of the CHP1_3.SQL script in SQL*Plus.

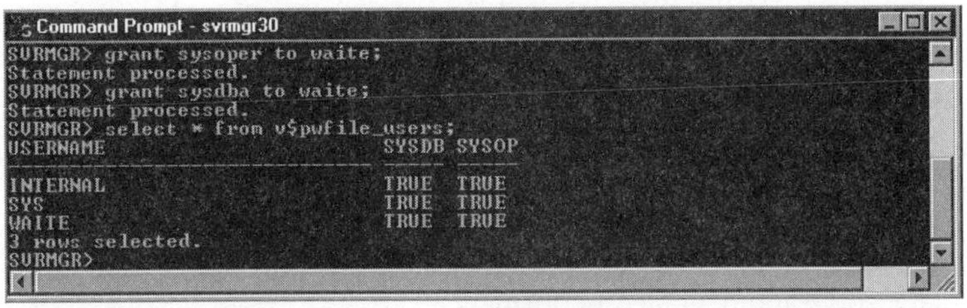

Figure 1.16 The results of the CHP1_4.SQL script in SQL*Plus.

NOTE

The script CHP1_4.SQL creates four rollback segments in four separate operations. Figure 1.16 shows only one of these operations to save space.

3. Use the START command to load and execute the CHP1_3.SQL script again to see the results of Step 2. The script and its results appear in Figure 1.17.

How It Works

Step 1 queries one data dictionary view and two dynamic performance tables that maintain information about the database's rollback segment configuration. The script in Step 2 uses the `create rollback segment` command to create a new rollback segment and makes the new rollback segment available to the Oracle8 server by using the `alter rollback segment` command to bring the rollback segment online. The final step is to repeat Step 1 to verify the successful creation of the new rollback segment.

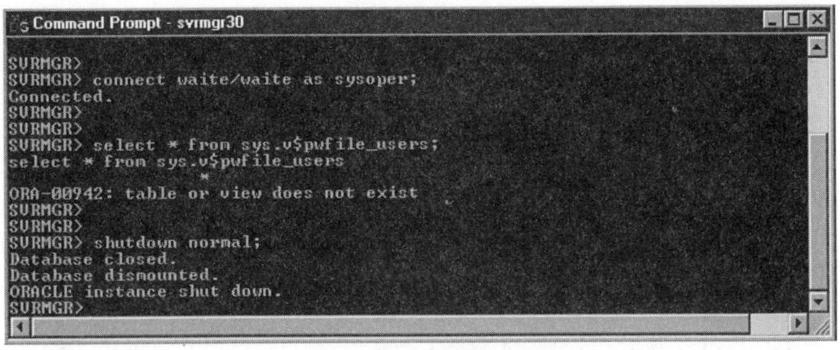

Figure 1.17 The results of the CHP1_3.SQL script in SQL*Plus after creating another rollback segment.

Unless the parallel option is enabled for an instance, public and private rollback segments are identical.

The rollback segment in the system tablespace is intended for special system transactions. If there are no other rollback segments or no available rollback segments, the Oracle8 server will assign user transactions to the SYSTEM rollback segment. Because Oracle8 often dynamically allocates and deallocates rollback segment storage, this situation can lead to fragmentation in the system tablespace and degraded performance.

COMPLEXITY
INTERMEDIATE

1.8 How do I...
Create and multiplex redo log groups?

Problem

I want to review the redo log configuration. I also want each redo log group to consist of more than one member to protect the database's redo logs from disk failures. How do I review and modify the redo log configuration?

Technique

The redo logs keep a running record of all database changes. They are used during recovery operations primarily to ensure that transactions committed since the last backup are re-applied to the database. This process is called *rolling forward*.

The LGWR process writes to redo log groups. There is at least one physical redo log file in each group. If there is more than one redo log file in a redo log group, the group is multiplexed. As soon as the DBA establishes this configuration, Oracle8 writes simultaneously to all members of the redo log group.

This How-To contains a query that accesses the dynamic performance tables V$LOG and V$LOGFILE (Figure 1.18 shows the structures of these) to summarize the current redo log configuration; the use of the `alter database` command to create additional redo log groups and members is also covered.

Steps

1. Run SQL*Plus and connect as the WAITE user account. Use the START command to load and execute the script in CHP1_5.SQL. The script appears here, and Figure 1.19 contains the script's output.

```
SQL> describe v$log
 Name                                  Null?    Type
 ------------------------------------- -------- ----
 GROUP#                                         NUMBER
 THREAD#                                        NUMBER
 SEQUENCE#                                      NUMBER
 BYTES                                          NUMBER
 MEMBERS                                        NUMBER
 ARCHIVED                                       VARCHAR2(3)
 STATUS                                         VARCHAR2(16)
 FIRST_CHANGE#                                  NUMBER
 FIRST_TIME                                     DATE

SQL> describe v$logfile
 Name                                  Null?    Type
 ------------------------------------- -------- ----
 GROUP#                                         NUMBER
 STATUS                                         VARCHAR2(7)
 MEMBER                                         VARCHAR2(513)

SQL>
```

Figure 1.18 The V$LOG and V$LOGFILE
dynamic performance tables.

```
SQL> start chp1_5
SQL>
SQL> SELECT vl.group#, members,
  2          vl.status groupstat,
  3          vf.member, vf.status filestat
  4  FROM v$log vl, v$logfile vf
  5  WHERE vf.group# = vl.group#;

 GROUP#   MEMBERS GROUPSTAT MEMBER                              FILESTAT
 -------- --------- --------- ----------------------------------- --------
        1         1 INACTIVE  D:\ORANT\DATABASE\LOG1ORCL.ORA
        2         1 CURRENT   D:\ORANT\DATABASE\LOG2ORCL.ORA

SQL>
SQL>
SQL>
SQL>
SQL> |
```

Figure 1.19 The results of the script CHP1_5.SQL in
SQL*Plus.

```
SQL> SELECT vl.group#, members,
  2          vl.status groupstat,
  3          vf.member, vf.status filestat
  4  FROM v$log vl, v$logfile vf
  5  WHERE vf.group# = vl.group#;
```

Line 1 returns the redo log group number and the number of members in
the group. Line 3 selects the physical filename of the redo log group
member. The status returned from both the V$LOG and V$LOGFILE
views indicates the status of the group and of the individual member,
respectively. Table 1.2 summarizes some of the most common values for
column STATUS in the V$LOG table.

Table 1.2 Common values of the STATUS column in the V$LOG dynamic performance table

UNUSED	Oracle8 has never written to this group.
CURRENT	This is the active group.
ACTIVE	Oracle8 has written to this log before; it is needed for instance recovery.
INACTIVE	Oracle8 has written to this log before; it is not needed for instance recovery.

2. Use the `alter database add logfile` command to add additional redo log groups to the database. Figure 1.20 shows the results of this command in the script CHP1_6.SQL. This script also calls CHP1_5.SQL to verify the success of the `alter database` command. Note that the status of the new log group (group 3) is UNUSED because Oracle8 has never written to this group.

3. Use the `alter database add logfile member` command to add additional redo log members to existing redo log groups. Figure 1.21 shows the results of this command. The script resides in CHP1_7.SQL, which also calls CHP1_5.SQL to verify that the new member was added successfully. Note that the status of the new log member is INVALID because Oracle has never written to it.

How It Works

Step 1 queries the data dictionary to summarize the current status of the redo log groups and members. In Figure 1.19, this query indicates that there are two redo log groups (the minimum) and that these groups are not multiplexed.

```
SQL>
SQL> alter database add logfile group 3
  2     'd:\orant\database\log3orcl.ora'
  3     size 200K;

Database altered.

SQL>
SQL> set termout off
SQL>
SQL> SELECT vl.group#, members,
  2          vl.status groupstat,
  3          vf.member, vf.status filestat
  4   FROM v$log vl, v$logfile vf
  5   WHERE vf.group# = vl.group#;

 GROUP#   MEMBERS GROUPSTAT MEMBER                          FILESTAT
-------- --------- --------- ------------------------------- --------
      1         1 INACTIVE  D:\ORANT\DATABASE\LOG1ORCL.ORA
      2         1 CURRENT   D:\ORANT\DATABASE\LOG2ORCL.ORA
      3         1 UNUSED    D:\ORANT\DATABASE\LOG3ORCL.ORA
```

Figure 1.20 Adding a redo log group with the `alter database` command in CHP1_6.SQL.

```
SQL> alter database add logfile member
  2     'd:\orant\database\log1orclm.ora'
  3     to group 1;

Database altered.

SQL>
SQL> set termout off
SQL>
SQL> SELECT vl.group#, members,
  2            vl.status groupstat,
  3            vf.member, vf.status filestat
  4   FROM v$log vl, v$logfile vf
  5   WHERE vf.group# = vl.group#;

 GROUP#  MEMBERS GROUPSTAT MEMBER                               FILESTAT
 ------- ------- --------- ----------------------------------- --------
       1       2 INACTIVE  D:\ORANT\DATABASE\LOG1ORCL.ORA
       1       2 INACTIVE  D:\ORANT\DATABASE\LOG1ORCLM.ORA INVALID
       2       1 CURRENT   D:\ORANT\DATABASE\LOG2ORCL.ORA
       3       1 UNUSED    D:\ORANT\DATABASE\LOG3ORCL.ORA
```

Figure 1.21 Multiplexing a redo log group with the `alter database` command in CHP1_7.SQL.

Comments

It is good practice to place redo log members of the same group on different disks so that a single disk failure will not destroy all redo information and make complete up-to-the-second recovery difficult or impossible. The LGWR process writes redo information nearly continuously in an OLTP environment, in addition, so spreading the members of the same group across disks will expedite LGWR operation.

Oracle8 does not permit specification of the size of a new redo log group member. It must be the same as the size of the existing members in the group.

The status of new log members remains INVALID until the group containing the new member becomes the current group. If you add a new member to the current group, the status of the new member remains INVALID until the group becomes current again.

COMPLEXITY
INTERMEDIATE

1.9 How do I...
Enable archive log mode?

Problem

I need to make sure that I can recover all changes to data contained within my Oracle8 instance. I know that I can do this by activating Archive Log mode. How do I determine whether my database is in Archive mode, and how do I activate and deactivate this capability?

Technique

The Oracle8 server stores all changes to the database, even uncommitted changes, in the redo log files. Without this ongoing record of database changes, the most complete recovery will only include database transactions committed prior to the last image backup. The complication is that the LGWR (log writer) process writes to the redo logs in a cyclic fashion. So, if the database includes two redo log files, LGWR starts to writes to the first redo log file until it is full, then writes to the second redo log file until it is full, and then writes to the first redo log file again, overwriting its contents.

The archive process preserves redo logs by copying them to a safe place after LGWR fills them. Use the `alter database` command to enable Archive Log mode for the database; then set parameters in the parameter initialization file to automate the archive process.

Steps

1. Select the LOG_MODE attribute from the V$DATABASE Dynamic Performance view. This brief command and its output are shown in Figure 1.22.

2. Use one of the database administration tools to shut down the instance.

3. Edit the parameter initialization file to assign values to the parameters LOG_ARCHIVE_START, LOG_ARCHIVE_DEST, and LOG_ARCHIVE_ FORMAT. Sample values for these parameters appear here:

```
log_archive_start = true            # if you want automatic
archiving
log_archive_dest  = c:\orant\database\archive  # archive
destination
log_archive_format = "ARCH%S.LOG"   # name format for archived
files
```

4. Use one of the database administration tools to restart and mount the database. Don't open the database yet.

Figure 1.22
Determining the
archive mode of the
database in SQL*Plus.

5. Issue the `alter database archivelog` command to put the database in ARCHIVELOG mode.

6. Use the `alter database open` command to open the database for normal operation.

7. Execute the command from step 1 to query the V$DATABASE table again to verify that the database is now operating in ARCHIVELOG mode.

8. From Server Manager or the SQL Worksheet in Enterprise Manager, issue the command `show parameter log_archive` to verify the values of the parameters set in step 3 (see Figure 1.23).

How It Works

Step 1 queries the V$DATABASE dynamic performance table data and reports the archive mode for the database. Figure 1.22 indicates that the database is not in ARCHIVELOG mode.

In Step 2, you prepare the database for the `alter database` command that cannot be issued when the database is open. In Step 3, you edit the parameter initialization file to enable automatic archiving. Without these modifications to the parameter file, the DBA must manually archive filled redo log files. Steps 5 and 6 establish ARCHIVELOG mode for the database and open it for production operation. Steps 7 and 8 verify the modifications made in the preceding steps. Figure 1.23 shows the results of these steps.

Comments

In almost all database installations, automatic archiving is the best configuration. The alternative, manual archiving, is only provided for special circumstances such as a media failure of the automatic archiving destination. If a database in

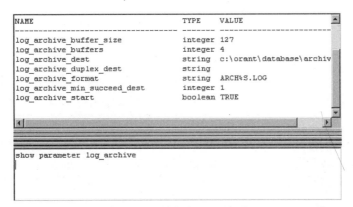

Figure 1.23 Verifying establishment of ARCHIVELOG mode in Enterprise Manager's SQL Worksheet utility.

Archive Log mode requires manual archiving, the database will halt if the database administrator neglects to manually archive filled redo logs when their status is inactive.

There are two special format parameters that appear in the LOG_ARCHIVE_ DEST parameter. The first is %t, for which the Oracle8 server will substitute the thread number. This is only meaningful in Oracle parallel server configurations. The second is %s, which Oracle8 will resolve to the log sequence number. Uppercase specifications of %S or %T instruct Oracle8 to left pad the resulting integer with zeros. Thus, a log_archive_format specification of ARCH%s.LOG becomes, for example, ARCH00454.LOG when the ARCH process copies log sequence number 454 to the archive destination specified in LOG_ARCHIVE_ DEST.

COMPLEXITY
BEGINNING

1.10 How do I...
Start the checkpoint process?

Problem

I suspect that checkpoint processing at our site will be intensive, and I would like to ease the workload on the LGWR process by enabling the CKPT process. How can I tell whether the CKPT process is currently running? How do I activate and deactivate the CKPT process?

Technique

The helpful CKPT process will not run unless the DBA requests it specifically. The show parameter command, issued from within one of the database administration tools, will reveal the current status of the CKPT process.

Steps

1. Start the Server Manager utility and connect as internal.

2. Enter the command show parameter checkpoint_process to find out whether the CKPT process is running. Figure 1.24 displays the results of this command and indicates that the CKPT process is not running.

3. Use one of the database administration tools to shut down the database.

4. Edit the parameter initialization file by locating the line specifying the checkpoint_process parameter (or adding a checkpoint_process line) and setting the parameter to the value TRUE.

5. Use one of the database administration tools to restart and open the database.

```
C:\>svrmgr30

Oracle Server Manager Release 3.0.2.0.1 - Beta

Copyright (c) Oracle Corporation 1994, 1995. All rights reserved.

Oracle8 Server Release 8.0.2.0.2 - Beta
With the distributed, heterogeneous, replication, objects
and parallel query options
PL/SQL Release 3.0.2.0.2 - Beta

SVRMGR> connect internal
Password:
Connected.
SVRMGR> show parameter checkpoint_process
NAME                                TYPE    VALUE
----------------------------------- ------- ----------------------
checkpoint_process                  boolean FALSE
SVRMGR>
```

Figure 1.24 Checking the value of the checkpoint_process parameter in Server Manager.

6. Use the `show parameter checkpoint_process` command from step 1 again to verify that the checkpoint process parameter is now set to TRUE.

How It Works

The `show parameter` command in step 1 and its output indicate that the CKPT process is not running.

Step 2 closes the database, a precursor for changing initialization parameters. In Step 3, you use any text editor to edit the parameter initialization file to enable the CKPT process. When the database opens in Step 5, the CKPT process will be ready to aid LGWR when checkpoints occur.

Comments

If it is possible to add one more background process to the server, the CKPT process is a worthwhile addition to most Oracle instances.

COMPLEXITY
INTERMEDIATE

1.11 How do I...
Enable product user profiles?

Problem

Whenever a user other than SYS or SYSTEM starts SQL*Plus, the Oracle8 server reports that product user profile information is not loaded. How do I eliminate this bothersome message? Also, I'd like to prevent some users from issuing certain SQL*Plus and SQL commands. How do I accomplish this using product user profiles?

Technique

Eliminate the SQL*Plus startup error message by running the Oracle-supplied script called PUPBLD.SQL. In the Windows NT environment, the default location of this script is the \ORANT\DBS subdirectory. Use standard INSERT statements to populate the PRODUCT_USER_PROFILE table and limit user access to various SQL and SQL*Plus commands.

Figure 1.25 shows the structure of the PRODUCT_USER_PROFILE table. Table 1.3 shows the columns in this table that must be populated to impose SQL*Plus and SQL command limits. Tables 1.4 and 1.5 list the SQL*Plus and SQL commands, respectively, which the PRODUCT_USER_PROFILES table can disable.

Table 1.3 PRODUCT_USER_PROFILE columns used to disable SQL*Plus and SQL commands

COLUMN NAME	DESCRIPTION	COLUMN VALUE
PRODUCT	Product name	SQL*Plus
USERID	User name (uppercase)	
ATTRIBUTE	Name of command to disable	(See Table 1.4)
CHAR_VALUE	Action to take	DISABLED

Table 1.4 SQL*Plus commands that can be disabled in PRODUCT_USER_PROFILE

COPY	EXIT	QUIT	SAVE	START
EDIT	GET	PASSWORD	SET	
EXECUTE	HOST	RUN	SPOOL	

Table 1.5 SQL commands that can be disabled in PRODUCT_USER_PROFILE

ALTER	DELETE	NOAUDIT	SET TRANSACTION
ANALYZE	DROP	RENAME	TRUNCATE
AUDIT	GRANT	REVOKE	UPDATE
CONNECT	INSERT	SELECT	BEGIN
CREATE	LOCK	SET ROLE	DECLARE

```
SQL> describe product_user_profile;
Name                              Null?     Type
--------------------------------- --------- ----
PRODUCT                           NOT NULL  VARCHAR2(30)
USERID                                      VARCHAR2(30)
ATTRIBUTE                                   VARCHAR2(240)
SCOPE                                       VARCHAR2(240)
NUMERIC_VALUE                               NUMBER(15,2)
CHAR_VALUE                                  VARCHAR2(240)
DATE_VALUE                                  DATE
LONG_VALUE                                  LONG
```

Figure 1.25 The PRODUCT_USER_PROFILE table described in SQL*Plus.

Steps

1. Run SQL*Plus and connect as the SYSTEM user account. Use the START command to load and execute the PUPBLD.SQL script.

2. While connected as SYSTEM, use an INSERT command to populate the PRODUCT_USER_PROFILE table with the appropriate values from Tables 1.3, 1.4, and 1.5. The script in CHP1_8.SQL that appears next, for example, will prevent the WAITE user from creating any objects through the SQL*Plus interface.

```
INSERT INTO product_user_profile
        (product,userid, attribute, char_value)
VALUES ('SQL*Plus', 'WAITE', 'CREATE', 'DISABLED');
```

3. Run SQL*Plus, connect as the WAITE user, and attempt to create any object. Now that product user profiles are enabled and the CREATE command is expressly disabled for the WAITE account, SQL*Plus will answer the CREATE command with the error message INVALID COMMAND; CREATE.

4. Run SQL*Plus, connect as the SYSTEM user, and use the START command to load and execute CHP1_9.SQL. This deletes any product user profile limitations established for the WAITE user so that scripts later in the book will not generate errors.

How It Works

PRODUCT_USER_PROFILE is actually a synonym. If the user is SYSTEM, this synonym resolves to the SQLPLUS_PRODUCT_PROFILE table. If the user is not SYSTEM, the synonym resolves to a view that queries the SQLPLUS_PRODUCT_PROFILE table. In Step 1, PUPBLD.SQL creates these views as well as the SQLPLUS_PRODUCT_PROFILE table that stores the product user profile data. Step 2 populates this table, and Step 3 displays the error message that Oracle8 displays when a user attempts to issue a disabled SQL*Plus command.

Comments

SQL*Plus reads only product profile information when a user starts the utility. Product user profile changes will not take effect for active SQL*Plus users until they terminate SQL*Plus and restart it. The contents of the PRODUCT_ USER_PROFILE table don't affect the SYSTEM user's interaction with SQL*Plus; SQL*Plus does not read this table when SYSTEM connects.

DBAs should fully document product user profiles and use them with caution. It can be difficult to trace the cause of the INVALID COMMAND SQL*Plus error if the DBA enables and forgets product user profile limits.

CHAPTER 2
SQL*PLUS

2

SQL*PLUS

How do I...

SQL*Plus is one of the most powerful tools used in developing applications for the Oracle database. SQL*Plus provides the most direct access to Oracle. Although it might seem that SQL*Plus is not user-friendly like graphical query tools, it provides a great deal of flexibility and runs on all platforms supporting Oracle. Unlike most graphical query tools, you can use SQL*Plus to manipulate data and create database objects.

SQL*Plus plays an important role in application development. It is a powerful prototyping tool that you can use to develop and test SQL statements before integrating them into your application. A working knowledge of SQL*Plus is strongly recommended for any developer using Oracle. In this chapter, you will learn how to make SQL*Plus an integral part of your development process. You will see examples of how SQL*Plus can help you develop Oracle applications efficiently.

2.1 Change the Format of Date Fields Returned in SQL*Plus

Date values are stored in the database with the year, month, day, year, hour, minute, and second. The value of a date column can be presented in a variety of formats using date functions. Also, time can be returned correctly for any time zone. If you query a date value without using a date function, the time portion of the date will not display and the format will be the default date format. This How-To presents the suite of date and time formatting returned in SQL*Plus.

2.2 Create and Use SQL*Plus Command Files

You can use SQL*Plus for many tasks, and most tasks consist of more than one step. SQL*Plus enables you to save a series of SQL, PL/SQL, and SQL*Plus commands in a file and run them as a single statement. SQL*Plus command files can be nested to create a complex sequence of events. This How-To explores how to create and use SQL*Plus command files.

2.3 Save Query Results and SQL Statements to a File

The more you work with Oracle, the easier it becomes to develop powerful SQL statements. But how can you avoid retyping the same SQL statement every time you need it? SQL*Plus enables you to save SQL statements and query results to files so they are available the next time you need them. This output can be edited, printed, or merged into a word processing document. This How-To guides you through the task of saving SQL statements and query results to files.

2.4 View and Modify SQL*Plus System Variables

Within SQL*Plus, system variables control the behavior of the SQL*Plus environment. In many ways, changing system variables is like executing commands. Changing the values of system variables changes the way SQL*Plus behaves when executing statements and retrieving records. In this How-To, you will learn to view and modify SQL*Plus system variables.

2.5 Prompt Users for Substitution Variables

User-defined variables give SQL*Plus a new level of flexibility. Developers can create variables that can be defined in SQL scripts or accepted from the user. This How-To explores creating user-defined variables in SQL*Plus and prompting users for values during runtime.

2.6 Pass Parameters to a SQL*Plus Script

As explained in How-To 1.5, a SQL*Plus script can contain substitution variables that the user enters at runtime. Another technique for increased flexibility is for parameters to be passed when calling a script. This How-To explores passing parameters to a SQL*Plus script during runtime.

2.7 Use SQL*Plus as a Report Writer

SQL*Plus commands and system variables enable you to format a report within SQL*Plus. You can create titles, change column headings, break on column changes, and even calculate totals. By using the formatting capabilities of SQL*Plus, you can create reports quickly and have greater control over the output of your queries. This How-To takes you through the different steps of formatting a report in SQL*Plus.

2.8 Use SQL*Plus to Write Repetitive Scripts

Almost everything you need to know about your Oracle database can be queried through SQL*Plus. Because SQL*Plus can write query output to files and command files can be executed by SQL*Plus, SQL*Plus can be used to create SQL statements. This How-To explores using queries to create SQL statements, which is the foundation for many other techniques discussed in the book.

COMPLEXITY
BEGINNING

2.1 How do I...
Change the format of date fields returned in SQL*Plus?

Problem

I need to format date and time values. The default representation of the date columns' type is not acceptable for my applications and reports. My applications need date and time values formatted in a variety of ways. How do I change the format of date and time values returned in SQL*Plus?

Technique

The TO_CHAR function converts a date value to character representations. You can use it within SQL statements or PL/SQL modules to present date values in more useful formats. The TO_CHAR function is overloaded in Oracle and has different uses, depending on the parameter list passed to the function. The syntax of the TO_CHAR function used to format date values is shown here:

```
TO_CHAR(date_value, 'format mask')
```

The NEW_TIME function displays the time portion of a date field relative to any two time zones. This is useful when displaying times in a zone other than where the data is stored. The syntax of the NEW_TIME function used to convert time among time zones is shown here:

```
NEW_TIME(date,zone_input,zone_output)
```

With the TO_CHAR function, the format mask specifies the format of the date when it is returned by the function. You can specify the output format any way you want by using valid date format models. Table 2.1 shows the valid date format models.

Table 2.1 Date format models

FORMAT	DESCRIPTION
MM	The number of the month (1–12).
RM	The month specified as a Roman numeral.
MON	The three-letter abbreviation of the month.
MONTH	The month fully spelled out.
D	The number of the day in the week.
DD	The number of the day in the month.
DDD	The number of the day in the year.
DY	The three-letter abbreviation of the day.
DAY	The day fully spelled out.
Y	The last digit of the year.
I	The last digit of the year, based on ISO standards.
YY	The last two digits of the year.
IY	The last two digits of the year, based on ISO standards.
YYY	The last three digits of the year.
IYY	The last three digits of the year, based on ISO standards.
YYYY	The full four-digit year.
IYYY	The four-digit year, based on ISO standards.
SYYYY	The year in a signed format, BC values represented negative.
Y,YYY	The year with a comma in the second position.
SCC or CC	The century; S prefixes BC dates with a -.
RR	The last two digits of the year used for year 2000 issues.
YEAR	The year spelled out.
SYEAR	The year spelled out; S prefixes BC dates with a -.
Q	The number of the quarter.
WW	The number of the week in the year.
W	The number of the week in the month.
IW	The week of the year, based on ISO standards (1–53).
J	The number of days since December 31, 4713 B.C.
HH or H12	The hour of the day (1–12).
HH24	The hour of the day (1–24).
MI	The minutes of the hour.
SS	The seconds of the minute.

FORMAT	DESCRIPTION
SSSSS	The seconds since midnight.
A.M.	A.M. or P.M. is displayed, depending on the time of day.
P.M.	A.M. or P.M. is displayed, depending on the time of day.
AM	AM or PM is displayed, depending on the time of day.
PM	AM or PM is displayed, depending on the time of day.
A.D.	B.C. or A.D. is displayed, depending on the date.
B.C.	(Same as A.D.)
AD	BC or AD is displayed, depending on the date.
BC	(Same as AD.)
fm	The prefix of MONTH or DAY to suppress padded spaces.
th	The suffix of the number format to cause th, st, or rd to be added to the end of the number.
sp	The suffix of a number to force the number to be spelled out.
spth	The suffix of a number to force it to be spelled out and given an ordinal suffix.
thsp	(Same as spth.)

You can use combinations of the format models with punctuation symbols to create an e42normous number of possibilities. In the ISO standards, a week starts on Monday and ends on Sunday. This means that a date can fall on the fifty-third week of the year in ISO standards, depending on whether January 1 is before a Friday.

The NEW_TIME function returns the time in `zone_input` as if it were in `zone_output`. For example, the time can be specified as Central standard, although th42e data is stored in Pacific standard time. The `zone_input` and `zone_output` can be specified any way you want by using valid time zone format models. Table 2.2 shows the valid time format models.

Table 2.2 Time format models

FORMAT	DESCRIPTION
AST/ADT	Atlantic (standard/daylight) time.
BST/BDT	Bering time.
CST/CDT	Central time.
EST/EDT	Eastern time.
GMT	Greenwich mean time.
HST/HDT	Alaska/Hawaii time.
MST/MDT	Mountain time.
NST	Newfoundland time.
PST/PDT	Pacific time.
YST/YDT	Yukon time.

Steps

1. Run SQL*Plus and connect as the WAITE user account. CHP2_1.SQL, shown in Figure 2.1, creates the SAMPLE2 table and inserts a sample record. The SAMPLE2 table will be used to show several of the available date formatting functions.

The SAMPLE2 table is created and populated with a single date value, which is queried in the examples using date formatting functions. The COLUMN commands contained in the script format the columns in the examples to make the output more readable. Run the file to create the sample table and sample record.

```
SQL>  START CHP2_1.sql

Table created.

1 row created.

Commit complete.
```

2. Load CHP2_2.SQL into the SQL buffer, shown in Figure 2.2. The file contains a query of the sample table that returns a date column in a variety of formats.

```
CREATE TABLE SAMPLE2 (
    DATEFLD     DATE);

INSERT INTO SAMPLE2 VALUES
    (TO_DATE('25-JAN-98 11:23:03','DD-MON-YY HH:MI:SS'));

COMMIT;

COLUMN MMDDYY FORMAT A8
COLUMN MMDDYYYY FORMAT A10
COLUMN DAY FORMAT A15
COLUMN MONTH FORMAT A15
COLUMN DY FORMAT A10
COLUMN DDD FORMAT A10
COLUMN WW FORMAT A5
COLUMN MON FORMAT A5
COLUMN YEAR FORMAT A20
COLUMN RM FORMAT A5
COLUMN CC FORMAT A5
COLUMN HH FORMAT A5
COLUMN HHPM FORMAT A10
COLUMN HH24 FORMAT A5
COLUMN MI FORMAT A5
COLUMN SS FORMAT A5
COLUMN SSSSS FORMAT A5
```

Figure 2.1 CHP2_1.SQL contains a SQL script to create the sample table used in this How-To.

```
SQL> GET C:\CHP2_2.SQL
  1  SELECT
  2      DATEFLD,
  3      TO_CHAR(DATEFLD,'MM/DD/YY') MMDDYY,
  4      TO_CHAR(DATEFLD,'MM/DD/YYYY') MMDDYYYY,
  5      TO_CHAR(DATEFLD,'DAY') DAY,
  6      TO_CHAR(DATEFLD,'MONTH') MONTH
  7  FROM
  8*     SAMPLE2
SQL> /

DATEFLD    MMDDYY    MMDDYYYY    DAY                 MONTH
---------- --------- ----------- ------------------- -------------
25-JAN-98  01/25/98  01/25/1998  SUNDAY              JANUARY

SQL> |
```

Figure 2.2 The output of CHP2_2.SQL within SQL*Plus.

Line 2 returns the date column in the default Oracle format. Lines 3 through 6 format the date in a variety of ways. Line 3 demonstrates the two-digit year format. Line 4 shows the day and month with the year in a four-digit format. Line 5 uses the DAY format mask to spell out the day of the week. Line 6 uses the MONTH format mask to spell out the month. Line 8 specifies that the sample table created in Step 1 is the source of the data.

3. Run the query to display the output. Figure 2.2 shows the output of the query within SQL*Plus.

The first three columns of the query display the date in the most commonly used formats. The DAY and MONTH columns show how the date can be converted and displayed in different formats. Both columns are shown in uppercase letters. If the format mask were specified in lowercase, or with only the first letter uppercase, the case of the output would change.

4. Load CHP2_3.SQL into the SQL buffer, shown in Figure 2.3. The query contained in the file presents more formats in which date values can be presented.

Line 2 displays the day of the week abbreviated in the three-digit format. Line 3 uses the DDD format mask to display the number of days from the beginning of the year. Line 4 uses the WW format mask to display the week of the year from 1 to 53. Line 5 uses the MON format mask to display the month in its three-digit abbreviation. Line 6 uses the YEAR format mask to display the year spelled out.

5. Run the statement to display the formatted results. Figure 2.3 shows the results of the query.

```
SQL> GET C:\CHP2_3.SQL
  1   SELECT
  2        TO_CHAR(DATEFLD,'DY') DY,
  3        TO_CHAR(DATEFLD,'DDD') DDD,
  4        TO_CHAR(DATEFLD,'WW') WW,
  5        TO_CHAR(DATEFLD,'MON') MON,
  6        TO_CHAR(DATEFLD,'YEAR') YEAR
  7   FROM
  8*      SAMPLE2
SQL> /

DY          DDD      WW    MON    YEAR
----------- -------- ----- ------ ---------------------
SUN         025      04    JAN    NINETEEN NINETY-EIGHT

SQL>
```

Figure 2.3 The output of CHP2_3.SQL within SQL*Plus.

The formats displayed by the query can be used for specific requirements within applications. Information such as the day of year or week of year can be useful in batch operations.

6. Load CHP2_4.SQL into the SQL buffer, shown in Figure 2.4. The query contained in the file displays format masks based on the year and the time portion of the date variable.

Line 2 uses the RM format mask to display the month of the year as a Roman numeral. Line 3 uses the CC format mask to format the century. Line 4 uses the HH format mask to display the hour of the day from 0 to 12. Line 5 uses the HH format mask with the PM modifier to display the hour of the time with AM or PM. Line 6 uses the HH24 format mask to display the hour in military time. Line 7 formats the minutes with the MI format mask. Line 8 uses the SS format mask to display the seconds. Line 9 uses the SSSSS format mask to display the number of seconds past midnight.

7. Run the statement to display the results.

```
SELECT
   TO_CHAR(DATEFLD,'RM') RM,
   TO_CHAR(DATEFLD,'CC') CC,
   TO_CHAR(DATEFLD,'HH') HH,
   TO_CHAR(DATEFLD,'HH PM') HHPM,
   TO_CHAR(DATEFLD,'HH24') HH24,
   TO_CHAR(DATEFLD,'MI') MI,
   TO_CHAR(DATEFLD,'SS') SS,
   TO_CHAR(DATEFLD,'SSSSS') SSSSS
FROM
   SAMPLE2
```

Figure 2.4 Date formats based on the year and time.

The results of the query show how year values can be presented as Roman numerals and the century can be calculated. The time formats contained in the query show that the time portion of the date column can be displayed in a variety of ways (see Figure 2.5).

8. Load CHP2_5 into the SQL buffer. The NEW_TIME function in the following statement returns the current time, converting the time of the system clock, which is on Greenwich mean time (GMT), to Eastern standard time (EST). This is shown in Figure 2.6.

9. Load CHP2_6 into the SQL buffer. This command returns the current time, converting the time of the system clock, which is on GMT, to Central standard time (CST). This is shown in Figure 2.7.

```
SQL> GET C:\CHP2_4.SQL
  1  SELECT
  2      TO_CHAR(DATEFLD,'RM') RM,
  3      TO_CHAR(DATEFLD,'CC') CC,
  4      TO_CHAR(DATEFLD,'HH') HH,
  5      TO_CHAR(DATEFLD,'HH PM') HHPM,
  6      TO_CHAR(DATEFLD,'HH24') HH24,
  7      TO_CHAR(DATEFLD,'MI') MI,
  8      TO_CHAR(DATEFLD,'SS') SS,
  9      TO_CHAR(DATEFLD,'SSSSS') SSSSS
 10  FROM
 11*     SAMPLE2
SQL> /

RM    CC    HH    HHPM        HH24  MI    SS    SSSSS
----- ----- ----- ----------- ----- ----- ----- -----
I     20    11    11 AM       11    23    03    40983

SQL>
```

Figure 2.5 The output of CHP2_4.SQL within SQL*Plus.

```
SQL> GET C:\CHP2_5
  1  SELECT
  2      TO_CHAR(NEW_TIME(DATEFLD,'GMT','EST'),'HH:MI:SS')
  3* FROM SAMPLE2
SQL> /

TO_CHAR(NEW_TIME(DATEFLD,'GMT','EST'),'HH:MI:SS')
-----------------------------------------------------------------
06:23:03

SQL>
```

Figure 2.6 The output of CHP2_5.SQL within SQL*Plus.

```
SQL> GET C:\CHP2_6
  1  SELECT
  2     TO_CHAR(NEW_TIME(DATEFLD,'GMT','CST'),'HH:MI:SS')
  3* FROM SAMPLE2
SQL> /

TO_CHAR(NEW_TIME(DATEFLD,'GMT','CST'),'HH:MI:SS')
------------------------------------------------------------
05:23:03

SQL>
```

Figure 2.7 The output of CHP2_6.SQL within
SQL*Plus.

Notice the one hour difference between the results from CHP2_5.SQL and
CHP2_6.SQL. The NEW_TIME function is important for database
operations that span time zones. Users in Japan, New York, and Hawaii
can get the date and time as it should appear in their individual time
zones.

How It Works

The TO_CHAR function is used to display a date value in a variety of formats.
You can use the format models shown in Table 2.1 to create date output in
almost any conceivable format. The opposite of the TO_CHAR function is the
TO_DATE function. Use the TO_DATE function to convert a character string to
the internal Oracle date format. Step 1 creates the sample table and data used
throughout this How-To. The sample table contains a date column and a single
record, which are queried in the later steps. Steps 2 through 9 present queries
that format the date column to present formatted output.

The NEW_TIME function converts and displays the time portion of a date
value. The valid format models of the `zone_input` and `zone_output` portions of
the function are shown in Table 2.2.

Comments

Date and time values can be formatted easily using the TO_CHAR function. The
power of the function can solve a variety of problems. You can use the date
formatting functions to write numbers as text. A common mistake is to
incorrectly select the date model MM for minutes; use MM only for months.

COMPLEXITY
BEGINNING

2.2 How do I...
Create and use SQL*Plus command files?

Problem

I know I can load a SQL statement into the SQL buffer from the disk using the GET command. I want to run a SQL*Plus command file from SQL*Plus without loading it into the SQL buffer first. This is important because my SQL*Plus command files contain formatting commands and multiple SQL statements. How do I run a SQL command file?

Technique

The START command executes a SQL*Plus command file. The START command can be substituted with the @ symbol, and the commands are interchangeable. When a START command is executed, each statement in the file is executed in order. Errors occurring in the file are displayed, and the file continues to run. SQL*Plus command files can be nested. START commands can be part of SQL*Plus command files to run the contents of other files. The technique of nesting command files can be used to set system variables as the result of queries.

Steps

1. Use CHP2_7.SQL as a SQL*Plus command file to create or replace the sample tables used throughout this chapter. The contents of the file show the structure of a SQL*Plus command file.

```
SET TERMOUT OFF
SPOOL CHP2_7.LOG
DROP TABLE DEPT2_1;
DROP TABLE EMP2_1;
CREATE TABLE DEPT2_1 (
    DEPTNO      NUMBER(6),
    DNAME       VARCHAR2(30));
CREATE TABLE EMP2_1 (
    EMPNO       NUMBER(6),
    ENAME       VARCHAR2(30),
    SALARY      NUMBER(12,2),
    DEPTNO      NUMBER(6));
INSERT INTO DEPT2_1
    VALUES (1, 'MARKETING');
INSERT INTO DEPT2_1
    VALUES (2, 'SALES');
```

continued on next page

continued from previous page

```
INSERT INTO DEPT2_1
    VALUES (3, 'ACCOUNTING');
INSERT INTO EMP2_1
    VALUES (1, 'SMITH, JOHN', 24000,1);
INSERT INTO EMP2_1
    VALUES (2, 'JONES, MARY', 42000,1);
INSERT INTO EMP2_1
    VALUES (3, 'BROWN, BILL', 36000,2);
INSERT INTO EMP2_1
    VALUES (4, 'CONWAY, JIM', 52000,3);
INSERT INTO EMP2_1
    VALUES (5, 'HENRY, JOHN', 22000,3);
INSERT INTO EMP2_1
    VALUES (6, 'SMITH, GARY', 43000,2);
INSERT INTO EMP2_1
    VALUES (7, 'BLACK, WILMA', 44000,2);
INSERT INTO EMP2_1
    VALUES (8, 'GREEN, JOHN', 33000,2);
INSERT INTO EMP2_1
    VALUES (9, 'JONHSON, MARY', 55000,3);
INSERT INTO EMP2_1
    VALUES (10, 'KELLY, JOHN', 20000,2);
COMMIT;
SPOOL OFF
SET TERMOUT ON
```

The first command is a SQL*Plus command that suppresses the output of
the statements when a script runs using the START command. The second
line writes the output generated by the statements to the file specified with
the SPOOL command. The two DROP TABLE statements remove the
sample tables if they already exist. The CREATE TABLE statements build
the sample tables, and the INSERT statements add data to the tables. For
more information on creating and modifying tables, see Chapter 4,
"Tables." The COMMIT statement saves the transactions to the database.
The SPOOL OFF statement stops the writing of the file, and the final
statement resets the TERMOUT system variable to ON.

2. Execute CHP2_7.SQL by using the START command. You must connect
to a database and have the privileges required to create tables. Chapter 3,
"Database Users," covers the creation of user accounts.

```
SQL>  START CHP2_7.sql
SQL>
```

Because the output of the file is suppressed with the first line of the file, no
information is in SQL*Plus when the file runs.

How It Works

The START command substituted with the @ symbol runs a file that can contain
SQL, PL/SQL, and SQL*Plus commands. The statements and commands in the
file are executed by SQL*Plus as if they were typed into SQL*Plus in order. If

you were to take a SQL*Plus command file and enter each line, it would behave exactly as if running the file. The command file CHP2_7.SQL contains SQL statements and SQL*Plus commands. The first line writes the output of the script to file CHP2_7.LOG. The next two lines remove the sample tables, if they exist. If they don't exist, errors will appear; however, you can ignore them. The two CREATE TABLE statements create two sample tables. The INSERT statements put sample data into the tables. The COMMIT statement saves the transactions to the database, and the last command closes the output file.

Comments

When you work with long SQL*Plus scripts, it is often easier to develop the script using a text editor such as Windows Notepad and run it with the START command. Although SQL*Plus has text editing capabilities, they can be difficult to use when working with large statements. If you run CHP2_7.SQL, you must be connected to an Oracle database and have privileges to create tables. If you are not sure what database access you have within your organization, contact your database administrator.

COMPLEXITY
BEGINNING

2.3 How do I...
Save query results and SQL statements to a file?

Problem

I often need to execute SQL statements more than once. When I write a long SQL statement or a SQL statement that I need to run repeatedly, I want to save it to a file so that I can run it later. I also need to write the results of my queries to a file so that I can edit and print their results. How do I save query results and SQL statements to a file?

Technique

One of the most powerful features of SQL*Plus is its capability to write query results, SQL statements, and the feedback from SQL statements to a file. These can be written to files to produce reports, can be imported into spreadsheets, or can run as command files. The results of long-running SQL*Plus scripts can be written to output files and checked later to ensure successful execution. The SPOOL command writes SQL*Plus output to a file. The syntax of the command is

```
SPO[OL] [file_name[.ext]|OFF|OUT]
```

If the full path of the output file is not specified, it is written to your working directory. If an extension is not specified, the extension .LST is appended to the filename. The SPOOL OFF command is used to stop the writing of output and close the file. The SPOOL OUT command stops the writing of the output and sends the output directly to the default printer. This is useful when creating reports with SQL*Plus.

The SQL*Plus SAVE command is used to save the SQL statement currently in the SQL buffer to a file. The SQL buffer contains the most recent SQL statement entered into SQL*Plus or retrieved from a file. As soon as SQL*Plus recognizes a statement as a SQL statement, it replaces the current statement in the SQL buffer with the new statement. Think of the SQL buffer as the Windows Clipboard for SQL*Plus. The SQL buffer can be saved to a file with the SAVE command, retrieved from a file with the GET command, and edited with a variety of SQL*Plus commands.

The syntax of the SAVE command is:

```
SAV[E] filename[.ext] [CRE[ATE]|REP[LACE]|APP[END]]
```

Characters and options shown in brackets ([]) are optional. Options separated with the pipe symbol (|) are exclusive. The default action of the SAVE command is to create a new file. If the file exists, the REPLACE or APPEND keyword is required. By default, SQL*Plus will save the file with the .SQL extension to identify it as a SQL*Plus file. If you want it saved with a different extension, you can specify one when you execute the SAVE command.

NOTE

The SUFFIX system variable can be modified to change the default extension from .SQL to another value. For more information on setting SQL*Plus system variables, see How-To 2.4.

Steps

1. CHP2_8.SQL, shown in Figure 2.8, contains a SQL script that includes the SPOOL command to save the results of a query to a file. The query contained in the file references a table created by CHP2_7.SQL. If you have not executed CHP2_7.SQL to create the sample tables (from How-To 2.2), run the file first using the START command.

The first line of the file contains the SPOOL command that writes the output of the subsequent statements to the file C:\TESTFILE.LST. The following three lines contain a simple query of the DEPT2_1 table created by CHP2_7.SQL. The SPOOL OFF command closes the output file. Execute CHP2_8.SQL with the START command.

```
SPOOL C:\TESTFILE.LST
SELECT DNAME
    FROM DEPT2_1
ORDER BY DNAME;
SPOOL OFF
```

Figure 2.8 CHP2_8.SQL
contains a SQL script
that includes the
SPOOL command.

```
SQL>  START CHP2_8.sql

DNAME
-------------------
MARKETING
ACCOUNTING
SALES
```

When the SQL file is executed, the SPOOL and SPOOL OFF commands
don't generate any output; however, they write the results of the query to
the file.

To save the current command in the SQL buffer, don't end the statement
with a semicolon. If the SQL statement is terminated with a semicolon,
SQL*Plus will attempt to execute it.

```
SQL> SELECT EMPNO, ENAME
2    FROM EMP
3    ORDER BY EMPNO
```

Unlike a SQL*Plus command, SQL statements can span multiple lines
without a line continuation character. The line continuation character for
SQL*Plus commands is the dash (-). You can begin a new line by pressing
[ENTER]. SQL*Plus automatically numbers the lines as they are entered. If
[ENTER] is pressed on an empty line, SQL*Plus returns to the SQL prompt.
The SQL statement entered remains in the SQL buffer until it is cleared,
replaced with another SQL statement, or SQL*Plus is exited.

2. Save the file with the SAVE command. If successful, SQL*Plus will notify
you that the file was created.

```
SQL> SAVE EMPQRY
Created file EMPQRY
```

The file is automatically created in the current working directory with the
.SQL extension. You can specify a complete path including a different
extension for the file. If the file already exists, an error message will be
returned.

3. Because a SQL*Plus command file can contain multiple SQL statements, the APPEND option enables you to add the contents of the SQL buffer to the end of an existing file. Save the contents of the SQL buffer to the same file with the SAVE command and the APPEND option.

```
SQL> SAVE EMPQRY APPEND
Appended file to empqry
```

If the file does not exist when an attempt to append to it is made, the file will be created.

How It Works

The SPOOL command is used within SQL*Plus to write the output generated to a file. CHP2_8.SQL demonstrates the process. The first line opens the file C:\TESTFILE.LST and instructs SQL*Plus to write a copy of all output to this file. Until spooling is stopped, all statements entered or displayed on the screen are written to the file. The last statement, SPOOL OFF, stops the spooling of the file and closes the file.

The SQL*Plus SAVE command is a SQL*Plus command (not a SQL statement). Executing it does not replace the contents of the SQL buffer. If the SAVE command is executed against Oracle using a different tool, an error will occur. Step 1 creates a SQL statement but does not execute it. Step 2 saves the contents of the SQL buffer created in Step 1 to a file using the SAVE command. Step 3 appends the contents of the SQL buffer to the end of an existing file by including the APPEND option with the SAVE command.

Comments

Writing the output of a query to a file is the basis for developing reports using SQL*Plus. Using the SPOOL command is an easy way to redirect output from SQL*Plus to a file. Many of the How-To's throughout the book use the SPOOL command.

When statements are entered into the SQL buffer, SQL*Plus expects only SQL or PL/SQL statements. SQL*Plus commands will not be saved in the SQL buffer. If you want the SQL script to contain formatting statements, use the INPUT command, which places all statements in the SQL buffer and does not analyze the statements as they are entered. Don't put a semicolon at the end of the SQL statement when using the INPUT command, or an error will occur.

COMPLEXITY
BEGINNING

2.4 How do I...
View and modify SQL*Plus system variables?

Problem

I know there are many SQL*Plus system variables and that these variables control the behavior of SQL*Plus. I often need to see the value of a variable and, if necessary, change it. How do I view and modify the values of the SQL*Plus system variables?

Technique

You can use the SHOW command to view the values of SQL*Plus system variables. The ALL keyword makes SQL*Plus show the value of all 68 system variables. System variables are changed with the SET command. Any system variable can be changed, and it will retain its new value throughout the SQL*Plus session.

Steps

1. View the values of the system variables by executing the SHOW ALL command. The trailing portion of the output is shown in Figure 2.9.

```
serveroutput OFF
showmode OFF
spool OFF
sqlcase MIXED
sqlcode 0
sqlcontinue "> "
sqlnumber ON
sqlprefix "#" (hex 23)
sqlprompt "SQL> "
sqlterminator ";" (hex 3b)
suffix "SQL"
tab ON
termout ON
time OFF
timing OFF
trimout ON
trimspool OFF
ttitle OFF and is the 1st few characters of the next SELECT statement
underline "-" (hex 2d)
user is "WAITE"
verify ON
wrap : lines will be wrapped
SQL> |
```

Figure 2.9 The result of the SHOW ALL command.

2. Display the value of a single system variable by replacing the ALL keyword with the name of the variable to display.

```
SQL>  SHOW FLUSH
flush ON
```

3. Change the value of the FLUSH system variable with the SET command. The FLUSH system variable can have the values ON or OFF. To change the value to OFF, execute the SET command specifying the system variable and the new value.

```
SQL>  SET FLUSH OFF
SQL>
```

How It Works

The SHOW and SET commands are the two commands used to maintain SQL*Plus system variables. Most system variables are restricted to specific values. If an attempt is made to change a system variable to an invalid value, an error is returned. Step 1 uses the SHOW ALL command to display all 68 system variables. Step 2 specifies a single system variable to display using the SHOW command. Step 3 uses the SET command to change the value of a system variable.

Comments

When the values of SQL*Plus system variables are changed, they are only changed for the duration of the current session. If SQL*Plus is exited, all the system variables will return to their default settings the next time SQL*Plus is started. If there are certain settings you want to change every time SQL*Plus is used, you can place them in a file and execute with the START command.

COMPLEXITY
ADVANCED

2.5 How do I...
Prompt users for substitution variables?

Problem

In many cases, I don't know the information I want to use in my SQL scripts but can get the information at runtime. I need to create my own user-defined variables that I can reference throughout my script. How do I prompt users for substitution variables?

Technique

User-defined variables can be created in SQL*Plus using the ACCEPT command. The execution of the script is halted, and the user is prompted to enter a value for the variable. After the user enters the value, the execution of the script continues at the line following the statement. When created, any references to the user-defined variable are replaced with the value entered. The format of the ACCEPT command is:

```
ACCEPT VARIABLE
```

After a user-defined variable has been created using either of these methods, it can be used throughout the SQL*Plus session by prefixing the variable name with an ampersand (&). The user will not be prompted for the value of the variable again, even if it is used as a substitution variable.

Steps

1. CHP2_9.SQL, shown in Figure 2.10, uses a complex method for defining user-defined variables.

The first line of the script sets the HEADING system variable to OFF to suppress the output of the headings generated by the query. The SPOOL statement contained in the second line opens a temporary file that is later executed. Lines 3 and 4 create a DEFINE statement using the result of a query of the DUAL table to dynamically generate a statement. The SPOOL OFF statement in line 5 terminates the creation of the temporary file. The SET HEADING ON statement restores the headings for subsequent queries. The last statement executes the temporary file using the START command. After the ACCEPT statement is executed, the variable can be used in other statements. Execute CHP2_9.SQL using the START command.

```
SQL>  START CHP2_9.sql
```

```
SET ECHO OFF
SET FEEDBACK OFF
SET HEADING OFF
SPOOL TEMP.SQL
SELECT 'DEFINE MYDATE = '||SYSDATE
     FROM DUAL;
SPOOL OFF
SET HEADING ON
START TEMP
```

Figure 2.10 CHP2_9.SQL contains a complex method for defining user-defined variables.

When this script is executed, the net result is that the MYDATE user-defined variable gets populated with the results of a query. If an error is returned from the SPOOL OFF statement, it might be ignored. The statement shown in the output of the query is executed by the START command in the last line of the script.

2. Use the MYDATE user-defined variable in a statement. Any reference to &MYDATE in a SQL statement or SQL*Plus command will be replaced with a string containing a system date.

```
SQL>  SELECT '&MYDATE' FROM DUAL;

'01-FEB-98
----------
01-FEB-98
```

How It Works

The first line of CHP2_9.SQL turns off the column headings for the next few statements. The second line uses the SPOOL command to create a file called TEMP.SQL. The SPOOL OFF command stops output to the TEMP.SQL file and closes the file. The command START TEMP runs the temporary command file to prompt the user for the MYDATE substitution variable. Because user-defined variables exist for the life of the SQL*Plus session, when Step 2 is executed, the user is not prompted for a value for &MYDATE.

Comments

This technique is invaluable for queries that are run several times with different search or select conditions. Instead of writing a new script each time a new value is needed, you can simply prompt the user at runtime.

COMPLEXITY
ADVANCED

2.6 How do I...
Pass parameters to a SQL*Plus script?

Problem

I have a script that pauses for users to enter substitution variables. I would like to pass values for the substitution variables on the command line so that the script does not prompt me to enter values. I need these parameters to be referenced throughout the script. How do I pass parameters to a SQL*Plus script?

Technique

User-defined variables, explained in How-To 1.5, can be passed as parameters on the command line. The execution of the script is not halted, and any references to the user-defined variables are replaced with the values passed. Several parameters can be passed in one command. The format of passing parameters is:

```
SQLPLUS USERNAME/PASSWORD PARAMETER1 [PARAMETER2 PARAMETER3 … ]
```

After a user-defined variable has been created using either of these methods, it can be used throughout the SQL*Plus session by prefixing the variable name with an ampersand (&). The user will not be prompted for the value of the variable again, even if it is used as a substitution variable.

Steps

1. CHP2_10.SQL, shown in Figure 2.11, uses two substitution variables to represent the owner and uses extents. The two variables can be defined by passing parameters.

The script can then be run, passing two parameters:

```
SQL> @CHP2_10 WAITE 5
```

The CHP2_10 script will replace the substitution variables in the order the parameters are passed. Thus, &1 is replaced with WAITE, and &2 is replaced with 5. The script will then display all objects owned by the WAITE with five or more extents.

How It Works

The command START or @ will call a script, passing any parameters along. If there are fewer parameters than there are substitution variables, execution is stopped until the user enters values for all remaining parameters. If there are extraneous parameters, the SQL script simply ignores them. The parameters are assigned to substitution variables in the order they are passed: &1 is replaced by the first parameter, &2 is replaced by the second parameter, and so on.

```
SELECT SEGMENT_NAME, EXTENTS
FROM DBA_SEGMENTS
WHERE OWNER = '&1' AND
      EXTENTS >= &2;
|
```

Figure 2.11 CHP2_10.SQL can be run with two parameters passed.

Comments

This technique is useful for writing scripts that call other scripts, passing values automatically. Operating-specific scripts can also be developed to pass environment variables into SQL scripts. This can be important for automatic monitoring scripts and maintenance scripts.

COMPLEXITY
INTERMEDIATE

2.7 How do I...
Use SQL*Plus as a report writer?

Problem

I am often called on to develop quick reports for top management. The query portion of the report is the most complicated part. I need to format the output of the query so it can be printed as a report. I know SQL*Plus has many report formatting functions. What are they and how do I use them?

Technique

SQL*Plus can be used as a reporting tool. SQL*Plus contains a complete set of formatting commands. System variables can be set to control the behavior of SQL*Plus while the report runs. In this section, you will go through the steps required to format a report. Because a report generated in SQL*Plus contains many SQL*Plus statements, it will be much easier to develop the report using Windows Notepad. Although SQL*Plus can be used to edit a SQL statement, I don't recommend it for complicated scripts.

Steps

1. Run SQL*Plus and connect as the WAITE user account. Execute CHP2_7.SQL, using the START command to create the sample tables used in this How-To.

```
SQL> START CHP2_7.sql
SQL>
```

2. Launch Windows Notepad and create the SQL statement that is the basis for the report. The SQL statement shown in Figure 2.12 is the basis for the report presented in this How-To.

Save the file to the working directory of SQL*Plus. Use the START command to run the SQL command file. Figure 2.13 displays the unformatted output of CHP2_11.SQL in SQL*Plus.

```
SELECT DEPT2_1.DEPTNO,
       DEPT2_1.DNAME,
       EMP2_1.EMPNO,
       EMP2_1.ENAME,
       EMP2_1.SALARY
FROM DEPT2_1, EMP2_1
WHERE
       EMP2_1.DEPTNO = DEPT2_1.DEPTNO
ORDER BY
       DEPT2_1.DEPTNO,
       EMP2_1.EMPNO;
```

Figure 2.12 CHP2_11.SQL
contains the query that is the
basis for the report.

```
SQL> START C:\CHP2_11.SQL

  DEPTNO DNAME                              EMPNO ENAME
--------- ----------------------------  --------- --------------------
        1 MARKETING                           1 SMITH, JOHN
        1 MARKETING                           2 JONES, MARY
        2 SALES                               3 BROWN, BILL
        2 SALES                               6 SMITH, GARY
        2 SALES                               7 BLACK, WILMA
        2 SALES                               8 GREEN, JOHN
        2 SALES                              10 KELLY, JOHN
        3 ACCOUNTING                          4 CONWAY, JIM
        3 ACCOUNTING                          5 HENRY, JOHN
        3 ACCOUNTING                          9 JOHNSON, MARY
SQL> |
```

Figure 2.13 The unformatted output of CHP2_11.SQL.

Because no formatting commands have been executed, the output is
unacceptable as a report. The next step formats the columns of the report.

3. Change the column headings to descriptions that are more meaningful to
the user. Column headings are formatted in SQL*Plus using the COLUMN
command. Insert these lines at the beginning of the file:

```
COLUMN DEPTNO FORMAT 9999 HEADING "Dept"
COLUMN DNAME FORMAT A15 HEADING "Department|Name"
COLUMN EMPNO FORMAT 9999 HEADING " "
COLUMN ENAME FORMAT A15 HEADING "Employee|Name" TRUNCATE
COLUMN SALARY FORMAT $999,999 HEADING "Salary"
```

CHP2_12.SQL shows the script as it should look after this step. Carefully
note the different formats a column can have. DEPTNO and EMPNO are
formatted as four-digit numbers; SALARY is formatted as money
containing a dollar sign and commas. DNAME and ENAME are formatted
as 15-character text strings. The TRUNCATE clause at the end of the
COLUMN command for the ENAME column truncates the output if it is
longer than 15 characters; otherwise, the output would be wrapped within

a 15-character column. The `Employee|Name` heading contains the heading separator character. This causes the heading to be printed as:

```
Employee
Name
```

You can view the current value of the heading separator character with the SHOW HEADSEP command.

4. Save the file and run it with the START command. Figure 2.14 shows the output of CHP2_12.SQL with formatted columns.

The output is starting to look very much like a report. In the next step, a title is added to the beginning and end of each page, and the row count at the end of the query is removed.

5. Add the commands to provide a title for the report. CHP2_13.SQL contains the script as it will look after this step. The title can be printed at the bottom or top of each page by using the BTITLE and TTITLE commands, respectively. The following commands are added to the beginning of the file to create a top and bottom title:

```
TTITLE CENTER 'Salary Report' SKIP 1 LINE
BTITLE LEFT 'Page: ' format 999 sql.pno
SET LINESIZE 80
SET FEEDBACK OFF
```

The TTITLE command creates a title for the top of each page. The SKIP 1 LINE clause makes the report skip one line after printing the title. The CENTER clause centers the title, based on the width of the line represented by the LINESIZE system variable. If the title requires multiple lines, they are appended to the TTITLE command. For example:

```
TTITLE CENTER 'Salary Report' SKIP 1 LINE LEFT 'CHAP2-SQL'
```

```
SQL> START C:\CHP2_12.SQL

          Department          Employee
Dept Name                     Name                 Salary
---- ----------------  ----- -----------------  ----------
   1 MARKETING             1 SMITH, JOHN        $24,000
   1 MARKETING             2 JONES, MARY        $42,000
   2 SALES                 3 BROWN, BILL        $36,000
   2 SALES                 6 SMITH, GARY        $43,000
   2 SALES                 7 BLACK, WILMA       $44,000
   2 SALES                 8 GREEN, JOHN        $33,000
   2 SALES                10 KELLY, JOHN        $20,000
   3 ACCOUNTING            4 CONWAY, JIM        $52,000
   3 ACCOUNTING            5 HENRY, JOHN        $22,000
   3 ACCOUNTING            9 JONHSON, MARY      $55,000
SQL>
```

Figure 2.14 The output of CHP2_12.SQL in SQL*Plus.

centers the Salary Report line, skips one line, and left-justifies CHAP2-SQL on the next line. The BTITLE command creates a title for the bottom of each page. The `sql.pno` variable used in this statement always represents the current page number. The SET LINESIZE 80 command sets the width of the line to 80 characters. The SET FEEDBACK OFF command eliminates the row count from the end of the query.

6. Save the file and run the script to generate the report as it looks after Step 5. Figure 2.15 shows the output of CHP2_12.SQL after the titles are created for the report.

The output of the query is beginning to look like a report. In the next step, common data are grouped together to give the report a more pleasing appearance.

7. Add the lines required to group repeating values within SQL*Plus. In the query, data is ordered by DEPTNO and DNAME. In the output of the query, there is repeating DEPTNO and DNAME data. The BREAK command groups together repeating occurrences of values. Adding the following statements to the file will group the output on the DEPTNO and DNAME fields. CHP2_13.SQL shows how the script will look after this step.

BREAK ON DEPTNO ON DNAME ON REPORT SKIP 1

The SKIP 1 clause leaves a blank line in the report after each grouping. You can vary the number of lines skipped or change the number to SKIP 1 PAGE to move to the top of a new page after each data group.

8. Save the file and run the report to show the results after the last step. Figure 2_16 shows the output of CHP2_13.SQL within SQL*Plus.

```
                              Salary Report

CHAP2-SQL
        Department             Employee
Dept Name                      Name              Salary
---- ----------------  -----  ---------------  ---------
   1 MARKETING             1  SMITH, JOHN       $24,000
   1 MARKETING             2  JONES, MARY       $42,000
   2 SALES                 3  BROWN, BILL       $36,000
   2 SALES                 6  SMITH, GARY       $43,000
   2 SALES                 7  BLACK, WILMA      $44,000
   2 SALES                 8  GREEN, JOHN       $33,000
   2 SALES                10  KELLY, JOHN       $20,000
   3 ACCOUNTING            4  CONWAY, JIM       $52,000
   3 ACCOUNTING            5  HENRY, JOHN       $22,000
   3 ACCOUNTING            9  JONHSON, MARY     $55,000
```

Figure 2.15 The output of CHP2_12.SQL containing titles and formatted output.

```
                                Salary Report
CHAP2-SQL
       Department                Employee
Dept Name                        Name              Salary
----- ----------------  -----   ----------------  --------
    1 MARKETING              1   SMITH, JOHN        $24,000
                            2   JONES, MARY        $42,000
    2 SALES                  3   BROWN, BILL        $36,000
                            6   SMITH, GARY        $43,000
                            7   BLACK, WILMA       $44,000
                            8   GREEN, JOHN        $33,000
                           10   KELLY, JOHN        $20,000
    3 ACCOUNTING             4   CONWAY, JIM        $52,000
                            5   HENRY, JOHN        $22,000
                            9   JONHSON, MARY      $55,000
```

Figure 2.16 The output of CHP2_13.SQL
containing additional formatting.

In the next step, the salaries are totaled for each of the departments and a grand total calculated for the report.

9. Add the lines required to provide totals and subtotals. The COMPUTE command enables calculations to be created for grouped data. The following statement calculates the sum of the SALARY column for each distinct occurrence of DEPTNO and generates a grand total for the report. The CHP2_14.SQL file contains the final results of this operation.

```
COMPUTE SUM OF SALARY ON DEPTNO REPORT
```

10. Save the file and run the report. Figure 2.17 shows the final output of this process.

In addition to calculating the sum of columns, the group calculations shown in Table 2.3 can be performed.

Table 2.3 Compute functions

COMPUTE CLAUSE	RESULTS
AVG	Average.
COUNT	Count, not NULL columns only.
MAX	The largest value.
MIN	The smallest value.
STD	The standard deviation.
SUM	The sum.
VAR	The variance.
NUM	Count, including NULL columns.

```
                              Salary Report

CHAP2-SQL
          Department                Employee
   Dept Name                        Name                Salary
   ----- -----------------   -----  -----------------  ----------
       1 MARKETING               1 SMITH, JOHN          $24,000
                                 2 JONES, MARY          $42,000
                                                      ----------
   ***** ***************
   sum                                                  $66,000
       2 SALES                   3 BROWN, BILL          $36,000
                                 6 SMITH, GARY          $43,000
                                 7 BLACK, WILMA         $44,000
                                 8 GREEN, JOHN          $33,000
                                10 KELLY, JOHN          $20,000
   ***** ***************
   sum                                                 $176,000
       3 ACCOUNTING              4 CONWAY, JIM          $52,000
                                 5 HENRY, JOHN          $22,000
                                 9 JONHSON, MARY        $55,000
   ***** ***************
   sum                                                 $129,000
                                                      ----------
   sum                                                 $371,000
   Page:     1
   SQL> |
```

Figure 2.17 Running CHP2_14.SQL shows the
results of the report creation process.

How It Works

A report created with SQL*Plus can be a large query formatted using SQL*Plus
commands and controlled with system variables. Table 2.4 contains the commands used most often in formatting reports.

Table 2.4 Report formatting commands

COMMAND	DEFINITION
BREAK ON	Controls where spaces are placed between sections and where to break for subtotals and totals.
BTITLE	Sets the bottom title for each page of the report.
COLUMN	Sets the heading and format of a column.
COMPUTE	Makes SQL*Plus compute a variety of totals.
REMARK	Identifies the words that follow as comments.
SAVE	Saves the contents of the SQL buffer to a file.
SET LINESIZE	Sets the width of a line in characters for the report.
SET NEWPAGE	Sets the number of lines between pages of a report.
SPOOL	Tells SQL*Plus to write output to a file.
START	Tells SQL*Plus to execute a file.
TTITLE	Sets the title for each page of the report.

Step 1 creates the sample tables that are queried in the How-To. Step 2 presents a query that is formatted in the How-To. Steps 3 and 4 use the COLUMN command to format the columns retrieved by the query. Steps 5 and 6 use the TTITLE and BTITLE commands to create titles for the report. Steps 7 and 8 use the BREAK command to group common data together. Steps 9 and 10 use the COMPUTE command to create subtotals and totals for the report.

Comments

SQL*Plus is a valid tool for creating reports using the Oracle database. In many cases, you will end up using SQL*Plus to prototype the SQL statement used in your report writer.

COMPLEXITY
INTERMEDIATE

2.8 How do I...
Use SQL*Plus to write repetitive scripts?

Problem

I need to run a SQL statement for each table in the database. It is a great deal of work to type in a statement for each table. I know that I can save the results of a query to a file and that I can run a file. How do I use SQL*Plus to write repetitive scripts?

Technique

The data dictionary contains just about everything you ever wanted to know about the structure of your database. Oracle enables you to concatenate text using the concatenation operator. By concatenating the keywords required by the statement you want to add to the query output, you can build a series of SQL statements based on a query. Because any string can be concatenated with the results of a query, the output of the query can be forced into the format of a SQL statement.

Steps

1. Run SQL*Plus and connect as the WAITE user account. Remove the column headings. A heading can be suppressed by setting the HEADING system variable to OFF.

```
SQL> SET HEADING OFF
SQL>
```

2. Remove the row count feedback by setting the FEEDBACK system variable to OFF. The FEEDBACK variable controls the row count displayed at the end of a query. The extra line of information will cause an error in the SQL script. Execute a SET command to turn off row feedback.

```
SQL>  SET FEEDBACK OFF
SQL>
```

3. Widen the output line. SQL*Plus attempts to make it easier to read the output of a query by wrapping the lines. When creating a SQL statement with a query, the default line length might be too small. The LINESIZE system variable determines the length of a line. The maximum value of LINESIZE is operating-system–dependent. In Microsoft Windows, the maximum value is 32,000.

```
SQL>  SET LINESIZE 132
SQL>
```

4. Construct the query that creates SQL statements. To do this, concatenate the keywords the statement requires to the table name as it is retrieved from the database. Figure 2.18 shows CHP2_15.SQL, which contains a query. Run the query once to check for syntax errors before writing the output to a file. Running the statement verifies the output.

Because there are no column headings and no row count, the output is a sequence of SQL statements without the undesirable statements.

5. Write the output to a file. The SPOOL command is used to create the output file.

```
SQL>  SPOOL CMDS.SQL
SQL>
```

```
SET HEADING OFF
SET FEEDBACK OFF
SELECT 'DROP TABLE '||TABLE_NAME||';'
   FROM USER_TABLES;
```

Figure 2.18 CHP2_15.SQL contains a query that creates SQL statements.

SQL*Plus commands, query results, and SQL*Plus feedback are written to the CMDS.SQL file. When spooling begins, only statements that produce SQL statements are desired. Be sure to execute all necessary SQL*Plus commands prior to executing the SPOOL command. Unfortunately, there will be a couple undesired lines because the slash and the SPOOL OFF commands are written to the file. These lines will create runtime errors, which can be ignored, or you can use any text editor to remove the unwanted lines from the file.

6. Execute the SQL statement from CHP2_15.SQL. This time when the query is executed, the results will be written to the CMDS.SQL file.

```
SQL>  /
```

7. Stop writing to the file by executing the SPOOL OFF command. SPOOL OFF stops the spooling operation and closes the output file.

```
SQL>  SPOOL OFF
```

A file that runs like a SQL*Plus command file is created. Figure 2.19 shows the results of the operation.

How It Works

Every SQL statement begins with keywords—such as SELECT COUNT(*) FROM, DROP TABLE, or INSERT INTO—and ends with a semicolon. The string concatenation function (||) enables static text to be combined with the query output to create a SQL statement. The capability of SQL*Plus to write query output to a text file and execute the file enables you to dynamically build SQL scripts as the output from a query. Step 1 suppresses the headings usually displayed by the query. Step 2 suppresses the row count feedback displayed at the end of a query. Step 3 widens the length of the line to ensure that the output fits on a single line. Step 4 creates and runs a query to create the desired SQL statements. Step 5 begins writing the output of the query to a file. Step 6 runs the query, and Step 7 ends the spooling process.

```
DROP TABLE DEPT2_1;
DROP TABLE EMP2_1;
DROP TABLE SAMPLE2;
```

Figure 2.19 The results of the query.

Comments

Using SQL*Plus to create SQL commands is a very useful feature. If you look to this technique whenever you need to execute a large number of statements on the database, you will greatly increase your productivity. This technique is used in many places throughout the book.

CHAPTER 3
DATABASE USERS

3

DATABASE USERS

How do I...

What good is an application if nobody can use it? The management of user accounts and roles is fundamental to the development and maintenance of multiuser database applications. Each person using an Oracle database must have a user account. Users should not share accounts, and each user account should have a password to protect the database from unauthorized access. A *privilege* is the permission to perform a task on the database or to access another user's database object. A *system privilege* enables the user to perform an action, such as create a session or create a table. An *object privilege* enables the user to access a specific object such as a table, view, or stored procedure. Within an organization, people perform different functions. A *role* is a group of related privileges that can be granted to user accounts as a single privilege. The structure of roles within Oracle enables database security to be modeled around the organization. A role can be defined at a high level, such as a person using the system, or at a more detailed level, such as an accountant, payroll clerk, or supervisor. Within a production system, user accounts and roles are usually managed by the database administrator.

3.1 Create a User Account

Users are the reason applications are developed. Creating user accounts is a fundamental task in delivering a new application. This How-To takes you through the steps of creating a new Oracle user account.

3.2 Grant and Determine User Disk Quotas

Disk space is a limited resource. In environments where users or developers can create their own data objects, it is important to restrict the amount of disk space a user account's objects can occupy. This How-To explores the method used to restrict a user account's disk space.

3.3 Summarize Basic User Account Information

Many times, it is important to learn the various attributes of a user account: the date the account was created, the date and time that the password will expire, the date that the account was locked, the default profile, the default and temporary tablespaces, and other attributes. This How-To guides you through the steps to find information on a particular user account.

3.4 Determine Who Is Logged On

One of the most frequent tasks of an Oracle database administrator is learning which users are connected to the database at any given time. This How-To shows you how to determine who is logged on.

3.5 Kill a User's Session

Is it possible to kill a user's session with SQL*Plus? Although the Session Manager is perfectly capable of performing this task, you might not always want to leave SQL*Plus to kill a session. This How-To demonstrates the power of SQL*Plus by using it to query the active sessions on the database and terminate a user's session.

3.6 Determine User Defaults

When a user connects to the database, the session acquires specific default privileges and system limitations. Also, both permanent and temporary objects the user creates are placed in default tablespaces. This How-To describes the technique for determining these user defaults.

3.7 Determine User System Privileges

As a part of maintaining user accounts, it is necessary to determine which system privileges have been granted to them. User accounts can be granted privileges directly or through roles. This How-To presents methods for identifying the system privileges and roles granted to a user account.

3.8 Determine User Object Privileges

Each user account can be set up to have different SELECT, INSERT, UPDATE, DELETE, and ALTER privileges to any or all objects in the database. For security reasons, it is important to know which objects can be viewed or modified by which users. This How-To shows you the method for determining user object privileges.

3.9 Create, Modify, and Associate User Profiles

User account defaults and profiles define the default location of database objects and the quantity of usable database resources. This How-To covers the management of user defaults and the creation and assignment of user profiles.

COMPLEXITY

BEGINNING

3.1 How do I...
Create a user account?

Problem

After developing my application, I need to create user accounts for the people who will use it. I also want to create user accounts within the development environment to test my application with different sets of privileges. How do I create a new user account in Oracle?

Technique

The CREATE USER statement is used to create a new user account in an Oracle database. User accounts can be created by using SQL*Plus. This How-To focuses on using SQL*Plus to create user accounts because it is portable across all database platforms. In this How-To, you will create user accounts that appear throughout the examples here and later in this chapter. The syntax of the CREATE USER statement is shown in Figure 3.1.

```
CREATE USER username
    {{IDENTIFIED [BY password] | EXTERNALLY } |
        DEFAULT TABLESPACE tablespace |
        TEMPORARY TABLESPACE tablespace |
        QUOTA integer ON tablespace
        PROFILE profile }
```

Figure 3.1 CREATE USER syntax.

The CREATE USER statement is a SQL statement and ends with a semicolon. The DEFAULT TABLESPACE clause identifies where objects created by the user account will reside if a tablespace is not specified in the CREATE statement. The TEMPORARY TABLESPACE clause identifies where temporary data will reside when required by operations performed by the user account. The QUOTA clause, which can occur many times within the statement, specifies the amount of disk space the user account's objects can occupy in a given tablespace. The PROFILE clause identifies the profile the user account uses to control resources available, such as the number of concurrent sessions and the maximum CPU time per call.

Steps

1. Run SQL*Plus and connect as the WAITE user account created by the installation script. Load CHP3_1.SQL into the SQL buffer. The file contains a CREATE USER statement to create a new user account.

```
SQL> GET CHP3_1.sql
  1  CREATE USER FRED
  2*     IDENTIFIED BY NEWUSER
```

Line 1 contains the CREATE USER keywords and specifies the name of the new user account. The IDENTIFIED BY clause contained in line 2 specifies the password required when the user account connects to the database. Because no modifying clauses are specified, the user account is created with default properties. Although the user account is created, it has no permission to do anything with the database. How-To 3.7 covers how to determine privileges of user accounts.

2. Execute the statement to create the user account.

```
SQL> /

User Created.
```

3. Load CHP3_2.SQL into the SQL buffer. The file contains a DROP USER statement to remove the user account FRED from the system.

```
SQL> GET CHP3_2.sql
  1* DROP USER FRED
```

Line 1 contains the DROP USER keywords and specifies the user account to be removed. If the user account owns database objects, the CASCADE clause must be specified to remove all the user account's objects from the database. An example of this would be DROP USER FRED CASCADE.

4. Run CHP3_2.SQL to remove the user account.

```
SQL> /

User dropped.
```

How It Works

The CREATE USER statement is used to create new user accounts in the database. Executing the CREATE USER statement does not create an account that can use an application or even connect to the database. The user account must be granted system privileges to use the system and object privileges to access database objects. The DROP USER statement is used to remove a user account from the system. If the user account owns objects, the CASCADE clause must be included to remove the objects owned by the user account. A user account cannot be removed if objects remain. Steps 1 and 2 create a new user account, and Steps 3 and 4 remove the account.

Comments

The SQL*Plus method for creating user accounts is important because it is portable across all platforms. If you create a large number of user accounts, you might find it easier to create the statements in Windows Notepad or another text editor and run all the statements as a single script. Roles define a group of related privileges. When creating a new user account, keep in mind that it has no privileges until they are granted. Privileges can be granted directly to a user account or indirectly through roles. The file CHP3_1.SQL contains all the statements required to build the user accounts used in this chapter. The examples later in this chapter assume these user accounts exist. How-To's 3.2, 3.7, 3.8, and 3.9 describe how to grant privileges to user accounts.

COMPLEXITY
INTERMEDIATE

3.2 How do I...
Grant and determine user disk quotas?

Problem

Some developers in my organization like to create huge tables when they test their applications. Because we have a limited amount of space in the database, I need to limit the amount of disk space a user account can occupy. How can I restrict a user account's disk space?

Technique

The QUOTA clause of the ALTER USER statement is used to restrict the disk space of an existing user account. The disk space can be restricted for a new user account by specifying a QUOTA clause in the CREATE USER statement. A user account is restricted storage by tablespace.

Steps

1. Run SQL*Plus and connect to the database as the WAITE user account. CHP3_3.SQL, shown in Figure 3.2, contains three ALTER USER statements to restrict disk usage in the SYSTEM tablespace.

The three CREATE USER statements create the user accounts that will be restricted by the ALTER USER statements. The user account WILMA is restricted to 10MB, BETTY to 500KB, and BARNEY to 100,000 bytes in the SYSTEM tablespace.

2. Execute CHP3_3.SQL to create the user accounts and restrict their disk space.

```
SQL>  START CHP3_3.sql

User created.

User created.

User created.

User altered.

User altered.

User altered.
```

How It Works

The QUOTA clause of the CREATE USER and ALTER USER statements limits the amount of disk space a user account's objects can occupy. The first three statements in CHP3_3.SQL create user accounts that will be restricted by the following statements. The first ALTER USER account restricts the WILMA user account to 10MB, represented with the statement 10M. The user account BETTY is restricted to 500KB, represented by 500K. If M or K is not specified, the statement interprets the value in bytes. The BARNEY user account is restricted to 100,000 bytes.

```
CREATE USER WILMA IDENTIFIED BY NEWUSER;
CREATE USER BETTY IDENTIFIED BY NEWUSER;
CREATE USER BARNEY IDENTIFIED BY NEWUSER;

ALTER USER WILMA
        QUOTA 10M ON SYSTEM;
ALTER USER BETTY
        QUOTA 500K ON SYSTEM;
ALTER USER BARNEY
        QUOTA 100000 ON SYSTEM;
```

Figure 3.2 CHP3_3.SQL creates three user accounts and restricts their disk usage.

Comments

Creating disk quotas is mainly an issue for developers and users running decision support applications that create summary tables. The UNLIMITED TABLESPACE privilege gives a user account unlimited space within all tablespaces and ignores the quotas placed on the user account. For example, ALTER USER WILMA QUOTA UNLIMITED ON SYSTEM would give the WILMA user account unlimited space on the SYSTEM tablespace, and GRANT UNLIMITED TABLESPACE TO WILMA would give unlimited space on all tablespaces to the WILMA user account.

COMPLEXITY
BEGINNING

3.3 How do I...
Summarize basic user account information?

Problem

I need to see information on each user in the database, including the date the account was created, the date and time that the password will expire, the date that the account was locked, the default profile, and the default and temporary tablespaces. How do I summarize basic user account information?

Technique

The DBA_USERS view contains information on all accounts. By querying the DBA_USERS view, you can obtain various attributes of each user account.

Steps

1. Run SQL*Plus and connect as the WAITE user account. Run the CHP3_4.SQL script, shown in Figure 3.3. By executing the script, you will see basic user account information for each user account of the Oracle database. Figure 3.4 shows a sample output from the CHP3_4.SQL script.

```
SELECT USERNAME, ACCOUNT_STATUS, LOCK_DATE, EXPIRY_DATE,
       DEFAULT_TABLESPACE, TEMPORARY_TABLESPACE, CREATED, PROFILE
FROM DBA_USERS;
```

Figure 3.3 CHP3_4.SQL can obtain basic user account information.

```
USERNAME                            ACCOUNT_STATUS                      LOCK_DATE
----------------------------------  ----------------------------------  ----------
EXPIRY_DA DEFAULT_TABLESPACE                    TEMPORARY_TABLESPACE
--------- ------------------------------------  ------------------------------------
CREATED   PROFILE
--------- ------------------------------------
WAITE                               OPEN
          USER_DATA                             TEMPORARY_DATA
20-AUG-97 DEFAULT

DEMO                                OPEN
          USER_DATA                             TEMPORARY_DATA
13-FEB-97 DEFAULT

SCOTT                               OPEN
          USER_DATA                             TEMPORARY_DATA
13-FEB-97 DEFAULT

SQL> |
```

Figure 3.4 Sample output from the CHP3_4.SQL script.

How It Works

The CHP3_4.SQL script queries the DBA_USERS view, reporting on user account information.

For the DBA_USERS view, the USERNAME column contains the username of the account.

The ACCOUNT_STATUS column shows whether an account is OPEN, LOCKED, or EXPIRED. An OPEN account enables the user to log on to the database. A LOCKED account prevents the user from logging on to the database until the lock is removed by a database administrator. An account becomes locked either manually by the database administrator or when a user enters an incorrect password more times than the defined limit allows. An EXPIRED account will not enable a user to log on to the database until the password is changed. An account is set to EXPIRED when the password for the user account goes for a defined amount of time without changing.

The LOCK_DATE column contains the date and time that the user has been locked out of the database. A null value indicates that the user has not been locked out.

The EXPIRY_DATE column contains the date and time that the password for the user account will expire. The user must change the password before the EXPIRY_DATE, or he or she will not be able to connect to the database. This column is derived from adding the date and time that the password was last changed to the number of days required before a password change must occur.

The DEFAULT_TABLESPACE column contains the tablespace that all objects created by the user account will be placed in, unless otherwise specified.

The TEMPORARY_TABLESPACE column contains the tablespace that will be used to create temporary sorting tables. These temporary tables are created when a user issues a statement with a GROUP BY, ORDER BY, or another group function and the sort area for the user is not large enough to process the statement.

The CREATED column contains the date and time that the user account was created.

The PROFILE column contains the profile to which the user account is assigned. The DEFAULT profile is used by all users unless defined otherwise.

Comments

The PASSWORD column, not included in the CHP3-4.SQL script, contains the encoded password for the user account. It is impossible to decode the password, but it can be set in another user account. This is done by using the VALUES clause of the ALTER USER *USERNAME* IDENTIFIED BY command.

In the CHP3_4.SQL script, only the date portion of the date fields are being returned. You can also retrieve the time portion using `TO_CHAR(EXPIRY_DATE, 'DD-MON-YY HH:MI:SS')` or `TO_CHAR(CREATE_DATE, 'DD-MON-YY HH:MI:SS')`. For the majority of cases, the time is not needed.

The DEFAULT_TABLESPACE should not be SYSTEM, except for the SYS user. If the DEFAULT_TABLESPACE is set to SYSTEM for a user account, any object created by that user without specifying a tablespace will be created in SYSTEM. Only vital data dictionary objects should be placed in the SYSTEM tablespace.

COMPLEXITY

INTERMEDIATE

3.4 How do I...
Determine who is logged on?

Problem

I need to see which users are logged on to the database. If possible, I would also like to see more information on those users, such as name and program. How do I determine who is logged on?

Technique

By querying the V$SESSION view, you can determine who is logged on, as well as information such as the time of logon, the program running, and the operating system username. The V$SESSION view, which is owned by the SYS user account, can be viewed with any user that has been granted DBA, such as the WAITE account.

Steps

1. Run SQL*Plus and connect as the WAITE user account. Run the CHP3_5.SQL script, shown in Figure 3.5. This shows all users currently logged on to the database. The output of the script is shown in Figure 3.6.

```
COLUMN USERNAME FORMAT A10
COLUMN SCHEMANAME FORMAT A15
COLUMN PROGRAM FORMAT A15
SELECT USERNAME, SCHEMANAME, PROGRAM, LOGON_TIME, OSUSER, STATUS
FROM V$SESSION;
```

Figure 3.5 CHP3_5.SQL shows the current users logged on to the database.

USERNAME	SCHEMANAME	PROGRAM	LOGON_TIM	OSUSER	STATUS
	SYS	ORACLE80.EXE	28-OCT-97	UNKNOWN	ACTIVE
	SYS	ORACLE80.EXE	28-OCT-97	UNKNOWN	ACTIVE
	SYS	ORACLE80.EXE	28-OCT-97	UNKNOWN	ACTIVE
	SYS	ORACLE80.EXE	28-OCT-97	UNKNOWN	ACTIVE
	SYS	ORACLE80.EXE	28-OCT-97	UNKNOWN	ACTIVE
	SYS	ORACLE80.EXE	28-OCT-97	UNKNOWN	ACTIVE
	SYS		28-OCT-97		ACTIVE
WAITE	WAITE		28-OCT-97		ACTIVE
SQL>					

Figure 3.6 Sample output from CHP3_5.SQL.

How It Works

The V$SESSION is a dynamic virtual table that holds information about each user logged on. By issuing a SELECT query against this virtual table, various aspects about each user account can be determined. The system username, the schema that the user is connected to, the date and time the user logged on, the program running (if any are applicable), and the operating system username can all be found in this virtual table.

The WAITE user has SELECT privileges to this view through the DBA permissions. Oracle keeps track of each user as they log on and off the database. The Monitor Session option in Server Manager runs off the V$SESSION view, and it can also be queried from within SQL*Plus.

Comments

When querying the V$SESSION view to determine the number of users, be sure to note that background processes, as well as the user issuing the query itself, are included in the total.

If the status column appears as KILLED, that session is marked by the database to be removed. Locks, memory, and all other resources held by that session will be released when the background processes remove the session from the database.

COMPLEXITY
ADVANCED

3.5 How do I...
Kill a user's session?

Problem

When developing applications, I have occurrences of runaway and unwanted processes. When a query runs for an unacceptable amount of time, I want to terminate the process. When I get a call from a user or developer wanting a session killed, I don't want to leave SQL*Plus. How can I kill a user's session using SQL*Plus?

Technique

To kill a user's session using SQL*Plus, you must be connected to the database as a user with the ALTER SYSTEM privilege. The SYS and SYSTEM users have this privilege by default. The V$SESSION view contains information about sessions connected to the database. Figure 3.7 and Figure 3.8 show the description of the V$SESSION view in SQL*Plus.

The V$SESSION view can be queried to find out what sessions a user has running on the database. The ALTER SYSTEM KILL USER statement is used to terminate a user's session through SQL*Plus. It requires the session identifier (SID) and the process serial number as part of the command.

```
SQL> DESC V$SESSION
 Name                                      Null?    Type
 ----------------------------------------- -------- ----
 SADDR                                              RAW(4)
 SID                                                NUMBER
 SERIAL#                                            NUMBER
 AUDSID                                             NUMBER
 PADDR                                              RAW(4)
 USER#                                              NUMBER
 USERNAME                                           VARCHAR2(30)
 COMMAND                                            NUMBER
 TADDR                                              VARCHAR2(8)
 LOCKWAIT                                           VARCHAR2(8)
 STATUS                                             VARCHAR2(8)
 SERVER                                             VARCHAR2(9)
 SCHEMA#                                            NUMBER
 SCHEMANAME                                         VARCHAR2(30)
 OSUSER                                             VARCHAR2(15)
 PROCESS                                            VARCHAR2(9)
 MACHINE                                            VARCHAR2(64)
 TERMINAL                                           VARCHAR2(16)
 PROGRAM                                            VARCHAR2(64)
 TYPE                                               VARCHAR2(10)
 SQL_ADDRESS                                        RAW(4)
```

Figure 3.7 The first screen of the V$SESSION data dictionary view description.

```
SQL_HASH_VALUE                 NUMBER
PREV_SQL_ADDR                  RAW(4)
PREV_HASH_VALUE                NUMBER
MODULE                         VARCHAR2(48)
MODULE_HASH                    NUMBER
ACTION                         VARCHAR2(32)
ACTION_HASH                    NUMBER
CLIENT_INFO                    VARCHAR2(64)
FIXED_TABLE_SEQUENCE           NUMBER
ROW_WAIT_OBJ#                  NUMBER
ROW_WAIT_FILE#                 NUMBER
ROW_WAIT_BLOCK#                NUMBER
ROW_WAIT_ROW#                  NUMBER
LOGON_TIME                     DATE
LAST_CALL_ET                   NUMBER
PDML_ENABLED                   VARCHAR2(3)
FAILOVER_TYPE                  VARCHAR2(13)
FAILOVER_METHOD                VARCHAR2(10)
FAILED_OVER                    VARCHAR2(3)

SQL>
```

Figure 3.8 The second part of the V$SESSION
data dictionary view description.

Steps

1. Run SQL*Plus and connect as the SYS or SYSTEM user account. Load
CHP3_6.SQL into the SQL buffer with the GET command. The file
contains a SQL statement that can be used to determine session
information for a user. The USERNAME column identifies which user
owns the session. Determine the SID and serial number for the session to
be killed.

```
SQL> GET CHP3_6.sql
  1  SELECT SID, SERIAL#, STATUS
  2     FROM V$SESSION
  3*    WHERE USERNAME = 'WAITE'
```

Line 1 returns the SID, serial number, and status of the session. Line 2
specifies the V$SESSION data dictionary view as the source of the query.
Line 3 causes records to be returned only for the WAITE user account.

2. Run the query to return the active connections.

```
SQL> /

SID   SERIAL# STATUS
----- ------- ------
  9         3 ACTIVE
 11        26 INACTIVE
```

The output from the query gives the information needed in the next step
to kill the process.

Notice that the STATUS column was queried. This column is important
because a user can have more than one session, and only the right one
should be terminated. A common example of multiple sessions is when
Oracle Reports creates a separate session any time a report is run.

3. Load CHP3_7.SQL into the SQL buffer. The ALTER SYSTEM statement contained in the file contains the KILL SESSION keywords to kill an Oracle session.

```
SQL> GET CHP3_7.sql
  1  ALTER SYSTEM
  2*   KILL SESSION '&sid,&serial'
```

Line 1 contains the ALTER SYSTEM keywords required to kill an Oracle session through SQL*Plus. Line 2 contains the KILL SESSION option and specifies the SID and serial number with the &SID and &SERIAL substitution variables.

4. Run the statement supplying the SID and serial number of the session to be killed for the &SID and &SERIAL substitution variables.

```
SQL> /
Enter value for sid: 11
Enter value for serial: 26
old   2:     kill session '&sid, &serial'
new   2:     kill session '11,26'

System Altered
```

After the statement has been executed, the session is terminated.

How It Works

The V$SESSION view is a virtual performance view. It is constantly changing as the dynamics of the system change. There are many of these views that can be queried at any time. Many performance monitoring tools regularly query these views to provide online monitoring of the system. The ALTER SYSTEM statement enables a user with the ALTER SYSTEM privilege to make changes to the system immediately. As soon as this statement is executed, the user's session will be killed. Steps 1 and 2 query the V$SESSION view to get information about the session to be killed. The SID and SERIAL# columns are required to kill a session with the ALTER SYSTEM statement. Steps 3 and 4 execute an ALTER SYSTEM statement to kill the session.

Comments

Unwanted or runaway sessions can steal CPU and other system resources from your system. Terminating processes through SQL*Plus is one of the ways to keep them from robbing your system of performance. It is important to develop a strategy for monitoring process utilization and performance. The V$ views enable you to create your own programs for monitoring database resources.

COMPLEXITY
INTERMEDIATE

3.6 How do I...
Determine user defaults?

Problem

When a user connects to the database, the session acquires specific default privileges and system limitations. When any new objects such as tables are created, they are put into the users default tablespace. Also, any sorting processes that need temporary objects are placed in default tablespaces. How do I determine user defaults?

Technique

By querying the DBA_USERS view, you can determine the temporary tablespace, the default tablespace, and the assigned profile.

Steps

1. Execute the CHP3_8.SQL script, shown in Figure 3.9, to query the DBA_USERS view. When prompted, enter the username for whom you want to determine the user default. Figure 3.10 shows a sample result.

How It Works

Each user has several defaults that are assigned when the user logs on to the database. The TEMPORARY_TABLESPACE column of the DBA_USERS view determines where temporary sort segments will be created by Oracle in the

```
COLUMN PROFILE FORMAT A10
COLUMN TEMPORARY_TABLESPACE FORMAT A22
SELECT USERNAME, TEMPORARY_TABLESPACE, DEFAULT_TABLESPACE, PROFILE
FROM DBA_USERS
WHERE USERNAME = '&USERNAME';|
```

Figure 3.9 CHP3_8.SQL determines user defaults.

```
SQL> START C:\CHP3_8.SQL
Enter value for username: WAITE
old    3: WHERE USERNAME = '&USERNAME'
new    3: WHERE USERNAME = 'WAITE'

USERNAME    TEMPORARY_TABLESPACE    DEFAULT_TABLESPACE          PROFILE
----------  ----------------------  --------------------------  ----------
WAITE       TEMPORARY_DATA          USER_DATA                   DEFAULT
SQL> |
```

Figure 3.10 Sample results of running the CHP3_8.SQL script.

event that memory cannot be allocated into the sort area. The size of the temporary segments will be determined by the default storage parameters defined for the temporary tablespace.

The DEFAULT_TABLESPACE column of the DBA_USERS view determines where objects are stored when created by the user without specifying another tablespace. All objects are stored in the DEFAULT_TABLESPACE location, with the exception of functions, stored procedures, and packages. These are always stored within the data dictionary in the SYSTEM tablespace.

The PROFILE column of the DBA_USERS view determines which profile is assigned to a user. The profile stores all limitations to the user, such as disk space, CPU quotas, and maximum connection time.

Comments

The process of creating, modifying, and associating user profiles is discussed in How-To 3.9. Granting and determining user disk quotas are explained in How-To 3.2.

COMPLEXITY
INTERMEDIATE

3.7 How do I...
Determine user system privileges?

Problem

Because a user account's privileges are the sum of its directly granted privileges and its role privileges, it's hard to tell whether a user account has a specific privilege. How do I determine which system privileges have been granted to a user account?

Technique

The DBA_ROLE_PRIVS view contains the roles granted to user accounts, and the DBA_SYS_PRIVS view contains system privileges granted to user accounts. The ROLE_SYS_PRIVS view can be used with the other views to calculate the effective privileges of a user account. Figure 3.11 describes the data dictionary views within SQL*Plus.

Steps

1. Run SQL*Plus and connect as the WAITE user account. CHP3_9.SQL, shown in Figure 3.12, creates the sample user accounts and roles used throughout both this How-To and How-To 3.9.

```
SQL> DESC DBA_SYS_PRIVS
 Name                              Null?    Type
 ------------------------------    -------- ----
 GRANTEE                           NOT NULL VARCHAR2(30)
 PRIVILEGE                         NOT NULL VARCHAR2(40)
 ADMIN_OPTION                               VARCHAR2(3)

SQL> DESC ROLE_SYS_PRIVS
 Name                              Null?    Type
 ------------------------------    -------- ----
 ROLE                              NOT NULL VARCHAR2(30)
 PRIVILEGE                         NOT NULL VARCHAR2(40)
 ADMIN_OPTION                               VARCHAR2(3)

SQL>
```

Figure 3.11 User system privileges data dictionary views.

The first statement creates the TERRI user account with a CREATE USER statement. The second statement creates the ROOFER role, and the third statement creates the DEPT3_1 table. The first GRANT statement grants all privileges on the DEPT3_1 table to the TERRI user account. The second GRANT statement grants the CONNECT and RESOURCE default roles, along with the ROOFER role, to the TERRI user account. Run the file to create the sample objects.

SQL> START CHP3_9.sql

User created.

Role created.

Table created.

Grant succeeded.

Grant succeeded.

```
CREATE USER TERRI IDENTIFIED BY NEWUSER;

CREATE ROLE ROOFER;

CREATE TABLE DEPT03 (
     DEPT_NO     NUMBER(5),
     DEPT_NAME   VARCHAR2(30));

GRANT ALL ON DEPT03 TO TERRI;

GRANT CONNECT, RESOURCE, ROOFER TO TERRI;
|
```

Figure 3.12 CHP3_9.SQL creates the sample objects used in this How-To.

2. Load CHP3_10. SQL into the SQL buffer. The file contains a query used to determine the system privileges granted directly to a user.

```
SQL> GET CHP3_10.sql
  1  SELECT PRIVILEGE, ADMIN_OPTION
  2     FROM SYS.DBA_SYS_PRIVS
  3* WHERE GRANTEE = '&GRANTEE'
```

Line 1 returns the PRIVILEGE granted to the user account, along with the ADMIN_OPTION column. Line 2 specifies the SYS.DBA_SYS_PRIVS data dictionary view as the source of the query. Line 3 returns data for the user account specified by the &GRANTEE substitution variable.

3. Execute the query for the TERRI user account, and replace the &GRANTEE substitution variable with TERRI.

```
SQL> /
Enter value for GRANTEE: TERRI

PRIVILEGE                                ADM
------------------------------------     ---
UNLIMITED TABLESPACE                     NO
```

The only system privileges granted to TERRI are from the CONNECT and RESOURCE system roles. This produces only the UNLIMITED TABLESPACE privilege in the DBA_SYS_PRIVS view, which does not accurately represent TERRI's system privileges. The ROLE_SYS_PRIVS view must be included in the query to show system privileges granted through roles.

4. Load CHP3_11. SQL (shown in Figure 3.13) into the SQL buffer with the GET command. The file contains a statement that queries privileges from both the DBA_SYS_PRIVS and ROLE_SYS_PRIVS views. The DBA_ROLE_PRIVS view is used to determine which roles the user account has been granted.

```
SELECT PRIVILEGE, ADMIN_OPTION
FROM
   DBA_SYS_PRIVS
WHERE
   GRANTEE = '&GRANTEE'
UNION
SELECT PRIVILEGE, ROLE_SYS_PRIVS.ADMIN_OPTION
   FROM
   ROLE_SYS_PRIVS, DBA_ROLE_PRIVS
WHERE
   ROLE_SYS_PRIVS.ROLE = DBA_ROLE_PRIVS.GRANTED_ROLE AND
   DBA_ROLE_PRIVS.GRANTEE = '&GRANTEE'
ORDER BY 1
```

Figure 3.13 CHP3_11.SQL queries privileges from both the DBA_SYS_PRIVS and ROLE_SYS_PRIVS views.

Lines 1 through 5 return the system privileges granted directly to a user account by querying the DBA_SYS_PRIVS data dictionary view. Lines 7 through 12 return system privileges granted to the user account through roles. The UNION operator in line 6 connects the two queries to generate a single result.

5. Execute the statement for the TERRI user account by replacing the &GRANTEE substitution variable with TERRI each time you are prompted to do so. Because the system privileges provided by the CONNECT and RESOURCE roles display, the output of the query is more useful in determining the privileges of the user account. Figure 3.14 shows the execution of this step in SQL*Plus.

6. Load the file CHP3_12.SQL into the SQL buffer. The file contains a query used to determine the roles granted to a user account. The DBA_ROLE_PRIVS view contains roles granted to user accounts. The DBA_ROLE_PRIVS view was used in Step 4 to determine the system privileges provided to a user account through a role.

```
SQL> GET CHP3_12.sql
  1   SELECT GRANTED_ROLE, DEFAULT_ROLE
  2      FROM DBA_ROLE_PRIVS
  3*  WHERE GRANTEE = '&GRANTEE'
```

Line 1 returns the role granted to the user account and its status as a default role. If a role is a default role, it is enabled automatically when the user account connects to the database. Line 2 specifies the DBA_ROLE_PRIVS data dictionary view as the source of the query. Line 3 specifies the user account granted access to the role with the &GRANTEE substitution variable.

7. Execute the query for the TERRI user account by specifying TERRI for the substitution variable.

```
PRIVILEGE                                       ADM
----------------------------------------------- ---
ALTER SESSION                                   NO
CREATE CLUSTER                                  NO
CREATE DATABASE LINK                            NO
CREATE PROCEDURE                                NO
CREATE SEQUENCE                                 NO
CREATE SESSION                                  NO
CREATE SYNONYM                                  NO
CREATE TABLE                                    NO
CREATE TRIGGER                                  NO
CREATE TYPE                                     NO
CREATE VIEW                                     NO
UNLIMITED TABLESPACE                            NO

12 rows selected.

SQL>
```

Figure 3.14 The system privileges granted to a user account.

```
SQL>  /
Enter value for 1: TERRI

GRANTED_ROLE                 DEF
--------------------------   ---
CONNECT                      YES
RESOURCE                     YES
ROOFER                       YES
```

CHP3_13.sql contains a SQL*Plus report to print all system privileges granted directly or indirectly to a user account. The report can be run by executing a START command.

```
COLUMN OBJECT FORMAT A20 HEADING 'OBJECT/PRIV'
COLUMN PRIVILEGE FORMAT A10
COLUMN A FORMAT A6 HEADING ' ' TRUNCATE
COLUMN B FORMAT A6 HEADING ' ' TRUNCATE
COLUMN C FORMAT A6 HEADING ' ' TRUNCATE
COLUMN D FORMAT A6 HEADING ' ' TRUNCATE
COLUMN E FORMAT A6 HEADING ' ' TRUNCATE
COLUMN F FORMAT A6 HEADING ' ' TRUNCATE
COLUMN G FORMAT A6 HEADING ' ' TRUNCATE
SELECT PRIVILEGE OBJECT,
  DECODE(ADMIN_OPTION,'YES','ADMIN',NULL) A,
  NULL B, NULL C, NULL D, NULL E, NULL F, NULL G
FROM
  DBA_SYS_PRIVS
WHERE
   GRANTEE = '&&GRANTEE'
UNION
  SELECT PRIVILEGE OBJECT,
  DECODE(ROLE_SYS_PRIVS.ADMIN_OPTION,'YES','ADMIN',NULL) A,
      NULL B, NULL C, NULL D, NULL E, NULL F, NULL G
FROM
    ROLE_SYS_PRIVS, DBA_ROLE_PRIVS
   WHERE
     ROLE_SYS_PRIVS.ROLE = DBA_ROLE_PRIVS.GRANTED_ROLE AND
     DBA_ROLE_PRIVS.GRANTEE = '&&GRANTEE'
GROUP BY UP.OWNER, UP.TABLE_NAME
   ORDER BY 1;
```

8. Run the report for the TERRI user account. Figure 3.15 shows the results of the operation in SQL*Plus.

How It Works

Step 1 creates the user account, role, and table used throughout this How-To. Steps 2 and 3 list the system roles granted directly to a user account by querying DBA_SYS_PRIVS. The query used in Steps 4 and 5 includes the system privileges provided by roles granted to the user account. Steps 6 and 7 list the roles granted to a user account. Step 8 presents and runs the CHP3_13.SQL file, which displays a report of all privileges granted to a user account either directly or through roles.

```
OBJECT/PRIV
-----------------------------------------------------------------------
ALTER SESSION
CREATE CLUSTER
CREATE DATABASE_LINK
CREATE PROCECDURE
CREATE SEQUENCE
CREATE SESSION
CREATE TABLE
CREATE TRIGGER
CREATE VIEW
UNLIMITED TABLESPACE
DEPT03             ALTER  INDEX  SELECT  INSERT  UPDATE  DELETE  REFERE

12 rows selected.

SQL>
```

Figure 3.15 The output of the formatted query contained in CHP3_13.SQL.

Comments

The data dictionary views provide information about privileges granted to a user account. Most views used in this How-To are DBA views. There is a complete set of corresponding USER views that enable a user account to query its own privileges. USER_ROLE_PRIVS contains roles granted to the user account, and USER_SYS_PRIVS contains system privileges granted to a user account.

COMPLEXITY
INTERMEDIATE

3.8 How do I...
Determine user object privileges?

Problem

I want to determine what object privileges have been granted to a user account. Because a user account's object privileges are the sum of its directly granted privileges and its role privileges, it's hard to tell whether a user account has a specific object privilege, such as SELECT, INSERT, UPDATE, DELETE, and ALTER. How do I determine the user's object privileges?

Technique

The DBA_TAB_PRIVS view contains object privileges granted directly to user accounts. The ROLE_TAB_PRIVS view can be used with other views to calculate the effective object privileges of a user account. Determining the privileges granted to a role can become complicated when role grants become nested. If roles have not been granted other roles, it is easy to determine the privileges granting a role provides. This How-To discusses both possibilities.

Steps

1. Run SQL*Plus and connect as the WAITE user account. CHP3_9.SQL creates the sample user accounts and roles used in this How-To. The script is explained in How-To 3.8. If you have not done so already, run the file to create the sample objects.

```
SQL> START CHP3_9.sql

User created.

Role created.

Table created.

Grant succeeded.

Grant succeeded.
```

2. Load CHP3_14.SQL into the SQL buffer. The file contains a query used to determine the object privileges granted directly to a user account. The DBA_TAB_PRIVS view contains all object privileges granted directly to user accounts.

```
SQL>  GET CHP3_14.sql
  1    SELECT OWNER ||'.'|| TABLE_NAME OBJECT,
  2        PRIVILEGE FROM
  3        DBA_TAB_PRIVS
  4*   WHERE GRANTEE = '&GRANTEE'
```

Line 1 concatenates the owner of the object and the object name to return the object in the format most often used to represent it. Line 2 returns the privilege granted to the object. Line 3 specifies the DBA_TAB_PRIVS data dictionary view as the source of the query. Line 4 specifies the user account granted the privileges with the &GRANTEE substitution variable.

3. Execute the query for the TERRI user account by replacing the &GRANTEE substitution variable with TERRI. The TERRI user account has been granted privileges directly on the table, so the DBA_TAB_PRIVS view contains data for the user account. If all object privileges were granted to the user account through roles, the query would return no rows.

```
SQL>  /
Enter value for 1: TERRI

OBJECT                          PRIVILEGE
-----------------------------   ----------------------------
WAITE.DEPT03                    DELETE
WAITE.DEPT03                    INDEX
```

continued on next page

continued from previous page

WAITE.DEPT03	INSERT
WAITE.DEPT03	SELECT
WAITE.DEPT03	UPDATE
WAITE.DEPT03	REFERENCES
WAITE.DEPT03	ALTER

7 rows selected.

4. Load CHP3_15.SQL (shown in Figure 3.16) into the SQL buffer with the GET command. This file contains a query used to determine object privileges granted to the user account through roles.

Line 1 returns the owner and table name on which the user account was granted privileges through a role. ROLE_TAB_PRIVS and DBA_ROLE_PRIVS views are specified in line 3 as the source of the query. The WHERE clause in lines 4 through 6 joins the views and returns only records specified by the &GRANTEE substitution variable.

5. Execute the query for the TERRI user account by replacing the &GRANTEE substitution variable in both locations with TERRI. The user account's privileges are listed one per row, making the output difficult to read. CHP3_16.SQL, shown in the next step, formats the data as an easy-to-read report.

```
SQL> /
Enter value for grantee: TERRI
old    6:      DP.GRANTEE = '&GRANTEE'
new    6:      DP.GRANTEE = 'TERRI'
Enter value for grantee: TERRI
old   12:      UP.GRANTEE = '&GRANTEE'
new   12:      UP.GRANTEE = 'TERRI'

no rows selected
```

6. CHP3_16.SQL contains a SQL*Plus report to print all privileges granted directly or indirectly to a user account. The report can be run by executing a START command.

```
SELECT RP.OWNER||'.'||RP.TABLE_NAME, PRIVILEGE
FROM
   ROLE_TAB_PRIVS RP, DBA_ROLE_PRIVS DP
WHERE
   RP.ROLE = DP.GRANTED_ROLE AND
   DP.GRANTEE = '&GRANTEE'
```

Figure 3.16 CHP3_15.SQL determines object privileges granted to the user through roles.

```
COLUMN OBJECT FORMAT A20 HEADING 'OBJECT/PRIV'
COLUMN PRIVILEGE FORMAT A10
COLUMN A FORMAT A6 HEADING ' ' TRUNCATE
COLUMN B FORMAT A6 HEADING ' ' TRUNCATE
COLUMN C FORMAT A6 HEADING ' ' TRUNCATE
COLUMN D FORMAT A6 HEADING ' ' TRUNCATE
COLUMN E FORMAT A6 HEADING ' ' TRUNCATE
COLUMN F FORMAT A6 HEADING ' ' TRUNCATE
COLUMN G FORMAT A6 HEADING ' ' TRUNCATE
SELECT RP.OWNER ||'.'|| RP.TABLE_NAME OBJECT,
      DECODE(SUM(DECODE(PRIVILEGE,'ALTER',1,0)),1,'ALTER',NULL) A,
      DECODE(SUM(DECODE(PRIVILEGE,'INDEX',1,0)),1,'INDEX',NULL) B,
      DECODE(SUM(DECODE(PRIVILEGE,'SELECT',1,0)),1,'SELECT',NULL)
C,
      DECODE(SUM(DECODE(PRIVILEGE,'ALTER',1,0)),1,'INSERT',NULL)
D,
      DECODE(SUM(DECODE(PRIVILEGE,'UPDATE',1,0)),1,'UPDATE',NULL)
E,
      DECODE(SUM(DECODE(PRIVILEGE,'DELETE',1,0)),1,'DELETE',NULL)
F,
DECODE(SUM(DECODE(PRIVILEGE,'REFERENCE',1,0)),1,'REFERENCE',NULL)
G
  FROM
     ROLE_TAB_PRIVS RP, DBA_ROLE_PRIVS DP
 WHERE
   RP.ROLE = DP.GRANTED_ROLE AND
   DP.GRANTEE = '&&GRANTEE'
   GROUP BY RP.OWNER, RP.TABLE_NAME
UNION
 SELECT
UP.OWNER ||'.'|| UP.TABLE_NAME,
    DECODE(SUM(DECODE(PRIVILEGE,'ALTER',1,0)),1,'ALTER',NULL) A,
    DECODE(SUM(DECODE(PRIVILEGE,'INDEX',1,0)),1,'INDEX',NULL) B,
    DECODE(SUM(DECODE(PRIVILEGE,'SELECT',1,0)),1,'SELECT',NULL) C,
    DECODE(SUM(DECODE(PRIVILEGE,'ALTER',1,0)),1,'INSERT',NULL) D,
    DECODE(SUM(DECODE(PRIVILEGE,'UPDATE',1,0)),1,'UPDATE',NULL) E,
    DECODE(SUM(DECODE(PRIVILEGE,'DELETE',1,0)),1,'DELETE',NULL) F,
    DECODE(SUM(DECODE(PRIVILEGE,'DELETE',1,0)),1,'REFERENCE',NULL)
G
  FROM
    DBA_TAB_PRIVS UP
  WHERE
    UP.GRANTEE = '&&GRANTEE'
  GROUP BY UP.OWNER, UP.TABLE_NAME
  ORDER BY 1;
```

Run the report for the TERRI user account. Figure 3.17 shows the results of the operation in SQL*Plus.

How It Works

Step 1 creates the user account, role, and table used throughout this How-To. Steps 2 and 3 list the object privileges granted directly to a user account by

```
old  13:     DP.GRANTEE = '&&GRANTEE'
new  13:     DP.GRANTEE = 'TERRI'
old  28:     UP.GRANTEE = '&&GRANTEE'
new  28:     UP.GRANTEE = 'TERRI'

OBJECT/PRIV
-------------------- ------ ------ ------ ------ ------ ------ ------
WAITE.DEPT83         ALTER  INDEX  SELECT INSERT UPDATE DELETE REFERE

SQL>
```

Figure 3.17 The output of the formatted query contained in CHP3_16.SQL.

querying DBA_TAB_PRIVS. Steps 4 and 5 include object privileges granted to the user account through roles. Step 6 presents and runs the CHP3_15.SQL file, which displays a report of all object privileges granted to a user account either directly or through roles.

Comments

The data dictionary views provide information about privileges granted to a user account. Most views used in this How-To are DBA views. There is a complete set of corresponding USER views that enable a user account to query its own privileges. USER_TAB_PRIVS contains the object privileges granted to the connected user account. USER_ROLE_PRIVS contains roles granted to the user account.

COMPLEXITY
INTERMEDIATE

3.9   How do I...
Create, modify, and associate user profiles?

Problem

When I create user accounts in the database, they have some high limits on the amount of CPU time they can use and the number of sessions to which they can connect. When a user or developer creates a table, it is created in an undesirable location. How can I create, modify, and associate user profiles?

Technique

The PROFILE clause in the CREATE USER and ALTER USER statements enables a profile to be specified for user accounts. A profile restricts the use of database resources for user accounts assigned to it. The CREATE PROFILE statement creates a new profile. The syntax of the CREATE PROFILE statement is shown in Figure 3.18.

```
CREATE PROFILE profile LIMIT
   { SESSION_PER_USER            { integer | UNLIMITED | DEFAULT } |
     CPU_PER_SESSION             { integer | UNLIMITED | DEFAULT } |
     CPU_PER_CALL                { integer | UNLIMITED | DEFAULT } |
     CONNECT_TIME                { integer | UNLIMITED | DEFAULT } |
     IDLE_TIME                   { integer | UNLIMITED | DEFAULT } |
     LOGICAL_READS_PER_SESSION   { integer | UNLIMITED | DEFAULT } |
     LOGICAL_READS_PER_CALL      { integer | UNLIMITED | DEFAULT } |
     COMPOSITE_LIMIT             { integer | UNLIMITED | DEFAULT } |
     IDLE_TIME                   { integer | UNLIMITED | DEFAULT } |
     PRIVATE_SGA                 { integer } }
```

Figure 3.18 The syntax of the CREATE PROFILE statement.

After a profile has been created, it can be assigned to new user accounts with the PROFILE clause of the CREATE USER statement. It can also be assigned to existing user accounts by executing an ALTER USER statement.

The default tablespace specifies where data objects will be created when the location is not specified in a CREATE statement. The temporary tablespace specifies the tablespace used when temporary storage is required by an operation the user account executes. The ALTER USER statement is used to change the default tablespace and the temporary tablespace of a user account. The syntax of the ALTER USER statement is shown in Figure 3.19.

Steps

1. Run SQL*Plus and connect as the WAITE user account. The CREATE PROFILE privilege is required to perform this step. Any user account with the DBA role has this privilege. Load CHP3_17.SQL into the SQL buffer with the GET command. The statement contained in CHP3_17.SQL creates a profile restricting the number of concurrent sessions a user account can have connected to the database. Because no other parameters are specified, they are assumed to be the default.

```
SQL> GET CHP3_17.sql
  1   CREATE PROFILE WAITE_PROFILE
  2*      LIMIT SESSIONS_PER_USER 4
```

Line 1 contains the CREATE PROFILE keywords and specifies the name of the profile to be created. Line 2 limits the number of sessions per user account to four.

```
ALTER USER name
  { PROFILE profilename |
    DEFALT TABLESPACE tablespace |
    TEMPORARY TABLESPACE tablespace |
    IDENTIFIED BY new_password }
```

Figure 3.19 The syntax of the ALTER USER statement.

2. Run the statement from the SQL buffer.

```
SQL>  /

Profile created.
```

3. Load CHP3_18.SQL into the SQL buffer. The file contains an ALTER USER statement to assign the new profile to the WAITE user account.

```
SQL> GET CHP3_18.sql
  1   ALTER USER WAITE
  2*      PROFILE WAITE_PROFILE
```

Line 1 contains the ALTER USER keywords, and line 2 contains the PROFILE clause to specify a new profile.

4. Execute the statement to modify the user account.

```
SQL>  /

User Altered
```

The WAITE user account is limited to four concurrent sessions by the profile.

How It Works

A profile limits resources allocated to a user account. A profile is like a role in that it groups user accounts into defined categories. A profile can be created by any user account with the CREATE PROFILE privilege and is assigned to a user account with a CREATE USER or ALTER USER statement. Steps 1 and 2 create a profile limiting the number of concurrent connections of a user account to four. Steps 3 and 4 assign the new profile to the WAITE user account.

Comments

A profile should be created for users and developers within the database. When developing applications, a developer might have many concurrent connections, which can drain resources.

CHAPTER 4
TABLES

4

TABLES

How do I...

Tables are the fundamental data storage objects within a relational database. Without tables, your applications would have no need for Oracle or any relational database. Tables are composed of one or more columns, which define what type of data may be stored, and whether the data is a string of characters, a number, a date, a binary object, or an external file. Tables may relate to each other, bound by common columns, which define Oracle as a relational database.

This chapter covers the creation and manipulation of tables within Oracle. Most likely, the Data Definition Language (DDL) statements used to manipulate production database tables in your organization are maintained and executed by the database administrator. Techniques used to design and build tables are important to both application developers and database administrators.

4.1 Create a Table

The most basic and important elements of a database are tables. Usually, all data used by applications and user accounts are stored within tables. This How-To explains the steps and syntax needed to create a regular table.

4.2 Determine All of the Tables Owned by a Particular User

Applications can contain many tables, and there can be several applications within a database. With many users and tables in an Oracle database, it is important to know which users own which tables. This How-To explains the methods used to determine which tables are owned by a particular user.

4.3 Put Comments on a Table and its Columns

Comments can be stored in the data dictionary to describe tables and their columns. The data dictionary is the set of internal Oracle tables that define everything within the database environment. Comments should always be stored in the data dictionary to provide a central repository for information about the schema. The better the database is documented, the easier future maintenance of the applications will be. This How-To covers the process of creating comments on tables and columns.

4.4 Recreate CREATE TABLE Statements

After a table has been altered a few times, the original scripts used to create it may look nothing like the table in production. The best way to re-create the scripts needed to rebuild a table is to query the data dictionary. This How-To covers the task of building CREATE TABLE statements from the data dictionary using SQL*Plus.

4.5 Determine a Table's Initial Size Parameters

Before creating a table, it is important to determine how much storage space will be needed, as well as knowing how quickly and how large the table will eventually grow. Without this information, performance on the table may be adversely affected. Also, storage for the table may be either wasted or not enough. This How-To takes you through the steps of determining a table's initial size parameters.

4.6 Use the ANALYZE Command to Determine Access Statistics

Oracle's Cost Based Optimizer can greatly improve query performance. Objects must have statistics gathered for the CBO to work. This How-To shows the steps needed to use the ANALYZE command to gather statistics on database objects.

4.7 Create a Table from Another Table

Tables can be created from a query of one or more other tables or views. The table can be populated with data when it is created. This How-To covers the methods used to create a table as the result of a query.

4.8 Interpret the Format of ROWID

ROWIDs are pseudo-columns of Oracle tables that are used to quickly access records. They contain information such as file, block, and object location, and uniquely identify records within a table. This How-To describes the ROWID formats and shows how to interpret the ROWID format.

4.9 Create an Index-Organized Table

One option to improve performance of accessing a table that would have a primary key is to create an index-organized table. These tables are stored like an index in the B-tree structure. This limits some Oracle capabilities on the table, but improves speed and saves storage. This How-To describes the process of creating an index-organized table and discusses its advantages and disadvantages.

4.10 Partition a Table

Oracle provides partitioned tables, a powerful feature that allows for greater storage flexibility and table availability. This How-To covers the methods used to create a partitioned table.

COMPLEXITY
BEGINNING

4.1 How do I...
Create a table?

Problem

I am just starting to create my database and need objects to put my data into. How do I create a table?

Technique

Tables are the fundamental part of every database. They contain columns that define how data is to be kept and formatted. The CREATE TABLE command is used to create tables. There are numerous options for this command, and this How-To will focus on the creation of a regular, stand-alone table. The comments section will describe some additional options for the CREATE TABLE command. The basic syntax for creating a table is shown in Figure 4.1.

Steps

1. Connect to SQL*Plus as the Waite user account. Run the CHP4_1.SQL script, shown in Figure 4.2, to create a sample table.

```
SQL> /

Table Created.
```

2. To see the description of the table, enter DESC TABLE_NAME.

```
SQL> DESC EMPLOYEE04
Name                    Null?      Type
-----------------       ---------  ----
EMPLOYEE_NAME           NOT NULL   VARCHAR2(30)
SALARY                             NUMBER
JOB_DESCRIPTION                    VARCHAR2(100)
DATE_EMPLOYED                      DATE
```

How It Works

CHP4_1.SQL contains a sample CREATE TABLE command. In the example, the EMPLOYEE04 table is created in the USERS tablespace. The columns of the

```
CREATE TABLE [schema_name.] table_name
   [ { column datatype [NOT NULL] }
   [ TABLESPACE tablespace_name
      | PCTFREE integer
      | PCTUSED integer
      | INITRANS integer
      | MAXTRANS integer
      | STORAGE ( INITIAL integer [ K | M ]
                | NEXT integer [ K | M ]
                | PCTINCREASE integer
                | MINEXTENTS integer
                | MAXEXTENTS integer ) ]
```

Figure 4.1 The basic syntax for creating a table.

```
CREATE TABLE EMPLOYEE04
(EMPLOYEE_NAME   VARCHAR2(30) NOT NULL,
 SALARY          NUMBER,
 JOB_DESCRIPTION VARCHAR2(100),
 DATE_EMPLOYED   DATE)
TABLESPACE USER_DATA PCTFREE 10, PCTUSED 90
STORAGE ( INITIAL 1M NEXT 500K PCTINCREASE 50
         MINEXTENTS 1 MAXEXTENTS 100);
```

Figure 4.2 CHP4_1.SQL, used to create a sample table.

table will be EMPLOYEE_NAME, SALARY, JOB_DESCRIPTION, and DATE_EMPLOYED.

Initially, one megabyte of space will be allocated to the table, as specified in the INITIAL storage clause. If the initial one megabyte fills up with data, Oracle will create an additional extent, sized 500K, as specified in the NEXT storage clause. If this 500K space is in turn filled with data, another extent will be created, 50% larger, as specified in the PCTINCREASE option. In this case, 500K*1.5 = 750K will be allocated.

Within each block, whose size is determined when the database is created, Oracle will add a record to another block when over ten percent of the block is filled. This is determined in the PCTFREE option. Also, Oracle will signal that there is free space within the block to add records when the block is less than ninety percent filled. This is determined in the PCTUSED option.

Comments

It is important to know data modeling techniques so that you can determine what columns your tables will contain. This discussion is too lengthy for a How-To, but there are several good books on the subject.

Other more advanced options for table creation include: Index-Organized table creation (described in How-To 4.9), constraint creation (described in How-To 6.1 and How-To 6.2), nested table options, cluster creation, parallel query options, and external LOBs. A table column that is defined as a LOB (Large Object) may contain up to four gigabytes of data and is accessed with the DBMS_LOB package.

COMPLEXITY
BEGINNING

4.2 How do I...
Determine all of the tables owned by a particular user?

Problem

I need an easy way to determine the names of all the tables owned by a user account when creating my application. I have access to a large number of tables and I cannot always remember their names. How can I determine all of the tables owned by a particular user?

Technique

The tables available to a user account can be queried from the data dictionary. The USER_TABLES data dictionary view contains all tables owned by the user account connected to the database. The ALL_TABLES view contains all tables for which the connected user account has privileges. By querying this view for a particular owner, you can determine that owner's tables. Figure 4.3 shows most of the columns in the ALL_TABLES data dictionary view. For a full explanation of the ALL_TABLES view, see How-To 4.6.

The OWNER column contains the name of the user account whose schema contains the table. The TABLE_NAME column contains the name of the table. When a table from another user account's schema is referenced, both the owner and table name must be provided unless a synonym is used.

Steps

1. Connect to SQL*Plus as the WAITE user account. You can also use any account with CREATE TABLE privileges. Load CHP4_2.SQL in the SQL buffer. The query contained in the file returns all tables owned by the connected user account.

```
SQL> GET CHP4_2.sql
  1  SELECT TABLE_NAME
  2    FROM USER_TABLES
  3* ORDER BY TABLE_NAME

SQL>
```

Line 1 contains the TABLE_NAME column in the select list of the query. Line 2 specifies the USER_TABLES data dictionary view as the source of the query. The ORDER BY clause in line 3 returns the results ordered by TABLE_NAME.

2. Execute the query to view the tables owned by the WAITE user account. The tables shown as the results of the query were created by CHP1_1.SQL in Chapter 1 and CHP4_1.SQL in Chapter 4. Your results may vary depending on the tables you have created for the WAITE user account.

Name	Null?	Type
OWNER		VARCHAR2(30)
TABLE_NAME		VARCHAR2(30)
TABLESPACE_NAME		VARCHAR2(30)
PCT_FREE		NUMBER
PCT_USED		NUMBER
INI_TRANS		NUMBER
MAX_TRANS		NUMBER
INITIAL_EXTENT		NUMBER
NEXT_EXTENT		NUMBER
MIN_EXTENTS		NUMBER
MAX_EXTENTS		NUMBER
PCT_INCREASE		NUMBER
FREELISTS		NUMBER
FREELIST_GROUPS		NUMBER

Figure 4.3 Part of the ALL_TABLES view.

```
SQL>  /

TABLE_NAME
------------------------------
DEPT01
EMP01
EMPLOYEE04
```

3. Load CHP4_3.SQL into the SQL buffer. The file contains a query of the ALL_TABLES data dictionary view to return all tables that the connected user account owns or has privileges to use. The OWNER column is included in the select list in order to determine which user account owns the table.

```
SQL> GET CHP4_3.sql
  1  SELECT OWNER, TABLE_NAME
  2    FROM ALL_TABLES
  3* ORDER BY OWNER, TABLE_NAME
```

Line 1 contains the select list of the query. The OWNER and TABLE_NAME columns are returned by the query. Line 2 specifies the ALL_TABLES data dictionary view as the source of the query. The ORDER BY clause contained in line 3 orders the output by OWNER and TABLE_NAME.

4. Execute the query. Because the WAITE user account was granted the DBA role by the installation script, every table in the database will be included in the query. The output of the query has been abbreviated in order to conserve space.

```
SQL>  /

OWNER                          TABLE_NAME
------------------------------ ------------------------------
SYS                            TRIGGER$
SYS                            UET$
SYS                            UNDO$
SYS                            USER$
SYS                            VIEW$
WAITE                          DEPT01
WAITE                          EMPLOYEE04

7 rows selected.
```

How It Works

The USER_TABLES and ALL_TABLES data dictionary views contain information about the tables to which a user account has access. The USER_TABLES view contains information about the tables in the user account's schema. The ALL_TABLES view contains all tables on which the user account has privileges. Steps 1 and 2 query the TABLE_NAME column from the USER_TABLES view to show all tables owned by the current user account. Steps 3 and 4 show all tables the user account owns in addition to the tables to which it has been granted privileges. The ALL_TABLES view is queried in steps 3 and 4.

Comments

If you own all of the tables you work with, the USER_TABLES view is the fastest way to determine the names of the tables. The USER_TABLES view only contains tables owned by the connected user account.

COMPLEXITY
BEGINNING

4.3 How do I...
Put comments on a table and its columns?

Problem

With the large number of tables used in our applications and the number of developers working in our organization, it is important that we document tables and their columns contained in the database. How do I put comments on tables and their columns?

Technique

The COMMENT statement is used to create comments on tables and columns. The comments are stored in the data dictionary and can be queried through the ALL_TAB_COMMENTS and ALL_COL_COMMENTS data dictionary views. Figure 4.4 shows the syntax of the COMMENT statement.

If the user account connected to the database is not the owner of the table, the user account must have the COMMENT ANY TABLE system privilege in order to put a comment on the table.

```
COMMENT ON
  { TABLE table |
    COLUMN table.column }
    IS 'text'
```

Figure 4.4 The syntax of the COMMENT statement.

Steps

1. Run SQL*Plus and connect to the WAITE user account. CHP4_4.SQL, shown in Figure 4.5, creates a sample table that is used throughout this How-To.

Run the file to create the sample table.

```
SQL> START CHP4_4.sql

Table created.
```

2. Load CHP4_5.SQL into the SQL buffer. The file contains a statement to put a comment on the DEPT4 table created in the previous step.

```
SQL> GET CHP4_5.sql
 1  COMMENT ON TABLE DEPT04 IS
 2* 'Departments in the Organization.'
```

The COMMENT statement is used to put a comment on either a table or a column. Line 1 presents the required keywords and identifies the DEPT04 table as the recipient of the comment. Line 2 specifies the comment placed on the table.

3. Execute the statement to create the comment.

```
SQL>  /

Comment created.
```

4. Load CHP4_6.SQL into the SQL buffer. The file contains a query to view the comment created in the previous step.

```
SQL>  GET CHP4_6.sql
 1   SELECT COMMENTS
 2    FROM USER_TAB_COMMENTS
 3*  WHERE TABLE_NAME = 'DEPT04'
```

The query returns the COMMENTS column from the USER_COMMENTS data dictionary view. The WHERE clause in line 3 only returns records for the sample table created in Step 1.

```
CREATE TABLE DEPT04 (
    DEPT_NO    NUMBER(5),
    DNAME      VARCHAR2(30));
```

Figure 4.5 CHP4_4.SQL creates a sample table for this How-To.

5. Execute the query to view the comment created in Steps 2 and 3.

```
SQL>  /

COMMENTS
------------------------------------------------
Departments in the Organization.
```

6. Load CHP4_7.SQL into the SQL buffer. The file contains a statement to create a comment on the DNAME column of the DEPT4_4 table.

```
SQL>  GET CHP4_7.sql
  1    COMMENT ON COLUMN DEPT04.DNAME IS
  2     'The name of the department.'
```

Line 1 contains the COMMENT keywords and specifies the table and column name receiving the comment. Both the table and column name must be specified in the statement. If the table name is not included, the COMMENT statement will fail.

7. Execute the statement to create the comment on the column.

```
SQL>  /

Comment created.
```

8. Load CHP4_8.SQL into the SQL buffer. The file contains a statement to query the comment created in Steps 6 and 7 (see Figure 4.6).

Line 1 specifies that the COMMENTS column is returned by the query. The FROM clause in line 2 specifies the USER_COL_COMMENTS data dictionary view as the source of the query. The WHERE clause in lines 3 through 5 returns records for the DNAME column of the sample table created in Step 1.

9. Execute the statement to view the comment.

```
SQL>  /

COMMENTS
------------------------------------------------
The name of the department
```

```
SELECT COMMENTS
FROM USER_COL_COMMENTS
WHERE
  TABLE_NAME = 'DEPT04' AND
  COLUMN_NAME = 'DNAME'
```

Figure 4.6 CHP4_8.SQL queries the comment on the DNAME column of the DEPT04 table.

How It Works

Step 1 creates the sample table DEPT04, commented in later steps in this How-To. Steps 2 and 3 create a comment on the DEPT04 table using the COMMENT statement. The comment is stored in the COM$ table owned by the SYS user account and can be queried through the ALL_TAB_COMMENTS and USER_TAB_COMMENTS data dictionary views. Steps 4 and 5 query the comment created in Steps 2 and 3 using the USER_TAB_COMMENTS data dictionary view. Steps 6 and 7 create a comment on the DNAME column of the DEPT04 table. Column comments are also stored in the COM$ table, but are queried from the ALL_COL_COMMENTS and USER_COL_COMMENTS views. Steps 8 and 9 query the comments created using the USER_COL_COMMENTS view.

Comments

It is important to document the tables and columns in your database. Create comments on tables and columns in order to improve the maintainability of your database and applications. Table and column comments can be used within your application by querying the data dictionary views.

COMPLEXITY
ADVANCED

4.4 How do I...
Recreate CREATE TABLE statements?

Problem

I need a SQL script to re-create one or more tables. I do not have any of the original statements used to create the tables. I know I can use the DESCRIBE command in SQL*Plus to list all the columns in the table, but I have many tables and the output of the DESCRIBE statement does not look like a CREATE TABLE statement. How can I generate scripts to re-create these tables?

Technique

The data dictionary view USER_TABLES contains all of the tables owned by a user account. The USER_TAB_COLUMNS data dictionary view contains each of the columns in the table. Unless the CREATE TABLE statement requires tablespace and storage information, only columns from the USER_TAB_COLUMNS view are needed. Figure 4.7 shows the columns in the USER_TAB_COLUMNS data dictionary view.

```
Name                               Null?      Type
-----------------------------------  --------  ----
TABLE_NAME                         NOT NULL   VARCHAR2(30)
COLUMN_NAME                        NOT NULL   VARCHAR2(30)
DATA_TYPE                                     VARCHAR2(30)
DATA_TYPE_MOD                                 VARCHAR2(3)
DATA_TYPE_OWNER                               VARCHAR2(30)
DATA_LENGTH                        NOT NULL   NUMBER
DATA_PRECISION                                NUMBER
DATA_SCALE                                    NUMBER
NULLABLE                                      VARCHAR2(1)
COLUMN_ID                          NOT NULL   NUMBER
DEFAULT_LENGTH                                NUMBER
DATA_DEFAULT                                  LONG
NUM_DISTINCT                                  NUMBER
LOW_VALUE                                     RAW(32)
HIGH_VALUE                                    RAW(32)
DENSITY                                       NUMBER
NUM_NULLS                                     NUMBER
NUM_BUCKETS                                   NUMBER
LAST_ANALYZED                                 DATE
SAMPLE_SIZE                                   NUMBER
PACKED                                        VARCHAR2(1)
CHARACTER_SET_NAME                            VARCHAR2(44)
```

Figure 4.7 The USER_TAB_COLUMNS data dictionary view.

The TABLE_NAME column contains the name of the table to which the column belongs. The COLUMN_NAME column contains the name of the column as it was defined when the table was created. The DATA_TYPE column contains the datatype of the column.

Steps

1. Run SQL*Plus and connect as the WAITE user account. CHP4_9.SQL, shown in Figure 4.8, contains a CREATE TABLE statement that will be rebuilt in this How-To.

2. Run the file to create the sample table.

```
SQL> START CHP4_9.sql

Table dropped.

Table created.
```

3. Turn off the heading and trailing statements and widen the length of the output line by setting the SQL*Plus environment variables.

```
DROP TABLE DEPT04;
CREATE TABLE DEPT04 (
    DEPT_NO       NUMBER(8,0),
    DEPT_NAME     VARCHAR2(30),
    CREATION_DATE DATE);
```

Figure 4.8 CH4_9.SQL contains a CREATE TABLE statement.

```
SQL> SET HEADING OFF
SQL> SET LINESIZE 132
SQL> SET FEEDBACK OFF
```

The SET HEADING OFF command removes any column headings from the output generated by the query. The SET LINESIZE 132 command ensures that the output generated by the query does not wrap to multiple lines for a single row. The SET FEEDBACK OFF command suppresses the row counter that displays the number of rows returned by the query and the end of the output.

4. Load CHP4_10.SQL (seen in Figure 4.9) into the SQL buffer. This file contains a statement to query column information for the table we are trying to re-create.

Lines 1 through 4 contain the columns returned by the query. The TABLE_NAME column contains the name of the table. COLUMN_ID represents the order of the column in the table. COLUMN_NAME contains the name of the column. DATA_TYPE contains the data type of the column. Lines 5 and 6 contain the FROM clause of the query, specifying the USER_TAB_COLUMNS data dictionary view as the source of the query. The WHERE clause in line 8 returns records for the sample table created in Step 1. The ORDER BY clause in line 8 organizes the records in the order of the columns in the table.

5. Run the statement to display the results of the query.

```
SQL>   /
1      DEPT_NO           NUMBER
2      DEPT_NAME         VARCHAR2
3      CREATION_DATE     DATE
```

This query looks somewhat like the SQL*Plus DESCRIBE statement. In the next step, the data will be formatted to look more like a SQL statement.

6. Load CHP4_11.SQL (seen in Figure 4.10) into the SQL buffer. The file contains a statement to begin formatting the output to look like a SQL statement.

```
SELECT
  COLUMN_ID,
  COLUMN_NAME,
  DATA_TYPE
FROM
  USER_TAB_COLUMNS
WHERE TABLE_NAME = 'DEPT04'
ORDER BY COLUMN_ID
```

Figure 4.9 CHP4_10.SQL queries column information for the table to be re-created.

```
SELECT DECODE(COLUMN_ID,1,'CREATE TABLE '||
  TABLE_NAME||' (', '    '),
  COLUMN_NAME,
  DATA_TYPE
FROM USER_TAB_COLUMNS
  WHERE TABLE_NAME = 'DEPT04'
ORDER BY COLUMN_ID
```

Figure 4.10 CHP4_11.SQL begins to format the output into a SQL statement.

Lines 1 and 2 use the DECODE function to concatenate the CREATE TABLE keywords and the tablename to the beginning of the first output line. The COLUMN_ID field represents the order of the columns in the table. The DECODE function works like an in-line IF statement. If COLUMN_ID = 1, then display the keywords; otherwise, display a blank space.

7. Run the query to display the output from the previous step.

```
SQL>  /

    CREATE TABLE DEPT04 ( DEPT_NO    NUMBER
               DEPT_NAME           VARCHAR2
               CREATION_DATE       DATE
```

The results are starting to look like a DDL statement. The CREATE TABLE keywords and the name of the table are only displayed on the first line of output.

8. Load CHP4_12.SQL (seen in Figure 4.11) into the SQL buffer. The query contained in this file handles the different data types possible in a table. The CHAR, VARCHAR2, and NUMBER data types require a length, scale, or precision modifier. All other data types do not require any more information. The DECODE function is used to put the correct modifiers with the data type. In Step 8, this statement will be combined with the statement created in the previous steps.

```
SELECT DATA_TYPE||DECODE(DATA_TYPE,
  'VARCHAR2','('||TO_CHAR(DATA_LENGTH)||')',
  'NUMBER','('||TO_CHAR(DATA_PRECISION)||
          ','||TO_CHAR(DATA_SCALE)||')',
  'CHAR','('||TO_CHAR(DATA_LENGTH)
  ||')')
FROM USER_TAB_COLUMNS
WHERE TABLE_NAME = 'DEPT04'
ORDER BY COLUMN_ID
|
```

Figure 4.11 CHP4_12.SQL handles datatypes of a table with the DECODE function.

Lines 1 through 6 create a single column of output, creating the datatype of a column with the proper length, scale, and precision. Line 2 handles the VARCHAR2 datatype by concatenating the DATA_LENGTH column to the datatype. Lines 3 and 4 handle the NUMBER datatype by concatenating the DATA_PRECISION and DATA_SCALE columns to the datatype. Line 5 handles the CHAR datatype by concatenating the DATA_LENGTH column to the datatype.

9. Run the statement to view the output from the previous step.

```
SQL>   /

NUMBER(8,0)
VARCHAR2(30)
DATE
```

Using the DECODE function to handle the possible data types generated is an important part of the statement. The query created in this step replaces the DATA_TYPE column in the previous query.

10. CHP4_13.SQL, shown in Figure 4.12, contains a combination of the two queries. When the queries are combined, the column name in the statement becomes long. To make the statement more readable, the columns are aliased and formatted in SQL*Plus.

Run the file using the START command.

```
SQL>   START CHP4_13.sql

CREATE TABLE DEPT04 (          DEPT_NO         NUMBER(8,0),
                               DEPT_NAME       VARCHAR2(30),
                               CREATION_DATE   DATE,
```

Note that the ending parenthesis and the semicolon are missing. Although this looks easy to correct, it is the most complicated part of the process. A parenthesis and semicolon must be placed only after the last column of the

```
COLUMN A FORMAT A30
COLUMN B FORMAT A20
COLUMN C FORMAT A20
SELECT DECODE(COLUMN_ID,1,'CREATE TABLE '||TABLE_NAME||' (',' ') A,
       COLUMN_NAME B,
       DATA_TYPE||DECODE(DATA_TYPE, 'VARCHAR2',
                   '('||TO_CHAR(DATA_LENGTH),
           'NUMBER','('||TO_CHAR(DATA_PRECISION)||
                   ','||TO_CHAR(DATA_SCALE),
           'CHAR','('||TO_CHAR(DATA_LENGTH))||')'||', ' C
FROM USER_TAB_COLUMNS
WHERE TABLE_NAME = 'DEPT04'
ORDER BY COLUMN_ID;
```

Figure 4.12 CHP4_13.SQL combines two queries to build the basis of a CREATE TABLE statement.

table. The last column in the table is the column with the largest COLUMN_ID. The steps that follow will correct this problem.

11. Load CHP4_14.SQL (shown in Figure 4.13) into the SQL buffer. The file contains a query of USER_TAB_COLUMNS, which returns the highest numbered column in the table.

The query returns the value required, but it must be used as part of a DECODE statement within the query. The MAX function is a GROUP function. It works on all rows of the query and returns a single value. The query used to build the CREATE TABLE statements must return one row for each column in the table. This is not consistent with the use of a group function. To get around the problem, the table must be joined with itself, executing a GROUP statement on only one instance of the table. The next step shows a simplified version of this concept.

12. Load CHP4_15.SQL (seen in Figure 4.14) into the SQL buffer. The file contains a query that joins a table with itself to execute a GROUP BY function as part of a multirow query.

Line 1 selects the largest COLUMN_ID column from one instance of the table and the COLUMN_ID value from the other. Line 3 contains the same table twice in the FROM clause. The first instance of the table has the alias T1 and the second has T2. Oracle will treat them as two separate tables. Line 5 joins the two instances of the table together using the TABLE_NAME column. Line 6 forces the query to run for only the

```
SELECT MAX(COLUMN_ID)
FROM
  USER_TAB_COLUMNS
WHERE
  TABLE_NAME = 'DEPT04'
```

Figure 4.13 CHP4_14.SQL queries the USER_TAB_COLUMNS, returning the highest numbered column.

```
SELECT MAX(T2.COLUMN_ID), T1.COLUMN_ID
FROM
  USER_TAB_COLUMNS T1, USER_TAB_COLUMNS T2
WHERE
  T1.TABLE_NAME = T2.TABLE_NAME
  AND T1.TABLE_NAME = 'DEPT04'
GROUP BY T1.COLUMN_ID
ORDER BY T1.COLUMN_ID
```

Figure 4.14 CHP4_15.SQL joins a table with itself to execute a GROUP BY function.

DEPT04 table. Line 7 contains a GROUP BY clause that is required to group data by the T1 instance of the table.

13. Execute the query to show a group by result on each line.

```
SQL>   /
```

```
        3            1
        3            2
        3            3
```

A number now exists that can be compared with the current COLUMN_ID to determine whether it is the last column in the table.

13. CHP4_16.SQL, shown in Figure 4.15, contains a SQL statement recreating a CREATE TABLE statement for a single table. Notice the additional DECODE function on the NUMBER type. This is to prevent parentheses from appearing when there is no precision defined for the column.

14. Execute the query using the START command.

```
SQL>   START CHP4_16.sql
```

```
CREATE TABLE DEPT04 (         DEPT_NO           NUMBER(8,0),
                             DEPT_NAME          VARCHAR2(30),
                             CREATION_DATE      DATE);
```

How It Works

Steps 1 and 2 create the DEPT04 sample table, used in this How-To. Step 3 sets the HEADING and FEEDBACK system variables to OFF to remove unwanted heading and trailing statements from the query results. Steps 4 and 5 query the column name and data type from the USER_TAB_COLUMNS view. The view contains all columns for tables owned by the current user account. Steps 6 and 7 use the DECODE function to format the query by concatenating the CREATE

```
SELECT DECODE(T1.COLUMN_ID,1,'CREATE TABLE '||T1.TABLE_NAME||
          ' (',' ') A,
       T1.COLUMN_NAME B,
       T1.DATA_TYPE||DECODE(T1.DATA_TYPE, 'VARCHAR2',
          '('||TO_CHAR(T1.DATA_LENGTH)||')',
       'NUMBER',DECODE(T1.DATA_PRECISION,NULL,NULL,
          '('||TO_CHAR(T1.DATA_PRECISION)||','||
       TO_CHAR(T1.DATA_SCALE)||')'),
       'CHAR','('||TO_CHAR(T1.DATA_LENGTH)||')')||
             DECODE(T1.COLUMN_ID,
             MAX(T2.COLUMN_ID), ');',',') C
FROM USER_TAB_COLUMNS T1, USER_TAB_COLUMNS T2
WHERE T1.TABLE_NAME = T2.TABLE_NAME AND
      T1.TABLE_NAME = 'DEPT04'
GROUP BY T1.COLUMN_ID, T1.TABLE_NAME, T1.DATA_TYPE,
         T1.DATA_LENGTH, T1.DATA_SCALE, T1.COLUMN_NAME,
         T1.DATA_PRECISION
ORDER BY T1.COLUMN_ID;
```

Figure 4.15 CHP4_16.SQL contains a SQL script to re-create the CREATE TABLE statement.

TABLE keywords to the beginning of the first column. Steps 8 and 9 use the DECODE function to create the scale and precision modifier for each of the columns. Step 10 uses the results from the prior steps to create a query with results very much like a CREATE TABLE statement. After these steps, a closing parenthesis and semicolon are all that is needed by the statement. Steps 11 through 13 present the method for joining a table to itself to determine the last column of the table. Step 14 puts this all together to create a final query.

Comments

It is not necessary to rewrite this script every time you need to re-create a table, or even type it in once. This book contains SQL scripts that you can use to re-create CREATE TABLE statements. SQL*Plus is a powerful tool for managing your database. Looking to the data dictionary and SQL*Plus to solve this type of problem saves you many hours. Re-creating CREATE TABLE statements would be a tedious job if done manually.

COMPLEXITY
BEGINNING

4.5 How do I...
Determine a table's initial size parameters?

Problem

I would like to know how large to make a table before I create one. I also know that the table will eventually grow in the coming months and want to plan accordingly so that I do not use too much or too little storage space. How do I determine a table's initial size parameters?

Technique

By using the formulas provided by this How-To, you can calculate the INITAL, NEXT, PCTFREE, and PCTUSED values before creating a table. These values can then be used by the CREATE TABLE command to create a table with properly sized parameters.

Steps

Determining how large a table must be will depend on several factors. Ideally, the entire table should fit within one extent. An *extent* is a collection of database blocks that comprise part or all of a table. When a table is created, the size of the INITIAL extent is defined. When data is added to the table, it creates the records within the INITIAL extent. If the INITIAL extent gets filled with data, Oracle allocates another extent, whose size is based upon the NEXT extent storage clause. For performance reasons, it is generally best to be sure that all database blocks for the table are contained within one extent. Thus, the INITAL storage clause should be large enough to contain every record, along with all overhead space.

1. Determine how large a block is set to for your Oracle instance. This is set at database creation time and cannot be changed without re-creating the entire database. CHP4_17.SQL contains a sample script to determine the database block size, by querying the V$PARAMETER view. Connect to SQL*Plus as the WAITE account, and run CHP4_17.SQL.

```
SQL> GET CHP4_17.sql
  1  SELECT VALUE
  2  FROM V$PARAMETER
  3  WHERE NAME = 'db_block_size'
SQL> /
VALUE
--------------------------------
4096
SQL>
```

2. Oracle inserts records into a block until it runs out of available space. The available space is determined by subtracting overhead and from the blocksize, and multiplying by the PCTFREE percentage. Follow the formula in Figure 4.16.

For example, if a block is 4096 bytes, there are 190 overhead bytes, and PCTFREE is 90; then the total available space for Oracle records is (4096-190)*.9 (about 3515 bytes).

3. Now that the available space for records within each block has been determined, you must find out the size in bytes of an average record. There is no clear method to determine this before the table has data. However, DESCRIBE the table and try to deduce the total bytes by looking at the number and types of columns. For example, the EMPLOYEE04 table is described in Figure 4.17.

For an example, the EMPLOYEE_NAME column can average 20 bytes, the SALARY 2 bytes (number field = 2 bytes), JOB_DESCRIPTION 40 bytes, DATE_EMPLOYED 7 (date field = 7 bytes). The total is 69. Each column will need an additional byte for an internal separator. Also, add 5 bytes

```
Available space in block =
(db_block_size - overhead) * (PCTFREE / 100)
```

Figure 4.16 This is the general formula for determining available space for Oracle records in a block.

```
SQL> desc employee04
 Name                               Null?    Type
 ----------------------------------- --------- ----
 EMPLOYEE_NAME                      NOT NULL VARCHAR2(30)
 SALARY                                      NUMBER
 JOB_DESCRIPTION                             VARCHAR2(100)
 DATE_EMPLOYED                               DATE

SQL> |
```

Figure 4.17 The description of
EMPLOYEE04.

overhead for each record. Thus, the total will be 78 bytes for each record, on average.

4. Now that both the available space within a block and the average size of a block is known, you can determine how many records fit within a block. This is determined by the formula in Figure 4.18.

For example, assume there are 3515 available bytes within a block for record storage, and a record averages 78 bytes. There will be 3515/78, or about 45 records, that will fit within a block.

5. Now, you can easily determine the INITIAL storage parameter. The table will be the total size of all blocks. This is determined by knowing the total number of records you expect for the table (including growth over several months), the block size, and the number of records that will fit within a block. Figure 4.19 shows the formula for determining this.

In our ongoing example, we will assume one million records. Thus, the INITIAL extent should be (4096 × 1000000) / 45, or 91022222 bytes. When issuing the CREATE TABLE command, you may specify 91022222, 88889K, or 87M.

The NEXT extent determines how large an extent Oracle will obtain if the INITIAL extent ever is filled. This is an arbitrary number and will depend on how large you want to incrementally expand your table. If you do not

```
Number of rows in block =

(usable space in block ) / (average length of record)
```

Figure 4.18 The formula for determining
the number of records that will fit within
a block.

```
INITIAL storage parameter =

(db_block_size) * (number of records) /
(records that will fit within a block)
```

Figure 4.19 The formula for determining
the INITIAL storage parameter.

know this, set the NEXT parameter to ten percent of the INITIAL storage parameter.

6. The PCTFREE parameter determines how much free space within each block will be reserved for expansion of existing records. If you do not anticipate much inserts, updates, or deletes, set the PCTFREE to a low value such as 10. If you anticipate your records to grow or shrink in size, such as when adding text to a text field, set the PCTFREE higher, such as 30 or 40.

7. The PCTUSED parameter determines how much space must be freed up by deleting records in a block before Oracle inserts into it. This parameter is used by Oracle to determine which blocks have space to insert. The larger this is set, the more records can fit within a block. However, this increases the chances of *row chaining*, which occurs when a record is updated and the new record size cannot fit into the remaining space of the block. Oracle would then have to "chain" the record, storing part of the record within one block and part of the record within another. This will adversely affect the performance of the table. If you do not know what you want to set PCTUSED to, start by subtracting PCTFREE from 100. So, if your PCTFREE is 10, set PCTUSED to 90.

How It Works

Step 1 determines how large the block size is. Step 2 determines the average space available within each block. Step 3 determines the average record size. Step 4 determines the number of records that will fit within a block. Step 5 brings all previous steps together to determine the INITIAL storage parameter. Step 6 shows how to determine the PCTFREE clause. This is important to prevent row chaining. Step 7 shows how to determine the PCTUSED parameter, also useful in preventing row chaining.

You should strive to fit all records within the INITIAL extent. Be sure to predict how large your table will grow within six or twelve months, and size accordingly. If a table grows into several extents, Oracle will be encumbered with overhead, and performance on the table will degrade. This is especially true for tables with over five extents.

The overhead of a block is determined by adding 57 to the product of 23 and the INITRANS parameter. By default, the INITRANS is one. So, the general overhead of a block is roughly 80 bytes. Due to other factors, the overhead for each block in reality reaches about 90–100 bytes.

Comments

After creating the table and populating it with data, you can see if the table was sized properly. Look to see how many extents the table has by issuing
`SELECT SEGMENT_NAME, EXTENTS FROM DBA_SEGMENTS WHERE SEGMENT_NAME =`

'table_name';. If the EXTENTS column is greater than one, you sized the INITIAL storage clause too small.

You cannot specify PCTFREE and PCTUSED so that they add up to more than 100.

To see if the table was sized too small, analyze the table and look at the number of blocks used versus blocks free. If too many blocks are free, and you do not expect your table to grow, the INITIAL storage clause was sized too large. How-To 4.6 describes how to use the ANALYZE command to gather these statistics.

COMPLEXITY
BEGINNING

4.6 How do I...
Use the ANALYZE command to determine access statistics?

Problem

I am using Oracle's Cost Based Optimizer by operating in CHOOSE mode, and want to improve query performance. I know that my objects must have statistics gathered on them for the CBO to work. How do I use the ANALYZE command to determine access statistics?

Technique

Use the ANALYZE TABLE command to gather statistics on a table and all associated indexes. The syntax of several different ANALYZE commands are shown in Figure 4.20. These will be used to gather and remove statistics for Oracle's Cost Based optimizer.

There are two main options of the ANALYZE table command: ESTIMATE and COMPUTE. ESTIMATE looks at a sample of records in a table and determines various statistics about the data of the table, which is explained later in this How-To. Although ESTIMATE looks at only a sample of data, usually 25% or less, COMPUTE looks at every record in a table. Although this takes considerably more time, the statistics that it gathers may be more accurate. Which method to use will depend on which is more important—the speed to collect statistics or the accuracy of the statistics.

```
ANALYZE TABLE table_name ESTIMATE STATISTICS SAMPLE x PERCENT;
ANALYZE TABLE table_name COMPUTE STATISTICS;
ANALYZE TABLE table_name DELETE STATISTICS;
```

Figure 4.20 Syntax of the ANALYZE TABLE command.

Steps

1. Connect to SQL*Plus as the WAITE account. If you have not done so already, create the EMPLOYEE04 table by running the CHP4_1.SQL script. At this point, there will be no records in the table. To get a better grasp of how statistics on tables work, create some sample data in the table.

2. Run CHP4_18.SQL, shown in Figure 4.21, to create sample data.

```
SQL> START CHP4_18.sql
1 row created.
1 row created.
2 rows created.
4 rows created.
8 rows created.
16 rows created.
SQL>
```

3. At this point, 32 records will be in the EMPLOYEE04 table but no statistics. Run CHP4_19.SQL to estimate statistics, sampling 25% of the records.

```
SQL> GET CHP4_19.sql
  1  ANALYZE TABLE EMPLOYEE04
  2  ESTIMATE STATISTICS SAMPLE 25 PERCENT;
SQL> /
Table analyzed.
SQL>
```

4. Now that the table has been analyzed, you may view the statistics that have been gathered. Run the CHP4_20.SQL script to see a few statistics.

```
SQL> GET CHP4_20.sql
  1  SELECT NUM_ROWS, AVG_SPACE, SAMPLE_SIZE, AVG_ROW_LEN
  2  FROM DBA_TABLES
  3  WHERE TABLE_NAME = 'EMPLOYEE04'
SQL> /
NUM_ROWS AVG_SPACE SAMPLE_SIZE AVG_ROW_LEN
-------- --------- ----------- -----------
      32      1574          25          45
SQL>
```

```
INSERT INTO EMPLOYEE04 VALUES ('TEST EMPLOYEE',45000,
                               'TEST DESCRIPTION',sysdate);
INSERT INTO EMPLOYEE04 SELECT * FROM EMPLOYEE04;
INSERT INTO EMPLOYEE04 SELECT * FROM EMPLOYEE04;
INSERT INTO EMPLOYEE04 SELECT * FROM EMPLOYEE04;
INSERT INTO EMPLOYEE04 SELECT * FROM EMPLOYEE04;
INSERT INTO EMPLOYEE04 SELECT * FROM EMPLOYEE04;
```

Figure 4.21 CHP4_18.SQL inserts sample data into the EMPLOYEE04 table.

How It Works

CHP4_18.SQL inserts sample records into the EMPLOYEE04 table. First, it creates one record. Then, it inserts into the table by selected all records from itself, several times. Thus, the first time the INSERT INTO EMPLOYEE04 SELECT * FROM EMPLOYEE04 command is issued, there is one record, so one record is inserted. The next time the statement is executed, there are two records in the table, so two records will be inserted. This method is a good process to quickly add sample data to a table.

CHP4_19.SQL uses the option SAMPLE 25 PERCENT. This will be much quicker than the COMPUTE option, but will potentially not be as accurate for the Cost Based Optimizer.

The statistics may be seen by querying the DBA_TABLES view, whose columns are described in Table 4.1. The CHP4_20.SQL script selects just a few of these columns, which can be expanded by any of the DBA_TABLES columns.

Table 4.1 Explanation of the DBA_TABLES view

COLUMN NAME	DESCRIPTION
OWNER	User account that created the table.
TABLE_NAME	Name of the table.
TABLESPACE_NAME	Tablespace in which the table resides.
CLUSTER_NAME	Name of the cluster for which the table belongs, if any.
IOT_NAME	The parent Index-Organized table, if any.
PCT_FREE	Percentage of space to keep free within each block of the table.
PCT_USED	Percentage of space to use within each block of the table before allocating a new block.
INI_TRANS	Initial number of transactions within each block.
MAX_TRANS	Maximum number of concurrent transactions that can use the block.
INITIAL_EXTENT	Size, in bytes, allocated for the first extent of the table.
NEXT_EXTENT	Size, in bytes, allocated for subsequent extents.
MIN_EXTENTS	Minimum number of extents to allocate when creating or truncating the table.
MAX_EXTENTS	Maximum number of extents.
PCT_INCREASE	Percent that each extent past the INITIAL and NEXT will increase in size by.
FREELISTS	Number of freelist buffers allocated for the table; set to the maximum number of concurrent insert processes you predict for the table.
FREELIST_GROUPS	Parallel Server option to determine number of freelist groups for all instances inserting into the table.
LOGGING	YES or NO value to determine if logging is used. If not, the table can be loaded in direct mode, created "AS SELECT ... FROM table_b", and other options quicker.
BACKED_UP	Specifies whether a table has been backed up since last modified.
NUM_ROWS	Number of records in the table. This is one of the most important statistics for the CBO.
BLOCKS	Number of used blocks of the table.

COLUMN NAME	DESCRIPTION
EMPTY_BLOCKS	Number of blocks that contain no data.
AVG_SPACE	Average free space in the table.
CHAIN_CNT	Number of chained rows.
AVG_ROW_LEN	Average length, in bytes, of a row.
AVG_SPACE_FREELIST_BLOCKS	Average freespace of blocks on a freelist.
NUM_FREELIST_BLOCKS	Number of blocks on a freelist.
DEGREE	Parallel Query option that indicates the number of instances the table is to be scanned across.
INSTANCES	Number of instances the table is to be scanned across.
CACHE	Y or N: if the table will be cached in the buffer cache.
TABLE_LOCK	ENABLED or DISABLED: is table locking enabled?
SAMPLE_SIZE	Shows what percent estimate was used in the ESTIMATE clause of the ANALYZE command.
LAST_ANALYZED	Date and time the table was last analyzed. Important to see if statistics need to be refreshed.
PARTITIONED	YES or NO: is the table partitioned.
IOT_TYPE	IOT or IOT_OVERFLOW or <NULL>: determines if this is an index-organized table (or overflow of one). <NULL> indicates a normal table.
TEMPORARY	Y or N: is the table temporary?
NESTED	YES or NO: is this a nested table?
BUFFER_POOL	DEFAULT or other pool name: displays the default buffer pool in which the object will be placed.

It is important to note that statistics are not automatically generated. You must either manually refresh table and index statistics, or set up a process that will do this automatically. It is recommended to refresh statistics after objects change more than about five percent of their data.

Analyzing tables will automatically analyze all indexes on the table.

Comments

Another method to analyze statistics is to issue `EXECUTE DBMS_UTILITY.ANALYZE_SCHEMA(schema_name, option);`, where the options are COMPUTE, ESTIMATE, or DELETE.

Do not analyze data dictionary objects owned by SYS. Oracle Corp. has tuned the database to use the rule-based optimizer for these internal tables, and by analyzing them, the database will access the data dictionary in cost-based mode, possibly affecting performance.

The user account must have the ANALYZE ANY or be the owner of the table/index/cluster to analyze an object.

ANALYZE can also be used to determine chained rows of a table, using the LIST CHAINED ROWS INTO chained_rows option. This is helpful in determining if the PCTFREE/PCTUSED storage parameters are set properly. You must run the UTLCHAIN.SQL script before this option may be used.

Using the COMPUTE option against a table is an intensive operation. Be sure to have sufficient free space in the default temporary tablespace for the user account issuing the command. The space should be as large as the object being analyzed.

COMPLEXITY
INTERMEDIATE

4.7 How do I...
Create a table from another table?

Problem

When developing applications, I like to make a backup of a table before making untested operations on the table. To do this, I want to create a new table from the existing table and make a copy of all of the rows. In our production environment, we want to create summary tables that are complicated queries of other tables. How do I create a table as a query from another table?

Technique

The CREATE TABLE statement is used to create new tables. The CREATE TABLE statement allows a query to be specified as the source of the columns and rows for the table. If the query used in the CREATE TABLE statement returns rows, the rows are inserted into the new table when it is created. If the query does not return rows, the table is created containing no rows. Complex queries can be used to create a table. A column alias is required if Oracle cannot create a valid column name from the column in the query.

Steps

1. Connect to SQL*Plus as the WAITE user account. CHP4_21.SQL, shown in Figure 4.22, creates the sample tables used in this How-To and populates them with data.

The DEPT04 table is created by the CREATE TABLE statement and populated with one record. In the steps that follow, a new table will be created by querying the sample table. The EMP04 table is created and populated with three records. The final example in the How-To creates a new table by joining the DEPT04 and EMP04 table. Run the file to create the sample table and populate it with data.

```
DROP TABLE DEPT04;
CREATE TABLE DEPT04 (
     DEPTNO      NUMBER(5),
     DNAME       VARCHAR2(30));

DROP TABLE EMP04;
CREATE TABLE EMP04 (
     EMPNO       NUMBER(5),
     DEPTNO      NUMBER(5));

INSERT INTO DEPT04 VALUES (1,'SALES');
INSERT INTO EMP04 VALUES(1,1);
INSERT INTO EMP04 VALUES(2,1);
INSERT INTO EMP04 VALUES(3,1);
COMMIT;
```

Figure 4.22 CHP4_21.SQL
creates the sample tables
used in How-To 4.7.

```
SQL> START CHP4_21.sql

Table Dropped.

Table Created.

Table Dropped.

Table Created.

1 row created.

1 row created.

1 row created.

1 row created.

1 row created.

Commit complete.
```

2. Load CHP4_22.SQL into the SQL buffer. The file contains a CREATE
TABLE statement that makes a new table as a query of the table created in
Step 1.

```
SQL> GET CHP4_22.sql
  1   CREATE TABLE NDEPT04
  2*  AS SELECT * FROM DEPT04
```

The CREATE TABLE keywords presented in line 1 are used to create a new
table in the database. The table name, NDEPT04, is specified in line 1.
Line 2 contains a query that specifies the columns to be created and the
initial data populated in the table.

3. Execute the statement to create the new table.

```
SQL> /

Table Created.
```

The table is created, but Oracle does not tell you how many rows were inserted. In order to get the number of rows, COUNT(*) can be queried from the new table.

4. Load CHP4_23.SQL into the SQL buffer. The file contains a statement to create a new table with the same columns as the original table, but with none of the data.

```
SQL> GET CHP4_23.sql
  1   CREATE TABLE N2DEPT04
  2    AS SELECT * FROM DEPT04
  3* WHERE 1 = 0
```

Line 1 contains the CREATE TABLE keywords used to create a new table. The query contained in lines 2 and 3 define the columns for the new table, but the WHERE clause in line 3 doesn't create any records in the table.

5. Execute the statement to create the new table.

```
SQL> /

Table Created.
```

6. Load CHP4_24.SQL (seen in Figure 4.23) into the SQL buffer. The file contains a query to create summary data from multiple tables.

Line 1 contains the required keywords and specifies the name of the new table. The query contained in lines 2 through 3 defines the columns of the new table and creates the initial records. Lines 2 and 3 define the columns returned by the query and created in the new table. An alias is required on all calculated fields so that a valid column name can be created. The NO_EMPLOYEES alias in line 3 tells the CREATE TABLE statement what to name the column. Functions such as COUNT are reserved words and

```
CREATE TABLE N3DEPT04 AS
   SELECT D.DEPTNO, D.DNAME,
          COUNT(*) NO_EMPLOYEES
   FROM
          DEPT04 D, EMP04 E
   WHERE
          D.DEPTNO = E.DEPTNO
   GROUP BY
          D.DEPTNO, DNAME
|
```

Figure 4.23 CHP4_24.SQL creates summary data from multiple tables.

cannot be used as the column name in the new table. Lines 4 and 5 contain the FROM clause and specify the two sample tables created in step 1 as the source of the query. The WHERE clause in lines 6 and 7 joins the two tables used in the query. The GROUP BY clause in lines 8 and 9 is required by the COUNT function specified in line 3.

7. Execute the statement to create the new table.

```
SQL> /

Table Created.
```

8. Describe the new table using the SQL*Plus DESCRIBE statement. The columns created in the new table will have the datatypes of the source table. The datatype of calculated fields will have a datatype based on the operator used in the SELECT statement. The description of the new table is shown in Figure 4.24.

9. Load CHP4_25.SQL into the SQL buffer. The file contains a statement to create a table with custom storage parameters and tablespace information.

```
SQL> GET CHP4_25.sql
  1   CREATE TABLE N4DEPT04
  2      STORAGE (
  3         INITIAL 1M
  4         NEXT 1M)
  6      AS SELECT * FROM DEPT04
```

Line 1 defines the new table created by the statement with the CREATE TABLE keywords. Lines 2 through 5 contain custom storage parameters that define how the table will be created in the database. The INITIAL clause specifies how much storage is allocated when the table is first created. The NEXT clause specifies how much storage will be allocated when the first allocated storage is used. Line 5 contains the query used to create the table.

10. Run the statement to create the table. The table is created with the storage parameters defined by the STORAGE clause.

```
SQL> /
Table created.
```

```
SQL> desc n3dept04
 Name                            Null?    Type
 ------------------------------- -------- ----
 DEPTNO                                   NUMBER(5)
 DNAME                                    VARCHAR2(30)
 NO_EMPLOYEES                             NUMBER

SQL>
```

Figure 4.24 The description of the table created by a multiple table query.

How It Works

Step 1 creates the sample tables used by this How-To. Steps 2 and 3 create a new table with all of the columns and data from the DEPT04 table created in Step 1. The CREATE TABLE statement includes an AS SELECT clause to create the new table from the results of the query. Steps 4 and 5 create a new table as a query without moving any data into the table. The WHERE 1 = 0 clause in the SELECT statement ensures that no rows will be returned by the query, but still creates the table. Steps 6 and 7 create a new table as a complex query from multiple tables. An alias is required for all calculated fields to give the column a name in the new table. Step 8 describes the table created in the previous two steps using the DESCRIBE command. The data type of the calculated column is the result type of the expression. Steps 9 and 10 create a new table as a query containing a STORAGE clause. The STORAGE clause is usually at the end of the CREATE TABLE statement, unless the table is created from a query.

Comments

Creating a table as a query from one or more additional tables or views is a very useful technique that can be used to create summary tables that can dramatically improve the performance of summary data queries. The Parallel Query Option in Oracle8 dramatically improves the performance of CREATE TABLE statements with SELECT clauses on multiprocessor computers.

COMPLEXITY
INTERMEDIATE

4.8 How do I...
Interpret the format of ROWID?

Problem

I need to use the ROWID pseudo-column for fast retrieval and location of records. I also need to determine where my actual data resides within a tablespace. How do I interpret the format of ROWID?

Technique

Use the various DBMS_ROWID functions to extract information about the ROWID pseudo-column. There are two ROWID formats: extended and restricted. Restricted is used mostly to be backward-compatible with Oracle7. The extended format takes advantage of new Oracle8 features.

Table 4.2 shows the components of the extended ROWID format, and Table 4.3 shows the components of the restricted ROWID format.

Table 4.2 Description of the extended format for ROWID (10 bytes)

PORTION	DESCRIPTION
000000	6-character object number (base-64 encoded)
fff	3-character relative file number (base-64 encoded)
bbbbbb	6-character block number in file (base-64 encoded)
sss	3-character slot within the block (base-64 encoded)

Table 4.3 Description of the restricted format for ROWID (6 bytes)

PORTION	DESCRIPTION
bbbbbbbb	6-character block (hexidecimal encoded)
rrrr	4-character row number in block (hexidecimal encoded)
ffff	4-character file number (hexidecimal encoded)

Steps

1. Connect to SQL*Plus as the Waite account. If you have not already done so, create the EMPLOYEE04 table by running the CHP4_1.SQL. Also, if you have not already done so, insert sample data into the EMPLOYEE04 table by running the CHP4_18.SQL script.

The DBMS_ROWID package has several procedures and functions to interpret the ROWIDs of records. Table 4.4 shows the DBMS_ROWID functions, most of which will be explained in this How-To.

Table 4.4 The DBMS_ROWID functions

FUNCTION	DESCRIPTION
ROWID_BLOCK_NUMBER	The block number that contains the record; 1 = extended ROWID.
ROWID_OBJECT	The object number of the object that contains the record.
ROWID_RELATIVE_FNO	The relative file number contains the record.
ROWID_ROW_NUMBER	The row number of the record.
ROWID_TO_ABSOLUTE_FNO	The absolute file number; you need to input rowid_val, schema, and object; the absolute file number is returned.
ROWID_TO_EXTENDED	Converts the ROWID from restricted to extended; you need to input restr_rowid, schema, object; the extended number is returned.
ROWID_TO_RESTRICTED	Converts the ROWID from extended to restricted.
ROWID_TYPE	0 = restricted ROWID, 1 = extended.
ROWID_VERIFY	Verifies if the ROWID can be extended; 0 = can be converted to extended format; 1= cannot be converted to extended format.

2. Run the CHP4_26.SQL script to retrieve ROWID information on each
record.

```
SQL> GET CHP4_26.sql
  1  select
  2      b.object_name||'.'||
  3      dbms_rowid.rowid_relative_fno(a.rowid)||'.'||
  4      dbms_rowid.rowid_block_number(a.rowid)||'.'||
  5      dbms_rowid.rowid_row_number(a.rowid)||'.'||
  6      '- type '||
  7
decode(dbms_rowid.rowid_type(a.rowid),0,'RESTRICTED',1,'EXTENDED')
  8  from employee04 a, all_objects b
  9  where dbms_rowid.rowid_object(a.rowid) = b.object_id
SQL> /

EMPLOYEE04.2.1493.0.- type EXTENDED
EMPLOYEE04.2.1493.1.- type EXTENDED
EMPLOYEE04.2.1493.2.- type EXTENDED
EMPLOYEE04.2.1493.3.- type EXTENDED
EMPLOYEE04.2.1493.4.- type EXTENDED
EMPLOYEE04.2.1493.5.- type EXTENDED
EMPLOYEE04.2.1493.6.- type EXTENDED
EMPLOYEE04.2.1493.7.- type EXTENDED
EMPLOYEE04.2.1493.8.- type EXTENDED
EMPLOYEE04.2.1493.9.- type EXTENDED
EMPLOYEE04.2.1493.10.- type EXTENDED
EMPLOYEE04.2.1493.11.- type EXTENDED
EMPLOYEE04.2.1493.12.- type EXTENDED
EMPLOYEE04.2.1493.13.- type EXTENDED
EMPLOYEE04.2.1493.14.- type EXTENDED
EMPLOYEE04.2.1493.15.- type EXTENDED
EMPLOYEE04.2.1493.16.- type EXTENDED
EMPLOYEE04.2.1493.17.- type EXTENDED
EMPLOYEE04.2.1493.18.- type EXTENDED
EMPLOYEE04.2.1493.19.- type EXTENDED
EMPLOYEE04.2.1493.20.- type EXTENDED
EMPLOYEE04.2.1493.21.- type EXTENDED
EMPLOYEE04.2.1493.22.- type EXTENDED
EMPLOYEE04.2.1493.23.- type EXTENDED
EMPLOYEE04.2.1493.24.- type EXTENDED
EMPLOYEE04.2.1493.25.- type EXTENDED
EMPLOYEE04.2.1493.26.- type EXTENDED
EMPLOYEE04.2.1493.27.- type EXTENDED
EMPLOYEE04.2.1493.28.- type EXTENDED
EMPLOYEE04.2.1493.29.- type EXTENDED
EMPLOYEE04.2.1493.30.- type EXTENDED
EMPLOYEE04.2.1493.31.- type EXTENDED

31 rows selected.
```

How It Works

The DBMS_ROWID functions provide information such as block, row, relative
file number, and absolute file number on each ROWID in a table. The ROWID is

a pseudo-column that has a unique value associated with each record of the database.

CHP4_26.SQL will display the object name, the relative file number that contains the record, the block that contains the record, the row of the record, and the ROWID type. The ROWID type is determined by using the DBMS_ROWID.ROWID_TYPE function. If the function returns 0, the ROWID is restricted. If the function returns 1, the ROWID is extended. The object name is determined by joining the ALL_OBJECTS view with the result of the DBMS_ROWID.ROWID_OBJECT function.

Comments

The DBMS_ROWID package is created by the $ORACLE_HOME /RDBMS/ADMIN/DBMSUTIL.SQL script. This script is automatically run when the Oracle instance is created. This program is a good source to learn more about ROWID information.

The functions for DBMS_ROWID will return a NULL if the input is NULL.

COMPLEXITY
INTERMEDIATE

4.9 How do I...
Create an index-organized table?

Problem

I want to improve my performance when accessing my table that contains a primary key. I also want to save storage space by creating my table as an index-organized table. How do I create an index-organized table?

Technique

An index-organized table is created by using the ORGANIZATION INDEX clause of the CREATE TABLE command. The basic syntax to create an index-organized table is shown in Figure 4.25.

All index-organized tables are stored in the B-tree structure based on the primary key. This structure is used for Oracle indexes. The difference is that

```
CREATE TABLE table_name
  ( { column_name datatype [, ] }
      CONSTRAINT constraint_name
      PRIMARY KEY ({ column_name [, ] } ) )
  ORGANIZATION INDEX TABLESPACE tablespace_name
  [ PCTTHRESHOLD 25 ] [INCLUDING column_name]
  [ OVERFLOW TABLESPACE overflow_tablespace ]
```

Figure 4.25 The basic syntax of creating an index-organized table.

non-key columns are stored in the B-tree structure. Thus, queries and updates to the table based on the primary key are improved by using this object format. A full table scan will return records in the order of the primary key, much like a clustered table.

Steps

1. Connect to SQL*Plus as the Waite user account. Run the CHP4_27.SQL script, shown in Figure 4.26, to create a sample index-organized table.

```
SQL> START CHP4_27.sql

Table Created.
```

How It Works

Note that the TEMP tablespace is not usually used for overflow tablespaces. For simplicity, TEMP was used; it is recommended to have an additional tablespace for overflow data.

The ORGANIZATION INDEX clause of the CREATE TABLE command will create an index-organized table. CHP4_27.SQL shows a simple create statement.

The PCTTHRESHOLD clause specifies what percentage of the block should be reserved for a record. If the record is larger than that defined in PCTTHRESHOLD, the portion of the record exceeding the threshold will be stored in the tablespace defined in the OVERFLOW clause. If no OVERFLOW clause is specified, all rows that contain even a portion exceeding the PCTTHRESHOLD are rejected completely and are not inserted into the index-organized table.

The INCLUDING clause, if specified, determines the column that will divide the table into the index portion and the overflow portion. Each column after the INCLUDING column is stored in the overflow portion of the index-organized table.

Storage is reduced, because the primary key becomes part of the table and is not stored as a separate index, and ROWIDs are not stored as they are in primary keys.

```
CREATE TABLE CUST04
  ( LAST_NAME      VARCHAR(30),
    SSN            INTEGER,
    SALARY         INTEGER,
    CUSTOMER_NOTES VARCHAR(2000),
    CONSTRAINT PK_CUST04 PRIMARY KEY (LAST_NAME, SSN) )
ORGANIZATION INDEX TABLESPACE USER_DATA
PCTTHRESHOLD 25 INCLUDING SALARY
OVERFLOW TABLESPACE TEMPORARY_DATA;
```

Figure 4.26 CHP4_27.SQL creates a sample index-organized table.

Comments

Index-organized tables may not contain a column of the LONG datatype. They may not have constraints (except for the primary key), nor any additional indexes.

As of Oracle8.0.3, index-organized tables may not be clustered, replicated, partitioned, or distributed.

Each index-organized table must contain a primary key. The primary key uniquely defines a record; ROWIDs are not used.

The PCTTHRESHOLD clause, if defined, must be 0 to 50.

COMPLEXITY
BEGINNING

4.10 How do I...
Partition a table?

Problem

I am creating a very large table and would like to improve access to the table by using a partitioned table. Also, I would like to perform maintenance such as restoring data, data loading, and statistical analysis on one part of a table, while the rest of the table is available for use by users. How do I partition a table?

Technique

Partitioning a table allows it to be split into several independent pieces, each with potentially differing storage parameters. One advantage is that large tables become more manageable. Each partition may be analyzed, exported, truncated, loaded, and so on. Also, if one partition of a table goes offline, users may still access and update data in other partitions of that table. Partitioning is transparent to the users and applications.

The PARTITION BY option of the CREATE TABLE command is used to create table partitions. Oracle allows multiple partitions with potentially different storage parameters, including tablespace. The syntax for this is shown in Figure 4.27.

```
CREATE TABLE table_name
( { column_name data_type [NOT NULL] [ , ] } )
PARTITION BY RANGE ( { partition_column [ , ] } )
(PARTITION partition_name1 VALUES [LESS|GREATER] THAN range_numbers1)
[TABLESPACE tablespace_name1]
[STORAGE (storage_parameter1 storage_value1, ...)],
(PARTITION partition_name2 VALUES [LESS|GREATER] THAN range_numbers2)
[TABLESPACE tablespace_name2]
[STORAGE (storage_parameter2 storage_value2, ...)],
...)
```

Figure 4.27 The syntax of SQL to create a partitioned table.

Steps

1. Connect to SQL*Plus as the WAITE user account.

2. Create the table, specifying a range partition, and listing all partitions and storage parameters. CHP4_28.SQL, in Figure 4.28, shows an example of creating a partitioned table.

3. Run the CHP4_28.SQL script, which will create the EMP04 table, with partitions stored in the USER, TEMP, and SYSTEM tablespaces. Each partition will also have its own storage parameters.

4. To demonstrate that Oracle will store records in the correct partition, insert one record for each partition. Run CHP4_29.SQL, shown in Figure 4.29, to insert one record into each partition. For example, the INSERT command will place a record within the first partition, which contains employees with salaries less than $25,000.

5. Query the ROWIDs of each record to see if they are placed in different datafiles. Run the CHP4_30.SQL script, shown in Figure 4.30, to retrieve this information.

```
DROP TABLE EMP04;
CREATE TABLE EMP04
(EMPLOYEE_NAME    VARCHAR2(30) NOT NULL,
 SALARY          NUMBER,
 JOB_DESCRIPTION VARCHAR2(100),
 DATE_EMPLOYED   DATE
)
PARTITION BY RANGE(SALARY)
   (PARTITION LOW_SALARY VALUES LESS THAN (25000)
            TABLESPACE USER_DATA
            STORAGE (INITIAL 50K NEXT 50K),
    PARTITION MEDIUM_SALARY VALUES LESS THAN (50000)
            TABLESPACE USER_DATA
            STORAGE (INITIAL 100K NEXT 100K),
    PARTITION LARGE_SALARY VALUES LESS THAN (150000)
            TABLESPACE TEMPORARY_DATA|
            STORAGE (INITIAL 50K NEXT 50K),
    PARTITION OUTRAGEOUS_SALARY VALUES LESS THAN (9999999999)
            TABLESPACE SYSTEM
            STORAGE (INITIAL 10K NEXT 10K));
```

Figure 4.28 CHP4_28.SQL shows the syntax to create a partitioned table.

```
INSERT INTO EMP04 VALUES('JOE THE INTERN',20000,'INTERN WORK',SYSDATE);
INSERT INTO EMP04 VALUES('BRENDAN',35000,'DEVELOPER',SYSDATE);
INSERT INTO EMP04 VALUES('CHRISTOPHER',100000,'SALES MANAGER',SYSDATE);
INSERT INTO EMP04 VALUES('ETHAN',1250000,'PRESIDENT AND CEO',SYSDATE);
```

Figure 4.29 CHP4_29.SQL will insert one record into each partition of the EMP04 table.

```
SELECT EMPLOYEE_NAME, SALARY,
DBMS_ROWID.ROWID_RELATIVE_FNO(ROWID) FROM EMP04;
```

Figure 4.30 CHP4_30.SQL retrieves
the ROWIDs of the partition
records.

```
SQL> START CHP4_30.sql
JOE THE INTERN    20000    2
BRENDAN           35000    2
CHRISTOPHER      100000    3
ETHAN           1250000    4
```

How It Works

The CREATE TABLE command has an optional PARTITION BY clause to create partitioned tables. Step 1 creates a sample partitioned table. Step 2 inserts values into the partitioned table, placing records within each partition. Step 3 retrieves records with their ROWIDs, showing that the records are indeed placed within different tablespaces.

Partitioned tables have several advantages over regular tables. If one part of the partition is unavailable, the other parts are available for select, insert, update, and delete. Only those records that are contained within the down partition will be unavailable. Also, a lock may be obtained on one partition while the others are available for data manipulation. This may greatly improve the availability of the records of a table.

Each partition may have its own storage parameters, such as INITIAL, NEXT, PCTFREE, PCTUSED, and so on. This is important, because one partition may have one record and another one million records. By allowing individual partitions to have different storage parameters, Oracle allows great flexibility in storage and performance tuning.

Each partition may be stored in different tablespaces. This is beneficial for availability if a tablespace is offline. This is also beneficial for performance, as a table may have multiple drives reading and/or writing in parallel.

The SQL*Loader import, export, and analyze commands can be performed on one or more partitions at a time. This can dramatically improve performance, as one part of a partition may be loading, locked, or unavailable, while other parts are available for use.

Comments

In the example, the SYSTEM and TEMP tablespaces were chosen for storage of partition parts. In reality, you would not want to put any objects in these tablespaces. They were included to show a simple example of how to put partition parts into separate tablespaces.

The column keys may not be of the LONG, RAW, or ROWID datatypes.

A partition key may have more than one column, as long as the columns are separated by commas in both the definition and the range specification.

CHAPTER 5

INDEXES

5

INDEXES

How do I...

Indexes are important objects used for data integrity and improving database performance. An index works as a "look-up" guide to directly locate a record, similar to how someone would look up a subject in the index of a book. Strategically placed indexes can improve query performance dramatically, decreasing result times from hours to seconds. Indexes are also useful to enforce business rules within the database, especially uniqueness within a column or group of columns. An index is separate from the data it is based upon, and so the index may be dropped or modified without affecting the underlying data. Once created, Oracle updates all relevant indexes during data manipulation. There are several types of indexes, such as bitmap indexes, regular indexes, partitioned indexes, and index-organized tables, each with its own unique advantages and disadvantages. This chapter covers the creation and manipulation of indexes within Oracle, and describes the pros and cons of each type of index.

5.1 Determine All of the Indexes on a Particular Table

The most commonly used method to improve data queries is the creation of indexes. Many times, it is important to know how a table has been indexed. This How-To explains the steps used to see which indexes exist on a table.

5.2 Determine All of the Indexes Owned by a Particular User

When a database contains many applications and/or user accounts, there may be a large number of indexes. It is important to keep track of owners, indexes, and tables. This How-To explains the steps used to see all indexes of one user account.

5.3 Determine an Index's Initial Size Parameters

Before creating an index, it is important to determine how much storage space will be needed, as well as to know how quickly and how large the table that the index is based upon will eventually grow. This information is important to make the index fit within a single extent, which is important for performance reasons. Also, if not sized properly, the index will either waste disk space or need more space. This How-To takes you through the steps of determining an index's initial size parameters.

5.4 Detect Unbalanced Indexes

When a table is heavily inserted to, updated, or deleted from, its indexes may become fragmented or unbalanced. An unbalanced index has many records clumped close together on the index tree due to their similar indexed values. When an index is unbalanced, parts of an index are accessed more frequently than others, from which disk contention may occur, creating a bottleneck in performance. It is important to periodically examine all indexes to determine if they have become unbalanced. This How-To takes you through the steps of detecting unbalanced indexes.

5.5 Rebuild Unbalanced Indexes

How-To 5.4 shows how to detect unbalanced indexes. For performance reasons, these indexes should be rebuilt to improve the disk throughput. This How-To takes you through the steps of rebuilding any unbalanced indexes, as well as providing suggestions for fast index rebuilding.

5.6 Enforce Uniqueness via an Index

Unique indexes may be created that ensure that the values of the indexed columns are unique for each record. This fulfills business rules and is created from a primary or unique constraint. A unique index may also be created manually with no corresponding constraint. Any attempt to add or update a record that duplicates the values of any other record will fail with an error. This How-To describes the steps used to create a unique index.

5.7 Partition an Index

When an index is partitioned, it allows for greater storage flexibility and index availability. A partitioned index may be split into several parts, each one residing on different tablespaces and with different storage options. This How-To covers the methods used to create a partitioned index.

5.8 Create a Bitmapped Index

Regular indexes are appropriate to improve query speed for columns that have many different values. When columns have only a few distinct values, such as TRUE/FALSE, a regular index will worsen performance, both on selecting data and on manipulating data. A bitmapped index, however, is ideal for such a situation. Not only will performance improve with these low-cardinality cases, the bitmapped indexes are stored in a much more compact format than regular indexes, saving disk space. This How-To describes the steps used to create a bitmapped index.

COMPLEXITY
BEGINNING

5.1 How do I...
Determine all of the indexes on a particular table?

Problem

The most commonly used method to improve data queries is the creation of indexes. Many times, it is important to know how a table has been indexed. How do I determine all of the indexes on a particular table?

Technique

The DBA_INDEXES data dictionary view contains information on each index within the database. By querying this view, you can determine which indexes exist on which tables. In this How-To, a sample table and indexes will be created. Then, the process of determining the indexes on the table will be shown.

Steps

1. For regular indexes to exist, you must first create a table. Connect to SQL*Plus as the WAITE account and run CHP5_1.SQL, which will create a sample table used throughout this How-To.

```
SQL> GET CHP5_1.sql
  1   CREATE TABLE EMPLOYEE05
  2   (EMPLOYEE_NAME    VARCHAR2(30) NOT NULL,
  3    SSN              NUMBER,
  4    SALARY           NUMBER,
  5    STATE            VARCHAR2(2),
  6    JOB_DESCRIPTION  VARCHAR2(100),
  7    DATE_EMPLOYED    DATE)
  8   TABLESPACE USER_DATA PCTFREE 10, PCTUSED 90
  9   STORAGE ( INITIAL 1M NEXT 500K PCTINCREASE 50
 10            MINEXTENTS 1 MAXEXTENTS 100);
SQL> /

Table Created.
```

2. Now that you have created the EMPLOYEE05 table, you are ready to create some sample indexes. A discussion of sizing indexes is discussed in How-To 5.3. CHP5_2.SQL contains a CREATE INDEX command that will create an index on the SSN column of the EMPLOYEE05 table. The SSN column was chosen for an index because employees are selected by their SSN in this example, and an index will speed up such queries. Run CHP5_2.SQL to create the SSN_INDEX index.

```
SQL> GET CHP5_2
  1   CREATE INDEX SSN_INDEX
  2   ON EMPLOYEE05 (SSN)
  3   TABLESPACE USER_DATA
SQL> /

Index Created.
```

3. At this point, the EMPLOYEE05 table has been created with an index on the SSN column. CHP5_3.SQL, shown in Figure 5.1, contains a script that will list all indexes on a table.

```
SELECT INDEX_NAME, OWNER, TABLE_NAME
FROM DBA_INDEXES
WHERE OWNER='&owner' AND
      TABLE_NAME='&table_name'
ORDER BY OWNER, TABLE_NAME, INDEX_NAME;
```

Figure 5.1 CHP5_3.SQL contains a query on the DBA_INDEXES view that will determine the indexes for a table and owner.

4. When the script is run, the user will be prompted for an owner and table name. Enter WAITE for the owner, and EMPLOYEE05 for the table. This is shown in Figure 5.2. The script can be run for any owner and any table, making it a simple, yet valuable, tool for a developer or database administrator.

How It Works

The DBA_INDEXES data dictionary view contains information on each index in the database. Step 1 runs the CHP5_1.SQL to create the EMPLOYEE05 sample table. Step 2 runs the CHP5_2.SQL to create an index on the EMPLOYEE05 table. Step 3 queries the DBA_INDEXES data dictionary view for the WAITE owner and the EMPLOYEE05 table. The result is a list of all indexes on the EMPLOYEE05 table.

Comments

Indexes may improve the performance of SELECT statements. They will slow down inserts, updates, and deletes, as any of these manipulations on the table will also be performed on the index. Five thousand record inserts on a table, for instance, will also result in 5,000 index inserts, slowing performance. Be sure to understand what the index will be used for, and determine if the trade-off is worthwhile.

The impact of an index on a query will depend on the cardinality of the columns that the index is comprised of. For instance, a column that only contains "True" or "False" as values (low cardinality) will be a poor choice for a regular index. A column with many possible values, such as Social Security numbers (high cardinality), will be a good choice for a regular index. How-To 5.8 explains how to create a bitmapped index, which is better suited for low cardinality columns.

```
SQL> START C:\CHP5_3.SQL
Enter value for owner: WAITE
old   3: WHERE OWNER='&owner' AND
new   3: WHERE OWNER='WAITE' AND
Enter value for table_name: EMPLOYEE05
old   4:        TABLE_NAME='&table_name'
new   4:        TABLE_NAME='EMPLOYEE05'

INDEX_NAME                           OWNER                          TABLE_NAME
--------------------------------     --------------------------     ----------------
NAME_SSN_INDEX                       WAITE                          EMPLOYEE05
SSN_INDEX                            WAITE                          EMPLOYEE05

SQL> |
```

Figure 5.2 A sample run of the CHP5_3.SQL script.

5.2 How do I...
Determine all of the indexes owned by a particular user?

Problem

My database has several owners, tables, and indexes. For better organization and management, I need to see what indexes are owned by each of the database's user accounts. How do I determine all of the indexes owned by a particular user?

Technique

The DBA_INDEXES data dictionary view contains information on each index within the database. How-To 5.1 describes how to determine the indexes on a table. By querying the same data dictionary view, but providing different WHERE clause conditions, you can determine which indexes exist that are owned by a user account.

Steps

1. Connect to SQL*Plus as the WAITE user account. If you have not created the EMPLOYEE05 table, run the CHP5_1.SQL script to create it. Also, if you have not created the SSN_INDEX on the EMPLOYEE05 table, run the CHP5_2.SQL script to create it.

2. Run the CHP5_4.SQL script, shown in Figure 5.3, to determine which indexes exist for a given user account.

```
SELECT INDEX_NAME, OWNER, TABLE_NAME
FROM DBA_INDEXES
WHERE OWNER='&owner'
ORDER BY OWNER, TABLE_NAME, INDEX_NAME;
```

Figure 5.3 The CHP5_4.SQL script contains a query on the DBA_INDEXES view that will determine which indexes are owned by a particular user account.

```
BLOCK HEADER SIZE = 113 + ( 24 * INITRANS )
```

Figure 5.4 The CHP5_4.SQL script
results for the SYS user account.

When the script is run, the user will be prompted for an owner. Enter
WAITE for the owner. This interaction is shown in Figure 5.4. The script
can be run for any owner in the database. Because there is only one index
for the WAITE user account at this point, the query result appears
identical to the result from How-To 5.1.

3. Run the CHP5_4.SQL script again, passing SYS as the owner. The result,
part of which is shown in Figure 5.4, has many more indexes than the
WAITE user account.

How It Works

This How-To works very similarly to How-To 5.1. The DBA_INDEXES data
dictionary view contains information on each index in the database. If not
already created, you can create the EMPLOYEE05 sample table by running
CHP5_1.SQL. Also, the SSN_INDEX sample index on the EMPLOYEE05 table is
created if it does not already exist.

First, CHP5_4.SQL queries the DBA_INDEXES data dictionary view for the
WAITE owner. The result is a list of all indexes on the EMPLOYEE05 table,
identical to that of How-To 5.1 because there is just one index. The
CHP5_4.SQL script is run again for the SYS account, and many indexes are
returned.

Comments

The CHP5_4.SQL script will order the index list by OWNER first, then
TABLE_NAME, and finally INDEX_NAME. This will improve readability across
several index owners.

COMPLEXITY

INTERMEDIATE

5.3 How do I...
Determine an index's initial size parameters?

Problem

I am about to create an index on one of my tables and would like to know how
large to make the INITIAL storage parameter. I also know that the table will

eventually grow in the coming months and would like to plan accordingly so that I do not use too much or too little storage space. How do I determine an index's initial size parameters?

Technique

In order to determine the INITIAL storage parameter of an index, you first need some basic information about the database and the index. For the calculations, you need to know the number of records in the table that the index is based upon, with a 6–12 month growth period. Also, you will need to determine the average length of all indexed columns, as well as the database block size. All of these steps are described in this How-To.

Calculating the average length of all indexed columns is similar to the process of determining the average record length when creating a table. This is explained in How-To 4.5. The difference is that the ROWID is stored within the index, and the bytes required for overhead are different.

Steps

1. Connect to the database as the WAITE user account. The first step is to determine the database block size. You can determine this by connecting to SQL*Plus and executing the CHP5_5.SQL script, as shown here.

```
SQL> GET CHP5_5
  1   SELECT VALUE
  2   FROM V$PARAMETER
  3   WHERE NAME = 'db_block_size';
SQL> /
VALUE
--------------------
4096

1 row selected.
```

Within each block of size **db_block_size** bytes, there will be a block header, index column length, and an index value size.

2. The block header size is calculated by the formula in Figure 5.5. By default, this value is 113 bytes.

3. Now that the block header size has been determined, the available space within each block must be determined. This process is similar to the one

```
BLOCK HEADER SIZE = 113 + ( 24 * INITRANS )
```

Figure 5.5 The calculation used to determine block header size.

```
AVAILABLE SPACE WITHIN EACH BLOCK =
(DB_BLOCK_SIZE - BLOCK_HEADER_SIZE) -
(DB_BLOCK_SIZE - BLOCK_HEADER_SIZE) * (PCTFREE / 100) )
```

Figure 5.6 The calculation used to determine available space within each block.

used for tables, explained in How-To 4.5. The factors are the database block size and the PCTFREE parameter for the index. The formula for calculating the available space within each block is shown in Figure 5.6.

For example, if a block is 4096 bytes, there are 161 overhead bytes, and PCTFREE is 90; then the total available space for Oracle records is (4096-161) × .9 (about 3486 bytes).

4. Now that the available space for indexes within each block has been determined, you must find out the size in bytes of an average index entry. There is no clear method to determine this before the table has data. However, do a "DESCRIBE" on the table and try to deduce the total bytes. For example, the EMPLOYEE05 table is described in Figure 5.7.

We will create an index on the SSN column. So, for an example, the SSN column can average 9 bytes. Each indexed column will need an additional byte for an internal separator. Also, the ROWID is stored along with each index entry. The Oracle8 formatted ROWID is 8 bytes. Two additional bytes for overhead are added. The formula for calculating index space for an entry is shown in Figure 5.8. In our example, the total will average 20 bytes for each index entry on SSN.

```
SQL> desc employee05
 Name                             Null?     Type
 -------------------------------- --------- ----
 EMPLOYEE_NAME                    NOT NULL  VARCHAR2(30)
 SSN                                        NUMBER
 SALARY                                     NUMBER
 STATE                                      VARCHAR2(2)
 JOB_DESCRIPTION                            VARCHAR2(100)
 DATE_EMPLOYED                              DATE

SQL>
```

Figure 5.7 The description of EMPLOYEE05.

```
INDEX ENTRY LENGTH =
2 + 8 + (NUMBER OF COLUMNS IN INDEX number of indexes) +
(TOTAL LENGTH OF ALL INDEXED COLUMNS)
```

Figure 5.8 The calculation used to determine the length of an index entry.

5. Now that both the available space within a block and the average size of an index entry are known, you can determine how many index records will fit within a block. This is determined by the formula in Figure 5.9.

In our example, the available space within each block was determined to be 3,486 bytes, and the average index entry length was determined to be 20 bytes. Thus, 3486/20, or about 174 index entries can fit within one block.

6. The final step to determine the INITIAL extent of the index is to determine how many total blocks the index will comprise of, and use that in the CREATE INDEX statement. The index will be the total size of all blocks. This is determined by knowing the total number of records you expect for the table (including growth over several months), the block size, and the number of records that will fit within a block. Note that the true size of the index depends on the number of records that do not contain NULL values within the indexed columns. Figure 5.10 shows the formula for determining this.

In our ongoing example, we will assume that there will be one million records. Of these, 750000 records will contain an SSN value (the other 250000 have NULL SSN values). Thus, the INITIAL extent for an index on the SSN column should be (4096 × 750000)/174, or 17655172 bytes. When issuing the CREATE INDEX command, you may specify 17655172, 17242K, or 17M.

7. Just as with a table, the NEXT extent of an index determines how large an extent Oracle will obtain if the INITIAL extent is ever filled. This is an arbitrary number and will depend on how large you want to incrementally expand your table. If you do not know this, set the NEXT parameter to ten percent of the INITIAL storage parameter.

The PCTFREE parameter determines how much free space within each block will be reserved for expansion of existing records. If you do not anticipate many

```
AVERAGE INDEX RECORDS PER DATABASE BLOCK =
(AVAILABLE SPACE WITHIN EACH BLOCK) / (INDEX ENTRY LENGTH)
```

Figure 5.9 The calculation used to determine how many index records will fit within a block.

```
INITIAL EXTENT OF AN INDEX =
(DB_BLOCK_SIZE * (NUMBER OF RECORDS WITH NON-NULL INDEX COLUMNS) ) /
(AVERAGE INDEX RECORDS PER DATABASE BLOCK)
```

Figure 5.10 The formula for determining the INITIAL storage parameter of an index.

inserts, updates, or deletes, set the PCTFREE to a low value such as 10. If you anticipate the data within the indexed columns to grow or shrink in size, such as when adding text to an indexed text field, set the PCTFREE to a higher value such as 30 or 40. Otherwise, you will get an unbalanced index. Identifying and fixing such indexes will be described in How-To 5.4 and How-To 5.5.

How It Works

Step 1 determines the `db_block_size` for the database. Step 2 determines the block header size. Step 3 calculates the available space within each block. Step 4 determines the length of an average index entry. This information is used in step 5 to determine how many index records will fit within a database block. The final calculation is done in Step 6 to determine the INITIAL extent size of the index. Step 7 provides general information to determine the NEXT and PCTFREE storage parameters of an index.

Comments

When calculating the index entry size, there is usually 5% additional space for index branch information. This is insignificant unless the data length is known with certainty, in which case you should add 5% to your INITIAL extent.

It is best for performance to create the index in a tablespace other than that of the corresponding table. This will reduce disk contention.

PCTUSED cannot be specified for indexes.

COMPLEXITY
ADVANCED

5.4 How do I...
Detect unbalanced indexes?

Problem

I have indexes on tables that are heavily inserted to, updated, or deleted from. I know that it is important to periodically examine all of my indexes to determine if they have become unbalanced. How do I detect unbalanced indexes?

Technique

An unbalanced index has many records clumped close together on the index tree due to their similar indexed values. When an index is unbalanced, parts of an index are accessed more frequently than others, from which disk contention may occur, creating a bottleneck in performance. Statistics can be gathered on an index by issuing ANALYZE INDEX *INDEX_NAME* COMPUTE|ESTIMATE STATISTICS. The statistics appear in the USER_INDEXES, ALL_INDEXES_, and

DBA_INDEXES data dictionary views. Also, additional statistics can be placed into the INDEX_STATS virtual table by using the VALIDATE INDEX *INDEX_NAME* statement.

Steps

1. Connect to SQL*Plus as the WAITE user account. If you have not created the EMPLOYEE05 table, run the CHP5_1.SQL script to create it. Also, if you have not created the SSN_INDEX on the EMPLOYEE05 table, run the CHP5_2.SQL script to create it.

Initially, the EMPLOYEE05 table will have no records, and neither will the index have index entries. To determine statistics, you must either validate the index or generate statistics. This must be done manually, unless a program is written to automatically gather statistics. This How-To will demonstrate both methods.

2. Gather statistics on the SSN_INDEX. Run the CHP5_6.SQL script to generate statistics. When prompted for an owner, enter WAITE; and when prompted for an index, enter SSN_INDEX. This script may be reused for any index in the database. For large indexes (over one hundred thousand records in the underlying table), use ESTIMATE instead of COMPUTE for faster response time.

```
SQL> GET CHP5_6
  1  ANALYZE INDEX &owner..&index_name
  2  COMPUTE STATISTICS
SQL> /
Enter value for owner: WAITE
Enter value for index_name: SSN_INDEX

Index Analyzed.

SQL>
```

3. At this point, statistics will indicate that the index is well-balanced, because there are no records in the underlying EMPLOYEE05 table. You can determine statistics by querying the DBA_INDEXES data dictionary view. Later in this How-To is the description and explanation of the DBA_INDEXES view. Run the CHP5_7.SQL script to gather statistics on how balanced the index is. Enter SSN_INDEX for the INDEX_NAME, and WAITE for the owner.

```
SQL> GET CHP5_7.sql
  1 SELECT BLEVEL, DECODE(BLEVEL,0,'OK BLEVEL',1,'OK BLEVEL',
  2                         2,'OK BLEVEL',3,'OK BLEVEL',
  3                         4,'OK BLEVEL','BLEVEL IS TOO HIGH') OK
  4 FROM DBA_INDEXES
  5 WHERE INDEX_NAME='&index_name' AND
  6       OWNER='&owner'
SQL> /
```

```
Enter name for index_name: SSN_INDEX
Enter name from owner: WAITE

HEIGHT      OK
------      ----------
0           OK BLEVEL

1 row selected.
```

You can see that the BLEVEL 0 is okay. The BLEVEL (or branch level) is part of the B-Trieve index format and relates to the number of times Oracle has to narrow its search on the index while searching for a particular record. In some cases, a separate disk hit is requested for each BLEVEL. If the BLEVEL were to be more than four, it is recommended to rebuild the index, as shown in How-To 5.5.

4. At this point, only the BLEVEL has been investigated. To further determine if an index is unbalanced, further statistics should be gathered. To do this, use the VALIDATE INDEX command by running CHP5_8.SQL. Enter SSN_INDEX for the INDEX_NAME and WAITE for the OWNER.

```
SQL> GET CHP5_8.SQL
  1  VALIDATE INDEX &owner..&index_name
SQL> /
Enter value for owner: WAITE
Enter value for index_name: SSN_INDEX

Index analyzed.

SQL>
```

5. At this point, the INDEX_STATS virtual table is populated with current statistics for the SSN_INDEX index. Query information on the deleted leaf rows, as compared to the total rows by running the CHP5_9.SQL script. Again, enter SSN_INDEX for index_name. The INDEX_STATS table does not contain an OWNER column and assumes you are looking for statistics for indexes created by your active session only.

```
SQL> GET CHP5_9.sql
  1  SELECT DEL_LF_ROWS*100 /
  2         DECODE((DEL_LF_ROWS+LF_ROWS),0,
  3         1,(DEL_LF_ROWS+LF_ROWS)) PCT_DELETED,
  4         (LF_ROWS-DISTINCT_KEYS)*100 /
  5         DECODE(LF_ROWS,0,1,LF_ROWS) DISTINCTIVENESS
  6  FROM INDEX_STATS
  7  WHERE NAME = '&index_name'
SQL> /
Enter value for index_name: SSN_INDEX

PCT DELETED       DISTINCTIVENESS
-------------     -----------------
          0                     0

SQL>
```

The PCT_DELETED column shows what percent of leaf entries (index entries) have been deleted and remain unfilled. The more deleted entries that exist on an index, the more unbalanced the index becomes. If the PCT_DELETED is 20% or higher, the index is a candidate for rebuilding. If you are more stringent and have time to rebuild indexes more frequently, then do so if the value is higher than 10%.

The distinctiveness column shows how often a value for the column(s) of the index is repeated on average. For example, if a table has 10000 records and 9000 distinct SSN values, the formula would result in $(10000 - 9000) \times 100 / 10000 = 10$. This shows a good distribution of values. If, however, the table has 10000 records and only two distinct SSN values, the formula would result in $(10000 - 2) \times 100 / 10000 = 99.98$. This shows that there are very few distinct values as a percentage of total records in the column. Such columns are not candidates for a rebuild but are good candidates for bitmapped indexes. A full discussion of bitmapped indexes is detailed in How-To 5.8.

How It Works

Step 1 creates the sample table and index used in this How-To. Step 2 gathers statistics on the SSN_INDEX index and places them in the DBA_INDEXES data dictionary view. Step 3 analyzes the height of the index to determine if the index is unbalanced. Step 4 validates the index, putting additional statistics into the INDEX_STATS virtual table. Step 5 reviews the statistics and determines if the index is unbalanced in a different way from Step 3. It also determines if the index is a candidate for a bitmapped index.

Table 5.1 gives the description of the INDEX_STATS data dictionary view.

Table 5.1 Explanation of the INDEX_STATS view

COLUMN NAME	DESCRIPTION
HEIGHT	Height of B-Tree
BLOCKS	Blocks allocated to the index
NAME	Index name
PARTITION_NAME	Partition name, if the index is partitioned
LF_ROWS	Number of leaf rows
LF_BLKS	Number of leaf blocks
LF_ROWS_LEN	Total length of all leaf rows
LF_BLK_LEN	Total usable space in leaf block
BR_ROWS	Number of branch rows
BR_BLKS	Number of branch blocks
BR_ROWS_LEN	Total length of all branch rows
BR_BLK_LEN	Total length of all branch blocks
DEL_LF_ROWS	Number of deleted leaf rows left unfilled

COLUMN NAME	DESCRIPTION
DEL_LF_ROWS_LEN	Total length of all unfilled deleted leaf rows
DISTINCT_KEYS	Number of distinct keys
MOST_REPEATED_KEY	Number of times the most-used key is repeated
BTREE_SPACE	Total B-Tree space
USED_SPACE	Total allocated space
PCT_USED	Percent of total allocated space that is being used
ROWS_PER_KEY	Average number of rows for keys
BLKS_GETS_PER_ACCESS	Average blocks read when searching for an index entry

Table 5.2 shows the description of the DBA_INDEXES data dictionary view.

Table 5.2 Explanation of the DBA_INDEXES view

COLUMN NAME	DESCRIPTION
OWNER	User account that created the index.
INDEX_NAME	Name of the index.
INDEX_TYPE	Type of index (NORMAL, LOB, CLUSTER, and so on).
TABLE_OWNER	Owner of the index's table.
TABLE_NAME	Name of the index's table.
TABLE_TYPE	Type of the index's table (TABLE, CLUSTER, and so on).
UNIQUENESS	Uniqueness status (UNIQUE, NONUNIQUE).
TABLESPACE_NAME	Tablespace in which the index resides.
INI_TRANS	Initial number of transactions within each block.
MAX_TRANS	Maximum number of concurrent transactions that can use the block.
INITIAL_EXTENT	Size, in bytes, allocated for the first extent of the table.
NEXT_EXTENT	Size, in bytes, allocated for subsequent extents.
MIN_EXTENTS	Minimum number of extents to allocate when creating or rebuilding the index.
MAX_EXTENTS	Maximum number of extents.
PCT_INCREASE	Percent that each extent past the INITIAL and NEXT will increase in size by.
PCT_THRESHOLD	Threshold percentage of block space defined for each index entry.
INCLUDE_COLUMN	(Index organized table only) The last indexed column to be included in the top index portion.
FREELISTS	Number of freelist buffers allocated for the table. Set to the maximum number of concurrent insert processes you predict for the index.
FREELIST GROUPS	Parallel Server option to determine number of freelist groups for all instances inserting into the index.
PCT_FREE	Percentage of space to keep free within each block of the index.
LOGGING	YES or NO value to determine if logging is used. If not, the underlying table can be loaded in direct mode, created AS SELECT ... FROM table_b, and other options quicker.

continued on next page

continued from previous page

COLUMN NAME	DESCRIPTION
BLEVEL	B-Tree level. This shows the depth of the index from branch to leaf.
LEAF_BLOCKS	Number of leaf blocks in the index.
DISTINCT_KEYS	Number of distinct keys in the index. This is important for determining if bitmapped indexes should be used.
AVG_LEAF_BLOCKS_PER_KEY	Average leaf blocks per key.
AVG_DATA_BLOCKS_PER_KEY	Average data blocks per key.
CLUSTERING_FACTOR	Amount of "order" in the underlying table.
STATUS	Index status (VALID, or INVALID, DIRECT_LOAD).
NUM_ROWS	Number of rows used. This does not include NULL values from the underlying table.
SAMPLE_SIZE	Shows what percent estimate was used in the ESTIMATE clause of the ANALYZE command (0 if COMPUTE was used).
LAST_ANALYZED	Date and time the table was last analyzed. Important to see if statistics need to be refreshed.
DEGREE	(Partitioned indexes only) Number of threads per instance.
INSTANCES	(Partitioned, Parallel Server indexes only) Number of instances across which the indexes are to be scanned.
PARTITIONED	Determines if the index is partitioned (YES or NO).
TEMPORARY	Determines if the index is temporary (Y or N).
GENERATED	Did Oracle generate the index name (Y) or the user (N).
BUFFER_POOL	DEFAULT or other pool name: displays the default buffer pool in which the index will be placed.

It is important to note that statistics are not automatically generated. You must either manually refresh table and index statistics, or set up a process that will do this automatically. It is recommended to refresh statistics after objects change more than about five percent of their data.

Comments

You can also gather index statistics by estimating or computing statistics on the table of which the index is based upon. Oracle will automatically generate statistics on the indexes of the table.

Once you log out of the database, all data from the INDEX_STATS virtual table is removed.

COMPLEXITY
BEGINNING

5.5 How do I...
Rebuild unbalanced indexes?

Problem

I have found an index that is unbalanced, after following the steps in How-To 5.4. For performance reasons, I want these indexes to be rebuilt. How do I rebuild unbalanced indexes?

Technique

Use the ALTER INDEX *INDEX_NAME* REBUILD command (UNRECOVER-ABLE is an option). With indexes, you can always rebuild them because they are driven by table data. Thus, you should always use UNRECOVERABLE, especially for large indexes. The only loss with this option is that the index is unrecoverable in the event of a crash, but it can be rebuilt easily.

Steps

1. Connect to SQL*Plus as the WAITE user account. Assume that the EMPLOYEE05 table has been in use for a while, and hundreds of thousands of records have been inserted, deleted, and updated. This might cause the index SSN_INDEX to become unbalanced. For this How-To, we will pretend that the index needs to be rebuilt.

The syntax of the ALTER INDEX ... REBUILD command is shown in Figure 5.11.

2. Run the CHP5_10.SQL script to rebuild an index. The script will prompt you for an owner and an index name. For this How-To, enter WAITE for the OWNER, and SSN_INDEX for the INDEX_NAME. This interaction is shown in Figure 5.12.

```
ALTER INDEX owner.index_name REBUILD [UNRECOVERABLE];
```

Figure 5.11 The syntax of the ALTER INDEX ... REBUILD command.

```
Enter value for owner: WAITE
Enter value for index_name: SSN_INDEX
old   1: ALTER INDEX &owner..&index_name REBUILD UNRECOVERABLE
new   1: ALTER INDEX WAITE.SSN_INDEX REBUILD UNRECOVERABLE

Index altered.

SQL>
SQL>
```

Figure 5.12 A sample run-through of
CHP5_10.SQL, which rebuilds an index.

How It Works

Any index may be rebuilt by running the CHP5_10.SQL script. The user is
prompted for the owner and index name, which is then rebuilt.

The UNRECOVERABLE option is used to improve performance. This option
bypassed redo usage and reduces sorting processing while rebuilding the index.
The larger the index is, the more effective the UNRECOVERABLE option
becomes. The only negative aspect is that the index may become corrupt if the
database were to crash during the rebuild. This really does not matter, as you
can simply re-create or rebuild the index when the database is brought back up.
As long as the table that the index is based upon remains intact, an index can
always be re-created.

Comments

The REBUILD option of the ALTER INDEX command saves you from
remembering storage parameters, dropping the index, and writing a CREATE
INDEX statement.

COMPLEXITY
BEGINNING

5.6   How do I...
Enforce uniqueness via an index?

Problem

My business rules require that each record in a table have unique values in
certain columns. I want to enforce this rule by making a unique index. I know
that this will also improve performance when querying data. How do I enforce
uniqueness via an index?

Technique

Use the UNIQUE clause of the CREATE INDEX command to create unique
indexes. A unique index will ensure that no two records will have the same
values in the columns that comprise the index. Any attempt to add a new record

that contains duplicate values will be rejected. Also, any attempt to alter the data contained in the indexed columns will be rejected.

Steps

1. Connect to SQL*Plus as the WAITE user account. If you have not created the EMPLOYEE05 table, run the CHP5_1.SQL script to create it. The description of the EMPLOYEE05 table appears in Figure 5.13.

The decision of which columns to make unique, if any, will depend on the business rules of your application. For example, it may not make sense to make the STATE column unique, as there may be more than one employee from a given state. It may also not make sense to make the EMPLOYEE_NAME column unique, as there may be two employees with the same name. Also, there may be two different possible employee names for a Social Security number (if you store nicknames, for example). In this How-To, we will create a unique index on the combination of EMPLOYEE_NAME and SSN columns for the EMPLOYEE05 table.

2. Create the unique index on the EMPLOYEE_NAME and SSN columns by running CHP5_11.SQL.

```
SQL> GET CHP5_11.sql
  1  CREATE UNIQUE INDEX name_ssn_index
  2  ON EMPLOYEE05 (EMPLOYEE_NAME, SSN)
SQL> /

Index created.
```

3. At this point, Oracle will automatically reject any records that duplicate the combination of EMPLOYEE_NAME and SSN. Insert a sample record into the EMPLOYEE05 table by running CHP5_12.SQL.

```
SQL> GET CHP5_12.sql
  1  INSERT INTO EMPLOYEE05
  2  VALUES ('AARON LIPMAN',111111111,100000,
  3          'CA','Photocopy Boy', sysdate)
SQL> /

1 row created.
```

```
SQL> desc employee05
 Name                             Null?    Type
 -------------------------------- -------- ----
 EMPLOYEE_NAME                    NOT NULL VARCHAR2(30)
 SSN                                       NUMBER
 SALARY                                    NUMBER
 STATE                                     VARCHAR2(2)
 JOB_DESCRIPTION                           VARCHAR2(100)
 DATE_EMPLOYED                             DATE

SQL> |
```

Figure 5.13 The description of the EMPLOYEE05 table.

4. At this point, there will be a new record in the table. If, however, you try to insert another record containing the same EMPLOYEE_NAME and SSN, Oracle will reject the statement and return an error. Run CHP5_13.SQL to create such a record.

```
SQL> GET CHP5_13.sql
  1   INSERT INTO EMPLOYEE05
  2   VALUES ('AARON LIPMAN',111111111,25000,
  3           'MA','Student Intern', sysdate)
SQL> /

INSERT INTO EMPLOYEE05
            *
ERROR at line 1:
ORA-00001: unique constraint (WAITE.NAME_SSN_INDEX) violated
```

You can see that Oracle automatically rejected the insert attempt.

How It Works

Step 1 creates the EMPLOYEE05 table used in this How-To. Step 2 creates the unique index on the EMPLOYEE_NAME and SSN columns together on the EMPLOYEE05 table. Step 3 inserts a sample record into the table. Step 4 tries to enter a record with duplicate EMPLOYEE_NAME and SSN values. Oracle rejects this attempt due to the existence of the unique key NAME_SSN_INDEX.

Comments

Unique keys are automatically created when a primary key constraint or a unique key constraint are created on the table. How-To 6.1 describes how to add such a primary key constraint.

COMPLEXITY
INTERMEDIATE

5.7 How do I...
Partition an index?

Problem

I am creating a very large index and want to improve access to the table by using a partitioned index. Also, I want to perform index maintenance such as generating statistics, restoring index parts, and data loading on one part of an index, while the rest of the index is available for use by users. How do I partition an index?

Technique

Use the PARTITION clause of the CREATE INDEX or ALTER INDEX command to create a partitioned index. A partitioned index, like a partitioned table, allows for multiple partitions with potentially different storage parameters, including tablespaces. There are two methods to define a partitioned index: LOCAL and GLOBAL. A LOCAL partitioned index is based upon the underlying partitioned table. It is partitioned with the same ranges of the table, and repartitions itself automatically as the underlying table is repartitioned. This is the preferred method in most cases, as the partition logic is driven by the underlying table. The syntax for creating a local partitioned index is shown in Figure 5.14.

A GLOBAL partitioned index allows for flexibility in defining partitioning ranges. If you want to partition your index more finely or differently than the underlying table, define your index as GLOBAL. The syntax for creating a GLOBAL partitioned index is shown in Figure 5.15.

The PARTITION BY RANGE clause, specified only with the global index, defines which columns are to be used to base the partition ranges upon. As with a partitioned table, the column list specifies the columns on which the index is partitioned.

The PARTITION clauses specify the individual partition names, their storage parameters, and their tablespaces. For LOCAL indexes, each index partition must correspond one-to-one with the underlying table's partitions.

The VALUES LESS THAN clause specifies the upper bounds for the partitions. This can only be defined in a GLOBAL index. All LOCAL indexes automatically are assigned to the range of the corresponding table partition. Be sure to include a sufficiently large MAXVALUE for the last partition.

```
CREATE INDEX index_name
ON table_name (column_name1, [column_name2,] ... )
[TABLESPACE tablespace_name]
LOCAL
    (PARTITION partition_name1 [TABLESPACE tablespace_name1]
    [STORAGE (storage_parameter1 storage_value1, ...)],
    PARTITION partition_name2 [TABLESPACE tablespace_name2]
    [STORAGE (storage_parameter2 storage_value2, ...)] ...)
```

Figure 5.14 The syntax of SQL to create a local partitioned index.

```
CREATE INDEX index_name
ON table_name (column_name1, [column_name2,] ... )
PARTITION BY RANGE (partition_column1, [partition_column2,] ...)
    (PARTITION partition_name1 VALUES [LESS|GREATER] THAN range_numbers1)
    [STORAGE (storage_parameter1 storage_value1, ...)],
    (PARTITION partition_name2 VALUES [LESS|GREATER] THAN range_numbers2)
[TABLESPACE tablespace_name2]
[STORAGE (storage_parameter2 storage_value2, ...)],
...)
[TABLESPACE tablespace_name]
```

Figure 5.15 The syntax of SQL to create a global partitioned index.

Steps

1. Connect to SQL*Plus as the WAITE user account. Create a partitioned table that will be used as a basis for the partitioned index by running CH5_14.SQL, as shown in Figure 5.16. For more information on partitioned tables, refer to How-To 4.10.

2. The EMP05 table, with partitions stored in the USER, TEMP, and SYSTEM tablespaces. Each partition of the table will also have its own storage parameters. Now, run the CHP5_15.SQL script, shown in Figure 5.17, to

```
SQL> GET C:\CHP5_14.SQL
  1  CREATE TABLE EMP05
  2  (EMPLOYEE_NAME    VARCHAR2(30) NOT NULL,
  3   SALARY          NUMBER,
  4   JOB_DESCRIPTION VARCHAR2(100),
  5   DATE_EMPLOYED   DATE
  6  )
  7  PARTITION BY RANGE(SALARY)
  8     (PARTITION LOW_SALARY VALUES LESS THAN (25000)
  9                 TABLESPACE USER_DATA
 10                 STORAGE (INITIAL 50K NEXT 50K),
 11        PARTITION MEDIUM_SALARY VALUES LESS THAN (50000)
 12                 TABLESPACE USER_DATA
 13                 STORAGE (INITIAL 100K NEXT 100K),
 14        PARTITION LARGE_SALARY VALUES LESS THAN (150000)
 15                 TABLESPACE TEMPORARY_DATA
 16                 STORAGE (INITIAL 50K NEXT 50K),
 17        PARTITION OUTRAGEOUS_SALARY VALUES LESS THAN (9999999999)
 18                 TABLESPACE SYSTEM
 19*                STORAGE (INITIAL 10K NEXT 10K))
SQL> /

Table created.

SQL> |
```

Figure 5.16 CHP5_14.SQL shows the syntax to create a partitioned table.

```
SQL> GET C:\CHP5_15.SQL
  1  CREATE INDEX EMP05_PART_INDEX
  2  ON EMP05 (EMPLOYEE_NAME)
  3  LOCAL (PARTITION LOW_SALARY
  4               TABLESPACE USER_DATA
  5               STORAGE (INITIAL 10K NEXT 10K),
  6        PARTITION MEDIUM_SALARY
  7               TABLESPACE USER_DATA
  8               STORAGE (INITIAL 20K NEXT 20K),
  9        PARTITION LARGE_SALARY
 10               TABLESPACE TEMPORARY_DATA
 11               STORAGE (INITIAL 10K NEXT 10K),
 12        PARTITION OUTRAGEOUS_SALARY
 13               TABLESPACE SYSTEM
 14*              STORAGE (INITIAL 1K NEXT 1K))
SQL> /

Index created.

SQL> |
```

Figure 5.17 CHP5_15.SQL creates a local partitioned index.

create a LOCAL partitioned index. The EMP05 table has four partitions, and so the index must have four partitions. Note that for this LOCAL index, the ranges are not specified, as they will inherit the ranges for the underlying EMP05 table.

How It Works

The CREATE INDEX command has an optional PARTITION clause to create partitioned indexes. Step 1 describes the difference between local and global partitioned indexes. Step 2 creates the EMP05 partitioned table to be used as a basis for the partitioned index. Step 3 creates the EMP05_PART_INDEX local partitioned index using the underlying value ranges from the underlying EMP05 partitioned table.

Partitioned indexes have several advantages over regular indexes. As with partitioned tables, if one part of the partition is unavailable, the other parts are available for select, insert, update, and delete. Only those records that are contained within the down partition will be unavailable. Also, index partitions may be rebuilt one at a time and structures validated. Index partitions may also be spread across multiple tablespaces, with varying storage parameters. All of these features greatly improve the availability and maintenance of index.

Comments

In the example, the SYSTEM and TEMP tablespaces were chosen for storage of partition parts. In reality, you would not want to put any objects in these tablespaces. They were included to show a simple example of how to put partition parts into separate tablespaces.

You cannot truncate an index partition; however, the ALTER TABLE TRUNCATE PARTITION statement truncates the matching partition in each local index.

As with partitioned tables, the indexes columns may not be of the LONG, RAW, or ROWID datatypes.

There may be up to 64,000 partitions on any index.

COMPLEXITY
INTERMEDIATE

5.8   How do I...
Create a bitmapped index?

Problem

I want to create an index on some columns that do not have many distinct values. Using a regular index will slow my performance in querying data. I know that bitmapped indexes are much more effective, both from a performance perspective and a storage perspective. How do I create a bitmapped index?

Technique

A bitmap index is ideal for when indexed columns have only a few distinct values, such as TRUE/FALSE. Regular indexes will worsen performance in such cases, both on selecting data and on manipulating data. The bitmapped indexes will be stored in a much more compact format than regular indexes.

Use the BITMAP clause of the CREATE INDEX command to create bitmap indexes. A bitmap index will greatly improve query performance on columns with low cardinality—columns with few distinct values as compared to the number of records. This How-To will show how to determine if it is appropriate to create a bitmap index and then will describe the steps used to create one.

Steps

1. Before creating a bitmap index, it important to know what a bitmap index is and if using one will improve performance. Bitmap indexes are ideal for columns that have few distinct values relative to the total number of records in a table. Regular indexes are the opposite; they perform better when there are more distinct values.

Due to the different internal structure of the index, it is stored in a much more compressed format. This dramatically reduces the space required to store the index when compared to traditional B-Tree indexes. Bitmap indexes usually require much less space than the data itself for storage. Bitmap indexes are, however, poor candidates for tables that frequently insert, update, or delete data in the indexed columns, as there will be more overhead in maintaining the bitmap indexes than traditional indexes.

A bitmap index is comprised of one bitmap for each distinct value the column(s) have. Each bitmap is comprised of 0 or 1, depending if the corresponding column contains the value associated with the bitmap. For example, assume a table has a column that contains the values Oracle6, Oracle7, and Oracle8. There are three records of each value. The bitmap will look something like that shown in Figure 5.18.

The first record can be seen by looking vertically at the first 0/1 bit of each line. In the previous example, the first three records have 1 by Oracle6, and 0 by Oracle7 and Oracle8. This means that the first three records

Figure 5.18 An example of a bitmap.

contain the value Oracle6. Oracle stores the data in binary format and performs Boolean math operations on the bitmaps. This provides for dramatic performance and storage improvements. You can now also see why it takes much processing to update bitmap data when altering data. Just by adding a new distinct value, Oracle would have to create a new bitmap for all records.

2. Connect to SQL*Plus as the WAITE user account and create the PLAYER05 table by running CHP5_16.SQL, as shown in Figure 5.19.

3. The PLAYER05 table is used to keep track of major and minor league baseball players. Some of the columns have high cardinality, such as the LAST_NAME column. They are good candidates for regular indexes. Other columns have low cardinality, such as POSITION, which in baseball can be limited to: 1B, 2B, 3B, SS, RF, CF, LF, RP, LP, DH, and UT. Another candidate would be THROWING_ARM, which would be limited to L or R. The best bitmap index would be on both the POSITION and THROWING_ARM columns. By running the CHP5_17.SQL script, this index is created, as shown in Figure 5.20.

4. The bitmap PLAYER_BITMAP_INDEX is successfully created on the PLAYER05 table. It is best to create an index after data is already in the table. Queries on the players' position and throwing arm will benefit greatly from this bitmap index. For instance, to find out how many left-

```
SQL> GET C:\CHP5_16.SQL
  1  CREATE TABLE PLAYER05
  2    (LAST_NAME      VARCHAR2(50) NOT NULL,
  3     FIRST_NAME     VARCHAR2(25) NOT NULL,
  4     POSITION       VARCHAR2(2) NOT NULL,
  5     THROWING_ARM   CHAR(1) NOT NULL)
  6* TABLESPACE USER_DATA
SQL> /

Table created.

SQL>
```

Figure 5.19 CHP5_16.SQL creates the PLAYER05 table, used to explain bitmap indexes.

```
SQL> GET C:\CHP5_17.SQL
  1  CREATE BITMAP INDEX PLAYER_BITMAP_INDEX
  2* ON PLAYER05 (POSITION, THROWING_ARM)
SQL> /

Index created.

SQL> |
```

Figure 5.20 CHP5_17.SQL creates the PLAYER_BITMAP_INDEX index.

```
SELECT * FROM PLAYER05
WHERE POSITION='SS' AND
      THROWING_ARM='L'
|
```

Figure 5.21 CHP5_18.SQL
contains a sample query on
the PLAYER05 table that uses
the PLAYER_BITMAP_INDEX.

handed shortstops, you would issue the CHP5_18.SQL query shown in Figure 5.21. There is no reason to run the query in the How-To as there are no records in the table; if there were many records in the database, you would notice a performance improvement with the query for the bitmap index.

Queries like the one shown in Figure 5.21 are used often in data warehouse applications. Typically, bitmap indexes are used more often in query-intensive applications such as data warehouses and data mining, and are used less in OLTP applications where data is updated often.

How It Works

Step 1 describes when it is appropriate to use bitmap indexes, and explains their difference from regular indexes. Step 2 creates the PLAYER05 table, which is then used to show good and bad column candidates for bitmap indexes. Step 3 creates a bitmap index, PLAYER_BITMAP_INDEX, on the concatenation of POSITION and THROWING_ARM. Step 4 shows a sample query on the PLAYER05 table that will utilize the bitmap index.

The CHP5_21.SQL query shown in Figure 5.21 will perform faster than a regular index because Oracle will search for records with the SS position bit set to 1, and with the L throwing arm bit set to 1. This is a quick Boolean math function handled internally by the Oracle engine.

Comments

You can create local bitmap indexes on partitioned tables, just as you can with other types of indexes.

There is no clearly defined cardinality of which bitmap indexes should be used. This will depend on how the data is spread among the possible values, the number of distinct keys, and the number of records in the table. Testing is the best method to determine if query speed is improved. A rule of thumb is if there are over one hundred records for each possible value, then bitmap indexes will improve query performance.

CHAPTER 6
CONSTRAINTS

6

CONSTRAINTS

How do I...

You can define constraints to enforce business rules on data in your tables and to ensure validity of data. Constraints also provide a means of defining how tables relate to each other. It is possible to enforce business rules programmatically in your application instead of using constraints, but this is a costlier approach. Constraints move much of the work away from the applications to the database. All data in tables must conform to the rules specified by the underlying constraints. An integrity constraint imposed on a table is a watchdog that ensures that SQL statements that modify data in a table satisfy conditions imposed by the constraint. A referential integrity constraint, however, enforces master-detail relationships between tables.

6.1 Create a Primary Key Constraint

A primary key is a set of columns that uniquely identifies the rows in a table. The task of creating a primary key is essential to enforcing referential integrity at the database level. Creating a primary key establishes a unique index on the table, which can increase the performance of applications using the table. This How-To covers the process of creating a primary key on a table.

6.2 Add a Foreign Key Constraint

Referential integrity constraints within Oracle are used to enforce business rules specified in the data model. It is critical that data in the database follow the rules developed when the database was designed. There are also situations when hierarchical relationships within a single table have to be implemented. This How-To covers the topic of creating referential integrity constraints using foreign key constraints.

6.3 Add a Column Check Constraint

Check constraints allow the database to perform important validation tasks. Adding a check constraint to a table ensures that applications will not create invalid data in the table. It also lets the database perform some of the work the application would normally do. This How-To takes you through the different methods used to create column check constraints.

6.4 Create a Table Constraint

A column constraint can enforce rules on the column in which it is defined, whereas, a table constraint can operate on multiple columns in the table. Complex validation logic involving multiple columns can be easily implemented using table constraints. This How-To explains how this is accomplished with the use of table constraints.

6.5 Determine Foreign Key Dependencies

Constraints on tables can be queried from data dictionary views. The USER_CONSTRAINTS and USER_CONS_COLUMNS data dictionary views provide information about constraints to which a user account has access. This information can be used to determine foreign key dependencies between tables and columns that relate them. This How-To covers the topic of listing integrity constraint definitions in the database.

6.6 Enable, Disable, and Enforce Constraints

Constraints implement rules within the database. There are times, such as during database maintenance or batch operations, that constraints can be temporarily violated. Constraints can be disabled and enabled so that batch operations and system maintenance can be performed. Enforcing a disabled constraint is much faster than enabling it. This How-To explains how constraints are enabled, disabled, and enforced.

6.7 Add Cascading Delete Functionality

A cascading delete functionality is necessary to maintain referential integrity and to ensure data consistency between related tables during row deletes. In a cascade delete, when rows containing referenced key values are deleted, all rows in child tables with dependent foreign key values are also deleted. This How-To covers the topic of adding a cascade delete functionality for complete referential integrity.

6.8 Create a Sequence to Generate a Unique Number

A *sequence* generates a unique sequential number in an Oracle session. Sequences can be created with a wide variety of options. Numeric primary keys and unique keys can be easily generated using sequences. Various sequence operations such as creating a sequence, altering a sequence, retrieving the sequence value, and listing sequence information are all covered. This How-To explains how a sequence can be used to generate a unique number for a primary key before inserting a record in a table.

6.9 Determine Integrity Violations

In most situations, constraints have to be disabled for batch operations to upload data into tables. In order to enable a constraint after a data load, rows that violate the constraint have to be either deleted or updated. Integrity violating rows in a table can be identified while enabling the constraint. This How-To illustrates how this is handled.

6.10 Create a Deferred Constraint

Constraints are always checked at the end of each SQL statement that modifies data. Oracle8 allows you to defer checking constraints for validity until the end of the transaction. If any data entered during the transaction violates the constraint upon commit, the transaction is rolled back. This How-To discusses the specifics of using deferred constraints for better performance.

COMPLEXITY
BEGINNING

6.1 How do I...
Create a primary key constraint?

Problem

In my data model, I have defined a primary key for all of my tables. I want to create primary keys in the database to enforce uniqueness. How do I create a primary key constraint on a table?

Technique

You can create a primary key constraint with the table as part of a CREATE TABLE statement, or later using the ALTER TABLE statement. Within a CREATE TABLE statement, a PRIMARY KEY clause is used to define the columns contained in the primary key. A named primary key can be created in the CREATE TABLE statement using the CONSTRAINT...PRIMARY KEY clause. Within an ALTER TABLE statement, a primary key can be created with the ADD PRIMARY KEY clause, or a named primary key with the ADD CONSTRAINT...PRIMARY KEY clause. Care must be taken to define NOT NULL constraints for columns of a table that absolutely require values at all times. A UNIQUE constraint ensures that no two rows of a table have duplicate values in a specific column or a set of columns. A UNIQUE NOT NULL constraint will disallow null values as well as duplicates. If the columns that are part of the primary key do not explicitly contain NOT NULL constraints, Oracle will automatically apply a NOT NULL constraint to each column comprising the primary key, and a UNIQUE index is created on the primary key columns. A UNIQUE NOT NULL constraint is inherently implied with a primary key. When defining a column using the CREATE TABLE or ALTER TABLE statements, you can specify a default value for a column by using a DEFAULT keyword.

Steps

1. Run SQL*Plus and connect as the WAITE user account. Run the statement in the CHP6_1.SQL file to create the table and primary key. The file contains a CREATE TABLE statement that creates a table with a primary key. Although it is a good idea to create a primary key for every table, doing so is optional. Figure 6.1 shows the results of running the statement in SQL*Plus.

```
SQL> START CHP6_1
SQL> SET ECHO ON
SQL> CREATE TABLE CUST06 (
  2    COMPANY_ID   NUMBER(10) NOT NULL,
  3    CUST_ID      NUMBER(10) NOT NULL,
  4    CUST_NAME    VARCHAR2(60),
  5    PHONE        NUMBER(10) UNIQUE,
  6    LAST_UPD_DT  DATE DEFAULT SYSDATE,
  7                 PRIMARY KEY (COMPANY_ID, CUST_ID));

Table created.

SQL>
```

Figure 6.1 CHP6_1.SQL creates the CUST06 table with a primary key.

Line 1 contains the CREATE TABLE keywords used to create a new table. Lines 2 through 6 identify the columns that make up the table. In line 4, although not a column defining the primary key, a NOT NULL constraint on the CUST_NAME column ensures that a value is entered for the CUST_NAME column for every row of the CUST06 table. The UNIQUE keyword contained in line 5 eliminates duplication of phone numbers. You can also explicitly define a DEFAULT value for a column as in line 6. When inserting a row into the CUST06 table, if a value is not given for the LAST_UPD_DT column, a default value of SYSDATE will be used as its column value in the inserted row. Line 7 defines the primary key as a concatenated key containing two columns. Note that line 6 was terminated with a comma.

2. Run the commands in the CHP6_2.SQL file. This file uses an ALTER TABLE statement to create a named constraint. Figure 6.2 shows the use of the ALTER TABLE command in SQL*Plus.

The first command is an ALTER TABLE statement with the DROP PRIMARY KEY keywords to drop the primary key on table CUST06. This is necessary before we re-create a primary key for the CUST06 table using the ALTER TABLE syntax. The ALTER TABLE keywords specifies that table CUST06 is to be modified. The ADD CONSTRAINT clause contained in line 2 is used to add a named constraint to the table. Line 3 identifies the constraint as a primary key constraint. COMPANY_ID and CUST_NO columns make up the primary key of the table.

3. Run the statement in the CHP6_3.SQL file. It uses the CONSTRAINT keyword to create named constraints, within a CREATE TABLE statement used to create a new table. The CONSTRAINT keyword can be used to specify a corresponding index, in addition to its use to assign a name to a constraint. Figure 6.3 shows the results of the operation in SQL*Plus.

```
SQL> START CHP6_2
SQL> SET ECHO ON
SQL> ALTER TABLE CUST06
  2           DROP PRIMARY KEY;

Table altered.

SQL> ALTER TABLE CUST06
  2           ADD CONSTRAINT PKEY_CUST
  3           PRIMARY KEY (COMPANY_ID, CUST_ID);

Table altered.

SQL> |
```

Figure 6.2 CHP6_2.SQL demonstrates the use of the ALTER TABLE command.

```
SQL> START CHP6_3
SQL> SET ECHO ON
SQL> CREATE TABLE COMPANY06 (
  2  COMPANY_ID   NUMBER(10)
  3               CONSTRAINT PKEY_COMPANY PRIMARY KEY
  4               USING INDEX TABLESPACE USER_DATA,
  5  COMPANY_NAME VARCHAR2(60)
  6               CONSTRAINT UNQ_COMP_NAME UNIQUE,
  7  COUNTRY      VARCHAR2(40));

Table created.

SQL>
```

Figure 6.3 CHP6_3.SQL creates a table with a named primary key.

Line 1 contains the CREATE TABLE keyword used to create a new table. Line 2 and 3 use the CONSTRAINT keyword to create a named primary key. Line 4 specifies the tablespace to be used to create a unique index for the primary key. A named UNIQUE constraint is created in line 6. It should be noted that UNIQUE constraints do not prevent null values from being inserted.

4. Run the CHP6_4.SQL file, which contains an ALTER TABLE statement to modify the datatype and provide a default value for the COUNTRY column. Figure 6.4 shows the results of the command in SQL*Plus.

A default value can be specified for a column in the MODIFY clause of an ALTER TABLE statement. Line 2 presents the MODIFY clause to add a default value to the COMPANY06 table. If the inserted value contains NULL, it will not be converted to the default. Whenever a row is inserted into the table without the column specified in the column list of the INSERT statement, the default value will be inserted into the column. Note that the datatype was modified from a VARCHAR2(40) to a VARCHAR2(30). If there are any existing rows in the COMPANY06 table with the COUNTRY column value that will not fit into the new datatype, you will get an ORA-01401 error: `inserted value too large for column`.

The ALTER TABLE...ADD syntax can be used to add an additional column to a table. An ALTER TABLE...DROP syntax cannot be used to drop columns from the table. An ALTER TABLE...MODIFY cannot be used to

```
SQL> START CHP6_4
SQL> SET ECHO ON
SQL> ALTER TABLE COMPANY06
  2  MODIFY (COUNTRY VARCHAR2(30) DEFAULT 'USA');

Table altered.

SQL>
```

Figure 6.4 CHP6_4.SQL modifies an existing column of a table.

modify an existing constraint on a table. The constraint has to be dropped using the ALTER TABLE...DROP statement and created anew with an ALTER TABLE...ADD statement.

How It Works

Steps 1 creates a primary key on a table when it is created with the CREATE TABLE statement. The primary key is specified by the PRIMARY KEY clause of the statement. The columns that are a part of the primary key must be declared as NOT NULL, or the NOT NULL constraint will be created automatically on each column. A SQL statement would fail if the primary key columns contained NULL data. Step 1 displays the use of the DEFAULT keyword to specify a default value for a column. System-generated names are assigned to the NOT NULL and UNIQUE constraints defined in Step 1. Step 2 presents a statement used to create a primary key on an existing table. The ALTER TABLE statement is used with the ADD CONSTRAINT clause to create a primary key with a specified name. Step 3 demonstrates the use of the CONSTRAINT keyword to create a named primary key constraint and a named unique constraint. Step 4 shows the use of the ALTER TABLE...MODIFY statement to change the datatype and specify a default value for a column using the DEFAULT keyword.

Comments

The columns within a primary key cannot be NULL. Creating a primary key on a table will create NOT NULL constraints on the columns included in the key. A primary key can contain 16 columns at most, and the total size of a key value in bytes should be less than half the block size of the database. The LONG and LONG RAW datatypes cannot be included in a primary key. Only one primary key can be defined for a table, but a table can have multiple unique keys. Declaring primary keys generally improves performance, especially if the primary key consists of a single column and furthermore if the column is of integer datatype.

A unique constraint is implied by the primary key, and Oracle automatically creates a unique index on the columns contained in the primary key. With Oracle8, you can also use non-unique indexes to enforce unique and primary key constraints. Non-unique indexes are not dropped when the constraint is disabled, as would happen with unique indexes.

If a name is not specified by the user when creating a constraint, Oracle generates a unique constraint name in the form SYS_Cn, where n is an integer. A user-assigned constraint name will not change during a system export and import, whereas an Oracle-generated constraint name will typically change. Although it is not necessary, naming constraints makes it much easier to administer them as user-defined names are usually easier to remember and understand. A constraint should be named whenever it needs to be referenced after it is defined. This is also very useful because whenever a constraint is violated, the constraint name will be included as a part of the error message to easily diagnose the error.

Default values should be used whenever you know a column should default to a specific value. The datatype of the default value created must match the datatype of the column. The column must also be long enough to hold the value created. A DEFAULT expression cannot contain references to other columns.

To create constraints on a table, the user account must have the ability to create tables (CREATE TABLE or CREATE ANY TABLE privilege); or the ability to alter tables (ALTER TABLE or ALTER ANY TABLE privilege).

COMPLEXITY
BEGINNING

6.2   How do I...
Add a foreign key constraint?

Problem

I have many applications updating the same sets of data. I want to ensure that the business rules governing the relationships between data in tables is enforced. It is important that no application can create data that violates the data relationships in our data model. Each application currently checks to ensure that new data and changes to existing data are valid. I want to enforce referential integrity at the database level using foreign keys. How do I add foreign key constraints?

Technique

Referential integrity is a feature of Oracle that ensures that all references to external objects within each database object are valid. Referential integrity is enforced by using a combination of primary keys and foreign keys. A primary key consists of one or more columns that uniquely identifies a row in a table. A primary key can be created in the CREATE TABLE statement or added later with an ALTER TABLE statement. The primary key ensures that each row in the table is unique. How-To 6.1 covered the creation of primary keys. A *foreign* key defines the columns in a table that must exist as a *primary* key of the same or another table. A foreign key can also reference a *unique* key of the same or another table. A foreign key references a referenced key (primary key or unique key) and not table columns directly. A foreign key constraint can be created in the CREATE TABLE statement or added later with an ALTER TABLE statement.

Steps

1. Run SQL*Plus and connect as the WAITE user account. Run the SQL in the CHP6_5.SQL file, shown in Figure 6.5, which contains the statements to create the two sample tables used in this How-To. The DEPT06 and EMP06 tables created in the script will be related by the common DEPT_NO column. The DEPT_NO column of the DEPT06 table is the primary key for the table and will be referenced by the same field in the EMP06 table. Thus, in achieving referential integrity, the primary key constraint of the DEPT06 table is referenced as a foreign key in the EMP06 table.

```
SQL> START CHP6_5
SQL> SET ECHO OFF

Table created.

Table created.
```

The CREATE TABLE keyword is used to create two new tables, DEPT06 and EMP06. The DEPT_NO in the EMP06 table is defined as NOT NULL, to ensure that there is no employee without a department. Observe the use of the CONSTRAINT clause to create a named primary key in the DEPT06 table and a named foreign key in the EMP06 table. The CONSTRAINT clause is optional in both tables. Finally, using the REFERENCE clause, this foreign key is bound to the primary key of the DEPT06 table. The DEPT_NO column of the DEPT06 on which the primary is defined is explicitly referred to as - `REFERENCES DEPT06(DEPT_NO)` - in the EMP06 table. The column name could have been omitted in the REFERENCES clause as - `REFERENCES DEPT06` -, and Oracle will automatically bind the foreign key with the default primary key of the DEPT06 table.

2. Run the statements in the CHP6_6.SQL file. This file contains two ALTER TABLE statements: the first ALTER TABLE statement to drop the existing foreign key created in step 1, and a second one to create a foreign key constraint between the two tables. Any value for the DEPT_NO field in the EMP06 table must have a corresponding record in the DEPT06 table. Figure 6.6 shows the results of running the two ALTER TABLE statements in SQL*Plus.

```
SET ECHO OFF
CREATE TABLE DEPT06 (
    DEPT_NO     NUMBER(4)
                CONSTRAINT PKEY_DEPT PRIMARY KEY,
    DEPT_NAME VARCHAR2(15));
CREATE TABLE EMP06 (
    EMP_NO      NUMBER(6) PRIMARY KEY,
    EMP_NAME    VARCHAR2(15) NOT NULL,
    MGR_NO      NUMBER(6),
    DEPT_NO     NUMBER(4) NOT NULL
                CONSTRAINT FKEY_DEPT
                REFERENCES DEPT06(DEPT_NO));
```

Figure 6.5 CHP6_5.SQL creates the sample tables used in How-To 6.2.

```
SQL> START CHP6_6
SQL> SET ECHO ON
SQL> ALTER TABLE EMP06
  2            DROP CONSTRAINT FKEY_DEPT;

Table altered.

SQL> ALTER TABLE EMP06
  2            ADD CONSTRAINT FKEY_DEPT
  3            FOREIGN KEY (DEPT_NO)
  4            REFERENCES DEPT06;

Table altered.

SQL>
```

Figure 6.6 CHP6_6.SQL drops and re-creates the foreign key.

The first command is an ALTER TABLE statement with the DROP CONSTRAINT keywords to drop the foreign key from the EMP06 table. This is necessary before we create the same foreign key for the EMP06 table using the ALTER TABLE syntax. The ADD CONSTRAINT clause contained in line 2 is used to add a named constraint to the table. The CONSTRAINT clause is optional and can be omitted if you have no need for the foreign key to have a specific name. Line 3 contains the FOREIGN KEY clause to create a foreign key on the DEPT_NO column of the EMP06 table. Line 4 makes this foreign key reference the default primary key of the DEPT06 table.

3. Run the CHP6_7.SQL file, which contains an INSERT statement to attempt to insert a record into the EMP06 table. Because there are no rows in DEPT06 table, the foreign key reference to the DEPT_NO in the DEPT06 will fail. Figure 6.7 shows the results of running the statement in SQL*Plus.

An ORA-02291 error is generated and the name of the constraint violated appears in the error message. For a statement inserting invalid data to succeed, the constraint must be disabled. How-To 6.4 explores the topic of disabling constraints. Also, if a record corresponding to the foreign key had existed in the DEPT06 table beforehand, then the statement will run successfully. This is demonstrated by running the CHP6_8.SQL to insert records in the proper order as shown in Figure 6.8.

```
SQL> START CHP6_7
SQL> SET ECHO ON
SQL> INSERT INTO EMP06
  2    VALUES(1, 'JOE SHMOE', NULL, 1);
INSERT INTO EMP06
            *
ERROR at line 1:
ORA-02291: integrity constraint (WAITE.FKEY_DEPT) violated - parent key not f

SQL>
```

Figure 6.7 CHP6_7.SQL attempts to insert an invalid record.

```
SQL> START CHP6_8
SQL> SET ECHO ON
SQL> INSERT INTO DEPT06
  2    VALUES(1, 'ACCT DEPT');

1 row created.

SQL> INSERT INTO EMP06
  2    VALUES(1, 'JOE SHMOE', NULL, 1);

1 row created.

SQL>
```

Figure 6.8 CHP6_8.SQL inserts
records in the proper order.

A record is first inserted into the DEPT06 table. The value of the primary
key of the DEPT06 record is then used as the foreign key while inserting a
record in the EMP06 table. Applications must be designed to insert
records in a parent table before the child table.

How It Works

Step 1 creates the tables used throughout this How-To. A primary key on the
DEPT06 table is also created. A primary key must exist on the master table
before creating a foreign key in the detail table. While creating the EMP06 table,
both a primary and foreign key are created. The foreign key references the
primary key of the DEPT06 table. In order to create a record in the EMP06 table,
there must be a corresponding record in the DEPT06 table. In Step 3, inserting
an invalid record into the EMP06 table is attempted initially. This is followed by
presenting the proper method of inserting records in tables with a master-detail
relationship.

While being referenced by one or more records in the EMP06 table, if you try
to delete that record from the DEPT06 table before deleting the referencing
EMP06 records, an ORA-02292 error will occur. The delete operation in a
master table is only possible if there are no rows in the detail table that refer to
the rows being deleted from the master table, or if the foreign key relationship is
defined using the ON DELETE CASCADE option (refer to How-To 6.7).

A foreign key can reference the primary key of the same table. This can be
used to enforce hierarchical relationships within a single table. For instance,
each manager is also an employee, so the MGR_NO column can be made as a
foreign key referencing the EMP_NO column of the EMP06 table. This is termed
as a self-referential integrity constraint.

Comments

Referential integrity helps ensure validity of data. It is not necessary that
columns of the parent (master) and child (detail) tables have the same names,
but they must be of the exact same datatype. Composite foreign keys are limited
to 16 columns just like composite primary keys. If the column list is not

included in the REFERENCES clause when defining a foreign key, the primary key of the specified table will be referenced by default. As rows in the child table reference the key in the *parent table*, it is not possible to UPDATE the parent key or DELETE that parent table record, without first deleting the referencing record from the child table. This functionality is also known as UPDATE RESTRICT and DELETE RESTRICT, respectively. If an INSERT or UPDATE is issued on the *child table*, foreign keys must have a value of the referenced key already existing in the parent table, or NULL. Unlike a primary key, a NOT NULL constraint is not implicit with a foreign key and has to be explicitly defined with a foreign key, if required. A referenced key can be referred by any number of foreign keys.

The application must have knowledge of constraints, regardless of how integrity is enforced in the database. The application must submit transaction statements in the proper order, in accordance with the referential integrity constraints. The application must also handle exceptions resulting from integrity violations. Referential integrity implemented through applications instead of foreign keys results in better performance, keeping in mind that a foreign key constraint necessitates an additional read.

There must be privileges, too. The user account must either be the owner of the parent table, or have the REFERENCES privilege to the columns of the primary key of the parent table. And to create the foreign key constraints in the child table, the user account must have the ability to create tables (CREATE TABLE or CREATE ANY TABLE privilege); or the ability to alter the child table (ALTER TABLE or ALTER ANY TABLE privilege). These privileges have to be explicitly granted to the creator of the constraint and cannot be obtained via a role.

NOTE

Oracle does not automatically create non-unique indexes on foreign keys. It is a good idea to explicitly create non-unique indexes on all foreign keys for improved performance and concurrency control.

COMPLEXITY
ADVANCED

6.3 How do I...
Add a column check constraint?

Problem

In our systems, we want to ensure that the values in some columns fall within allowable ranges. Our applications can verify the values within the data, but I want to ensure that no invalid data can be created. I have heard that column check constraints can be used to easily enforce integrity rules at the column level. How do I use column check constraints to validate data?

Technique

When a table is created using the CREATE TABLE statement, a CHECK clause can be specified after a column to create a column check constraint. The syntax is:

```
CREATE TABLE tablename (
  columnname datatype [CONSTRAINT constraint_name] CHECK (condition));
```

The CONSTRAINT clause is optional and can be used to create a named constraint. The *condition* following the CHECK keyword is a Boolean expression that is evaluated using the values in the row being inserted or updated. Column check constraints are very flexible to use, but there are some restrictions that should be kept in mind while designing column check constraints. Restrictions on expressions in a column check constraint are as follows:

✔ A column check constraint expression cannot reference other columns.

✔ Use of sequences and queries is disallowed in the expression.

✔ The expression cannot call system functions: SYSDATE, UID, USER, and USERENV.

✔ The expression cannot reference pseudo-columns: CURRVAL, NEXTVAL, LEVEL, PRIOR, and ROWNUM.

Steps

1. Run SQL*Plus and connect as the WAITE user account. Run the SQL in the CHP6_9.SQL file, as shown in Figure 6.9, which contains a statement to create a table with a column check constraint.

Line 1 contains the CREATE TABLE keywords used to create a new table. Lines 2 through 4 define the columns that make up the table. The CHECK clause in line 5 requires that the value of the SAL column be less than 10,000 whenever a record is inserted or updated. Note that there is no comma after the SAL column definition and the check constraint is a part of it. A named constraint is created as a result of the CONSTRAINT clause before the CHECK keyword. It is generally a good practice to name

```
SQL> START CHP6_9
SQL> SET ECHO ON
SQL> CREATE TABLE BONUS06 (
  2     ENAME      VARCHAR2(30),
  3     JOB        VARCHAR2(30),
  4     SAL        NUMBER(10,2)
  5                CONSTRAINT CHK_SALARY CHECK (SAL < 10000));

Table created.

SQL>
```

Figure 6.9 CHP6_9.SQL creates a table with a column check constraint.

constraints whenever possible, for easier tracking of constraints in the database. Check constraints can be viewed by querying the USER_CONSTRAINTS data dictionary view, which is discussed in How-To 6.5.

2. Run the CHP6_10.SQL file in SQL*Plus. The INSERT statement contained in the file attempts to insert a row into the BONUS06 table. The statement will fail because the value being inserted into the SAL column is such that the expression defining the column check constraint evaluates to FALSE. Figure 6.10 shows the results of running the statement in SQL*Plus.

The VALUES clause in lines 3 and 4 attempt to insert a row into the BONUS06 table with a value of the SAL column greater than that is allowed by the constraint. This results in an ORA-02290 error as a value in the SAL column violates the column check constraint created in Step 1.

NOTE

The Boolean expression defining a check constraint can evaluate to true, false, or unknown. The constraint is violated only if the expression evaluates to false, and not with true or unknown. If a value of NULL was used as a value for the SAL column in this example, the expression evaluates to unknown, and the row will be inserted. To avoid conditions like this, a NOT NULL constraint should be placed before the CHECK keyword:

```
SAL NUMBER(10,2) NOT NULL CHECK (SAL < 10000)
```

Alternatively, the constraint can also be written as:

```
SAL NUMBER(10,2) CHECK (SAL < 10000 AND SAL IS NOT NULL)
```

How It Works

Step 1 creates a table with a column check constraint. A column check constraint can be created for columns only with a CREATE TABLE statement and not with an ALTER TABLE statement. Step 2 attempts to insert an invalid

```
SQL> START CHP6_10
SQL> SET ECHO ON
SQL> INSERT INTO BONUS06
  2    (ENAME, JOB, SAL)
  3  VALUES
  4    ('JOE SHMOE', 'TEST CLERK', 12000);
INSERT INTO BONUS06
            *
ERROR at line 1:
ORA-02290: check constraint (WAITE.CHK_SALARY) violated

SQL>
```

Figure 6.10 CHP6_10.SQL attempts to violate the check constraint.

row into the table. The error message displayed in Step 2 contains the constraint name created when the constraint was added. A NOT NULL constraint is a type of a column CHECK constraint.

Comments

A column check constraint restricts the range of valid values for a column. Multiple column check constraints are allowed with any column definition. The check expression defining the check constraint cannot reference any other columns in the same or another table. Check constraints force the database to do some of the work your applications normally would do. If an application fails to check for invalid values, you can be assured that the database will catch the error. Table check constraints enforce more sophisticated integrity rules on multiple columns and are discussed in the next How-To.

COMPLEXITY
INTERMEDIATE

6.4 How do I...
Create a table constraint?

Problem

I need to use check constraints on tables to reduce redundant validation code from my applications. I want to create table check constraints to perform these validation checks automatically in the database, whenever a statement inserts or updates a row in the table. I know that column check constraints can be used on individual columns, but I want to specify a business rule that spans multiple columns of the table. How do I use table constraints to validate data?

Technique

When a table is created using the CREATE TABLE statement, a table constraint can be specified independently, that is, not a part of any column definition. Consequently, multiple columns can be included in the definition of a table constraint. Table constraints and column definitions can appear in any order, such as the following:

```
CREATE TABLE tablename (
column_definition,
table_constraint);
```

The `table_constraint` while defining a table check constraint contains the following:

```
[CONSTRAINT constraint_name] CHECK(condition)
```

The CONSTRAINT clause is optional and can be used to create a named constraint. The *condition* following the CHECK keyword is a Boolean expression, but unlike the column check constraint; a table check constraint expression can reference any columns in the table in which it is defined. Any column constraint can be defined using the table constraint syntax. A NOT NULL constraint can be implemented as a CHECK constraint by defining a table check constraint using the CHECK *COLUMN_NAME* IS NOT NULL syntax. For restrictions on check constraints, refer to the previous How-To. An ALTER TABLE statement allows table constraints to be created for an existing table.

Steps

1. Run SQL*Plus and connect as the WAITE user account. Run the CHP6_11.SQL file in SQL*Plus, as shown in Figure 6.11. The file contains a statement to create a table with a table check constraint.

Line 1 contains the CREATE TABLE keywords used to create a new table. Lines 2 through 4 define the columns that make up the table. The CHECK clause in line 5 defines a table check constraint that enforces a rule on the two salary columns in the same expression, to specify a range of valid salaries. The expression within parentheses must evaluate to TRUE for a record to be inserted or updated. As you can see, multiple table columns can be included in the check expression of a table check constraint. Note the comma at the end of line 4, preceding the CHECK clause. If the comma is omitted an ORA-02438 error would occur, as Oracle would treat it as a column check constraint and column constraints cannot reference other columns. When the table is created, a constraint will be added to the USER_CONSTRAINTS data dictionary view and given a name generated by the database. To create a named table check constraint, simply use a CONSTRAINT clause before the CHECK clause. Check constraints can be viewed by querying the USER_CONSTRAINTS data dictionary view.

```
SQL> START CHP6_11
SQL> SET ECHO ON
SQL> CREATE TABLE SALGRADE06 (
  2     GRADE      VARCHAR2(30),
  3     HISAL      NUMBER(10,2),
  4     LOSAL      NUMBER(10,2),
  5        CONSTRAINT CHK_HI_LO CHECK (LOSAL >= 0 AND HISAL < 10000));

Table created.

SQL> |
```

Figure 6.11 CHP6_11.SQL creates a table with a table constraint.

2. Run SQL*Plus and connect as the WAITE user account. Run the CHP6_3.SQL file to create the COMPANY06 table if you do not have this table in your current schema. Now run the commands in the CHP6_12.SQL file. The existing constraint on the COMPANY06 table is dropped, and then an ALTER TABLE statement is issued to add a table check constraint to the COMPANY06 table. Remember, an ALTER statement can be used to create table constraints and not column constraints. Figure 6.12 shows the results of running the two ALTER TABLE statements in SQL*Plus.

Using the ALTER TABLE syntax, the existing column constraint on the COMPANY06 table (which was created in Step 3 of How-To 6.1) is dropped before re-creating it as a table constraint. Line 1 contains the ALTER TABLE keywords used to modify a table. Line 2 contains the ADD CONSTRAINT clause used to add a named primary key as a table constraint. While creating a primary key, an index is also created for it. Line 3 dictates the tablespace name (following the USING INDEX keywords) to be used for creating the index. Lines 4 through 7 are the storage specifications for the index being created. The USING INDEX and STORAGE clauses are optional. Note the explicit tablespace and storage specifications for the index that needs to be created for the primary key. Similar specifications can be included with a primary or unique key definition as a column constraint. In either case, if such a specification is omitted, Oracle will automatically create indexes in the default tablespace using the default storage specification.

3. Run the CHP6_13.SQL file. The INSERT statement contained in the file attempts to insert a row into the BONUS06 table. The statement will fail because the value being inserted into the SAL column is negative, which makes the expression defining the table check constraint evaluate to FALSE. Figure 6.13 shows the results of running the statement in SQL*Plus.

```
SQL> START CHP6_12
SQL> SET ECHO ON
SQL> ALTER TABLE COMPANY06
  2     DROP CONSTRAINT PKEY_COMPANY;

Table altered.

SQL> ALTER TABLE COMPANY06
  2     ADD CONSTRAINT PKEY_COMPANY PRIMARY KEY (COMPANY_ID)
  3        USING INDEX TABLESPACE USER_DATA
  4        STORAGE(INITIAL 5K
  5              NEXT 5K
  6              MAXEXTENTS 50
  7              PCTINCREASE 5);

Table altered.

SQL>
```

Figure 6.12 CHP6_12.SQL drops an re-creates the table constraint.

```
SQL> START CHP6_13
SQL> SET ECHO ON
SQL> INSERT INTO SALGRADE06
  2    (GRADE, HISAL, LOSAL)
  3  VALUES
  4    ('GRADE 1', 5000, -4);
INSERT INTO SALGRADE06
            *
ERROR at line 1:
ORA-02290: check constraint (WAITE.CHK_HI_LO) violated


SQL>
```

Figure 6.13 CHP6_13.SQL attempts to violate
the table check constraint.

The VALUES clause in lines 3 and 4 attempt to insert a row into the
BONUS06 table with a negative value for the SAL column, and this is pro-
hibited by the constraint. This results in an ORA-02290 error as a value in
the SAL column violates the table check constraint created in step 2.

How It Works

Step 1 creates a table with a table check constraint. A table check constraint can
be created within a CREATE TABLE statement. Step 2 creates a table check
constraint on an existing table using an ALTER TABLE statement with an ADD
CONSTRAINT clause. The constraint is added at the table level, because check
constraints on columns cannot be created with the ALTER TABLE statement.
Step 3 attempts to insert an invalid row into the table. The error message
displayed in Step 3 contains the constraint name created when the constraint
was added. The note in the previous How-To, where the Boolean expression
defining the constraint evaluates to unknown with NULL values applies to table
check constraints as well, and care should be taken to avoid such situations.

In Steps 1 and 2 of How-To 6.1, the composite primary key on the CUST06
table is defined at the table level as a table constraint. The columns comprising
the primary key are defined before defining the CUST06 table's primary key as a
table constraint. The constraint definition could have preceded column
definitions comprising the composite primary key, as column definitions and
table constraint definitions can appear in any order.

Comments

Composite primary, foreign, and unique keys have to be implemented as table
constraints. Table constraints can reference multiple columns. A table can have
multiple FOREIGN KEY and CHECK constraints. A single column can be
referenced by several table constraints in that table. Multiple check constraints
should be designed carefully to have no conflicts within themselves. It is better
to have multiple check constraints, each with a simple expression rather than
having a single check constraint with a complex expression. If there is an

integrity violation, an error message is returned by Oracle identifying the constraint. This error message can be used to quickly identify the violated business rule as each constraint implements a single business rule.

Whenever integrity rules can be evaluated based on logical expressions, check constraints should be used. Triggers (Chapter 13) can also be used to enforce complex business constraints that are not definable using declarative constraints.

COMPLEXITY
BEGINNING

6.5 How do I...
Determine foreign key dependencies?

Problem

I want to list information about the constraints in the database. I need to determine the constraint name, the type of constraint, and the status of the constraint. I also need to find out the table and columns on which the constraint is defined. I know that all this information can be obtained from data dictionary views. How do I list information about constraints to determine foreign key dependencies in the database?

Technique

Constraint information can be queried from the USER_CONSTRAINTS or ALL_CONSTRAINTS data dictionary views. Columns associated with constraints can be viewed from the USER_CONS_COLUMNS or ALL_CONS_COLUMNS views. When the primary key is created, a unique index is placed on the table that can be listed from the USER_INDEXES view. Table 6.1 shows the columns in the USER_CONSTRAINTS view and details on how to interpret the value of the CONSTRAINT_TYPE column to find out the type of constraint definition.

Table 6.1 Columns in the USER_CONSTRAINTS view

COLUMN	DESCRIPTION
OWNER	Owner of the constraint
CONSTRAINT_NAME	Name of the constraint
CONSTRAINT_TYPE	Type of constraint definition
TABLE_NAME	Name of the table associated with the constraint
SEARCH_CONDITION	Search condition used for CHECK constraints
R_OWNER	Owner of the table referenced by a FOREIGN KEY constraint

continued on next page

continued from previous page

COLUMN	DESCRIPTION
R_CONSTRAINT_NAME	Name of the constraint referenced by a FOREIGN KEY constraint
DELETE_RULE	Delete rule for a referential constraint: CASCADE or NO ACTION
STATUS	Status of constraint: ENFORCED, ENABLED, or DISABLED
DEFERRABLE (Oracle8)	Indicates whether the constraint is deferrable
DEFERRED (Oracle8)	Indicates whether the constraint was initially deferred
GENERATED (Oracle8)	Indicates whether the constraint name is system generated
LAST_CHANGE (Oracle8)	Indicates when the constraint was last enabled or disabled
VALIDATED (Oracle8)	Indicates whether all data obeys the constraint: VALIDATED or NOT VALIDATED

Steps

1. Run SQL*Plus and connect as the WAITE user account. Run the CHP6_14.SQL file. The USER_CONSTRAINTS view is queried to display information about constraints created in this chapter.

```
SQL> START CHP6_14
SQL> SET ECHO ON
SQL> COLUMN CONSTRAINT_NAME FORMAT A15
SQL> COLUMN TABLE_NAME FORMAT A10
SQL> COLUMN R_CONSTRAINT_NAME FORMAT A17
SQL> COLUMN SEARCH_CONDITION FORMAT A30
SQL> SELECT
  2     CONSTRAINT_NAME,
  3     TABLE_NAME,
  4     CONSTRAINT_TYPE,
  5     R_CONSTRAINT_NAME,
  6     SEARCH_CONDITION,
  7     STATUS
  8  FROM
  9     USER_CONSTRAINTS
 10  ORDER BY 1, 2;
```

Figure 6.14 shows the results of the query. The COLUMN commands at the top format column lengths, before running the statement. The columns returned by the query show you the name of the constraint, the type of constraint, and the name of the referenced key—if it is a foreign key constraint. The CONSTRAINT_NAME column contains the unique name of the constraint. Use Table 6.2 to recognize the type of constraint from the character displayed under the CONSTRAINT_TYPE column. The query displays PRIMARY KEY constraints on tables created in previous sections. NOT NULL constraints show up as CHECK constraints with a value of "C" under the constraint type column listing. Most importantly, the FOREIGN KEY constraint in table EMP06 shows a dependency on the PRIMARY KEY constraint of DEPT06, through the

R_CONSTRAINT_NAME column value. As all CHECK constraints and NOT NULL constraints have a value of "C" in the CONSTRAINT_TYPE column, the SEARCH_CONDITION column can be used to distinguish between the two. As you might note, for NOT NULL constraints, the SEARCH_CONDITION is clearly identified by *COLUMN_NAME* IS NOT NULL. For CHECK constraints, this column would display the user-defined condition that was specified while defining the constraint. The STATUS column contains the state of the constraint: ENABLED, DISABLED, or ENFORCED. By including the DELETE_RULE column in the preceding query, any missing cascade delete rules can be easily found. Delete cascades are examined in section 6.7.

Table 6.2 Values for the CONSTRAINT_TYPE column

CHARACTER	CONSTRAINT TYPE
C	Check constraint (including NOT NULL)
P	PRIMARY KEY constraint
R	FOREIGN KEY constraint
U	UNIQUE constraint
V	WITH CHECK OPTION constraint for views

2. Run the CHP6_15.SQL file, which contains a SELECT statement to query the USER_CONS_COLUMNS table and list columns on which constraints

```
  7   FROM
  8     USER_CONSTRAINTS
  9   WHERE TABLE_NAME LIKE '%06'
 10   ORDER BY 1, 2;

CONSTRAINT_NAME  TABLE_NAME C R_CONSTRAINT_NAME SEARCH_CONDITION
---------------  ---------- - ----------------- ----------------
CHK_HI_LO        SALGRADE06 C                   LOSAL >= 0 AND HISAL < 10000
CHK_SALARY       BONUS06    C                   SAL < 10000
FKEY_DEPT        EMP06      R PKEY_DEPT
PKEY_COMPANY     COMPANY06  P
PKEY_CUST        CUST06     P
PKEY_DEPT        DEPT06     P
SYS_C001008      CUST06     C                   COMPANY_ID IS NOT NULL
SYS_C001009      CUST06     C                   CUST_ID IS NOT NULL
SYS_C001010      CUST06     U
SYS_C001016      EMP06      C                   EMP_NAME IS NOT NULL
SYS_C001017      EMP06      C                   DEPT_NO IS NOT NULL
SYS_C001018      EMP06      P
UNQ_COMP_NAME    COMPANY06  U

13 rows selected.

SQL>
```

Figure 6.14 Results of the query on the USER_CONSTRAINTS view.

are defined for a specified table. Columns of the USER_CONS_COLUMNS view are listed in Table 6.3.

```
SQL> START CHP6_15
SQL> SET ECHO ON
SQL> SET DEFINE ON
SQL> SET VERIFY ON
SQL> SELECT
  2     CONSTRAINT_NAME,
  3     COLUMN_NAME
  4  FROM
  5     USER_CONS_COLUMNS
  6  WHERE TABLE_NAME = UPPER('&TABLE_NAME')
  7  ORDER BY 1;
```

Provide EMP06 as the value for the table name substitution variable. Figure 6.15 shows the results of the query for the EMP06 table created earlier in this chapter. The columns returned by the query show you the name of the constraint followed by the name of the participating column. The USER_CONSTRAINTS and USER_CONS_COLUMNS views can be joined in a single SELECT statement for a detailed reporting of constraints and their constituent columns.

```
SQL> START CHP6_15
SQL> SET ECHO ON
SQL> SET DEFINE ON
SQL> SET VERIFY ON
SQL> COLUMN COLUMN_NAME FORMAT A12
SQL> SELECT
  2     CONSTRAINT_NAME,
  3     COLUMN_NAME
  4  FROM
  5     USER_CONS_COLUMNS
  6  WHERE TABLE_NAME = UPPER('&TABLE_NAME')
  7  ORDER BY 1;
Enter value for table_name: EMP06
old   6: WHERE TABLE_NAME = UPPER('&TABLE_NAME')
new   6: WHERE TABLE_NAME = UPPER('EMP06')

CONSTRAINT_NAME  COLUMN_NAME
---------------- ------------
FKEY_DEPT        DEPT_NO
SYS_C001016      EMP_NAME
SYS_C001017      DEPT_NO
SYS_C001018      EMP_NO

SQL>
```

Figure 6.15 Results of the query on the USER_CONS_COLUMNS view.

Table 6.3 Columns in the USER_CONS_COLUMNS view

CONSTRAINT_TYPE	DESCRIPTION
OWNER	Owner of the constraint
CONSTRAINT_NAME	Name of the constraint
TABLE_NAME	Name of the table associated with the constraint
COLUMN_NAME	Name of the associated column or attribute
POSITION	Position of column or attribute in definition

How It Works

The USER_CONSTRAINTS and USER_CONS_COLUMNS data dictionary views contain information about constraints in the database. The TABLE_NAME column can be used in the WHERE clause of a query to either view, for returning information about constraints on a specific table. Step 1 executes a query on the USER_CONTRAINTS view to list information about all constraints in the database that are accessible to you. Foreign key dependencies are then deciphered from the output resulting from the query. Step 2 executes a query on the USER_CONS_COLUMNS view to list the names of constraints on a specified table along with the names of the columns that they act upon.

Comments

A simple query to the USER_CONSTRAINTS and USER_CONS_COLUMNS data dictionary views will provide you with valuable information about constraints in the database. If data manipulation statements are running into integrity violation exceptions, query the data dictionary to verify that they behave in conformance with the foreign key dependencies and also comply with other constraints defined on tables. With Oracle8, important new columns to the USER_CONSTRAINTS view are DEFERRABLE and DEFERRED, which indicate the mode of deferred constraints. Noteworthy is the new VALIDATED column, if included in the query would display whether the data in any table is valid or not. This can be used to troubleshoot data problems. As with other views, a prefix of ALL_ instead of USER_ will allow you to query constraints created by another user, by specifying the OWNER in the WHERE clause of the query.

6.6 How do I...
Enable, disable, and enforce constraints?

Problem

In order to manipulate data in some batch processing functions within our organization, I need to disable constraints. Without disabling the constraints, programs cannot perform any tasks that violate referential integrity, even temporarily. After the batch processes have completed, I need to enable the constraints. I know that with Oracle8, a constraint can be enforced before enabling it. How do I enable, disable, and enforce constraints?

Technique

You must know the name of the constraint in order to enable, disable, or enforce it. As explained in the previous How-To, names of constraints on tables owned by the current user account can be queried as the CONSTRAINT_NAME column from the USER_CONSTRAINTS data dictionary view. The STATUS column of the view lists the current state of these constraints. When a new constraint is created, its state defaults to ENABLED. A constraint can be disabled right upon creation by having a DISABLE keyword after the constraint definition as in:

```
CREATE TABLE DEPT06 (
        DEPT_NO NUMBER(4) PRIMARY KEY DISABLE,
        .......);
```

or while adding a new constraint with an ALTER TABLE statement:

```
ALTER TABLE DEPT06
        ADD PRIMARY KEY DEPT_NO DISABLE;
```

An ALTER TABLE statement can be used to change the state of a constraint anytime after creation of the constraint.

Steps

1. Run SQL*Plus and connect as the WAITE user account. If you have not run the CHP6_5.SQL script before, run it to create the EMP06 and DEPT06 tables. Now run the CHP6_16.SQL file, which contains an ALTER TABLE statement to disable the foreign key constraint in the EMP06 table. The name of the constraint was obtained from the query in the previous How-To. Figure 6.16 shows the results of running the statement in SQL*Plus.

```
SQL> START CHP6_16
SQL> SET ECHO ON
SQL> ALTER TABLE EMP06
  2  DISABLE CONSTRAINT
  3    FKEY_DEPT;

Table altered.

SQL>
```

Figure 6.16 CHP6_16.SQL
disables the foreign key in
the EMP06 table.

The DISABLE CONSTRAINT clause instructs Oracle to disable the
constraint specified in line 3. If the constraint is already disabled,
the statement will not return an error. After a constraint is disabled, the
database does not check to ensure that an operation follows the rules of
the constraint. If an operation is performed that violates a disabled
constraint, the data must be corrected before the constraint can be
enabled, or an ORA-02298 error will occur while enabling the constraint.
To perform a cascade disable, that is, disable a primary key and any
foreign keys dependent on it, use the CASCADE keyword as DISABLE
PRIMARY KEY CASCADE.

2. Run the CHP6_17.SQL file in SQL*Plus. This file is similar to the one
used in step 1 of the previous How-To to view constraint information from
the USER_CONSTRAINTS view.

```
SQL> SET ECHO ON
SQL> COLUMN CONSTRAINT_NAME FORMAT A15
SQL> COLUMN TABLE_NAME FORMAT A10
SQL> COLUMN R_CONSTRAINT_NAME FORMAT A17
SQL> COLUMN SEARCH_CONDITION FORMAT A30
SQL> SELECT
  2    CONSTRAINT_NAME,
  3    TABLE_NAME,
  4    CONSTRAINT_TYPE,
  5    R_CONSTRAINT_NAME,
  6    STATUS
  7  FROM
  8    USER_CONSTRAINTS
  9  ORDER BY 1, 2;
```

Figure 6.17 shows the results of the query. The STATUS column contains
the state of the constraint: ENABLED, DISABLED, or ENFORCED. The
constraint FKEY_DEPT is shown as DISABLED because it was disabled in
Step 1. When a constraint is disabled, it cannot be used to create new
constraints. For example, a foreign key constraint requires a primary key
constraint on the parent table. If the primary key constraint on the parent
table has been disabled, the foreign key cannot be created.

```
  7  FROM
  8    USER_CONSTRAINTS
  9  ORDER BY 1, 2;

CONSTRAINT_NAME   TABLE_NAME  C  R_CONSTRAINT_NAME  STATUS
----------------  ----------  -  -----------------  --------
CHK_HI_LO         SALGRADE06  C                     ENABLED
CHK_SALARY        BONUS06     C                     ENABLED
FKEY_DEPT         EMP06       R  PKEY_DEPT          DISABLED
PKEY_COMPANY      COMPANY06   P                     ENABLED
PKEY_CUST         CUST06      P                     ENABLED
PKEY_DEPT         DEPT06      P                     ENABLED
SYS_C001008       CUST06      C                     ENABLED
SYS_C001009       CUST06      C                     ENABLED
SYS_C001010       CUST06      U                     ENABLED
SYS_C001016       EMP06       C                     ENABLED
SYS_C001017       EMP06       C                     ENABLED
SYS_C001018       EMP06       P                     ENABLED
UNQ_COMP_NAME     COMPANY06   U                     ENABLED

13 rows selected.

SQL>
```

Figure 6.17 Results of the query on the USER_SEQUENCES view after a constraint is disabled.

3. Run the command in CHP6_18.SQL file, which contains an ALTER TABLE statement to enforce the foreign key constraint in the EMP06 table, which was disabled in Step 1. Figure 6.18 shows the results of running the statement in SQL*Plus.

The constraint is enforced after running the statement. Both enabled or disabled constraints can be sent into an enforced state of trance. An ALTER TABLE statement that attempts to enforce an integrity constraint will not fail if there are rows in the table that violate any integrity constraint defined with the table. But after the constraint is enforced, it wont allow anymore integrity violating rows to be inserted or updated that would have been possible if the constraint was in a disabled state. Enforcing the constraint changes the STATUS column of the USER_CONSTRAINTS view to ENFORCED, which can be viewed by running the CHP6_17.SQL file in SQL*Plus.

```
SQL> START CHP6_18
SQL> SET ECHO ON
SQL> ALTER TABLE EMP06
  2  ENFORCE CONSTRAINT
  3    FKEY_DEPT;

Table altered.

SQL>
```

Figure 6.18 CHP6_18.SQL enforces the foreign key in the EMP06 table.

Oracle8 introduces this new constraint state of enforced. It is a partially enabled constraint with an intermediate **enable novalidate** state as it does not check existing table data for validity, whereas an enabled constraint is in an **enable validate** state.

4. Run the command in CHP6_19.SQL file, which contains an ALTER TABLE statement to enable the foreign key constraint in the EMP06 table, which was enforced in step 2. Figure 6.19 shows the results of running the statement in SQL*Plus.

The constraint is enabled after running the statement. A constraint that is either in a disabled or an enforced state can be enabled using the above command. Enabling the constraint changes the STATUS column of the USER_CONSTRAINTS view to ENABLED. This can be verified by running the CHP6_17.SQL file in SQL*Plus. An ALTER TABLE statement that attempts to enable an integrity constraint may fail if there are rows in the table that violate any integrity constraint defined with the table. Consequently, the constraint is not enabled and the statement is rolled back.

How It Works

Step 1 executes an ALTER TABLE statement with a DISABLE CONSTRAINT clause to disable a constraint. Step 2 to view the constraint status by querying the USER _CONSTRAINTS view after it has been disabled. Step 3 demonstrates how to enforce a constraint with the ENFORCE keyword in the ALTER TABLE statement. Step 4 enables the constraint by using an ALTER TABLE statement with the ENABLE CONSTRAINT clause.

Comments

Constraints should be used whenever possible to ensure data integrity. Enabled constraints can cause problems in batch processes or during system maintenance, as not a single row violating a constraint can be inserted into the corresponding table. In data warehouse configurations, temporarily disabling integrity constraints might be necessary to upload valid OLTP data. Disabling a constraint makes it possible to insert rows violating constraints. These rows are

```
SQL> START CHP6_19
SQL> SET ECHO ON
SQL> ALTER TABLE EMP06
  2  ENABLE CONSTRAINT
  3    FKEY_DEPT;

Table altered.

SQL>
```

Figure 6.19 CHP6_19.SQL enables the foreign key in the EMP06 table.

known as constraint exceptions. The data in the tables affected by the constraint must be valid before the constraint is enabled. Oracle will not allow the constraint to be enabled if the data in the table violates the constraint. The rows that violate the constraint must be either deleted or updated before enabling the constraint. All rows violating constraints can be examined from an exceptions table, which is examined in How-To 6.9.

In Oracle8, a disabled constraint can be enforced using the ENFORCE keyword with the ALTER TABLE statement. A table with enforced constraints can contain invalid data, but it disallows adding new invalid data to it. Validation is not required when enforcing a constraint, which makes it much faster than enabling a constraint. Enforced constraints can then be enabled at leisure to validate data in the tables. Thus, ENFORCED is an interim state of a constraint, before it gets reincarnated when the constraint is enabled using the ENABLE keyword.

Prior to Oracle8, disabling a unique or primary key constraint caused the corresponding unique index to be dropped. When enabling a disabled constraint, an index had to be re-created. This resulted into a long time to get the primary key constraint enabled for large tables. With Oracle8, the index does not need to be rebuilt when the constraint is re-enabled. Also, unique and primary keys can use non-unique indexes as mentioned earlier in How-To 6.1. The non-unique index has to be created manually, and the constraint must be created in a disabled state. An existing index is used when the constraint is enabled.

Validation takes place when enabling a disabled constraint. To ensure that no new data is entered while data is being validated, Oracle puts exclusive locks on the table. All this might have a negative impact on the availability and performance of a system while enabling disabled constraints. Enforced constraints are handy in such situations, as no locks are required during validation. Consequently, concurrent operations can be allowed on tables with enforced constraints, and enforced constraints can be enabled concurrently unlike disabled constraints that have to enabled serially. As the table does not need to be exclusively locked, users can read and modify data while an enforced constraint is enabled.

In order to enable, disable, or enforce a constraint, the user account must either be the owner of the table, or have the ALTER TABLE or ALTER ANY TABLE privilege.

COMPLEXITY
INTERMEDIATE

6.7 How do I...
Add cascading delete functionality?

Problem

I get an error when my application tries to delete data from parent tables, as records in the parent table are referenced by records from other child tables. I know that when I use referential integrity constraints, I need to have a cascade delete functionality to automatically delete all dependent records from the child table, whenever I delete referenced records from the parent table. How do I add a cascading delete functionality?

Technique

The ON DELETE CASCADE is an important feature of the foreign key constraint. The ON DELETE CASCADE can be optionally specified in the REFERENCES clause while defining a foreign key constraint. If it is not specified, a parent table record cannot be deleted until all referencing child table records are deleted first. The ON DELETE CASCADE option allows deletions of parent table rows, as Oracle will automatically delete corresponding rows in the child table that have references to the parent table record being deleted. As no constraint specification is allowed in the ALTER TABLE...MODIFY clause, it cannot be used to add an ON DELETE CASCADE option to an already existing foreign key constraint. The constraint has to be dropped and created again with the ALTER TABLE...ADD syntax or the entire table can be created anew with a CREATE TABLE statement.

Steps

1. Run SQL*Plus and connect as the WAITE user account. CHP6_20.SQL, shown in Figure 6.20, drops the EMP06 table and creates the table again, this time with the ON DELETE CASCADE option, and also creates sample data used in this How-To.

```
SQL> START CHP6_20
SQL> SET ECHO OFF

Table dropped.

Table created.

1 row created.

1 row created.

1 row created.
```

When a department is deleted from the DEPT06 parent table, all associated records in the EMP06 child table should also be deleted. Sample records are created in both tables to demonstrate the process.

2. Run the statements in CHP6_21.SQL to query the DEPT06 and EMP06 tables, as shown in Figure 6.21.

```
SET ECHO OFF
DROP TABLE EMP06;
CREATE TABLE EMP06 (
    EMP_NO     NUMBER(6) PRIMARY KEY,
    EMP_NAME   VARCHAR2(15) NOT NULL,
    MGR_NO     NUMBER(6),
    DEPT_NO    NUMBER(4) NOT NULL
               CONSTRAINT FKEY_DEPT
               REFERENCES DEPT06(DEPT_NO)
               ON DELETE CASCADE);
INSERT INTO DEPT06 VALUES (10, 'MARKETING');
INSERT INTO EMP06 VALUES (1, 'JANE SMITH', NULL, 10);
INSERT INTO EMP06 VALUES (2, 'JOE SHMOE', NULL, 10);
```

Figure 6.20 CHP6_20.SQL creates the sample tables used in How-To 6.7.

```
SQL> START CHP6_21
SQL> SET ECHO ON
SQL> SELECT * FROM DEPT06;

 DEPT_NO DEPT_NAME
--------- ----------------
       1 ACCT DEPT
      10 MARKETING

SQL> SELECT * FROM EMP06;

  EMP_NO EMP_NAME            MGR_NO   DEPT_NO
--------- ---------------- --------- ---------
       1 JANE SMITH                        10
       2 JOE SHMOE                         10

SQL>
```

Figure 6.21 CHP6_21.SQL queries the DEPT06 and EMP06 tables.

There are two records in the EMP06 pointing to the DEPT06 record with DEPT_NO=10. Now execute the CHP6_22.SQL file, as shown in Figure 6.22, to delete the record in the DEPT06 parent table with DEPT_NO=10.

As the ON DELETE CASCADE option was specified in Step 1 while defining the foreign key constraint on EMP06 table, the two records in the EMP06 table pointing to the DEPT06 record with DEPT_NO=10 are deleted by Oracle automatically. Confirm this by running CHP6_21.SQL to query both tables again, as shown in Figure 6.23.

The record with a DEPT_NO=10 was deleted from the DEPT06 table. The corresponding two records in the EMP06 table with a DEPT_NO=10 were also automatically deleted.

How It Works

Cascading deletes can be defined with the ON DELETE CASCADE while creating a foreign key constraint. Properly defined cascade deletes ensure referential integrity is maintained in the database whenever DELETE statements are issued against referenced tables. Step 1 creates the EMP06 table with an ON DELETE CASCADE defined with its foreign key constraint. Step 2 demonstrates the automatic deletion of associated child table records from the EMP06 table, by deleting a record from the DEPT06 parent table.

```
SQL> START CHP6_22
SQL> SET ECHO ON
SQL> DELETE DEPT06
  2  WHERE  DEPT_NO = 10;

1 row deleted.

SQL>
```

Figure 6.22 CHP6_22.SQL deletes a referenced record from the DEPT06 table.

```
SQL> START CHP6_21
SQL> SET ECHO ON
SQL> SELECT * FROM DEPT06;

   DEPT_NO DEPT_NAME
---------- ------------------
         1 ACCT DEPT

SQL> SELECT * FROM EMP06;

no rows selected

SQL>
```

Figure 6.23 After a referenced record is deleted from the DEPT06 table.

Comments

Cascading deletes are ideal for enforcing referential integrity, and defining them with foreign key constraints is fairly easy. The cascading deletes come to action only when a DELETE statement is issued on a parent table record. Cascading deletes can be also performed by using DELETE triggers. See How-To 13.5 for a thorough discussion on how DELETE triggers can be used for cascading deletes. Depending on the size of tables, complexity of relationships, and performance requirements, cascading deletes can be implemented using different approaches: in the application itself, or ON DELETE CASCADE with foreign key constraints, or DELETE triggers.

COMPLEXITY

INTERMEDIATE

6.8 How do I...
Create a sequence to generate a unique number?

Problem

I need to generate a sequential number in my application. The number will be used as the primary key value of a table and has to be unique. How do I create a sequence to generate a unique number for a primary key before inserting a record in a table, and how do I change the behavior of an existing sequence?

Technique

The CREATE SEQUENCE statement is used to create a new sequence. The ALTER SEQUENCE statement is used to change the values of certain sequence parameters. There is no direct way to change the value of a sequence. In order to change the value of a sequence, the sequence must be dropped and re-created with the new parameters. Information about sequences contained in the database can be queried from the USER_SEQUENCES and ALL_SEQUENCES data dictionary views.

The CURRVAL pseudo-column within a sequence allows a sequence value to be queried without incrementing it. The CURRVAL pseudo-column cannot be queried until a NEXTVAL pseudo-column is queried for the sequence during the session. This keeps an application from using a sequence value created by another user or application.

Steps

1. Run SQL*Plus and connect as the WAITE user account. Execute the CHP6_23.SQL file, which contains a CREATE SEQUENCE statement to create a new sequence:

```
SQL> START CHP6_23
  1  CREATE SEQUENCE NEW_SEQ06;

Sequence created.
```

The CREATE SEQUENCE keywords are required to create a new sequence. Because no other options are specified, the sequence will contain default values for all the parameters (see Table 6.4) and start with 1. The NEW_SEQ06.NEXTVAL pseudo-column can be queried within an application to increment the sequence and return the next value of the sequence.

Table 6.4 Options available with CREATE SEQUENCE/ALTER SEQUENCE

KEYWORD	PURPOSE
INCREMENT BY n	Increment value for sequence counter, positive for ascending sequence or negative for descending sequence (default +1).
START WITH n	First sequence number to be generated; cannot be used in ALTER SEQUENCE (default 1).
MAXVALUE n	Highest number the sequence will generate; (default -1 for descending sequence).
NOMAXVALUE	Maximum value of 10^{27} for an ascending sequence or -1 for a descending sequence (default).
MINVALUE n	Lowest number the sequence will generate (default 1 for ascending sequence).
NOMINVALUE	Minimum value of 1 for an ascending sequence or $-(10^{26})$ for a descending sequence (default).
CYCLE	Sequence restarts after reaching MAXVALUE or MINVALUE (not default).
NOCYCLE	Error when MAXVALUE hit for ascending sequence and MINVALUE hit for descending sequence (default).
CACHE n	Number of pre-allocated sequence values kept in memory (default 20).
NOCACHE	Sequence values are not pre-allocated (not default).
ORDER	Guarantees sequence numbers are generated in the order of requests, required for parallel mode operation (not default).
NOORDER	No specific order to sequence number generation (default).

2. Run the CHP6_24.SQL file, as shown in Figure 6.24, which contains a CREATE SEQUENCE statement to generate descending numbers.

```
SQL> START CHP6_24
SQL> CREATE SEQUENCE NEG_SEQ06
  2    START WITH 1000
  3    MAXVALUE 1000
  4    INCREMENT BY -1;

Sequence created.

SQL>
```

Figure 6.24 CHP6_24.SQL
creates a sequence with
negative increments.

Line 1 contains the keywords required to create the sequence and give it a name. The START WITH clause contained in line 2 specifies that the sequence starts at 1,000. The MAXVALUE clause specified in line 2 provides the largest value the sequence can contain, and the negative number in the INCREMENT BY clause in line 4 creates a descending sequence. The first value returned when the sequence is queried will be 1,000, because it was specified in the START WITH clause. The negative value in the INCREMENT BY clause decreases the sequence each time it is queried.

3. Run the CHP6_25.SQL file, which contains two ALTER SEQUENCE statements: one to change the maximum value of an ascending sequence and another to change the minimum value of a descending sequence. Figure 6.25 shows the results of running the two statements in SQL*Plus.

Both statements fail as the current value of a sequence has to be changed to satisfy either ALTER SEQUENCE, and Oracle does not allow the current value of a sequence to be changed in an ALTER statement. An ALTER SEQUENCE statement is issued in a similar fashion as the CREATE SEQUENCE, except that START WITH is not available. To change the value of a sequence, you must DROP and CREATE it again.

```
SQL> START CHP6_25
SQL> ALTER SEQUENCE NEW_SEQ06
  2    MINVALUE 100;
ALTER SEQUENCE NEW_SEQ06
*
ERROR at line 1:
ORA-04007: MINVALUE cannot be made to exceed the current value

SQL> ALTER SEQUENCE NEG_SEQ06
  2    MAXVALUE 900;
ALTER SEQUENCE NEG_SEQ06
*
ERROR at line 1:
ORA-04009: MAXVALUE cannot be made to be less than the current value

SQL>
```

Figure 6.25 Illegal use of ALTER SEQUENCE statements.

4. Run the CHP6_26.SQL file, which contains two ALTER SEQUENCE statements: one to modify the minimum and maximum values associated with the ascending sequence and another to remove the minimum value from the descending sequence. Figure 6.26 shows the results of running the two statements in SQL*Plus.

In the first ALTER SEQUENCE statement, line 1 contains the keywords required to modify the parameters of a sequence. Lines 2 and 3 use the MINVALUE and MAXVALUE keywords to affect the sequence parameter values. In the second ALTER SEQUENCE statement, line 2 removes the minimum value of the sequence by specifying the NOMINVALUE clause. Other sequence parameter values are left unchanged by the both statements. Whenever a MAXVALUE or MINVALUE specification is explicitly provided, NOMAXVALUE and NOMINVALUE defaults get overridden respectively.

5. Run the CHP6_27.SQL file, which contains queries to the NEXTVAL and CURRVAL pseudo-columns of the NEW_SEQ06 sequence. CURRVAL returns the current value of the sequence, while NEXTVAL increments the sequence and returns the new value. Figure 6.27 shows the results of queries in SQL*Plus.

```
SQL> START CHP6_26
SQL> ALTER SEQUENCE NEW_SEQ06
  2    MINVALUE 0
  3    MAXVALUE 10000;

Sequence altered.

SQL> ALTER SEQUENCE NEG_SEQ06
  2    MAXVALUE 10000
  3    NOMINVALUE;

Sequence altered.

SQL>
```

Figure 6.26 Legal use of ALTER SEQUENCE statements.

```
SQL> START CHP6_27
SQL> SET ECHO ON
SQL> SELECT NEW_SEQ06.NEXTVAL
  2  FROM DUAL;

  NEXTVAL
----------
        1

SQL> SELECT NEW_SEQ06.CURRVAL
  2  FROM DUAL;

  CURRVAL
----------
        1

SQL>
```

Figure 6.27 Results of queries on NEXTVAL and CURRVAL pseudo-columns.

The DUAL system table is used as the source of both queries and always returns a single value. Once the NEXTVAL pseudo-column is retrieved from the sequence in the current session, the CURRVAL pseudo-column can be used to retrieve the same number repeatedly. The value returned will always be the last value returned by the NEXTVAL pseudo-column in the same session.

6. Run the CHP6_28.SQL file, as shown in Figure 6.28, which contains a query to display sequence information from your current schema.

The columns returned by the query on the USER_SEQUENCES view show you the name of the sequence, the minimum and maximum values, and how the sequence counter is incremented. The columns C and O in the listing stand for CYCLE_FLAG and ORDER_FLAG, and have a value of N as a sequence is created with a NOCYCLE and NOORDER by default. The LAST_NUMBER column contains the last sequence number written to disk. If a sequence uses caching, the number written to disk is the last number placed in the sequence cache. This number is likely to be greater than the last sequence number that was actually used. This value is not continuously updated during database operation and is intended for use after a warm start or import. The CURRVAL and NEXTVAL pseudo-columns should always be used to retrieve the sequence value, which guarantee that a unique sequence value is always returned in an Oracle session. The USER_SEQUENCES and ALL_SEQUENCES views contain the sequences available to a user. The ALL_SEQUENCES view contains sequences owned by the user account and those granted to the user account.

7. If you have not run the CHP6_3.SQL script so far, you must run it to create the COMPANY06 table before you run the CHP6_29.SQL file, which contains an INSERT statement that uses a sequence to generate a unique number for the primary key of the COMPANY06 table. Figure 6.29 shows the results of running the statement in SQL*Plus.

```
SQL> START CHP6_28
SQL> SET ECHO ON
SQL> COLUMN SEQUENCE_NAME FORMAT A14
SQL> SELECT *
  2  FROM USER_SEQUENCES;

SEQUENCE_NAME  MIN_VALUE MAX_VALUE INCREMENT_BY C O CACHE_SIZE LAST_NUMBER
-------------- --------- --------- ------------ - - ---------- -----------
NEG_SEQ06      -1.00E+26     10000           -1 N N         20        1000
NEW_SEQ06              0     10000            1 N N         20          21

SQL>
```

Figure 6.28 Results of the query on USER_SEQUENCES view.

```
SQL> START CHP6_29
SQL> SET ECHO ON
SQL> INSERT INTO COMPANY06
  2  VALUES (NEW_SEQ06.NEXTVAL, 'INDIGO SOFTWARE', 'USA');

1 row created.

SQL>
```

Figure 6.29 CHP6_29.SQL uses NEXTVAL in an INSERT statement.

The NEXTVAL pseudo-column of the NEW_SEQ06 sequence is used within an INSERT statement. In the event that multiple requests to insert records in the same table came in parallel, a unique value for the COMPANY_ID column is guaranteed for each request.

How It Works

Step 1 creates a sequence with default values for parameters. When a sequence is created with default values, it starts with 1 and has no upper limit. In Step 2, a descending sequence is created. Steps 3 and 4 demonstrate modifying parameters associated with sequences. In Step 5, sequential values are queried from a sequence using the NEXTVAL and CURRVAL pseudo-columns. The USER_SEQUENCES view is queried in Step 6, to display information about sequences created in the first two steps. Step 7 demonstrates how a sequence can be used for generating a unique primary key within an INSERT statement.

Comments

Sequences are the best way to generate integer keys in Oracle, and sequential numbered primary keys result in improved performance. After creating a sequence, privileges need to be granted to user accounts or roles just like tables. The ALTER SEQUENCE statement can be used to change most of the parameters set for a sequence, but not the value of a sequence. The ALL_SEQUENCES and USER_SEQUENCES data dictionary views provide information about sequences in the database. If you need to list information about the sequences in your current schema, use the USER_SEQUENCES view. If you need to know about sequences to which you have been granted privileges, use the ALL_SEQUENCES view. To retrieve the value of a sequence, the NEXTVAL pseudo-column must be queried before the CURRVAL pseudo-column can be queried within the session. One sequence can be used for many tables, or a separate sequence can be created for each table requiring generated keys.

To create a sequence, you must have a CREATE SEQUENCE or CREATE ANY SEQUENCE privilege. To alter a sequence, you must have the ALTER SEQUENCE or ALTER ANY SEQUENCE privilege. Once the sequence is created, it can be used by the current user account or any user account granted SELECT privileges.

COMPLEXITY
ADVANCED

6.9 How do I...
Determine integrity violations?

Problem

In order to upload data into the database in batch operations, I have to disable constraints. After the load operation completes, I cannot enable constraints, due to constraint violating rows being inserted during the load. How do I identify exactly which rows violate integrity constraints?

Technique

If a row of a table does not satisfy any constraint defined with the table, this row is called as an *exception* to the constraint. Even if there is a single row in exception, the constraint cannot be enabled. An error is returned and the constraint remains disabled. In order to enable the constraint, exceptions to the constraint must be either deleted or updated to comply with the constraint.

Oracle can automatically report exceptions through an exception table. The EXCEPTIONS option in the ENABLE clause of a CREATE TABLE or ALTER TABLE statement can be used to specify an exception table to identify rows violating a constraint. A query on the specified exception table returns the ROWID, table owner, table name, and the constraint name for all exception rows.

Steps

1. As a prerequisite, run CHP6_20.SQL if you have not done this before. This will create the EMP06 table and insert some sample data in it. Run the statements in the CHP6_30.SQL file. This file contains an ALTER TABLE statement to disable the primary key on the EMP06 table. This is followed by an INSERT statement to insert a row with a duplicate primary key. Figure 6.30 shows the results of the operation in SQL*Plus.

In demonstrating this How-to, a row with a duplicate key needs to be inserted. This can be done only after disabling the constraint with the ALTER TABLE statement (refer to How-To 6.6). This is succeeded by inserting a row with a primary key equal to that of a record already existing in the table. No error is reported as the primary key is disabled. Now, there are multiple records with the EMP_NO value of 1 in the EMP06 table.

```
SQL> START CHP6_30
SQL> SET ECHO ON
SQL> ALTER TABLE EMP06
  2     DISABLE PRIMARY KEY;

Table altered.

SQL> INSERT INTO EMP06
  2     VALUES (1, 'JOE SHMOE', NULL, 1);

1 row created.

SQL> INSERT INTO EMP06
  2     VALUES (1, 'BILL DOE', NULL, 1);

1 row created.

SQL> |
```

Figure 6.30 CHP6_30.SQL inserts a
duplicate row in the EMP06 table.

2. Run the statements in the CHP6_31.SQL file. The first statement is a
CREATE TABLE statement to create an exceptions table. An ALTER TABLE
statement is then used to specify this exceptions table to report exception
rows encountered when enabling the constraint. Figure 6.31 illustrates the
method of using an exceptions table to trap integrity violations.

In the first command, line 1 contains the CREATE TABLE keywords to
create a table named WAITE_EXCEPTIONS. From line 2 through 5,
columns of the table are created in line with expectations of any exception
table that must typically have four columns—ROWID, table owner, table
name, and constraint name, in that order—and must have the same
datatypes and lengths as used in the WAITE_EXCEPTIONS table.

In the second command, the ALTER TABLE statement has an
EXCEPTIONS option in the ENABLE clause, to specify the
WAITE_EXCEPTIONS table to log information about constraint

```
SQL> START CHP6_31
SQL> SET ECHO ON
SQL> CREATE TABLE WAITE_EXCEPTIONS (
  2    ROW_ID            ROWID NOT NULL,
  3    OWNER             VARCHAR2(30) NOT NULL,
  4    TABLE_NAME        VARCHAR2(30) NOT NULL,
  5    CONSTRAINT_NAME   VARCHAR2(30) NOT NULL);

Table created.

SQL> ALTER TABLE EMP06
  2    ENABLE PRIMARY KEY
  3    EXCEPTIONS INTO WAITE_EXCEPTIONS;
ALTER TABLE EMP06
*
ERROR at line 1:
ORA-02437: cannot enable (WAITE.SYS_C001034) - primary key violated

SQL> |
```

Figure 6.31 CHP6_31.SQL creates an exceptions table
for a primary key.

exceptions in the EMP06 table. The statement ends up with an error as expected, as a record with a duplicate key was intentionally inserted in Step 1. While attempting to enable the primary key, information about exception rows is placed by Oracle in the WAITE_EXCEPTIONS table.

3. Run the CHP6_32.SQL to query the WAITE_EXCEPTIONS table to report constraint exceptions. Another variation of the query lists actual rows from the EMP06 table using ROWIDs from the WAITE_EXCEPTIONS table. Figure 6.32 shows the output from the queries as displayed in SQL*Plus.

4. Run the CHP6_33.SQL file in SQL*Plus, as shown in Figure 6.33, to correct the exceptions reported for the EMP06 table.

The offending row is deleted from the EMP06 table followed by deleting the corresponding entries from the WAITE_EXCEPTIONS exception report table. A COMMIT transaction statement is issued to ensure changes to tables by the DELETE statements are made permanent. The primary key of the EMP06 is now enabled successfully using an ALTER TABLE statement.

How It Works

Step 1 executes an ALTER TABLE statement to disable a primary key before inserting an invalid row into a table. Step 2 creates an exception table by using the CREATE TABLE statement and issues an ALTER TABLE statement to specify the exception table in the EXCEPTIONS option of ENABLE clause. Step 3

```
SQL> @CHP6_32
SQL> SET ECHO ON
SQL> COLUMN TABLE_OWNER FORMAT A11
SQL> COLUMN TABLE_NAME FORMAT A10
SQL> COLUMN CONSTRAINT_NAME FORMAT A15
SQL> SELECT *
  2   FROM WAITE_EXCEPTIONS;

ROW_ID                    OWNER                               TABLE_NAME CONSTRAINT_NAME
------------------------- ----------------------------------- ---------- ---------------
0000271E.0000.0001 WAITE                                      EMP06      SYS_C002405
0000271E.0002.0001 WAITE                                      EMP06      SYS_C002405
0000271E.0003.0001 WAITE                                      EMP06      SYS_C002405
00002A4D.0000.0001 WAITE                                      EMP06      SYS_C002397
00002A4D.0002.0001 WAITE                                      EMP06      SYS_C002397

SQL> SELECT EMP06.*
  2   FROM EMP06, WAITE_EXCEPTIONS
  3   WHERE EMP06.ROWID = WAITE_EXCEPTIONS.ROW_ID;

    EMP_NO EMP_NAME              MGR_NO     DEPT_NO
---------- -------------------- --------- ---------
         1 JANE SMITH                           10
         1 JOE SHMOE                             1
         1 BILL DOE                              1

SQL>
```

Figure 6.32 Results of the query on WAITE_EXCEPTIONS table.

```
SQL> @CHP6_33
SQL> SET ECHO ON
SQL> DELETE FROM EMP06
  2     WHERE EMP_NAME = 'BILL DOE'
  3     OR EMP_NAME = 'JANE SMITH';

2 rows deleted.

SQL> DELETE FROM WAITE_EXCEPTIONS
  2     WHERE TABLE_NAME = 'EMP06';

5 rows deleted.

SQL> COMMIT;

Commit complete.

SQL> ALTER TABLE EMP06
  2     ENABLE PRIMARY KEY
  3     EXCEPTIONS INTO WAITE_EXCEPTIONS;

Table altered.

SQL>
```

Figure 6.33 CHP6_33.SQL corrects the integrity exceptions.

queries the integrity violating rows from the exception table. Step 4 fixes integrity exceptions before successfully enabling the primary key using an ALTER TABLE statement.

Comments

An exception is a row in a table that violates an integrity constraint. If an exception table is specified and the constraint is being enabled, a row is inserted automatically in the exception table for each exception. If there are any exceptions, the constraint remains disabled. Exceptions from multiple constraints can be channeled to the same exception table. Exception rows can be either deleted or updated to correct integrity violations, and corresponding rows in the exception table have to be deleted explicitly. As a special case for index-only tables where rows are identified by the primary key and not the ROWID, the BUILD_EXCEPTIONS_TABLE procedure in the DBMS_IOT package is used to create the exceptions table.

COMPLEXITY
ADVANCED

6.10 How do I...
Create a deferred constraint?

Problem

I have an application that needs to update the primary key of a parent table. To maintain the master-detail relationship, foreign keys in child tables must also be updated. I cannot perform this operation unless I disable the underlying constraints. Disabling constraints for every cascading update operation is not practical apart from the fact that enabling constraints after such updates is slow as we have large tables. I know that with Oracle8 there is a powerful new functionality of deferred constraints that permit cascade updates without having to disable constraints. How do I create a deferred constraint?

Technique

Deferred constraints is a new Oracle8 feature that allows constraint checking to be deferred until the end of the transaction. For any *deferred* constraint, the system checks that it is satisfied on commit in contrast to an *immediate* constraint that is checked at the end of each statement. Deferred constraints ensure that constraint processing time remains constant as the database grows in size and complexity. Multiple related tables can be manipulated in an arbitrary order within a transaction. When the transaction is committed, constraint checking on foreign keys is done to determine referential integrity violations. While performing bulk insert or update operations on a single table, constraint checking of primary key, NOT NULL, and check constraints can be deferred until the end of the transaction. A deferrable constraint can be specified with the constraint definition in the CREATE TABLE statement or can be added later using an ALTER TABLE statement. In a transaction, the SET CONSTRAINT statement can be issued to change the constraint mode of a deferrable constraint to deferred or immediate. A non-deferrable constraint is always in an immediate mode and cannot be set to a deferred mode.

Steps

1. Run SQL*Plus and connect as the WAITE user account. CHP6_34.SQL, shown in Figure 6.34, drops the EMP06 table and creates the table again with a DEFERRABLE foreign key constraint, and also creates sample data used in this How-To.

```
SQL> START CHP6_34
SQL> SET ECHO OFF
```

```
Table dropped.

Table created.

1 row deleted.

1 row created.

1 row created.

1 row created.

1 row created.
```

Any table or column constraint can be defined as deferrable. In this example, we choose to create a deferrable foreign key constraint. The DEFERRABLE keyword means that the constraint will not be checked until the transaction is committed. A constraint can be specified to be NOT DEFERRABLE, which means that for every single row being manipulated, the constraint will be checked. NOT DEFERRABLE is the default. When you specify a constraint to be DEFERRABLE, you can additionally specify the initial state of the constraint. With the INITIALLY DEFERRED keywords, the transaction is started in a deferred mode, and constraint checking is postponed until a SET CONSTRAINT IMMEDIATE statement is issued, or the end of transaction signaled by a COMMIT statement. With the INITIALLY IMMEDIATE keywords, the constraint starts in a non-deferred mode, that is, the constraint is checked immediately after each statement. The default is INITIALLY IMMEDIATE. An ALTER TABLE statement can be used to add a deferred constraint to an existing table.

2. Note that the foreign key constraint on EMP06 table is still not in a DEFERRED mode, even though it was defined as DEFERRABLE. As no initial state was specified in the constraint definition, the constraint starts

```
SET ECHO OFF
DROP TABLE EMP06;
CREATE TABLE EMP06 (
    EMP_NO      NUMBER(6) PRIMARY KEY,
    EMP_NAME    VARCHAR2(15) NOT NULL,
    MGR_NO      NUMBER(6),
    DEPT_NO     NUMBER(4) NOT NULL
                CONSTRAINT FKEY_DEPT
                REFERENCES DEPT06(DEPT_NO) DEFERRABLE);
INSERT INTO DEPT06 VALUES (10, 'SALES');
INSERT INTO DEPT06 VALUES (20, 'BILLING');
INSERT INTO EMP06 VALUES (1, 'JANE SMITH', NULL, 10);
INSERT INTO EMP06 VALUES (2, 'JOE SHMOE', NULL, 20);
```

Figure 6.34 CHP6_34.SQL creates the sample tables used in How-To 6.10.

with the default mode of INITIALLY IMMEDIATE. Run the CHP6_35.SQL file, as shown in Figure 6.35, which contains a SET CONSTRAINT statement to set the initial state of the constraint to DEFERRED.

The SET CONSTRAINT statement is used to change the mode of a constraint. SET CONSTRAINT is followed by the name of constraint it needs to act upon. You can use SET CONSTRAINT (with an optional trailing S for plural purists) with a list of constraint names separated by commas to change the states of multiple deferrable constraints in communion using a single statement. The ALL keyword can also be used instead of the constraint names to apply the change to all deferrable constraints at once. The DEFERRED keyword indicates that the conditions specified by the deferrable constraint are checked when the constraint state is changed to IMMEDIATE, or the transaction is committed with COMMIT.

3. Run the CHP6_36.SQL file, which contains an UPDATE statement to modify a primary key value in the DEPT06 table that is being referenced by a record in the EMP06 table. The results of the operation are shown in Figure 6.36.

```
SQL>
SQL> START CHP6_35
SQL> SET ECHO ON
SQL> SET CONSTRAINT FKEY_DEPT DEFERRED;

Constraint set.

SQL>
```

Figure 6.35 CHP6_35.SQL sets the constraint to DEFERRED mode.

```
SQL> START CHP6_36
SQL> UPDATE DEPT06 SET DEPT_NO = 30
  2  WHERE DEPT_NO = 20;

1 row updated.

SQL> SELECT * FROM EMP06
  2  ORDER BY DEPT_NO;

  EMP_NO EMP_NAME              MGR_NO   DEPT_NO
  ------ -------------------- -------- ---------
       1 JANE SMITH                         10
       2 JOE SHMOE                          20

SQL> SELECT * FROM DEPT06
  2  ORDER BY DEPT_NO;

 DEPT_NO DEPT_NAME
 ------- ---------
       1 ACCT DEPT
      10 SALES
      30 BILLING

SQL>
```

Figure 6.36 CHP6_36.SQL manipulates a primary key value in the DEPT06 table.

Because the foreign key was deferred in the previous step, the UPDATE statement succeeds in modifying the DEPT_NO value of a record that is referenced in the EMP06 table. Had the constraint not been deferred, such a statement would fail. As the deferred mode initiated by the SET CONSTRAINT DEFERRED statement is effective, this interim state where the foreign key constraint is violated is allowed by the system.

With Oracle7, you would have to disable the foreign key constraint or add temporary rows to the EMP06 table to avoid constraint violations. Disabling and enabling the constraint leaves a time window in between where the table is unprotected. Adding temporary rows is an equally undesirable solution with extraneous complexity in the application.

4. Run the statement in file CHP6_37.SQL to query the USER_CONSTRAINTS view. Figure 6.37 shows the results of the query. The DEFERRABLE column contains the mode of the constraint— DEFERRABLE or NOT DEFERRABLE, depending on the way it was created.

The FKEY_DEPT is correctly shown as a DEFERRABLE constraint. The current state of the constraint can be queried from the DEFERRED column of the USER_CONSTRAINTS view. The last column has a value of VALIDATED that indicates that constraints are in an enabled state. When a constraint is either disabled or enforced after it was disabled, you will see a NOT VALIDATED value in this column, as validation takes place only when the constraint is enabled. Only after validation has completed successfully and the constraint is enabled, this column will show a value of VALIDATED.

5. Run the CHP6_38.SQL file, as shown in Figure 6.38, which contains a SET CONSTRAINT statement to set the state of all deferred constraints to IMMEDIATE.

```
SQL> START CHP6_37
SQL> SET ECHO ON
SQL> SELECT CONSTRAINT_NAME, TABLE_NAME, DEFERRABLE, DEFERRED, VALIDATED
  2  FROM USER_CONSTRAINTS
  3  WHERE TABLE_NAME IN ('EMP06', 'DEPT06');

CONSTRAINT_NAME TABLE_NAME DEFERRABLE      DEFERRED  VALIDATED
--------------- ---------- --------------- --------- ---------
PKEY_DEPT       DEPT06     NOT DEFERRABLE  IMMEDIATE VALIDATED
SYS_C001052     EMP06      NOT DEFERRABLE  IMMEDIATE VALIDATED
SYS_C001053     EMP06      NOT DEFERRABLE  IMMEDIATE VALIDATED
SYS_C001054     EMP06      NOT DEFERRABLE  IMMEDIATE VALIDATED
FKEY_DEPT       EMP06      DEFERRABLE      IMMEDIATE VALIDATED

SQL>
```

Figure 6.37 CHP6_37.SQL queries the USER_CONSTRAINTS view.

```
SQL> START CHP6_38
SQL> SET ECHO ON
SQL> SET CONSTRAINTS ALL IMMEDIATE;
set CONSTRAINTS ALL IMMEDIATE
*
ERROR at line 1:
ORA-02292: integrity constraint (WAITE.FKEY_DEPT) violated - child record fou

SQL> |
```

Figure 6.38 CHP6_38.SQL attempts to set constraints to
IMMEDIATE mode.

The SET CONSTRAINT statement is used to set the constraint mode to
either DEFERRED or IMMEDIATE in a transaction. The IMMEDIATE
keyword indicates that you want to check whether any constraints remain
violated before committing the transaction. The statement effectively
checks whether it is safe to issue a COMMIT statement. If the SET
CONSTRAINT statement fails due to any constraint violations, an ORA-
02292 error is returned by Oracle but the transaction is not rolled back.
The name of the constraint violated appears in the error message. This
gives an opportunity to examine and fix constraint violations. This SET
CONSTRAINT statement can be issued any number of times until it
succeeds when there are no remaining constraint violations.

6. Run the statements in the CHP6_39.SQL file. It has an UPDATE statement
to correct the data in the EMP06 table. A SET CONSTRAINT ALL
IMMEDIATE statement executes successfully after the constraint violating
row has been adjusted. A COMMIT is finally issued to complete the
transaction. Figure 6.39 displays the results of the operation in SQL*Plus.

If a COMMIT statement was issued before fixing the constraint violation,
the transaction would have been rolled back. The SET CONSTRAINT
mode lasts until another SET CONSTRAINT statement toggles the mode

```
SQL> START CHP6_39
SQL> SET ECHO ON
SQL> UPDATE EMP06 SET DEPT_NO = 30 WHERE DEPT_NO = 20;

1 row updated.

SQL> SET CONSTRAINTS ALL IMMEDIATE;

Constraint set.

SQL> COMMIT;

Commit complete.

SQL> |
```

Figure 6.39 CHP6_39.SQL sets the constraint to
IMMEDIATE mode.

or until the end of transaction. The ALTER SESSION statement provides an alternative means of setting the constraint mode and is equivalent to the SET CONSTRAINT ALL statement. The SET CONSTRAINT statement cannot be used in triggers.

How It Works

Step 1 creates the EMP06 table with a deferrable foreign key constraint. Step 2 actually sets the FKEY_DEPT constraint in the deferred mode by issuing a SET CONSTRAINT...DEFERRED statement. Step 3 updates the primary key value of a row in the DEPT06 table that is referenced as a foreign key value by a row in the EMP06 table. A primary key value must exist in the parent table before a foreign key in the child table can reference it. As constraint checking is in a deferred mode, the system does not complain about the foreign key constraint violation. Steps 4 queries the USER_CONSTRAINTS view to list relevant constraint information. Step 5 issues a SET CONSTRAINT...IMMEDIATE statement to set the constraint back to immediate mode. Constraints are checked at this point, and an error is returned due to the constraint violation that was intentionally introduced in Step 3. The constraint remains in deferred mode but the transaction is not rolled back. In order to satisfy the foreign key constraint, Step 6 updates the foreign key value to that of the new primary key value that was set in Step 3. A SET CONSTRAINT...IMMEDIATE statement now executes successfully. Subsequently, a COMMIT statement signals the end of the transaction and changes to data are made permanent.

Comments

Oracle8 allows constraint checking to be deferred until the end of the transaction. A deferred constraint is checked at the end of the transaction, and if any data still violates the constraint upon commit, the transaction is rolled back. By changing the constraint mode to immediate from deferred, constraint violations can be checked to see if it is safe to issue a commit or not. If there are constraint violations, an error is returned but the transaction is not rolled back. You can then correct the error before committing the transaction. Both deferrable and non-deferrable constraints can use non-unique indexes, thus eliminating redundant indexes.

CHAPTER 7
VIEWS

7

VIEWS

How do I...

A view is a logical table based on a query. Views themselves do not store data, but present data from other sources, such as tables and other views. To an application, a view looks and acts like a table. Data can be queried from a view, and in many cases, data can be inserted, updated, and deleted through a view. Views can be used to present data in a different format than how it is actually stored in the underlying tables. Views simplify the presentation of data by hiding the actual structure of the base tables, and can secure data at the row level by presenting a restricted subset of the underlying table to the user.

7.1 Create a View

A view can be created for several reasons. Views can be used to represent queries on tables or other views in a virtual table. Views are used mostly to make a subset of data, or to join several tables, all invisible to the user accounts. This is useful for increased data security and simplifying code. This How-To shows the method for creating views.

7.2 Determine All of the Views Owned by a Particular User

The views available to a user can be queried from the data dictionary through the USER_VIEWS and ALL_VIEWS data dictionary views. Because it is possible to have many views available, an easy method to determine the views available is presented in this How-To.

7.3 Determine if a View Can Be Updated

A view's data can be manipulated if the structure of the view meets certain criteria. A view cannot be updated if it joins tables, uses a DISTINCT operator, or contains a GROUP BY clause or group functions. This How-To presents SQL and PL/SQL statements to quickly determine if a view is updatable, without analyzing the structure of the view.

7.4 Create an Updatable Join View

Having the ability to update a view based upon more than one table allows for great flexibility in developing applications. If a table in a join view is key-preserved, it may be updated, depending on additional criteria. The ability to update object views are also available. This How-To describes the conditions that join views may be updatable, and steps through creating an updatable join view.

7.5 Simulate a Cross-Tab Query Using a View

A cross-tab query in Microsoft Access presents data from multiple rows on a single line. This type of query is useful for presenting data, such as monthly summary data, in a spreadsheet type format. This How-To presents a method to create a view that displays multiple records as a single record.

7.6 Re-Create CREATE VIEW Statements

It is often necessary to re-create the CREATE VIEW statements that were used to create views. Throughout the book, SQL*Plus and the data dictionary are used to re-create DDL statements with a complex query of the data dictionary. This How-To presents the queries used to rebuild CREATE VIEW statements from the data dictionary.

7.7 Implement Record Level Security Using Views

One of the most common uses of views is to restrict access to data from users. Users can have different views of the same data. A subset of the data in the base table can be shown by including a WHERE clause in the view, which restricts data that is based on the user account's name or privileges. This How-To presents methods for restricting access to data on the record level using views.

COMPLEXITY
BEGINNING

7.1 How do I...
Create a view?

Problem

I want to create views to improve the security of my data and to represent complex queries simply. I understand that views can be created to represent subsets of data or queries on tables and other views in a virtual table. How do I create views?

Technique

The CREATE VIEW statement creates views. The statement will show compilation errors when run, if they exist, but the view will still be created in the data dictionary. Use the CREATE VIEW statement to make a subset of data, or to join several tables, all invisible to the user accounts. This How-To will create a table, insert sample data into it, create a view limiting the data, and then retrieve the data through the view.

Steps

1. Run SQL*Plus and connect as the WAITE user account. Load CHP7_1.SQL into the SQL buffer. The file contains a CREATE TABLE statement to build the table that will be referenced in the first sample view.

```
SQL> GET CHP7_1.sql
  1   CREATE TABLE DEPT07 (
  2      DEPT_NO    NUMBER(10),
  3      DNAME      VARCHAR2(30),
  4*     MGR_ID     NUMBER(10))
```

The DEPT07 table contains all of the columns that will be referenced by the sample view. If it did not, the view would be invalid when created.

2. Execute the statement to create the table.

```
SQL>  /

Table created.
```

3. Load the CHP7_2.SQL into the SQL buffer and run it. The file contains a CREATE VIEW statement to create a view on the DEPT07 table.

```
SQL> GET CHP7_2.sql
  1   CREATE VIEW
  2      DEPT_VIEW07
  3   AS SELECT
```

continued on next page

continued from previous page

```
     4          DEPT_NO,
     5          DNAME,
     6          MGR_ID
     7     FROM DEPT07
     8     WHERE DEPT_NO=4
SQL>  /
```

View created.

The DEPT_VIEW07 view will show only records where the DEPT_NO=4. This type of view is useful for restricting data that users may see, on a record level.

4. Insert sample records into the DEPT07 table by running CHP7_3.SQL, which is shown in Figure 7.1.

```
SQL> START CHP7_3.sql
1 row created.
1 row created.
1 row created.
1 row created.
SQL>
```

5. Now, select everything from the view by running CHP7_4.SQL, as shown in Figure 7.2. You will see how the data is selected based on the restriction that the DEPT_NO=4.

```
INSERT INTO DEPT07 VALUES (1,'HUMAN RESOURCES',7500);
INSERT INTO DEPT07 VALUES (2,'MANUFACTURING',7653);
INSERT INTO DEPT07 VALUES (3,'SHIPPING',7570);
INSERT INTO DEPT07 VALUES (4,'INFORMATION TECHNOLOGY',7659);
|
```

Figure 7.1 CHP7_3.SQL inserts sample data into the DEPT07 table.

```
SQL> GET C:\CHP7_4.SQL
  1* SELECT * FROM DEPT_VIEW07
SQL> /

  DEPT_NO DNAME                                MGR_ID
--------- ------------------------------------ ---------
        4 INFORMATION TECHNOLOGY                 7659

SQL>
```

Figure 7.2 The DEPT_VIEW07 view selects data from DEPT07 where DEPT_NO=4.

How It Works

Steps 1 and 2 create the DEPT07 table that will be referenced by the view. Step 3 creates a view using a CREATE VIEW statement, based upon the DEPT07 table, restricting data to the records where DEPT_NO = 4. Step 4 inserts sample records into the DEPT07 table to demonstrate how a view may limit data seen by a user account. Step 5 selects records from the view, demonstrating that the view limits data returned to those records whose DEPT_NO = 4.

Views can be created to restrict data in any manner, or to join several tables in a simple or complex fashion. In a more advanced setup, views can also be used to select data across several databases, and the user accounts would view the data as if it were local.

Comments

Object views are useful when dealing with abstract data types and object-relational data. See How-To 7.5 to learn more about object views. Also, views that contain several tables may be inserted, updated, or deleted. How-To 7.4 shows how to create an updatable join view.

It is also possible to create a view that contains an invalid query. The query cannot contain syntax errors, but tables or columns referenced in the query do not have to exist. The FORCE option in the CREATE VIEW statement allows invalid views to be created.

COMPLEXITY
BEGINNING

7.2 How do I...
Determine all of the views owned by a particular user?

Problem

We have many views in our organization. I cannot always remember the names of the views to which I have access. Within our decision support applications, I want to present a list of the views a user has available to display data. How do I determine the views owned by a particular user account?

Technique

The USER_VIEWS data dictionary view contains views owned by the user account connected to the database. The ALL_VIEWS data dictionary view contains the views that a user account owns or has been granted privileges on. Either view can be queried to list the views available. Table 7.1 shows the columns available in the ALL_VIEWS data dictionary view.

Table 7.1 ALL_VIEWS data dictionary view

COLUMN NAME	DESCRIPTION
OWNER	Owner of the view
VIEW_NAME	Name of the view
TEXT_LENGTH	Length of the view's text
TEXT	The view's SELECT statement—stored in a LONG column
TEXT_TYPE_LENGTH	(*Object view*)—Length of the type clause of the view
TYPE_TEXT	(*Object view*)—The text of the type clause of the view
OID_TEXT_LENGTH	(*Object view*)—The length of the text of the WITH OID clause
OID_TEXT	(*Object view*)—The text of the WITH OID clause
VIEW_TYPE_OWNER	(*Object view*)—Owner of the typed view
VIEW_TYPE	(*Object view*)—The type of view

The columns pertinent to this How-To are the OWNER, VIEW_NAME, and TEXT columns. The OWNER column contains the owner of the view, and the VIEW_NAME column contains the view's name. The TEXT column contains the query used to generate the records returned by the view.

Steps

1. Run SQL*Plus and connect as the WAITE user account. Load CHP7_5.SQL into the SQL buffer. The file contains a query to list the views available to the user account.

```
SQL> GET CHP7_5.sql
  1 SELECT OWNER||'.'||VIEW_NAME
  2 FROM
  3* ALL_VIEWS
```

Line 1 concatenates the owner of the view with the name of the view to present the output in the `owner.objectname` format.

2. Run the statement to list the views. Since the WAITE user account was granted the DBA role by the installation script, every view in the database is listed. A portion of the results of the query are shown in Figure 7.3.

How It Works

The ALL_VIEWS data dictionary view contains information about the views to which a user account has access. Steps 1 and 2 query the ALL_VIEWS data dictionary view to list all the views to which the WAITE user account has been granted access. The OWNER and VIEW_NAME columns are concatenated to return a single column. If you want to list only the views owned by the connected user account, use the USER_VIEWS data dictionary view.

```
OWNER||'.'||VIEW_NAME
-------------------------------------------------------------
SYSTEM.AQ$DEF$_AQERROR
SYSTEM.DEF$_CALL
SYSTEM.PRODUCT_PRIVS
DEMO.SALES
WAITE.DEPT_VIEW07

845 rows selected.

SQL> |
```

Figure 7.3 A query of the ALL_VIEWS data
dictionary view.

Comments

Views can be used in many places, just like tables. Retrieving a list of available
views is a fairly easy process. If you are developing an application that needs to
include a list of view names, you can include the data dictionary views in your
application.

COMPLEXITY
INTERMEDIATE

7.3 How do I...
Determine if a view can be
updated?

Problem

We use views to make querying data easier. I know many views can be updated,
but I need a method to determine which ones they are. How do I determine if a
view can be updated?

Technique

A view cannot be updated in some cases if it joins tables, uses a DISTINCT
operator, or contains a GROUP BY clause or group functions. How-To 7.4 fully
describes how to update a join view. You can use the TEXT column in the
ALL_VIEWS data dictionary view to determine if any of these limitations exist in
the query. An easier way to determine if the view can be updated is to perform a
data management operation and trap the error if it occurs.

Steps

1. Run SQL*Plus and connect as the WAITE user account. CHP7_6.SQL,
shown in Figure 7.4, contains the statements used to build two tables and
two views that will test the code segment developed in this How-To.

```
CREATE TABLE TAB_A07 (
       FLD1     NUMBER(10));

CREATE TABLE TAB_B07 (
       FLD2     NUMBER(10));

CREATE VIEW VIEW_A07
       AS SELECT * FROM TAB_A07;

CREATE VIEW VIEW_B07
       AS SELECT FLD1, FLD2
          FROM TAB_A07, TAB_B07;
|
```

Figure 7.4 CHP7_6.SQL queries the
TEXT column of the ALL_VIEWS
data dictionary view.

The two tables, TAB_A07 and TAB_B07, are the source tables for the two views. The first view, VIEW0_A07, selects all of the columns from the TAB_A07 table and can be updated. The second view, VIEW_B07, joins the two sample tables and cannot be updated due to the join condition.

2. Run the statement to create the tables and views.

```
SQL>  START CHP7_6.sql

Table created.

Table created.

View created.

View created.
```

3. Load CHP7_7.SQL into the SQL buffer. The file contains an INSERT statement that tests if a data management statement can be performed on a view. Because the INSERT statement uses a query of the view, it is not necessary to know the structure of the view. The technique shown in this step will test all views.

```
SQL> GET CHP7_7
  1 INSERT INTO VIEW_B07
  2  SELECT * FROM VIEW_B07
  3*  WHERE 1 = 0
```

Line 1 specifies that records are inserted into VIEW_B07. Line 2 specifies that the records inserted are also queried from VIEW_B07. The WHERE clause in line 3 doesn't insert any rows, because 1 is never equal to 0. If an INSERT statement cannot be executed on the view, an error will occur when the statement is run.

4. Run the statement to attempt to insert a record into the view.

```
SQL>  /
insert into VIEW_B07 select * from VIEW_B07
*
ERROR at line 1:
ORA-01779: cannot modify a column which maps to a non key-
preserved table
```

The Oracle error ORA-01779 is returned when a data manipulation operation is attempted on a view where it is not allowed.

5. Load CHP7_8.SQL into the SQL buffer. The statement in the file creates a stored function to determine if a data manipulation operation can be performed on a view. For more information about the creation of stored functions, see How-To 10.4.

```
SQL>  GET CHP7_8.sql
  1 CREATE OR REPLACE FUNCTION CHECK_VIEW
  2   (VIEW_NAME IN VARCHAR2) RETURN BOOLEAN IS
  3 TMP VARCHAR2(60);
  4  CURSOR_HANDLE INTEGER;
  5  CNT INTEGER;
  6 BEGIN
  7  TMP := 'INSERT INTO '||VIEW_NAME;
  8  TMP := TMP||' SELECT * FROM '||VIEW_NAME;
  9  TMP := TMP||' WHERE 1 = 0';
 10 CURSOR_HANDLE := DBMS_SQL.OPEN_CURSOR;
 11 DBMS_SQL.PARSE(CURSOR_HANDLE, TMP, DBMS_SQL.V7);
 12 CNT := DBMS_SQL.EXECUTE(CURSOR_HANDLE);
 13 RETURN TRUE;
 14 EXCEPTION
 15  WHEN OTHERS
 16  THEN
 17  RETURN FALSE;
 18* END;
```

Lines 1 and 2 declare a stored function that is passed a view name and returns a Boolean value. Lines 3 through 5 create the temporary variables used by the function. Lines 7 through 10 put the type of INSERT statement shown in the prior steps into the TMP variable. Line 10 uses the OPEN_CURSOR function from the DBMS_SQL stored package to open a cursor that will execute the INSERT statement. The DBMS_SQL package allows dynamic SQL to be created and executed against the database. Because the view name is passed as a parameter, a fixed SQL statement cannot be created in the PL/SQL function. Line 11 parses the INSERT statement contained in the TMP variable by executing the PARSE procedure in the DBMS_SQL package. Line 12 executes the INSERT statement, using the EXECUTE function from the same package. Line 13 returns TRUE if an error does not occur. Lines 14 through 17 handle an error created if the INSERT statement fails, by returning FALSE.

6. Execute the statement to create the stored function.

```
SQL>  /

Function created.
```

7. Load CHP7_9.SQL into the SQL buffer. The file contains a PL/SQL statement to test the operation of the stored function created in the previous step.

```
SQL>  GET CHP7_9.sql
 1 DECLARE
 2  X BOOLEAN;
 3 BEGIN
 4  X := CHECK_VIEW('VIEW_A07');
 5 IF X THEN
 6  DBMS_OUTPUT.PUT_LINE('Can update VIEW_A07');
 7 ELSE
 8  DBMS_OUTPUT.PUT_LINE('Cannot update VIEW_A07');
 9 END IF;
10  X := CHECK_VIEW('VIEW_B07');
11 IF X THEN
12     DBMS_OUTPUT.PUT_LINE('Can update VIEW_B07');
13     ELSE
14      DBMS_OUTPUT.PUT_LINE('Cannot update VIEW_B07');
15     END IF;
16*    END;
```

Line 4 executes the TEST_CHECK function for TEST_VIEW1. Lines 5 through 9 display the results of the function call. Line 10 executes the TEST_CHECK function for TEST_VIEW2. Lines 11 through 15 display the results of the function call.

8. Set the SERVEROUTPUT system variable to ON with the SET command and execute the statement to test the function. TEST_VIEW1 is updatable, and TEST_VIEW2 is not.

```
SQL> SET SERVEROUTPUT ON
SQL> /

Can update VIEW_A07
Cannot update VIEW_B07

PL/SQL procedure successfully completed.
```

How It Works

Steps 1 and 2 create the two sample tables and two views used in the example. Steps 3 and 4 present a method for testing a view by inserting records into it with a SELECT statement. The INSERT statement will not create any rows in the table if successful and will fail if the operation is not allowed. Step 4 attempts to execute the INSERT statement and fails because VIEW_B07 cannot be updated.

Steps 5 and 6 create a stored function that is passed a view name, returning TRUE if the view data can be modified, FALSE if it cannot. The function uses the DBMS_SQL package to execute a dynamic SQL statement that tests the INSERT statement on the view. Steps 7 and 8 test the operation of the stored function created in steps 5 and 6.

Comments

The steps shown in this How-To test a view to determine if data management operations can be performed on the view. When the data in the view can be modified, views can provide benefits over using base tables in your applications. For more information, see How-To 7.4.

Also, by querying the DBA_UPDATABLE_VIEWS data dictionary view, you can determine all views that are and are not updatable.

COMPLEXITY
ADVANCED

7.4 How do I...
Create an updatable join view?

Problem

I want to create views based upon my tables and objects, and would like to allow the underlying tables to be modified. My application requires that the tables and objects can be inserted, updated, and deleted, yet I want to retain the flexibility and security of using views. How do I create an updatable join view?

Technique

When a view is based upon a single table or object, all Data Manipulation Language statements (DML) may be performed on the view such as insert, update, and delete, if the user account has proper permissions. However, when two or more tables are joined within a view, there are limitations on if and how the underlying tables may be inserted, updated, and deleted.

Only one table may be modified, and with certain restrictions. The most important condition is that the table being modified is key-preserved. A key-preserved table has all of its identifying unique key columns contained within the SELECT clause of the view text. For the view to be updatable, the resulting join must also uniquely define each record in the view. This How-To will provide examples that explain this important condition.

In addition to having to be key-preserved, the view must not contain certain clauses. These are the ROWNUM pseudocolumn, table hierarchies (START WITH; CONNECT BY), set operations (UNION, MINUS, and so on), grouping functions (DISTINCT; GROUP BY; HAVING), and math functions (COUNT, MAX, SUM, and so on).

To delete records, only one table in the resulting join may be key-preserved. If two or more tables are key-preserved, Oracle would not know which table to delete from, due to the ambiguity of the statement.

To insert records, all columns of the view must come from key-preserved tables. If a view has several columns from several tables, and at least one column is from an underlying non–key-preserved table, then Oracle would not be able to determine how to uniquely identify the record being inserted.

As with inserting records, to update records, all columns of the view must come from key-preserved tables. If a view has several columns from several tables, and at least one column is from an underlying non–key-preserved table, then Oracle would not be able to determine how to uniquely identify the record being updated.

Steps

1. Run SQL*Plus and connect as the WAITE user account. CHP7_10.SQL creates the PART07 and FACTORY07 tables. Run the script, as shown in Figure 7.5.

Notice that the FACTORY_NO column of the FACTORY07 table is defined as the primary key. If the FACTORY_NO column appears in the view, it will be an updatable key-defined view. Also, the PARTNO column of the PART07 table will be the key-defined column whose inclusion in the view is necessary for updating data.

2. Run the CHP7_11.SQL script to insert data into each table. The data will be used to describe how views may be updated. CHP7_11.SQL is shown in Figure 7.6.

```
SQL> START C:\CHP7_10.SQL
SQL> CREATE TABLE FACTORY07 (
  2        FACTORY_NO    NUMBER(10) PRIMARY KEY,
  3        FACTORY_NAME  VARCHAR2(20),
  4        LOCATION      VARCHAR2(200));

Table created.

SQL> CREATE TABLE PART07 (
  2        PARTNO        NUMBER(10) PRIMARY KEY,
  3        PART_NAME     VARCHAR2(20),
  4        PART_DESC     VARCHAR2(3000),
  5        QTY           NUMBER,
  6        FACTORY_NO    NUMBER(10),
  7        FOREIGN KEY (FACTORY_NO) REFERENCES
  8                      FACTORY07(FACTORY_NO));

Table created.

SQL>
```

Figure 7.5 CHP7_10.SQL creates the PART07 and FACTORY07 tables, which will be used to create an updatable join view.

```
INSERT INTO FACTORY07 VALUES (10,'HEADQUARTERS','CHICAGO, IL');
INSERT INTO FACTORY07 VALUES (20,'HORSE FARM','NEW YORK, NY');
INSERT INTO FACTORY07 VALUES (30,'SHIPPING PLANT','LOS ANGELES, CA');

INSERT INTO PART07 VALUES (1,'GLUE','GLUE SUPPLIES',2500,10);
INSERT INTO PART07 VALUES (2,'PAPER CLIP','PAPER CLIP SUPPLIES',1233,10);
INSERT INTO PART07 VALUES (3,'SCISSOR','CUTTING SUPPLIES',7659,10);
INSERT INTO PART07 VALUES (4,'TRAINER','HORSE TRAINER',8,20);
INSERT INTO PART07 VALUES (5,'HORSE','HORSE',325,20);
INSERT INTO PART07 VALUES (6,'SADDLE','HORSE SUPPLIES',400,20);
```

Figure 7.6 CHP7_11.SQL creates sample data for the
PART07 and FACTORY07 tables.

```
SQL> START CHP7_11.SQL
1 row created.
1 row created.
1 row created.
1 row created.
1 row created.
1 row created.
1 row created.
1 row created.
1 row created.
SQL>
```

3. Now that the two tables have data, run the CHP7_12.SQL script to create
the PART_VIEW07 view, which is a join of the PART07 and FACTORY07
tables. This process is shown in Figure 7.7.

4. The PART_VIEW07 view has been created. Note that because of the many-
to-one relationship between PART07 and FACTORY07, only the PART07
table may be updated. In our example, there are three records that exist
where the FACTORY_NO=20. If the entire operation were to move to
Tokyo, we would want to update all records to point to Japan. Because the
FACTORY07 is not a key-preserved table in this join view, the statement
will fail. Run CHP7_13.SQL to see the results.

```
SQL> GET C:\CHP7_12.SQL
  1  CREATE VIEW PART_VIEW07 AS
  2     SELECT PART07.PARTNO, PART07.PART_NAME, PART07.QTY,
  3            FACTORY07.FACTORY_NO, FACTORY07.LOCATION
  4  FROM PART07, FACTORY07
  5* WHERE PART07.FACTORY_NO = FACTORY07.FACTORY_NO
SQL> /

View created.

SQL>
```

Figure 7.7 CHP7_12.SQL creates the
PART_VIEW07 view, based on the join of the
PART07 and FACTORY07 tables.

```
SQL> GET CHP7_13.SQL
  1  UPDATE PART_VIEW07
  2  SET LOCATION='TOKYO, JAPAN'
SQL> /
SET LOCATION='TOKYO, JAPAN'
ERROR at line 2:
ORA-01779: cannot modify a column which maps to a non key-
preserved table
SQL>
```

5. You may, however, update the PART07 table, because it is a key-preserved table and also uniquely identifies each record in the PART_VIEW07 view. In our example, assume that all of the horses escaped, and we must update the PART07 to reflect this. Run the CHP7_14.SQL script to set the QTY=0 for the HORSE record.

```
SQL> GET CHP7_14.sql
  1  UPDATE PART_VIEW07
  2     SET QTY=0
  3  WHERE PART_NAME = 'HORSE'
SQL> /
1 row updated.
```

How It Works

Step 1 creates the PART07 and FACTORY07 tables. PART07 is uniquely defined by a primary key on PARTNO, and FACTORY07 is uniquely defined by a primary key on FACTORY_NO, and the two tables are joined by a many-to-one relationship based upon the FACTORY_NO column in each table. Step 2 inserts sample data into both tables. Step 3 creates the PART_VIEW07 view, based on a join of the two tables. Step 4 tries and fails to update a column on the FACTORY07 table, which is not a key-preserved table. Step 5 successfully updates the PART07 table through the view, because the PART07 table is key-preserved in the PART_VIEW07 view.

Comments

A view constructed by an outer join may be updatable if it is still key-preserved. Each record must be uniquely identifiable, and no keys may contain NULL values. For object views, you may also update them with INSTEAD OF triggers. See How-To 16.9 on the use of INSTEAD OF triggers.

You may create UNIQUE indexes on the key-preserved columns instead of PRIMARY/FOREIGN constraints shown in this How-To.

COMPLEXITY
ADVANCED

7.5 How do I...
Simulate a cross-tab query using a view?

Problem

In other applications such as Microsoft Access, I use a cross-tab query to view records horizontally. In my table, I have one record for each month. In my reports and inquiry screens, I want to display the data for a year horizontally, even though a record exists for each month. How do I simulate a cross-tab query using a view to present the combination of multiple records as a single row?

Technique

The DECODE function is a very powerful tool for creating advanced queries. DECODE works like an in-line IF...THEN...ELSE statement. It can be used to view data horizontally by returning a value if the row is in the correct column.

Steps

1. Run SQL*Plus and connect as the WAITE user account. The CHP7_15.SQL file, shown in Figure 7.8, builds a table that will be the basis for the cross-tab view and inserts sample data.

The CROSS_TAB table contains one row for each year, month combination. The VALUE column represents the value for the given month.

```
CREATE TABLE CROSS_TAB07 (
    YEAR     NUMBER(4),
    MONTH    NUMBER(2),
    VALUE    NUMBER(12,2));

INSERT INTO CROSS_TAB07 VALUES (1997,1,235);
INSERT INTO CROSS_TAB07 VALUES (1997,2,180);
INSERT INTO CROSS_TAB07 VALUES (1997,3,185);
INSERT INTO CROSS_TAB07 VALUES (1998,1,245);
INSERT INTO CROSS_TAB07 VALUES (1998,2,200);
INSERT INTO CROSS_TAB07 VALUES (1998,3,188);
COMMIT;
```

Figure 7.8 CHP7_15.SQL creates the sample objects used in How-To 7.5.

2. Run the command to create the table and build sample data.

```
SQL>  START CHP7_15.sql

Table created.

1 row created.

1 row created.

1 row created.

1 row created.

1 row created.

1 row created.

Commit complete.
```

3. Load CHP7_16.SQL into the SQL buffer. The file contains an SQL script to query the table created in the previous steps, displaying the data horizontally.

```
SQL>  GET CHP7_16.sql
  1 SELECT YEAR,
  2   SUM(DECODE(month,1,VALUE,0)) January,
  3   SUM(DECODE(month,2,VALUE,0)) February,
  4   SUM(DECODE(month,3,VALUE,0)) March
  5 FROM
  6   CROSS_TAB07
  7   GROUP BY YEAR
  8* ORDER BY YEAR
```

Line 1 begins the query statement and selects the YEAR column. The YEAR column is the only column not modified by a GROUP BY operator. Lines 2 through 4 return the values for the first three months. The DECODE function returns the VALUE if the MONTH column is correct for the column, otherwise it returns 0. The SUM operator displays one row for each year. Because 0 will be returned for each column whose month is not correct, the SUM operator doesn't affect the data besides grouping it as a single row. Line 7 groups the data by the YEAR column. Because the YEAR column retrieved in line 1 is not a GROUP BY expression, the GROUP BY clause in line 7 is required.

4. Run the query. Because sample data was created for two years, two rows will be returned by the query.

```
SQL> START CHP7_16.sql
     YEAR   JANUARY  FEBRUARY    MARCH
--------- --------- --------- ---------
     1997       235       180       185
```

```
          1998      245      200      188

2 rows selected.

SQL>
```

5. Load CHP7_17.SQL into the SQL buffer. The file contains a CREATE
VIEW statement to create the YEAR_VIEW07 view based on the query
shown in Step 3.

```
SQL>  GET CHP7_17.sql
  1   CREATE VIEW YEAR_VIEW07
  2   AS
  3   SELECT YEAR,
  4     SUM(DECODE(MONTH,1,VALUE,0)) January,
  5     SUM(DECODE(MONTH,2,VALUE,0)) February,
  6     SUM(DECODE(MONTH,3,VALUE,0)) March,
  7     SUM(DECODE(MONTH,4,VALUE,0)) April,
  8     SUM(DECODE(MONTH,5,VALUE,0)) May,
  9     SUM(DECODE(MONTH,6,VALUE,0)) June,
 10     SUM(DECODE(MONTH,7,VALUE,0)) July,
 11     SUM(DECODE(MONTH,8,VALUE,0)) August,
 12     SUM(DECODE(MONTH,9,VALUE,0)) September,
 13     SUM(DECODE(MONTH,10,VALUE,0)) October,
 14     SUM(DECODE(MONTH,11,VALUE,0)) November,
 15     SUM(DECODE(MONTH,12,VALUE,0)) December,
 16     SUM(VALUE) Total
 17   FROM
 18     CROSS_TAB07
 19*  GROUP BY YEAR
```

Lines 2 through 15 create a column for each month of the year. Line 16
creates a total for each year.

6. Run the statement to create the view.

```
SQL>  /

View created.
```

7. Look at the description of the view created with the DESCRIBE statement.
Figure 7.9 shows the results of the operation within SQL*Plus.

How It Works

The DECODE function works like an in-line IF statement and can be used
within a query to present records horizontally. Steps 1 and 2 create the tables
used in this How-To. Step 3 uses the DECODE function to transform data from
a vertical view to a horizontal view. For each column, the VALUE field is only
added to the column if the MONTH belongs in it. Steps 5 and 6 build a view
that hides the complexity of the query from the user. Step 7 shows that the view
represents the data as 12 columns instead of 12 separate rows.

```
SQL> DESC YEAR_VIEW07
 Name                                  Null?    Type
 ----------------------------------    ------   ----
 YEAR                                           NUMBER(4)
 JANUARY                                        NUMBER
 FEBRUARY                                       NUMBER
 MARCH                                          NUMBER
 APRIL                                          NUMBER
 MAY                                            NUMBER
 JUNE                                           NUMBER
 JULY                                           NUMBER
 AUGUST                                         NUMBER
 SEPTEMBER                                      NUMBER
 OCTOBER                                        NUMBER
 NOVEMBER                                       NUMBER
 DECEMBER                                       NUMBER
 TOTAL                                          NUMBER

SQL>
```

Figure 7.9 The description of the
YEAR_VIEW view in SQL*Plus.

Comments

The DECODE function technique uses a powerful feature of Oracle. Each time
the view is queried, many more rows from the base tables are queried than are
actually shown by the view. This may cause inadequate performance. Consider
creating summary tables to represent data of this type if the performance of your
views is unacceptable.

COMPLEXITY
INTERMEDIATE

7.6   How do I...
Re-create CREATE VIEW statements?

Problem

I need to re-create the CREATE VIEW statements used to develop some of the
views in our system. I know that we use SQL*Plus and the data dictionary to
rebuild other DDL statements throughout this book. How do I re-create
CREATE VIEW statements using the data dictionary?

Technique

The query used to rebuild CREATE VIEW statements uses the ALL_VIEWS data
dictionary view. The TEXT column contains the query used by the view to
return rows. The TEXT column is of the LONG datatype, which makes it harder
to work with in SQL*Plus. Many operators and functions cannot be used with
columns of the LONG datatype.

```
SET HEADING OFF
SET LONG 2000
SET FEEDBACK OFF

SELECT TEXT
FROM
    ALL_VIEWS
WHERE
    OWNER='&OWNER' AND
    VIEW_NAME = '&VIEW_NAME'
```

Figure 7.10 CHP7_18.SQL queries
the TEXT column of the
ALL_VIEWS data dictionary view.

Steps

1. Run SQL*Plus and connect as the WAITE user account. CHP7_18.SQL,
shown in Figure 7.10, depicts a query of the TEXT column in the
ALL_VIEWS data dictionary view.

The first three commands set SQL*Plus system variables to turn the
heading off, set the long data display to 2,000 characters, and turn
feedback off. This formats the output of the query and removes the query
heading and the feedback displayed when the query completes. Line 4
suppresses the verification of substitution variables. The query retrieves
the TEXT column from the ALL_VIEWS data dictionary view.

2. Run the CHP7_18.SQL script. Substitute the &OWNER substitution
variable with SYS and the &VIEW_NAME substitution variable with
DBA_CONSTRAINTS.

```
SQL>  START CHP7_18
Enter value for owner: SYS
Enter value for view_name: DBA_CONSTRAINTS

select ou.name, oc.name,
        decode(c.type#, 1, 'C', 2, 'P', 3, 'U',
            4, 'R', 5, 'V', 6, 'O', 7,'C', '?'),
        o.name, c.condition, ru.name, rc.name,
        decode(c.type#, 4,
            decode(c.refact, 1, 'CASCADE', 'NO ACTION'), NULL),
        decode(c.type#, 5, 'ENABLED',
        decode(c.enabled, NULL, 'DISABLED',
                    decode(bitand(c.defer, 4), 4, 'ENABLED',
                                    'ENFORCED'))),
        decode(bitand(c.defer, 1), 1, 'DEFERRABLE', 'NOT
                                    DEFERRABLE'),
        decode(bitand(c.defer, 2), 2, 'DEFERRED', 'IMMEDIATE'),
        decode(bitand(c.defer, 4), 4, 'VALIDATED', 'NOT
                                    VALIDATED'),
        decode(bitand(c.defer, 8), 8, 'GENERATED NAME', 'USER
                                    NAME'),
        decode(bitand(c.defer,16),16, 'BAD', null),
```

continued on next page

continued from previous page

```
            c.mtime
    from sys.con$ oc, sys.con$ rc, sys.user$ ou, sys.user$ ru,
        sys.obj$ o, sys.cdef$ c
    where oc.owner# = ou.user#
      and oc.con# = c.con#
      and c.obj# = o.obj#
      and c.type# != 8          /* don't include hash expressions */
      and c.rcon# = rc.con#(+)
      and rc.owner# = ru.user#(+)

SQL>
```

3. The CHP7_19.SQL file, shown in Figure 7.11, includes the CREATE OR REPLACE VIEW keywords. The keywords are not concatenated to the TEXT column because the column is of the LONG datatype. LONG columns cannot be concatenated to other columns and cannot use any of the character functions.

4. Spool the output of the query and run CHP7_19.SQL. Replace the &OWNER substitution variable with SYS and the &VIEW_NAME substitution variable with DBA_CONSTRAINTS.

```
SQL>  SPOOL VIEWS07.sql
SQL>  START CHP7_19.sql
Enter value for owner: SYS
Enter value for view_name: DBA_CONSTRAINTS

CREATE OR REPLACE TABLE DBA_CONSTRAINTS AS
select ou.name, oc.name,
       decode(c.type#, 1, 'C', 2, 'P', 3, 'U',
              4, 'R', 5, 'V', 6, 'O', 7,'C', '?'),
       o.name, c.condition, ru.name, rc.name,
       decode(c.type#, 4,
              decode(c.refact, 1, 'CASCADE', 'NO ACTION'), NULL),
       decode(c.type#, 5, 'ENABLED',
       decode(c.enabled, NULL, 'DISABLED',
                     decode(bitand(c.defer, 4), 4, 'ENABLED',
                                          'ENFORCED'))),
       decode(bitand(c.defer, 1), 1, 'DEFERRABLE', 'NOT
                                          DEFERRABLE'),
       decode(bitand(c.defer, 2), 2, 'DEFERRED', 'IMMEDIATE'),
       decode(bitand(c.defer, 4), 4, 'VALIDATED', 'NOT
                                          VALIDATED'),
       decode(bitand(c.defer, 8), 8, 'GENERATED NAME', 'USER
                                          NAME'),
       decode(bitand(c.defer,16),16, 'BAD', null),
       c.mtime
from sys.con$ oc, sys.con$ rc, sys.user$ ou, sys.user$ ru,
    sys.obj$ o, sys.cdef$ c
where oc.owner# = ou.user#
  and oc.con# = c.con#
  and c.obj# = o.obj#
  and c.type# != 8          /* don't include hash expressions */
  and c.rcon# = rc.con#(+)
  and rc.owner# = ru.user#(+)
```

```
SELECT 'CREATE OR REPLACE VIEW '||VIEW_NAME||' AS ',
       TEXT
FROM
       ALL_VIEWS
WHERE
       OWNER='&OWNER' AND
       VIEW_NAME='&VIEW_NAME'
```

Figure 7.11 CHP7_19.SQL returns the
CREATE VIEW statements.

5. Stop spooling the output file. The output file contains a CREATE OR
REPLACE VIEW statement that can build the view.

```
SQL> SPOOL OFF
SQL>
```

When the output file is closed, it can be run as a SQL*Plus command file
to rebuild the view queried from the data dictionary.

How It Works

A CREATE VIEW statement can be rebuilt by querying the ALL_VIEWS data
dictionary view. Steps 1 and 2 return the query used by a view from the
ALL_VIEWS data dictionary view. The value of the LONG system variable was
changed in order to display the entire value of the LONG column. Steps 3 and 4
build a CREATE OR REPLACE VIEW statement by adding the keywords to the
query. Step 5 spools the output to a file that can run as an SQL script and then
runs the query to build the statements.

Comments

Once again, the data dictionary is used to rebuild a DDL statement. The LONG
column in the ALL_TABLES view causes some problems in SQL*Plus. The
LONG system variable in SQL*Plus is used to set the size of long data queried
from the view. The LONG datatype prevents many operations from being
performed on the column.

COMPLEXITY
INTERMEDIATE

7.7 How do I...
Implement record level security using views?

Problem

We have certain tables that are used throughout the organization. We want all
users to work with the same table, but only see the data for their job function. I

know that I can use views to query selective data, but how do I restrict access to data on a record level using views?

Technique

The USER pseudo-column contains the account of the user connected to the database. Most pseudo-columns can be used in views. The USER pseudo-column can restrict access to certain users, and the SYSDATE pseudo-column can restrict access from old data. Subqueries can be used to produce lists of valid values within an IN operator.

Steps

1. Run SQL*Plus and connect as the WAITE user account. CHP7_20.SQL, shown in Figure 7.12, contains a CREATE TABLE statement for building a table that will be restricted by a view.

The SALES_ID column contains the name of the user account that creates the record. The ORDER_DATE column contains the date the order is placed, and the ORDER_DESC column describes the order.

2. Run the statement to create the table.

```
SQL> START CHP7_20.sql

Table created.
```

3. Load CHP7_21.SQL into the SQL buffer. The file contains a statement to restrict data based on the ORDER_DATE column. In this example, the customer service department can only work with orders that have an order date of today or later.

```
SQL> GET CHP7_21.sql
  1   CREATE OR REPLACE VIEW SALES_VIEW07 AS
  2   SELECT SALES_ID,
  3        ORDER_DATE,
  4        ORDER_DESC
  5   FROM
  6        SALES07
  7   WHERE
  8*       ORDER_DATE < SYSDATE
```

```
CREATE TABLE SALES07 (
   SALES_ID    VARCHAR2(10),
   ORDER_DATE  DATE,
   ORDER_DESC  VARCHAR2(60))
|
```

Figure 7.12 CHP7_20.SQL creates the sample table used in How-To 7.7.

Line 1 contains the CREATE OR REPLACE VIEW keywords to build the view and provides the name of the view. Lines 2 through 8 contain the query that generates the view's records. The WHERE clause in lines 7 and 8 specifies that the view will only return records where the ORDER_DATE column is less than the SYSDATE.

4. Run the statement to create the view.

```
SQL> /

View created.
```

5. Load CHP7_22.SQL into the SQL buffer. The file contains a statement to insert a sample record into the table.

```
SQL>  GET CHP7_22.sql
   1    INSERT INTO SALES07 (
   2        SALES_ID, ORDER_DATE, ORDER_DESC)
   3    VALUES
   4*     (USER, SYSDATE+5, 'FIVE DAYS LATER');
```

6. This statement inserts a record with an order date after today into the table. Even though the record will exist in the table, it will not appear in the view created in the previous steps. Run the statement to insert the record into the table and commit the transaction.

```
SQL>  /

1 row created.

SQL> COMMIT;

Commit complete
```

7. Query the record from the SALES07 table. Because the table is not restricted, the row will be displayed.

```
SQL> SELECT * FROM SALES07;

SALES_ID  ORDER_DATE  ORDER_DESC
--------  ----------  -----------------------------
WAITE     07-JAN-98   FIVE DAYS LATER
```

8. Query the record from the view. Because the view will not contain any rows with the ORDER_DATE column after the system date, no records will be retrieved.

```
SQL> SELECT * FROM SALES_VIEW07;

no rows selected.
```

9. Load CHP7_23.SQL into the SQL buffer. The file will replace the SALES_VIEW07 with a view that only returns rows with the SALES_ID column equal to the USER pseudo-column. Using the USER pseudo-column in the WHERE clause causes the view to return different results for each user account.

```
SQL> GET CHP7_23.sql
  1    CREATE OR REPLACE VIEW SALES_VIEW07 AS
  2    SELECT SALES_ID,
  3        ORDER_DATE,
  4        ORDER_DESC
  5    FROM
  6        SALES07
  7    WHERE
  8*       SALES_ID = USER
```

Line 1 contains the keywords required to create the view and specifies the name of the view. Lines 2 through 8 contain the query used to generate records for the view. The WHERE clause in lines 7 and 8 returns rows only where the SALES_ID field is equal to the user account.

10. Create the view that restricts records based on the user account.

```
SQL> /

View created.
```

11. Query the view to determine if the record created in steps 5 and 6 exists in the view.

```
SQL> SELECT * FROM SALES_VIEW07;

SALES_ID ORDER_DATE  ORDER_DESC
-------- ----------- -----------------------------
WAITE    07-JAN-98   FIVE DAYS LATER
```

How It Works

Steps 1 and 2 build a table that is the basis for the restricted view. Steps 3 and 4 create a view that only returns data if the ORDER_DATE column is less than SYSDATE. Steps 5 and 6 insert a record into the base table, which violates the WHERE clause of the view. Step 7 queries the table directly to display the data stored in it. Step 8 queries the view to show that the row is not returned by it. Steps 9 and 10 create a view that only lets a user whose account name is the same as the SALES_ID field display data. Step 11 queries the view to show that the user's data is returned by a query of the view.

Comments

Restricted views should be utilized to limit users to viewing data for their job function only. Restricting views can have a cascading effect. Restricting one table will have the effect of limiting the rows returned by other queries using the table.

CHAPTER 8
SECURITY

8

SECURITY

How do I...

Security is a major issue in the development of multi-user Oracle applications. Advances in technology have created tools that can access Oracle databases in more sophisticated ways. With ad hoc query tools becoming easier to use, it is important to ensure that only approved applications can query and modify data. Also, the management of user accounts and roles is fundamental to the development and maintenance of multi-user database applications. Users should not share accounts, and each user account should have a password to protect the database from unauthorized access. A role helps this organization by relating privileges that can be granted to user accounts with a single command. The structure of roles within Oracle enables database security to be modeled around the organization. This chapter explores topics related to enhancing security within your Oracle applications.

8.1 Grant System and Object Privileges

As part of maintaining user accounts, it is necessary to manage both the system and object privileges. System privileges enable user accounts to manage objects and privileges, create new accounts, and export the database, among other tasks. Object privileges enable user accounts to INSERT, UPDATE, DELETE, SELECT, drop, and manipulate objects such as tables, sequences, and indexes. User accounts can be granted privileges directly or through roles. This How-To shows methods for granting system and object privileges to a user account or role.

8.2 Create a Role

A role defines a group of related privileges and assigns user accounts a collection of privileges in a single step. Instead of user accounts being granted access to each object individually, they can be granted access to a role defining the complete set of privileges. This How-To takes you through the process of creating a new role.

8.3 Grant Roles to Users

When a user account is created, it must be granted access to the database and the objects required by the application. How-To 8.1 describes how privileges can be granted directly to the user account or indirectly through database roles. This How-To takes you through the process of granting roles to user accounts.

8.4 Enable and Disable Roles at Runtime

Ad hoc query tools pose a complicated problem in an Oracle environment. It is sometimes necessary to restrict users from data used in their applications. Do you really want your payroll clerks running ad hoc queries against your payroll data with Microsoft Access? This How-To explores the process of protecting sensitive data from ad hoc query tools by enabling and disabling roles at runtime.

8.5 Determine the Privileges Associated with a Role

Granting a role to a user account gives the user account all privileges assigned to that role. This How-To covers the task of determining which system and object privileges are assigned to a role, and it provides SQL statements to determine these privileges.

8.6 Determine a User's Access to a Particular Object

One of the many jobs of a database administrator is to determine which users have access to which objects. With proper access, a user account can INSERT, UPDATE, SELECT, or DELETE data for an object, even if the object is owned by another user account. This How-To describes how to determine the types of access, if any, that a user account has on a particular object.

8.7 Determine Which Users Have Access to a Particular Object

For any object in the database, each user account can have various privileges to modify the object or view data within the object. With proper access, a user account can ALTER, INSERT, UPDATE, SELECT, or DELETE for an object. Also, the user account can have SELECT privileges on a sequence and EXECUTE privileges on a package, procedure, or function. This How-To describes how to determine which users have access to a particular object, and their types of privileges.

8.8 Enable Database Auditing

Database auditing is a powerful method of monitoring activity within a database. Auditing can provide information on dozens of types of activities. It can monitor when a table is modified, altered, selected from, or granted to, along with a myriad of possibilities. Auditing can monitor when and how often a particular user logs in. Auditing can record every time a particular error occurs in the database, such as permission problems. This How-To describes often-used auditing options and how to enable database auditing.

8.9 View Audit Information

After database auditing has been enabled, and auditing data has been collected, it is important to know how to retrieve data from the audit trail. This How-To describes the technique to view the audit trail for the desired information of database activity.

8.10 Delete Audit Information

If database auditing has been enabled, data is entered into the audit trail each time an auditing event has transpired. Eventually, the audit data can take up significant space or might no longer be necessary to store. This How-To describes how to delete audit information.

8.11 Manage Passwords

Oracle8 provides a suite of password management and control that greatly improves the security of Oracle databases. The new capabilities ensure that passwords conform to company standards. This includes such options as forcing users to change their passwords every 30 days, locking users out of the database after a specified number of failed attempts, ensuring a password is a certain length, and other options. This How-To shows how to assign and change password enforcement to manage passwords.

COMPLEXITY
INTERMEDIATE

8.1 How do I...
Grant system and object privileges?

Problem

I want to grant system and object privileges to a user account. The system privileges will be used to enable users to create objects and other user accounts, for the capability to export the database, and for other privileges. The object privileges will be used to enable users to INSERT, UPDATE, DELETE, SELECT, drop, and manipulate objects such as tables, sequences, and indexes. How do I grant system and object privileges?

Technique

Use the GRANT command to grant both system and object privileges to a user account. Privileges can also be granted to roles. The syntax to grant privileges is

```
GRANT privilege TO [user, role, PUBLIC] [WITH ADMIN OPTION]
```

Around 100 system privileges exist in Oracle8, which can be listed by querying the SYSTEM_PRIVILEGE_MAP data dictionary view. A sample of frequently used system privileges is shown in Table 8.1. Many of the DROP privileges have corresponding ALTER and CREATE privileges, such as CREATE ANY INDEX.

Table 8.1 System privileges

SYSTEM PRIVILEGE	CAPABILITY TO...
ANALYZE ANY	Analyze any table of any user account
BECOME USER	Connect to the database as another user without knowing their password
DELETE ANY TABLE	Delete records from any table of any user account
DROP ANY CLUSTER	Drop any cluster from any user account
DROP ANY INDEX	Drop any index from any user account
DROP ANY PROCEDURE	Drop any procedure of any user account
DROP ANY ROLE	Drop any role from the database (be careful not to drop default roles)
DROP ANY SEQUENCE	Drop any sequence from any user account
DROP ANY SNAPSHOT	Drop any snapshot (and snapshot log) from any user account

SYSTEM PRIVILEGE	CAPABILITY TO...
DROP ANY SYNONYM	Drop any synonym from any user account
DROP ANY TABLE	Drop any table from any user account (be careful not to drop data dictionary tables)
DROP ANY TRIGGER	Drop any trigger from any user account
DROP ANY TYPE	Drop any object type from any user account
DROP ANY VIEW	Drop any view from any user account (be careful not to drop data dictionary views)
DROP PROFILE	Drop any profile
DROP PUBLIC DATABASE LINK	Drop any public database link
DROP PUBLIC SYNONYM	Drop any public synonym
DROP ROLLBACK SEGMENT	Drop any rollback segment
DROP TABLESPACE	Drop any tablespace (be VERY careful when giving this privilege out)
DROP USER	Drop any user
EXECUTE ANY PROCEDURE	Execute any procedure of any user account
EXECUTE ANY TYPE	Execute any object type
GRANT ANY PRIVILEGE	Grant any system privilege to any user, including DBA
GRANT ANY ROLE	Grant any role to any user account
INSERT ANY TABLE	Insert records into any table of any user account
LOCK ANY TABLE	Explicitly lock any table of any user account (having more users that have this privilege increases the chances of lock contention)
MANAGE TABLESPACE	Take tablespaces online/offline, and do tablespace hot backups
SELECT ANY SEQUENCE	Increment any sequence of any user account, or see the current value
SELECT ANY TABLE	Select data from any table of any user account
SYSDBA	Have full DBA privileges, which includes all system privileges previously listed
SYSOPER	Have instance capabilities such as database startup and shutdown

Steps

1. Run SQL*Plus and connect as the WAITE user account. CHP8_1.SQL, shown in Figure 8.1, creates the sample user accounts and roles used throughout this How-To.

The first statement creates the TERRI user account with a CREATE USER statement. The second statement creates the ROOFER role and the third statement creates the DEPT8 table. Run the file to create the sample objects.

```
SQL> START CHP8_1.sql

User created.

Role created.

Table created.
```

```
CREATE USER TERRI IDENTIFIED BY NEWUSER;

CREATE ROLE ROOFER;

CREATE TABLE DEPT8 (
    DEPT_NO    NUMBER(5),
    DEPT_NAME VARCHAR2(30));
```

Figure 8.1 CHP8_1.SQL creates the sample user account, role, and table for this How-To.

2. Run CHP8_2.SQL to grant privileges to the TERRI user account, as shown in Figure 8.2.

The first GRANT statement grants all object privileges on the DEPT8 table to the TERRI user account. This includes SELECT, INSERT, UPDATE, and DELETE. The second GRANT statement grants the CONNECT and RESOURCE default roles, along with the ROOFER role, to the TERRI user account. CONNECT is really the combination of eight system privileges: ALTER SESSION, CREATE CLUSTER, CREATE DATABASE LINK, CREATE SEQUENCE, CREATE SESSION, CREATE SYNONYM, CREATE TABLE, and CREATE VIEW. RESOURCE is the combination of five system privileges: CREATE CLUSTER, CREATE PROCEDURE, CREATE SEQUENCE, CREATE TABLE, and CREATE TRIGGER. Granting the CONNECT and RESOURCE roles is a simpler method than granting five or eight separate privileges.

3. System and object privileges can be granted to individual user accounts or to roles. Another option is to grant the privilege to PUBLIC. By doing so, every user account in the database has that privilege. Run the CHP8_3.SQL script, as shown in Figure 8.3, which grants object privileges for the DEPT8 table to PUBLIC.

```
SQL> START C:\CHP8_2.SQL

Grant succeeded.


Grant succeeded.

SQL>
```

Figure 8.2 CHP8_2.SQL contains one GRANT statement for object privileges and one for system privileges.

```
SQL> GET C:\CHP8_3.SQL
  1  GRANT SELECT, INSERT, UPDATE, DELETE
  2  ON DEPT8
  3* TO PUBLIC
SQL> /

Grant succeeded.

SQL>
```

Figure 8.3 CHP8_3.SQL grants object privileges to PUBLIC.

CHP8_3.SQL grants the SELECT, INSERT, UPDATE, and DELETE object privileges on the DEPT8 table to PUBLIC. All user accounts will be able to modify data, regardless of any other role or privilege they might have been granted. Unless a PUBLIC synonym is created for the DEPT8 table, all users will have to reference it as WAITE.DEPT8.

4. By using the WITH ADMIN OPTION clause of the GRANT command, you pass along the capability for other user accounts to grant the privilege. Run CHP8_4.SQL, shown in Figure 8.4, which grants the capability to drop any synonym with the admin option to TERRI.

The GRANT in CHP8_4.SQL empowers the TERRI user account to issue a similar grant to any other user account in the database. By default, the GRANT command does not pass along the capability for other users to grant privileges.

How It Works

Step 1 creates the user account, role, and table used throughout this How-To. Step 2 issues two GRANT statements to give the TERRI user object and system privileges. Step 3 uses the GRANT command to create privileges to PUBLIC, for which all user accounts in the database are affected. Step 4 demonstrates the WITH ADMIN OPTION clause, which enables other user accounts to propagate the privilege to other user accounts and roles.

```
SQL> GET C:\CHP8_4.SQL
  1  GRANT DROP ANY SYNONYM
  2  TO TERRI
  3* WITH ADMIN OPTION
SQL> /

Grant succeeded.

SQL> |
```

Figure 8.4 CHP8_4.SQL issues the GRANT command with the WITH ADMIN OPTION clause.

Comments

DBA_TAB_PRIVS contains the object privileges granted to the connected user account. DBA_ROLE_PRIVS contains roles granted to the user account and DBA_SYS_PRIVS contains system privileges granted to a user account. Also, SYSTEM_PRIVILEGE_MAP shows all available system privileges. See How-To's 8.2, 8.3, and 8.4 for additional information on roles, which make privilege management easier.

COMPLEXITY
BEGINNING

8.2 How do I...
Create a role?

Problem

In my application, I have groups of users who perform related functions. The number of people using my application is very large and I don't want to grant privileges on all the database objects to so many people. How do I create a role to represent a group of users?

Technique

Database roles should be created to represent related groups of privileges within the database. The CREATE ROLE statement is used to create a new role, the syntax of which is shown in Figure 8.2.

The IDENTIFIED BY clause defines a password for the role. When a role contains a password, the password must be supplied when enabling the role. When a new role is created, it has no privileges, which must be granted to the role in order for the role to have any effect on a user account. The CONNECT, RESOURCE, and DBA roles are provided by Oracle to supply different levels of access. User accounts with the CONNECT role have access to the database but cannot create their own objects. They can access other user account's objects to which they have been granted permission. User accounts with the RESOURCE role can create their own database objects. The DBA role gives the user account powerful privileges: complete access to the database and the capability to grant privileges to other user accounts.

Steps

1. Run SQL*Plus and connect as the WAITE user account. Load CHP8_5.SQL into the SQL buffer and run it, as shown in Figure 8.5.

```
SQL> GET C:\CHP8_5.SQL
  1* CREATE ROLE IS_DEV
SQL> /

Role created.

SQL>
SQL> |
```

Figure 8.5 CHP8_5.SQL creates a role.

The file contains a CREATE ROLE statement to create a new role and the CREATE ROLE keywords are required. A name must be specified for the role when it is created. After the role has been created, it must be granted privileges to be of any use. How-To 8.1 covers the processes of granting privileges to roles.

2. Load CHP8_6.SQL into the SQL buffer and run it, as shown in Figure 8.6. The file contains a CREATE ROLE statement, which creates a new role protected with a password.

Line 1 contains the CREATE ROLE keywords to create a new role and specify the name of the role. The IDENTIFIED BY clause in line 2 specifies an optional password that must be provided when the role is enabled.

3. Load CHP8_7.SQL into the SQL buffer and run it, as shown in Figure 8.7. The file contains a DROP ROLE statement to remove the role created in Steps 1 and 2.

```
SQL>
SQL> GET C:\CHP8_6.SQL
  1   CREATE ROLE ID_ADM
  2*     IDENTIFIED BY SECURE
  3  /

Role created.

SQL>
```

Figure 8.6 CHP8_6.SQL contains a CREATE ROLE statement to create a password-protected role.

```
SQL> GET C:\CHP8_7.SQL
  1* DROP ROLE IS_DEV
SQL> /

Role dropped.

SQL>
SQL>
SQL> |
```

Figure 8.7 CHP8_7.SQL uses the DROP ROLE statement to drop a role.

The DROP ROLE keywords presented in line 1 are required to remove a role from the database. The role to be removed must be specified in the statement. When one is removed, all user accounts that were granted the role immediately lose their privileges.

How It Works

The CREATE ROLE statement is used to create a new role in the database and Step 1 creates a new role using the CREATE ROLE statement. Step 2 creates a role containing a password that must be specified when the role is enabled. The IDENTIFIED BY clause creates a password for a role. Step 3 presents the DROP ROLE statement, which is used to remove an existing role. When a role is removed, the privileges provided by the role are removed immediately from the user account granted the role privileges.

Comments

Roles play a major part in the development of an organizational security model. In the early releases of Oracle, the CONNECT, RESOURCE, and DBA roles were used to administer security to user accounts. Access to tables and views was granted to each user account individually or to the PUBLIC user group, which enabled all user accounts access to the data. Roles increase the security capabilities of Oracle and reduce the maintenance required by the system administrator. A security model should be developed using roles that effectively protect your database.

COMPLEXITY
INTERMEDIATE

8.3 How do I...
Grant roles to users?

Problem

I have created user accounts and roles within my database. Each of my roles have differing system and object privileges. I need to assign users to my various roles. How do I grant roles to a user account?

Technique

User accounts are assigned to roles with the GRANT command. Both system and object privileges can be granted to user accounts and roles with the GRANT statement. This is described in How-To 8.1.

One or more privileges or roles can be granted to one or more user accounts with a single statement. The WITH ADMIN OPTION clause specifies that the grantee can grant this role to another user account or role.

By assigning unique sets of privileges to different roles, you can easily start to make a secure and easily managed environment for your applications. Instead of issuing GRANT commands to dozens or even thousands of users, you can assign them all to a role and issue a single GRANT command to that role. All users assigned to the role will then obtain that privilege.

Steps

1. Run SQL*Plus and connect as the WAITE user account. Run CHP8_8.SQL, shown in Figure 8.8, to create the sample user account and the role that will be used throughout this How-To.

The CREATE USER statement creates the SMITH user account, which is granted privileges in the following steps. The CREATE ROLE statement also creates the GENERAL role, which is granted privileges and granted to the user account. The DEPT8 table is created to have an object that can be granted privileges in the sample statements. Run the SQL script to create the objects.

2. Load CHP8_9.SQL into the SQL buffer and run it, as shown in Figure 8.9. The GRANT statement contained in the file grants CREATE SESSION and ALTER SESSION privileges to the sample role.

```
SQL> START C:\CHP8_8.SQL
SQL> CREATE USER SMITH IDENTIFIED BY NEWUSER;

User created.

SQL>
SQL> CREATE ROLE GENERAL;

Role created.

SQL>
SQL> DROP TABLE DEPT8;

Table dropped.

SQL>
SQL> CREATE TABLE DEPT8 (
  2      DEPT_NO    NUMBER(10),
  3      DEPT_NAME  VARCHAR2(30));

Table created.

SQL> |
```

Figure 8.8 CHP8_8.SQL creates the objects used in this How-To.

```
SQL>
SQL> GET C:\CHP8_9.SQL
  1  GRANT CREATE SESSION,
  2*     ALTER SESSION TO GENERAL
SQL> /

Grant succeeded.

SQL>
```

Figure 8.9 CHP8_9.SQL grants system privileges to the GENERAL role.

Line 1 contains the GRANT keyword, used to grant privileges to a user account or role. The CREATE SESSION and ALTER SESSION system privileges are granted to the GENERAL role, which was created in Step 1. Any user account granted this role can connect to the database after this statement is executed.

3. Load CHP8_10.SQL into the SQL buffer and run it, as shown in Figure 8.10. The GRANT statement contained in the file grants SELECT, INSERT, UPDATE, and DELETE privileges on the DEPT8 table created in step 1 to the TECHIE role created in step 1.

Line 1 contains the GRANT keyword and specifies that SELECT, INSERT, UPDATE, and DELETE privileges are granted on the object. Line 2 specifies that the privileges are granted on the DEPT8 table created in step 1. Line 3 then specifies that the GENERAL role is the recipient of the privileges.

4. Load CHP8_11.SQL into the SQL buffer and run it, as shown in Figure 8.11. The GRANT statement contained in the file grants the GENERAL role to the SMITH user account.

This statement grants the GENERAL role created in Step 1 to the SMITH user account created in Step 1. When the statement is executed, any privileges granted to the GENERAL role are available to the SMITH user account.

```
SQL> GET C:\CHP8_10.SQL
  1  GRANT SELECT, INSERT, UPDATE, DELETE
  2     ON DEPT8 TO
  3* GENERAL
SQL> /

Grant succeeded.

SQL> |
```

Figure 8.10 CHP8_10.SQL grants object privileges to the GENERAL role.

```
SQL> GET C:\CHP8_11.SQL
  1  GRANT GENERAL
  2*    TO SMITH
SQL> /

Grant succeeded.

SQL> |
```

Figure 8.11 CHP8_11.SQL grants object privileges to the GENERAL role.

How It Works

The GRANT statement is used to give privileges to user accounts or roles. Object
or system privileges can be granted to user accounts or roles, and role privileges
can be granted to them as well. Step 1 creates a user account, role, and table,
which are used throughout this How-To. Step 2 grants the GENERAL role
CREATE SESSION and ALTER SESSION privileges. User accounts granted this
role can connect to the database. Step 3 grants SELECT, INSERT, UPDATE, and
DELETE privileges to the GENERAL role for the DEPT8 table. Step 4 grants the
GENERAL role to the SMITH user account. The SMITH user account inherits all
system and object privileges that are granted to the GENERAL role.

Comments

As stated previously, privileges can be granted to a user account or role. It is
much easier to create roles and grant each privilege once to the role than to each
user account individually. If a database object is removed and then re-created, all
grants to the object must be re-created. If roles were not in use, then it would be
an arduous task to determine and re-create all privileges to each user account.

COMPLEXITY
ADVANCED

8.4 How do I...
Enable and disable roles at runtime?

Problem

Within my application, I control the information the users can view. With the
availability of easy-to-use ad hoc query tools, the users of my applications can
query and modify data from the database, but I cannot remove their user
accounts because they are valid users of the application. How do I restrict access
by enabling and disabling roles at runtime?

Technique

Password-protected roles are the key to restricting the access of ad hoc query tools. Access can be restricted at two levels. Ad hoc tools can be restricted from modifying data or totally restricted from viewing data. Applications using the tables must embed a SET ROLE statement or call the DBMS_SESSION.SET_ROLE procedure after connecting to the database. The password of the role must also be kept secret from the users of the application. Without the password of the role and the method for enabling it, users will have restricted access to the data.

Steps

1. Run SQL*Plus and connect as the WAITE user account. Run the CHP8_12.SQL script, shown in Figure 8.12, to create a sample table and users that will be restricted by the technique presented in this How-To.

2. Create the roles that control access to the data by running CHP8_13.SQL, as shown in Figure 8.13.

```
SQL> START C:\CHP8_12.SQL
SQL> DROP TABLE DEPT8;

Table dropped.

SQL>
SQL> CREATE TABLE DEPT8 (
  2      DEPT_NO      NUMBER(10),
  3      DEPT_NAME    VARCHAR2(30));

Table created.

SQL>
SQL> CREATE USER MARY IDENTIFIED BY CHAPTER8;

User created.

SQL>
```

Figure 8.12 CHP8_12.SQL creates the sample table and user account employed in How-To 8.4.

```
SQL> START C:\CHP8_13.SQL
SQL> CREATE ROLE SELECT_ROLE;

Role created.

SQL> CREATE ROLE UPDATE_ROLE IDENTIFIED BY SECURE;

Role created.

SQL> |
```

Figure 8.13. CHP8_13.SQL creates the roles used in this How-To.

3. The CHP8_13.SQL script assumes that ad hoc query tools are only restricted from modifying data, and so it creates two roles. The first is a default role with SELECT privileges in which users can query information without enabling additional roles. A second role provides all the privileges required to use the approved applications. The second role is a non-default, password-protected role, which must be enabled by the application to be used. If ad hoc query tools are totally restricted from the data, only create the password-protected role.

4. Grant privileges on the database objects to the roles by running CHP8_14.SQL, as shown in Figure 8.14.

5. Now, grant the role privileges to the users of the application. In the example, MARY is the only user of the application. If two roles are created in Step 2, grant both roles to the users.

```
SQL>  GRANT SELECT_ROLE, UPDATE_ROLE TO MARY;
Grant succeeded.
```

6. Remove the role with all privileges from the user account's default roles by running CHP8_15.SQL. This forces the user to enable the role in order to use it.

```
SQL>  GET CHP8_15.sql
  1   ALTER USER MARY
DEFAULT ROLE ALL EXCEPT UPDATE_ROLE;
User altered.
SQL>
```

7. Now insert program code to enable the role into applications capable of modifying data. The technique used to enable password-protected roles at runtime is to call the DBMS_SESSION.SET_ROLE procedure, whose syntax is shown in Figure 8.15.

```
SQL> START C:\CHP8_14.SQL
SQL> GRANT SELECT ON DEPT8 TO SELECT_ROLE;

Grant succeeded.

SQL>
SQL> GRANT SELECT, INSERT, UPDATE, DELETE
  2  ON DEPT8 TO UPDATE_ROLE;

Grant succeeded.

SQL>
```

Figure 8.14 CHP8_14.SQL grants privileges to the roles.

```
DBMS_SESSION.SET_ROLE ('
    rolename | {IDENTIFIED BY password] ')
|
```

Figure 8.15 The syntax of the
DBMS_SESSION.SET_ROLE procedure, used to
enable a role.

To enable the user to update the DEPT8 table from within a program, for
example, insert the code from CHP8_16.SQL, as shown in Figure 8.16.
The SET ROLE procedure in the DBMS_SESSION package enables
PL/SQL statements to execute a SET ROLE statement. Executing the SET
ROLE statement directly in PL/SQL causes an error.

How It Works

Step 1 creates a sample user account and table used throughout this How-To.
Step 2 creates the roles used to restrict access to the database. Step 3 grants the
privileges required on the database objects to the roles created in Step 2. Step 4
grants the users of the system the role privileges. Step 5 removes the password-
protected role as the default from system users. Step 6 is where code would be
inserted into applications that need to use the restricted table. The
DBMS_SESSION.SET_ROLE procedure is used within applications to enable
password-protected roles.

Comments

Password-protected roles can be used to restrict access from ad hoc query tools.
They can be used to disable INSERT, UPDATE, and DELETE privileges or to
disable all privileges. When SELECT privileges are restricted through password-
protected roles, side effects can occur. You must be very careful how you
develop your applications when restricting the SELECT privilege through roles.
Some development tools look at the database before running their first
statement.

```
SQL> START C:\CHP8_16.SQL
SQL> BEGIN
  2     DBMS_SESSION.SET_ROLE('UPDATE_ROLE IDENTIFIED BY SECURE');
  3  END;
  4  /

PL/SQL procedure successfully completed.

SQL>
```

Figure 8.16 CHP8_16.SQL enables the
UPDATE_ROLE for the MARY user account.

For example, Oracle Reports interprets the code in PL/SQL formatting triggers before executing the first statement of code. The SET ROLE procedure must be run before this occurs, but unfortunately, it cannot. If you are restricting SELECT privileges with the roles, you cannot use PL/SQL format triggers in Oracle Reports. You must also specify all the roles that should be enabled within a single SET ROLE statement. Otherwise, just the roles specified are enabled, and no others.

COMPLEXITY
INTERMEDIATE

8.5 How do I...
Determine the privileges associated with a role?

Problem

I want to determine which privileges have been granted to a role. This will let me see whether the role requires more privileges or whether it is the right role to grant a user account. How do I determine which privileges have been granted to a role?

Technique

The ROLE_TAB_PRIVS data dictionary view contains the object privileges granted to a role. The ROLE_ROLE_PRIVS view contains the roles granted to another role, and the ROLE_SYS_PRIVS view contains system privileges granted to a role. Determining the privileges granted to a role can become complicated when role grants become nested. If roles have not been granted other ones, it is easy to determine the privileges that granting a role provides. Figure 8.17 shows the description of the data dictionary views within SQL*Plus.

Steps

1. Run SQL*Plus and connect as the WAITE user account. If you were in SQL*Plus already from the previous How-To, then you must exit and run SQL*Plus again to enable all roles. CHP8_17.SQL, shown in Figure 8.18, creates a table and two roles that are used throughout this How-To.

```
SQL> DESC ROLE_TAB_PRIUS
 Name                                Null?    Type
 ----------------------------------- -------- ----
 ROLE                                NOT NULL VARCHAR2(30)
 OWNER                               NOT NULL VARCHAR2(30)
 TABLE_NAME                          NOT NULL VARCHAR2(30)
 COLUMN_NAME                                  VARCHAR2(30)
 PRIVILEGE                           NOT NULL VARCHAR2(40)
 GRANTABLE                                    VARCHAR2(3)

SQL> DESC ROLE_ROLE_PRIUS
 Name                                Null?    Type
 ----------------------------------- -------- ----
 ROLE                                NOT NULL VARCHAR2(30)
 GRANTED_ROLE                        NOT NULL VARCHAR2(30)
 ADMIN_OPTION                                 VARCHAR2(3)

SQL> DESC ROLE_SYS_PRIUS
 Name                                Null?    Type
 ----------------------------------- -------- ----
 ROLE                                NOT NULL VARCHAR2(30)
 PRIVILEGE                           NOT NULL VARCHAR2(40)
 ADMIN_OPTION                                 VARCHAR2(3)

SQL>
```

Figure 8.17 Role privilege data dictionary views.

```
CREATE ROLE WAITRESS;
CREATE ROLE BARTENDER;

DROP TABLE DEPT8;
CREATE TABLE DEPT8 (
    DEPT_NO     NUMBER(5),
    DEPT_NAME   VARCHAR2(30));

GRANT DELETE, INSERT, UPDATE, SELECT
    ON DEPT8 TO WAITRESS;
GRANT CONNECT TO BARTENDER;
```

Figure 8.18 CHP8_17.SQL creates the sample roles and objects used in this How-To.

The first statement creates the WAITRESS role and the second statement creates the BARTENDER role. The CREATE TABLE statement creates a table with privileges on it granted in the first GRANT statement. The second GRANT statement grants the CONNECT default role to the BARTENDER role.

2. Run the file to create the sample roles.

```
SQL> START CHP8_17.sql

Role created.

Role created.

Table dropped.

Table created.

Grant succeeded.

Grant succeeded.
```

3. Load CHP8_18.SQL into the SQL buffer. The file contains a query used to determine the object privileges granted to a role. The ROLE_TAB_PRIVS view contains all the object privileges granted to roles.

```
SQL> GET CHP8_18.sql
  1    SELECT OWNER||'.'||TABLE_NAME OBJECT,
  2       PRIVILEGE FROM
  3       DBA_TAB_PRIVS
  4*  WHERE GRANTEE = '&ROLE'
```

Line 1 concatenates the OWNER and TABLE_NAME columns to return the object in the format in which it is usually used. Line 2 returns the privilege granted to the object. Line 3 specifies the DBA_TAB_PRIVS data dictionary view as the source of the query. Line 4 causes information for the role specified by the &ROLE substitution variable to be returned.

3. Format the output of the column using the COLUMN command. Execute the query for the WAITRESS role created in Step 1 by replacing the &ROLE substitution variable with WAITRESS.

```
SQL>  COLUMN OBJECT FORMAT A30
SQL>  COLUMN PRIVILEGE FORMAT A30
SQL>  /
Enter value for 1: WAITRESS

old   4:    where role = '&ROLE'
new   4:    where role = 'WAITRESS'

OBJECT                          PRIVILEGE
------------------------------  ------------------------------
WAITE.DEPT8                     DELETE
WAITE.DEPT8                     INSERT
WAITE.DEPT8                     SELECT
WAITE.DEPT8                     UPDATE
```

4. Load CHP8_19.SQL into the SQL buffer and run it for the BARTENDER role to view roles granted to this role. Replace the &ROLE substitution variable with BARTENDER, as shown in Figure 8.19. The file contains a query that identifies roles granted to a role.

Lines 1 and 2 return the GRANTED_ROLE column from the ROLE_ROLE_PRIVS. Line 3 causes information to be returned for the role specified by the &ROLE substitution variable. The ROLE_ROLE_PRIVS view returns roles that have been granted to other roles.

5. Load CHP8_20.SQL into the SQL buffer and run it, as shown in Figure 8.20. Execute the statement for the CONNECT system role by specifying CONNECT as the &ROLE substitution variable. The file contains a query that identifies system privileges granted to a role.

```
SQL> START C:\CHP8_19.SQL
SQL> SELECT GRANTED_ROLE
  2     FROM ROLE_ROLE_PRIVS
  3  WHERE ROLE = '&ROLE'
  4  /
Enter value for role: BARTENDER
old   3: WHERE ROLE = '&ROLE'
new   3: WHERE ROLE = 'BARTENDER'

GRANTED_ROLE
-----------------------------------
CONNECT

SQL> |
```

Figure 8.19 CHP8_19.SQL contains a query to identify other roles granted to a role.

```
SQL> START C:\CHP8_20.SQL
SQL> SELECT PRIVILEGE, ADMIN_OPTION
  2  FROM
  3     ROLE_SYS_PRIVS
  4  WHERE
  5     ROLE = '&ROLE'
  6  /
Enter value for role: CONNECT
old   5:    ROLE = '&ROLE'
new   5:    ROLE = 'CONNECT'

PRIVILEGE                         ADM
-----------------------------     ---
ALTER SESSION                     NO
CREATE CLUSTER                    NO
CREATE DATABASE LINK              NO
CREATE SEQUENCE                   NO
CREATE SESSION                    NO
CREATE SYNONYM                    NO
CREATE TABLE                      NO
CREATE VIEW                       NO

8 rows selected.

SQL>
```

Figure 8.20 CHP8_20.SQL contains a query to identify system privileges granted to a role.

Line 1 returns the PRIVILEGE and ADMIN_OPTION columns. The ADMIN_OPTION contains YES if the privilege can be granted by users of the role to other user accounts and roles. Line 3 specifies the ROLE_SYS_PRIVS data dictionary view as the source of the query. Line 5 returns information for the role specified by the &ROLE substitution variable.

How It Works

The DBA_TAB_PRIVS data dictionary view contains object privileges granted to a role. ROLE_SYS_PRIVS contains system privileges granted to the role and ROLE_ROLE_PRIVS contains other roles granted to a role. Steps 1 and 2 list the object privileges granted to a role by querying the ROLE_TAB_PRIVS view. Steps 3 and 4 list the roles granted to a role by querying the ROLE_ROLE_PRIVS view. Step 5 queries ROLE_SYS_PRIVS to determine the system privileges granted to the role.

Comments

To determine the privileges granted to a role, take all the system and object privileges granted directly to it and add the privileges provided by other roles. The data dictionary is the source for information regarding privileges and roles. How-To's 8.1 through 8.7 provide additional information about privileges and roles.

COMPLEXITY
ADVANCED

8.6 How do I...
Determine a user's access to a particular object?

Problem

I need to determine whether a user has access to an object. It is important to know whether the user account can ALTER, INSERT, UPDATE, SELECT, or DELETE the data for this table. How do I determine a user's access to a particular object?

Technique

The DBA_TAB_PRIVS data dictionary view contains the object privileges granted to all users and roles. Despite having TAB in the name of the view, it is valid for tables, sequences, procedures, packages, functions, views, database links, and other objects.

The DBA_ROLE_PRIVS data dictionary view contains which user accounts are associated with roles. Object privileges can be granted directly to a user account, or indirectly through a role or through the PUBLIC default role. If roles have not been granted other roles, it is easy to determine a user account's access to an object. Figure 8.21 shows the description of the data dictionary views within SQL*Plus.

Steps

1. Run SQL*Plus and connect as the WAITE user account. Run CHP8_21.SQL to create the sample table, user account, and role that will be used with this How-To (see Figure 8.22).

```
SQL> DESC DBA_TAB_PRIVS
 Name                                    Null?     Type
 --------------------------------------- --------- ----
 GRANTEE                                 NOT NULL  VARCHAR2(30)
 OWNER                                   NOT NULL  VARCHAR2(30)
 TABLE_NAME                              NOT NULL  VARCHAR2(30)
 GRANTOR                                 NOT NULL  VARCHAR2(30)
 PRIVILEGE                               NOT NULL  VARCHAR2(40)
 GRANTABLE                                         VARCHAR2(3)

SQL> DESC DBA_ROLE_PRIVS
 Name                                    Null?     Type
 --------------------------------------- --------- ----
 GRANTEE                                           VARCHAR2(30)
 GRANTED_ROLE                            NOT NULL  VARCHAR2(30)
 ADMIN_OPTION                                      VARCHAR2(3)
 DEFAULT_ROLE                                      VARCHAR2(3)

SQL>
```

Figure 8.21 Table privilege and role association data dictionary views.

```
SQL> START C:\CHP8_21.SQL
SQL> DROP TABLE DEPT8;

Table dropped.

SQL>
SQL> CREATE TABLE DEPT8 (
  2     DEPT_NO     NUMBER(5),
  3     DEPT_NAME   VARCHAR2(30));

Table created.

SQL>
SQL> CREATE ROLE READ_ONLY;

Role created.

SQL> CREATE USER JODI IDENTIFIED BY JODI;

User created.

SQL>
```

Figure 8.22 Running CHP8_21.SQL creates the sample table, user account, and role used in this How-To.

2. Assign the JODI user account to the READ_ONLY role and grant privileges on the DEPT8 table to the JODI user account by running CHP8_22.SQL, as shown in Figure 8.23. The first statement assigns the READ_ONLY role to the JODI user account. The second statement grants UPDATE privileges on the DEPT8 table directly to the JODI user account. The third statement grants SELECT privileges on the DEPT8 table indirectly to the JODI user account by granting to the READ_ONLY role, of which the JODI account belongs. The fourth statement indirectly grants INSERT privileges on the DEPT8 table to the DEPT8 table by granting the privilege to PUBLIC. Granting to PUBLIC enables all user accounts to use the privilege.

3. At this point, all privileges have been granted for this How-To. There are several methods to determine access to an object. The first is by determining all privileges granted directly to a user account. Run CHP8_23.SQL and pass JODI for `username`, DEPT8 for `table_name`, and WAITE for `table_owner` as shown in Figure 8.24.

4. The second method to determine privileges granted for an object is to determine all PUBLIC grants for that object. Run CHP8_24.SQL and pass DEPT8 for `table_name`, and WAITE for `table_owner` as shown in Figure 8.25.

5. The third method to determine privileges granted for an object is to determine all privileges on the object granted to a role of which that the user account belongs. Run CHP8_25.SQL and pass JODI for `username`, DEPT8 for `table_name`, and WAITE for `table_owner` as shown in Figure 8.26. The inner select returns all roles of which the user belongs. The outer select determines whether those roles have been granted any object privileges for the desired object.

```
SQL> START C:\CHP8_22.SQL
SQL> GRANT READ_ONLY TO JODI;

Grant succeeded.

SQL> GRANT UPDATE ON DEPT8 TO JODI;

Grant succeeded.

SQL> GRANT SELECT ON DEPT8 TO READ_ONLY;

Grant succeeded.

SQL> GRANT INSERT ON DEPT8 TO PUBLIC;

Grant succeeded.

SQL> |
```

Figure 8.23 CHP8_22.SQL grants privileges both directly and indirectly to the JODI user account and assigns the READ_ONLY role to JODI.

```
SQL> GET C:\CHP8_23.SQL
  1  SELECT GRANTEE, PRIVILEGE
  2  FROM DBA_TAB_PRIVS
  3  WHERE GRANTEE = '&username' AND
  4        TABLE_NAME = '&table_name' AND
  5*       OWNER = '&table_owner'
SQL> /
Enter value for username: JODI
old   3: WHERE GRANTEE = '&username' AND
new   3: WHERE GRANTEE = 'JODI' AND
Enter value for table_name: DEPT8
old   4:       TABLE_NAME = '&table_name' AND
new   4:       TABLE_NAME = 'DEPT8' AND
Enter value for table_owner: WAITE
old   5:       OWNER = '&table_owner'
new   5:       OWNER = 'WAITE'

GRANTEE                          PRIVILEGE
------------------------------   ------------------------
JODI                             UPDATE

SQL>
```

Figure 8.24 CHP8_23.SQL determines the object privileges granted directly to a user account.

```
SQL> GET C:\CHP8_24.SQL
  1  SELECT GRANTEE, PRIVILEGE
  2  FROM DBA_TAB_PRIVS
  3  WHERE GRANTEE = 'PUBLIC' AND
  4        TABLE_NAME = '&table_name' AND
  5*       OWNER = '&table_owner'
SQL> /
Enter value for table_name: DEPT8
old   4:       TABLE_NAME = '&table_name' AND
new   4:       TABLE_NAME = 'DEPT8' AND
Enter value for table_owner: WAITE
old   5:       OWNER = '&table_owner'
new   5:       OWNER = 'WAITE'

GRANTEE                          PRIVILEGE
------------------------------   ------------------------
PUBLIC                           INSERT

SQL>
```

Figure 8.25 CHP8_24.SQL determines the object privileges granted indirectly to a user account through a PUBLIC grant.

6. It can be cumbersome to run several statements to determine the direct and indirect privileges for a user account on an object. All the previous three statements can be combined into one. Begin by running CHP8_26.SQL to determine the user's access to a particular object, shown in Figure 8.27. Pass WAITE for table_owner, DEPT8 for table_name, and JODI for username. In one statement, you can see whether the user account has access to the object directly, or through a role or PUBLIC.

```
SQL> START CHP8_26.SQL
Enter value for table_owner: WAITE
old   3: WHERE OWNER = '&table_owner' AND
new   3: WHERE OWNER = 'WAITE' AND
```

```
Enter value for table_name: DEPT8
old    4:        TABLE_NAME = '&table_name' and
new    4:        TABLE_NAME = 'DEPT8' and
Enter value for username: JODI
old    6:        GRANTEE = '&username' OR
new    6:        GRANTEE = 'JODI' OR
Enter value for username: JODI
old   10:              WHERE GRANTEE = '&username'))
new   10:              WHERE GRANTEE = 'JODI'))


GRANTEE                            PRIVILEGE
------------------------------     --------------------
PUBLIC                             INSERT
READ_ONLY                          SELECT
JODI                               UPDATE
```

```
SQL> GET C:\CHP8_25.SQL
  1  SELECT GRANTEE, PRIVILEGE
  2  FROM DBA_TAB_PRIVS
  3  WHERE GRANTEE IN (
  4             SELECT GRANTED_ROLE
  5             FROM DBA_ROLE_PRIVS
  6             WHERE GRANTEE = '&username') AND
  7        TABLE_NAME = '&table_name' AND
  8*       OWNER = '&table_owner'
SQL> /
Enter value for username: JODI
old    6:            WHERE GRANTEE = '&username') AND
new    6:            WHERE GRANTEE = 'JODI') AND
Enter value for table_name: DEPT8
old    7:        TABLE_NAME = '&table_name' AND
new    7:        TABLE_NAME = 'DEPT8' AND
Enter value for table_owner: WAITE
old    8:        OWNER = '&table_owner'
new    8:        OWNER = 'WAITE'

GRANTEE                            PRIVILEGE
--------------------------------   -----------------------
READ_ONLY                          SELECT
SQL>
```

Figure 8.26 CHP8_25.SQL determines the object privileges granted indirectly to a user account by granting to a role of which the user account belongs.

```
SELECT GRANTEE, PRIVILEGE
FROM DBA_TAB_PRIVS
WHERE OWNER = '&table_owner' AND
      TABLE_NAME = '&table_name' and
     (GRANTEE = 'PUBLIC' OR
      GRANTEE = '&username' OR
      GRANTEE IN
              (SELECT GRANTED_ROLE
               FROM DBA_ROLE_PRIVS
               WHERE GRANTEE = '&username'))
```

Figure 8.27 CHP8_26.SQL determines all object privileges granted to a particular object.

How It Works

Step 1 creates the sample table, user account, and role used in this How-To. Step 2 grants privileges both directly and indirectly to the JODI user account, and assigns the READ_ONLY role to JODI. Step 3 determines the object privileges granted directly to a user account. Step 4 determines the object privileges granted indirectly to a user account through a PUBLIC grant. Step 5 determines the object privileges granted indirectly to a user account by granting to a role of which the user account belongs. Step 6 determines all object privileges granted to a particular object by combining Steps 3 through 6 into one SELECT statement.

Comments

If an object privilege has been granted through a role that has been granted another role that the user account is assigned to, then discovering object privileges is more difficult. If this is the case, you would have to traverse the role structure and determine whether the user account belongs to a role that has privileges on the table. Also, if a user account owns an object, then that user account has all object privileges associated with it. All user accounts have all privileges, both system and object, that are granted to PUBLIC.

COMPLEXITY
ADVANCED

8.7   How do I...
Determine which users have access to a particular object?

Problem

I have a sensitive object in my database. It is important to know which users can ALTER, INSERT, UPDATE, SELECT, or DELETE the data if the object is a table, or which users can EXECUTE the object if it is a package, stored procedure, or function. How do I determine which users have access to a particular object?

Technique

User accounts are granted access to an object either indirectly through a grant or directly. By querying the DBA_TAB_PRIVS and DBA_ROLE_PRIVS data dictionary views, all users that have access to a particular object, along with their privileges, can be determined. The DBA_TAB_PRIVS data dictionary view contains the object privileges granted to all users and roles for tables, sequences, procedures, packages, functions, views, and database links among all other objects. The DBA_ROLE_PRIVS data dictionary view contains which user accounts are associated with roles. How-To 8.6 provides additional information about roles.

Steps

1. Run SQL*Plus and connect as the WAITE user account. If you have not already done so in How-To 8.6, run CHP8_21.SQL to create the sample table, user account, and role that will be used with this How-To.

2. Grant the object privileges to the JODI user account and role by running CHP8_22.SQL, if you have not already done so. The JODI user account is assigned to the READ_ONLY role. The first statement assigns the READ_ONLY role to the JODI user account. The second statement grants UPDATE privileges on the DEPT8 table directly to the JODI user account. The third statement grants SELECT privileges on the DEPT8 table indirectly to the JODI user account by granting to the READ_ONLY role, of which the JODI account belongs. The fourth statement indirectly grants INSERT privileges on the DEPT8 table to the DEPT8 table by granting the privilege to PUBLIC. Granting to PUBLIC enables all user accounts to use the privilege.

To determine which user accounts have access to an object, one of three conditions must be true. If PUBLIC has been granted, then ALL user accounts in the database have the privilege. If the user account has been explicitly granted a privilege, then the user has the privilege. Also, if a role has been granted a privilege, then all user accounts in that role have the privilege.

3. CHP8_27.SQL, shown in Figure 8.28, determines which users have access to a particular object. In the example, you will pass DEPT8 for `object_name` and WAITE for `object_owner`. If the query returns PUBLIC as a grantee, then all user accounts in the database have the corresponding privilege for the object.

```
SELECT GRANTEE, PRIVILEGE
FROM DBA_TAB_PRIVS
WHERE
        TABLE_NAME = '&object_name' AND
        OWNER = '&object_owner'
UNION
SELECT A.GRANTEE, B.PRIVILEGE
FROM DBA_ROLE_PRIVS A, DBA_TAB_PRIVS B
WHERE B.TABLE_NAME = '&object_name' AND
        B.OWNER = '&object_owner' AND
        A.GRANTED_ROLE = B.GRANTEE
```

Figure 8.28 CHP8_27.SQL determines which user accounts and roles have been directly or indirectly granted access to a particular object.

4. Run the script to get the results.

```
SQL> START CHP8_27.sql
Enter value for object_name: DEPT8
old    4:        TABLE_NAME = '&object_name' AND
new    4:        TABLE_NAME = 'DEPT8' AND
Enter value for object_owner: WAITE
old    5:        OWNER = '&object_owner'
new    5:        OWNER = 'WAITE'
Enter value for object_name: DEPT8
old    9: WHERE B.TABLE_NAME = '&object_name' AND
new    9: WHERE B.TABLE_NAME = 'DEPT8' AND
Enter value for object_owner: WAITE
old   10:        B.OWNER = '&object_owner' AND
new   10:        B.OWNER = 'WAITE' AND


GRANTEE                              PRIVILEGE
------------------------------- --------------------
JODI                                 SELECT
JODI                                 UPDATE
PUBLIC                               INSERT
READ_ONLY                            SELECT
WAITE                                SELECT

SQL>
```

How It Works

Step 1 creates the sample table, role, and user account used in this How-To. Step 2 assigns the user account to the role, and issues several grants, which are used to demonstrate selecting from data dictionary views. Steps 3 and 4 run the CHP8_27.SQL to query the DBA_ROLE_PRIVS and DBA_TAB_PRIVS data dictionary view.

Lines 1 through 5 query from the DBA_TAB_PRIVS, providing all users and roles (including PUBLIC). Because a role can be granted to several users, it is important to see all user accounts that belong to all roles returned in the query. Line 6 issues the UNION clause, which joins the query in lines 1 through 5 with the query in lines 7 through 11, which queries from both the DBA_TAB_PRIVS and the DBA_ROLE_PRIVS data dictionary views. A query similar to lines 1 through 5 is used, joining the two tables where the granted role of the DBA_ROLE_PRIVS equals the grantee of the DBA_TAB_PRIVS. The DBA_ROLE_PRIVS contains the GRANTED_ROLE and the GRANTEE columns, of which the GRANTED_ROLE column represents the role and the GRANTEE column represents the user account assigned to the role.

Comments

Several object privileges are available that can be returned from the CHP8_27.SQL query. The available object privileges in Oracle8 are: ALTER, AUDIT, COMMENT, DELETE, GRANT, INDEX, INSERT, LOCK, RENAME, SELECT, UPDATE, REFERENCES, EXECUTE, CREATE, READ, and WRITE. The CHP8_27.SQL query works well unless a user has been granted a privilege through a role that has been granted another role, which has been granted the object privilege. If this is the case, you would have to traverse the role structure, using the information gathered from CHP8_27.SQL as a list of all roles with access to the object.

COMPLEXITY
ADVANCED

8.8 How do I...
Enable database auditing?

Problem

I would like to closely monitor activity within my database. It is important to know how often a particular user logs in and I'd also like to know when a specific table is updated or altered. It is also important to know when another user account tries to select data and fails. How to I enable database auditing?

Technique

By using the AUDIT command, one can audit a wide range of activities within the database. One-hundred and fifty-nine different actions can be audited in Oracle8, which is too numerous to explain individually in this How-To. The actions fall into three general categories: object auditing (whenever an object is referenced by a user), privilege auditing (whenever a privilege is used or fails an attempt to be used), and statement auditing (when a statement is issued). The syntax of the AUDIT command is shown in Figure 8.29.

```
AUDIT audit_option
[ON schema.object ]
[BY username ]
[BY { SESSION | ACCESS } ]
[WHENEVER {SUCCESSFUL | NOT SUCCESSFUL } ]
```

Figure 8.29 The syntax of the AUDIT statement.

Object auditing can involve auditing statements on objects, such as CREATE INDEX, ALTER TABLE, GRANTs on an object, or DROP PUBLIC DATABASE LINK. Privilege auditing can involve auditing any system privilege, such as the SELECT ANY SEQUENCE privilege, the ALTER SYSTEM privilege, or the ALTER USER privilege. Statement auditing can record DDL or DML statements, based on a type of database object.

All audit statements can be specified for a particular user or all users with the BY username clause. If desired, they can also be specified to record to the audit trail only if a statement succeeds or fails, by the WHENEVER SUCCESSFUL or WHENEVER NOT SUCCESSFUL clause. The BY ACCESS and BY SESSION clause indicates how often the audit trail is updated by one session between login and logout. For example, if a user issues ten SELECT statements against an audited table, then one record will be recorded in the audit trail if BY SESSION was selected for the audit, and ten records if BY ACCESS.

Steps

1. To enable database auditing, you must first modify your initialization file and change the parameter AUDIT_TRAIL. To send the auditing events to the database audit trail, change the AUDIT_TRAIL parameter to DB. The audit records are then inserted into the AUD$ data dictionary table in the SYS user account. To send the auditing events to the operating system trail, change the AUDIT_TRAIL parameter to OS and the audit files will be located in the AUDIT_FILE_DEST directory. This directory by default is $ORACLE_HOME/RDBMS/AUDIT in UNIX, and \ORANT\DATABASE in Windows NT. The database must be shut down and restarted for auditing to take effect.

2. Run SQL*Plus and connect as the WAITE user account. Run CHP8_28.SQL to create a sample table to demonstrate auditing, as shown in Figure 8.30. The table contains Social Security and salary information, and by auditing the table, the database administrator can determine when and how users access and modify the table.

```
SQL> GET C:\CHP8_28.SQL
  1  CREATE TABLE SENSITIVE_DATA (
  2      EMP_NAME      VARCHAR2(50),
  3      SSN           VARCHAR2(11),
  4*     SALARY        NUMBER)
SQL> /

Table created.

SQL>
```

Figure 8.30 CHP8_28.SQL creates the SENSITIVE_DATA table to be used for this How-To.

3. Audit all SELECT, INSERT, UPDATE, and DELETE statements made against the SENSITIVE_DATA table by any user by running CHP8_29.SQL, as shown in Figure 8.31. The steps to view audit information for all examples in this How-To is explained in How-To 8.9.

4. Audit every time a user connects to the database as the WAITE account by running CHP8_30.SQL, as shown in Figure 8.32. This is good to track the time the WAITE user account logs in and logs out. If you are the only user with the WAITE password, this is also a good method to determine whether anyone else logs in to the database.

5. Audit each time a user attempts to DELETE records from the SENSITIVE_DATA table and fails, by running CHP8_31.SQL, as shown in Figure 8.33.

```
SQL> GET C:\CHP8_29.SQL
  1  AUDIT SELECT, INSERT, UPDATE, DELETE
  2* ON SENSITIVE_DATA
SQL> /

Audit succeeded.

SQL> |
```

Figure 8.31 CHP8_29.SQL starts auditing the SENSITIVE_DATA table for data modifications or queries.

```
SQL> GET C:\CHP8_30.SQL
  1* AUDIT SESSION BY WAITE
SQL> /

Audit succeeded.

SQL>
SQL> |
```

Figure 8.32 CHP8_30.SQL starts auditing whenever a user logs in as WAITE.

```
SQL> GET C:\CHP8_31.SQL
  1  AUDIT DELETE
  2      ON SENSITIVE_DATA
  3*     WHENEVER NOT SUCCESSFUL
SQL> /

Audit succeeded.

SQL> |
```

Figure 8.33 CHP8_31.SQL starts auditing whenever a user attempts to DELETE data from the SENSITIVE_DATA table and fails.

How It Works

Step 1 enables auditing within the database by modifying the initialization parameter file to set AUDIT_TRAIL to DB. Step 2 creates the SENSITIVE_DATA table to demonstrate auditing. Step 3 enables auditing for all SELECT, INSERT, UPDATE, and DELETE statements made against the SENSITIVE_DATA table by any user. Step 4 audits every time a user connects to the database as the WAITE account. Step 5 audits each time a user attempts to DELETE records from the SENSITIVE_DATA table and fails.

Comments

The SYS and INTERNAL accounts are never audited. If a user rolls back a transaction, the statement is still audited. A user account can only audit activity within their own account, unless they have AUDIT ANY privileges, and the DBA role contains them. Operating system audit trails are automatically generated in the $ORACLE_HOME/RDBMS/AUDIT directory, which keeps track of all instance startups, instance shutdowns, and connections to the database as a DBA user account. Even if auditing is not on, these files will be created. Be sure to periodically purge these files, or the file system eventually fills up. Many database administrators, even advanced DBAs, don't know about these files.

COMPLEXITY
INTERMEDIATE

8.9   How do I...
View audit information?

Problem

I have enabled database auditing, as described in How-To 8.8. I would like to analyze the audit trail to get information about database activity. How do I view audit information?

Technique

Look in the AUD$ table, known as the audit trail, which contains all auditing information, or look at the files in the AUDIT_FILE_DEST directory. When your Oracle8 database is created, the CATAUDIT.SQL script, located in the $ORACLE_HOME/rdbms/admin directory, is run through the CATALOG.SQL script. These scripts create several data dictionary views that make analyzing the AUD$ table easier, such as DBA_AUDIT_TRAIL (all audits), DBA_AUDIT_SESSION (session audits), and DBA_AUDIT_OBJECT (object and statement audits). By querying DBA_OBJ_AUDIT_OPTS, you can determine the audit options for all objects. By querying DBA_PRIV_AUDIT_OPTS, you can determine the audit options for sessions and privileges.

Steps

1. Connect to SQL*Plus as the WAITE account. If you have not already created the SENSITIVE_DATA table and AUDIT commands from How-To 8.8, do so now.

2. Ensure that auditing is working. The SYS.AUD$ table contains every audit entry. Because nothing has been done to create an audit entry, there should be nothing in the table. Do a count on the table to be sure:

```
SQL> SELECT COUNT(*) FROM SYS.AUD$;
COUNT(*)
--------
0

SQL>
```

Generate the first audit record by connecting to SQL*Plus again as the WAITE user. Step 4 from How-To 8.8 enabled auditing for each time someone connects as the WAITE user account. Again, do a count on the SYS.AUD$ table:

```
SQL> SELECT COUNT(*) FROM SYS.AUD$;
COUNT(*)
--------
1

SQL>
```

3. Create an additional audit record by running CHP8_32.SQL as shown in Figure 8.34. This script will SELECT from the SENSITIVE_DATA table, adding an audit trail entry as a result from the previous How-To.

4. At this point, two records are in the audit trail. To see the records, you can select from the DBA_AUDIT_SESSION view for session audits, and the DBA_AUDIT_OBJECT view for object audits. Load CHP8_33.SQL into the SQL buffer, and run it.

```
SQL> START CHP8_33.sql
1 SELECT USERNAME, TERMINAL, ACTION_NAME,
2 TO_CHAR (LOGOFF_TIME, 'DD-MON-YYYY HH:MI:SS') LOGOFF_TIME
3 FROM SYS.DBA_AUDIT_SESSION
SQL> /
USERNAME  TERMINAL  ACTION_NAME  LOGOFF_TIME
--------  --------  -----------  -----------
WAITE     WAITE     LOGON        10-JAN-1998 03:15:33
SQL>
```

```
SQL> GET C:\CHP8_32.SQL
  1* SELECT * FROM SENSITIVE_DATA
SQL> /

no rows selected

SQL>
SQL> |
```

Figure 8.34 CHP8_32.SQL selects from the
SENSITIVE_DATA table and by doing so
adds an audit trail entry.

This shows all the session auditing. Now, select from the
DBA_AUDIT_OBJECT view. Load CHP8_34.SQL into the SQL buffer, and
run it.

```
SQL> START CHP8_34.sql
1 SELECT USERNAME, TERMINAL,
2   ACTION_NAME, OBJ_NAME,
3   TO_CHAR (TIMESTAMP, 'DD-MON-YYYY HH:MI:SS') TIME
4 FROM SYS.DBA_AUDIT_OBJECT
SQL> /
USERNAME  TERMINAL    ACTION_NAME  OBJ_NAME      _   TIME
--------  --------    -----------  -----------       ---------------
-----
WAITE     ARI KAPLAN  SESSION REC  SENSITIVE_DATA   19-SEP-1997
12:47:26

SQL>
```

How It Works

Step 1 repeats How-To 8.8, if necessary. Step 2 ensures that auditing is
functioning by counting from the SYS.AUD$ table, adding an auditing record by
reconnecting as WAITE, and by counting again from the SYS.AUD$ table. Step 3
creates another audit record by selecting from the SENSITIVE_DATA table. Step
4 shows the session audit data by selecting from the DBA_AUDIT_SESSION
data dictionary view. It then shows the object audit data by selecting from the
DBA_AUDIT_OBJECT data dictionary view.

Comments

This How-To explains how to view data that has been created in the audit trail.
How-To 8.10 shows how to delete audit trail entries. To determine which object,
statements, and privileges are being audited, you can query the DBA_OBJ_
AUDIT_OPTS view, the ALL_DEF_AUDIT_OPTS view, or the DBA_PRIV_AUDIT_
OPTS view.

COMPLEXITY
ADVANCED

8.10 How do I...
Delete audit information?

Problem

I have had database auditing enabled for some time now, and the data audit data takes up significant space. Also, some of the audit information is no longer necessary. How do I delete audit information?

Technique

To disable a particular auditing event, but still enable auditing to continue for other auditing actions, use the NOAUDIT command. NOAUDIT is essentially the opposite of AUDIT. It turns off all object, statement, and system privilege auditing based on the auditing options selected. The syntax of the NOAUDIT command appears in Figure 8.35.

To disable auditing altogether from the database, modify the initialization file, and change the line with AUDIT_TRAIL from DB or OS to NONE. If you want to remove the auditing data dictionary views, run the $ORACLE_HOME/RDBMS/ADMIN/CATNOAUD.SQL script. To delete the audit data, you must either TRUNCATE the AUD$ data dictionary table or delete the unnecessary data from the table.

Steps

1. Connect to SQL*Plus as the WAITE account. If you have not already created the SENSITIVE_DATA table and AUDIT commands from How-To 8.8, do so now. Also, if you have not created audit trail entries from How-To 8.9, do so now.

2. Remove the auditing for people connecting to the database as the WAITE user account by running CHP8_35.SQL, shown in Figure 8.36.

3. Remove the auditing from the SENSITIVE_DATA table by running CHP8_36.SQL, shown in Figure 8.37.

```
NOAUDIT audit_option
{ON schema.object |  BY username }
[WHENEVER {SUCCESSFUL | NOT SUCCESSFUL } ]
```

Figure 8.35 The syntax of the NOAUDIT command.

```
SQL> GET C:\CHP8_35.SQL
  1* NOAUDIT session
SQL> /

Noaudit succeeded.

SQL> |
```

Figure 8.36 CHP8_35.SQL removes session auditing.

```
SQL> GET C:\CHP8_36.SQL
  1  NOAUDIT SELECT, INSERT, UPDATE, DELETE ON
  2* SENSITIVE_DATA
SQL> /

Noaudit succeeded.

SQL>
```

Figure 8.37 CHP8_36.SQL removes auditing from the SENSITIVE_DATA table.

4. To delete auditing data within the database, use the TRUNCATE command on the SYS.AUD$ data dictionary table. This is the only data dictionary table that you should modify. Load CHP8_37.SQL into the SQL buffer and run it.

```
SQL> GET CHP8_37.sql
1   TRUNCATE TABLE SYS.AUD$
SQL> /
Table truncated.
SQL>
```

5. To stop auditing altogether from the database, you must modify your initialization file and change the parameter AUDIT_TRAIL to NONE.

How It Works

Step 1 creates all objects, audit options, and audit trail entries. Step 2 removes auditing from users connecting as the WAITE user account. Step 3 removes auditing of SELECT, INSERT, UPDATE, and DELETE for the SENSITIVE_DATA table. Step 4 shows how to delete auditing data from the audit trail. Step 5 shows how to stop auditing altogether for the entire database.

Comments

To prevent the data in the audit trail for growing without bounds and taking up disk space, you can either delete data, turn off auditing options, or turn off auditing altogether. By default, Oracle8 audits every startup, shutdown, and connections as DBA user accounts into operating system files. The files are located by default in $ORACLE_HOME/RDBMS/AUDIT in UNIX, and \ORANT\DATABASE in Windows NT.

COMPLEXITY
ADVANCED

8.11 How do I...
Manage passwords?

Problem

I need to be able to assign password enforcement rules to conform to company standards, such as forcing users to change their passwords every 30 days. Other rules I would like to enforce are to ensure a user does not repeat a recently used password, and that a user is locked out of the database if they enter an invalid password a couple of times. How do I manage passwords?

Technique

Use the CREATE PROFILE command to enforce and modify password management. After creating a profile, assign it to a user account. View password information by querying the DBA_USERS data dictionary view for ACCOUNT_STATUS (unlocked, locked, expired), LOCK_DATE (when the account was locked), and EXPIRY_DATE (date and time when the account expires). You can also query the DBA_PROFILES view to see which password values are set for each profile.

Several new additions are included with the CREATE PROFILE and ALTER PROFILE commands, which are shown in Table 8.2.

Table 8.2 New profile options

PROFILE OPTION	DESCRIPTION
FAILED_LOGIN_ATTEMPTS	Locks account after the user enters an incorrect password for FAILED_LOGIN_ATTEMPTS times, cumulative.
PASSWORD_GRACE_TIME	Number (or fraction) of days that a user can login with an expired password until a password change occurs.
PASSWORD_LIFE_TIME	Number (or fraction) of days before a password expires.
PASSWORD_LOCK_TIME	Number (or fraction) of days that the user is locked out of the database after entering invalid passwords, greater than the # defined in FAILED_LOGIN_ATTEMPTS. UNLIMITED can also be specified, in which case the user is locked out of the database indefinitely until it is manually unlocked.
PASSWORD_REUSE_MAX	Number of times a user must change the password before it can be reused. For example, setting this to 3 requires a user must change the password to three other passwords before a password can be reused.
PASSWORD_REUSE_TIME	Number (or fraction) of days before a password can be reused. For example, you can set this to 365 so a year must pass before you can reuse a password.
PASSWORD_VERIFY_FUNCTION	Checks the password to see whether an intruder can easily break the password.

You can use either PASSWORD_REUSE_MAX or PASSWORD_REUSE_TIME, but not both.

The PASSWORD_VERIFY_FUNCTION comes with a default function, called verify_function, which verifies that each user's password meets minimum protection from intruders trying to guess it. This includes ensuring the password is greater than four characters, contains at least one digit, one character, and one punctuation mark, and is three characters or more different from the previous password. The password cannot be one of several predefined passwords: abcd, account, computer, database, oracle, password, user, or welcome.

Steps

1. Connect to SQL*Plus as the WAITE user account and run CHP8_37.SQL to create a profile. The profile enforces password control, which is shown in Figure 8.38.

The NORMAL_USERS profile forces the user to change their password after every 30 days. It also locks the account out of the database for one hour if the user tries to connect with an invalid password after three times.

2. Create the sample user account BRENDAN for this How-To by running CHP8_38.SQL, shown here:

```
SQL> GET CHP8_38.sql
1   CREATE USER BRENDAN
2   IDENTIFIED BY CLOVER
SQL> /

User created.

SQL>
```

```
SQL> GET C:\CHP8_37.SQL
  1   CREATE PROFILE NORMAL_USERS LIMIT
  2       PASSWORD_LIFE_TIME 30
  3       FAILED_LOGIN_ATTEMPTS 3
  4*      PASSWORD_LOCK_TIME 1/24
SQL> /

Profile created.

SQL>
```

Figure 8.38 CHP8_37.SQL creates a profile to enforce password control.

3. Assign the newly created NORMAL_USER profile to the user account by running CHP8_39.SQL, shown here:

```
SQL> GET CHP8_39.sql
1   ALTER USER BRENDAN
2   PROFILE NORMAL_USERS
SQL> /

User created.

SQL>
```

Now the BRENDAN user account is assigned to the x-profile, along with all the associated password security.

4. Another password control capability is to expire passwords to enforce users to change them on their first connection to the database. Run CHP8_40.SQL to expire the BRENDAN user's password:

```
SQL> GET CHP8_40.sql
1   ALTER USER BRENDAN
2   PASSWORD EXPIRE;
SQL> /

User altered.

SQL>
```

5. Query the DBA_USERS view to review user password expiration status by running CHP8_41.SQL. Pass BRENDAN for the username, as shown in Figure 8.39.

```
SQL> START C:\CHP8_41.SQL
SQL> COLUMN USERNAME FORMAT A14
SQL> COLUMN ACCOUNT_STATUS FORMAT A14
SQL> COLUMN LOCK_DATE FORMAT A14
SQL> COLUMN EXPIRY_DATE FORMAT A16
SQL> COLUMN PROFILE FORMAT A15
SQL> SELECT USERNAME, ACCOUNT_STATUS,
  2         TO_CHAR(LOCK_DATE,'DD-MON-YY') LOCK_DATE,
  3         TO_CHAR(EXPIRY_DATE,'DD-MON-YY') EXPIRY_DATE,
  4         PROFILE
  5  FROM DBA_USERS
  6  WHERE USERNAME = '&username'
  7  /
Enter value for username: BRENDAN
old   6: WHERE USERNAME = '&username'
new   6: WHERE USERNAME = 'BRENDAN'

USERNAME       ACCOUNT_STATUS LOCK_DATE      EXPIRY_DATE      PROFILE
-------------- -------------- -------------- ---------------- ---------------
BRENDAN        EXPIRED                       00-DECEMBER-00   NORMAL_USERS

SQL>
```

Figure 8.39 CHP8_41.SQL selects password status information for a user account.

6. Query the DBA_PROFILES view to see which password values are set for each profile, by running CHP8_42.SQL. The script is shown in Figure 8.40 and the results are shown in Figure 8.41. Pass NORMAL_USER when prompted for `profile_name`.

How It Works

Step 1 creates the NORMAL_USERS profile with sample password limitations. The profile forces the user to change their password after every 30 days, and locks the account out of the database for one hour if the user tries to connect with an invalid password after three times. Step 2 creates the BRENDAN sample user account. Step 3 associates the NORMAL_USERS profile to the BRENDAN user account. Step 4 expires the BRENDAN account's password, so that the next time BRENDAN logs in, the password must be changed. Step 5 queries the DBA_USERS view to review user password expiration status. Step 6 queries the DBA_PROFILES view to determine the password enforcement associated with a particular profile.

Comments

The default profile for all users has their password options set to those shown in Table 8.3. For example, the default PASSWORD_LOCK_TIME is 1/1440 and corresponds to 1 minute (1/1440 of a day).

```
COLUMN PROFILE FORMAT A15
COLUMN RESOURCE_NAME FORMAT A25
COLUMN RESOURCE_TYPE FORMAT A15
COLUMN LIMIT FORMAT A15
SELECT PROFILE, RESOURCE_NAME,
       RESOURCE_TYPE, LIMIT
FROM DBA_PROFILES
WHERE PROFILE = '&profile_name' AND
      RESOURCE_TYPE LIKE '%PASSWORD%'
|
```

Figure 8.40 CHP8_42.SQL selects password status information for a user account.

```
Enter value for profile_name: NORMAL_USERS
old    4: WHERE PROFILE = '&profile_name' AND
new    4: WHERE PROFILE = 'NORMAL_USERS' AND

PROFILE          RESOURCE_NAME              RESOURCE_TYPE     LIMIT
---------------  -------------------------  ----------------  ---------------
NORMAL_USERS     FAILED_LOGIN_ATTEMPTS      PASSWORD          3
NORMAL_USERS     PASSWORD_LIFE_TIME         PASSWORD          30
NORMAL_USERS     PASSWORD_REUSE_TIME        PASSWORD          DEFAULT
NORMAL_USERS     PASSWORD_REUSE_MAX         PASSWORD          DEFAULT
NORMAL_USERS     PASSWORD_VERIFY_FUNCTION   PASSWORD          DEFAULT
NORMAL_USERS     PASSWORD_LOCK_TIME         PASSWORD          .0416
NORMAL_USERS     PASSWORD_GRACE_TIME        PASSWORD          DEFAULT

7 rows selected.
```

Figure 8.41 The results of running CHP8_42.SQL.

Table 8.3 The default profile password options

PROFILE OPTION	DEFAULT VALUE
FAILED_LOGIN_ATTEMPTS	3
PASSWORD_GRACE_TIME	10
PASSWORD_LIFE_TIME	60
PASSWORD_LOCK_TIME	1/1440
PASSWORD_REUSE_MAX	UNLIMITED
PASSWORD_REUSE_TIME	1800
PASSWORD_VERIFY_FUNCTION	verify_function

CHAPTER 9
SPACE MANAGEMENT

9

SPACE MANAGEMENT

How do I...

Space management is one of the primary responsibilities for database administrators. Recent improvements in the Oracle server have simplified this task so that database space management does not consume so much of a DBA's time. These enhancements include unlimited extents, the capability to deallocate space in a segment, and the capability to coalesce fragmented space in a tablespace. The series of How-To's in this chapter explain how to use these features of the Oracle server to simplify space management.

9.1 Detect Objects Close to Maximum Extents

Application and user activity contribute to the growth of database tables and indexes. These objects can grow out of their first storage allocation or extent and, in fact, they can grow into multiple extents. Although the UNLIMITED extent option is available in Oracle8, DBAs can choose to limit the number of maximum extents for any object so that it cannot grow without restriction. This How-To explains detection of objects close to this physical limit on their growth so that the DBA can take action before the situation becomes problematic.

9.2 Detect Row Chaining and Migration in Tables

Oracle8 databases, or any databases really, do not perform at their best unless database tuners take steps to minimize physical input/output. The Oracle8 server stores data in blocks, where the size of a block is chosen at database creation time.

Sometimes parts of a single table row inhabit more than one block. If a modification increases a row's size beyond the capacity of its original data block, Oracle8 moves the row to another block and maintains a pointer to the row's new location in its original data block. This is called *row migration*.

Row chaining, in contrast, occurs when a table row is too large to fit in any database block. In either case, this "one row, many blocks" situation forces Oracle8 to perform extra physical I/O to access to chained or migrated rows. This How-to presents a method for detecting table rows that require more than one data block.

9.3 Correct Row Migration in Tables

The How-To 9.2 addressed detection of chained and migrated rows. Most of the time, Oracle users and DBAs cannot resolve row chaining. Row migration, however, is often reversible. This How-To outlines a method to ease row migration difficulties in Oracle8 databases.

9.4 Determine and Coalesce the Free Space in a Tablespace

When tablespaces run low on free space, the Oracle8 server can generate a plethora of error messages, including "unable to allocate initial extent" and "failed to extend." The Oracle8 data dictionary can help DBAs and privileged users identify which tablespaces are approaching conditions like these.

This How-To outlines a method to identify these kinds of tablespaces and also contains an explanation of the difference between free space and contiguous free space. Finally, this How-To describes how to use the ALTER_TABLESPACE command to coalesce fragmented free space in a tablespace.

9.5 Allocate Unlimited Extents for a Database Object

Oracle objects are composed of extents, and, until recently, the number of extents that the Oracle server could allocate to any object was limited. The addition of unlimited extents capability can considerably reduce space management efforts because it enables Oracle to dynamically allocate as many extents to an object as necessary.

9.6 Deallocate Unused Space in a Segment

Reclaim unused space in a segment used to require standard reorganization techniques: export the table, drop the table, re-create the table with different storage parameters, and import the data back into the table. This How-To focuses on the DEALLOCATE option of the ALTER TABLE statement, which enables dynamic release of unused segment space.

9.7 Configure Database Files to Extend Automatically

At the physical level, Oracle8 stores data in data files. The DBA specifies an initial size for data files during tablespace creation. The default data file behavior is to disallow any future object growth when the data file is full. The AUTOEXTEND capability for data files, however, enables them to grow indefinitely. The process of querying the data dictionary to determine the extension status of data files and enabling or disabling AUTOEXTEND capability is the subject of this How-To.

COMPLEXITY
ADVANCED

9.1 How do I...
Detect objects close to maximum extents?

Problem

I have created some database objects and have either accepted the default for the number of maximum extents or imposed a maximum extent limit of my own. I want to query my database periodically to determine whether any of these objects are close to a point where the maximum extent limit will not permit them to grow. How can I determine which tables and indexes are close to their limit for maximum extents?

Technique

The Oracle8 server allocates storage space in extents. The data definition language (DDL) commands that create tables and indexes can contain a storage clause specifying the size of the first extent, the next extent, and the amount by which to increase extents subsequent to the second extent. There is controversy regarding the advisability of confining database objects to a single extent. One philosophy holds that this practice minimizes input/output processing. Another school of thought maintains that the alleged I/O performance improvements don't justify the effort of confining objects to a single extent. In any case, there is no doubt that maximally extended objects are likely to cause problems.

The Oracle8 data dictionary view DBA_SEGMENTS contains the information you need to discover whether any database objects are close to the MAXEXTENTS limit. Table 9.1 contains a description of this data dictionary object.

Table 9.1 The DBA_SEGMENTS data dictionary view

COLUMN	COLUMN DESCRIPTION
OWNER	User name of the segment owner
SEGMENT_NAME	Name, if any, of the segment
SEGMENT_TYPE	Type of segment: INDEX PARTITION, TABLE PARTITION, TABLE, CLUSTER, INDEX, ROLLBACK, DEFERRED ROLLBACK, TEMPORARY, or CACHE
TABLESPACE_NAME	Name of the tablespace containing the q segment
HEADER_FILE	ID of the file containing the segment header
HEADER_BLOCK	ID of the block containing the segment header
BYTES	Size, in bytes, of the segment
BLOCKS	Size, in Oracle blocks, of the segment
EXTENTS	Number of extents allocated to the segment
INITIAL_EXTENT	Size, in bytes, of the initial extent of the segment
NEXT_EXTENT	Size, in bytes, of the next extent to be allocated to the segment
MIN_EXTENTS	Minimum number of extents allowed in the segment
MAX_EXTENTS	Maximum number of extents allowed in the segment
PCT_INCREASE	Percent by which to increase the size of the next extent to be allocated
FREELISTS	Number of process freelists allocated to the segment
FREELIST_GROUPS	Number of freelist groups allocated to the segment
RELATIVE_FNO	Relative file number of the segment header
PARTITION_NAME	Object partition name (Set to NULL for non-partitioned objects)

Steps

1. Run SQL*Plus, connect as the WAITE user, and use the SQL*Plus START command to run the script contained in CHP9_1.SQL. This script creates a partitioned table (see How-To 4.10 for an in-depth explanation of object partitioning in Oracle8) and is shown in Figure 9.1.

This example is contrived; it is unlikely that any developer would specify 3 for the maximum number of extents for the first partition of this table. Here, it will serve to illustrate the next step.

2. While still connected to SQL*Plus as the WAITE user, use the SQL*Plus START command to run the script contained in CHP9_2.SQL. The script will prompt for the substitution variable EXTLIMIT and will produce a report listing any database objects that are within EXTLIMIT extents of their maximum extent limit. The script and its output appear in Figure 9.2.

```
SQL> start chp9_1
SQL>
SQL> CREATE TABLE emp09
  2  (
  3    empno         NUMBER(4) NOT NULL,
  4    ename         VARCHAR2(10),
  5    job           VARCHAR2(9),
  6    mgr           NUMBER(4),
  7    hiredate      DATE,
  8    sal           NUMBER(7,2),
  9    comm          NUMBER(7,2),
 10    deptno        NUMBER(2)
 11  )
 12  PARTITION BY RANGE (empno)
 13  (
 14    PARTITION emp09p1
 15      VALUES LESS THAN (5000)
 16      storage (maxextents 3),
 17    PARTITION emp09p2
 18      VALUES LESS THAN (MAXVALUE)
 19  );

Table created.
```

Figure 9.1 Running the
CHP9_1.SQL script in SQL*Plus.

```
SQL> start chp9_2
SQL>
SQL> SELECT owner, segment_name, segment_type, max_extents,
  2           partition_name, sum(extents)
  3  FROM    dba_segments
  4  GROUP BY owner, segment_name, segment_type, max_extents,
  5           partition_name
  6  HAVING max_extents - sum(extents) <= &extlimit;
Enter value for extlimit: 5

OWNER SEGMENT_NAME SEGMENT_TYPE      MAX_EXTENTS PARTITION_NAME  SUM(EXTENTS)
----- ------------ ----------------- ----------- --------------- ------------
SCOTT DEPT         TABLE                       3                            1
SCOTT PK_DEPT      INDEX                       3                            1
SYS   1.522        CACHE                       0                            1
WAITE EMP09        TABLE PARTITION             3 EMP09P1                     1

SQL> |
```

Figure 9.2 The CHP9_2.SQL script reporting on objects close
to their maximum extent limit.

This script queries the DBA_SEGMENTS data dictionary view.
Experienced Oracle users will likely have familiarity with a script like this
one that they developed for use with previous versions of Oracle. The one
main difference is the inclusion of the PARTITION_NAME column that
supports Oracle8 object partitioning.

How It Works

The DBA_SEGMENTS view contains everything you need to produce a
meaningful report of all database objects that are close to maximum extension.
Notice in Figure 9.2, for example, that a table and an index that user SCOTT
owns, a CACHE object that user SYS owns, and the first partition of the EMP09
table created in Step 1 are all within five extents of their maximum extent limits.

Comments

Beginning with Oracle server release 7.3, DBAs can specify that objects grow through an unlimited number of extents. Tables and indexes featuring this option can grow until they consume all the available space in the tablespace. The script in step 2 will not fail, even in the presence of the UNLIMITED value for the MAXEXTENTS parameter. The value stored in the MAXEXTENTS attribute in the DBA_TABLES view in this case is still a number: 2147483645.

COMPLEXITY

INTERMEDIATE

9.2 How do I...

Detect row chaining and migration in tables?

Problem

I have reason to believe that my database is generating more I/O than it should. How can I find out whether particular tables are suffering from row chaining or row migration?

Technique

Row migration occurs when a database block does not contain enough free space to accommodate an update statement. Suppose, for example, that block number AAAAAB contains two rows. If a user issues an update statement that updates one of these rows, and the updated row no longer fits in block number AAAAAB, Oracle8 *migrates* the row. That is, the server moves the row to another block and maintains a pointer to the new block in the row's original block.

Row chaining, in contrast, occurs when no single database block is large enough to accommodate a particular row. This is common when a table contains several large CHAR or VARCHAR2 data types. If the database block size is 2048 bytes and a row is 3000 bytes long, for example, this row will not fit in any single database block; it will reside in multiple database blocks. An unpleasant side effect of both chaining and migration is that the Oracle8 server must read more than one database block to read a single row.

The ANALYZE command can reveal, on a table-by-table basis, which tables contain migrated and/or chained rows. A table to hold information about these migrated/chained rows must exist prior to using the ANALYZE command for this purpose, and you will build that table first.

Steps

1. Run SQL*Plus and connect as the WAITE user. Use the START command to load and execute the UTLCHAIN.SQL script to create the CHAINED_ROWS table. This script is supplied by Oracle corporation; under Windows NT it resides in the \ORANT\RDBMS80\ADMIN subdirectory. The results of this operation appear in Figure 9.3.

2. Use the START command to load and execute the CHP9_3.SQL script, which appears in Listing 9.1.

Listing 9.1 Creating the CHAIN and MIGRATE tables in the CHP9_3.SQL script

```
 1  DROP TABLE migrate09;
 2  --
 3  CREATE TABLE migrate09
 4    (attr1  char(900),
 5     attr2  char(200))
 6  PCTFREE 0
 7  PCTUSED 99;
 8  --
 9  INSERT INTO migrate09 (attr1) VALUES ('1');
10  INSERT INTO migrate09 (attr1) VALUES ('2');
11  --
12  UPDATE migrate09 set attr2 = 'a';
13  --
14  DROP TABLE chain09;
15  --
16  CREATE TABLE chain09
17    (attr1 char(2000),
18     attr2 char(2000));
19  --
20  insert into chain09 values ('a', 'b');
```

```
SQL> start d:\orant\rdbms80\admin\utlchain.sql

Table created.

SQL> describe chained_rows;
 Name                                    Null?    Type
 --------------------------------------- -------- ----
 OWNER_NAME                                       VARCHAR2(30)
 TABLE_NAME                                       VARCHAR2(30)
 CLUSTER_NAME                                     VARCHAR2(30)
 PARTITION_NAME                                   VARCHAR2(30)
 HEAD_ROWID                                       ROWID
 ANALYZE_TIMESTAMP                                DATE

SQL> |
```

Figure 9.3 Creating and describing the CHAINED_ROWS table in SQL*Plus.

In lines 3 through 7, the script creates a table called MIGRATE09. Script lines 16 through 18 create a second table called CHAIN09. The script also inserts two rows into CHAIN09 and one row into MIGRATE09.

The two tables CHAIN09 and MIGRATE09 are shown in Figure 9.4 and are composed of attributes of data type CHAR. Oracle8 will right-pad fields of this type with blanks so that they assume their maximum length. The values of PCTFREE and PCTUSED are not very realistic, but they do help to induce row migration for the purposes of this example.

3. Use the START command to load and execute the CHP9_4.SQL script to determine whether any chained or migrated rows exist in the CHAIN09 or MIGRATE09 tables.

How It Works

Step 1 creates the CHAINED_ROWS table in the WAITE account's default tablespace. Step 2 creates two tables that will subsequently suffer from row chaining, row migration, or both. In step 3, the CHP9_4.SQL script issues the ANALYZE command with the `list chained rows into` clause to insert the ROWIDs of any chained or migrated rows in the tables CHAIN09 or MIGRATE09 into the CHAINED_ROWS table. The final command in the script queries the CHAINED_ROWS table, exposing any chained or migrated rows. The script and its output appear in Figure 9.5.

The script results in Figure 9.5 indicate that there is one chained or migrated row in both the CHAIN09 and MIGRATE09 tables.

Comments

This How-To indicated rows in the CHAIN09 and MIGRATE09 tables that Oracle8 either chained or migrated. The next logical question is "Are the rows described in CHAINED_ROWS really chained rows, or might they be migrated rows?" More compelling still is this question: "How can I resolve this situation?" How-To 9.3 is the place to look for answers.

```
SQL> describe chain09
 Name                                     Null?    Type
 ---------------------------------------- -------- ----
 ATTR1                                             CHAR(2000)
 ATTR2                                             CHAR(2000)

SQL> describe migrate09
 Name                                     Null?    Type
 ---------------------------------------- -------- ----
 ATTR1                                             CHAR(900)
 ATTR2                                             CHAR(200)

SQL> |
```

Figure 9.4 Describing the CHAIN09 and MIGRATE09 tables in SQL*Plus.

```
SQL> start chp9_5
SQL>
SQL> analyze table migrate09
  2  list chained rows into chained_rows;

Table analyzed.

SQL>
SQL> analyze table chain09
  2  list chained rows into chained_rows;

Table analyzed.

SQL>
SQL> SELECT owner_name,table_name,head_rowid
  2  FROM chained_rows;

OWNER_NAME TABLE_NAME                          HEAD_ROWID
---------- --------------------------------    --------------------
WAITE      CHAIN09                             AAAAktAACAAAABkAAA
WAITE      MIGRATE09                           AAAAksAACAAAABYAAA

SQL>
```

Figure 9.5 Analyzing the CHAIN09 and
MIGRATE09 tables in SQL*Plus.

You can also detect the presence of chained rows by querying the system statistic called "table fetch continued row" in the V$SYSSTAT dynamic performance table. This table and a query to check for chained-row activity are displayed in Figure 9.6.

Running this query repeatedly and examining its results over time will help you ascertain that there is chained-row activity in the database. Unfortunately, the query only indicates that somewhere in the database, some chained rows exist, and some user or application has read them. In other words, with respect to row chaining, the V$SYSSTAT table only indicates that you have some more work to do. If you have no idea where the chained rows exist, then the best plan of attack is to use the ANALYZE command with the `list chained rows into` clause on a regular basis and examine the CHAINED_ROWS table.

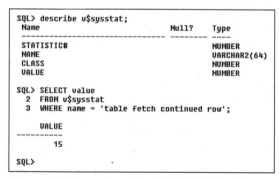

```
SQL> describe v$sysstat;
 Name                                Null?     Type
 ----------------------------------- --------- ----
 STATISTIC#                                    NUMBER
 NAME                                          VARCHAR2(64)
 CLASS                                         NUMBER
 VALUE                                         NUMBER

SQL> SELECT value
  2  FROM v$sysstat
  3  WHERE name = 'table fetch continued row';

    VALUE
 ----------
        15

SQL>
```

Figure 9.6 Querying the V$SYSSTAT table
to check for row chaining in SQL*Plus.

Proactive DBAs attempt to prevent chaining and migration. This is easy to say and hard to do unless the DBA has intimate knowledge of the data that will eventually reside in the database. Skillful use of the PCTFREE parameter in conjunction with awareness of the row changes caused by typical update statements can minimize or eliminate row migration. The difficult task is to quantify the typical update statement. A DBA seeking to prevent row migration must be armed with similar knowledge. Specifically, during database creation it must choose the database block size to accommodate the largest row that will ever be stored in any table. This is a tall order for most production database administrators.

COMPLEXITY
INTERMEDIATE

9.3 How do I...
Correct row migration in tables?

Problem

I have used the techniques in How-To 9.2 to analyze some database tables and have discovered that some of the tables in my database do indeed contain chained or migrated rows. How can I correct this state so that each table row resides entirely in a single block?

Technique

Using the sample tables from How-To 9.2, including the CHAINED_ROWS table, move the table rows in question to a temporary table, delete them from the original table, and copy them back to the original table from the temporary table.

Steps

1. Run SQL*Plus and connect as the WAITE user. Use the START command to load and execute the CHP9_3.SQL script and the CHP9_4.SQL script. See the previous How-To for an in-depth explanation of the SQL statements in these scripts.

2. While still in SQL*Plus, issue these two START commands to execute the CHP9_5 script for the CHAIN09 and MIGRATE09 tables: `start chp9_5 migrate09` and `start chp9_5 chain09`. This CHP9_5 script appears in Listing 9.2.

Listing 9.2 The CHP9_5 script attempts to correct row migration

```
 1  DROP TABLE temp;
 2  --
 3  CREATE TABLE temp AS
 4   SELECT * FROM &1
 5   WHERE rowid IN
 6    (SELECT head_rowid FROM chained_rows
 7     WHERE table_name = upper('&1'));
 8  --
 9  DELETE FROM &1
10  WHERE rowid IN
11    (SELECT head_rowid FROM chained_rows
12     WHERE table_name = upper('&1'));
13  --
14  INSERT INTO &1
15* SELECT * FROM temp;
```

The script makes multiple use of a single substitution variable that contains the name of the table containing the migrated rows. You'll call this the *target table* for the remainder of this discussion. The SQL function UPPER appears throughout the script to convert the target table name to uppercase. This is necessary if the user invokes this script with the table name in lowercase because the CHAINED_ROWS table stores the table name in uppercase.

Line 1 drops the table TEMP created by previous invocations of this script. Lines 3 through 8 recreate the TEMP table and populate it with any rows from the target table whose ROWIDs appear in the CHAINED_ROWS table. Lines 9 through 12 delete these same rows from the target table. Lines 14 and 15, finally, insert the problematic rows back into the target table.

3. While still in SQL*Plus, use the START command to load and execute the script CHP9_4.SQL. This script analyzes the CHAIN09 and MIGRATE09 tables again to help determine what effect, if any, the preceding steps had on these tables.

How It Works

Step 1 recreates the CHAIN09 and MIGRATE09 tables from the previous How-To. Step 2 attempts to correct row migration by essentially giving the Oracle8 server another chance to insert the offending rows, identified in the CHAINED_ROWS table, back into the target table. Step 3 analyzes the two sample tables after the curative measures applied in step 2. The results of the re-analysis of the two sample tables appear in Figure 9.7.

```
SQL> start chp9_5
SQL>
SQL> analyze table migrate09
  2  list chained rows into chained_rows;

Table analyzed.

SQL>
SQL> analyze table chain09
  2  list chained rows into chained_rows;

Table analyzed.

SQL>
SQL> SELECT owner_name,table_name,head_rowid
  2  FROM chained_rows;

OWNER_NAME TABLE_NAME                          HEAD_ROWID
---------- ----------------------------------- --------------------
WAITE      CHAIN09                             AAAAk7AACAAAABkAAB

SQL> |
```

Figure 9.7 Analyzing the CHAIN09 and
MIGRATE09 tables after an attempt to correct
row migration.

Notice that the CHAIN09 table is still listed in the CHAINED_ROWS table. Why? The answer is that even after the steps in this How-To gave Oracle8 another opportunity to insert this problematic row from the CHAIN09 table, the row still occupies more than one data block. Oracle8 did not migrate this row because of an update statement like the row from the MIGRATE09 table. Oracle8 chained this row because it contains 4000 bytes of data and the database block size is only 2048 bytes. The row is too large to fit in any database block; the DBA can move it to another table and re-insert it in the target table until the Oracle9 release date, and the row will still be chained.

Comments

Row migration can contribute to degraded database performance, but it is often resolvable using the preceding techniques. If it is not feasible to create a table to temporarily store the migrated rows, as in this How-To, then the export and import utilities can help resolve row migration problems. After the DBA resolves migrated row difficulties with one of these techniques, an increase in the PCTFREE parameter can decrease migration frequency in the future. (Recall that the value of this parameter is equal to the amount of database block space, expressed as a percent, that Oracle8 attempts to keep free for future updates.)

Row chaining is more problematic because the only way to address it is usually to rebuild the database with a larger database block size. This intricate process requires a full database export, database recreation, and database import. Moreover, if the database's primary function is online transaction processing, a larger block size can impede database operation. This performance degradation could more than offset any gains arising from elimination of row chaining. In general, this discussion emphasizes the need for benchmarking in a test environment to identify and assess unintended side effects of database parameter modifications.

COMPLEXITY
INTERMEDIATE

9.4 How do I...
Determine and coalesce the free space in a tablespace?

Problem

I administer some Oracle8 tablespaces that occasionally report space allocation errors. When this happens, I add data files to the tablespace or reorganize tables as needed to eliminate the problem. How do I monitor tablespace free space proactively so I can avoid space errors in the future?

Technique

The Oracle8 server maintains a data dictionary view, DBA_FREE_SPACE, that contains information about the amount of free space in a tablespace. Table 9.2 summarizes this view.

Table 9.2 The DBA_FREE_SPACE data dictionary view

COLUMN	COLUMN DESCRIPTION
TABLESPACE_NAME	Name of the tablespace containing the extent
FILE_ID	ID number of the file containing the extent
BLOCK_ID	Starting block number of the extent
BYTES	Size of the extent in bytes
BLOCKS	Size of the extent in Oracle blocks
RELATIVE_FNO	Relative file number of the first extent block

This view contains one row for each free extent in each tablespace. To report the total number of free bytes, the query need only use the SUM aggregate function, but this is not the most important measure of free space.

As users and applications create and delete database objects, the total amount of free space in a tablespace can become fragmented across multiple extents. Should this happen, users might not be able to create a new extent, even though the requested extent is smaller than the total amount of free space in a tablespace. Figure 9.8 illustrates a situation like this where a tablespace contains 90KB of free space, yet a DDL statement asking for an initial extent of 40KB will fail.

Allocated Extent	Free Extent 1 30 Kbytes	Free Extent 2 30 Kbytes	Free Extent 3 30 Kbytes	Allocated Extent

Figure 9.8 A tablespace with free space fragmentation.

Armed with an appreciation of contiguous free space, another data dictionary view, DBA_FREE_SPACE_COALESCED, is helpful when a DBA needs to determine the status of a tablespace's free space (see Table 9.3).

Table 9.3 The DBA_FREE_SPACE_COALESCED data dictionary view

COLUMN	COLUMN DESCRIPTION
TABLESPACE_NAME	Name of tablespace
TOTAL_EXTENTS	Total number of free extents in tablespace
EXTENTS_COALESCED	Total number of coalesced free extents in tablespace
PERCENT_EXTENTS_COALESCED	Percentage of coalesced free extents in tablespace
TOTAL_BYTES	Total number of free bytes in tablespace
BYTES_COALESCED	Total number of coalesced free bytes in tablespace
TOTAL_BLOCKS	Total number of free Oracle blocks in tablespace
BLOCKS_COALESCED	Total number of coalesced free Oracle blocks in tablespace
PERCENT_BLOCKS_COALESCED	Percentage of coalesced free Oracle blocks in tablespace

Steps

1. Run SQL*Plus and connect as the WAITE user. Use the START command to load and execute the CHP9_6.SQL script; the script and its output appear in Figure 9.9.

```
SQL> start chp9_11
SQL>
SQL> SELECT dfsc.tablespace_name,
  2         dfsc.total_extents,
  3         dfsc.total_bytes,
  4         dfsc.bytes_coalesced,
  5         max(dfs.bytes) LARGEST
  6  FROM dba_free_space_coalesced dfsc, dba_free_space dfs
  7  WHERE dfsc.tablespace_name = dfs.tablespace_name
  8  GROUP BY dfsc.tablespace_name, dfsc.total_extents,
  9         dfsc.total_bytes, dfsc.bytes_coalesced;

TABLESPACE_NAME  TOTAL_EXTENTS  TOTAL_BYTES  BYTES_COALESCED    LARGEST
---------------  -------------  -----------  ---------------    -------
RBS                          1      2322432          2322432    2322432
SYSTEM                       7     18375168         18375168    9371648
TEMP                         1      5240832          5240832    5240832
USERS                        2      4999168          1034240    3964928

SQL>
```

Figure 9.9 Reporting free space fragmentation.

This script reports the largest free space extent via the calculation in line 5 and also calculates the percentage of total free bytes that exist in coalesced space via the calculation in line 4.

2. To coalesce the adjacent free extents in a tablespace, issue the `ALTER TABLESPACE <tablespace name> COALESCE` command.

3. Rerun the script CHP9_6.SQL to observe improvements, if any, that the command in Step 2 made to the tablespace's free extents. The results of Steps 2 and 3 appear in Figure 9.10.

How It Works

Notice in Figure 9.9 that only 20 percent of the free bytes existed in coalesced space. Figure 9.10 reports that after completion of the ALTER TABLESPACE command with the COALESCE option, all the USER tablespace's free bytes exist in coalesced extents.

Comments

The COALESCE option of the ALTER TABLESPACE command is an attempt to address some of the shortcomings of the SMON process, which is supposed to be performing the same function every two hours. Unfortunately, the SMON processes data files by file number, and if a database includes many data files, SMON always shuts down before it has visited all the data files in large databases.

A natural question is this: "If the ALTER TABLESPACE command with the COALESCE really is coalescing free space, why, at the culmination of this command, are there still multiple extents of free space in the some of the

```
SQL> alter tablespace users coalesce;

Tablespace altered.

SQL> start chp9_11
SQL>
SQL> SELECT dfsc.tablespace_name,
  2          dfsc.total_extents,
  3          dfsc.total_bytes,
  4          round((dfsc.bytes_coalesced/dfsc.total_bytes)*100, 0) percent_coa
  5          max(dfs.bytes) LARGEST
  6   FROM dba_free_space_coalesced dfsc, dba_free_space dfs
  7   WHERE dfsc.tablespace_name = dfs.tablespace_name
  8   GROUP BY dfsc.tablespace_name, dfsc.total_extents,
  9          dfsc.total_bytes, dfsc.bytes_coalesced;

TABLESPACE_NAME  TOTAL_EXTENTS TOTAL_BYTES PERCENT_COALESCED    LARGEST
---------------  ------------- ----------- -----------------  ----------
RBS                          1     2322432               100     2322432
SYSTEM                       7    10375168               100     9371648
TEMP                         1     5240832               100     5240832
USERS                        1     4999168               100     4999168

SQL>
```

Figure 9.10 Attempting to correct free space fragmentation.

tablespaces?" The answer is that this version of the ALTER TABLESPACE command coalesces adjacent or contiguous free space extents (this sort of fragmentation, pictured in Figure 9.8, is sometimes referred to as *honeycomb* fragmentation). It does not collapse bubbles of free space into one extent when those bubbles are separated by allocated extents. Currently, DBAs can eliminate this type of fragmentation (sometimes called *bubble* fragmentation) only by exporting every object from the tablespace using the COMPRESS=Y flag on the export command, dropping and re-creating the tablespace, and importing all the objects back into the tablespace.

COMPLEXITY
INTERMEDIATE

9.5 How do I...
Allocate unlimited extents for a database object?

Problem

I administer an Oracle8 instance that frequently reports an inability to allocate new extents. This happens for database tables, indexes, and rollback segments. I have set the MAXEXTENTS storage parameter to the maximum value for the database block size. How can I avoid these "failure to extend" errors?

Technique

With the advent of Oracle version 7.3, DBAs and developers can set the value of the MAXEXTENTS storage parameter to UNLIMITED. The UNLIMITED specification is valid at object creation time, and Oracle8 users can easily convert existing objects, such as rollback segments, to unlimited format as well. This How-To focuses on converting a rollback segment to unlimited extent format.

Steps

1. Run SQL*Plus and connect as the WAITE user. Use the START command to load and execute the script CHP9_7.SQL, as shown in Figure 9.11.

A SQL*Plus substitution variable enables the user to pass the name of any rollback segment to the CHP9_7.SQL script. The first SQL statement takes the rollback segment offline, a required prerequisite to changing a rollback segment's MAXEXTENTS storage parameter. The next SQL statement modifies the rollback segment's storage clause. The third and final statement puts the rollback segment back online, making it available to the Oracle8 instance.

```
SQL> start chp9_7 rbs1
SQL>
SQL> ALTER ROLLBACK SEGMENT &1 OFFLINE;

Rollback segment altered.

SQL>
SQL> ALTER ROLLBACK SEGMENT &1
  2      STORAGE (MAXEXTENTS UNLIMITED);

Rollback segment altered.

SQL>
SQL> ALTER ROLLBACK SEGMENT &1 ONLINE;

Rollback segment altered.

SQL> |
```

Figure 9.11 Script CHP9_7.SQL
converts a rollback segment to
unlimited extents format.

2. Use the START command to load and execute the script CHP9_8.SQL,
which queries the DBA_ROLLBACK_SEGS data dictionary table to
confirm the successful completion of the operation in Step 1. This query
and its result appear in Figure 9.12.

How It Works

The script takes the rollback segment offline and changes the value of the
MAXEXTENTS storage parameter. Step 2 confirms the change in the Oracle8
data dictionary.

```
SQL> start chp9_8
SQL> SELECT segment_name, max_extents, status
  2  FROM   dba_rollback_segs;

SEGMENT_NAME                    MAX_EXTENTS STATUS
------------------------------- ----------- ----------------
SYSTEM                                  121 ONLINE
RBS1                             2147483645 ONLINE
RBS2                                    121 ONLINE
RBS3                                    121 ONLINE
RBS4                                    121 ONLINE
RBS5                                    121 ONLINE

6 rows selected.

SQL> |
```

Figure 9.12 Script CHP9_8.SQL queries the
DBA_ROLLBACK_SEGS data dictionary view in
SQL*Plus.

```
SQL>
SQL> CREATE TABLE unl_extents
  2      (attr1        number(5))
  3      STORAGE
  4        (INITIAL      5k
  5         NEXT         5k
  6         PCTINCREASE 0
  7         MAXEXTENTS UNLIMITED)
  8  ;

Table created.

SQL>
SQL> SELECT table_name, max_extents
  2  FROM   DBA_TABLES
  3  WHERE  table_name = 'UNL_EXTENTS' and owner = 'WAITE';

TABLE_NAME                       MAX_EXTENTS
-------------------------------- -----------
UNL_EXTENTS                       2147483645

SQL> |
```

Figure 9.13 Creating a table with unlimited extents.

Comments

To create a table in unlimited extent format, specify the MAXEXTENTS UNLIMITED option in the storage clause of the CREATE_TABLE statement. Figure 9.13 illustrates this operation.

Note that the queries in Figures 9.12 and 9.13 report the value of the MAXEXTENTS parameter as 2147483645. Apparently, the UNLIMITED value does not mean that the number of allowable extents is literally unlimited, but 2 billion extents should be adequate for most of us!

The initialization parameter COMPATIBLE must be at least 7.3.0.0 to enable you to take advantage of unlimited extents capability.

COMPLEXITY
INTERMEDIATE

9.6 How do I...
Deallocate unused space in a segment?

Problem

I suspect that the initial extent for some of my database objects is much too large. Also, the value of PCTINCREASE for some tables is so large it's likely that Oracle8 has allocated much more space than necessary to these tables. How can I find out whether there is unused space allocated to some objects in the database? If there is unused space, how can I transform the wasted space back into free space?

Technique

The UNUSED_SPACE procedure in the DBMS_SPACE package reveals some segment information absent from the Oracle8 data dictionary. Table 9.4 summarizes this procedure's input and output parameters. This How-To uses this procedure to return the total space and the unused space allocated to a segment.

Table 9.4 UNUSED_SPACE procedure parameters

PARAMETER NAME	PARAMETER TYPE	PARAMETER DESCRIPTION
segment_owner	IN	Owner of the target segment
segment_name	IN	Name of the target segment
segment_type	IN	Type of the segment to be analyzed (TABLE, INDEX, or CLUSTER)
total_blocks	OUT	Total number of blocks in the segment
total_bytes	OUT	Total number of bytes in the segment
unused_blocks	OUT	Number of blocks not used in the segment
unused_bytes	OUT	Number of bytes not used in the segment
last_used_extent_file_id	OUT	File ID of the last extent that contains data
last_used_extent_block_id	OUT	Block ID of the last extent containing data
last_used_block	OUT	Last block within the last extent containing data
partition_name	IN	Partition name of the target segment

The ALTER TABLE statement with the DEALLOCATE option can dynamically return unused space in database segments. Use this statement after the UNUSED_SPACE procedure indicates that some segments are larger than necessary.

Steps

1. Run SQL*Plus and connect as the WAITE user. Use the START command to load and execute the script CHP9_9.SQL. The script appears in Listing 9.3.

Listing 9.3 The script CHP9_9.SQL creates a nested table

```
2   DROP TABLE dept09;
3   DROP TYPE emp_t_table09;
4   DROP TYPE emp_t09;
5   CREATE TYPE emp_t09 AS OBJECT
6   (empno  number(4),
7    ename  varchar2(10)
8   );
9   CREATE TYPE emp_t_table09 AS TABLE OF emp_t09;
```

continued on next page

continued from previous page

```
10   CREATE TABLE dept09
11   (
12    deptno    number(2),
13    dname     varchar2(14),
14    emps      emp_t_table09
15   )
16   NESTED TABLE emps STORE AS dept_emps09
17   STORAGE
18     (INITIAL 50k
19      NEXT    50k
20     );
21   INSERT INTO dept09 VALUES
22   (
23    1, 'IT', emp_t_table09(emp_t09(1, 'JOE')
24                           emp_t09(2, 'JANE'))
25   );
```

This script creates a table called DEPT09 that contains a nested table column called EMPS (read more about nested tables in Chapter 16). These tables are similar to the EMP and DEPT tables traditionally found in the schema SCOTT.

The preceding DDL contains a new twist on these common tables using the nested table capability of the Oracle8 server. Lines 5 through 7 create an object type called EMP_T09 to describe an employee. Line 9 creates a table of the newly defined EMP_T09 type. Lines 10 through 20 create the DEPT09 table, which stores departments and, using the nested table, the employees who work in each department. Line 16 specifies the storage table to hold the nested table EMPS. This is an Oracle8 segment that users cannot query directly, although it does have its own physical storage parameters. In this case, the storage clause in lines 17 through 20 specifies 50KB for the size of the initial and next extents of the table DEPT. The storage table, EMPS09, inherits the default storage parameters for the tablespace. In lines 21 through 25, a single record is inserted into table DEPT for the Information Technology department. This department currently has two employees: Joe and Jane.

2. Although it is unlikely that the one now in the DEPT09 table has consumed all 50KB of the initial extent, the data dictionary does not contain information indicating how much space that single row requires. The script CHP9_10.SQL creates a stored procedure called SEGSPACE, which can reveal how much segment space is used and how much is free in any data segment; the script appears in Listing 9.4. Use the START command to load and execute the CHP9_10.SQL script.

Listing 9.4 The script CHP9_10.SQL creates the SEGSPACE procedure

```
 1  CREATE OR REPLACE PROCEDURE segspace
 2     (owner IN  varchar2,
 3      name  IN  varchar2,
 4      type  IN  varchar2
 5     )
 6  IS
 7  freespace  number(10);
 8  totalspace number(10);
 9  dummyn     number(10);
10  using      number(10);
11  needs      number(10);
12  BEGIN
13  dbms_space.unused_space(segment_owner => owner,
14                          segment_name => name,
15                          segment_type => type,
16                          total_blocks => dummyn,
17                          total_bytes => totalspace,
18                          unused_blocks => dummyn,
19                          unused_bytes => freespace,
20                          last_used_extent_file_id => dummyn,
21                          last_used_extent_block_id => dummyn,
22                          last_used_block => dummyn,
23                          partition_name => null);
24  using := round(totalspace/1024, 0);
25  needs := round((totalspace-freespace)/1024, 0);
26  dbms_output.put_line ('object ' || name || ' is allocated ' ||
27                          to_char(using) || 'k and is using ' ||
28                          to_char(needs) || 'k');
29  END;
```

SEGSPACE calls the UNUSED_SPACE procedure in lines 13 through 23, using named notation to pass the appropriate parameters. Lines 24 through 26 convert the values returned by the UNUSED_SPACE procedure from bytes to kilobytes. The PUT_LINE procedure that appears in lines 26 through 28 displays the object's name, how much space the object is using, and how much space is free.

3. Use the START command to load and execute the SEGSPACE procedure for the database objects you want to query for space consumption. Figure 9.14 contains the results of running script CHP9_11.SQL, which runs the SEGSPACE procedure against the DEPT09 table and the DEPT_EMPS09 storage table.

Notice that the type passed to the SEGSPACE procedure is TABLE for the DEPT_EMPS09 storage table and for the DEPT09 table.

```
SQL> start chp9_16
SQL>
SQL> execute segspace (owner=>'WAITE', name=>'DEPT09', type=>'TABLE');
object DEPT09 is allocated 50k and is using 4k

PL/SQL procedure successfully completed.

SQL> execute segspace (owner=>'WAITE',name=>'DEPT_EMPS09',type=>'TABLE');
object DEPT_EMPS09 is allocated 20k and is using 4k

PL/SQL procedure successfully completed.

SQL> |
```

Figure 9.14 Script CHP9_11.SQL checks the DEPT09 and DEPT_EMPS09 tables for unused space.

4. Use the ALTER TABLESPACE DEALLOCATE UNUSED command to free allocated but unused space. The script CHP9_12.SQL contains two invocations of this command, one for the DEPT09 table and one for the DEPT_EMPS09 storage table. The script and its output appear in Figure 9.15.

5. Run the UNUSED_SPACE procedure again for the resized tables. Figure 9.16 contains the results of the CHP9_11.SQL script when it runs after the deallocation operation in Step 4.

```
SQL> start chp9_17
SQL>
SQL> alter table dept09 deallocate unused keep 10k;

Table altered.

SQL> alter table dept_emps09 deallocate unused keep 5k;

Table altered.

SQL>
```

Figure 9.15 Script CHP9_12.SQL frees unused space in the DEPT09 table and the DEPT_EMPS09 storage table.

```
SQL> start chp9_16
SQL>
SQL> execute segspace (owner=>'WAITE', name=>'DEPT09', type=>'TABLE');
object DEPT09 is allocated 14k and is using 4k

PL/SQL procedure successfully completed.

SQL> execute segspace (owner=>'WAITE',name=>'DEPT_EMPS09',type=>'TABLE');
object DEPT_EMPS09 is allocated 10k and is using 4k

PL/SQL procedure successfully completed.

SQL>
```

Figure 9.16 Script CHP9_11.SQL checks the DEPT09 and DEPT_EMPS09 tables for unused space after the ALTER TABLESPACE DEALLOCATE command.

How It Works

Steps 2 and 3 summarize creation and use of the SEGSPACE procedure, which acts as a parameterized interface to the UNUSED_SPACE procedure in the Oracle-supplied package_DBMS_SPACE. Step 4 deallocates unused segment space using the ALTER TABLESPACE command with the DEALLOCATE option.

Comments

The alternative to the DEALLOCATE OPTION of the ALTER_TABLESPACE command is to re-create the table with a more appropriate storage clause or to create tablespaces with storage clauses tailored for the tablespace's planned contents. These are admirable goals, but even the most watchful DBA occasionally sizes a table incorrectly. The technique in the How-To provides a much more straightforward method of deallocating unused segment space if it becomes necessary to adjust a table in this way. Note that without the KEEP option in Step 4, the size of the initial extent or space allocated via the number of minimum extents is preserved throughout a deallocation attempt.

COMPLEXITY
INTERMEDIATE

9.7 How do I...
Configure database files to extend automatically?

Problem

I have sized my database files as carefully as I can, but I am concerned that they will run out of space during a crucial database operation. How can I tell the Oracle8 server to extend data files automatically without any DBA intervention?

Technique

Use the AUTOEXTEND option on the `create tablespace` or `alter database` commands to enable autoextend capability on data files. Through these statements you can also specify the size of the increment for Oracle8 to use when the server must autoextend a data file. Query the DBA_DATA_FILES data dictionary view to determine or confirm the autoextend status of data files. This view appears in Table 9.5.

Table 9.5 The DBA_DATA_FILES data dictionary view

COLUMN	COLUMN DESCRIPTION
FILE_NAME	Physical file name
FILE_ID	File number in database
TABLESPACE_NAME	Tablespace to which the file belongs
BYTES	File size in bytes
BLOCKS	File size in blocks
STATUS	File status: AVAILABLE or INVALID
RELATIVE_FNO	File number in tablespace
AUTOEXTENSIBLE	File can autoextend (YES or NO)
MAXBYTES	Limit on file's growth in bytes
MAXBLOCKS	Limit on file's growth in blocks
INCREMENT_BY	Autoextension increment in blocks

Steps

1. Run SQL*Plus and connect as the WAITE user. The script CHP9_13.SQL is operating-system–specific because it contains physical file names. Modify it as necessary for your operating system prior to execution. Use the START command to load and execute CHP9_13.SQL. The script and its output appear in Figure 9.17.

```
SQL> start chp9_12
SQL>
SQL> CREATE TABLESPACE auto09
  2    DATAFILE 'c:\orant\database\auto09.dat'
  3    SIZE 2M
  4    AUTOEXTEND ON
  5    NEXT 500k
  6    MAXSIZE 50M;

Tablespace created.

SQL>
SQL> ALTER DATABASE
  2    DATAFILE 'c:\orant\database\users.dat'
  3    AUTOEXTEND ON;

Database altered.

SQL> |
```

Figure 9.17 Script CHP9_13 creates an autoextensible data file and modifies an existing file to enable autoextension.

The first statement creates a new tablespace called AUTO09, which is a single data file. The initial size of the file is 2MB, but it can autoextend as necessary up to 50MB. The second SQL statement modifies an existing data file so that it can autoextend.

2. Use the START command to load and execute the CHP9_14.SQL script, which queries the DBA_DATA_FILES data dictionary view and lists all data files with autoextend capability. Figure 9.18 contains the script and its output.

How It Works

Step 1 illustrates two methods for enabling autoextend capability for a data file: The first is to create a tablespace consisting of an autoextending file, and the second is to modify an existing data file to autoextend. Step 2 queries the appropriate data dictionary view to confirm the success of Step 1.

Comments

The autoextension defaults do not serve every Oracle8 installation. Figure 9.18 shows that the defaults are accepted for the MAXSIZE and NEXT parameters in the USERS tablespace. Oracle8 set the values of these parameters to 8 gigabytes and 1 block, respectively.

Remember that it is a waste of time to enable autoextension for a data file residing on a full, or nearly full, device. Autoextension in this case fails because of inadequate space availability at the physical level. In such a situation, the options are to rename the data file using the `alter database rename...` statement or to add an additional autoextensible data file, residing on a less populated device, to the appropriate tablespace.

```
SQL> start chp9_13
SQL>
SQL> SELECT tablespace_name, file_name, bytes,
  2          autoextensible, maxbytes, increment_by
  3  FROM dba_data_files
  4  WHERE autoextensible = 'YES';

TABLESPACE  FILE_NAME                       BYTES AUT   MAXBYTES INCREMENT
----------- ------------------------------ -------- --- ---------- ---------
USERS       C:\ORANT\DATABASE\USERS.DAT    5242880 YES 8589930496         1
AUTO09      C:\ORANT\DATABASE\AUTO09.DAT   2097152 YES   52428800       250

SQL> |
```

Figure 9.18 Script CHP9_14 reports on all autoextensible data files.

It is tempting to combine the information in How-To's 9.5 and 9.7 so that database objects and data files can extend without limit. It would appear that this architecture frees DBAs from space management altogether! A database like this, however, will not run out of space until Oracle8 reaches a hardware limitation (usually, a full disk). When this happens, though, options for resolution are limited to freeing disk space, adding another disk, or reorganizing the database to move some data files to less populated media. These operations take time and will delay the offending database operation until the DBA resolves the space limitation. Paradoxically, the autoextend options can increase the need for space management monitoring, so use them with care.

CHAPTER 10

PL/SQL

10

PL/SQL

How do I...

Oracle PL/SQL is a procedural language extension to SQL. It is a sophisticated block-structured programming language that provides the flexibility of third-generation languages in addition to nonprocedural SQL constructs. PL/SQL includes a full range of datatypes, conditional structures, loop structures, and exception handling structures.

Two types of PL/SQL program units exist: anonymous blocks and stored subprograms. PL/SQL subprograms (functions and procedures) promote development of modular code. PL/SQL is tightly integrated with SQL, enabling SQL statements to be executed within PL/SQL programs and PL/SQL functions to be used within SQL statements. The PL/SQL runtime engine executes procedural statements and sends SQL statements to the SQL Statement Executor in the Oracle Server. This runtime engine can reside in the Oracle Server or in an application development tool like Oracle Forms.

This chapter presents techniques that provide a foundation to help you use PL/SQL effectively in developing better applications. All your PL/SQL applications written for Oracle7 will work in Oracle8.

10.1 Create Anonymous PL/SQL Blocks

A *block* is the basic unit of PL/SQL code, which can contain a mix of procedural constructs and SQL statements. All PL/SQL programs are made up of one or more blocks. Each block performs a unit of work within the application, and blocks can be nested to create modular code. The DBMS_OUTPUT package can be used in a PL/SQL block to print text messages in SQL*Plus and is commonly used to debug PL/SQL blocks. This How-To presents examples for creating PL/SQL blocks.

10.2 Achieve Conditional and Looping Control

PL/SQL has three types of IF constructs to control the execution of statements based on Boolean conditions. PL/SQL also contains three basic types of looping constructs. The simple LOOP construct performs a sequence of statements repeatedly until an EXIT statement terminates it. A numeric FOR loop performs a series of statements repeatedly for a specified number of iterations. The WHILE loop tests a Boolean expression and executes the statements as long as the expression evaluates to TRUE. This How-To introduces conditional and looping constructs in PL/SQL.

10.3 Create a Stored Procedure

A stored procedure is a named PL/SQL block stored in the database, making itself accessible to applications. Parameters can be passed to and from stored procedures, creating modular units of reusable code. A standalone statement is used to call a stored procedure in PL/SQL modules. This How-To presents the technique used to create a stored procedure and call it from a PL/SQL block.

10.4   Create a Stored Function

Parameters can be passed to and from a stored function, making it similar to a stored procedure, except that it must be invoked as part of an expression. The return value can be a standard datatype, record variable, and, since PL/SQL version 2.3, a cursor variable. This How-To presents the technique used to create a stored function and calls it from a PL/SQL block.

10.5   Create a Stored Package

A stored package groups related procedures and functions into a single package. Grouping related subprograms into packages extends an object-oriented approach to the development of stored procedures and functions. A package can contain its own local procedures, variables, and datatypes and expose only specified objects to the user. This How-To offers a framework for creating stored packages.

10.6   List Information About Stored Objects in the Database

The USER_OBJECTS data dictionary view can be queried to reveal useful information about stored objects. The USER_OBJECT_SIZE view lets you analyze the size of stored modules. The source code of stored modules can be queried from the USER_SOURCE view. Object dependencies can be listed from the USER_DEPENDENCIES view and the USER_ERRORS view can be used to display compilation errors. This How-To presents queries to examine stored objects.

10.7   Overload Procedures and Functions in Packages

Procedure and function overloading is a useful technique, enabling the same procedure or function to accept multiple parameter lists. Overloading is used extensively in Oracle to make procedures and functions work with parameters of varying datatypes. This How-To presents the method used to overload procedures and functions within packages.

10.8   Create Variables to Represent Database Records and Columns

The %TYPE and %ROWTYPE attributes define the datatype of a variable in the declarative section of a block. The %TYPE attribute declares a variable to represent a column within a table, ensuring that the variable datatype can handle the values in the column. The %ROWTYPE attribute creates a record variable representing all the columns in a record. This How-To uses these attributes to declare variables representing database records, columns, and rows.

10.9   Achieve Array Functionality with PL/SQL Index-By Tables

PL/SQL Index-By tables are similar to one-dimensional arrays in other procedural languages. The implementation of a PL/SQL Index-By table requires the creation of a datatype and a variable declaration of the datatype created. This How-To presents the method for creating a PL/SQL table and using it like an array.

10.10 Handle Predefined Exceptions and System Errors

Exception handlers in the exception section of a block handle system errors and user-defined errors. Unhandled exceptions cause abnormal termination of a PL/SQL block, and system errors cause predefined exceptions to occur. This How-To covers the process of handling predefined exceptions and system errors without predefined exceptions.

10.11 Handle User-Defined Exceptions and User-Defined Errors

An exception does not have to be a system error returned by Oracle. It is possible to create a user-defined exception, which can be raised and handled with a RAISE statement. User-defined exceptions enable you to treat a violation of business rules as an exception. The built-in procedure RAISE_APPLICATION_ERROR enables you to raise an exception with a user-defined error number and user-defined error message. When an exception occurs in a stored subprogram, the exception must be handled either in the subprogram or in the calling PL/SQL code. This How-To presents the method used to create, raise, and handle user-defined exceptions.

10.12 Rebuild Statements to Create Stored Modules

As you have done throughout the book, you can use the data dictionary and SQL*Plus to rebuild DDL statements. Because the source code for stored modules is contained in the data dictionary, it is possible to rebuild the statements used to create existing stored modules. This How-To presents a query to generate DDL statements to create stored modules in addition to a query that enables you to recompile stored modules in your schema.

COMPLEXITY
BEGINNING

10.1 How do I...
Create anonymous PL/SQL blocks?

Problem

I want to perform tasks not well-suited for SQL on the database, such as performing conditional logic and working with the procedural components available in PL/SQL. Because the PL/SQL block is the smallest logical unit of PL/SQL code, I want to start by creating a PL/SQL block to perform a simple action. How do I create anonymous PL/SQL blocks in Oracle?

Technique

PL/SQL is a block structured language. PL/SQL blocks are implemented using anonymous blocks, procedures, and functions. Unlike functions and procedures, no name is associated with an anonymous PL/SQL block and, hence, cannot be referenced from other PL/SQL blocks. Anonymous blocks are standalone; they neither take input parameters nor return values and can be nested within another PL/SQL block. The anonymous PL/SQL block is made up of three sections, of which two are optional (indicated by square brackets):

```
[DECLARE
   Declarative Section]
BEGIN
   Executable Section
[EXCEPTION
   Exception handling Section]
END;
```

The declarative section, started with the DECLARE statement, is where objects are declared. User-defined variables, datatypes, cursors, and PL/SQL subprograms local to the block are declared in this section. The objects within the declarative section are limited to the block and cannot be used outside it. The executable section starts with the BEGIN keyword and contains procedural and SQL statements that are executed when the block is run. Next, the exception section starts with the EXCEPTION keyword and contains exception handlers to handle errors that occur during processing. The error handling code in the exception section is executed only when an error occurs. A PL/SQL block is terminated with the END statement and a semicolon.

Steps

1. Run SQL*Plus and connect to the database as the WAITE user account. Run the CHP10_1.SQL file at the prompt. It has the simplest form of the anonymous block, one that does not have the optional declaration and exception sections. The PL/SQL block contained in the file calls the DBMS_OUTPUT.PUT_LINE to display a message in SQL*Plus. Figure 10.1 shows the code and the output of the anonymous PL/SQL block in SQL*Plus.

For the output of the DBMS_OUTPUT package to be displayed in SQL*Plus, the SERVEROUTPUT system variable must be set to ON. The anonymous block calls the PUT_LINE procedure in the DBMS_OUTPUT built-in package to display a text message in SQL*Plus. The PUT_LINE procedure is passed a string to be displayed within SQL*Plus and can accept DATE and NUMBER variables as well. To display data of other datatypes, a conversion function such as TO_CHAR must be used. Table 10.1 shows procedures in the DBMS_OUTPUT package.

```
SQL> START CHP10_1
SQL> SET SERVEROUTPUT ON
SQL> BEGIN
  2    DBMS_OUTPUT.PUT_LINE('HELLO WORLD');
  3  END;
  4  /
HELLO WORLD

PL/SQL procedure successfully completed.

SQL> SHOW ERRORS
No errors.
SQL>
```

Figure 10.1 The output of the
DBMS_OUPUT.PUT_LINE procedure.

Table 10.1 Procedures in the DBMS_OUTPUT package

PROCEDURE	DESCRIPTION
ENABLE	Enables message output (or SERVEROUTPUT ON)
DISABLE	Disables message output (or SERVEROUTPUT OFF)
PUT_LINE	Puts the output on a new line
PUT	Puts the output on the same line
NEW_LINE	Signals the beginning of a new line
GET_LINE	Retrieves a line from the buffer
GET_LINES	Retrieves an array of lines from the buffer

Note that line 4 in the file has a / signaling SQL*Plus to run the anonymous block after it has loaded the block into the SQL*Plus buffer. The DBMS_OUTPUT.PUT_LINE procedure is important because it is often used to debug PL/SQL code.

To debug a PL/SQL block with compilation errors, issue a SHOW ERRORS command at the SQL*Plus prompt; you can also include the SHOW ERRORS command at the end of the block in the line following the /, as shown in the preceding example. This makes SQL*Plus display any errors generated by the last module compiled in the current session. A blank line is left as the line following the /, to avoid a benign SQL*Plus error (**Input truncated to *n* characters**).

2. Run CHP10_2.SQL, which has a PL/SQL block that declares and uses a numeric variable. Figure 10.2 shows the code and output.

Lines 1 and 2 contain the declarative section of the block, which is started with the DECLARE keyword and continues until the BEGIN keyword. When declaring variables in PL/SQL, the datatype is specified after the variable name. Lines 4 and 5 contain the code segment executed when the block is run. The statement on line 4 sets the value of the variable ORDER_NO to the number 3000. The colon-equals operator (:=) is used to set a variable to a value in PL/SQL.

```
SQL> START CHP10_2
SQL> SET ECHO ON
SQL> SET SERUEROUTPUT ON
SQL> DECLARE
  2     ORDER_NO NUMBER(5);
  3  BEGIN
  4     ORDER_NO := 3000;
  5     DBMS_OUTPUT.PUT_LINE('ORDER_NO = ' || ORDER_NO);
  6  EXCEPTION
  7     WHEN OTHERS THEN
  8        NULL;
  9  END;
 10  /
ORDER_NO = 3000

PL/SQL procedure successfully completed.

SQL> |
```

Figure 10.2 Output of the anonymous block in CHP10_2.

Table 10.2 contains the operators used in PL/SQL, listed in the order of descending precedence; operators with higher precedence are evaluated first. Whenever the precedence of operators is in doubt or you need to override the default precedence, use the (and) expression delimiters around the expression that needs to be evaluated first.

Exceptions are handled in the exception section starting on line 6. The WHEN OTHERS exception handler in line 7 handles any exceptions not dealt with by other exception handlers and must be the last exception handler. The NULL statement in line 8 is a "do nothing" construct, and here it specifies that no action is taken for exceptions.

How-To's 10.11 and 10.12 cover the process of handling exceptions in detail. Both the declarative section and the exception section are optional. If you don't need any local variables for your block or you don't want to handle exceptions that occur, these sections can be removed.

Table 10.2 PL/SQL operators

OPERATOR	DESCRIPTION
**	Exponentiation
NOT†	Logical negation
+	Unary identity
-	Unary negation
*	Multiplication
/	Division
+	Addition
-	Subtraction

continued on next page

continued from previous page

OPERATOR	DESCRIPTION
¦ ¦	String concatenation
=	Equality
!=	Not equals
<>	Not equals
~=	Not equals
^=	Not equals
<	Less than
>	Greater than
<=	Less than or equal
>=	Greater than or equal
IS NULL	Comparison for null
LIKE	Comparison for match
BETWEEN	Range of values
IN	Set membership
AND	Conjunction
OR	Inclusion
:=	Assignment
=>	Association
..	Range operator

† Negation operator NOT can be used as IS NOT NULL, NOT LIKE, NOT BETWEEN, NOT IN.

3. Run the CHP10_3.SQL file that contains a nested PL/SQL block, which is a PL/SQL block declared inside another block. The block also presents the methods for creating comments within PL/SQL code. The nested block also declares constants and variables with a variety of datatypes. The output is shown in Figure 10.3.

```
22    WHEN OTHERS THEN
23        DBMS_OUTPUT.PUT_LINE('Outer block error.');
24    END;
25  /
ORDER NO = 26
CUST_NAME = JOE SHMOE
PI = 3.1416

PL/SQL procedure successfully completed.

SQL> |
```

Figure 10.3 Output of the nested block in CHP10_3.SQL.

```
SQL> START CHP10_3
SQL> SET ECHO ON
SQL> SET SERVEROUTPUT ON
SQL> DECLARE
  2     ORDER_DATE DATE;                -- Date variable
  3     ORDER_NO NUMBER := 24;          -- Initialized numeric variable
  4     PI CONSTANT NUMBER := 3.1416;   -- Numeric constant
  5     /* The declarative section of the outer block ends here. All the
  6        variables declared above have scope limited to the outer block */
  7  BEGIN
  8     ORDER_NO := 25;
  9     DECLARE                         -- Inner block begins here
 10       CUST_NAME VARCHAR2(30);       -- Character variable with a width of 20
 11     BEGIN
 12       ORDER_NO := 26;               -- Outer block variable used in inner block
 13       CUST_NAME := 'JOE SHMOE';
 14       DBMS_OUTPUT.PUT_LINE('ORDER NO = ' || ORDER_NO);
 15       DBMS_OUTPUT.PUT_LINE('CUST_NAME = ' || CUST_NAME);
 16       DBMS_OUTPUT.PUT_LINE('PI = ' || PI);
 17     EXCEPTION
 18       WHEN OTHERS THEN
 19         DBMS_OUTPUT.PUT_LINE('Inner block error.');
 20     END;                            -- Inner block ends here
 21  EXCEPTION
 22     WHEN OTHERS THEN
 23         DBMS_OUTPUT.PUT_LINE('Outer block error.');
 24  END;
 25  /
```

Lines 1 to 6 present the declarative section of the outermost block. Line 2 declares a DATE variable and also presents the syntax of a single line comment, specified with two dashes --. Line 3 declares a NUMBER variable and sets its default value to 24. Line 4 declares a constant numeric value. Lines 5 and 6 present the syntax for a multiline comment, which uses the same style as the C language and starts with /* and ends with */. The outer PL/SQL block begins on line 7 and ends on line 24. The nested inner block begins on line 9 and ends on line 20. The variables declared in the inner block are visible within the inner block but not in the outer block. Variables created in both the inner and outer blocks can be accessed in the inner block. The exception section defined in lines 17 through 19 only handles exceptions for the inner block. Any exceptions in the outer block are handled by the exception section defined in lines 21 through 23. Table 10.3 contains the PL/SQL scalar datatypes and subtypes available to all PL/SQL modules.

Table 10.3 PL/SQL scalar datatypes

NAME	TYPE	DESCRIPTION
DATE	Date	Date values with a format as in the database
BOOLEAN	Boolean	TRUE or FALSE
NUMBER	Numeric	Integer and real values that can be defined with a precision and scale
BINARY_INTEGER	Numeric	Signed integers, less storage than NUMBER
POSITIVE	Numeric	Subtype of BINARY_INTEGER, positive integer values
POSITIVEN	Numeric	Subtype of BINARY_INTEGER, positive integer values, null values not allowed
NATURAL	Numeric	Subtype of BINARY_INTEGER, non-negative integer values
NATURALN	Numeric	Subtype of BINARY_INTEGER, non-negative integer values, null values not allowed
SIGNTYPE	Numeric	-1, 0, or 1 values only
DECIMAL	Numeric	Subtype of NUMBER, decimal
DEC	Numeric	Same as DECIMAL
DOUBLE PRECISION		Subtype of NUMBER, real numbers with high precision
INTEGER	Numeric	Subtype of NUMBER, integer values only
INT	Numeric	Same as INTEGER
NUMERIC	Numeric	Same as NUMBER
REAL	Numeric	Same as NUMBER
SMALLINT	Numeric	Subtype of NUMBER, small range of integer
FLOAT	Numeric	Subtype of NUMBER, requires a binary precision but no scale
PLS_INTEGER	Numeric	Signed integers, faster than NUMBER and BINARY_INTEGER
VARCHAR2	Character	Variable-length character strings
CHAR	Character	Fixed-length character strings
CHARACTER	Character	Same as CHAR
LONG	Character	Variable-length byte strings
RAW	Character	Binary data or byte strings, no character set conversions
LONG RAW	Character	Binary data or byte strings
ROWID	Character	Consists of data object number, data file, data block, and row in the data block
NCHAR	Character	Fixed-length NLS character strings
NVARCHAR2	Character	Variable-length NLS character strings

† All PL/SQL character datatypes have a maximum limit of 32,767 bytes with the exception of ROWID, which is used to represent row addresses.

†† Table columns and PL/SQL datatypes can have different maximum limits; a VARCHAR2 database column can be up to 4000 bytes long.

The maximum width of a RAW column is 2000 bytes, whereas LONG and LONG RAW columns can hold as much as 2GB of data.

How It Works

Step 1 presents a simple PL/SQL block showing the basic structure of a block. In Step 2, the block contains a declarative section, an executable section, and an exception section. Both the declarative and exception sections are optional. Step 3 demonstrates how blocks can be nested in PL/SQL, and nesting is important when you need exceptions handled separately within each block. Both the outermost and innermost blocks can contain all three block sections. Step 3 also declares variables of a variety of scalar datatypes in a PL/SQL block.

Comments

The PL/SQL block is the fundamental structure in PL/SQL. Anonymous PL/SQL blocks provide control over scope and visibility of identifiers and exception handling. Anonymous blocks are not stored in the database, and typically they are constructed dynamically to be executed only once. You can nest anonymous blocks in the execution or exception section of a PL/SQL block but not in the declarative section. To declare a PL/SQL block in the declarative section, the block has to be a local subprogram—a function or procedure local to the block, which is addressed in How-To 10.4.

COMPLEXITY
BEGINNING

10.2 How do I...
Achieve conditional and looping control?

Problem

I need to use conditional statements like IF...THEN...ELSE, to control program behavior. I also need to perform looping operations within my PL/SQL blocks. How do I achieve conditional and looping control in PL/SQL?

Technique

Conditional Control

Three types of IF statements exist in PL/SQL. The IF statement shown next is the simplest and enables you to incorporate conditional logic in your code:

```
IF <boolean expression> THEN
   Sequence of statements
END IF;
```

The Boolean expression is an expression that evaluates to a Boolean value: TRUE, FALSE, or NULL. The statement evaluates the Boolean expression and executes the sequence of statements if the expression evaluates to TRUE. The second type is the IF...THEN...ELSE statement, shown next, which provides an alternate sequence of statements to execute if the Boolean expression evaluates to FALSE or NULL:

```
IF <boolean expression> THEN
   Sequence of statements
ELSE
   Alternate sequence of statements
END IF;
```

If the Boolean expression evaluates to TRUE, the first set of statements is executed; otherwise, the alternate statements are executed. The third type has an ELSIF construct that evaluates additional Boolean expressions when the first expression evaluates to FALSE or NULL. The syntax shown here presents the use of ELSIF:

```
IF <boolean expression> THEN
   First sequence of statements
ELSIF <alternate boolean expression> THEN
   Second sequence of statements
ELSE
   Third sequence of statements
END IF;
```

If the first Boolean expression evaluates to FALSE or NULL, the Boolean expression in the ELSIF clause is evaluated. If the alternate Boolean expression evaluates to TRUE, the alternate statements are executed. One or more ELSIF clauses can be included with the IF statement to simulate a case structure found in other programming languages. The final ELSE clause is optional.

Technique

Iterative Control

Four types of looping constructs exist in PL/SQL: simple loops, FOR loops, WHILE loops, and cursor FOR loops. Simple loops execute a sequence of statements repeatedly with no apparent end. The syntax of a simple loop is shown here:

```
LOOP
   Sequence of statements
END LOOP;
```

The loop will continue to execute until it encounters an EXIT statement. Some forms of the EXIT statement include a WHEN clause, which includes a Boolean expression to be evaluated. A FOR loop has a defined number of iterations performed and includes a loop counter that can be used within the loop. The syntax of a FOR loop is:

```
FOR loop counter IN [REVERSE] lower_bound..upper_bound LOOP
   Sequence of statements
END LOOP;
```

The loop is executed once for each value starting with the lower bound moving upwards to the upper bound. If the optional REVERSE keyword is used, the loop starts with the upper bound moving downwards to the lower bound. The WHILE loop evaluates a Boolean expression before each iteration. If the expression evaluates to TRUE, the statements in the loop are executed. If the expression evaluates to FALSE or NULL, execution is passed to the statement following the loop. The syntax of the WHILE loop is shown here:

```
WHILE <boolean expression> LOOP
    Sequence of statements
END LOOP;
```

If the Boolean expression evaluates to FALSE or NULL the first time it's evaluated, the statements will never be executed. The cursor FOR loop is explored in How-To 11.2.

Anonymous PL/SQL blocks and loops can be labeled using the <<label_name>> syntax to enable explicit references to variables as label_name.variable_name to avoid ambiguity when referencing a variable with the same name in a nested block or a nested loop:

```
<<LOOP_NAME>>          -- could be used before a FOR or WHILE loop as well
LOOP
    Sequence of statements
END LOOP LOOP_NAME;
```

Labels provide greater readability when using nested loops.

Technique

Sequential Control

With conditional and looping constructs, almost any logic can be coded, but PL/SQL also provides a GOTO statement in the rare event that you need to use it. The GOTO statement unconditionally transfers control to the labeled statement. The label must precede a start of a PL/SQL block or loop, or an executable statement. Otherwise, use a NULL statement after the label to avoid compilation errors. The GOTO statement and label can appear in any order within a block:

```
BEGIN
    ...
    <<DO_QUERY>>
    BEGIN
        SELECT * FROM ...
        ...
    END;
    ...
    GOTO DO_QUERY;
    ...
END;
```

Steps

1. Run SQL*Plus and connect as the WAITE user account and run the PL/SQL block contained in the CHP10_4.SQL file that demonstrates the use of a simple IF statement with an ELSE clause. Figure 10.4 shows the code and output in SQL*Plus.

Lines 1 and 2 contain the declarative section of the block. The variable declared in line 2 is evaluated within the IF statement in the executable section. Lines 3 through 10 contain the executable section of the block. Line 4 assigns a value of 3 to the variable X. The IF statement in line 5 evaluates the variable X using a Boolean expression. If the value of X is greater than 2, the statement in line 6 is executed; otherwise, the statement in line 8 is executed. The DBMS_OUTPUT stored package is used to display PL/SQL output in lines 6 and 8 in SQL*Plus.

Because X is assigned a value of 3 in line 4, the Boolean expression in line 5 evaluates to TRUE, displaying the first message.

2. Run the CHP10_5.SQL file as shown in Figure 10.5. The PL/SQL block contained in the file uses the IF...THEN...ELSIF...ELSE construct to perform conditional logic.

Lines 5 through 11 present the IF...ELSIF...ELSE construct. If the Boolean expression contained in line 5 evaluates to TRUE, line 6 is executed. Otherwise, the Boolean expression in line 7 is evaluated. If the expression evaluates to TRUE, line 8 is executed; otherwise, line 10 is executed.

Line 4 assigns the value 4 to the variable X. The expression in line 5 evaluates to FALSE, causing the expression on line 7 to be tested. Because X is greater than 3, the expression evaluates to TRUE, and the message in line 8 is displayed.

```
SQL> START CHP10_4
SQL> SET ECHO ON
SQL> SET SERUEROUTPUT ON
SQL> DECLARE
  2    X NUMBER;
  3  BEGIN
  4    X := 3;
  5    IF X > 2 THEN
  6      DBMS_OUTPUT.PUT_LINE('X IS GREATER THAN 2');
  7    ELSE
  8      DBMS_OUTPUT.PUT_LINE('X IS NOT GREATER THAN 2');
  9    END IF;
 10  END;
 11  /
X IS GREATER THAN 2

PL/SQL procedure successfully completed.

SQL>
```

Figure 10.4 CHP10_4.SQL uses a simple IF...THEN...ELSE construct.

```
SQL> START CHP10_5
SQL> SET ECHO ON
SQL> SET SERVEROUTPUT ON
SQL> DECLARE
  2     X NUMBER;
  3  BEGIN
  4     X := 4;
  5     IF X > 5 THEN
  6        DBMS_OUTPUT.PUT_LINE('X IS GREATER THAN 5');
  7     ELSIF X > 3 THEN
  8        DBMS_OUTPUT.PUT_LINE('X IS GREATER THAN 3 BUT NOT GREATER THAN 5');
  9     ELSE
 10        DBMS_OUTPUT.PUT_LINE('X IS NOT GREATER THAN 3');
 11     END IF;
 12  END;
 13  /
X IS GREATER THAN 3 BUT NOT GREATER THAN 5

PL/SQL procedure successfully completed.

SQL>
```

Figure 10.5 CHP10_5.SQL uses a IF...THEN...ELSIF...ELSE construct.

3. Run the CHP10_6.SQL file in SQL*Plus. The PL/SQL block contained in the file executes a simple loop, using the EXIT WHEN statement to break out of the loop. The code and output are shown in Figure 10.6.

Lines 5 through 9 present a simple loop that continues to perform iterations until the Boolean expression contained in line 8 evaluates to TRUE. The PUT_LINE function contained in the loop displays a value within SQL*Plus for each iteration of the loop.

The loop executes three times before the expression in the EXIT WHEN statement evaluates to TRUE. When the expression is TRUE, the loop is exited.

```
SQL> START CHP10_6
SQL> SET ECHO ON
SQL> SET SERVEROUTPUT ON
SQL> DECLARE
  2     I NUMBER;
  3  BEGIN
  4     I := 0;
  5     LOOP
  6        I := I + 1;
  7        DBMS_OUTPUT.PUT_LINE('THE VALUE OF I IS: ' || TO_CHAR(I));
  8        EXIT WHEN I = 3;
  9     END LOOP;
 10  END;
 11  /
THE VALUE OF I IS: 1
THE VALUE OF I IS: 2
THE VALUE OF I IS: 3

PL/SQL procedure successfully completed.

SQL>
```

Figure 10.6 The output generated by a simple LOOP.

4. Run the CHP10_7.SQL file in SQL*Plus. The PL/SQL block in the file contains a FOR loop, which counts from 1 to 3 and displays the loop index. The results of the operation are shown in Figure 10.7.

Lines 1 through 5 contain the execution section of the block. There is no declarative section because the loop counter variable is declared implicitly as an integer when a FOR loop is used. The loop counter variable cannot be referenced outside the FOR loop. The loop in lines 2 through 4 performs an iteration for each value between 1 and 3. Line 3 displays the value of the loop counter by calling the DBMS_OUTPUT.PUT_LINE procedure.

The loop is performed three times with the loop counter representing the number of the iteration performed.

5. Load CHP10_8.SQL into the SQL buffer. The PL/SQL block in the file uses a WHILE loop to perform iterations. The results of the operation are shown in Figure 10.8.

```
SQL> START CHP10_7
SQL> SET ECHO ON
SQL> SET SERVEROUTPUT ON
SQL> BEGIN
  2     FOR J IN 1..3 LOOP
  3         DBMS_OUTPUT.PUT_LINE('THE VALUE OF J IS: '||TO_CHAR(J));
  4     END LOOP;
  5  END;
  6  /
THE VALUE OF J IS: 1
THE VALUE OF J IS: 2
THE VALUE OF J IS: 3

PL/SQL procedure successfully completed.

SQL>
```

Figure 10.7 The output generated by a FOR loop.

```
SQL> START CHP10_8
SQL> SET ECHO ON
SQL> SET SERVEROUTPUT ON
SQL> DECLARE
  2      K NUMBER;
  3  BEGIN
  4      K := 1;
  5      WHILE K < 3 LOOP
  6          DBMS_OUTPUT.PUT_LINE(TO_CHAR(K)||' IS STILL LESS THAN 3');
  7          K := K + 1;
  8      END LOOP;
  9  END;
 10  /
1 IS STILL LESS THAN 3
2 IS STILL LESS THAN 3

PL/SQL procedure successfully completed.

SQL>
```

Figure 10.8 The output generated by a WHILE loop.

The variable declared in line 2 is used in the Boolean expression in the WHILE loop. The WHILE loop in lines 5 through 8 performs iterations as long as the value of K is less than 3. Line 6 displays a message using the DBMS_OUTPUT.PUT_LINE procedure, and line 7 increments the value of K. If line 7 does not exist, the loop is performed indefinitely.

The loop is executed two times because the value of K is less than 3 only for the first two iterations.

How It Works

The IF statement is used to perform conditional operations within PL/SQL by evaluating a Boolean expression and performing statements based on the result. Step 1 presents the basic IF...THEN...ELSE construct within a PL/SQL block. Step 2 uses the ELSIF clause to provide a case functionality.

PL/SQL contains four types of looping constructs, three of which are presented in this How-To. The simple loop presented in Step 3 performs a loop indefinitely until it encounters an EXIT statement. The FOR loop, presented in Step 4, performs a defined number of iterations, based on the value of a loop counter between a lower and upper bound. Bound values can be static or determined dynamically at runtime to provide a dynamic range, but they must evaluate to integers. The WHILE loop, presented in Step 5, evaluates a Boolean expression before each iteration of the loop. As long as the Boolean expression evaluates to TRUE, the loop is performed. If the expression never evaluates to TRUE, the statements contained in the loop are never performed. Loops can also be nested within other loops. An EXIT statement cannot be placed outside the loop, and multiple EXIT statements can be used in any loop.

Comments

Conditional statements give PL/SQL added flexibility not provided by SQL. As you develop applications using PL/SQL, you will find yourself using conditional statements often. Make use of the ELSIF clause instead of a nested IF statement, whenever possible. Looping operations are a fundamental part of procedural languages. You can choose a looping construct that best suits the type of operation in hand. GOTO statements should be used sparingly.

COMPLEXITY
INTERMEDIATE

10.3 How do I...
Create a stored procedure?

Problem

I have one anonymous PL/SQL block that performs operations on database objects, but because this block is not stored in the database, it has to be compiled every time before I run it. I want to be able to create a procedure that can accept and return parameters. I know that a stored procedure is compiled and stored in the database and can be called from other PL/SQL blocks. How do I create a stored procedure?

Technique

A stored procedure is created with the CREATE PROCEDURE statement and consists of two parts. The procedure specification defines the name of the procedure and its parameters. The procedure body contains the PL/SQL block, which is executed when the procedure is run. The procedure body has the same structure as the PL/SQL blocks presented in How-To 10.1. It contains a declarative section, an executable section, and an exception section. Like anonymous blocks, the declarative and exception sections are optional. The syntax used to create a simple stored procedure that does not contain any parameters is shown here:

```
CREATE [OR REPLACE] PROCEDURE procedure_name IS
    [Optional declarative section contains all local types, variables, constants,
    cursors and subprogram declarations. Note: There is no DECLARE statement.]
BEGIN
    Executable section is run when the procedure is executed.
[EXCEPTION
    Optional exception section to handle errors.]
END;
```

A stored procedure can contain parameters that can be passed into the procedure, back to the calling PL/SQL block, or in both directions. When a parameter is defined in the procedure specification, a name, the parameter mode, and the datatype have to be specified. The three possible parameter modes are IN (the default), which represents a parameter passed into the procedure; OUT, which represents a parameter passed back to the caller; or IN OUT, which represents a parameter passed in both directions. In the body of a subprogram, a parameter with an IN mode cannot be assigned a value, and a parameter with an OUT mode cannot be read from, or a compilation error will occur. A parameter can be defined with a default value to be used when the no value is specified for that parameter when calling the procedure. The AS keyword can be optionally used instead of the IS keyword. A sample procedure specification containing parameters is shown here:

```
CREATE OR REPLACE PROCEDURE Test_Proc
         (dept_no  IN VARCHAR2,
          mgr_id    OUT NUMBER,
          run_date IN DATE DEFAULT SYSDATE) IS
```

The third parameter shown in the example contains a default parameter. If a value for the run_date parameter is not specified, the current system date is used. The %TYPE attribute can be used to declare a parameter to have a datatype the same as a table column. The %ROWTYPE attribute can be used to declare a parameter to have a datatype the same as a table row or a cursor. Refer to How-To 10.8 for more information.

By default, the stored procedure is created in the current user account's schema. Provided you have the necessary privileges, a different schema name can be provided as *SCHEMA_NAME.PROCEDURE_NAME* in the CREATE PROCEDURE statement.

Positional and Named Notation

Parameter names in a subprogram (function or procedure) declaration are *formal* parameters, whereas variables placed in the parameter list of a subprogram call are *actual* parameters. When calling a subprogram, the association between actual and formal parameters can be indicated by using positional notation or named notation.

When a procedure is called from a PL/SQL block, positional notation matches the parameter value with the order of the parameters in the procedure specification. A sample call using positional notation is shown here:

```
TEST_PROC(12, mgr_variable);
```

Named notation lets you specify a name for the parameter value, to ensure that the parameter is correct. A sample call using named notation is shown here:

```
TEST_PROC(mgr_id => mgr_variable, dept_no => 12);
```

The assignment operator **=>** is used to relate the parameter name with its value. Named parameters ensure that the values are assigned correctly, irrespective of the order in which you specify parameters. Another way of calling using named notation is:

```
TEST_PROC(dept_no => 12, mgr_id => mgr_variable);
```

When using named notation, the order of parameters is not important. You can also mix positional and named notation within a single call:

```
TEST_PROC(12, mgr_id => mgr_variable);
```

With mixed notation, named notation cannot precede positional notation. Hence, the following procedure call is illegal:

```
TEST_PROC(mgr_id => mgr_variable, 12); -- this is illegal
```

Named notation is flexible because you can specify only a partial list of parameters and omit those parameters that have default values. When calling stored subprograms, greater readability is achieved by using named notation.

An ORA-6502 error occurs if there is a datatype mismatch between the formal and actual parameters, irrespective of the notation used.

Steps

1. Run SQL*Plus and connect as the WAITE user account and execute the CHP10_9.SQL file. It has a CREATE PROCEDURE statement contained in the file that creates a simple stored procedure, which receives a parameter and displays it. Figure 10.09 displays the results of the operation.

Lines 1 and 2 provide the procedure specification of the statement. The CREATE OR REPLACE clause instructs Oracle to create a new procedure if one does not exist or to replace the existing one. Line 2 specifies the name of the procedure and provides a parameter list. The parameter ORDER_NO is declared as an IN parameter of the NUMBER datatype. Lines 3 through 5 contain the procedure body. Line 4 displays the parameter passed to the procedure using the DBMS_OUTPUT.PUT_LINE procedure.

2. Run CHP10_10.SQL in SQL*Plus. The PL/SQL block contained in the file calls the stored procedure created in the previous steps. Figure 10.10 displays the results of the operation.

```
SQL> START CHP10_9
SQL> SET ECHO ON
SQL> CREATE OR REPLACE PROCEDURE
  2          FIRST_PROC10 (ORDER_NO IN NUMBER) AS
  3  BEGIN
  4          DBMS_OUTPUT.PUT_LINE('THE PARAMETER IS ' || TO_CHAR(ORDER_NO));
  5  END;
  6  /

Procedure created.

SQL>
```

Figure 10.9 CHP10_9.SQL creates a stored procedure.

```
SQL> START CHP10_10
SQL> SET ECHO ON
SQL> SET SERVEROUTPUT ON
SQL> BEGIN
  2          FIRST_PROC10(25);
  3  END;
  4  /
THE PARAMETER IS 25

PL/SQL procedure successfully completed.

SQL>
```

Figure 10.10 The results of a PL/SQL block calling a stored procedure.

Line 2 calls the stored procedure created in the previous steps and passes it a parameter of 25. When the procedure is executed, the statements contained in the executable section of the procedure are run on the server.

The message displayed by the DBMS_OUTPUT.PUT_LINE procedure contained in the stored procedure is displayed in SQL*Plus. The number displayed in the output line is passed to the stored procedure as a parameter.

3. Run CHP10_11.SQL in SQL*Plus. The statement contained in the file creates a stored procedure demonstrating OUT parameters, default parameters, and the declaration of variables within a stored procedure. Figure 10.11 displays the results of the operation.

Lines 1 and 2 present the procedure specification. Lines 2 through 4 declare the name of the procedure and specify the parameter list.

Three parameters are passed to the procedure. The first parameter is an IN parameter of the VARCHAR2 datatype. Notice that no length is specified with the datatype. Be sure not to specify a length for a parameter, or an error will occur, but you can use the %TYPE and %ROWTYPE attributes to specify parameters with constrained datatypes.

A default value of NULL is specified for the first parameter. A NOT NULL constraint cannot be specified on a parameter. The second parameter is an OUT parameter, which is passed back to the caller. The third parameter is an IN parameter, with a default value specified using a syntax different than the first parameter. The default value is used whenever the procedure is called without a value for that parameter. Line 5 declares a local variable for the stored procedure and assigns a default value to the variable. Note that a NOT NULL constraint can be placed on a variable, but it must be assigned a default value in the declaration. The DECLARE clause is not

```
SQL> START CHP10_11
SQL> SET ECHO ON
SQL> CREATE OR REPLACE PROCEDURE
  2      SECOND_PROC10 (IN_STRING  IN  VARCHAR2 DEFAULT NULL,
  3                     OUT_STRING OUT VARCHAR2,
  4                     IN_NUMBER  IN  NUMBER := 1) AS
  5      LOCAL_VAR VARCHAR2(30) NOT NULL := 'SECOND_PROC10';
  6  BEGIN
  7      OUT_STRING := LOCAL_VAR || ': ' || IN_STRING || ' ' || IN_NUMBER;
  8  END;
  9  /

Procedure created.

SQL>
```

Figure 10.11 CHP10_11.SQL demonstrates default parameters and OUT parameters.

used in named PL/SQL blocks. Lines 6 through 8 define the procedure body. The statement in line 7 sets the value of the OUT parameter to a value based on the parameters passed to the procedure. Note the implicit conversion of a number to a string when concatenating input parameters to form the return string. Whenever the procedure is called, the value of the OUT parameter is passed back to the caller.

4. Run CHP10_12.SQL in SQL*Plus. The PL/SQL block contained in the file runs the stored procedure created in the previous steps, demonstrating the use of parameters. The results of the operation are displayed in Figure 10.12.

Lines 1 and 2 contain the declarative section of the block. The variable declared in line 2 receives the value passed back through the OUT parameter from the procedure when it is called. Lines 4 and 5 pass two parameters to the stored procedure using positional notation. PL/SQL assigns the values to the parameters based on their location in the parameter list. Because the third parameter in the procedure is optional, the default value is used. Line 6 displays the results of the OUT parameter using the DBMS_OUTPUT.PUT_LINE procedure. Lines 7 through 9 call the same procedure using named notation. The name of the parameter is provided with the value that enables the parameters to be specified in any order. Line 10 displays the value returned by the called procedure.

Both calls to the stored procedure generate valid output. It does not matter whether position notation or named notation is used within your code, as long as the stored procedure can identify the values assigned to the parameters.

```
SQL> START CHP10_12
SQL> SET ECHO ON
SQL> SET SERVEROUTPUT ON
SQL> DECLARE
  2      LOCAL_STRING    VARCHAR2(30);
  3  BEGIN
  4      SECOND_PROC10 ('HELLO WORLD',
  5                     LOCAL_STRING);
  6      DBMS_OUTPUT.PUT_LINE(LOCAL_STRING);
  7      SECOND_PROC10 (IN_STRING   => 'HELLO WORLD',
  8                     IN_NUMBER   => 2,
  9                     OUT_STRING  => LOCAL_STRING);
 10      DBMS_OUTPUT.PUT_LINE(LOCAL_STRING);
 11  END;
 12  /
SECOND_PROC10: HELLO WORLD 1
SECOND_PROC10: HELLO WORLD 2

PL/SQL procedure successfully completed.

SQL>
```

Figure 10.12 The results of calling the CHP10_12 stored procedure.

How It Works

Stored procedures are created with the CREATE PROCEDURE statement. Step 1 creates a simple procedure that receives a parameter and displays it using DBMS_OUTPUT.PUT_LINE. Step 2 runs the stored procedure created in the first step and displays its output. Step 3 creates a stored procedure with three parameters, of which two are assigned default values. A parameter can be optionally assigned a default value in the procedure specification. Step 4 presents the two methods used to pass parameters to the stored procedure. The first call to the procedure uses positional notation, which sets the parameter values based on their position in the list. The second call to the procedure uses the named notation.

The RETURN statement at the end of a procedure is implicit. A procedure can have explicit RETURN statements anywhere in the body to immediately return control back to the caller. The RETURN statement in a procedure cannot contain an expression.

Comments

Stored procedures enable your applications to perform business functions on the server, resulting in dramatic improvement in performance. Stored procedures promote code reuse and easier maintenance. Stored subprograms provide modularity and abstraction because they can be referenced from different applications without the application knowing the internal workings of the subprogram. They can improve performance because of reduced network traffic, better execution speed, and memory usage, as well as smaller application size.

NOTE

A stored procedure is marked with a valid or invalid state, depending on whether errors were encountered during compilation. Only valid stored procedures can be referenced. If any schema object (procedure, function, package specification, table, view, sequence, or synonym) referenced by a procedure has changed, the state of the procedure becomes invalid. All functions, procedures, and packages referencing an invalid procedure are also marked invalid.

Irrespective of state, all stored procedures are stored in the database. When an application calls a procedure, Oracle loads it into the shared pool (SGA) if it is not already in the shared pool. A valid procedure is executed immediately and, for an invalid procedure, Oracle automatically recompiles the procedure. If the recompilation succeeds, the procedure is marked as valid and execution continues. Otherwise, Oracle returns a runtime error.

continued on next page

continued from previous page

In a complex system, you must ensure that all referenced objects are compiled before the referencing procedures to ensure that they are all marked valid. Object dependencies and state information can be queried from the USER_DEPENDENCIES and USER_OBJECTS data dictionary views. This is demonstrated in How-To 10.6.

To create stored procedural objects (procedures, functions, and packages), the user account must have the capability to create them with the CREATE PROCEDURE or the CREATE ANY PROCEDURE privilege or to alter them with the ALTER PROCEDURE or ALTER ANY PROCEDURE privilege. Privileges have to be explicitly granted and cannot be obtained through roles. To execute a stored procedural object, a different user (other than the object owner) must be granted EXECUTE privilege on that object or must have an EXECUTE ANY PROCEDURE system privilege. Users are not required to have privileges to the objects referenced by the subprogram. Previously granted EXECUTE privileges on an existing stored procedural object are preserved while replacing it with the OR REPLACE clause.

COMPLEXITY
INTERMEDIATE

10.4 How do I...
Create a stored function?

Problem

In my PL/SQL program, there is repetitive code that could be better designed using functions. I want to create a stored function that returns a result after performing some operations. I also want to create some local procedures and functions within a PL/SQL block. How do I create a stored function?

Technique

Stored functions are similar to stored procedures, except that a stored function returns a value and must be called as part of an expression. A function is a named PL/SQL block, which contains a declarative, an execution, and an exception section. The declarative and exception sections are optional. For more information about the sections of a PL/SQL block, see How-To 10.1. The structure of a stored function is shown here:

```
CREATE [OR REPLACE] FUNCTION function_name (parameter list) IS
    [Optional declarative section contains all local types, variables, constants,
    cursors and subprogram declarations. Note: There is no DECLARE statement.]
```

```
BEGIN
    Executable section which is run when the function is executed.
    A RETURN statement must be specified to return a value.
[EXCEPTION
    Optional exception section to handle errors that may occur.]
END;
```

A stored function can accept parameters like a stored procedure (more information on passing parameters is covered in How-To 10.2). It must contain a RETURN statement to return a value back to the calling expression. When created, the stored function can be used in expressions in other PL/SQL blocks executed by the function owner or any user account granted EXECUTE privileges to the stored function.

Ever since the release of PL/SQL version 2.1, stored functions can be called from SQL statements with certain limitations. Stored functions can be used like system functions presented in Chapter 2, but they must meet certain conditions, depending on how they are used. Parameters used in these functions must use positional notation. They cannot be OUT or IN OUT parameters and are limited to only those datatypes supported by SQL. No stored function used in a SQL statement can modify data, and no procedures or functions called by the function can modify data. These rules are automatically enforced by checking the function body of a standalone stored function, but for functions defined in a package, the RESTRICT_REFERENCES pragma should be used in the package specification to enforce these rules, as explained in How-To 10.5.

Local subprograms (procedures and functions) can be specified in the declarative section of a PL/SQL block and remain local to the block; they can be called only from the executable section of the same block. Except that the CREATE OR REPLACE keywords cannot be used, a local procedure or function specified in the declarative section of a PL/SQL block has the same structure as stored procedures and functions. They all contain a header, a declarative section, an executable section, and an exception section. Local subprograms can reference other local subprograms as long as the referenced subprogram is declared before the referencing subprogram, or at least a forward declaration is provided for the referenced subprogram. All type, variable, and cursor declarations for the PL/SQL block must precede local subprogram declaration.

Steps

1. Run SQL*Plus, connect as the WAITE user account, and execute the CHP10_13.SQL file. It has a CREATE OR REPLACE FUNCTION statement to create a stored function, or you can replace it if it already exists in the database. It receives a single string parameter and returns a string. The results of the operation are displayed in Figure 10.13.

```
SQL> START CHP10_13
SQL> SET ECHO ON
SQL> CREATE OR REPLACE FUNCTION
  2      FIRST_FUNC10 (IN_STRING VARCHAR2) RETURN VARCHAR2 AS
  3  BEGIN
  4      RETURN IN_STRING || ' IS THE PARAMETER';
  5  END;
  6  /

Function created.

SQL>
```

Figure 10.13 CHP10_13.SQL creates a stored function.

Lines 1 and 2 contain the function specification. Line 2 specifies the name of the function, its parameter, and the datatype of the value the function returns. All functions must include a returned datatype, which must be contained in the function specification. Lines 3 through 5 specify the body of the function. Line 4 uses the RETURN statement to return the value of the input parameter concatenated with a text string. A RETURN statement must be executed when the function is run, and a RETURN statement in a function must contain an expression. It is possible for a function to contain more than one RETURN statement, but only one can be executed each time the function is called.

2. Run the CHP10_14.SQL file in SQL*Plus. The PL/SQL block contained in the file executes the stored function and displays the value returned. The results of the operation are displayed in Figure 10.14.

Lines 1 and 2 contain the declarative section of the anonymous block. Line 2 declares a variable assigned the value returned by the function created in the previous steps. Line 4 calls the stored function, passing a string as a parameter, and it assigns the return value to the local variable created in line 2. Line 5 displays the string returned by the function.

When the PL/SQL block is executed, the stored function modifies the parameter passed and returns a string, which is displayed in SQL*Plus using the DBMS_OUPUT.PUT_LINE procedure.

```
SQL> START CHP10_14
SQL> SET ECHO ON
SQL> SET SERVEROUTPUT ON
SQL> DECLARE
  2      VALUE_RETURNED VARCHAR2(80);
  3  BEGIN
  4      VALUE_RETURNED := FIRST_FUNC10('HELLO WORLD');
  5      DBMS_OUTPUT.PUT_LINE(VALUE_RETURNED);
  6  END;
  7  /
HELLO WORLD IS THE PARAMETER

PL/SQL procedure successfully completed.

SQL>
```

Figure 10.14 The results of calling the CHP10_14 stored function.

3. Run the CHP10_15.SQL file in SQL*Plus. A function is declared within the declarative section of the anonymous PL/SQL block. Figure 10.15 shows the output of the block in SQL*Plus.

Lines 1 through 5 contain the declarative section of the block. Lines 2 through 5 declare a function local to the block. Line 2 contains the function specification for the local function. Lines 3 through 5 contain the executable section of the local function. Line 4 returns the string 'WORLD' when the function is called. Lines 6 through 8 contain the executable section for the main PL/SQL block. Line 7 uses the local function as a parameter to the DBMS_OUTPUT.PUT_LINE procedure to display the string returned by the function.

The string returned by the local function is displayed by the DBMS_OUTPUT.PUT_LINE procedure in SQL*Plus.

4. Run the CHP10_16.SQL file in SQL*Plus. The PL/SQL block in the file contains both a procedure and a function defined in the declarative section of the code. Figure 10.16 shows the output of the nested calls in the PL/SQL block.

The module demonstrates a local procedure calling a local function, all within the declarative section of a PL/SQL block. Lines 2 through 5 create a local function returning a string when it is called. Lines 6 through 9 define a local procedure that calls the local function. Lines 10 through 12 contain the execution section of the block, which calls the CALL_HELLO procedure, which in turn calls the HELLO_WORLD function.

Because the function is defined before the procedure in the declarative section, the function is visible to the procedure. An error would occur if the order of the procedure and function were reversed—if the procedure

```
SQL> START CHP10_15
SQL> SET ECHO ON
SQL> SET SERVEROUTPUT ON
SQL> DECLARE
  2      FUNCTION HELLO_WORLD RETURN VARCHAR2 IS
  3      BEGIN
  4          RETURN 'HELLO WORLD';
  5      END;
  6  BEGIN
  7      DBMS_OUTPUT.PUT_LINE(HELLO_WORLD);
  8  END;
  9  /
HELLO WORLD

PL/SQL procedure successfully completed.

SQL>
```

Figure 10.15 The results of CHP10_15.SQL in SQL*Plus.

```
SQL> START CHP10_16
SQL> SET ECHO ON
SQL> SET SERVEROUTPUT ON
SQL> DECLARE
  2      FUNCTION HELLO_WORLD RETURN VARCHAR2 IS
  3      BEGIN
  4          RETURN 'HELLO WORLD';
  5      END;
  6      PROCEDURE CALL_HELLO IS
  7      BEGIN
  8          DBMS_OUTPUT.PUT_LINE(HELLO_WORLD);
  9      END;
 10  BEGIN
 11      CALL_HELLO;
 12  END;
 13  /
HELLO WORLD

PL/SQL procedure successfully completed.

SQL>
```

Figure 10.16 The results of CHP10_16.sql in SQL*Plus.

were defined before the function it calls. This can be resolved by a *forward declaration*, which consists of a subprogram specification terminated by a semicolon. In this case, you would have a forward declaration for the function as

FUNCTION HELLO RETURN VARCHAR2;

before the procedure definition, followed by the function definition. The forward declaration of the function enables it to be referenced in the procedure before it is defined.

The output displayed in SQL*Plus is generated by a local procedure calling a local function. The visibility of local procedures and functions depends on the order in which they are declared in the declarative section. Only after a declaration or forward declaration is provided for a local subprogram is it visible to other local subprograms.

5. Run the CHP10_17.SQL file in SQL*Plus, as shown in Figure 10.17. The file contains a local function declared in the declarative section of a stored procedure. This local function is complicated and generates words from numbers.

In the first block, lines 2 through 16 define a function local to the PL/SQL block. Lines 2 and 3 declare the local function. The function receives a numeric parameter and returns a string. The purpose of the function is to convert a number between 1 and 99 to a text representation. Line 4 declares the TMP variable in the local function. The variable holds the result of a DUAL table query using the TO_CHAR and TO_DATE functions to convert a numeric value to its text representation, shown in line 10. The conditional statement in line 6 returns a NULL value if the parameter is outside the acceptable range. Lines 17 through 19 contain the

```
SQL> START CHP10_17
SQL> SET ECHO ON
SQL> SET SERVEROUTPUT ON
SQL> CREATE OR REPLACE PROCEDURE SPELL_IT10 (IN_NUMBER IN NUMBER) AS
  2      FUNCTION SPELL_NUMBER (IN_NUM IN NUMBER)
  3          RETURN VARCHAR2 IS
  4      TMP VARCHAR2(30);
  5      BEGIN
  6        IF IN_NUM >= 100 OR IN_NUM < 1 THEN
  7          RETURN NULL;
  8        ELSE
  9          SELECT
 10            TO_CHAR(TO_DATE(LPAD(TO_CHAR(IN_NUM),4,'0'),'YYYY'),'YEAR')
 11              INTO TMP
 12          FROM
 13              DUAL;
 14          RETURN TMP;
 15        END IF;
 16      END;
 17  BEGIN
 18      DBMS_OUTPUT.PUT_LINE(SPELL_NUMBER(IN_NUMBER));
 19  END;
 20  /

Procedure created.

SQL>
```

Figure 10.17 CHP10_17.SQL creates a stored procedure with a local function.

executable section for the main block. Line 18 uses the local function within the DBMS_OUTPUT.PUT_LINE procedure to display the output generated by the function.

An easier way to execute a stored procedure instead of using the anonymous block is to use the EXECUTE SQL*Plus command, which effectively wraps the BEGIN and END statements around the statement that calls the stored procedure. The stored procedure is invoked in SQL*Plus using the EXECUTE command (or EXEC for short):

```
SQL> EXECUTE SPELL_IT10(22);
TWENTY-TWO

PL/SQL procedure successfully completed.

SQL> EXECUTE SPELL_IT10(17);
SEVENTEEN

PL/SQL procedure successfully completed.

SQL> EXEC SPELL_IT10(75);
SEVENTY-FIVE

PL/SQL procedure successfully completed.
```

Each of the three values converted with the local function of the stored procedure are displayed in SQL*Plus. This step illustrates how you can use local subprograms in stored functions and procedures to simplify coding.

How It Works

Stored functions are similar to stored procedures because they execute a PL/SQL block on the server. Unlike stored procedures, stored functions return a value and must be used in an expression. They can also return simple datatypes or record variables. Step 1 presents a stored function that receives one parameter and returns a VARCHAR2 result. Step 2 executes the function created in Step 1. Step 3 creates a stored function in the declarative section of the anonymous PL/SQL block and calls it in the execution section. Step 4 illustrates the method of calling a local subprogram from another local subprogram, both of which are defined in the declarative section of a PL/SQL block. Step 5 shows the use of nested subprograms by defining local subprograms within the declarative section of a stored subprogram.

Comments

Stored functions return a single value and, unlike stored procedures, must be used in expressions. Although it is possible to return more than one value from a stored function by using OUT parameters, this is not recommended because it creates code that is difficult to read and maintain.

Functions and procedures should always be used to make your code more modular. If there is a piece of code that is repeated in a PL/SQL block, consider putting it in a local function or procedure. If it should be accessible to other applications, consider creating a stored function or procedure in the database. Stored functions can be used just like built-in functions in PL/SQL expressions and even in SQL statements. Columns returned by a query can be used as parameters for stored functions, to generate complex output from queries. Stored functions cannot be used in SQL statements if they modify data in the database.

COMPLEXITY
INTERMEDIATE

10.5 How do I...
Create a stored package?

Problem

I want to group related stored procedures and functions and let them share variables. I know that stored packages enable me to group related procedures and functions and have performance advantages. How do I create a stored package?

Technique

A *stored package* is a group of related procedures and functions stored together that share common variables as well as local procedures and functions.

A package contains two separate parts. First, the package specification contains information about the package contents. Procedures, functions, cursors, datatypes, and variables visible to the package user are all declared in the package specification. Second, the package body contains the code for the objects declared in the package specification and objects local to the package. The package specification and package body are compiled separately and stored in the data dictionary as two separate objects. The package body is optional and does not need to be created if the package specification does not contain any procedures or functions. The executable section in the package body is optional. The executable section in a package body is referred to as the initialization section because it contains initialization code that is executed whenever the package is run for the first time in a session. Objects within the package body but not declared in the package specification are treated as local objects in a package and are accessible only to subprograms in the package body.

NOTE

To call a packaged function from a SQL statement, the PRAGMA RESTRICT_REFERENCES must follow the function declaration in the package specification. This is used to assure that the function does not modify data. The syntax used for PRAGMA RESTRICT_REFERENCES is:

```
PRAGMA RESTRICT_REFERENCES (function_name, WNDS);
```

Additionally, the WNPS, RNDS, RNPS optional arguments separated by commas can also be specified, if necessary. See Table 10.4 to decode the meaning of these arguments.

Table 10.4 PRAGMA RESTRICT_REFERENCES arguments

ARGUMENT	DESCRIPTION
WNDS	Writes no database state
RNDS	Reads no database state
WNPS	Writes no package state
RNPS	Reads no package state

Steps

1. Run SQL*Plus and connect as the WAITE user account. Run the CHP10_18.SQL file, which contains the code to create a package specification. The results are shown in Figure 10.18.

Line 1 contains the keywords required to create the package specification. Lines 2 through 7 declare the procedures, functions, and variables visible to users of the package. Line 2 declares a procedure and line 3 declares a function. Lines 4 through 6 declare package variables available to procedures and functions within the package, as well as to users of the package.

The package body creates the procedures and functions declared in the package specification. The package can be used only after creating a package body.

2. Run the CHP10_19.SQL file in SQL*Plus. The file contains the code required to create the package body for the package developed in the previous step. The results are shown in Figure 10.19.

```
SQL> START CHP10_18
SQL> SET ECHO ON
SQL> CREATE OR REPLACE PACKAGE FIRST_PACKAGE10 IS
  2        PROCEDURE PROC10 (X NUMBER);
  3        FUNCTION FUN10 RETURN VARCHAR2;
  4        VAR1 NUMBER;
  5        VAR2 VARCHAR2(30);
  6        VAR3 BOOLEAN;
  7    END FIRST_PACKAGE10;
  8    /

Package created.

SQL>
```

Figure 10.18 CHP10_18.SQL creates a package specification.

```
SQL> START CHP10_19
SQL> SET ECHO ON
SQL> CREATE OR REPLACE PACKAGE BODY FIRST_PACKAGE10 IS
  2        PROCEDURE PROC10 (X NUMBER) IS
  3        BEGIN
  4            VAR1 := X;
  5        END;
  6        FUNCTION FUN10 RETURN VARCHAR2 IS
  7        BEGIN
  8            VAR2 := 'HELLO';
  9            RETURN VAR2||' '||TO_CHAR(VAR1);
 10        END;
 11    BEGIN
 12        DBMS_OUTPUT.PUT_LINE('First time in package FIRST_PACKAGE10');
 13    END FIRST_PACKAGE10;
 14    /

Package body created.

SQL>
```

Figure 10.19 CHP10_19.SQL creates the package body.

Line 1 presents the keywords required to create a package body. The procedures and function declared in the package specification must be contained in the package body, or errors occur. Lines 2 through 5 create the procedure declared in the package specification. Line 4 references a package variable created in the package specification. Package variables are global throughout the package. Lines 6 through 10 create the function declared in the package specification. Line 12 contains code that is run the first time a user executes the package in a session. Line 13 ends the block creating the package body.

The creation of the package body makes the package available to the current user or any account granted an EXECUTE privilege.

3. Run the CHP10_20.SQL file in SQL*Plus. The PL/SQL block in the file calls the procedures and functions in the stored package. The results are shown in Figure 10.20.

Line 2 assigns a value directly to a package variable. Variables defined in the package specification can be used by any user account with EXECUTE privilege on the package. Line 3 calls the package procedure, passing the required variable. Line 4 calls the package function in the DBMS_OUTPUT.PUT_LINE procedure to display the output of the function in SQL*Plus.

The package code displaying a message in SQL*Plus is executed when the package is executed for the first time in a user session. The call to the package procedure assigns a value to a package variable, which the package function returns. This chain of events displays the parameter passed to the package procedure in SQL*Plus. A stored package enables you to share variables between subprograms and to create global variables.

```
SQL> START CHP10_20
SQL> SET ECHO ON
SQL> SET SERVEROUTPUT ON
SQL> BEGIN
  2      FIRST_PACKAGE10.VAR3 := TRUE;
  3      FIRST_PACKAGE10.PROC10(1);
  4      DBMS_OUTPUT.PUT_LINE(FIRST_PACKAGE10.FUN10);
  5  END;
  6  /
First time in package FIRST_PACKAGE10
HELLO 1

PL/SQL procedure successfully completed.

SQL>
```

Figure 10.20 Results of executing the procedure in the package.

How It Works

As stated earlier, a stored package requires two separate blocks: the package specification and the package body. Step 1 creates a package specification, which contains a procedure, function, and three variables. Variables defined in a package specification are global to the package and the session. Whenever a package variable is changed, the value is retained until it is changed again or until the session is terminated. Step 2 creates the package body. Each of the procedures and functions declared in the package specification are created in the package body. Failure to do so generates an error. The procedure and function both use the package variables created in the package specification. The procedure sets a package variable to a value and the function displays its value, showing how variables can be shared using packages. Step 3 presents a PL/SQL block that uses the stored package and executes it to display the package operation.

Comments

Stored packages let you group common procedures and functions and share variables between them. There are many benefits to packaging stored subprograms. When a stored package is accessed, the entire package is moved into the SGA and prepared to run. Any time you have related procedures that are likely to run together, they should be grouped in a stored package.

COMPLEXITY

INTERMEDIATE

10.6 How do I...
List information about stored objects in the database?

Problem

I want to list information about stored objects owned by a particular user account. I also need to view the size of subprograms and the associated source code. To ensure that they are compiled in the right order, I need to know dependencies between them. How do I list information about stored objects in the database?

Technique

• The USER_OBJECTS, USER_OBJECT_SIZE, USER_SOURCE, USER_DEPEND-ENCIES, and USER_ERRORS data dictionary views supply a lot of information about stored objects created by a user account. To query objects (to which you have the necessary access privileges) created by a different user account, replace USER_ with ALL_ for the view name in your query and specify the OWNER in the WHERE clause of the query.

The STATUS column of the USER_OBJECTS view tells you whether a given object is valid. Query the USER_OBJECT_SIZE view to show all stored objects in your schema and their sizing data. The TEXT column of the USER_SOURCE view contains a row for each line of source code in the stored module, and the LINE column represents the line number in the module. As the name suggests, a query on the USER_DEPENDENCIES view provides information about object dependencies in the system. From the REFERENCED_NAME column, a list of names of all objects that are referenced by a particular stored object can be found. The USER_ERRORS view can be queried to look up error information for modules that failed to compile. In all these views (except the USER_OBJECTS view), the NAME column represents the name of the stored object, and the TYPE column denotes the type of stored module. Object types for stored modules are PROCEDURE, FUNCTION, PACKAGE, and PACKAGE BODY. In the USER_OBJECTS view, the corresponding columns are named OBJECT_NAME and OBJECT_TYPE.

Steps

1. Run SQL*Plus and connect as the WAITE user account. It is assumed that you have run the files from the previous How-To's in this chapter. CHP10_21.SQL, as shown in Figure 10.21, queries the USER_OBJECTS data dictionary view to display stored object information if it is a function, procedure, package specification, or a package body. Columns of the USER_OBJECTS view are listed in Table 10.5.

Line 1 specifies that the name of the object, its type, and state to be listed for each record are returned by the query. Line 2 specifies that the

```
SQL> START CHP10_21
SQL> SET ECHO ON
SQL> COLUMN OBJECT_NAME FORMAT A20
SQL> SELECT OBJECT_NAME, OBJECT_TYPE, STATUS
  2  FROM   USER_OBJECTS
  3  WHERE  OBJECT_TYPE IN
  4         ('FUNCTION', 'PROCEDURE', 'PACKAGE', 'PACKAGE BODY');

OBJECT_NAME          OBJECT_TYPE      STATUS
-------------------- ---------------- -------
FIRST_FUNC10         FUNCTION         VALID
FIRST_PACKAGE10      PACKAGE          VALID
FIRST_PACKAGE10      PACKAGE BODY     VALID
FIRST_PROC10         PROCEDURE        VALID
SECOND_PROC10        PROCEDURE        VALID
SPELL_IT10           PROCEDURE        VALID

6 rows selected.

SQL>
```

Figure 10.21 Results of the query on USER_OBJECTS view.

USER_OBJECTS view is the data source. The WHERE clause in line 3 specifies that object type should be FUNCTION, PROCEDURE, PACKAGE, or PACKAGE BODY.

Table 10.5 Columns of the USER_OBJECTS view

COLUMN	DESCRIPTION
OBJECT_NAME	Name of the object
SUBOBJECT_NAME	Name of the subobject, if it is a subobject
OBJECT_ID	A unique object number
DATA_OBJECT_ID	Same as the object number for TABLE and INDEX object types
OBJECT_TYPE	Type of object: FUNCTION, PROCEDURE, PACKAGE, PACKAGE BODY, TRIGGER, TABLE, INDEX, SEQUENCE, SYNONYM
CREATED	Timestamp telling when the object was created as a DATE column
LAST_DDL_TIME	Timestamp telling when a DDL command was last applied to the object
TIMESTAMP	Timestamp for creation of the object as a VARCHAR2 column
STATUS	Object status: VALID or INVALID
TEMPORARY	Indicates whether the object is temporary (Y or N)
GENERATED	Indicates whether the object was generated by the system (Y or N)

2. Run the CHP10_22.SQL file in SQL*Plus. The size of the source code, parsed code, compiled code, and error code (if there is a compilation error) is queried from the USER_OBJECT_SIZE view. The code and results are shown in Figure 10.22. Columns of the USER_OBJECT_SIZE view are listed in Table 10.6.

Lines 1 and 2 return all size columns for each record returned by the query and also return the total of all size columns as a separate column. Line 3 specifies that USER_OBJECT_SIZE view is the data source. The total amount of space in bytes taken up by the stored module in the USER_DATA table space is summed up under the TOTAL_SIZE column.

Table 10.6 Columns of the USER_OBJECT_SIZE view

COLUMN	DESCRIPTION
NAME	Name of the object
TYPE	Type of the object: FUNCTION, PROCEDURE, PACKAGE, PACKAGE BODY
SOURCE_SIZE	Size of the source code (in bytes)
PARSED_SIZE	Size of the parsed code (in bytes)
CODE_SIZE	Size of the compiled code (in bytes)
ERROR_SIZE	Size of the error messages (in bytes)

```
SQL> COLUMN PARSED_SIZE HEADING 'PARSED|SIZE'
SQL> COLUMN CODE_SIZE HEADING 'CODE|SIZE'
SQL> COLUMN ERROR_SIZE HEADING 'ERROR|SIZE'
SQL> COLUMN TOTAL_SIZE HEADING 'TOTAL|SIZE'
SQL> SELECT USER_OBJECT_SIZE.*,
  2         SOURCE_SIZE + PARSED_SIZE +
  3         CODE_SIZE + ERROR_SIZE "TOTAL_SIZE"
  4  FROM   USER_OBJECT_SIZE
  5  WHERE  TYPE IN
  6         ('FUNCTION', 'PROCEDURE', 'PACKAGE', 'PACKAGE BODY');

                                  SOURCE    PARSED      CODE     ERROR     TOTAL
NAME                TYPE            SIZE      SIZE      SIZE      SIZE      SIZE
-----------------   -------------  ------   -------   -------   -------   -------
FIRST_PROC10        PROCEDURE        134       447       236         0       817
SECOND_PROC10       PROCEDURE        298       817       313         0      1428
FIRST_FUNC10        FUNCTION         122       373       192         0       687
SPELL_IT10          PROCEDURE        469      1235       610         0      2314
FIRST_PACKAGE10     PACKAGE          170       532       219         0       921
FIRST_PACKAGE10     PACKAGE BODY     240         0       323         0       563

6 rows selected.

SQL>
```

Figure 10.22 Results of the query on USER_OBJECT_SIZE view.

3. The CHP10_23.SQL file contains a query to the USER_SOURCE data dictionary view to display the source code of the sample stored procedure created in step 1 of How-To 10.3. The USER_SOURCE view contains a row for each line of source code in the TEXT column. Run the query to display the results, as shown in Figure 10.23. Columns of the USER_SOURCE view are listed in Table 10.7.

Line 1 returns the line number and a single line of code for each record returned by the query. Line 2 specifies that USER_SOURCE view is the data source. The WHERE clause in line 3 specifies that source code for the sample stored procedure created in step 1 of How-To 10.3 will be returned.

```
SQL> START CHP10_23
SQL> SET ECHO ON
SQL> COLUMN LINE FORMAT 990
SQL> COLUMN TEXT FORMAT A70
SQL> SELECT LINE, TEXT
  2  FROM USER_SOURCE
  3  WHERE NAME = 'FIRST_PROC10';

LINE TEXT
---- -------------------------------------------------------------------------
   1 PROCEDURE
   2     FIRST_PROC10 (ORDER_NO IN NUMBER) AS
   3 BEGIN
   4     DBMS_OUTPUT.PUT_LINE('THE PARAMETER IS ' || TO_CHAR(ORDER_NO));
   5 END;

SQL>
```

Figure 10.23 Results of the query on USER_SOURCE view.

Table 10.7 Columns of the USER_SOURCE view.

COLUMN	DESCRIPTION
NAME	Name of the object
TYPE	Type of the object: FUNCTION, PROCEDURE, PACKAGE, PACKAGE BODY
LINE	Line number in the source code
TEXT	Text of a line in the source code

The code contained in the sample stored procedure is displayed exactly as it was entered. The case of the characters and the code indentation is preserved in the USER_SOURCE data dictionary view.

4. Run the CHP10_24.SQL file in SQL*Plus. The file first creates a stored procedure that references a stored procedure created in Step 1 of How-To 10.3, and then a SELECT statement to query the USER_DEPENDENCIES table and to list all objects referenced by a dependent object specified by the user in SQL*Plus. The code and results are shown in Figure 10.24. Columns of the USER_DEPENDENCIES view are listed in Table 10.8.

Lines 1 through 3 return the name, type, and owner for each referenced object. Line 4 specifies that USER_DEPENDENCIES view is the data source. THIRD_PROC10 is provided as the value for the object name substitution variable for which referenced object details are returned. The USER_DEPENDENCIES and ALL_OBJECTS views can be joined in a

```
SQL> CREATE OR REPLACE PROCEDURE THIRD_PROC10 AS
  2  BEGIN
  3    FIRST_PROC10(1);
  4  END;
  5  /

Procedure created.

SQL> SHOW ERRORS
No errors.
SQL> COLUMN REFERENCED_NAME FORMAT A16
SQL> COLUMN REFERENCED_TYPE FORMAT A16
SQL> COLUMN REFERENCED_OWNER FORMAT A16
SQL> SELECT REFERENCED_NAME, REFERENCED_TYPE, REFERENCED_OWNER
  2  FROM    USER_DEPENDENCIES
  3  WHERE   NAME = UPPER('&1');
Enter value for 1: THIRD_PROC10
old   3: WHERE   NAME = UPPER('&1')
new   3: WHERE   NAME = UPPER('THIRD_PROC10')

REFERENCED_NAME  REFERENCED_TYPE  REFERENCED_OWNER
---------------  ---------------  ----------------
FIRST_PROC10     PROCEDURE        WAITE
STANDARD         PACKAGE          SYS

SQL>
```

Figure 10.24 Results of the query on USER_DEPENDENCIES view.

single SELECT statement for detailed reporting of referenced or dependent objects along with their state information.

Table 10.8 Columns of the USER_DEPENDENCIES view

COLUMN	DESCRIPTION
NAME	Name of the object
TYPE	Type of the object: FUNCTION, PROCEDURE, PACKAGE, PACKAGE BODY
REFERENCED_OWNER	Owner of the referenced object
REFERENCED_NAME	Name of the referenced object
REFERENCED_TYPE	Object type of the referenced object
REFERENCED_LINK_NAME	Name of link to the remote referenced object
SCHEMAID	Identity of the schema of the object

How It Works

The USER_OBJECTS view lists information about all objects in the user's schema. Step 1 queries the USER_OBJECTS view to list the name, type, and status of PL/SQL modules created in the previous How-To's. Step 2 uses the USER_OBJECT_SIZE view to find out the code size of stored modules. Step 3 queries the USER_SOURCE view to display the source code of a stored module. Step 4 lists objects referenced by a particular object by querying the USER_DEPENDENCIES view.

Comments

As mentioned earlier in a note in How-To 10.3, if a referenced object has changed, the dependent object is invalidated. Oracle automatically tries to recompile an invalid module before referencing it. This runtime compilation of invalidated modules can result in degradation of performance. To avoid automatic recompilation of invalid modules, you can manually compile them beforehand by using information from the USER_OBJECTS view. How-To 10.13 presents a technique used to recompile stored modules.

When a stored module is called, Oracle checks to see whether it is present in the SGA. If not, it loads the compiled code in the SGA. If the available space in the SGA is insufficient, Oracle swaps some modules existing in the SGA disk to make room for loading the called stored module. If you have large modules in the system, frequent swapping might occur, which can severely affect the performance of the system because of increased I/O. Occasionally, you might run out of buffer space while compiling immoderately sized source code. Care should be taken to identify overly large modules and modularize them into smaller units. The USER_OBJECT_SIZE comes in handy if you need to find out information about the size of modules in the system.

The source code contained in the data dictionary always contains the same code used during the latest compilation of a module. If you have questions about the validity of the source files used to create the stored modules, query the USER_SOURCE view to compare the source code. The SQL*Plus LIST command can display the source code of the last module compiled in the current session, as long as you have not executed any other SQL statements after the compilation.

To keep track of dependencies between stored objects in the database, the USER_DEPENDENCIES view can be used to see any objects that reference or depend on a particular object. In a complex system, this information can be used to build DDL scripts that compile all dependent stored modules whenever a referenced stored module is modified.

The SQL*Plus SHOW ERRORS command shows errors only for the most recent stored module that you attempted to compile. If a SQL script is used to create or compile stored modules, the command will not show errors generated for all modules. Thus, it is a good programming practice to have a SHOW ERRORS command in the script after each module compilation. The USER_ERRORS view can also be queried to show errors for all modules that were compiled.

COMPLEXITY
INTERMEDIATE

10.7 How do I...
Overload procedures and functions in packages?

Problem

I want to create procedures and functions with different parameter lists, depending on their use. I know that within a package I can declare the same procedure or function many times, as long as the parameter lists are different with each declaration. How do I overload procedures and functions in packages?

Technique

PL/SQL enables more than one procedure or function in a package to have the same name but with different parameter lists. This feature is useful in situations in which you want the same subprogram to accept different parameters. Each combination of subprogram name and parameter list must be unique within the package. The datatypes of the parameters make them unique if the subprogram names are the same. Variable names have no impact on the uniqueness of the parameter lists. Subprograms can be overloaded within a package or even in the declarative section of a PL/SQL block.

Steps

1. Run SQL*Plus and connect as the WAITE user account. Run CHP10_25.SQL, which contains a package specification that declares overloaded procedures. The code and results are shown in Figure 10.25.

Line 1 presents the keywords required to create a package specification. Lines 2 through 4 define the same procedure with three different parameter lists. When the package body is created, each of the procedure declarations listed in the package specification must be created. The datatypes of the parameters in the overloaded procedures must be unique, so that the PL/SQL runtime engine can match it with the procedure headers to determine which procedure definition needs to be executed. After the package specification is created, each of the procedures must be created in the package body, or an error will occur.

2. Run CHP10_26.SQL in SQL*Plus. The code created in the file creates the package body for the package developed in the previous step. The code and results are shown in Figure 10.26.

Line 1 provides the keywords necessary to create or replace the package body. Lines 2 though 5 create the first specification of the procedure. Lines 6 through 9 create the second specification of the overloaded procedure, and lines 10 through 13 create the third specification. Using the DBMS_OUTPUT package, each of the three overloaded procedures displays a message indicating which specification was executed. When the package is created, the user can call the package procedures with any of the parameter lists specified. The instance of the procedure used depends on the parameter list provided.

3. Run CHP10_27.SQL in SQL*Plus. The PL/SQL module in the file calls the overloaded procedure with the three different parameter lists. Figure 10.27 shows the results of the three procedure calls in SQL*Plus.

```
SQL> START CHP10_25
SQL> SET ECHO ON
SQL> CREATE OR REPLACE PACKAGE SECOND_PACKAGE10 IS
  2      PROCEDURE PROC10 (X NUMBER);
  3      PROCEDURE PROC10 (X VARCHAR2, Y NUMBER);
  4      PROCEDURE PROC10 (X VARCHAR2);
  5  END SECOND_PACKAGE10;
  6  /

Package created.

SQL>
```

Figure 10.25 CHP10_25.SQL declares over-loaded procedures.

```
SQL> START CHP10_26
SQL> SET ECHO ON
SQL> CREATE OR REPLACE PACKAGE BODY SECOND_PACKAGE10 IS
  2      PROCEDURE PROC10 (X NUMBER) IS
  3      BEGIN
  4          DBMS_OUTPUT.PUT_LINE('FIRST SPECIFICATION USED');
  5      END;
  6      PROCEDURE PROC10 (X VARCHAR2, Y NUMBER) IS
  7      BEGIN
  8          DBMS_OUTPUT.PUT_LINE('SECOND SPECIFICATION USED');
  9      END;
 10      PROCEDURE PROC10 (X VARCHAR2) IS
 11      BEGIN
 12          DBMS_OUTPUT.PUT_LINE('THIRD SPECIFICATION USED');
 13      END;
 14  END SECOND_PACKAGE10;
 15  /

Package body created.

SQL>
```

Figure 10.26 CHP10_26.SQL creates the code for overloaded procedures.

```
SQL> START CHP10_27
SQL> SET ECHO ON
SQL> SET SERVEROUTPUT ON
SQL> BEGIN
  2      SECOND_PACKAGE10.PROC10('X');
  3      SECOND_PACKAGE10.PROC10(1);
  4      SECOND_PACKAGE10.PROC10('X',1);
  5  END;
  6  /
THIRD SPECIFICATION USED
FIRST SPECIFICATION USED
SECOND SPECIFICATION USED

PL/SQL procedure successfully completed.

SQL>
```

Figure 10.27 The results of calling overloaded procedures.

Line 2 calls the overloaded procedure passing a VARCHAR2 parameter, executing the third version of the procedure from the package. Line 3 calls the procedure passing a NUMBER parameter to the function, executing the first version. Line 4 passes a VARCHAR2 and a NUMBER parameter to the procedure, executing the second version of the procedure.

When the procedure is called with dissimilar parameter lists, a different procedure body is executed each time, depending on the parameters passed. The DBMS_OUTPUT.PUT_LINE statement in each procedure version identifies the one used.

How It Works

Step 1 presents a package specification declaring three procedures with the same name but different parameter lists. Step 2 presents the package body containing the overloaded procedures. Each procedure defined in the package specification must be created in the package body, or an error will occur. The DBMS_OUTPUT.PUT_LINE procedure displays a message from each procedure to identify the specification executed. Step 3 calls the procedures with different parameters, executing different instances.

Comments

Overloading procedures and functions can simplify your applications by expanding the capabilities of a module. Most built-in PL/SQL functions are good examples of overloading. The built-in function TO_CHAR is overloaded, for example, because it can accept a variety of parameters with different datatypes performing the same function.

COMPLEXITY
INTERMEDIATE

10.8 How do I...
Create variables to represent database records and columns?

Problem

I need to declare variables in my PL/SQL code to represent columns retrieved from the database. Errors can occur if I don't create the variable with the correct datatype and column width. If the column changes in the table, my code needs to be modified. I want to create variables to represent columns. I also want to create structures to represent records in my PL/SQL code. How do I create variables to represent records and columns?

Technique

In PL/SQL, it is possible to declare the datatype of a variable as the datatype of a table column using the %TYPE attribute. The %TYPE attribute ensures that the datatype of the variable is suitable for handling the column. The usage of the %TYPE attribute is shown here:

```
variable_name table_name.column_name%TYPE;
```

A separate variable is declared for each table column, using the %TYPE attribute. A single variable can be created to represent the entire row, by using the %ROWTYPE attribute. Variables declared with the %ROWTYPE attribute are structures containing all the columns in the table. The usage of the %ROWTYPE attribute is shown here:

```
variable_name table_name%ROWTYPE;
```

When a variable is declared using the %ROWTYPE attribute, its components are referenced using the syntax *VARIABLE_NAME.COLUMN_NAME*. When using cursors, the %ROWTYPE attribute can be used to declare a variable representing the columns returned by a cursor as:

```
variable_name cursor_name%ROWTYPE;
```

This is particularly useful when you are not dealing with all the columns of a table but only those returned by the cursor. Obviously, the cursor declaration has to appear before using the %ROWTYPE attribute with the cursor_name. Refer to Chapter 11 for more information on the use of cursors. You can also define a PL/SQL record type as

```
TYPE record_type IS
    RECORD
    (field_name1 datatype1 [NOT NULL] [DEFAULT default_value1],
     field_name2 datatype2 [NOT NULL] [DEFAULT default_value2],
     ...
     field_namen datatypen [NOT NULL] [DEFAULT default_valuen]);
```

where **record_type** is the name of the datatype representing the record. The **field_name** is the name of the field within the record, and **data_type** represents the datatype of the field. A NOT NULL constraint and a DEFAULT initial value for each field in the record can be optionally specified. A DEFAULT value must be provided for any NOT NULL fields in the record.

Steps

1. Run SQL*Plus and connect as the WAITE user account. CHP10_28.SQL, as shown in Figure 10.28, creates the sample table used in this How-To. Run the file to create the sample table and data.

The DEPT10 table created by the script contains two columns used to define column and record type variables in the following steps.

```
SQL> START CHP10_28
SQL> SET ECHO ON
SQL> CREATE TABLE DEPT10 (
  2         DEPT_NO   NUMBER(5),
  3         DEPT_NAME VARCHAR2(30));

Table created.

SQL>
SQL> INSERT INTO DEPT10
  2         VALUES (1, 'Marketing');

1 row created.

SQL>
```

Figure 10.28 CHP10_28.SQL creates a sample table used in How-To 10.8.

2. Run the CHP10_29.SQL file in SQL*Plus. The PL/SQL block contained in the file uses the %TYPE attribute when declaring variables to represent database columns. The code and results are shown in Figure 10.29.

Lines 1 through 3 contain the declarative section of the block. Lines 2 and 3 declare variables using the %TYPE attribute. The D_NO and D_NAME variables are declared with the datatype of the DEPT_NO and DEPT_NAME columns in the sample table, even though the datatypes are not specified. Lines 4 through 9 contain the execution section of the block. The query contained in lines 5 through 7 selects a record from the sample table and puts the results in the variables declared with the %TYPE attribute. Even though the datatype is not known to the programmer when the module is created, the %TYPE attribute ensures its correctness. The DBMS_OUTPUT package is used in lines 8 and 9 to display the values returned by the query. The exception section contained in lines 10 through 12 handles the exception raised if no data is returned by the query.

3. Run the CHP10_30.SQL file in SQL*Plus. The PL/SQL block contained in the file declares a record variable using the %ROWTYPE attribute (see Figure 10.30).

Lines 1 and 2 contain the declarative section of the block. Line 2 uses the %ROWTYPE attribute to declare a record variable representing all the columns in the DEPT10 table. Lines 3 through 8 contain the executable section of the block. The query defined in lines 4 through 6 retrieves a record from the sample table in Step 1 and places the columns in the

```
SQL> START CHP10_29
SQL> SET ECHO ON
SQL> SET SERVEROUTPUT ON
SQL> DECLARE
  2     D_NO    DEPT10.DEPT_NO%TYPE;
  3     D_NAME  DEPT10.DEPT_NAME%TYPE;
  4  BEGIN
  5     SELECT DEPT_NO, DEPT_NAME
  6     INTO   D_NO, D_NAME
  7     FROM   DEPT10;
  8     DBMS_OUTPUT.PUT_LINE('DEPT_NO = ' || TO_CHAR(D_NO));
  9     DBMS_OUTPUT.PUT_LINE('DEPT_NAME = ' || D_NAME);
 10  EXCEPTION
 11     WHEN NO_DATA_FOUND THEN
 12          DBMS_OUTPUT.PUT_LINE('No records found in the DEPT10 table');
 13  END;
 14  /
DEPT_NO = 1
DEPT_NAME = Marketing

PL/SQL procedure successfully completed.

SQL>
```

Figure 10.29 CHP10_29.SQL demonstrates use of the %TYPE attribute.

```
SQL> START CHP10_30
SQL> SET ECHO ON
SQL> SET SERVEROUTPUT ON
SQL> DECLARE
  2     D   DEPT10%ROWTYPE;
  3  BEGIN
  4     SELECT DEPT_NO, DEPT_NAME
  5     INTO   D.DEPT_NO, D.DEPT_NAME
  6     FROM   DEPT10;
  7     DBMS_OUTPUT.PUT_LINE('DEPT_NO = ' || TO_CHAR(D.DEPT_NO));
  8     DBMS_OUTPUT.PUT_LINE('DEPT_NAME = ' || D.DEPT_NAME);
  9  EXCEPTION
 10     WHEN NO_DATA_FOUND THEN
 11         DBMS_OUTPUT.PUT_LINE('No records found in the DEPT10 table');
 12  END;
 13  /
DEPT_NO = 1
DEPT_NAME = Marketing

PL/SQL procedure successfully completed.

SQL>
```

Figure 10.30 CHP10_30.SQL demonstrates use of the %ROWTYPE attribute.

components of the record variable. Line 5 shows how the columns of a record-type variable are referenced using dot notation. Lines 7 and 8 use the DBMS_OUTPUT package to display the values contained in the components of the record variable. The exception section contained in lines 9 through 11 handles the exception if no data is returned by the query.

4. Run the CHP10_31.SQL file in SQL*Plus. The PL/SQL block contained in the file declares a record variable of a user-defined RECORD type (see Figure 10.31).

```
SQL> START CHP10_31
SQL> SET ECHO ON
SQL> SET SERVEROUTPUT ON
SQL> DECLARE
  2     TYPE DEPT_REC IS RECORD (
  3            DEPT_NO    NUMBER(5),
  4            DEPT_NAME  VARCHAR2(30));
  5     D DEPT_REC;
  6  BEGIN
  7     SELECT DEPT_NO, DEPT_NAME
  8     INTO   D.DEPT_NO, D.DEPT_NAME
  9     FROM   DEPT10;
 10     DBMS_OUTPUT.PUT_LINE('DEPT_NO = ' || TO_CHAR(D.DEPT_NO));
 11     DBMS_OUTPUT.PUT_LINE('DEPT_NAME = ' || D.DEPT_NAME);
 12  EXCEPTION
 13     WHEN NO_DATA_FOUND THEN
 14         DBMS_OUTPUT.PUT_LINE('No records Found in the DEPT10 table');
 15  END;
 16  /
DEPT_NO = 1
DEPT_NAME = Marketing

PL/SQL procedure successfully completed.

SQL>
```

Figure 10.31 CHP10_31.SQL uses a variable of a RECORD type.

Lines 2 through 5 contain the declarative section of the block. A user-defined composite type is defined in lines 2 through 4 using the TYPE IS RECORD syntax. Line 5 declares a record variable of the newly defined record type. Lines 6 through 11 contain the executable section of the block. The query defined in lines 7 through 9 retrieves a record from the sample table created in Step 1 and places the columns in the fields of the record variable. Line 8 shows how the columns of a record-type variable are referenced using dot notation. Lines 10 and 11 use the DBMS_OUTPUT package to display the values contained in the components of the record variable. The exception section contained in lines 12 through 14 handles the exception if the query fails to return a row from the table.

How It Works

The %TYPE attribute can be used to declare variables of the datatype contained in the column of a table. This enables you to declare variables without knowing the datatype of the value it will receive. The %ROWTYPE attribute enables you to declare a composite datatype containing all the columns in a table. Step 1 creates a sample table used in the following steps. Step 2 demonstrates the use of the %TYPE attribute by declaring variables to represent the columns in the sample table. Step 3 uses the %ROWTYPE attribute to declare a composite variable containing all the columns in the sample table. Step 4 uses the TYPE IS RECORD syntax to define a record type and then declare a record variable of that record type. A PL/SQL record type can contain another table or a record with composite fields.

Comments

It is good practice to use the %TYPE and %ROWTYPE attributes whenever you create a variable to represent a table column or create multiple variables to represent an entire record. Using the %TYPE and %ROWTYPE attributes ensures that your PL/SQL code will continue to work if the structure of the table or datatypes of a column change. A record type variable provides a means to group logically related variables to be treated as a single unit. Records can be passed as parameters to subprograms.

COMPLEXITY
INTERMEDIATE

10.9 How do I...
Achieve array functionality with PL/SQL Index-By tables?

Problem

I need to use arrays in my PL/SQL code, but PL/SQL does not contain array structures. I know that PL/SQL tables exist, and I want to use them the same way arrays are used. How do I achieve array functionality with PL/SQL Index-By tables?

Technique

One-dimensional arrays can be simulated in PL/SQL, using PL/SQL Index-By tables. You can define tables of PL/SQL datatypes or user-defined datatypes. To create a table of user-defined datatypes, the user-defined datatype must be defined before declaring a table of that datatype. A two-step process is required to create a PL/SQL table: Define a datatype for the Index-By table and then declare variables of that datatype. The syntax used to define an Index-By table is shown here:

```
TYPE type_name IS
    TABLE OF data_type
    INDEX BY BINARY_INTEGER;
```

type_name is the name of the datatype representing the table and data_type represents the datatype of the elements contained in the table. The INDEX BY BINARY_INTEGER clause is required when creating an Index-By table. In PL/SQL versions 2.3 and later, you can use record variables as elements of a table. When a datatype is defined to represent the table, variables of the new datatype can be declared.

Steps

1. Run SQL*Plus and connect as the WAITE user account. The code in the CHP10_32.SQL file and the resulting output is shown in Figure 10.32. The PL/SQL block contained in the file uses a FOR loop to define a PL/SQL table and fill it with data. When the table is filled, a second FOR loop moves through the table, displaying the values contained.

Lines 1 through 5 contain the declarative section of the PL/SQL block. The TYPE statement started in line 2 creates a datatype called ARRAY_TYPE, which defines a table of numbers. Line 4 presents the required INDEX BY

```
SQL> START CHP10_32
SQL> SET ECHO ON
SQL> SET SERVEROUTPUT ON
SQL> DECLARE
  2      TYPE ARRAY_TYPE IS
  3          TABLE OF NUMBER
  4              INDEX BY BINARY_INTEGER;
  5      MY_ARRAY ARRAY_TYPE;
  6  BEGIN
  7      FOR I IN 1..4 LOOP
  8          MY_ARRAY(I) := I * 2;
  9      END LOOP;
 10      FOR I IN 1..4 LOOP
 11          DBMS_OUTPUT.PUT_LINE('MYARRAY(' || I || ') = '
 12                                  || TO_CHAR(MY_ARRAY(I)));
 13      END LOOP;
 14  END;
 15  /
MYARRAY(1) = 2
MYARRAY(2) = 4
MYARRAY(3) = 6
MYARRAY(4) = 8

PL/SQL procedure successfully completed.

SQL>
```

Figure 10.32 CHP10_32.SQL demonstrates use of a PL/SQL table.

BINARY_INTEGER clause to create the index for the table. Table declarations must use BINARY_INTEGER indexes. Line 5 declares a variable of the table type defined in the previous lines. Lines 6 through 14 contain the execution section of the block. The FOR loop contained in lines 7 through 9 populates the first 10 values of the table with a calculated value. The FOR loop contained in lines 10 through 13 loops through the table, displaying the values contained in the records.

When the block is executed, the PL/SQL table is created and populated with elements. When the table is populated, the values of the table are displayed within SQL*Plus.

2. Run CHP10_33.SQL, which has a PL/SQL block that declares a cursor and uses the columns returned by the cursor as a basis for defining a user-defined TABLE type. The code and output are shown in Figure 10.33.

Lines 1 through 8 contain the declarative section of the PL/SQL block. Line 2 defines a cursor to query the DEPT10 table. The TYPE statement in line 3 creates a new datatype called DEPT_TYPE. Line 4 specifies that the new datatype is a table of records corresponding with the columns returned by the cursor. The INDEX BY BINARY_INTEGER clause in line 5 is necessary to define an Index-By table. Line 6 declares a record variable of the cursor type that will serve as a placeholder for fetching rows from the cursor. Line 7 declares a variable of the newly defined table type. Lines 9 through 16 contain the execution section of the block. The FOR loop contained in lines 10 through 15 fetches all rows from the DEPT10 table.

```
SQL> START CHP10_33
SQL> SET ECHO ON
SQL> SET SERVEROUTPUT ON
SQL> DECLARE
  2     CURSOR DEPT_CURS06 IS SELECT * FROM DEPT10;
  3     TYPE DEPT_TYPE IS
  4        TABLE OF DEPT_CURS06%ROWTYPE
  5           INDEX BY BINARY_INTEGER;
  6     C DEPT_CURS06%ROWTYPE;
  7     D DEPT_TYPE;
  8     I BINARY_INTEGER := 1;
  9  BEGIN
 10     FOR C IN DEPT_CURS06 LOOP
 11        D(I) := C;
 12        DBMS_OUTPUT.PUT_LINE('DEPT_NO = ' || TO_CHAR(D(I).DEPT_NO));
 13        DBMS_OUTPUT.PUT_LINE('DEPT_NAME = ' || D(I).DEPT_NAME);
 14        I := I + 1;
 15     END LOOP;
 16  END;
 17  /
DEPT_NO = 1
DEPT_NAME = Marketing

PL/SQL procedure successfully completed.

SQL>
```

Figure 10.33 A table of cursor type in CHP10_33.SQL.

A row is first fetched from the DEPT10 table into the record variable in line 10. Line 11 shows how records of the same type can be directly assigned without using a dot notation. The Index-By table is populated with rows returned by the cursor through the cursor type record variable as the mediator. After each row is fetched from the database table into the Index-By table, the column values contained in the Index-By table are displayed in SQL*Plus, using the DBMS_OUTPUT.PUT_LINE procedure.

When the block is executed, the PL/SQL Index-By table is initialized and populated with elements. As the table becomes populated, the values of columns are displayed in SQL*Plus.

How It Works

Index-By tables are similar to one-dimensional arrays and are referenced like arrays of records. Index-By tables can be created using any of the standard PL/SQL datatypes. In PL/SQL version 2.3 and later, you can even use record variables in PL/SQL tables.

To use an Index-By table, a datatype for the table must first be defined. When the datatype is defined, variables of the new datatype can be declared. Steps 1 and 2 show how you can use an Index-By table like an array. A datatype is defined in the declarative section of the block with the TYPE statement. Step 1 defines a table to contain values of the NUMBER datatype, whereas step 2 defines a table to contain records of a cursor type. Any built-in datatype or user-defined datatype can be specified in the TABLE OF clause.

In contrast to record types, Index-By tables cannot contain a table or a record with composite fields. The INDEX BY BINARY_INTEGER clause is required in all Index-By table definitions. When the table variable is declared, it can be referenced like an array by specifying an index value in parentheses to represent an element in the table. Elements of Index-By tables are initialized with null values automatically during declaration.

Comments

Array processing is a common need in procedural languages. PL/SQL Index-By tables can be used like one-dimensional arrays within your code. If your requirements include two-dimensional arrays, this requires considerably more effort. You can define a table type based on a column using the %TYPE attribute, based on a database table or cursor using the %ROWTYPE attribute, or by using a RECORD type. If you are running PL/SQL version 2.3 or later, additional support of record variables in PL/SQL tables lets you create array-type structures to represent records returned by a query. Refer to How-To 10.9 for more information on creating variables of user-defined record types. PL/SQL tables can be passed as parameters to subprograms. Other new datatypes such as Varrays and Nested Tables are addressed in Chapter 16.

COMPLEXITY
BEGINNING

10.10 How do I...
Handle predefined exceptions and system errors?

Problem

Any time an exception occurs in my PL/SQL block, it terminates the block. I need to handle exceptions in all my PL/SQL code to ensure that unexpected errors don't terminate the program. When exceptions occur, I want to be sure that runtime errors are handled gracefully. How do I handle exceptions in PL/SQL?

Technique

The exception section of each PL/SQL block can handle one or more exceptions. The EXCEPTION keyword identifies the beginning of the exception section. If an exception occurs and an exception handler does not exist in the exception section to handle it, an unhandled exception error occurs and execution of the module is terminated. Handlers are listed in the exception section following the WHEN clause, as shown here:

```
EXCEPTION
    WHEN first_exception THEN
      <code to handle first exception>
    WHEN second_exception THEN
       <code to handle second exception>
    ...
    WHEN OTHERS THEN
       <code to handle any other system exceptions>
END;
```

Predefined exceptions are system exceptions that correspond to the most common Oracle runtime errors. Identifiers for predefined exceptions are defined in the STANDARD package, and these predefined exceptions are listed in Table 10.9. Exception handlers can appear in any order in the EXCEPTION section, except for the OTHERS exception handler, which appears as the last one. The exception handling code for OTHERS handles all other exceptions for which no exception handler is explicitly specified in the EXCEPTION section.

Table 10.9 Predefined exceptions.

EXCEPTION NAME	ORACLE ERROR	DESCRIPTION
ACCESS_INTO_NULL[1]	ORA-6530	Assign values to attributes of an uninitialized object.
COLLECTION_IS_NULL[1]	ORA-6531	With an uninitialized collection, assign values to elements, or apply collection methods other than EXISTS.
CURSOR_ALREADY_OPEN	ORA-6511	Open a cursor that is already open.
DUP_VAL_ON_INDEX	ORA-0001	Violate a unique constraint.
INVALID_CURSOR	ORA-1001	Use an invalid cursor.
INVALID_NUMBER	ORA-1722	Conversion of a string to a number failed.
LOGIN_DENIED	ORA-1017	Invalid username/password.
NO_DATA_FOUND	ORA-1403	No row returned by a SELECT INTO statement. Reference a deleted element in a nested table. Reference an initialized element in an Index-By table.
NOT_LOGGED_ON	ORA-1010	Attempt to perform a database operation when not connected.
PROGRAM_ERROR	ORA-6501	Internal error.
ROWTYPE_MISMATCH[2]	ORA-6504	Host variable and cursor variable have incompatible types.
STORAGE_ERROR	ORA-6500	PL/SQL runs out of memory.
SUBSCRIPT_BEYOND_COUNT[1]	ORA-6533	Reference a collection using an index number larger than the number of elements in the collection.
SUBSCRIPT_OUTSIDE_LIMIT[1]	ORA-6532	Reference a collection using an illegal index number (a negative index number for example).
TIMEOUT_ON_RESOURCE	ORA-0051	Timeout occurred.
TOO_MANY_ROWS	ORA-1422	More than one row returned by a SELECT INTO statement.
TRANSACTION_BACKED_OUT[3]	ORA-0061	Transaction rolled back because of deadlock.

EXCEPTION NAME	ORACLE ERROR	DESCRIPTION
VALUE_ERROR	ORA-6502	Arithmetic, conversion, truncation, or size-constraint error.
ZERO_DIVIDE	ORA-1476	Attempt to divide by zero.

[1] Exception predefined in PL/SQL 3.0 and later.

[2] Exception predefined in PL/SQL 2.2 and later.

[3] Exception predefined only in PL/SQL 2.0 and 2.1.

NOTE

If a system error that is not a predefined exception needs to be handled, an exception identifier can be defined and linked to the error, using the PRAGMA EXCEPTION_INIT statement in a block's declarative section. The syntax of the statement is shown here:

```
PRAGMA EXCEPTION_INIT(exception_name, error_number);
```

Errors specified in the EXCEPTION_INIT statement are negative. Remember to include the minus sign (-) when defining the error, because error numbers are negative numbers.

Steps

1. Run SQL*Plus and connect as the WAITE user account. The PL/SQL block in the CHP10_34.SQL file generates an exception intentionally by assigning a character value to a numeric variable.

If the PL/SQL block does not contain an exception section, the block terminates abnormally. An Oracle error and its description are displayed whenever an unhandled exception occurs, but here the exception is handled in the exception section of the block by catching it as a predefined exception. Figure 10.34 displays the code and results of the operation in SQL*Plus.

Lines 1 and 2 contain the declarative section of the block. Line 4 attempts to set the numeric variable defined in line 2 to a character value, which is an illegal operation. If there is no exception handler defined to handle the error, the program terminates abnormally. The exception section starting on line 6 is executed whenever an exception occurs. The VALUE_ERROR exception is handled in lines 7 and 8.

The Oracle error generated by line 4 is handled by the exception handler in lines 7 and 8. The only way for this code to execute is for the exception to occur. If a different exception occured, it would not be handled, and the execution of the block would still be terminated abnormally. This can be

```
SQL> START CHP10_34
SQL> SET ECHO ON
SQL> SET SERVEROUTPUT ON
SQL> DECLARE
  2     X NUMBER;
  3  BEGIN
  4     X := 'YYYY';
  5     DBMS_OUTPUT.PUT_LINE('IT WORKS');
  6  EXCEPTION
  7     WHEN VALUE_ERROR THEN
  8         DBMS_OUTPUT.PUT_LINE('VALUE_ERROR EXCEPTION HANDLER');
  9  END;
 10  /
VALUE_ERROR EXCEPTION HANDLER

PL/SQL procedure successfully completed.

SQL>
```

Figure 10.34 CHP10_34.SQL uses a predefined exception.

avoided by including a WHEN OTHERS exception handler as a catchall for all other Oracle errors.

2. Run the CHP10_35.SQL file in SQL*Plus. The PL/SQL block contained in the file creates an exception for an Oracle error not that is not predefined. The code and output are shown in Figure 10.35.

Lines 1 through 3 contain the declarative section for the block. Line 2 declares an exception to identify an Oracle error for which a predefined exception does not exist. The statement contained in line 4 is a compiler directive to associate the newly defined exception with an Oracle error. When the Oracle error defined in the EXCEPTION_INIT procedure is encountered, the exception associated with it is raised. Lines 6 through 9 attempt an illegal query of a ROWID from a view. The error encounter is the one defined by the BAD_ROWID exception. Lines 11 and 12 handle

```
SQL> START CHP10_35
SQL> DECLARE
  2     BAD_ROWID EXCEPTION;
  3     V_ROWID ROWID;
  4     PRAGMA EXCEPTION_INIT(BAD_ROWID,-01445);
  5  BEGIN
  6     SELECT ROWID
  7        INTO V_ROWID
  8     FROM ALL_VIEWS
  9        WHERE ROWNUM = 1;
 10  EXCEPTION
 11     WHEN BAD_ROWID THEN
 12        DBMS_OUTPUT.PUT_LINE('CANNOT QUERY ROWID FROM THIS VIEW');
 13     WHEN OTHERS THEN
 14        DBMS_OUTPUT.PUT_LINE('SOME OTHER ERROR');
 15  END;
 16  /
CANNOT QUERY ROWID FROM THIS VIEW

PL/SQL procedure successfully completed.

SQL>
```

Figure 10.35 CHP10_35.SQL uses the PRAGMA EXCEPTION directive.

the exception by displaying a message within SQL*Plus. Lines 13 and 14 handle any other system error that might occur during execution.

When the Oracle error ORA-01445 occurs in line 6 of the PL/SQL block, the user-defined exception handler processes the error and terminates the program normally.

How It Works

Errors are handled in PL/SQL blocks by exception handlers in the exception section. If a PL/SQL block does not handle exceptions when they occur, an error is generated and the program is terminated abnormally. Step 1 presents a PL/SQL block with an exception handler for the VALUE_ERROR exception. When this exception occurs, the exception handler causes the program to display a message before it terminates normally. Step 2 presents the technique for handling system errors that are not predefined. An exception is declared, and the PRAGMA EXCEPTION_INIT directive is used to associate an Oracle error with the exception. The WHEN OTHERS exception handler handles exceptions not dealt with by a specific error handler.

Comments

It is important to handle exceptions within your PL/SQL code. Exceptions can occur for a variety of reasons and can cause your code to terminate abnormally. You should attempt to handle exceptions specifically and not rely on the WHEN OTHERS exception to handle all your errors. The WHEN OTHERS exception handler must be placed last in the exception section. An exception raised in the declarative section because of an illegal assignment cannot be handled by a handler in the exception section and is propagated to the calling environment.

COMPLEXITY

INTERMEDIATE

10.11 How do I...
Handle user-defined exceptions and user-defined errors?

Problem

I want to create and use my own exception within the code to treat certain situations like an exception. When certain business rules are violated within a PL/SQL block, I want to invoke the user-defined exception. I also want to know how to create exceptions with a user-defined error number and user-defined error message. How do I create and handle user-defined exceptions?

Technique

A user-defined exception can be declared in the declarative section of a PL/SQL block and raised using the RAISE statement. When an exception is raised, execution is passed to the exception section of the block. The exception handler created for the user-defined exception is executed any time the exception is raised. The RAISE statement can also be used to manually invoke a predefined exception.

The built-in procedure RAISE_APPLICATION_ERROR enables you to raise an exception with a user-defined error number and user-defined error message. As seen in How-To 10.10, an exception can be declared in the declarative section of a block, which can be associated with an error code by using the EXCEPTION_INIT pragma compiler directive.

Whenever a predefined or user-defined exception is raised inside a subprogram and there is no exception handler, control is immediately passed to the calling block. Even if the values of the OUT and IN OUT parameters have been modified in the subprogram, they are not returned back to the caller. If the calling block also does not have a handler for the exception, control is propagated back to the calling environment. A handler must exist in the subprogram or the calling block to trap and handle the exception.

Steps

1. Run SQL*Plus and connect as the WAITE user account and run CHP10_36.SQL, which contains a PL/SQL block that makes use of a user-defined exception. The code and resulting output are shown in Figure 10.36.

```
SQL> START CHP10_36
SQL> SET ECHO ON
SQL> SET SERVEROUTPUT ON
SQL> DECLARE
  2      SALARY_CODE VARCHAR2(1);
  3      INVALID_SALARY_CODE EXCEPTION;
  4  BEGIN
  5      SALARY_CODE := 'X';
  6      IF SALARY_CODE NOT IN ('A','B','C') THEN
  7          RAISE INVALID_SALARY_CODE;
  8      END IF;
  9      DBMS_OUTPUT.PUT_LINE('EVERYTHING IS OK');
 10  EXCEPTION
 11      WHEN INVALID_SALARY_CODE THEN
 12          DBMS_OUTPUT.PUT_LINE('SQLCODE = ' || SQLCODE || ' ' ||
 13                               'SQLERRM = ' || SQLERRM);
 14  END;
 15  /
SQLCODE = 1 SQLERRM = User-Defined Exception

PL/SQL procedure successfully completed.

SQL>
```

Figure 10.36 CHP10_36.SQL uses a user-defined exception.

Lines 1 though 3 contain the declarative section of the block. Line 3 declares an exception variable that can be raised in the executable section of the block and handled in the exception section. Lines 4 through 9 contain the executable section of the block. Line 5 sets the value of a variable to X. Lines 6 through 8 evaluate the value of the variable. If the value of the variable is not in a list of valid values, the RAISE statement raises the exception in line 7. Lines 10 through 14 contain the exception section of the block. Lines 11 and 10 handle the user-defined exception and display the error code and error message using the SQLCODE and SQLERRM built-in functions.

The user-defined exception is raised in the block and handled by the exception handler in lines 11 and 10. The message displayed in SQL*Plus is generated by this exception handler. The error code of 1 stands for a user-defined exception as the error message confirms.

2. Run CHP10_37.SQL in SQL*Plus, as shown in Figure 10.37. The sample stored procedure calls the RAISE_APPLICATION_ERROR system procedure to return a user-defined error code and error message to the calling module. The exception the stored procedure generates can be caught as a user-defined exception in the calling block.

3. Run the CHP10_38.SQL file in SQL*Plus. The PL/SQL block in the file calls the stored procedure created in the last step and handles the error returned. The code and output are shown in Figure 10.38.

Lines 1 through 3 contain the declarative section of the block. Line 2 declares an exception to handle the error generated by the stored procedure. Line 3 associates the error code returned by the stored procedure with the name of the exception, by using a PRAGMA EXCEPTION directive. Lines 4 through 6 contain the executable section of the block. Line 5 executes the stored procedure. Any errors generated by the stored procedure must be handled, or the PL/SQL block terminates abnormally. The exception handler in lines 8 to 10 handles the exception generated as a result of calling the stored procedure.

```
SQL> START CHP10_37
SQL> CREATE OR REPLACE PROCEDURE STORED_PROC10 AS
  2  BEGIN
  3      RAISE_APPLICATION_ERROR(-20001,'Fatal Error.');
  4  END;
  5  /

Procedure created.

SQL>
```

Figure 10.37 The stored procedure in CHP10_37.SQL returns a user-defined error code.

```
SQL> START CHP10_38
SQL> SET ECHO ON
SQL> SET SERVEROUTPUT ON
SQL> DECLARE
  2     INVALID_SP_CALL EXCEPTION;
  3     PRAGMA EXCEPTION_INIT(INVALID_SP_CALL,-20001);
  4  BEGIN
  5     STORED_PROC10;
  6     DBMS_OUTPUT.PUT_LINE('NO ERROR OCCURRED');
  7  EXCEPTION
  8     WHEN INVALID_SP_CALL THEN
  9          DBMS_OUTPUT.PUT_LINE('SQLCODE = ' || SQLCODE || ' ' ||
 10                         'SQLERRM = ' || SQLERRM);
 11  END;
 12  /
SQLCODE = -20001 SQLERRM = ORA-20001: Fatal Error.

PL/SQL procedure successfully completed.

SQL>
```

Figure 10.38 CHP10_38.SQL handles the user-defined error code.

The exception created in the declarative section handles the error generated by the stored procedure. The user-defined error number and user-defined error message specified in the call to RAISE_APPLICATION_ERROR procedure in the previous step are now displayed in SQL*Plus, using the SQLCODE and SQLERRM functions.

How It Works

A user-defined exception can be declared in the declarative section of a block and raised using the RAISE statement. When the exception is raised, the associated exception handler is executed. Step 1 presents a PL/SQL block employing a user-defined exception to exit the executable section of the code. If a user-defined exception is raised in the executable section but not handled in the exception section, an error occurs and the block terminates abnormally.

Step 2 creates a stored procedure that returns a user-defined error code and error message, when an exception is raised by calling the RAISE_APPLICATION_ERROR procedure. In Step 3, an exception is declared in the declarative section of a PL/SQL block and associated with a user-defined error code by using the PRAGMA EXCEPTION_INIT compiler directive. The exception generated when the stored procedure is called is handled by a user-defined exception handler in the calling block.

Comments

If a business situation arises such that you need to gracefully exit a PL/SQL block, consider generating a user-defined exception by using the RAISE statement in an IF statement. Alternatively, you can use the

RAISE_APPLICATION_ERROR procedure to generate an exception with a user-defined error code. The user-defined error code has to be in the range of -20,000 to -20,999. An exception raised in the exception section cannot be handled by another handler in the exception section and is propagated to the calling environment.

COMPLEXITY
ADVANCED

10.12 How do I...
Rebuild statements to create stored modules?

Problem

I need a technique to rebuild the CREATE statements that originally built the stored modules in my database. I also need to generate DDL statements to recompile all (or invalid) stored modules in the database. How do I generate DDL scripts to accomplish this?

Technique

The USER_SOURCE data dictionary view contains the source code for all the modules in a user account's schema. Each record in the view represents a single line of source code in a stored module. The LINE column contains the line number within the module, and the TEXT column contains the line of code. To list the source code of stored modules, the TEXT column should be queried from the view ordered by the TYPE and LINE columns. The TYPE column must be included, as package specifications and package bodies have the same name. The CREATE OR REPLACE keywords are prefixed to the first line of the source code using the DECODE function to generate rebuild statements.

Refer to How-To 10.6 to identify the need to manually recompile invalidly stored modules to avoid runtime compilation. The name and type of stored modules can be queried from the USER_OBJECTS data dictionary view. The ALTER keyword is prefixed with the COMPILE keyword as a suffix, to generate commands to force recompilation of stored modules. To recompile only invalid objects, a WHERE clause can be used in the query to return objects with an invalid status as `WHERE STATUS = 'INVALID'`.

By default, both the package specification and the package body are compiled with the ALTER...PACKAGE...COMPILE command. Optionally, the PACKAGE keyword to compile the package specification only, or the BODY keyword to compile the package body only, can be specified as the keyword following the COMPILE keyword.

Steps

1. Run CHP10_39.SQL in SQL*Plus. The query contained in the file generates a CREATE OR REPLACE statement for all stored modules in the current user account's schema. The HEADING SQL*Plus variable is set to OFF to suppress the heading output and run the query. Figure 10.39 shows the query used.

The DECODE function prefixes the first line of source code for each stored module with the CREATE OR REPLACE keywords. The first line of code is identified by a value of 1 in the LINE column. The ORDER BY clause ensures that the output of the source code for each module is in the correct order and that each module is separated. Including the TYPE column in the ORDER BY clause ensures that the order is correct for stored packages (a package specification and body have the same object name).

To save the DDL statements created by the query, include a SPOOL command to write the output to a file.

2. If you don't want to rebuild the stored modules but simply recompile them, run the CHP10_40.SQL file in SQL*Plus. The query contained in the file generates an ALTER COMPILE statement for each stored module in the user's schema and saves it in a script file. The HEADING, FEEDBACK, and TERMOUT SQL*Plus variables are set to OFF to suppress the column headings, row count, and output of query to screen. The script file is then invoked to compile the stored modules. Figure 10.40 shows the contents of the CHP10_40.SQL file.

The ALTER keyword is prefixed, and the COMPILE keyword is suffixed for each object queried from the USER_OBJECTS view. The output is a list of DDL statements that are saved to a file. The WHERE clause ensures that the objects returned by the query are stored modules in the user account's schema. Note that PACKAGE BODY objects are excluded; both the package specification and body are compiled by default with an

```
SET ECHO ON
SET HEADING OFF
SELECT
    DECODE(LINE,1,'CREATE OR REPLACE '||TEXT, TEXT)
FROM
    USER_SOURCE
ORDER BY NAME, TYPE, LINE;
/
```

Figure 10.39 CHP10_39.SQL generates rebuild statements.

```
SET ECHO OFF HEADING OFF FEEDBACK OFF TERMOUT OFF
SPOOL C:\TEMP\RECOMPILE.SQL
SELECT 'ALTER ' || OBJECT_TYPE || ' '
           || OBJECT_NAME || ' COMPILE;', 'SHOW ERRORS'
FROM
      USER_OBJECTS
WHERE
      OBJECT_TYPE IN ('FUNCTION', 'PROCEDURE', 'PACKAGE');
SPOOL OFF
SET ECHO ON HEADING ON FEEDBACK ON TERMOUT ON
START C:\TEMP\RECOMPILE.SQL
```

Figure 10.40 CHP10_40.SQL generates recompile statements.

ALTER…PACKAGE…COMPILE statement. When the commands are spooled to the command file, the file is run using the START command to recompile the stored modules.

The ALTER and COMPILE keywords in the query are used to create valid DDL statements. To recompile invalid stored modules, include a WHERE clause in the preceding query, to return only those modules that have an INVALID status in the USER_OBJECTS view. The query adds a SHOW ERRORS command after each compile statement to display any errors during compilation of a stored module.

How It Works

Step 1 presents a query using the DECODE function to concatenate the CREATE OR REPLACE keywords to the beginning of the first line. The query generates DDL statements for rebuilding stored modules. In Step 2, a query on the USER_OBJECTS view is used to generate DDL statements to recompile stored modules.

Comments

There might be times when you want to rebuild a stored module from the source code or recompile invalid modules in the database. Use the USER_SOURCE and USER_OBJECTS data dictionary views to create the necessary DDL statements. Refer to the Comments section of How-To 10.3 to identify system privileges that are required to execute the DDL statements.

QUERYING DATA

11

QUERYING DATA

How do I...

One of the most powerful features of Oracle is the sophisticated way it retrieves data from the database. Querying data can be as simple as retrieving all records from a single table or as complex as querying the hierarchy of tree-structured data.

Many of the topics covered in this chapter are common to all relational databases supporting SQL, whereas others are specific to Oracle, such as cursors that maintain the set of rows returned from a query temporarily and manipulate the rows one at a time. Oracle comes with powerful functions and packages to enhance SQL. Using its power to create sophisticated queries within your application means that records don't need to be manipulated within your application. This chapter also explores methods of querying data from the database.

11.1 Issue Single Record Queries with Implicit Cursors

If you don't explicitly define a cursor for a SELECT query, then Oracle creates an implicit one. An implicit cursor automatically performs the OPEN, FETCH, and CLOSE steps that must be specified with an explicit cursor. Several limitations, however, exist when using implicit cursors. This How-To describes how to issue queries with implicit cursors.

11.2 Issue Multiple Record Queries with Explicit Cursors

Using explicit cursors is a more controlled approach to querying data within PL/SQL than with implicit cursors. Control of processing each record returned from the SELECT statement of the cursor is possible. Also, additional exception handling processes can be implemented with explicit cursors. This How-To describes how to create a basic explicit cursor to query multiple records.

11.3 Use Cursor Attributes to Monitor Cursor State

Four attributes can be used with both implicit and explicit cursors: %FOUND, %ISOPEN, %NOTFOUND, and %ROWCOUNT, which return useful information about the execution of a cursor. These attributes can be used in expressions by appending the attribute to the cursor name. This How-To pertains to the use of cursor attributes to monitor the state of a cursor in PL/SQL.

11.4 Use Cursor Parameters to Enhance Cursor Reusability

Parameters can be passed to a cursor just as you would pass parameters to a stored procedure. Rather than reference PL/SQL variables directly in a cursor declaration, a cursor that accepts a parameter list is much easier to read and maintain, in addition to the benefits of reusability of the cursor within the PL/SQL block. This How-To presents the techniques for using cursor parameters to enhance cursor reusability.

11.5 Use Cursor Variables for More Flexibility

A cursor is tied to a static query, but cursor variables are dynamic because you can associate different queries with a cursor variable as long as the columns returned by each query match the declaration of the cursor variable. Cursor variables are like pointers and are very useful in passing result sets between stored subprograms. This How-To explores the use of cursor variables for more flexibility.

11.6 Use Wildcards in a Query

You don't always know the exact spelling of values in a character field, and to cope with this, wildcards enable you to query information without knowing the exact value of a field. The LIKE operator in Oracle is a powerful tool for pattern matching. In Oracle, the percent sign (%) is the wildcard and can represent any number of characters. The underscore (_) character is a position marker. It can represent any single character in its position. This How-To covers the process of using wildcards in a query.

11.7 Lock Rows When I Query Them

If you are planning to update a row after it has been queried, it is important to lock the row to prevent other users from unexpectedly updating it. The FOR UPDATE clause in a query locks the record it returns, until a COMMIT statement is executed or the session is terminated. This How-To presents the method for locking records with a query.

11.8 Prevent the Selection of Duplicate Rows

Sometimes a query returns duplicate records based on its selection criteria. If you are looking for all the unique values contained in a column, you can remove duplicate values by using the DISTINCT operator in a query. This How-To covers the technique used to prevent duplicate results in a query.

11.9 Traverse a Tree Structure

Data can be stored in a hierarchical structure within a table. An example is the reporting structure within an organization. Oracle provides support for a hierarchical structure through the CONNECT BY clause. This How-To presents the method for navigating a tree structure in Oracle.

COMPLEXITY
BEGINNING

11.1 How do I...
Issue single record queries with implicit cursors?

Problem

I want to select one record into a variable within my PL/SQL routine. Also, I don't want to explicitly step through the OPEN, FETCH, and CLOSE steps that must be specified with an explicit cursor. How do I issue single record queries with implicit cursors?

Technique

If a PL/SQL routine uses a SELECT statement but does not explicitly define a cursor, that SELECT statement is considered an implicit cursor. For more information on explicit cursors, see How-To 11.2.

After the implicit cursor has run, you can find additional information about the results of the query. The cursor attributes are SQL%ISOPEN, SQL%FOUND, SQL%NOTFOUND, and SQL%ROWCOUNT. They are fully covered in How-To 11.3.

With an implicit cursor, the query must return exactly one row. The values of the cursor attributes always refer to the most recently executed SQL statement. If no rows are returned, or more than one row is returned, then an error is returned, and control of the flow moves to the exception portion of the PL/SQL routine.

Steps

1. Run SQL*Plus and connect as the WAITE user account. CHP11_1.SQL, shown in Figure 11.1, creates the sample table used in this How-To.

2. The DEPT11 sample table contains two columns, DEPT_NO and DEPT_NAME, and is populated with three records. Run the file to create the sample table with its data.

```
SQL> START CHP11_1

Table created.

1 row inserted.

1 row inserted.

1 row inserted.

1 row inserted.

SQL>
```

CHP11_2.SQL, shown in Figure 11.2, has a PL/SQL routine that queries the DEPT11 table for a single record.

3. Run CHP11_2.SQL to execute the PL/SQL routine that uses an implicit cursor.

```
SQL> START CHP11_2.sql
The Department Name is Marketing
PL/SQL procedure successfully completed.
```

```
SET ECHO OFF
DROP TABLE DEPT11;
CREATE TABLE DEPT11 (
    DEPT_NO    NUMBER(10),
    DEPT_NAME VARCHAR2(30));

INSERT INTO DEPT11 VALUES
    (1,'Marketing');

INSERT INTO DEPT11 VALUES
    (2, 'Sales');

INSERT INTO DEPT11 VALUES
    (3, 'I/S');

INSERT INTO DEPT11 VALUES
    (4, 'Finance');
```

Figure 11.1 CHP11_1.SQL creates the DEPT11 sample table and data used in this How-To.

```
SET ECHO ON SERVEROUTPUT ON
DECLARE
    DEPARTMENT_NAME VARCHAR2(30);
BEGIN
    SELECT DEPT_NAME INTO DEPARTMENT_NAME
    FROM DEPT11
    WHERE DEPT_NO = 1;
    DBMS_OUTPUT.PUT_LINE ('The Department Name is '||DEPARTMENT_NAME);
END;
/
```

Figure 11.2 CHP11_2.SQL uses an implicit cursor to select one record from the DEPT11 table.

How It Works

Steps 1 and 2 create the DEPT11 table used throughout this chapter and populate it with sample data. Step 3 runs CHP11_2.SQL, which executes a PL/SQL routine that uses an implicit cursor. Line 1 has the SET ECHO ON SERVEROUTPUT ON statement, which enables Oracle to pass text back to the SQL*Plus screen. Without setting this, the user will not have messages from the PL/SQL routine displayed. Lines 2 and 3 declare a variable, DEPARTMENT_NAME, for the PL/SQL routine that will be assigned the value for the department name. Line 4 contains the BEGIN statement, which is necessary for the PL/SQL construct. Lines 5-7 contain the cursor. The cursor is simply a SELECT statement with an additional INTO clause, which assigns the DEPT_NAME to the DEPARTMENT_NAME variable. Line 8 gives a message back to the user account, using the DBMS_OUTPUT.PUT_LINE procedure. Line 9 contains the END statement, also necessary for the PL/SQL construct.

Comments

Implicit cursors work well for queries that return exactly one row. In our example, if one additional record is added to the DEPT11 table, with DEPT_NO=1, then the cursor has returned more than one row, which causes a TOO_MANY_ROWS error. To use implicit cursors, you must be sure that at no point in the future will the query return more than one record. Explicit cursors allow for multiple records to be returned and add greater flexibility to PL/SQL routines (for information on using explicit cursors, see How-To 11.2). INSERT and UPDATE statements automatically use implicit cursors.

COMPLEXITY
BEGINNING

11.2 How do I...
Issue multiple record queries with explicit cursors?

Problem

I need to query multiple records within PL/SQL. I would like more control over querying data within PL/SQL than I have with implicit cursors. After the results of the query have been moved into PL/SQL, I need to be able to navigate through the record set. How do I issue multiple record queries with explicit cursors?

Technique

To perform a multiple record query in PL/SQL, a cursor must be used. A *cursor* is a pointer to an area in the Process Global Area (PGA) on the server called the *context area*. Explicit cursors can be defined only by using PL/SQL, which is an extension of SQL. When a query is executed on the server, the set of rows the query returns is contained in the context area and can be retrieved to the client application through operations on a cursor.

The general flow of the PL/SQL routine is to define a cursor using a SELECT statement, OPEN the cursor, repeatedly FETCH data, and then CLOSE the cursor.

The OPEN command executes the SELECT query of the cursor. How-To's 11.4 and 11.5 give more detail on the OPEN command. When the FETCH command is used, the values of the record returned from the cursor are pushed into variables. This is where PL/SQL and explicit cursors have great value. Other tables can be updated based on the values of the variables. Other procedures or packages can also be called and programs started, among other possibilities. In this How-To, the results of the query are returned to the user. The CLOSE command is used to release memory associated with the cursor and generally to end the PL/SQL routine.

Steps

1. Connect to SQL*Plus as the WAITE user account. If you have not already run CHP11_1.SQL from How-To 11.1, run it now to create the DEPT11 table and populate it with sample data.

2. After the DEPT11 table has been created, run the CHP11_3.SQL file, as shown in Figure 11.3. The PL/SQL block contained in the file demonstrates the use of an explicit cursor.

```
SQL> START CHP11_3.sql
DEPT_NO = 1 DEPT_NAME = Marketing
DEPT_NO = 2 DEPT_NAME = Sales
DEPT_NO = 3 DEPT_NAME = I/S
DEPT_NO = 4 DEPT_NAME = Finance

PL/SQL procedure successfully completed.

SQL>
```

The four records present in the DEPT11 table are fetched in a loop and the column values are displayed, but when the %FOUND attribute evaluates to FALSE, the loop is exited.

```
SET ECHO ON SERVEROUTPUT ON
DECLARE
  CURSOR DEPT_CURS IS SELECT * FROM DEPT11;
  DEPT_REC DEPT_CURS%ROWTYPE;
BEGIN
  OPEN DEPT_CURS;
  FETCH DEPT_CURS INTO DEPT_REC;
  WHILE DEPT_CURS%FOUND LOOP
    DBMS_OUTPUT.PUT_LINE('DEPT_NO = ' || DEPT_REC.DEPT_NO ||
                         ' DEPT_NAME = ' || DEPT_REC.DEPT_NAME);
    FETCH DEPT_CURS INTO DEPT_REC;
  END LOOP;
  CLOSE DEPT_CURS;
END;
/
```

Figure 11.3 An explicit cursor that queries the DEPT11 table.

How It Works

Lines 2 and 3 contain the declarative section of the block. An explicit cursor is defined in line 2, and line 3 uses the %ROWTYPE attribute to declare a record variable representing all the columns returned by the cursor. Alternatively, you can use DEPT11%ROWTYPE to mean the same thing. Lines 5 through 12 contain the executable section of the block. Line 5 opens the cursor, and the loop in lines 7 through 11 fetches the next row from the result set. The first FETCH statement in line 6 is necessary to set the %FOUND attribute before entering the WHILE loop, which tests the attribute value on each entry into the loop.

After a FETCH is issued to retrieve the next row from the cursor, the %FOUND attribute is set to TRUE, if the FETCH was successful, and FALSE otherwise. The WHILE loop continues as long as the %FOUND attribute evaluates to TRUE. For each row that is fetched, the column values are displayed in lines 8 and 9. If the FETCH fails to retrieve a row from the cursor, the %FOUND attribute is set to FALSE and the loop is exited. Line 12 closes the cursor to release system resources used by the cursor. Although not a recommended practice, you can use the Boolean NOT operator for negation. NOT *CURSOR_NAME*%FOUND is equivalent to %NOTFOUND, and NOT *CURSOR_NAME*%NOTFOUND is equivalent to %FOUND.

Comments

This How-To shows some examples of how much more flexible explicit cursors are than implicit cursors. Much of the rest of this chapter provides more coverage of explicit cursors and PL/SQL. How-To 11.3 describes how to use cursor attributes, such as %FOUND, in more detail. How-To 11.4 shows how explicit cursor parameters can enhance reusability. How-To 11.5 shows how to use cursor variables.

COMPLEXITY
INTERMEDIATE

11.3 How do I...
Use cursor attributes to monitor cursor state?

Problem

When I query records from tables and views using cursors, I need to know whether the query returned any rows or not and the number of rows fetched by the cursor. I also need to know whether the cursor is already open before opening a cursor. In some cases, if I issue an UPDATE statement on a single record, I want to know if there is no matching record in the table so that I can insert a record in the table. How do I use cursor attributes to monitor cursor state?

Technique

Cursors have four attributes: %FOUND, %ISOPEN, %NOTFOUND, and %ROWCOUNT. Table 11.1 explains the meaning of each attribute. A cursor attribute appended to the cursor name acts like a built-in variable that can be tested to find out information about the execution of the cursor. How-To's 11.1 and 11.2 demonstrate the use of explicit cursors to execute a multi-row query and how an implicit cursor is used by Oracle in executing a SELECT...INTO, INSERT, UPDATE, or DELETE statement. Cursor attributes can be used with both implicit and explicit cursors, but differences exist in terms of which attributes can be meaningfully used with implicit cursors.

Table 11.1 Cursor attributes

ATTRIBUTE	MEANING
%FOUND	Boolean attribute that returns TRUE if the record returned by the last fetch attempt is successful
%NOTFOUND	Boolean attribute that always returns the opposite of %FOUND
%ISOPEN	Boolean attribute that returns TRUE if the cursor is open
%ROWCOUNT	Numeric attribute that returns the number of records fetched from the cursor

With explicit cursors, more than one row can be returned by the query that forms the result set. As rows are fetched one at a time from the result set, the number of rows currently fetched is returned by the %ROWCOUNT attribute. The %FOUND attribute is TRUE if the previous fetch returned a row and is FALSE otherwise. Vice versa, the %NOTFOUND attribute is TRUE if the previous fetch did not return a row and FALSE otherwise. The %ISOPEN attribute yields TRUE if the cursor is open, FALSE otherwise.

With an implicit cursor, the query must return exactly one row, and the values of the cursor attributes always refer to the most recently executed SQL statement. Oracle uses a cursor named SQL as the implicit cursor, and the attributes of the SQL cursor are set to NULL whenever an implicit cursor is opened. The implicit cursor is automatically closed after execution of the SQL statement, so SQL%ISOPEN always returns FALSE.

If a SELECT...INTO statement returns more than one row, the TOO_MANY_ROWS exception is raised; and if no rows are returned, the NO_DATA_FOUND exception is raised. Naturally, the SQL%ROWCOUNT has to be 1 for the SELECT...INTO statement to execute successfully. Similarly, the SQL%FOUND and SQL%NOTFOUND attributes have no meaningful use with a SELECT...INTO statement. If the TOO_MANY_ROWS exception is raised, the %ROWCOUNT is still 1 and not the actual number of rows returned by the query. Neither the NO_DATA_FOUND exception is raised, nor the SQL%NOTFOUND set to TRUE, however, if the SELECT...INTO statement uses SQL group functions, such as AVG or SUM, which always return a value or NULL.

Steps

1. If you have not already created the DEPT11 table and populated it with sample data in How-To 11.1, then run SQL*Plus, connect as the WAITE user account, and run CHP11_1.SQL.

2. Run the CHP11_4.SQL file in SQL*Plus (see Figure 11.4). The PL/SQL block contained in the file demonstrates the use of %FOUND and %ROWCOUNT attributes of an implicit cursor.

Until a DML statement is executed, the SQL%FOUND and SQL%ROWCOUNT attributes of the implicit SQL cursor are NULL. Line 2 deletes two records from the DEPT11 table. After the DELETE statement successfully deletes rows from the DEPT11 table, the SQL%FOUND attribute is set to TRUE. The SQL%ROWCOUNT attribute is set to the number of rows deleted. The IF statement in line 4 checks the value of the SQL%FOUND attribute, and if TRUE, the message in line 5 displays the number of rows deleted.

Because two records are deleted from the DEPT11 table, the SQL%FOUND attribute evaluates to TRUE, and the number of rows deleted is displayed in SQL*Plus.

3. Run the CHP11_5.SQL file in SQL*Plus (see Figure 11.5). The PL/SQL block contained in the file demonstrates the use of the SQL%NOTFOUND attribute of an implicit cursor after an UPDATE statement fails to match any rows.

```
SQL> START C:\CHP11_4.SQL
SQL> SET ECHO ON SERVEROUTPUT ON
SQL> BEGIN
  2     DELETE FROM DEPT11
  3     WHERE DEPT_NO > 2;
  4     IF SQL%FOUND THEN
  5        DBMS_OUTPUT.PUT_LINE(SQL%ROWCOUNT || ' rows deleted
  6     END IF;
  7  END;
  8  /
2 rows deleted.

PL/SQL procedure successfully completed.

SQL> |
```

Figure 11.4 CHP11_4.SQL shows the %FOUND and %ROWCOUNT attributes of an implicit cursor.

```
SQL> START C:\CHP11_5.SQL
SQL> BEGIN
  2     UPDATE DEPT11
  3        SET DEPT_NAME = 'Tech Support'
  4        WHERE DEPT_NO = 3;
  5     IF SQL%NOTFOUND THEN
  6        INSERT INTO DEPT11
  7        VALUES (3, 'Tech Support');
  8     END IF;
  9  END;
 10  /

PL/SQL procedure successfully completed.

SQL> |
```

Figure 11.5 CHP11_5.SQL
shows the %NOTFOUND
attribute of an implicit cursor.

The SQL%NOTFOUND attribute of the implicit SQL cursor is NULL at
the beginning. Lines 2 through 4 attempt to update a record in the
DEPT11 table. The record is non-existent because it was deleted from the
table in Step 2. Because no rows are affected by the UPDATE statement,
the SQL%NOTFOUND attribute is set to TRUE. Lines 5 to 8 ensure that,
if the UPDATE statement failed because of a non-existent record, then that
record gets inserted into the table. Run a simple query on the DEPT11
table to check whether the record is actually inserted.

```
SQL> SELECT * FROM DEPT11;

DEPT_NO DEPT_NAME
-------- -----------------------------
      1 Marketing
      2 Sales
      3 Tech Support
```

Because no records are to be updated in the DEPT11 table, the
SQL%NOTFOUND attribute evaluates to TRUE and the record is inserted
into the DEPT11 table, as seen from the query results.

4. The %FOUND attribute of an explicit cursor is explained in How-To 11.2.
For an example of using the %FOUND attribute to loop through records
of an explicit cursor, please see How-To 11.2.

5. The PL/SQL block contained in the CHP11_6.SQL file, shown in Figure
11.6, demonstrates the use of the %NOTFOUND and %ISOPEN attributes
of an explicit cursor.

```
SET ECHO ON SERVEROUTPUT ON
DECLARE
  CURSOR DEPT_CURS IS SELECT DEPT_NAME FROM DEPT11
                      FOR UPDATE OF DEPT_NAME;
  DEPT_NAME DEPT11.DEPT_NAME%TYPE;
BEGIN
  OPEN DEPT_CURS;
  LOOP
    FETCH DEPT_CURS INTO DEPT_NAME;
    EXIT WHEN DEPT_CURS%NOTFOUND;
    IF DEPT_CURS%ROWCOUNT = 3 THEN
       UPDATE DEPT11 SET DEPT_NAME = 'MIS'
       WHERE CURRENT OF DEPT_CURS;
    END IF;
  END LOOP;
  CLOSE DEPT_CURS;
END;
/
```

Figure 11.6 CHP11_6.SQL shows the
%NOTFOUND and %ISOPEN attributes
of an explicit cursor.

Lines 2 and 3 contain the declarative section of the block. An explicit cursor is defined in line 2, and line 3 uses the %ROWTYPE attribute to declare a record variable representing all the columns returned by the cursor. Lines 5 through 12 contain the executable section of the block. Line 5 opens the cursor, and the loop in lines 6 through 11 fetch the rows from the cursor. In line 7, after a FETCH is issued to retrieve the next row from the cursor, the %NOTFOUND attribute is set to FALSE if the FETCH was successful, TRUE otherwise. For each row that is fetched, the column values are displayed in lines 9 and 10. If the FETCH failed to retrieve a row from the cursor, the %NOTFOUND attribute is set to TRUE and the loop is immediately exited in line 8 as the condition in the EXIT WHEN statement is satisfied.

Line 12 closes the cursor to release system resources used by the cursor. Lines 13 through 17 contain the exception section of the block. If an error occurred while processing, the %ISOPEN attribute is checked to see whether the cursor is open, to close the cursor before exiting the block. It is a good programming practice to include code to close any open cursors in the execution section as well as in the exception section, just in case an error occurred during execution. When a cursor is closed, system resources taken up by the cursor are released.

The three records present in the DEPT11 table are fetched in a loop and the column values are displayed, but when the %NOTFOUND attribute evaluates to TRUE, the loop is exited.

6. Run the CHP11_7.SQL file in SQL*Plus (see Figure 11.7). The PL/SQL block contained in the file explores the use of the %ROWCOUNT attribute of an explicit cursor and demonstrates the use of the UPDATE...WHERE CURRENT OF statement while using cursors.

```
SQL> START C:\CHP11_7.SQL
SQL> SET ECHO ON SERVEROUTPUT ON
SQL> DECLARE
  2     CURSOR DEPT_CURS IS SELECT DEPT_NAME FROM DEPT11
  3                  FOR UPDATE OF DEPT_NAME;
  4     DEPT_NAME DEPT11.DEPT_NAME%TYPE;
  5  BEGIN
  6     OPEN DEPT_CURS;
  7     LOOP
  8       FETCH DEPT_CURS INTO DEPT_NAME;
  9       EXIT WHEN DEPT_CURS%NOTFOUND;
 10       IF DEPT_CURS%ROWCOUNT = 3 THEN
 11          UPDATE DEPT11 SET DEPT_NAME = 'MIS'
 12          WHERE CURRENT OF DEPT_CURS;
 13       END IF;
 14     END LOOP;
 15     CLOSE DEPT_CURS;
 16  END;
 17  /

PL/SQL procedure successfully completed.

SQL>
```

Figure 11.7 The %ROWCOUNT and
UPDATE...WHERE CURRENT OF roundup.

Lines 2 to 4 contain the declarative section of the block. An explicit cursor is defined in line 2 and 3. Note the use of the FOR UPDATE OF clause of the SELECT statement in line 3 while declaring a cursor for update operations. Line 4 uses the %TYPE attribute to declare a variable representing the DEPT_NAME column of the DEPT11 table. Line 6 opens the cursor, and the loop in lines 7 through 14 fetch the rows from the cursor. In line 8, after a FETCH is issued to retrieve the next row from the cursor, the %NOTFOUND attribute is set to FALSE if the FETCH was successful and TRUE otherwise. The %ROWCOUNT is set to 0 after the cursor has been opened, but no fetch has been done. For each row fetched, the %ROWCOUNT is incremented by 1.

When the %ROWCOUNT reaches 3, as checked for in line 10, an UPDATE statement is issued in lines 11 and 12 using the WHERE CURRENT OF clause, to update the row that was fetched most recently. It is not necessary to use the %ROWCOUNT when using the WHERE CURRENT OF clause. This is just an example where two techniques are shown in a single step. If the FETCH fails to retrieve a row from the cursor, the %NOTFOUND attribute is set to TRUE, and the loop is immediately exited in line 9 as the condition in the EXIT WHEN statement is satisfied. Line 15 closes the cursor to release system resources used by the cursor. You can query the DEPT11 table to see whether the intended row is updated.

How It Works

INSERT, UPDATE, DELETE, and SELECT...INTO statements are executed by Oracle using the SQL cursor. Cursor attributes can be applied to the SQL cursor. The SQL%ISOPEN always returns FALSE. Step 1 creates the sample table and data, and Step 2 shows the use of SQL%ROWCOUNT and SQL%FOUND after executing a DELETE statement. The SQL%NOTFOUND attribute is checked in Step 3 after executing an UPDATE statement, and if set to TRUE, a record is inserted into the DEPT11 table. With a SELECT...INTO statement, if more than one record is returned by the statement, the TOO_MANY_ROWS exception is raised; if no records are returned, the NO_DATA_FOUND exception is raised. Hence, the SQL cursor attributes have no meaningful use when using a SELECT...INTO statement. Step 4 makes use of the %FOUND attribute of an explicit cursor to check whether a record is returned after executing the FETCH statement. Step 5 uses %NOTFOUND, which is the exact opposite of %FOUND and is used to exit the loop if no more remaining rows are to be fetched from the cursor. Step 6 demonstrates the use of the %ROWCOUNT attribute and exemplifies the declaration of an update cursor and the use of the UPDATE...WHERE CURRENT OF statement.

Comments

You can use cursor attributes only in procedural statements, not in SQL statements. Cursor attributes are set to NULL before the implicit SQL cursor is opened for executing a SQL statement. Cursor attribute values refer to the most recently executed SQL statements.

Note that after you execute a SQL statement, call a stored procedure, and then check the values of the SQL cursor attributes, they might not be what you expect. This is because if the stored procedure executed any SQL statements, the values of the SQL cursor attributes refer to the results of the execution of the SQL statement in the stored procedure. As a workaround, you can save values of the relevant cursor attributes in PL/SQL variables before calling the stored procedure. The INVALID_CURSOR predefined exception is raised if you try to use cursor attributes with an explicit cursor that has not been opened or if the cursor has been closed. Cursor attributes can also be used with cursor variables, which is the topic of discussion of How-To 11.5.

COMPLEXITY
INTERMEDIATE

11.4 How do I...
Use cursor parameters to enhance cursor reusability?

Problem

I need to use the same cursor to fetch different results, depending on the values of variables in the PL/SQL block. If I use PL/SQL variables in the cursor declaration itself, I have to write the same cursor several times, each time tying it up with a set of variables. I need to pass parameters to the cursor so that I can write the cursor once and pass parameters to it whenever I open the cursor. How do I use cursor parameters to enhance cursor reusability?

Technique

Passing parameters to cursors is similar to passing parameters to stored procedures and functions. The only difference is that OUT and IN OUT mode parameters cannot be specified with cursors. Parameters passed to a cursor are specified along with their datatypes while defining the cursor. The syntax used to define a cursor with parameters is:

```
CURSOR cursor_name [(parameter_name1 datatype1[, parameter_name2 datatype2]...)]
IS query;
```

The scope of parameters is limited to the cursor definition. In other words, they cannot be accessed in the PL/SQL block in which the cursor is defined. The parameters passed can be used in the query to control the output generated. Typically, the parameters passed to the cursor are used in the WHERE clause of the SELECT statement, but they can be referenced anywhere in the query defining the cursor. Default values can be specified for the parameters using the DEFAULT keyword or using the := notation.

The OPEN statement is used to open the cursor and pass parameter values to the cursor. The syntax for opening a cursor that takes parameters looks like:

```
OPEN cursor_name [(parameter_value1[, parameter_value2]...)];
```

If parameters have default values in the cursor definition, the cursor can be opened without specifying any parameters. After the OPEN statement is executed, the query is performed using the parameter values provided in the OPEN statement, and the result set can be fetched using the FETCH statement. A cursor FOR loop can be used in a similar fashion to implicitly open a cursor that takes parameters.

If you are using packages, cursors can be packaged just like stored subprograms. You can separate the cursor declaration in the package header from the cursor definition in the package body. This way, you can change the cursor body without having to change the cursor declaration. The cursor declaration in the package header uses the following syntax:

```
CURSOR cursor_name [(parameter_name1 datatype1[, parameter_name2 datatype2]...)]
RETURN return_type;
```

return_type must represent a scalar datatype or a PL/SQL user-defined record or a row in a table.

Steps

1. Run SQL*Plus and connect as the WAITE user account. If you have not done so already, run the CHP11_1.SQL file from step 1 of How-To 11.1. The DEPT11 table is created with some sample data.

2. The next step demonstrates the method used to create a cursor with parameters. Run the CHP11_8.SQL in SQL*Plus, and the PL/SQL block contained in the file creates a cursor with parameters. Cursor parameters enable the same cursor to be used with variable information in the query. The results of the operation are shown in Figure 11.8.

```
SQL> START C:\CHP11_8.SQL
SQL> DECLARE
  2      CURSOR DEPT_CURS (IN_DEPT_NO NUMBER) IS
  3          SELECT DEPT_NO,
  4                 DEPT_NAME
  5          FROM DEPT11
  6          WHERE DEPT_NO > IN_DEPT_NO;
  7      DEPT_REC DEPT11%ROWTYPE;
  8  BEGIN
  9      OPEN DEPT_CURS(2);
 10      LOOP
 11          FETCH DEPT_CURS INTO DEPT_REC;
 12          EXIT WHEN DEPT_CURS%NOTFOUND;
 13          DBMS_OUTPUT.PUT_LINE(DEPT_REC.DEPT_NAME);
 14      END LOOP;
 15      CLOSE DEPT_CURS;
 16  END;
 17  /
MIS

PL/SQL procedure successfully completed.

SQL>
```

Figure 11.8 CHP11_8.SQL demonstrates a cursor with parameters.

Lines 2 through 7 contain the declarative section of the block. The cursor defined in lines 2 to 6 uses a parameter, which is used in the WHERE clause in line 6 to control the output of the query. A default value for the parameter can be supplied using the := operator or DEFAULT keyword as with stored procedures. Line 7 uses the %ROWTYPE attribute to declare a record variable representing all columns of the DEPT11 table. Line 9 opens the cursor and passes 2 as a parameter to the cursor. A result set that matches the selection criteria in the WHERE clause of the query is then ready to be fetched from the cursor. The loop in lines 10 through 14 fetches rows from the cursor and displays the DEPT_NAME column value in SQL*Plus.

The two records with DEPT_NO values greater than two are returned by the cursor. The DEPT_NAME column value is displayed after each record is fetched from the cursor. When the %NOTFOUND attribute evaluates to TRUE, the loop is exited.

3. Run the CHP11_9.SQL in SQL*Plus, as shown in Figure 11.9. The PL/SQL block contained in the file uses a FOR loop to fetch the result set of a cursor with parameters.

```
SQL> START C:\CHP11_9.SQL
SQL> SET ECHO ON SERVEROUTPUT ON
SQL> DECLARE
  2      CURSOR C1 (VIEW_PATTERN VARCHAR2) IS
  3          SELECT VIEW_NAME
  4              FROM ALL_VIEWS
  5          WHERE VIEW_NAME LIKE VIEW_PATTERN || '%' AND
  6                  ROWNUM <= 5
  7          ORDER BY VIEW_NAME;
  8  BEGIN
  9      FOR VNAME IN C1('DBA_') LOOP
 10          DBMS_OUTPUT.PUT_LINE(VNAME.VIEW_NAME);
 11      END LOOP;
 12  END;
 13  /
DBA_2PC_NEIGHBORS
DBA_2PC_PENDING
DBA_ANALYZE_OBJECTS
DBA_AUDIT_DBA
DBA_AUDIT_EXISTS

PL/SQL procedure successfully completed.

SQL>
```

Figure 11.9 CHP11_9.SQL uses a FOR loop for a cursor with parameters.

The cursor defined in lines 2 through 7 contains a parameter used in the WHERE clause in line 5. When the cursor is opened, the parameter must be supplied or an error will occur. Lines 9 through 13 contain the executable section of the block. In line 11, the cursor opened by the FOR loop passes a character parameter to the cursor, which is used in the WHERE clause when the query is executed.

When using a FOR loop to process records returned by the cursor, the cursor is opened and closed implicitly by the FOR loop. This is why the cursor does not have to be opened or closed explicitly using the OPEN and CLOSE calls, as with other loop structures. Also, note that each record returned by the cursor into the VNAME record variable is not declared explicitly in the declarative section. The cursor FOR loop contained in lines 10 through 12 loops through each record in the cursor and displays the VIEW_NAME column using the DBMS_OUTPUT.PUT_LINE procedure.

The parameter passed to the opened query causes only the records beginning with DBA_ to be returned by the query and displayed in SQL*Plus.

How It Works

A cursor is defined in the declarative section along with the parameters and their datatypes, followed by the query to be executed. Within the executable section, the parameters are passed when the cursor is opened—in the OPEN statement or in a FOR loop. Step 1 creates the DEPT11 table used for this How-To. Step 2 demonstrates the process of passing parameters to a cursor in the OPEN statement while opening the cursor. The process of opening the cursor with parameters can also be consolidated by using a cursor FOR loop to process a cursor. Step 3 demonstrates the operation of a cursor FOR loop. Note that the OPEN, FETCH, and CLOSE calls are eliminated while using cursor FOR loops. Cursors enable parameters to be specified, providing greater flexibility and promoting their reuse in similar queries.

Comments

Parameters can be passed to a query by specifying them with their datatypes with the cursor name. If the cursor is going to be used in several places in a PL/SQL block with different values in the WHERE clause for each invocation, that cursor is a good candidate to use parameters with. Using parameters makes the cursor more reusable because the result set is not tied to any variables used in the PL/SQL block. Coding for a cursor can be greatly simplified by using a FOR loop to process a cursor. Whenever possible, use cursors containing parameters so you can reuse cursors in your code.

COMPLEXITY

INTERMEDIATE

11.5 How do I...
Use cursor variables for more flexibility?

Problem

I need to declare a cursor variable in my PL/SQL code to associate it with different cursors dynamically. I want to assign new cursors to the cursor variable and pass the cursor variable as a parameter to stored procedures and functions. How do I create cursor variables for more flexibility?

Technique

A cursor is tied to a static query, whereas a cursor variable is dynamically associated with a query at runtime. If you associate different queries with a cursor variable, columns returned by each query must match the return type of the cursor variable. A cursor variable is similar to a cursor because you can fetch the current row from the result set by using the FETCH statement. Think of a cursor variable as a pointer to which you can assign new queries. The real advantage of using cursor variables is that you can pass them as parameters to functions and procedures.

In PL/SQL, you can use the REF type modifier to construct a reference (or pointer) to an object. The datatype of the pointer is `ref_object_type`, where `ref` is simply a short form for REFERENCE and `object_type` is the name of an existing object type. Because a cursor variable is a pointer to a cursor, it has a datatype of REF CURSOR. Creating references to other object types is covered in Chapter 16.

Two steps are required to create cursor variables. First, you define a REF CURSOR type; then, you declare cursor variables of that type. You can define REF CURSOR types using the syntax:

```
TYPE ref_cursor_type IS REF CURSOR RETURN return_type;
```

`ref_cursor_type` is a new datatype used in subsequent declarations of cursor variables, and `return_type` is a record type corresponding with the columns returned by any cursor associated with the cursor variable. Refer to How-To 10.8 for more information on record types. The RETURN clause is optional, and when included, it causes the cursor variable to be strongly typed. A weakly typed cursor variable can be defined by omitting the RETURN clause as:

```
TYPE ref_cursor_type IS REF CURSOR;
```

Columns returned by a query must match the return type of a strongly typed cursor variable or else a compilation error occurs. Any query, however, can be associated with a weakly typed cursor variable. After the type is defined, cursor variables can be declared like any other variables, for example:

```
DECLARE
    cv_ref_ref_cursor_type;
```

The OPEN FOR statement is used to open a cursor variable and associate a query with it. The syntax for opening a cursor variable is:

```
OPEN cv_ref FOR query;
```

The following steps show how you can control cursor variables in your PL/SQL programs.

Steps

1. Run SQL*Plus and connect as the WAITE user account. CHP11_10.SQL, shown in Figure 11.10, creates the sample tables and data used in this How-To. Run the file to create the sample table and data. The DEPT11 and EMP11 tables created by the script are used in the following steps.

```
SQL>  START CHP11_10.sql

Table created.

1 row created.

1 row created.

Table created.

1 row created.
```

```
SET ECHO OFF
DROP TABLE DEPT11;
CREATE TABLE DEPT11 (
    DEPT_NO    NUMBER(10),
    DEPT_NAME VARCHAR2(20));

INSERT INTO DEPT11 VALUES
    (1,'Marketing');

INSERT INTO DEPT11 VALUES
    (2, 'Sales');

CREATE TABLE EMP11 (
    EMP_NO    NUMBER(10),
    EMP_NAME VARCHAR2(30));

INSERT INTO EMP11 VALUES
    (1,'Joe Shmoe');
```

Figure 11.10 CHP11_10.SQL creates the sample tables and data used in How-To 11.5.

2. Run the CHP11_11.SQL file in SQL*Plus, as shown in Figure 11.11. The PL/SQL block contained in the file uses a cursor variable to fetch records from the DEPT11 table.

Line 2 defines a cursor reference type using the REF CURSOR keywords. The cursor reference is strongly typed as the record type that must be returned by any cursor associated with the cursor variable defined using the RETURN clause. A cursor variable of the cursor reference type is declared in line 3. A record variable corresponding with all columns of the DEPT11 table is declared in line 4. Lines 6 and 7 open a cursor variable by associating it with a query on the DEPT11 table. Note the use of the FOR keyword in the OPEN statement. The loop in lines 8 through 13 is used to fetch records from the cursor variable. There is no difference in this loop if you use either a cursor or a cursor variable.

3. Run the CHP11_12.SQL file in SQL*Plus. The package example contained in the file uses a procedure to associate the cursor variable to point to one of two different cursors, based on the value of a selector parameter. Figure 11.12 shows the results of the operation.

First, a package specification is created. A cursor reference type is defined in line 2 of the package specification. A weakly typed cursor reference is defined by omitting the RETURN clause after the REF CURSOR keywords. Lines 3 and 4 declare the procedure contained in the package.

```
SQL> START C:\CHP11_11.SQL
SQL> DECLARE
  2    TYPE DEPT_CU_TYPE IS REF CURSOR RETURN DEPT11%ROWTYPE;
  3    DEPT_CU DEPT_CU_TYPE;
  4    DEPT_REC DEPT11%ROWTYPE;
  5  BEGIN
  6    OPEN DEPT_CU FOR
  7    SELECT * FROM DEPT11;
  8    LOOP
  9      FETCH DEPT_CU INTO DEPT_REC;
 10      EXIT WHEN DEPT_CU%NOTFOUND;
 11      DBMS_OUTPUT.PUT_LINE(DEPT_REC.DEPT_NO || ' ' ||
 12                            DEPT_REC.DEPT_NAME);
 13    END LOOP;
 14    CLOSE DEPT_CU;
 15  END;
 16  /
1 Marketing
2 Sales

PL/SQL procedure successfully completed.

SQL>
```

Figure 11.11 CHP11_11.SQL shows the use of a strongly typed cursor variable.

```
SQL> START C:\CHP11_12.SQL
SQL> CREATE OR REPLACE PACKAGE EMP_OR_DEPT11 AS
  2    TYPE CU_TYPE IS REF CURSOR;
  3    PROCEDURE OPEN_CU (CU  IN OUT CU_TYPE,
  4                       TBL IN INTEGER);
  5  END EMP_OR_DEPT11;
  6  /

Package created.

SQL> CREATE OR REPLACE PACKAGE BODY EMP_OR_DEPT11 AS
  2    PROCEDURE OPEN_CU (CU  IN OUT CU_TYPE,
  3                       TBL IN INTEGER) IS
  4    BEGIN
  5      IF TBL = 1 THEN
  6        OPEN CU FOR SELECT * FROM DEPT11;
  7      ELSIF TBL = 2 THEN
  8        OPEN CU FOR SELECT * FROM EMP11;
  9      END IF;
 10    END OPEN_CU;
 11  END EMP_OR_DEPT11;
 12  /

Package body created.
```

Figure 11.12 CHP11_12.SQL creates a package to implement a weakly typed cursor reference.

Second, the package body is created using the CREATE OR REPLACE PACKAGE BODY keywords. Note that the cursor variable is an IN OUT parameter to the procedure. In lines 6 and 8, the cursor variable is associated with a query on the DEPT11 table or the EMP11 table depending on the value of the TBL parameter. Because the cursor reference is weakly typed, cursors returning different record types can be associated with the cursor variable. The next step makes use of this package.

4. Run the CHP11_13.SQL file in SQL*Plus, as shown in Figure 11.13. The PL/SQL block contained in the file calls the OPEN_CV procedure to open the cursor variable and point it to a query on either the EMP11 or DEPT11 table. For the sake of simplicity, a single row is fetched from the cursor variable in each case.

Line 2 declares a cursor variable of the cursor reference type defined in the package specification of the previous step. A record variable corresponding with columns of the DEPT11 table is declared in line 3, and a record variable corresponding with columns of the EMP11 table is declared in line 4. Line 6 calls the OPEN_CV procedure to open a cursor variable by associating it with a query on the DEPT11 table. A record is fetched from the cursor variable, and column values are displayed. Line 10 closes the cursor variable before reopening it by calling the OPEN_CV procedure in line 11 to point it to a query on the EMP11 table. The first record in the EMP11 table is fetched using the cursor variable, and column values are displayed.

```
SQL> START C:\CHP11_13.SQL
SQL> SET ECHO ON SERVEROUTPUT ON
SQL> DECLARE
  2     CV EMP_OR_DEPT11.CV_TYPE;
  3     DEPT_REC DEPT11%ROWTYPE;
  4     EMP_REC EMP11%ROWTYPE;
  5  BEGIN
  6     EMP_OR_DEPT11.OPEN_CV(CV, 1);
  7     FETCH CV INTO DEPT_REC;
  8     DBMS_OUTPUT.PUT_LINE(DEPT_REC.DEPT_NO || ' ' ||
  9                          DEPT_REC.DEPT_NAME);
 10     CLOSE CV;
 11     EMP_OR_DEPT11.OPEN_CV(CV, 2);
 12     FETCH CV INTO EMP_REC;
 13     DBMS_OUTPUT.PUT_LINE(EMP_REC.EMP_NO || ' ' ||
 14                          EMP_REC.EMP_NAME);
 15     CLOSE CV;
 16  END;
 17  /
1 Marketing
1 Joe Shmoe

PL/SQL procedure successfully completed.

SQL> |
```

Figure 11.13 CHP11_13.SQL shows the use of a weakly typed cursor variable.

How It Works

The REF CURSOR keywords are used to define a cursor reference type, and cursor variables of that type can then be declared. If the REF CURSOR type is defined in a package, you can declare cursor variables of that cursor reference type in any PL/SQL block, function, or procedure.

Columns returned by a query must match the return type of a strongly typed cursor variable, whereas a weakly typed cursor variable can be associated with any query. This enables you to declare cursor variables without knowing the cursor it will receive.

Three steps are required to control a cursor variable: OPEN FOR, FETCH, and CLOSE. Cursor variables follow the same scoping and instantiation rules as any other variables declared in a block.

Step 1 creates the sample tables used in the following steps. Step 2 demonstrates the use of a strongly typed cursor variable. Columns returned by an associated query must be type-compatible with the return type of the cursor variable or else a compilation error occurs. Step 3 creates a package to implement a weakly typed cursor reference. Step 4 shows the use of a weakly typed cursor variable. If the records fetched from the cursor variable don't match that of the receiving record variable, a ROW_MISMATCH predefined exception is raised. This exception can be trapped to try a fit into a record variable with the expected datatypes of columns returned. If you try to fetch, close, or apply cursor attributes to a cursor variable that is not open, the INVALID_CURSOR predefined exception is raised.

Comments

It is a good practice to use strongly typed cursor variables types because they are less error-prone: The compiler lets you associate a strongly typed cursor variable only with type-compatible queries. Weakly typed cursor variables are more flexible, however, because the compiler lets you associate a weakly typed cursor variable with any query. Cursor variables are available to every PL/SQL client and can be bind variables. The associated query can reference bind variables as well.

The %FOUND, %NOTFOUND, %ROWCOUNT, and %ISOPEN cursor attributes (refer to How-To 11.3) can be used with cursor variables, which cannot be declared in a package because they don't have a persistent state. Parameters cannot be passed to a cursor variable, nor can you associate a FOR UPDATE query with a cursor variable. Cursor variables cannot be used with dynamic SQL, a NULL value cannot be assigned to a cursor variable, and collection elements cannot store cursor variable values. Always remember that creating a cursor variable creates a pointer, not an object.

COMPLEXITY

INTERMEDIATE

11.6 How do I...
Use wildcards in a query?

Problem

I want to use wildcard characters in some of my queries. As an example, I want to return all records in which the first three letters of the person's last name are *JON*. The user of the system does not always know the exact spelling of the data in a character field, and pattern matching is necessary. How do I use wildcards in a query?

Technique

Oracle contains two special characters used in pattern matching operations. The percent sign (%) is used to specify any number of unknown characters. The underscore (_) is a placeholder character and can be replaced by only one character in the specified location.

Wildcard characters must be used with the LIKE operator. If a wildcard character is used with an equal sign (=), it is taken literally. The LIKE operator specifies that wildcards can be used in the specified string. If the LIKE operator is used and no wildcards are specified, it is equivalent to the equal sign.

Steps

1. Run SQL*Plus and connect as the WAITE user account. CHP11_14.SQL, shown in Figure 11.14, creates the sample tables and data used in this How-To.

The sample table is populated with data to demonstrate the use of wildcard characters. Run the file to create the sample table and data.

```
SQL>  START CHP11_14.sql

Table created.

1 row created.

1 row created.

1 row created.

1 row created.

1 row created.

Commit complete.
```

2. Load CHP11_15.SQL into the SQL buffer. The file contains a query that uses a wildcard character to return all rows in which the first three letters of the LAST_NAME column are *JON*.

```
SQL> GET CHP11_15.sql
  1   SELECT
  2     LAST_NAME,
  3     FIRST_NAME
  4   FROM
  5     EMP11
  6   WHERE
  7*    LAST_NAME LIKE 'JON%'
```

```
CREATE TABLE EMP11 (
    LAST_NAME    VARCHAR2(20),
    FIRST_NAME   VARCHAR2(20));

INSERT INTO EMP11
    VALUES ('JONSON','BILL');
INSERT INTO EMP11
    VALUES ('JONES','MARY');
INSERT INTO EMP11
    VALUES ('KAPLAN','EVA');
INSERT INTO EMP11
    VALUES ('SMITH','HARRY');
INSERT INTO EMP11
    VALUES ('JOLES','MEIR');
COMMIT;
```

Figure 11.14 CHP11_14.SQL creates the sample objects used in How-To 11.6.

Lines 2 and 3 specify the columns returned by the query. Line 5 specifies the source table for the data. Line 7 uses the LIKE operator and the % wildcard character in the WHERE clause of the query. The query returns all records in which the LAST_NAME column begins with the letters *JON*.

3. Run the statement to view the results.

```
SQL>  /

LAST_NAME              FIRST_NAME
------------------     --------------------
JONSON                 BILL
JONES                  MARY
```

4. Load CHP11_16.SQL into the SQL buffer. The file contains a query that uses the _ wildcard character to replace a single letter in a string.

```
SQL> GET CHP11_16.SQL
  1   SELECT
  2       LAST_NAME
  3   FROM
  4       EMP11
  5   WHERE
  6*      LAST_NAME LIKE 'JO_ES'
```

The _ wildcard character in line 6 specifies that only the third letter in the name can be replaced in the query. The first two letters in the LAST_NAME column must be *JO* and the final two letters must be *ES*. The column must also be five characters long.

5. Run the statement to display the results.

```
SQL>  /

LAST_NAME
-------------------------
JONES
JOLES
```

How It Works

Step 1 creates the sample table and records used in this How-To. Steps 2 and 3 use the % wildcard character to replace any number of characters. The query returns all records in which a column begins with a specific string. Steps 4 and 5 use the _ wildcard character to specify that only a single character can be replaced in the query.

Comments

Wildcard characters make it easier to find data in a table. The % character is equivalent to the * character in UNIX or DOS. Remember to use the LIKE operator when working with wildcard characters or else they will be treated as literal values.

COMPLEXITY
INTERMEDIATE

11.7 How do I...
Lock rows when I query them?

Problem

In my programs, I have procedures that perform queries and later update the results. I need to ensure that other users cannot update the records while the procedures are processing data. How do I lock rows when I query them?

Technique

The FOR UPDATE clause of a SELECT statement locks the rows returned by the query until a COMMIT statement is executed. When the FOR UPDATE clause is used in a query, another user cannot update, delete, or lock the rows until the lock is released. If the rows you are attempting to query for update are locked, the query will wait until the lock is released, unless the NO WAIT clause is specified.

Steps

1. Run SQL*Plus and connect as the WAITE user account. CHP11_17.SQL, shown in Figure 11.15, creates the sample tables used in this How-To.

```
DROP TABLE DEPT11;
CREATE TABLE DEPT11 (
    DEPT_NO     NUMBER(5),
    DEPT_NAME   VARCHAR2(20));

DROP TABLE EMP11;
CREATE TABLE EMP11 (
    EMP_NO      NUMBER(5),
    EMP_NAME    VARCHAR2(20),
    DEPT_NO     NUMBER(5));

INSERT INTO DEPT11
    VALUES (25, 'MARKETING');
INSERT INTO DEPT11
    VALUES (26, 'SALES');
INSERT INTO EMP11
    VALUES (1, 'BILL SMITH', 25);
INSERT INTO EMP11
    VALUES (2, 'MARY ROBERTS', 26);

COMMIT;
```

Figure 11.15 CHP11_17.SQL creates the sample tables used in How-To 11.7.

The sample table is a simple table containing the departments in an organization. Data used to demonstrate the locking capabilities of the FOR UPDATE clause is created. Run the file to create the sample table and data.

```
SQL>  START CHP11_17.sql

Table dropped.

Table created.

Table dropped.

Table created.

1 row inserted.

1 row inserted.

1 row inserted.

Commit complete.
```

2. Load CHP11_18.SQL into the SQL buffer. The file contains a query that locks the rows as they are queried.

```
SQL> GET CHP11_18.sql
  1  SELECT DEPT_NO
  2  FROM
  3     DEPT11
  4  WHERE
  5     DEPT_NO = 25
  6* FOR UPDATE
```

Lines 4 and 5 specify the WHERE clause identifying which rows the query will retrieve. Line 6 tells Oracle to lock the rows retrieved by the query.

3. Run the query to return the results and lock the rows.

```
SQL>  /

DEPT_NO
-------
     25
```

4. Load CHP11_19.SQL into the SQL buffer. The file contains a query of multiple tables but only locks one of them.

```
SQL>  GET CHP11_19.sql
  1  SELECT DEPT11.DEPT_NO, EMP_NO
  2     FROM DEPT11, EMP11
  3  WHERE
  4     DEPT11.DEPT_NO = EMP11.DEPT_NO
  5* FOR UPDATE OF DEPT11.DEPT_NO
```

The FROM clause in line 2 specifies the two tables used in the query. Line 4 contains the join condition between the two tables. Line 5 specifies that only DEPT11 will have rows returned by the query locked. Rows from EMP11 will not be locked and can be updated by another process.

5. Run the query to lock the rows.

```
SQL>  /

DEPT_NO    EMP_NO
--------- ---------
       25         1
       26         2
```

The query locks the DEPT11 records returning the two rows.

6. Execute a COMMIT statement to unlock the rows. When rows are locked using the SELECT statement with a FOR UPDATE clause, they remain locked until a COMMIT or ROLLBACK statement is executed or until the session is terminated.

```
COMMIT;
```

How It Works

Step 1 creates two sample tables and records used throughout this How-To. Steps 2 and 3 use the FOR UPDATE clause in a SELECT statement to lock all rows returned by the query. The query only has a single source table, so the FOR UPDATE clause knows which table to lock. Steps 4 and 5 demonstrate a query from multiple tables, only one of which is locked. The table name is specified in the FOR UPDATE clause, telling Oracle to lock only that table. If the table name is not specified in the clause, records from both tables are locked. Step 6 unlocks any locked records by executing a COMMIT statement.

Comments

If you are planning to update a record that will be first returned by a query, it is a good idea to lock the record to prevent other users from updating it. Remember to unlock the record if you decide not to commit the changes you make.

COMPLEXITY
INTERMEDIATE

11.8 How do I...
Prevent the selection of duplicate rows?

Problem

In some of my queries, duplicate rows are returned. Even though the records are valid for the query, I don't want to return duplicate rows from the query. In many cases, I want to view the unique values within a column. How do I prevent the selection of duplicate rows and present unique results?

Technique

The DISTINCT operator causes only unique rows to be returned by a query. If any column in the query makes the row unique, the row is returned. The keyword is placed at the beginning of the select list and needs to be specified only once in the query.

Steps

1. Run SQL*Plus and connect as the WAITE user account. CHP11_20.SQL, shown in Figure 11.16, creates the sample tables and records used in this How-To.

```
DROP TABLE EMP11;
CREATE TABLE EMP11 (
    EMP_NO     NUMBER(10),
    EMP_NAME   VARCHAR2(20),
    DEPT_NO    NUMBER(5));

INSERT INTO EMP11
    VALUES (1, 'BILL', 1);
INSERT INTO EMP11
    VALUES (2, 'TED', 1);
INSERT INTO EMP11
    VALUES (3, 'MARY', 2);
INSERT INTO EMP11
    VALUES (4, 'JOHN', 2);
COMMIT;
```

Figure 11.16 CHP11_20.SQL creates the sample objects used in How-To 11.8.

The data created in the sample table contains duplicate values for some of the columns. When the data is queried using the DISTINCT operator, the duplicate column values are eliminated. Run the statement to create the table and data.

```
SQL> START CHP11_20.sql

Table dropped.

Table created.

1 row created.

1 row created.

1 row created.

1 row created.

Commit complete.
```

2. Load CHP11_21.SQL into the SQL buffer. The file contains a query of the sample table that does not use the DISTINCT keyword to eliminate duplicate rows.

```
SQL> GET CHP11_21.sql
  1   SELECT
  2      DEPT_NO
  3   FROM
  4      EMP11
  5*  ORDER BY DEPT_NO
```

Line 2 specifies the column returned by the query. Line 4 presents the sample table as the source of the data, and line 5 specifies the order of the resulting data.

3. Run the statement to show the results.

```
SQL>  /

  DEPT_NO
----------
        1
        1
        2
        2
```

If the purpose of the query is to display the unique department numbers, the duplicate data makes the query results hard to read. Even though each record contains a unique employee, the DEPT_NO column is duplicated among records. If the source table contains hundreds of records, the results of this query are unreadable.

4. Load CHP11_22.SQL into the SQL buffer. The file contains a query that returns unique department numbers by specifying the DISTINCT keyword before the select list.

```
SQL> GET CHP11_22.sql
  1    SELECT
  2        DISTINCT DEPT_NO
  3    FROM
  4        EMP11
  5* ORDER BY DEPT_NO
```

Line 2 uses the DISTINCT keyword to prevent the query from returning duplicate department numbers. The remaining lines of the query are identical to the query presented in Step 2.

5. Run the statement to display the results.

```
SQL> /

   DEPT_NO
----------
         1
         2
```

Regardless of the number of rows in the table, only distinct departments are returned by the query. The DISTINCT keyword applies to all columns following it in the select list.

6. Load CHP11_23.SQL into the SQL buffer. The query returns two columns after the DISTINCT operator.

```
SQL> GET CHP11_23.sql
  1  SELECT
  2      DISTINCT DEPT_NO, EMP_NO
  3  FROM
  4      EMP11
  5* ORDER BY DEPT_NO
```

Line 2 specifies two columns to be returned by the query. The DISTINCT keyword will cause distinct DEPT_NO, EMP_NO combinations to be returned by the query.

7. Run the query to display the results.

```
DEPT_NO       EMP_NO
----------  ----------
         1           1
         1           2
         2           3
         2           4
```

Even though duplicate DEPT_NO columns are returned by the query, all the rows returned are distinct.

How It Works

The DISTINCT keyword is used to prevent queries from returning duplicate rows. Step 1 creates the sample tables and records used throughout this How-To. Steps 2 and 3 query the records in the table without using the DISTINCT keyword. Steps 4 and 5 use the DISTINCT keyword to return distinct DEPT_NO columns from the sample table. Steps 6 and 7 show the results of a query with two columns specified in a select list using the DISTINCT keyword.

Comments

The DISTINCT operator is useful in analyzing data in a table. When you use the DISTINCT keyword, keep in mind that it affects the entire select list. You don't need to specify the keyword for each column in the list. The keyword is useful within subqueries to limit the number of rows to be processed by the query.

COMPLEXITY
ADVANCED

11.9 How do I...
Traverse a tree structure?

Problem

In my application, I have a table containing data in a hierarchical structure. I need to create a query that navigates the tree structure to create a report. I have not been able to generate a simple query to traverse a tree structure. How do I traverse a tree structure in a query?

Technique

The CONNECT BY clause in a query provides support for hierarchical data structures. Unfortunately, using the CONNECT BY clause can be confusing. Navigating a tree structure requires two clauses. The START WITH clause identifies where the query begins in the tree structure. The CONNECT BY PRIOR clause identifies the parent/child relationship between key fields. The format of the query is shown here:

```
SELECT fields
FROM table
START WITH column = value
CONNECT BY PRIOR parent primary key = child foreign key;
```

An additional WHERE clause or an ORDER BY clause is not allowed by Oracle in a query using the CONNECT BY structure.

Steps

1. Run SQL*Plus and connect as the WAITE user account. CHP11_24.SQL, shown in Figure 11.17, creates the sample table and data used in this How-To.

The sample table contains names of employees for an organization. Each record contains an EMP_NO column to uniquely identify each employee and a MGR_NO column to identify his or her manager. If the MGR_NO column is NULL, the employee is at the top of the corporate structure. Run the file to create the sample table and data.

```
SQL> START CHP11_24.SQL

Table dropped.

Table created.
```

2. Load CH11_25.SQL into the SQL buffer. The file contains a query of the sample table for the hierarchical structure of the data.

```
SQL> GET CHP11_25.sql
   1   SELECT
   2      LPAD(' ',4*(LEVEL-1))||EMP_NAME EMP_NAME
   3   FROM
   4      EMP11
   5   START WITH MGR_NO IS NULL
   6*  CONNECT BY PRIOR EMP_NO = MGR_NO
```

```
DROP TABLE EMP11;
CREATE TABLE EMP11 (
   EMP_NO     NUMBER(5),
   EMP_NAME   VARCHAR2(15),
   MGR_NO     NUMBER(5));

SET TERMOUT OFF
INSERT INTO EMP11 VALUES (1, 'JONES, TOM', NULL);
INSERT INTO EMP11 VALUES (2, 'MAX, DAVID', 1);
INSERT INTO EMP11 VALUES (3, 'LANGER, KEITH', 2);
INSERT INTO EMP11 VALUES (4, 'LIPMAN, AARON', 2);
INSERT INTO EMP11 VALUES (5, 'LIMDI, MADHUR', 2);
INSERT INTO EMP11 VALUES (6, 'GREENE, RACHEL', 3);
INSERT INTO EMP11 VALUES (7, 'KAPLAN, TODD', 3);
INSERT INTO EMP11 VALUES (8, 'YELLOW, STEVE', 4);
INSERT INTO EMP11 VALUES (9, 'RED, MIKE', 5);
INSERT INTO EMP11 VALUES (10, 'KAPLAN, JODI', 9);
```

Figure 11.17 CHP11_24.SQL creates the sample table and data used in How-To 11.9.

Line 2 uses the LEVEL pseudo-column to left-pad the EMP_NAME column with four spaces for each level of the hierarchy. The START WITH clause in line 5 begins the tree navigation for records in which the MGR_NO column is NULL. Because a NULL MGR_NO column represents an employee at the top of the corporate structure, you want the tree navigation to start there. The CONNECT BY PRIOR clause identifies that the EMP_NO column of the previous level joins to the MGR_NO column from the next level down.

3. Run the statement to display the results of the query. The results of the query are shown in Figure 11.18.

The query used the LEVEL pseudo-column to indent the results of the query and display the records in the tree structure. Because the JONES, TOM record contained no MGR_NO column, the query results begin with that column. The CONNECT BY PRIOR clause causes the tree to be navigated beginning at the record.

How It Works

Step 1 creates the sample table and records used in this How-To. Steps 2 and 3 present a query using the START WITH and CONNECT BY PRIOR clauses to navigate the data's hierarchical structure. The START WITH clause identifies the root of the tree structure and the CONNECT BY PRIOR clause identifies the columns linking the hierarchy. The LEVEL pseudo-column is used in the select list to indent the results based on the level of the tree structure.

Comments

A hierarchical structure of data is definitely not easy to work with. The CONNECT BY PRIOR clause in a query enables Oracle to perform this task. Remember to include the START WITH clause, and also keep in mind that the ordering of the columns in the CONNECT BY prior clause is important.

```
SQL> /

EMP_NAME
------------------------------------------------------------
JONES, TOM
    MAX, DAVID
        LANGER, KEITH
            GREENE, RACHEL
            KAPLAN, TODD
        LIPMAN, AARON
            YELLOW, STEVE
        LIMDI, MADHUR
            RED, MIKE
                KAPLAN, JODI

10 rows selected.

SQL> |
```

Figure 11.18 The results of CHP11_25.SQL in SQL*Plus.

BUILT-IN PACKAGES

12

BUILT-IN PACKAGES

How do I...

Built-in packages are provided by Oracle to extend the functionality of the database. Oracle's modular approach allows new features to be added while maintaining compatibility with existing versions. Built-in packages contain functions and procedures that perform many tasks that would otherwise be impossible, or at least very difficult, to execute. With each new release, Oracle extends the functionality of the database by including new built-in packages. Many of the How-To's presented in this chapter require PL/SQL versions 2.1, 2.2, 2.3, or 3.0. The PL/SQL version required to perform each one is provided at the beginning of the How-To.

12.1 Execute Dynamic SQL with DBMS_SQL

The ability to execute dynamic SQL statements within PL/SQL greatly extends the tasks you can perform. The DBMS_SQL package, available in PL/SQL version 2.1 and higher, enables you to create, parse, and send a SQL statement to the database at runtime. This enables you to build SQL statements based on the results of actions or queries performed at runtime. This How-To presents the technique used to execute dynamic SQL statements.

12.2 Submit Scheduled Jobs with DBMS_JOB

It is likely that within one or more of your applications, you need to perform some process at a regularly scheduled interval or need to schedule a program to be executed later. The DBMS_JOB package, available in PL/SQL version 2.2 and higher, enables you to schedule a single or recurring job. This How-To explores the use of the DBMS_JOB package to schedule programs within Oracle.

12.3 Communicate Between Sessions with DBMS_PIPE

Messages can be sent between Oracle processes by using the DBMS_PIPE package. Named pipes referenced by one or more processes can be created in the database. This How-To presents the method used to pass messages between processes using DBMS_PIPE.

12.4 Monitor the Database Asynchronously with DBMS_ALERT

It is sometimes necessary to perform an action when an event occurs in the database or to broadcast an event to other processes. The DBMS_ALERT package allows events to be recognized and their notification to occur asynchronously within the database. This How-To explores using the DBMS_ALERT package within Oracle.

12.5 Read and Write Operating System Files with UTL_FILE

The UTL_FILE package, available in PL/SQL version 2.3 and higher, enables you to read and write operating system files through PL/SQL. Files can be written on the server system by creating stored procedures or functions that use the UTL_FILE package. Files can also be written on the client system by using the UTL_FILE package in client-side PL/SQL modules.

12.6 Use Comma Separated Lists with DBMS_UTILITY

Comma separated lists can be moved in and out of PL/SQL tables using procedures in the DBMS_UTILITY package. The COMMA_TO_TABLE procedure converts a comma separated list into a PL/SQL table, and the TABLE_TO_COMMA procedure converts a PL/SQL table into a comma separated list. This How-To presents the method used to work with comma separated lists in PL/SQL.

12.7 Manage large objects with DBMS_LOB

Oracle8 supports the definition, creation, deletion, and updates of LOBs. The DBMS_LOB package allows piecewise random access to LOB data. Functions and procedures in the DBMS_LOB package allow read and write operations on Oracle Large Object (LOBs) datatypes: BLOB, CLOB and NCLOB as well as read-only access to BFILEs. This How-To presents techniques to manage LOBs.

COMPLEXITY
INTERMEDIATE

12.1 How do I...
Execute dynamic SQL with DBMS_SQL?

AVAILABILITY: PL/SQL VERSION 2.1 AND HIGHER.

Problem

I want to run a DDL statement in my PL/SQL block but I get a compilation error. Sometimes the SQL statement to be executed needs to be constructed at runtime by using the results of another query. I also want to invoke a PL/SQL procedure dynamically as the name of the procedure is returned by a query at runtime. How do I execute dynamic SQL statements in PL/SQL?

Technique

Dynamic SQL is supported by the DBMS_SQL package, which you can use to write stored procedures or functions and anonymous PL/SQL blocks that generate and execute dynamic SQL statements. Dynamic SQL statements are not embedded in your source program but are stored in strings that are built at runtime. Both data manipulation language (DML) and data definition language (DDL) statements can be executed dynamically using the DBMS_SQL package.

Essentially, SQL and PL/SQL can be generated on-the-fly and then executed. With this powerful technique, redundant code can be generated by PL/SQL code itself. Using dynamic SQL, for instance, enables you to create a procedure that manipulates a table whose name is not known until runtime. The DBMS_SQL package also allows a SQL statement to be created, parsed, and executed dynamically at runtime. Table 12.1 shows the functions and procedures in the DBMS_SQL package.

Table 12.1 Functions/procedures in the DBMS_SQL package

NAME	TYPE	DESCRIPTION
OPEN_CURSOR	Function	Opens a cursor and returns a cursor ID to be used in all other calls.
PARSE	Procedure	Parses the statement for syntax.

continued on next page

continued from previous page

NAME	TYPE	DESCRIPTION
BIND_VARIABLE	Procedure	Binds a value to an input variable.
DEFINE_COLUMN	Procedure	Binds a variable to a cursor column.
EXECUTE	Function	Executes the cursor.
EXECUTE_AND_FETCH	Function	Executes the cursor and fetch rows.
FETCH_ROWS	Function	Fetches the rows from the cursor.
VARIABLE_VALUE	Procedure	Retrieves the value of a output bind variable.
COLUMN_VALUE	Procedure	Retrieves a column value from the cursor into an output variable.
CLOSE_CURSOR	Procedure	Closes the cursor after processing.

When executing *query* (SELECT) statements with the DBMS_SQL package, the first step is to create a cursor with the OPEN_CURSOR function. The PARSE procedure is then used to parse the SQL statement and prepares it for execution. Use the BIND_VARIABLE procedure to bind values to any input variables. Column values from the cursor can be returned to the local PL/SQL module by binding local variables to columns, using the DEFINE_COLUMN procedure. The EXECUTE function executes the cursor once it has been parsed. Use the FETCH_ROWS function to fetch records, and the COLUMN_VALUE procedure to retrieve the column values to local variables. After the processing is done, the cursor is closed using the CLOSE_CURSOR procedure. The EXECUTE and FETCH_ROWS calls can be combined into a single call by using the EXECUTE_AND_FETCH function.

When executing *non-query* DDL and DML statements or PL/SQL blocks using the DBMS_SQL package, the steps are simpler than the above steps. First of all, create a cursor with the OPEN_CURSOR function and bind any input variables, using the BIND_VARIABLE procedure. The query-related calls to DEFINE_COLUMN, FETCH_ROWS, and COLUMN_VALUE are eliminated. After executing the cursor using the EXECUTE procedure, retrieve the values any output bind variables with the VARIABLE_VALUE procedure, only if the statement being executed is an anonymous PL/SQL block. Finally, close the cursor using the CLOSE_CURSOR procedure.

Steps

1. Run SQL*Plus and connect as the WAITE user account. Run the CHP12_1.SQL file to create the sample table and data used in this How-To.

```
SQL> START CHP12_1
SQL> SET ECHO ON
SQL> CREATE TABLE DEPT12 (
  2        DEPT_NO    NUMBER(5),
  3        DEPT_NAME VARCHAR2(30));
```

```
Table created.
SQL>
SQL> INSERT INTO DEPT12
  2        VALUES (1, 'Marketing');

1 row created.
```

2. Run the CHP12_2.SQL file in SQL*Plus, which contains PL/SQL code that uses the DBMS_SQL package to execute an INSERT statement using dynamic SQL. The technique to associate placeholders (input bind variables) with actual PL/SQL variables, to construct general purpose DML statements is established through this exercise. The results of the operation are shown in Figure 12.1.

Line 2 declares a variable containing a handle for the cursor when it is created. Line 7 executes the OPEN_CURSOR function in the DBMS_SQL package to create a cursor and return its handle into a PL/SQL variable. The INSERT statement to be executed is parsed for syntax errors using the PARSE procedure in lines 8 and 9. The PARSE procedure is passed the cursor handle, the SQL statement, and the DBMS_SQL.V7 constant. These lines could be replaced by any valid SQL statement to be executed dynamically.

The bind variables in the INSERT statement are associated with actual PL/SQL variables in lines 10 and 11. Line 12 uses the EXECUTE function in the DBMS_SQL package to execute the SQL statement, which processes

```
SQL> START CHP12_2
SQL> SET SERVEROUTPUT ON
SQL> DECLARE
  2      CURSOR_ID INTEGER;
  3      ROWS_INSERTED INTEGER;
  4      D_NO NUMBER := 10;
  5      D_NAME VARCHAR2(10) := 'Sales';
  6  BEGIN
  7      CURSOR_ID := DBMS_SQL.OPEN_CURSOR;
  8      DBMS_SQL.PARSE(CURSOR_ID, 'INSERT INTO DEPT12 VALUES
  9                      (:DEPT_NO, :DEPT_NAME)', DBMS_SQL.V7);
 10      DBMS_SQL.BIND_VARIABLE(CURSOR_ID, ':DEPT_NO', D_NO);
 11      DBMS_SQL.BIND_VARIABLE(CURSOR_ID, ':DEPT_NAME', D_NAME);
 12      ROWS_INSERTED := DBMS_SQL.EXECUTE(CURSOR_ID);
 13      DBMS_SQL.CLOSE_CURSOR(CURSOR_ID);
 14      DBMS_OUTPUT.PUT_LINE(ROWS_INSERTED || ' row created.');
 15  EXCEPTION
 16  WHEN OTHERS THEN
 17      DBMS_SQL.CLOSE_CURSOR(CURSOR_ID);
 18      DBMS_OUTPUT.PUT_LINE(SQLERRM);
 19  END;
 20  /
1 row created.

PL/SQL procedure successfully completed.

SQL> |
```

Figure 12.1 CHP12_2.SQL runs an INSERT statement using dynamic SQL.

and returns the number of rows if it is an INSERT, UPDATE, or DELETE statement. Line 13 closes the cursor. The number of rows processed by the EXECUTE function is displayed in SQL*Plus using the DBMS_OUTPUT.PUT_LINE procedure.

Lines 15 through 18 handle any exceptions occurring with a WHEN OTHERS exception handler. If an exception occurred in a function or procedure of the DBMS_SQL package, it must be handled by an exception handler in the local PL/SQL block. The cursor is closed in the event of an exception to free system resources taken up by the cursor. Line 18 prints the SQLCODE and SQLERRM to help debug the cause of the error.

3. Load the CHP12_3.SQL file in SQL*Plus, as shown in Figure 12.2. The file contains an anonymous PL/SQL block that performs a dynamic query and returns the column values to local variables.

In line 8, the SELECT statement to query the DEPT12 table is stored in a string variable. The variables used to retrieve the columns are declared in lines 4 and 5. Line 9 opens a cursor for the process, using the OPEN_CURSOR function. Line 10 parses the query statement using the PARSE procedure. Lines 11 and 12 use the DEFINE_COLUMN procedure to identify the variables that will hold column values returned by the query. Line 13 executes the statement and builds the cursor. The LOOP statement from lines 14 through 22 processes the rows of the cursor by

```
SQL> START CHP12_3
SQL> SET SERVEROUTPUT ON
SQL> DECLARE
  2     TMP_STR    VARCHAR2(60);
  3     CURSOR_ID INTEGER;
  4     DEPT_NO    NUMBER;
  5     DEPT_NAME VARCHAR2(30);
  6     CNT        NUMBER;
  7  BEGIN
  8     TMP_STR := 'SELECT DEPT_NO, DEPT_NAME FROM DEPT12';
  9     CURSOR_ID := DBMS_SQL.OPEN_CURSOR;
 10     DBMS_SQL.PARSE(CURSOR_ID, TMP_STR, DBMS_SQL.V7);
 11     DBMS_SQL.DEFINE_COLUMN(CURSOR_ID, 1, DEPT_NO);
 12     DBMS_SQL.DEFINE_COLUMN(CURSOR_ID, 2, DEPT_NAME, 30);
 13     CNT := DBMS_SQL.EXECUTE(CURSOR_ID);
 14     LOOP
 15         IF DBMS_SQL.FETCH_ROWS(CURSOR_ID) = 0 THEN
 16             EXIT;
 17         ELSE
 18             DBMS_SQL.COLUMN_VALUE(CURSOR_ID, 1, DEPT_NO);
 19             DBMS_SQL.COLUMN_VALUE(CURSOR_ID, 2, DEPT_NAME);
 20             DBMS_OUTPUT.PUT_LINE(TO_CHAR(DEPT_NO) || ' - ' || DEPT_NAME);
 21         END IF;
 22     END LOOP;
 23     DBMS_SQL.CLOSE_CURSOR(CURSOR_ID);
 24  END;
 25
```

Figure 12.2 CHP12_3.SQL executes a SELECT statement dynamically.

executing the FETCH_ROWS function shown in line 15. If the function returns 0, there are no more records to retrieve and the loop is exited. The COLUMN_VALUE procedures in lines 18 and 19 are used to move column values returned by the cursor to local variables.

4. Run the PL/SQL block to display the results. Figure 12.3 shows the results of the operation.

5. Run the CHP12_4.SQL file in SQL*Plus. The file contains an anonymous PL/SQL block that executes another anonymous PL/SQL block dynamically and retrieves the values of output variables. Figure 12.4 shows the results of the operation.

```
23     DBMS_SQL.CLOSE_CURSOR(CURSOR_ID);
24  END;
25  /
1 - Marketing
10 - Sales

PL/SQL procedure successfully completed.

SQL>
```

Figure 12.3 Results of the
dynamic query in CHP12_3.SQL.

```
SQL> START CHP12_4
SQL> SET SERVEROUTPUT ON
SQL> DECLARE
  2     TMP_STR    VARCHAR2(300);
  3     CURSOR_ID  INTEGER;
  4     DEPT_NO    NUMBER := 10;
  5     DEPT_NAME  VARCHAR2(30);
  6     CNT        NUMBER;
  7  BEGIN
  8     TMP_STR := 'BEGIN SELECT DEPT_NAME
  9                        INTO :D_NAME
 10                        FROM DEPT12
 11                        WHERE DEPT_NO = :D_NO;
 12                END;';
 13     CURSOR_ID := DBMS_SQL.OPEN_CURSOR;
 14     DBMS_SQL.PARSE(CURSOR_ID, TMP_STR, DBMS_SQL.V7);
 15     DBMS_SQL.BIND_VARIABLE(CURSOR_ID, ':D_NO', DEPT_NO);
 16     DBMS_SQL.BIND_VARIABLE(CURSOR_ID, ':D_NAME', DEPT_NAME, 30);
 17     CNT := DBMS_SQL.EXECUTE(CURSOR_ID);
 18     DBMS_SQL.VARIABLE_VALUE(CURSOR_ID, ':D_NAME', DEPT_NAME);
 19     DBMS_SQL.CLOSE_CURSOR(CURSOR_ID);
 20     DBMS_OUTPUT.PUT_LINE(TO_CHAR(DEPT_NO) || ' - ' || DEPT_NAME);
 21  END;
 22  /
10 - Sales

PL/SQL procedure successfully completed.

SQL>
```

Figure 12.4 CHP12_4.SQL runs an anonymous block
dynamically.

The input and output bind variables used in the block are declared in lines 4 and 5. In lines 8 through 12, the anonymous block containing a query to the DEPT12 table is stored in a string variable. Note that both the input and output bind variables are identified by calling the BIND_VARIABLE procedure in lines 15 and 16. In line 16, the last argument in the call to BIND_VARIABLE for an output bind variable specifies the maximum length. Line 17 executes the anonymous block. The VARIABLE_VALUE procedure in line 18 retrieves the column value returned by the query in the anonymous block, into the output bind variable. All other calls are similar to those in Step 3.

How It Works

The DBMS_SQL package is used to execute dynamic SQL statements and return the results to the local PL/SQL code. The OPEN_CURSOR function is used to open a cursor and return its handle, which is used in all subsequent calls. The cursor handle and SQL statement (or an anonymous PL/SQL block) are passed to the PARSE procedure to catch any syntactical errors. The EXECUTE function is then used to execute the statement after it has been parsed. The CLOSE_CURSOR procedure is used to close the cursor after processing is completed.

For queries, to return values from the cursor back to the PL/SQL code, the DEFINE_COLUMN procedure identifies which local variable receives which column. The FETCH_ROWS function actually returns the record. The COLUMN_VALUE procedure is used to move column values from the cursor to variables, for each variable that was defined using the DEFINE_COLUMN procedure. The COLUMN_VALUE procedure should be called only after a successful call to FETCH_ROWS or EXECUTE_AND_FETCH. Only if you are executing an anonymous PL/SQL block, use the VARIABLE_VALUE procedure to retrieve the value of each output variable.

Step 2 executes a DML statement that does not return any values to the local PL/SQL code. Instead, it accepts input variables that are defined using the BIND_VARIABLE procedure. Step 2 also presents exception handling routines in a PL/SQL module using dynamic SQL. When dynamic SQL is used, the local PL/SQL module is expected to handle any exceptions that occur. Steps 3 and 4 present a dynamic SELECT statement. The DEFINE_COLUMN procedure binds columns returned by the query to local variables. The FETCH_ROWS procedure retrieves the records and the COLUMN_VALUE procedure moves the column values to local variables. In Step 5, an anonymous PL/SQL block is executed dynamically. Both input and output bind variables are specified using the BIND_VARIABLE procedure. The value of the output variable is retrieved using the VARIABLE_VALUE procedure.

Additional functions supported by the DBMS_SQL package for error reporting and DBMS_SQL cursor management are listed in Table 12.2 along with a description and where they should be called.

Table 12.2 Additional functions in the DBMS_SQL package

NAME	TYPE	DESCRIPTION
LAST_ERROR_POSITION	Function	Returns byte offset in the SQL statement where the error occurred. Called after PARSE.
LAST_ROW_COUNT	Function	Returns number of rows fetched from a cursor. Called after FETCH_ROWS or EXECUTE_AND_FETCH.
LAST_ROW_ID	Function	Returns ROWID of the last record fetched. Called after FETCH_ROWS or EXECUTE_AND_FETCH.
LAST_SQL_FUNCTION_CODE	Function	Returns function code for the SQL statement being executed.
IS_OPEN	Function	Returns TRUE if the cursor is open, FALSE otherwise.

When using variables of the CHAR, RAW, or ROWID datatypes, and to issue a call to the BIND_VARIABLE, DEFINE_COLUMN, COLUMN_VALUE or VARIABLE_VALUE procedure, you would use the name of the procedure suffixed with the datatype. For example, use the BIND_VARIABLE_ROWID procedure to bind a variable of the ROWID datatype. As a special case for variables of the LONG datatype, the DEFINE_COLUMN_LONG and COLUMN_VALUE_LONG procedures must be used. To use PL/SQL arrays as input/output variables, use the BIND_ARRAY and DEFINE_ARRAY procedures.

Comments

Ever since the release of PL/SQL 2.1, DBMS_SQL package implements dynamic SQL and PL/SQL, which can be called from other PL/SQL blocks. It is perhaps one of the most valuable advancements in Oracle for the application developer. Anonymous PL/SQL blocks, queries, DML, and DDL statements can be handled using the DBMS_SQL package. The ability to dynamically create SQL statements and PL/SQL blocks, as well as parse and execute them at runtime, adds a new dimension to application development.

The DBMS_SQL package helps you to create general purpose procedures. Dynamic SQL is a powerful feature but should be used with care and only when such a need occurs in an application. You might want to issue a UPDATE TABLE statement, for example, from within a stored procedure. OCI and Oracle precompilers are other tools that can perform dynamic SQL and PL/SQL, and are even more powerful than DBMS_SQL.

The privileges are that the DBMS_SQL package is owned by SYS, but operations are performed with the privileges of the caller. Thus, a user executing SQL or PL/SQL through DBMS_SQL should have direct privileges to the objects in question. If the caller is an anonymous PL/SQL block, executing a subprogram (procedure or function) dynamically, the subprogram is run using the privileges of the current user account. But if the caller is a stored subprogram, the called subprogram is run using the privileges of the owner of the calling stored subprogram.

12.2   How do I...
Submit scheduled jobs with DBMS_JOB?

AVAILABILITY: PL/SQL VERSION 2.2 AND HIGHER.

Problem

In our application, I have some processes that need to be run regularly to update data and perform calculations. The operating system can schedule jobs, but we want our database applications to be operating system independent. How do I schedule programs within Oracle?

Technique

The DBMS_JOB package allows stored procedures to be run periodically, providing a means to manage background batch processes. The DBMS_JOB package contains procedures to control job scheduling. Table 12.1 lists the procedures embodied in the DBMS_JOB package.

Table 12.3 Procedures in the DBMS_JOB package

PROCEDURE	DESCRIPTION
ISUBMIT	Submits a new job with a specified job number.
SUBMIT	Submits a new job. Returns a unique job number.
REMOVE	Removes an existing job from the job queue.
CHANGE	Changes one or more job attributes.
WHAT	Changes the program on which the job is to run.
NEXT_DATE	Changes when an existing job is to be run.
INTERVAL	Changes the interval that the job runs.
BROKEN	Sets the broken flag. Terminates scheduling of a job.
RUN	Executes a job immediately (even if it is broken).
USER_EXPORT	Produces the text of a call to re-create the specified job.

The SUBMIT procedure is used to send a job to the queue along with parameters specifying how often it should run. Each job submitted to the queue is given a unique job number for identification. Alternatively, the ISUBMIT procedure is used to submit a job with a specified job number. To remove a job from the queue, use the REMOVE procedure, but a running job cannot be stopped with the REMOVE procedure.

The WHAT, NEXT_DATE, and INTERVAL procedures are used to alter a single characteristic of a job, while the CHANGE procedure allows changes to more than one job characteristic in a single call. The BROKEN procedure can be used to mark the job status as broken and the job will not be run again. You can use the RUN procedure in the DBMS_JOB package to force a job to run immediately (even a broken job). If the job completes successfully, the job status is marked as not broken. In order to mark the job as broken again, the BROKEN procedure has to be called explicitly. Jobs currently in the queue can be viewed by querying the USER_JOBS data dictionary view. Important columns of the USER_JOBS view are listed in Table 12.4.

Table 12.4 Important columns in the USER_OBJECTS view

COLUMN	DESCRIPTION
JOB	Job number.
LOG_USER	USER who submitted the job.
PRIV_USER	USER whose privileges apply to the job.
SCHEMA_USER	Schema used.
LAST_DATE	Date when this job was last successfully run.
LAST_SEC	Same as LAST_DATE.
THIS_DATE	Date when this job started running.
THIS_SEC	Same as THIS_DATE.
NEXT_DATE	Date when the job will next run.
NEXT_SEC	Same as NEXT_DATE.
TOTAL_TIME	Seconds spent by the system running this job.
BROKEN	If Y, this job will not be run.
INTERVAL	A date function to calculate NEXT_DATE.
FAILURES	Number of times job failed after the last successful run.
WHAT	PL/SQL code that the job runs.

Steps

1. Run SQL*Plus and connect as the WAITE user account. CHP12_5.SQL, shown in Figure 12.5, creates a table and a stored procedure used in this How-To. The stored procedure is executed using the DBMS_JOB package and inserts a record into the table each time it runs.

```
SET ECHO ON
CREATE TABLE LOG_TABLE12 (
    RUN_DATE    DATE);

CREATE OR REPLACE PROCEDURE LOG_PROC12 AS
BEGIN
    INSERT INTO LOG_TABLE12
        VALUES (SYSDATE);
    COMMIT;
END LOG_PROC12;
/
```

Figure 12.5 CHP12_5.SQL creates a log table and a stored procedure used in How-To 12.2.

The script creates a table containing a date column. The stored procedure created inserts a record with the date and time into the table each time it runs. Note the COMMIT statement at the end of the stored procedure, which enables you to determine when the stored procedure was last executed by querying the table.

2. Run CHP12_6.SQL file in SQL*Plus. The PL/SQL code contained in the file schedules the stored procedure to run every other minute throughout the day. The results of the operation are shown in Figure 12.6.

Line 2 declares a variable to be passed the job number as an OUT parameter from the SUBMIT function. Lines 4 through 9 call the DBMS_JOB.SUBMIT procedure to schedule the procedure. The first parameter, shown in line 5, is an OUT parameter that returns the job number. Unique job numbers are generated from the SYS.JOBSEQ sequence. The second parameter (string for WHAT), shown in line 6,

```
SQL> START CHP12_6
SQL> SET SERVEROUTPUT ON
SQL> DECLARE
  2     JOB_NUM INTEGER;
  3  BEGIN
  4     DBMS_JOB.SUBMIT (
  5            JOB_NUM,
  6            'LOG_PROC12;',
  7            SYSDATE + (1/1440),
  8            'SYSDATE + (1/1440)',
  9            FALSE);
 10     DBMS_OUTPUT.PUT_LINE('JOB NUMBER = '||TO_CHAR(JOB_NUM));
 11  EXCEPTION
 12     WHEN OTHERS THEN
 13        DBMS_OUTPUT.PUT_LINE(SQLERRM);
 14  END;
 15  /
JOB NUMBER = 1

PL/SQL procedure successfully completed.

SQL> |
```

Figure 12.6 CHP12_6.SQL uses the DBMS_JOB.SUBMIT procedure to submit a job.

specifies the procedure scheduled to run. The third parameter (value for NEXT_DATE), shown in line 7, is the date and time at which the job will next run.

The value of the parameter is the current date and time, plus one minute. If the value of the parameter is before SYSDATE, the job will never begin running. The fourth parameter (string for INTERVAL), shown in line 8, specifies a date function to calculate the time for the next execution of the job. This date function is evaluated before the job starts running and each time thereafter when the job completes successfully. The new date and time is then used as a value for NEXT_DATE. To execute a job only once, use 'null' for the INTERVAL parameter.

The last parameter, shown in line 9, specifies that the procedure called should be parsed when it is submitted (FALSE is the default). If TRUE, parsing is deferred until the procedure is run for the first time. Line 10 displays the unique job number returned by the SUBMIT procedure.

3. Run CHP12_7.SQL in SQL*Plus, as shown in Figure 12.7. The query contained in the file queries the USER_JOBS data dictionary view to show the scheduled jobs for the current user account.

The JOB column specified in line 2 returns the job number of the scheduled job. The NEXT_DATE column specified in line 3 is formatted with the TO_CHAR function to display both the date and time portions of the date. The value contained in the NEXT_DATE column is the next date the procedure will be executed. The function specified to calculate the next execution time of the job while submitting it is listed under the INTERVAL column. The BROKEN column in line 5 is a flag denoting whether the job is broken or not. Broken jobs are not scheduled to run again. The WHAT column shown in line 4 returns PL/SQL code that the job runs, of which only the name of the procedure to be executed is extracted for display.

```
SQL> START CHP12_7
SQL> COLUMN NEXT_DATE FORMAT A17
SQL> COLUMN INTERVAL FORMAT A30
SQL> COLUMN WHAT FORMAT A13
SQL> SELECT
  2     JOB,
  3     TO_CHAR(NEXT_DATE, 'MM/DD/YY HH24:MI:SS') NEXT_DATE,
  4     INTERVAL,
  5     BROKEN,
  6     WHAT
  7  FROM
  8     USER_JOBS;

   JOB NEXT_DATE         INTERVAL                        B WHAT
---------- ----------------- ------------------------------ - -------------
     1 11/01/97 22:44:44 SYSDATE + (1/1440)             N LOG_PROC12;

SQL>
```

Figure 12.7 Results of the query on USER_JOBS view.

4. The CHP12_8.SQL file queries the table created in Step 1. Each time the scheduled job is run, a record is inserted into the table. Run the statement to view records inserted into the table. Figure 12.8 displays the results of the query.

Line 2 returns the RUN_DATE column formatted with the TO_CHAR function to display the date and time the procedure was last executed. The FROM clause in lines 3 and 4 specifies that the table created in Step 1 is the source of data.

5. The REMOVE procedure is used to delete a job from the queue. To remove the job scheduled, simply execute the REMOVE procedure in the DBMS_JOB package. Pass the job number returned by the job created in Step 2 as a parameter to the REMOVE procedure.

```
SQL> EXEC DBMS_JOB.REMOVE(61);

PL/SQL successfully completed.
```

The REMOVE procedure receives the job number as its only parameter. The query to the USER_JOBS view used in Step 3 can be used to determine the job number. Once the DBMS_JOB.REMOVE procedure has been executed, the job will be no longer scheduled to run. In order to start the job again, the SUBMIT function must be executed.

How It Works

The DBMS_JOB package contains a complete set of procedures for managing job scheduling within Oracle. The SUBMIT procedure is used to submit a job for execution either once, or repeatedly. After jobs have been scheduled, the REMOVE procedure is used to remove a scheduled job from the queue. Jobs scheduled for execution by the user connected to the database can be found in the USER_JOBS data dictionary view.

```
SQL> START CHP12_8
SQL> SELECT
  2      TO_CHAR(RUN_DATE,'MM/DD/YY HH24:MI:SS') RUN_DATE
  3  FROM
  4      LOG_TABLE12;

RUN_DATE
-----------------------------------------------------------------------------
11/01/97 22:44:44
11/01/97 22:45:44
11/01/97 22:46:44

SQL>
```

Figure 12.8 Results of the query on the log table.

Step 1 creates a sample table and stored procedure used in this How-To. The log table contains a DATE field used to track the execution times of the sample stored procedure. The stored procedure inserts the system date and time into the table each time it runs. Step 2 schedules the sample procedure to be executed every other minute, by specifying SYSDATE + 1/1440 as the execution interval time. Step 3 queries the USER_JOBS data dictionary view to display information about the job scheduled in the prior step. Step 4 queries the log table to view how often the scheduled job is running. The longer the job is allowed to run, the more the records are created in the sample table. Step 5 uses the REMOVE procedure from the DBMS_JOB package to cancel execution of the scheduled job.

Comments

The DBMS_JOB package lets you schedule batch processes independent of the operating system. Background processes in job queues are run by SNP processes. The number of SNP processes that Oracle runs in the background are specified as the JOB_QUEUE_PROCESSES=n parameter in the INIT<SID>.ORA file. Since the default is 0, make sure that you have this parameter set to the number of SNP processes you want Oracle to run; otherwise, no jobs will be executed.

The JOB_QUEUE_INTERVAL parameter in the INIT<SID>.ORA file is used to specify the interval in seconds for the SNP processes to check for new jobs in the job queue. Jobs can be exported and imported, and job numbers remain the same. The retry interval for running a failed job is doubled each time starting from the first retry interval of one minute. If attempts to run a job fails 16 times in a row, it is marked as broken and stops running. The USER_JOBS, ALL_JOBS, and DBA_JOBS provide information about jobs in the job queue. The DBA_JOBS_RUNNING view can be queried to list currently running jobs. Whenever possible, it is best to have Oracle schedule jobs because the scheduling code is portable to any platform Oracle runs on.

COMPLEXITY
INTERMEDIATE

12.3 How do I...
Communicate between sessions with DBMS_PIPE?

AVAILABILITY: PL/SQL VERSION 2.1 AND HIGHER.

Problem

I need a method to allow Oracle processes to communicate. I want to be able to send a message and have the other process read it when it's ready. How do I communicate between Oracle sessions?

Technique

The DBMS_PIPE built-in package allows communication between processes using named pipes. One or more sessions connected to the same database instance can write to and read from a pipe asynchronously. Table 12.5 shows the functions and procedures in the DBMS_PIPE package.

Table 12.5 Functions/procedures in the DBMS_PIPE package

MODULE	TYPE	DESCRIPTION
CREATE_PIPE	Function	Explicitly creates a new pipe.
PACK_MESSAGE	Procedure	Adds an item to the message buffer.
SEND_MESSAGE	Function	Sends the contents of the message buffer to a pipe.
RECEIVE_MESSAGE	Function	Receives a message from the pipe into the message buffer.
NEXT_ITEM_TYPE	Function	Returns the datatype of the next item in the buffer.
UNPACK_MESSAGE	Procedure	Reads the next item from the message buffer.
REMOVE_PIPE	Function	Removes a pipe.
PURGE	Procedure	Purges contents of a pipe.
RESET_BUFFER	Procedure	Clears the message buffer.
UNIQUE_SESSION_NAME	Function	Returns a unique session name.

In PL/SQL version 2.2 and higher, a pipe can be public or private. A public pipe can be accessed by all users and does not need to be created explicitly. However, you can create a public pipe explicitly using the CREATE_PIPE function by setting the `private_flag` parameter to FALSE. A private pipe must be created explicitly using the CREATE_PIPE function. Access to a private pipe is restricted to sessions connected with the same user account as the pipe creator, or a user connected as SYSDBA or INTERNAL. An explicitly created public or private pipe should be removed with the REMOVE_PIPE function, or else the pipe remains in memory until the database instance is shutdown. The CREATE_PIPE and REMOVE_PIPE procedures are supported in PL/SQL 2.2 and higher.

The first time a pipe is used with the SEND_MESSAGE or RECEIVE_MESSAGE functions, it will be created automatically as a public pipe. To send a message through the pipe, add data items to the local message buffer using the PACK_MESSAGE procedure and then send the message to the pipe using the SEND_MESSAGE function. To read a message from a pipe, use the RECEIVE_MESSAGE procedure to receive the message and then the UNPACK_MESSAGE procedure to read each message item.

Steps

1. Run SQL*Plus and connect as the WAITE user account. Run the CHP12_9.SQL file, as shown in Figure 12.9. The statement in the file packs a message and puts it into a pipe. A new public pipe is implicitly created as it is referenced for the first time.

```
SQL> START CHP12_9
SQL> SET ECHO ON SERUEROUTPUT ON
SQL> DECLARE
  2     STATUS NUMBER;
  3  BEGIN
  4     DBMS_PIPE.PACK_MESSAGE('THIS IS THE MESSAGE');
  5     STATUS := DBMS_PIPE.SEND_MESSAGE('WAITE_PIPE');
  6     IF STATUS != 0 THEN
  7        DBMS_OUTPUT.PUT_LINE('ERROR SENDING THE MESSAGE, ' ||
  8                             'STATUS = ' || STATUS);
  9     ELSE
 10        DBMS_OUTPUT.PUT_LINE('MESSAGE SENT SUCCESSFULLY');
 11     END IF;
 12  END;
 13  /
MESSAGE SENT SUCCESSFULLY

PL/SQL procedure successfully completed.

SQL>
```

Figure 12.9 CHP12_9.SQL sends a message to a pipe.

The variable declared in line 2 receives the value returned by the SEND_MESSAGE function. Line 4 uses the PACK_MESSAGE procedure to pack the message passed as a parameter, preparing it for delivery. Line 5 uses the SEND_MESSAGE function to send the message to the specified pipe, which is created implicitly. If the value returned by SEND_MESSAGE is not 0, an error occurred and the corresponding status code is displayed; otherwise, a happy message is written to the screen.

2. Run SQL*Plus, creating a second session to the database with the WAITE user account. Load CHP12_10.SQL into the SQL buffer. The PL/SQL code within the file reads the message from the pipe created in the prior step and displays it onscreen. The results of the operation are shown in Figure 12.10.

```
SQL> START CHP12_10
SQL> SET ECHO ON SERUEROUTPUT ON
SQL> DECLARE
  2     STATUS NUMBER;
  3     MESSAGE VARCHAR2(80);
  4  BEGIN
  5     STATUS := DBMS_PIPE.RECEIVE_MESSAGE('WAITE_PIPE');
  6     IF STATUS = 0 THEN
  7        DBMS_PIPE.UNPACK_MESSAGE(MESSAGE);
  8        DBMS_OUTPUT.PUT_LINE(MESSAGE);
  9     ELSE
 10        DBMS_OUTPUT.PUT_LINE('NO DATA FOUND IN PIPE, ' ||
 11                             'STATUS = ' || STATUS);
 12     END IF;
 13  END;
 14  /
THIS IS THE MESSAGE

PL/SQL procedure successfully completed.

SQL>
```

Figure 12.10 CHP12_10.SQL receives a message from a pipe.

Line 2 declares a variable containing the status of the pipe when the RECEIVE_MESSAGE function is executed. Line 3 declares the variable receiving the message from the pipe. Line 5 executes the RECEIVE_MESSAGE function to receive the next message from the specified pipe. If the value returned is 0, the pipe contains a message. Line 7 uses the UNPACK_MESSAGE procedure to retrieve the message from the buffer and put it in a local variable. Line 8 displays the message using the PUT_LINE procedure of the DBMS_OUTPUT package. If a message was not successfully received from the pipe, lines 10 and 11 generate a message onscreen. The message sent to the pipe by the first process is read, unpacked, and displayed by the second process.

3. Run CHP12_11.SQL in SQL*Plus, as shown in Figure 12.11. The PL/SQL block in the file explicitly creates a new private pipe. This Step primarily demonstrates the method used to create a private pipe. If you want to simply use a public pipe created implicitly by the system, jump to Step 5.

Line 2 declares a variable to handle the results of the CREATE_PIPE function. Line 3 declares an exception variable for handling the error that occurs when the pipe already exists. Line 4 declares a PRAGMA to link the exceptions declared in line 3 with the Oracle error occurring when the pipe exists. Line 6 executes the CREATE_PIPE function to create a private pipe with the name WAITE_PIPE. Line 7 sets the PRIVATE_FLAG to TRUE in order to create a private pipe.

No two pipes in the database can have the same name. An ORA-23322 error will occur if another user has created a private pipe (or a public pipe with pending messages) and has the same name specified in the

```
SQL> START CHP12_11
SQL> SET ECHO ON SERVEROUTPUT ON
SQL> DECLARE
  2      STATUS NUMBER;
  3      PIPE_EXISTS EXCEPTION;
  4      PRAGMA EXCEPTION_INIT(PIPE_EXISTS, -23322);
  5  BEGIN
  6      STATUS := DBMS_PIPE.CREATE_PIPE(PIPENAME => 'WAITE_PIPE',
  7                                 PRIVATE => TRUE);
  8      IF STATUS = 0 THEN
  9          DBMS_OUTPUT.PUT_LINE('PRIVATE PIPE CREATED');
 10      END IF;
 11  EXCEPTION
 12      WHEN PIPE_EXISTS THEN
 13          DBMS_OUTPUT.PUT_LINE(SQLERRM);
 14  END;
 15  /
PRIVATE PIPE CREATED

PL/SQL procedure successfully completed.

SQL>
```

Figure 12.11 CHP12_11.SQL creates a new private pipe.

CREATE_PIPE function. If an ORA-23322 is raised, the exception handler in lines 12 and 13 displays a message. As the WAITE_PIPE pipe does not contain any pending messages in the pipe after Step 2, the public pipe is automatically removed and re-created as a private pipe.

4. Because the pipe was created explicitly in Step 3, it has to be removed using the REMOVE_PIPE function.

```
SQL> VARIABLE STATUS NUMBER
SQL> EXEC :STATUS := DBMS_PIPE.REMOVE_PIPE('WAITE_PIPE')

PL/SQL procedure successfully completed.

SQL> PRINT STATUS

     X

----------

     0
```

At the SQL*Plus prompt, a bind variable is created using the VARIABLE command. The REMOVE_PIPE function in the DBMS_PIPE package is executed to remove the pipe specified. The bind variable receives the value returned by the REMOVE_PIPE function. The function returns 0 if the pipe is removed successfully; otherwise, an error occurred. The PRINT command is issued to check the value of the bind variable. To clear the contents of a pipe instead of removing it, use the PURGE procedure.

5. The example presented in this step and the next requires two sessions connected to the same database. This can be performed with two SQL*Plus sessions in a 32-bit environment, such as Windows NT or Windows 95, or using two computers connected to the same database. Run SQL*Plus and connect as the WAITE user account, and run the CHP12_12.SQL file in this first session. The PL/SQL code in the file uses a loop to read messages from a public pipe. The module appears to hang until the first message is sent to the pipe. Figure 12.12 shows SQL*Plus waiting for the first message.

Line 2 declares the variable used to receive the status from the RECEIVE_MESSAGE function. Line 3 declares the variable that receives each item of the message from the buffer. The variable in line 4 holds the value of the total number of items to be read from the message. Line 6 uses the RECEIVE_MESSAGE function to receive the complete message from the NEW_PIPE pipe. Because the pipe has not been created explicitly, it will be created as a public pipe the first time it is read. The first item in the message is a count of the total items contained in the message, which is read in line 9. Lines 10 through 13 contain a FOR loop to read message items. Line 11 uses the UNPACK_MESSAGE procedure to

```
SQL> START CHP12_12
SQL> DECLARE
  2      STATUS NUMBER(10);
  3      MESSAGE VARCHAR2(80);
  4      ITEM_COUNT INTEGER;
  5  BEGIN
  6      STATUS := DBMS_PIPE.RECEIVE_MESSAGE('NEW_PIPE');
  7      IF STATUS = 0 THEN
  8          DBMS_PIPE.UNPACK_MESSAGE(ITEM_COUNT);
  9          DBMS_OUTPUT.PUT_LINE(ITEM_COUNT);
 10          FOR I IN 1..ITEM_COUNT LOOP
 11              DBMS_PIPE.UNPACK_MESSAGE(MESSAGE);
 12              DBMS_OUTPUT.PUT_LINE(MESSAGE);
 13          END LOOP;
 14      ELSE
 15          DBMS_OUTPUT.PUT_LINE('ERROR RECEIVING THE MESSAGE ' ||
 16                              ', STATUS = ' || STATUS);
 17      END IF;
 18  END;
 19  /
```

Figure 12.12 The first process waits for a message from a pipe.

retrieve the next item from the message. Lines 15 and 16 display the error status code if a problem occurred while reading the message from the pipe.

6. Run SQL*Plus and connect as the WAITE user account to create a second session, and run CHP12_13.SQL, as shown in Figure 12.13. The PL/SQL code in the file sends 10 messages to the public pipe to be displayed by the second session.

Line 4 puts the first message item with the count of items in the message so that the receiving process will know how many items to read from the message. Lines 5 through 7 perform a loop 10 times, using the

```
SQL> START CHP12_13
SQL> DECLARE
  2      STATUS NUMBER;
  3  BEGIN
  4      DBMS_PIPE.PACK_MESSAGE(10);
  5      FOR I IN 1..10 LOOP
  6          DBMS_PIPE.PACK_MESSAGE('THIS IS MESSAGE '||TO_CHAR(I));
  7      END LOOP;
  8      STATUS := DBMS_PIPE.SEND_MESSAGE('NEW_PIPE');
  9      IF STATUS != 0 THEN
 10          DBMS_OUTPUT.PUT_LINE('ERROR SENDING THE MESSAGE ' ||
 11                              ', STATUS = ' || STATUS);
 12      END IF;
 13  END;
 14  /

PL/SQL procedure successfully completed.

SQL>
```

Figure 12.13 The second process sends a message to a pipe.

PACK_MESSAGE procedure to add each message item to the local message buffer. The SEND_MESSAGE function in line 8 is used to send the message to the pipe.

7. Now watch the first session. When the process in the second session is executed, the ten message items are displayed in the first session before it terminates. Figure 12.14 show the results in the first session after the process in the second session has executed.

Alternatively, you can pack and send each item as a complete message by calling the PACK_MESSAGE procedure followed by calling SEND_MESSAGE function in a loop that executes ten times. On the other end, you can execute a block that issues READ_MESSAGE followed by UNPACK_MESSAGE in a loop that runs ten times.

How It Works

Named pipes can be either public or private. Message items are packed into a message with the PACK_MESSAGE procedure and the message is sent to a pipe with the SEND_MESSAGE function. Messages are received with the RECEIVE_MESSAGE function and items in the message are unpacked with the UNPACK_MESSAGE procedure.

Step 1 packs and sends a message via the named pipe using the PACK_MESSAGE and SEND_MESSAGE procedures. Step 2 the message in the pipe is read using the RECEIVE_MESSAGE and UNPACK_MESSAGE procedures. Step 3 creates a private pipe called WAITE_PIPE by executing the CREATE_PIPE function. Step 4 removes the pipe created in Step 3. Step 5 employs a session to run a PL/SQL module using a loop to continuously check a public pipe for messages.

```
17      END IF;
18  END;
19  /
10
THIS IS MESSAGE 1
THIS IS MESSAGE 2
THIS IS MESSAGE 3
THIS IS MESSAGE 4
THIS IS MESSAGE 5
THIS IS MESSAGE 6
THIS IS MESSAGE 7
THIS IS MESSAGE 8
THIS IS MESSAGE 9
THIS IS MESSAGE 10

PL/SQL procedure successfully completed.

SQL>
```

Figure 12.14 The first session after it has received messages through the pipe.

When a message is received, the module runs a loop depending on the item count, which is the first item in the message. Step 6 executes a PL/SQL module to create a message in which the first item is the item count followed by the message items. After the message is built in the buffer, it is sent to the pipe. The PACK_MESSAGE and UNPACK_MESSAGE procedures are overloaded to accept VARCHAR2, NUMBER, and DATE variables. Use a conversion function for any other datatypes. To recognize the datatype of the next item in the buffer, use the NEXT_ITEM_TYPE function. An ORA-06558 is raised by the PACK_MESSAGE procedure if the buffer size exceeds 4096 bytes. An ORA-06656 is generated by the NEXT_ITEM_TYPE function if the buffer contains no more items, and ORA-06659 if the item requested is of the wrong datatype (see Table 12.6).

Table 12.6 Return values of the NEXT_ITEM_TYPE function

RETURN VALUE	DATATYPE
0	No more items
6	NUMBER
9	VARCHAR2
11	ROWID
12	DATE
23	RAW

With multiple sessions using the same pipe, a session can pack its unique session name returned by the UNIQUE_SESSION_NAME function as a message item to identify the sender of the message. A user-defined protocol can be further worked upon by two sessions that wish to communicate with each other, for example, using the unique session name as the pipe name.

Comments

Messages sent over pipes are buffered in the system global area (SGA). There can be multiple readers and writers of the same pipe, but the communicating sessions must be in the same instance. Messages in pipes are lost when the instance is shut down. Pipes currently being used in the system can be queried from the V$DB_PIPES data dictionary view.

Pipes are an effective way to communicate asynchronously between processes. Unlike the DBMS_ALERT package presented in How-To 12.4, a COMMIT statement does not need to be executed in order to send the message. When two processes need to communicate, the DBMP_PIPE package provides benefits over the DBMS_ALERT package. When many processes are interested in messages sent by another process, the DBMS_ALERT package is preferable.

The Privileges are that users with the EXECUTE ANY PROCEDURE can access the DBMS_PIPE package. Other users must be granted EXECUTE privilege on the DBMS_PIPE package by the DBA and security can be further tightened by using private pipes.

COMPLEXITY
INTERMEDIATE

12.4 How do I...
Monitor the database asynchro-
nously with DBMS_ALERT?

AVAILABILITY: PL/SQL VERSION 2.1 AND HIGHER.

Problem

I want my application to be alerted when certain events take place in the database. I do not want to continuously query an object to determine if the event has occurred; I want to be notified by the database. How do I execute an action based on an event in the database?

Technique

The DBMS_ALERT package is used to alert a session when an event occurs in the database. The receiving session registers for notifications from an alert, and the alert signals the session when the event occurs. Table 12.7 shows the procedures in the DBMS_ALERT package.

Table 12.7 The DBMS_ALERT package

NAME	TYPE	DESCRIPTION
REGISTER	Procedure	Registers the session to receive messages from an alert.
WAITONE	Procedure	Waits for a signal from a specific alert.
WAITANY	Procedure	Waits for any of the alerts registered for the session.
SIGNAL	Procedure	Signals an alert causing messages to be sent to registered sessions.
SET_DEFAULTS	Procedure	Sets the polling interval.
REMOVE	Procedure	Removes the session from receiving notifications from an alert.
REMOVEALL	Procedure	Removes the session from all alert registrations.

The REGISTER procedure is used by applications to register interest in an alert. The name of the alert is passed as an IN parameter. A session may register interest in more than one alerts.

Once an alert has been registered, the WAITONE procedure can be used to wait for a signal from a specific alert or the WAITANY procedure can be used to wait for a signal from any of the alerts for which the session is registered.

The SIGNAL procedure notifies all sessions that have registered on the alert and optionally sends a message to each session. A COMMIT statement must be issued after calling the SIGNAL procedure for the call to the SIGNAL procedure to become effective.

If the transaction rolls back, the SIGNAL call has no effect. If the alerted session has blocked in a WAITONE/WAITANY call, the call returns and execution resumes with the next statement. If the alert was signaled before issuing a call to the WAITONE/WAITANY procedure, the call returns immediately. Multiple sessions can concurrently signal on the same alert. If the SIGNAL procedure was called more than once for an alert before the receiving end issued a WAITONE/WAITANY call, then the message received will be from the last SIGNAL call.

A polling loop is not required in most cases, except by the WAITANY call when a SIGNAL call remains uncommitted longer than a second, and to check for alerts from another instance when the database is running in parallel mode. The polling loop interval defaults to one second but can be changed by calling the SET_DEFAULTS procedure.

Steps

1. Run SQL*Plus and connect as the WAITE user account. This How-To requires two connections to the same database. This can be performed with two SQL*Plus sessions in a 32-bit environment, such as Windows NT or Windows 95, or can be performed using two computers connected to the same database. The first connection will register its interest in an alert and wait for the alert to fire. Run the CHP12_14.SQL file in SQL*Plus. Figure 12.15 shows the operation in SQL*Plus before the alert is fired.

Set the SERVEROUTPUT system variable to ON to display the output using the DBMS_OUTPUT.PUT_LINE procedure. The STATUS variable declared in line 2 returns the status of the WAITONE procedure call to the module. The MESSAGE variable declared in line 3 returns the message sent by the session signaling the alert. Line 5 executes the REGISTER procedure to register interest in the WAITE_ALERT alert. Line 6 executes the WAITONE procedure, making the module wait for the alert to fire.

```
SQL> START CHP12_14
SQL> SET ECHO ON SERVEROUTPUT ON
SQL> DECLARE
  2      STATUS NUMBER;
  3      MESSAGE VARCHAR2(100);
  4  BEGIN
  5      DBMS_ALERT.REGISTER('WAITE_ALERT');
  6      DBMS_ALERT.WAITONE('WAITE_ALERT', MESSAGE, STATUS, 1000);
  7      IF STATUS = 1 THEN
  8          DBMS_OUTPUT.PUT_LINE('TIMEOUT OCCURED');
  9      ELSE
 10          DBMS_OUTPUT.PUT_LINE(MESSAGE);
 11      END IF;
 12  END;
 13  /
```

Figure 12.15 The first session waits for an alert.

The first IN parameter is the alert name on which the procedure is waiting. The second parameter is an OUT parameter returning the message sent when the alert is signaled. The third parameter is also an OUT parameter returning the status of the procedure call. A value of 0 identifies that an alert was fired; a value of 1 means that the timeout occurred. The last IN parameter is the timeout in seconds.

If timeout is not specified, it defaults to DBMS_ALERT.MAXWAIT, which is 1,000 days. Line 7 checks the status variable and displays the timeout message if it occurred or the alert message if fired. When the PL/SQL block is executed, it hangs until another session fires the alert.

2. Establish another SQL*Plus session to the same database and connect as the WAITE user account. This session will be used to fire alerts that are received by the first session. The SIGNAL procedure in the DBMS_ALERT package is used to fire an alert.

```
SQL> EXEC DBMS_ALERT.SIGNAL('WAITE_ALERT', 'THE ALERT HAS FIRED');

PL/SQL procedure successfully completed.

SQL> COMMIT;

Commit complete.
```

At the SQL*Plus prompt, execute the SIGNAL procedure from the DBMS_ALERT package. The first parameter identifies the alert fired. The second parameter is optional and specifies a message sent to all processes receiving the alert. Then issue a COMMIT statement to commit the transaction. Because the DBMS_ALERT package uses tables and database triggers to provide its functionality, it requires a COMMIT to be executed before the alerts are fired.

Watch the first session after executing the statements in the second session. The first session displays the message sent by the alert. Figure 12.16 shows the message displayed in the first session.

```
  8        DBMS_OUTPUT.PUT_LINE('TIMEOUT OCCURED');
  9     ELSE
 10        DBMS_OUTPUT.PUT_LINE(MESSAGE);
 11     END IF;
 12  END;
 13  /
THE ALERT HAS FIRED

PL/SQL procedure successfully completed.

SQL>
```

Figure 12.16 The first session after the alert is fired.

3. Use the first session to run CHP12_15.SQL in SQL*Plus, as shown in Figure 12.17. The PL/SQL statement in the file uses the WAITANY procedure to wait for more than one alert to fire.

The ALERT_NAME variable defined in line 4 returns the name of the alert fired to the PL/SQL module. Lines 6 through 8 register three alerts that the module waits for. CANCEL_ALERT terminates the module when the alert name is checked in line 15. As soon as one of the other alerts is fired, the alert name and message are displayed by line 18. Until the CANCEL_ALERT alert is not signaled, the loop continues to block in the call to the WAITONE procedure and waits for any of the registered alerts to fire.

4. Use the second session to execute CHP12_16.SQL, watching the results in the first session. CHP12_16.SQL executes the SIGNAL procedure for firing alerts to be displayed by the first session. Figure 12.18 shows the operation performed in the second session. Figure 12.19 shows its results in the first session.

5. When the session is no longer interested in an alert, it should remove the alert using the REMOVE procedure. Unregistering an alert frees up resources used. Run the CHP12_17.SQL file in SQL*Plus, as shown in Figure 12.20, to remove the alerts registered in this How-To.

```
SQL> START CHP12_15
SQL> SET ECHO ON SERVEROUTPUT ON
SQL> DECLARE
  2     STATUS NUMBER;
  3     MESSAGE VARCHAR2(100);
  4     ALERT_NAME VARCHAR2(30);
  5  BEGIN
  6     DBMS_ALERT.REGISTER('ALERT_ONE');
  7     DBMS_ALERT.REGISTER('ALERT_TWO');
  8     DBMS_ALERT.REGISTER('CANCEL_ALERT');
  9     LOOP
 10       DBMS_ALERT.WAITANY(ALERT_NAME, MESSAGE, STATUS);
 11       IF STATUS = 1 THEN
 12          DBMS_OUTPUT.PUT_LINE('TIMEOUT OCCURED');
 13          EXIT;
 14       ELSE
 15          IF ALERT_NAME = 'CANCEL_ALERT' THEN
 16             EXIT;
 17          ELSE
 18             DBMS_OUTPUT.PUT_LINE(ALERT_NAME || ': ' || MESSAGE);
 19          END IF;
 20       END IF;
 21     END LOOP;
 22  END;
 23  /
```

Figure 12.17 The first session waits on multiple alerts.

```
SQL> START CHP12_16
SQL> SET ECHO ON
SQL> BEGIN
  2         DBMS_ALERT.SIGNAL('ALERT_ONE','THE FIRST ALERT HAS FIRED');
  3         DBMS_ALERT.SIGNAL('ALERT_TWO','THE SECOND ALERT HAS FIRED');
  4         DBMS_ALERT.SIGNAL('CANCEL_ALERT','WE ARE DONE');
  5      COMMIT;
  6   END;
  7   /

PL/SQL procedure successfully completed.

SQL>
```

Figure 12.18 The second session fires multiple alerts.

```
 21         END LOOP;
 22   END;
 23   /
ALERT_ONE: THE FIRST ALERT HAS FIRED
ALERT_TWO: THE SECOND ALERT HAS FIRED

PL/SQL procedure successfully completed.

SQL>
```

Figure 12.19 The first session
after receiving multiple alert
signals.

```
SQL> START CHP12_17
SQL> BEGIN
  2         DBMS_ALERT.REMOVE('WAITE_ALERT');
  3         DBMS_ALERT.REMOVE('ALERT_ONE');
  4         DBMS_ALERT.REMOVE('ALERT_TWO');
  5         DBMS_ALERT.REMOVE('CANCEL_ALERT');
  6   END;
  7   /

PL/SQL procedure successfully completed.

SQL>
```

Figure 12.20 Cleanup of alerts
registered in this How-To.

How It Works

The SIGNAL procedure of the DBMS_ALERT package is used to fire an alert on the database. Sessions that expressed an interest in the alert by executing the REGISTER function receive the alert when they execute the WAITONE or WAITANY procedures. The WAITONE procedure waits for a specific alert to fire and the WAITANY procedure waits for any of the registered alerts to fire.

This How-To requires two SQL*Plus sessions connected to the same database. Step 1 registers interest in an alert and execute the WAITONE procedure to wait for it to fire. Step 2 establishes a second connection to the database and fires the alert by executing the SIGNAL procedure.

When the alert is fired, the PL/SQL module in the first session displays the alert message and terminates. Step 3 registers three alerts and executes the WAITANY procedure within a loop to receive alerts as they are fired. When a specific alert is fired, the module is terminated. Step 4 fires alerts from the second session to display the results in the first session. Step 5 removes the alerts registered in this How-To. The SYS.DBMS_ALERT_INFO table can be queried to list information about registered alerts in the system.

Comments

The DBMS_ALERT package is useful in providing asynchronous notification of database events. The DBMS_ALERT package uses tables and triggers requiring that commits be executed before the alert is fired. This can cause problems in development environments, such as Developer/2000, which manages commits at the form level. If you do not commit the form, the alert will not fire. If your application does not require transaction based alerts, then using the DBMS_PIPE package discussed in How-To 12.3 may provide a better alternative.

Typically, the DBMS_ALERT package is used for one-way communication, whereas the DBMS_PIPE package is used for two-way communication. The DBMS_PIPE package internally uses the DBMS_LOCK and the DBMS_PIPE packages.

The privileges here include access being permitted to users with the EXECUTE ANY PROCEDURE or they are granted EXECUTE privileges on the DBMS_ALERT package.

COMPLEXITY
INTERMEDIATE

12.5 How do I...
Read and write operating system files with UTL_FILE?

AVAILABILITY: PL/SQL VERSION 2.3 AND HIGHER.

Problem

I need a method to read and write operating system files from within PL/SQL. I want to read and write files from within stored procedures and functions. How do I read and write operating system files?

Technique

The UTL_FILE built-in package is available with PL/SQL 2.3 and higher. The package enables you to both read and write operating system files. UTL_FILE modules can be called from within stored modules or client-side modules. Table 12.8 shows the modules that make up the UTL_FILE database package.

Table 12.8 The UTL_FILE database package

NAME	TYPE	DESCRIPTION
FOPEN	Function	Opens the specified file.
IS_OPEN	Function	Returns TRUE if the file is currently open.
GET_LINE	Procedure	Gets the next line from the file.
PUT_LINE	Procedure	Writes a line to the file after appending the line terminator.
PUT	Procedure	Writes a line to the file without appending the line terminator.
PUTF	Procedure	Writes a formatted line to the file without appending the line terminator.
NEW_LINE	Procedure	Terminates current line and begins a new line.
FFLUSH	Procedure	Writes all data from the buffer to the file.
FCLOSE	Procedure	Closes the specified file.
FCLOSE_ALL	Procedure	Closes all open files.

In order to read a file you first have to declare a file handle, which is used to reference the file in the other procedures. Next, you must open the file with a call to FOPEN. The file can be opened to read, write, or append. The PUT_LINE, PUT, and PUTF procedures are used to write data to the file, which is closed using the FCLOSE procedure. The GET_LINE procedure is used to read a line of data and places it in a VARCHAR2 variable.

The locations of directories accessible to UTL_FILE must be defined using the utl_file_dir parameter in the INIT<SID>.ORA initialization file. Only exact directories listed in the INIT<SID>.ORA file are accessible. Subdirectories of accessible directories are not automatically accessible unless you specify utl_file_dir = * in your INIT<SID>.ORA file; then all directories are accessible to UTL_FILE.

After changing the INIT<SID>.ORA file, the Oracle instance must be brought down and back up for the changes to be effective. Ensure that the Oracle owner has read and write permissions on these directories.

Steps

1. Run SQL*Plus and connect as the WAITE user account. Run the CHP12_18.SQL file, as shown in Figure 12.21. The file contains PL/SQL code to open a file and write two lines to it.

```
SQL> START CHP12_18
SQL> DECLARE
  2      FILE_HANDLE UTL_FILE.FILE_TYPE;
  3  BEGIN
  4      FILE_HANDLE := UTL_FILE.FOPEN('C:\TEMP', 'CHP12.TXT', 'W');
  5      UTL_FILE.PUT_LINE(FILE_HANDLE, 'HELLO WORLD');
  6      UTL_FILE.PUTF(FILE_HANDLE, '%s AT CHAPTER %s\n', USER, 12);
  7      UTL_FILE.FCLOSE(FILE_HANDLE);
  8  EXCEPTION
  9      WHEN UTL_FILE.WRITE_ERROR THEN
 10         RAISE_APPLICATION_ERROR(-20100, 'WRITE ERROR.');
 11         UTL_FILE.FCLOSE(FILE_HANDLE);
 12      WHEN UTL_FILE.INVALID_OPERATION THEN
 13         RAISE_APPLICATION_ERROR(-20101, 'INVALID OPERATION.');
 14         DBMS_OUTPUT.PUT_LINE(SQLERRM);
 15         UTL_FILE.FCLOSE(FILE_HANDLE);
 16  END;
 17  /

PL/SQL procedure successfully completed.

SQL>
```

Figure 12.21 CHP12_18.SQL writes a line to a file.

Line 2 declares a file handle variable, the datatype of the file handle defined in the UTL_FILE package. Line 4 uses the FOPEN function to open the file CHP12.TXT in the C:\TEMP directory. The file handle returned by FOPEN is used in all subsequent calls. The W parameter specifies that the file is opened in write mode. If A is specified, the file is opened in append mode; R opens the file in a read mode.

Line 5 calls PUT_LINE to write a line of text to the file and line 6 calls PUTF to write a formatted line of text to the file. The maximum size for the buffer in any PUT_LINE procedure is 1,023 bytes. If an error occurred while writing to the file, the exception handler in lines 9 to 11 is raised. If the file was already opened for read by another process in the system, the exception handler in lines 12 to 14 is raised.

Line 7 closes the file using the FCLOSE procedure. Check the C:\TEMP directory to view the contents of the CHP12.TXT file. On UNIX, file permissions on a file created using the UTL_FILE package are rw-r--r--. If the UTL_FIL.INVALID_PATH EXCEPTION is raised, verify that you do not have a slash (\ or /) at the end of the directory path in either the INIT<SID>.ORA file or your code.

2. Run the CHP12_19.SQL file in SQL*Plus. The PL/SQL block in the file reads the line of data written in the previous step. Figure 12.22 shows the results of the operation in SQL*Plus.

Line 2 declares a VARCHAR2 variable which receives the data when read from the file. Line 3 declares the file handle controlling access to the file. Line 5 opens the file for reading by using the FOPEN function and passing

```
SQL> START CHP12_19
SQL> SET ECHO ON SERVEROUTPUT ON
SQL> DECLARE
  2      DATA_LINE VARCHAR2(80);
  3      FILE_HANDLE UTL_FILE.FILE_TYPE;
  4  BEGIN
  5      FILE_HANDLE := UTL_FILE.FOPEN('C:\TEMP', 'CHP12.TXT', 'R');
  6      UTL_FILE.GET_LINE(FILE_HANDLE, DATA_LINE);
  7      DBMS_OUTPUT.PUT_LINE(DATA_LINE);
  8      UTL_FILE.GET_LINE(FILE_HANDLE, DATA_LINE);
  9      DBMS_OUTPUT.PUT_LINE(DATA_LINE);
 10      UTL_FILE.FCLOSE(FILE_HANDLE);
 11  EXCEPTION
 12      WHEN UTL_FILE.READ_ERROR THEN
 13          RAISE_APPLICATION_ERROR(-20200, 'READ ERROR.');
 14          UTL_FILE.FCLOSE(FILE_HANDLE);
 15      WHEN UTL_FILE.INVALID_OPERATION THEN
 16          RAISE_APPLICATION_ERROR(-20201, 'INVALID OPERATION.');
 17          UTL_FILE.FCLOSE(FILE_HANDLE);
 18  END;
 19  /
HELLO WORLD
WAITE AT CHAPTER 12

PL/SQL procedure successfully completed.

SQL>
```

Figure 12.22 CHP12_19.SQL reads a line from the file.

'R' as the second parameter. Lines 6 and 8 use the GET_LINE procedure to read a line from the file. The maximum size for the buffer in any GET_LINE procedure is 1,022 bytes. If an error occurred while reading the file, the exception handler in lines 12 to 14 is raised. If the file is already opened for write by another process in the system, the exception handler in lines 15 to 17 is raised. Lines 7 and 9 use the PUT_LINE procedure from the DBMS_OUTPUT package to display the line read from the file. Line 10 closes the file by executing the FCLOSE procedure.

How It Works

The UTL_FILE package is used to read and write operating system files. The directories specified by the utl_file_dir parameter are valid for reading and writing for all users of the UTL_FILE package. It should be noted that this can override operating system permissions.

The FOPEN function is used to open a file, and the PUT_LINE, PUT, and PUTF procedures are used to write data to a file. The GET_LINE procedure is used to read a line from a file. Finally, the file handle is closed by calling FCLOSE to free any resources associated with the file.

Step 1 opens an operating system file and writes a single line to it. Step 2 opens the same file and reads the line from it and displays it in SQL*Plus. If an error occurred while calling a function or procedure in the UTL_FILE package an exception is raised. Exceptions defined in the UTL_FILE package are listed in Table 12.9. In addition, the NO_DATA_FOUND or VALUE_ERROR predefined exceptions can also be raised by the UTL_FILE package.

Table 12.9 UTL_FILE package exceptions

EXCEPTION	DESCRIPTION
INVALID_PATH	Invalid filename or directory.
INVALID_MODE	Invalid OPEN_MODE parameter in FOPEN call.
INVALID_FILEHANDLE	Invalid file handle.
INVALID_OPERATION	File could not be opened or operated on.
READ_ERROR	Read operation failed.
WRITE_ERROR	Write operation failed.
INTERNAL_ERROR	Unspecified internal error.

The FLCOSE_ALL procedure does not change the state of open file handles, even though it closes all open file handles. The IS_OPEN function returns TRUE for a file handle that was closed by calling FCLOSE_ALL. Discretion is advised.

Comments

Reading and writing operating system files is very useful and expands the capabilities of PL/SQL. The UTL_FILE package runs on the server side and is only available in PL/SQL 2.3 and above. The client-side TEXT_IO package provided with the Oracle Procedure Builder is similar to the UTL_FILE package.

COMPLEXITY
INTERMEDIATE

12.6 How do I...
Use comma separated lists with DBMS_UTILITY?

AVAILABILITY: PL/SQL VERSION 2.1 AND HIGHER.

Problem

I need a method to convert a comma separated list into a format I can easily use in PL/SQL. Some of our applications receive data in a comma separated format, and others are required to produce output in this format. Parsing character strings in PL/SQL can require a lot of code. How do I use PL/SQL built-in packages to use comma separated lists?

Technique

The DBMS_UTILITY package contains two procedures for working with comma separated lists. The COMMA_TO_TABLE procedure converts a comma separated list into a PL/SQL table. Once the list is in a PL/SQL table, it becomes easy to work with. The specification for the procedure is shown here:

```
DBMS_UTILITY.COMMA_TO_TABLE (list IN varchar2,
        tablen OUT binary_integer,
        tab OUT uncl_array);
```

The list parameter contains the comma separated list moved to the table by the procedure. The TABLEN parameter is an OUT parameter, which returns the number of elements moved to the table. The TAB parameter returns the PL/SQL table containing the list to the calling module. The UNCL_ARRAY datatype is defined in the package and must be used in the procedure to declare the table variable. A variable can be defined as a datatype in a package by specifying the package name with the datatype. If you are working with a PL/SQL table and wish to move the values into a comma separated list, the TABLE_TO_COMMA procedure can be used. The specification for the procedure is shown here:

```
DBMS_UTILITY.TABLE_TO_COMMA (tab IN uncl_array,
        tablen OUT binary_integer,
        list OUT varchar2);
```

The TAB parameter specifies the table to be converted to a comma separated list. The TABLEN parameter is an OUT parameter returning the number of items moved to the list, and the LIST parameter returns the character string containing the comma separated list. Functions and procedures in the DBMS_UTILITY package provide a variety of useful utilities as listed in Table 12.10.

Table 12.10 DBMS_UTILITY miscellaneous functions/procedures

NAME	TYPE	DESCRIPTION
COMMA_TO_TABLE	Procedure	Converts a comma-separated list of names into a PL/SQL table of names.
TABLE_TO_COMMA	Procedure	Converts a PL/SQL table of names into a comma-separated list of names.
GET_TIME	Function	Finds the current time in the hundredths of a second.
GET_PARAMETER_VALUE	Function	Gets value of the specified parameter.
FORMAT_CALL_STACK	Function	Displays the current call stack.
FORMAT_ERROR_STACK	Function	Displays the current error stack.
COMPILE_SCHEMA	Procedure	Compiles all functions, procedures, and packages in the specified schema.
ANALYZE_SCHEMA	Procedure	Analyzes all tables, clusters, and indexes in a schema.
ANALYZE_DATABASE	Procedure	Analyzes all tables, clusters, and indexes in a database.
ANALYZE_PART_OBJECT	Procedure	Analyzes the schema object for each partition, in parallel.
EXEC_DDL_STATEMENT	Procedure	Executes the given DDL statement.
IS_PARALLEL_SERVER	Function	Returns TRUE if the database is running in parallel server mode, FALSE, or otherwise.
NAME_RESOLVE	Procedure	Gets RESOLVE the specified object name.
NAME_TOKENIZE	Procedure	Calls the parser to return a tokenized string.
MAKE_DATA_BLOCK_ADDRESS	Function	Creates a data block address from a file number and a block number.

continued on next page

continued from previous page

NAME	TYPE	DESCRIPTION
DATA_BLOCK_ADDRESS_FILE	Function	Gets the file number part of a data block address.
DATA_BLOCK_ADDRESS_BLOCK	Function	Gets the block number part of a data block address.
GET_HASH_VALUE	Function	Computes the hash value of a given string.
PORT_STRING	Function	Returns a string identifying the version of Oracle and the operating system.
DB_VERSION	Procedure	Returns the database version.

Steps

1. Run SQL*Plus and connect as the WAITE user account. CHP12_20, shown in Figure 12.23, creates the sample table and data used in the example. The sample table contains three columns and the sample data is converted to a comma separated list using PL/SQL tables. Run the script to create the sample table and its data.

```
SQL>  START CHP12_20

Table created.

1 row created.

1 row created.

1 row created.

Commit complete.
```

```
SET ECHO OFF
DROP TABLE DEPT12;
CREATE TABLE DEPT12 (
     DEPT_NO    NUMBER(10),
     DEPT_NAME  VARCHAR2(30),
     LOCATION   VARCHAR2(20));

INSERT INTO DEPT12 VALUES
     (1,'Marketing','Chicago');

INSERT INTO DEPT12 VALUES
     (2, 'Sales','Tampa');

INSERT INTO DEPT12 VALUES
     (3, 'I/S', 'New York');
```

Figure 12.23
CHP12_20.SQL creates the
sample table and data
used in this How-To.

2. Run the CHP12_21.SQL file in SQL*Plus, as shown in Figure 12.24. The PL/SQL code contained in the file converts a comma-separated list into a PL/SQL table and displays its contents.

Line 1 declares a variable of the UNCL_ARRAY datatype created in the DBMS_UTILITY package. In order to pass the table as a parameter to the COMMA_TO_TABLE procedure, it must be declared as this datatype. Line 2 declares a variable to be passed the number of elements processed in the list. Line 3 declares the variable containing the comma separated list. Line 6 moves a sample list into the COMMA_STRING variable. Line 7 calls the COMMA_TO_TABLE procedure.

The first parameter contains the list to be processed. The last two parameters are both OUT parameters used to return values from the procedure. The CNT variable receives the number of elements processed, and the MT_TABLE variable contains the PL/SQL table.

Lines 8 through 10 loop through each element in the table and display its values. Each element in the list is displayed as a separate line.

3. Run the CHP12_22.SQL file in SQL*Plus. The PL/SQL code contained in the file reads records from the sample table, places the records in a PL/SQL table, and returns them as a comma-separated list. Figure 12.25 shows the results of the PL/SQL module in SQL*Plus.

Lines 2 through 6 declare a cursor to query the sample table created in Step 1. Line 7 declares a variable of the UNCL_ARRAY datatype, defined in the DBMS_UTILITY package. Line 8 declares a variable used as an OUT

```
SQL> START CHP12_21
SQL> SET ECHO ON SERVEROUTPUT ON
SQL> DECLARE
  2    MY_TABLE  DBMS_UTILITY.UNCL_ARRAY;
  3    CNT         BINARY_INTEGER;
  4    COMMA_STRING VARCHAR2(250);
  5  BEGIN
  6    COMMA_STRING := 'Illinois,Iowa,Indiana,Kentucky,Maryland,Montan
  7    DBMS_UTILITY.COMMA_TO_TABLE(COMMA_STRING,CNT,MY_TABLE);
  8    FOR I IN 1..CNT LOOP
  9      DBMS_OUTPUT.PUT_LINE(MY_TABLE(I));
 10    END LOOP;
 11  END;
 12  /
Illinois
Iowa
Indiana
Kentucky
Maryland
Montana

PL/SQL procedure successfully completed.

SQL>
```

Figure 12.24 CHP12_21.SQL converts a comma-separated list into a PL/SQL table.

```
SQL> START CHP12_22
SQL> SET ECHO ON SERVEROUTPUT ON
SQL> DECLARE
  2     CURSOR C1 IS
  3        SELECT DEPT_NO,
  4               DEPT_NAME,
  5               LOCATION
  6        FROM DEPT12;
  7     OUTPUT_TABLE DBMS_UTILITY.UNCL_ARRAY;
  8     CNT BINARY_INTEGER;
  9     OUTPUT_STRING VARCHAR2(80);
 10     COUNTER INTEGER := 0;
 11  BEGIN
 12     FOR I IN C1 LOOP
 13        OUTPUT_TABLE(COUNTER+1) := I.DEPT_NO;
 14        OUTPUT_TABLE(COUNTER+2) := I.DEPT_NAME;
 15        OUTPUT_TABLE(COUNTER+3) := I.LOCATION;
 16        COUNTER := COUNTER+3;
 17     END LOOP;
 18     DBMS_UTILITY.TABLE_TO_COMMA(OUTPUT_TABLE,CNT,OUTPUT_STRING);
 19     DBMS_OUTPUT.PUT_LINE(OUTPUT_STRING);
 20  END;
 21  /
1,Marketing,Chicago,2,Sales,Tampa,3,I/S,New York

PL/SQL procedure successfully completed.

SQL>
```

Figure 12.25 CHP12_22.SQL converts contents of the sample table into a comma-separated list.

parameter and passes the number of elements processed by the procedure. Line 9 declares a variable used as an OUT parameter and returns the comma separated list from the procedure. Line 10 declares a variable tracking the current element in the PL/SQL table. The loop defined in lines 12 through 17 processes each record contained in the cursor. Lines 13 through 15 move the values in the columns next to the records in the PL/SQL table. Line 16 increments the counter. Line 18 uses the TABLE_TO_COMMA function to move the records in the PL/SQL table into the character string as comma separated values. Line 19 displays the comma separated list to the screen.

How It Works

The TABLE_TO_COMMA and COMMA_TO_TABLE procedures in the DBMS_UTILITY package can be used to work with comma separated lists in PL/SQL. The PL/SQL table used must be declared of the type UNCL_ARRAY, defined in the DBMS_UTILITY package. Step 1 creates a sample table with data used to demonstrate the procedures. Steps 2 and 3 present a PL/SQL module, which converts a comma separated list into a PL/SQL table using the COMMA_TO_TABLE procedure. Once the list is moved into the table, it can be manipulated easily within the PL/SQL code. Steps 4 and 5 present a PL/SQL module, which queries a database table and converts the results to a comma separated character string by using the TABLE_TO_COMMA procedure.

Comments

Working with comma separated lists can be difficult without the use of the DBMS_UTILITY package because you would have to use character functions and parse the comma separated list with PL/SQL code.

The COMMA_TO_TABLE procedure is useful for creating a PL/SQL table from a comma separated list. Because a PL/SQL table works like a one-dimensional array, it is perfect for handling lists.

COMPLEXITY
ADVANCED

12.7 How do I...
Manage large objects with DBMS_LOB?

AVAILABILITY: PL/SQL VERSION 3.0 AND HIGHER.

Problem

I need to store large blocks containing unstructured data such as text, graphic images, video clips, and sound waveforms in the database. Our applications must be able to randomly access these large objects (LOBs) of data efficiently. I know that the DMBS_LOB package allows efficient access to LOBs. How do I use the DBMS_LOB package to manage LOBs?

Technique

LOBs support random access to data and can have a maximum size of up to four gigabytes as compared to the LONG scalar datatype, which supports only sequential access and has a maximum size of two gigabytes.

There are four LOB datatypes: A *BLOB* contains unstructured binary data. A CLOB contains single-byte character data. A *NCLOB* contains fixed width single or multi-byte NLS character data. A *BFILE* is a BLOB stored as an external file outside the database. A *BFILE* is read-only supporting only random (non-sequential) reads. The source and destination buffers are of the RAW datatype for BLOB and BFILE, and VARCHAR2 datatype for CLOB and NCLOB.

For LOB operations, Oracle uses pointers called as LOB locators that specify the location of the LOB stored out-of-line. The LOB locator for a BFILE is a pointer to the location of the binary file in the operating system. Locators cannot span transactions or sessions and all LOBs, except BFILEs, can participate in transactions. The DBMS_LOB package can be used to manipulate LOBs. The functions and procedures in the DBMS_LOB package are listed in Tables 12.11, 12.12, and 12.13.

Table 12.11 DBMS_LOB procedures to modify BLOB, CLOB, NLOB values

NAME	TYPE	DESCRIPTION
APPEND	Procedure	Appends the contents of source LOB to destination LOB.
COPY	Procedure	Copies the source LOB to destination LOB partially or fully.
ERASE	Procedure	Clears the LOB partially or fully.
TRIM	Procedure	Trims the LOB to the new length.
WRITE	Procedure	Writes data from a buffer to LOB.

Table 12.12 DBMS_LOB functions/procedures to read/examine LOB values

NAME	TYPE	DESCRIPTION
COMPARE	Function	Compares two LOBs partially or fully.
GETLENGTH	Function	Returns length of the LOB.
INSTR	Function	Searches for a pattern in the LOB.
READ	Procedure	Reads data from LOB into a buffer.
SUBSTR	Function	Returns a partial LOB value.

Table 12.13 DBMS_LOB functions/procedures specific to BFILEs

NAME	TYPE	DESCRIPTION
FILEOPEN	Function	Opens the specified BFILE file.
FILEISOPEN	Function	Returns TRUE if the file is currently open.
FILEEXISTS	Function	Checks for the actual existence of the file.
FILEGETNAME	Procedure	Returns the name of the BFILE file.
FILECLOSE	Procedure	Closes the specified BFILE file.
FILECLOSEALL	Procedure	Closes all open BFILE files.

In this How-To, examples are provided for each DBMS_LOB routine to illustrate their use in the following steps.

Steps

1. Run SQL*Plus and connect as the WAITE user account. Run CHP12_23.SQL, as shown in Figure 12.26, which creates the sample table with LOB type columns and inserts sample data into it. The sample table contains an integer column as the primary key and four LOB columns of BLOB, CLOB, NCLOB, and BFILE datatypes. Run the script to create the sample table and data.

```
SQL> START CHP12_23
SQL> SET ECHO ON SERVEROUTPUT ON
SQL> CREATE TABLE LOB_TABLE12 (
  2    IDX_VALUE INTEGER PRIMARY KEY,
  3    BLOB_OBJ  BLOB,
  4    CLOB_OBJ  CLOB,
  5    NCLOB_OBJ NCLOB,
  6    BFILE_OBJ BFILE);

Table created.

SQL> CREATE OR REPLACE DIRECTORY DIR12 AS 'C:\TEMP';

Directory created.

SQL> INSERT INTO LOB_TABLE12 VALUES
  2         (1, EMPTY_BLOB(), EMPTY_CLOB(), EMPTY_CLOB(),
  3          BFILENAME('DIR12', 'BFILE1.DAT'));

1 row created.

SQL> INSERT INTO LOB_TABLE12 VALUES
  2         (2, NULL, 'WAITE CLOB SAMPLE', NULL,
  3          BFILENAME('DIR12', 'BFILE2.DAT'));

1 row created.

SQL>
```

Figure 12.26 CHP12_23.SQL creates a sample
table and data used in this How-To.

In the CREATE TABLE statement, line 2 declares the primary key. Lines 3
to 6 declare a locator for each of the BLOB, CLOB, NCLOB, and BFILE
datatypes. Additionally, you can specify a LOB storage clause, and the
NOCACHE and NOLOGGING options with the CREATE TABLE
statement as discussed in Chapter 4.

The first INSERT statement uses the EMPTY_BLOB() and EMPTY_CLOB()
functions to initialize the BLOB column with an empty BLOB locator and
the CLOB and NCLOB columns with empty CLOB locators. In the second
INSERT statement, the CLOB column is initialized with a locator that
points to an LOB value containing the string specified in the statement.

An LOB column must contain a locator that points to an empty or
populated value before you can write any data to the LOB. The
BFILENAME() function is used to associate a BFILE column with an
external file. The first parameter to the BFILENAME() function is the
directory_alias and the second one is the *filename*. The *directory_alias* is
created beforehand with the CREATE OR REPLACE DIRECTORY
statement to create a directory object. BFILENAME() does not check for
the existence of the physical directory, however, until actual file access is
performed.

2. Run the CHP12_24.SQL file in SQL*Plus. The PL/SQL block in the file
writes a line of text to a CLOB. Figure 12.27 shows the results of the
operation in SQL*Plus.

```
SQL> START CHP12_24
SQL> DECLARE
  2     CLOB_LOCKED  CLOB;
  3     NUM_BYTES    INTEGER;
  4     WRITE_OFFSET INTEGER;
  5     BUFFER       VARCHAR2(20) := 'CHARACTER LOB SAMPLE';
  6  BEGIN
  7     SELECT CLOB_OBJ
  8       INTO CLOB_LOCKED
  9     FROM LOB_TABLE12
 10       WHERE IDX_VALUE = 1 FOR UPDATE;
 11     NUM_BYTES    := LENGTH(BUFFER);
 12     WRITE_OFFSET := 1;
 13     DBMS_LOB.WRITE(CLOB_LOCKED, NUM_BYTES, WRITE_OFFSET, BUFFER);
 14     COMMIT;
 15  END;
 16  /

PL/SQL procedure successfully completed.

SQL>
```

Figure 12.27 CHP12_24.SQL writes text to a CLOB.

Line 2 declares the CLOB locator controlling access to the CLOB object. Line 5 declares a VARCHAR2 buffer to hold character data that needs to be written to the CLOB object. Lines 7 through 10 select a CLOB locator for writing by using the FOR UPDATE clause in the SELECT statement. Line 11 uses the LENGTH function to determine the number of bytes in the buffer to be written to the CLOB. The variable in line 12 is the offset in the CLOB at which the buffer contents are written. Line 13 calls the WRITE procedure in the DBMS_LOB package to write the contents of the buffer to the CLOB. Line 14 issues a COMMIT to complete the transaction and release the lock on the row that was acquired due to the FOR UPDATE clause of the SELECT statement.

3. Run the CHP12_25.SQL file in SQL*Plus. The PL/SQL block in the file demonstrates the use of the GETLENGTH function in the DBMS_LOB package to find out the length of a CLOB value. Figure 12.28 shows the results of the operation in SQL*Plus.

Line 2 declares the CLOB locator controlling access to the CLOB object. Lines 4 through 7 query the CLOB locator from the sample table. Lines 8 and 9 display the length of the CLOB value pointed by the CLOB locator using the DBMS_LOB.GETLENGTH function and display it in SQL*Plus.

4. Run the CHP12_26.SQL file in SQL*Plus. The PL/SQL block in the file reads a line of text from a CLOB. Figure 12.29 shows the results of the operation in SQL*Plus.

Line 2 declares the CLOB locator controlling access to the CLOB object. Line 3 declares a bind variable for the CLOB locator. Lines 8 through 11 query the CLOB locator from the sample table. Line 12 reads 20 bytes

```
SQL> START CHP12_25
SQL> DECLARE
  2      CLOB_VAR  CLOB;
  3   BEGIN
  4       SELECT CLOB_OBJ
  5         INTO CLOB_VAR
  6       FROM LOB_TABLE12
  7         WHERE  IDX_VALUE = 1;
  8       DBMS_OUTPUT.PUT_LINE('SIZE OF THE CLOB OBJECT = ' ||
  9                      DBMS_LOB.GETLENGTH(CLOB_VAR));
 10   END;
 11   /
SIZE OF THE CLOB OBJECT = 20

PL/SQL procedure successfully completed.

SQL>
```

Figure 12.28 CHP12_25.SQL prints the length of the CLOB.

```
SQL> START CHP12_26
SQL> DECLARE
  2      CLOB_VAR      CLOB;
  3      CLOB_VAR2     CLOB;
  4      NUM_BYTES     INTEGER := 20;
  5      READ_OFFSET   INTEGER := 1;
  6      BUFFER        VARCHAR2(20);
  7   BEGIN
  8       SELECT CLOB_OBJ
  9         INTO CLOB_VAR
 10       FROM LOB_TABLE12
 11         WHERE IDX_VALUE = 1;
 12       DBMS_LOB.READ(CLOB_VAR, NUM_BYTES, READ_OFFSET, BUFFER);
 13       DBMS_OUTPUT.PUT_LINE(BUFFER);
 14       NUM_BYTES := 10;
 15       CLOB_VAR2 := CLOB_VAR;
 16       DBMS_LOB.READ(CLOB_VAR2, NUM_BYTES, READ_OFFSET, BUFFER);
 17       DBMS_OUTPUT.PUT_LINE(BUFFER);
 18   END;
 19   /
CHARACTER LOB SAMPLE
CHARACTER

PL/SQL procedure successfully completed.

SQL>
```

Figure 12.29 CHP12_26.SQL reads text from a CLOB.

starting at offset 1 from the CLOB. Line 13 displays the retrieved text in SQL*Plus. Line 16 uses the bind variable to retrieve only the first 10 bytes from the CLOB. Line 17 displays the partially retrieved text in SQL*Plus.

5. Run the CHP12_27.SQL file in SQL*Plus, as shown in Figure 12.30. The PL/SQL block in the file exposes some more LOB manipulation techniques that you will typically need to use.

Line 2 declares the CLOB locator controlling access to the CLOB object. In line 4, the EMPTY_CLOB() function is used to initialize a CLOB locator to point to an empty CLOB. Lines 5 through 8 update the CLOB locator in

```
SQL> START CHP12_27
SQL> DECLARE
  2     CLOB_VAR CLOB;
  3  BEGIN
  4     CLOB_VAR := EMPTY_CLOB();
  5     UPDATE LOB_TABLE12
  6        SET CLOB_OBJ = CLOB_VAR,
  7            BLOB_OBJ = EMPTY_BLOB()
  8        WHERE IDX_VALUE = 2;
  9     UPDATE LOB_TABLE12
 10        SET CLOB_OBJ = (SELECT CLOB_OBJ
 11                          FROM LOB_TABLE12
 12                          WHERE IDX_VALUE = 1)
 13        WHERE IDX_VALUE = 2;
 14  END;
 15  /

PL/SQL procedure successfully completed.

SQL>
```

Figure 12.30 More LOB manipulation techniques.

the sample table using the empty CLOB initialized in line 4, and also sets the BLOB value to an empty BLOB. Line 9 through 13 are used to copy the CLOB value from one record to another. Alternatively, the COPY procedure in the DBMS_LOB package can also be used.

6. Run the CHP12_28.SQL file in SQL*Plus, as shown in Figure 12.31. The PL/SQL block in the file reads the contents of a BFILE and writes it to a BLOB.

```
SQL> START CHP12_28
SQL> DECLARE
  2     FIL BFILE;
  3     BLB BLOB;
  4     AMT BINARY_INTEGER;
  5     BUF RAW(4000);
  6  BEGIN
  7     SELECT BLOB_OBJ INTO BLB
  8     FROM LOB_TABLE12 WHERE IDX_VALUE = 1 FOR UPDATE;
  9     SELECT BFILE_OBJ INTO FIL
 10     FROM LOB_TABLE12 WHERE IDX_VALUE = 1;
 11     DBMS_LOB.FILEOPEN(FIL, DBMS_LOB.FILE_READONLY);
 12     AMT := DBMS_LOB.GETLENGTH(FIL);
 13     DBMS_LOB.READ(FIL, AMT, 1, BUF);
 14     DBMS_LOB.WRITE(BLB, AMT, 1, BUF);
 15     DBMS_LOB.FILECLOSE(FIL);
 16  EXCEPTION
 17     WHEN NO_DATA_FOUND THEN
 18          DBMS_OUTPUT.PUT_LINE('END OF FILE REACHED. CLOSING FILE');
 19          DBMS_LOB.FILECLOSE(FIL);
 20  END;
 21  /

PL/SQL procedure successfully completed.

SQL>
```

Figure 12.31 CHP12_28.SQL reads from a BFILE and writes to a BLOB.

Line 2 declares the BFILE locator for file operations. Line 3 declares the BLOB locator controlling access to the BLOB object. Line 5 declares a buffer of the RAW datatype as we are dealing with binary data here. Lines 7 and 8 select a BLOB locator for writing by using the FOR UPDATE clause in the SELECT statement. Lines 9 and 10 select the BFILE locator for reading the contents of the external file.

Ensure that the file BFILE1.DAT exists in the C:\TEMP directory. This file could be an image or any other file with binary contents that you'll want to store in the database as a BLOB object.

Line 11 opens the BFILE locator by calling the FILEOPEN procedure. Line 12 calls the GETLENGTH function, which returns the total number of bytes in the BFILE. Lines 13 reads the complete BFILE into the RAW buffer. Line 14 writes contents of the buffer to the BLOB. Line 15 closes the BFILE locator using the FILECLOSE procedure. The exception handler in lines 17 to 19 is raised if the call to the READ procedure in line 13 fails if it tries to read beyond the end of file. Because the RAW datatype has a maximum limit of 32,767 bytes, if you are uploading a file larger than that, use a buffer of a suitable size and do the read and write in a loop, incrementing the starting position for the next read and write by the number of bytes read.

7. Run the CHP12_29.SQL file in SQL*Plus, as shown in Figure 12.32. The PL/SQL block in it compares the contents of two BFILEs.

```
SQL> START C:\CHP12_29
SQL> DECLARE
  2     FIL_1  BFILE;
  3     FIL_2  BFILE;
  4     RESULT INTEGER;
  5  BEGIN
  6     SELECT BFILE_OBJ INTO FIL_1 FROM LOB_TABLE12 WHERE IDX_VALUE = 1;
  7     FIL_2 := BFILENAME('DIR12', 'BFILE2.DAT');
  8     DBMS_LOB.FILEOPEN(FIL_1);
  9     DBMS_LOB.FILEOPEN(FIL_2);
 10     RESULT := DBMS_LOB.COMPARE(FIL_1, FIL_2,
 11                             DBMS_LOB.GETLENGTH(FIL_1));
 12     IF (RESULT != 0) THEN
 13        DBMS_OUTPUT.PUT_LINE('THE TWO FILES ARE DIFFERENT');
 14     ELSE
 15        DBMS_OUTPUT.PUT_LINE('THE TWO FILES ARE THE SAME');
 16     END IF;
 17     DBMS_LOB.FILECLOSEALL();
 18  END;
 19  /
THE TWO FILES ARE DIFFERENT

PL/SQL procedure successfully completed.

SQL>
```

Figure 12.32 CHP12_29.SQL compares two BFILEs.

Line 2 and 3 declare the BFILE locators for file operations on the two external files. Line 6 selects the BFILE locator for reading the contents of the external file. BFILEs are read-only. Line 7 creates a new BFILE locator by calling the BFILENAME procedure and passing the directory alias (created in Step 1) and the filename. Line 10 calls the COMPARE procedure in the DBMS_LOB package to compare the contents of the two files. In addition to passing the BFILE locators, the length of the first BFILE is passed as the third parameter in line 11 by calling the GETLENGTH function. A return code of 0 means that the two files were the same; otherwise, they are different. Line 17 closes all open BFILE locators in the block by calling the FILECLOSEALL procedure of the DBMS_LOB package.

How It Works

The DBMS_LOB package is used to manage LOBs, which include functions and procedures to read, write, append, copy, and erase LOBs. The directory alias for all accessible directories must be created before performing any operations on BFILEs. Oracle must also have permissions to access these files.

Step 1 creates the sample table with columns of LOB datatypes and inserts data into it. The EMPTY_CLOB() and EMPTY_BLOB() functions are used within an INSERT statement to create LOB locators pointing to empty LOB values. Any read/write operations will fail if the LOB was initialized to NULL instead.

Step 2 performs a CLOB write operation and Step 3 displays the length of the CLOB in SQL*Plus. Step 4 reads data from the CLOB and displays it. Step 5 shows the use of EMPTY_CLOB() and EMPTY_BLOB() in PL/SQL and copies LOB data by nesting a SELECT statement in an UPDATE statement.

The COPY and ERASE procedures in the DBMS_LOB package provide an easier means of achieving the same effect as you can specify the number of bytes and the starting offset within the LOB. The APPEND procedure appends one LOB to another, but both have to be of the same LOB datatype.

Step 6 reads a BFILE into a buffer and writes the contents of the buffer to a BLOB column, which is useful in uploading binary data files to be stored as BLOBs in the database. Step 7 uses the COMPARE function to compare the contents of two BFILEs.

Comments

The DBMS_LOB package in PL/SQL 3.0 provides routines to access and manipulate portions of LOBs or complete LOBs. All DBMS_LOB routines work based on LOB locators. For the successful completion of DBMS_LOB routines, you must provide an input locator that represents a LOB which already exists in the database tablespaces or external file system.

For internal LOBs, you must first use SQL DDL to define tables that contain LOB columns, and subsequently SQL DML to initialize or populate the locators in these LOB columns. For external LOBs, you must ensure that a DIRECTORY object that represents a valid, existing physical directory has been defined, and physical files exist with read permission for Oracle.

Once the LOBs are defined and created, you can then SELECT a LOB locator into a local PL/SQL LOB variable and use this variable as an input parameter to DBMS_LOB for manipulation of the LOB value.

CHAPTER 13
TRIGGERS

13

TRIGGERS

How do I...

Database triggers execute when a specific DML operation on a table is performed. Triggers can be used to ensure that specific business rules related to a table are performed when records are inserted, updated, or deleted. As triggers are stored in the database and tied to the table, they fire regardless of which application performed the operation.

You can use database triggers to ensure the integrity and consistency of data. Like stored procedures and functions, triggers are a fundamental part of application partitioning. Moving business rules from the application code to the database ensures that the business rules are enforced and performance improved. Triggers are typically used for auditing and event logging purposes, as well as security authorizations, to prevent invalid transactions, data replication, and most importantly to enforce complex integrity constraints.

Triggers should be used to augment the power of declarative integrity constraints functionality, which is already built into Oracle (refer to Chapter 6). The INSTEAD-OF triggers provide a way of updating object views as well as relational views, which will be examined in Chapter 16.

13.1 Create a Database Trigger?

Database triggers ensure that an action is performed when a table is modified. They can be used to enforce business rules regardless of the source of the operation. This How-To demonstrates the creation of database triggers and the different types of triggers that can be created.

13.2 Use Column Values Within Database Triggers?

It is almost always necessary to use the column values from the table containing the trigger. The :NEW and :OLD pseudo-records allow the column values to be used within a database trigger. If a statement within a trigger requires a value from the updated or new record, then :NEW is used. If a statement requires the value of a column before it was modified, then :OLD is used. This How-To explores the use of column values within database triggers.

13.3 Fire Triggers Selectively Using Trigger Predicates?

Instead of writing three different triggers for INSERT, UPDATE, and DELETE operations, you might want to write a single trigger that handles any DML operation on a given table. The trigger body can use conditional predicates to recognize the type of DML operation that caused the trigger to fire. This How-To presents the use of trigger predicates to conditionally execute code within the trigger.

13.4 Perform Cascading Deletes with Database Triggers?

There will be situations when you will want to use database triggers to delete the data related to a record deleted from a table. If you want to delete a record referenced as the foreign key to a record in another table, the delete operation must be cascaded through the data model. This How-To presents the method for deleting related data using database triggers.

13.5 Disable and Enable Triggers?

Database triggers will fire whenever a table is modified. You need to disable database triggers in order to perform management tasks or to perform batch operations. When a trigger is disabled, it will not fire when the triggering event occurs on the table. This How-To presents the method used to disable and enable triggers when necessary.

13.6 List Information About Triggers?

Information about a trigger, including its name, status, owner, and triggering event, can be queried from the data dictionary through the USER_TRIGGERS and ALL_TRIGGERS data dictionary views. This How-To presents the method and queries used to display information about database triggers.

13.7 Rebuild CREATE TRIGGER Statements?

The CREATE TRIGGER statements used to create database triggers can be rebuilt using the data dictionary and SQL*Plus. This How-To presents the method and SQL scripts used to rebuild the CREATE TRIGGER statement for a specified trigger.

COMPLEXITY

INTERMEDIATE

13.1 How do I...
Create a database trigger?

Problem

I need to create database triggers on the tables used by my application. I also want to use triggers to enforce business rules, manage redundancy, and perform cascading deletes. I want to create triggers that execute once when a statement is executed or for each row modified in the table. How do I create a database trigger on a table?

Technique

The CREATE TRIGGER statement is used to create a database trigger on a table. Each trigger is given a name and can be programmed to execute before or after an event on a table. The syntax used to create a trigger is as follows:

```
CREATE [OR REPLACE] TRIGGER trigger_name
{BEFORE | AFTER} triggering_event ON table_name
[REFERENCING {NEW AS|OLD AS} qualifier name]
[FOR EACH ROW]
[WHEN (expression)]
[DECLARE
    Optional declarative section contains all local types,
    variables, constants, cursors and subprogram declarations.]
BEGIN
    Executable section of the trigger.
[EXCEPTION
    Optional exception section to handle errors.]
END;
```

The triggering_event following the BEFORE or AFTER keyword can be an INSERT, UPDATE, or DELETE event or a combination of any of these three events. Any combination of triggering events can be included in the same database trigger. The name of each trigger must be unique within its schema.

There are two types of triggers: statement triggers and row triggers. A statement trigger executes only once for the triggering statement, irrespective of the number of rows affected. A row trigger is created by specifying the FOR EACH ROW option, which causes the trigger to fire once to each row created, modified, or deleted by the triggering statement. If the option is not included, the trigger is considered to be a statement trigger. The possible trigger types that can be created on a table are shown in Table 13.1.

Table 13.1 Possible trigger types allowed on a given table

NAME	FUNCTION
BEFORE INSERT	Fires once before an INSERT statement
BEFORE INSERT FOR EACH ROW	Fires before each new record is created
AFTER INSERT	Fires once after an INSERT statement
AFTER INSERT FOR EACH ROW	Fires after each new record is created
BEFORE UPDATE	Fires once before an UPDATE statement
BEFORE UPDATE FOR EACH ROW	Fires before each record is updated
AFTER UPDATE	Fires once after an UPDATE statement
AFTER UPDATE FOR EACH ROW	Fires after each record is updated
BEFORE DELETE	Fires once before a DELETE statement
BEFORE DELETE FOR EACH ROW	Fires before each record is deleted
AFTER DELETE	Fires once after a DELETE statement
AFTER DELETE FOR EACH ROW	Fires after each record is deleted

An optional WHEN clause can be used to restrict the records for which a row trigger fires. The WHEN clause contains a Boolean expression, which is evaluated for each row that is affected by the trigger. If the expression evaluates to FALSE for a given row, the trigger body is not executed for that row. The optional REFERENCING clause can be used to avoid name conflicts with the NEW and OLD qualifiers.

Steps

1. Run SQL*Plus and connect as the WAITE user account. Run CHP13_1.SQL, as shown in Figure 13.1, to create a sample table displaying the triggers created in this How-To.

The sample table, DEPT13, is a simple table with three columns. In the steps that follow, triggers will be created on the table and the capabilities of triggers will be demonstrated.

2. Run the CHP13_2.SQL file in SQL*Plus. The CREATE TRIGGER statement contained in the file creates a simple trigger that fires before a record is created. The results of the operation are shown in Figure 13.2.

The CREATE OR REPLACE TRIGGER keywords create the trigger with the specified trigger name that must be unique within the schema. Because the CREATE OR REPLACE keywords are used, another trigger with the same

```
SQL> START CHP13_1
SQL> SET ECHO ON
SQL> CREATE TABLE DEPT13 (
  2         DEPT_NO     NUMBER(5),
  3         DEPT_NAME   VARCHAR2(30),
  4         LOCATION    VARCHAR2(30));

Table created.

SQL> INSERT INTO DEPT13
  2        VALUES (1, 'MARKETING', 'NEW YORK');

1 row created.

SQL> INSERT INTO DEPT13
  2        VALUES (2, 'ACCOUNTING', 'CHICAGO');

1 row created.

SQL>
```

Figure 13.1 CHP13_1.SQL creates
the sample table and data used in
this How-To.

```
SQL> START CHP13_2
SQL> CREATE OR REPLACE TRIGGER DEPT_BI_13
  2  BEFORE INSERT ON DEPT13
  3  DECLARE
  4     X NUMBER(10);
  5  BEGIN
  6     DBMS_OUTPUT.PUT_LINE('BEFORE INSERT TRIGGER FIRED');
  7  END;
  8  /

Trigger created.

SQL>
```

Figure 13.2 CHP13_2.SQL creates a BEFORE
INSERT trigger.

name in the schema will be replaced, regardless of the table the trigger is
on. However, a trigger name can have the same name as that of a table or
procedure.

Line 2 specifies the triggering statement with the BEFORE INSERT ON
clause, which makes the trigger fire after the INSERT operation takes place
on the DEPT13 table. Lines 3 and 4 present the syntax used to declare
variables for database triggers, even though the variable created is not
used. Unlike stored procedures, the DECLARE statement is used at the
beginning of the declarative section, when creating database triggers. Lines
5 through 7 contain the executable section of the trigger. The only
executable line in the trigger displays a message that the trigger has fired,
by using the PUT_LINE procedure of the DBMS_OUTPUT package.

The trigger is automatically enabled when created. Any new data added to
the table after the trigger is created will make it fire. The next step creates
a trigger that only fires when the data meets certain criteria.

3. Run the CHP13_3.SQL file in SQL*Plus, as shown in Figure 13.3. The CREATE TRIGGER statement contained in the file creates a trigger that fires after new records are inserted into the table. It also includes a WHEN clause restricting when the trigger is fired.

Line 1 is the CREATE TRIGGER statement to create the new trigger. Line 2 specifies the triggering event and the trigger will fire after a new record is inserted. The FOR EACH ROW clause in line 3 ensures the trigger will fire once for each new row created. Line 4 specifies a WHEN clause making the trigger fire only when the DEPT_NO column of the new record is greater than three. The NEW represents the new record inserted into the table. The expression in the WHEN clause must evaluate to a Boolean TRUE or FALSE. Lines 5 through 7 contain the trigger body. The PUT_LINE procedure from the DBMS_OUTPUT package shown in line 6 will display a message when the trigger is fired.

Now two triggers are on the sample table. The first trigger will fire any time a new record is inserted into the table. The trigger just created will only fire when the DEPT_NO column is greater than three, and only after the record has been successfully inserted. The next step creates a trigger that fires when records in the table are updated.

4. Run the CHP13_4.SQL in SQL*Plus, as shown in Figure 13.4. The CREATE TRIGGER statement contained in the file creates a trigger that executes when the DEPT_NAME column in the DEPT13 table is updated.

Line 1 is the CREATE TRIGGER clause. Line 2 specifies the triggering event. The trigger fires whenever the DEPT_NAME column is updated but after the record is updated. If the OF DEPT_NAME clause is not on the trigger, the trigger fires when any table column is updated. The FOR EACH ROW clause in line 3 causes the trigger to execute once for each record updated. Lines 4 through 6 present a trigger body displaying a message when the trigger fires.

```
SQL> START CHP13_3
SQL> CREATE OR REPLACE TRIGGER DEPT_AIR_13
  2   AFTER INSERT ON DEPT13
  3   FOR EACH ROW
  4   WHEN (NEW.DEPT_NO > 3)
  5   BEGIN
  6     DBMS_OUTPUT.PUT_LINE('AFTER INSERT TRIGGER FIRED');
  7   END;
  8   /

Trigger created.

SQL>
```

Figure 13.3 CHP13_3.SQL creates a AFTER INSERT FOR EACH ROW trigger.

```
SQL> START CHP13_4
SQL> CREATE OR REPLACE TRIGGER DEPT_AUR_13
  2  AFTER UPDATE OF DEPT_NAME ON DEPT13
  3  FOR EACH ROW
  4  BEGIN
  5    DBMS_OUTPUT.PUT_LINE('AFTER UPDATE TRIGGER FIRED');
  6  END;
  7  /

Trigger created.

SQL>
```

Figure 13.4 CHP13_4.SQL creates an AFTER
UPDATE FOR EACH ROW trigger.

5. Run the CHP13_5.SQL in SQL*Plus, as shown in Figure 13.5. The
CREATE TRIGGER statement contained in the file creates a trigger that
executes after a DELETE statement has executed successfully.

Line 1 creates the trigger with the name DEPT_AD_13. Line 2 specifies
that the trigger will execute after the DELETE statement has run. The
absence of a FOR EACH ROW clause means the statement will fire only
once when the DELETE statement is executed, regardless of the number of
rows deleted. Lines 3 through 5 contain the trigger body. The statement
contained in line 4 displays a message when the trigger fires.

The sample table created in Step 1 now contains four database triggers. In
the following steps, the data in the tables will be manipulated to make the
triggers fire.

6. Run the CHP13_6.SQL in SQL*Plus. The SERVEROUTPUT SQL*Plus
variable is set to ON to display the output from the triggers within
SQL*Plus. The INSERT statement contained in the file inserts a record
into the sample table. Figure 13.6 displays the results of the operation.

The INSERT statement creates a new record with a DEPT_NO value of 5.
The BEFORE INSERT trigger will fire, but the AFTER INSERT statement
will not, due to the WHEN clause contained in the statement.

```
SQL> START CHP13_5
SQL> CREATE OR REPLACE TRIGGER DEPT_AD_13
  2  AFTER DELETE ON DEPT13
  3  BEGIN
  4    DBMS_OUTPUT.PUT_LINE('AFTER DELETE TRIGGER FIRED');
  5  END;
  6  /

Trigger created.

SQL>
```

Figure 13.5 CHP13_5.SQL creates a AFTER
DELETE statement trigger.

```
SQL> START CHP13_6
SQL> SET SERVEROUTPUT ON
SQL> INSERT INTO DEPT13
  2        VALUES (3, 'I/S', 'SAN HOSE');
BEFORE INSERT TRIGGER FIRED

1 row created.

SQL>
```

Figure 13.6 CHP13_6.SQL
inserts a record to fire the
INSERT trigger.

One message is displayed because only the BEFORE INSERT trigger fires. The WHEN clause in the AFTER INSERT trigger prevents it from firing, because the value of the DEPT_NO column is not greater than 5. The next step creates a record that does not prevent the AFTER INSERT trigger from firing.

7. Run the CHP13_7.SQL file in SQL*Plus. The INSERT statement contained in the file creates a new record which has a DEPT_NO column greater than 5. Because the record created will have a DEPT_NO column value greater than 5, both the BEFORE INSERT and AFTER INSERT triggers will fire. Figure 13.7 shows the results in SQL*Plus.

Both the BEFORE INSERT and AFTER INSERT triggers are fired because the value of the DEPT_NO column does not prevent the AFTER INSERT trigger from firing. In the next step, an UPDATE statement will be used to fire the BEFORE UPDATE trigger.

8. Run the CHP13_8.SQL file in SQL*Plus. The UPDATE statement contained in the file updates each of the records in the table. The UPDATE statement will make the AFTER UPDATE trigger fire for each revised row, because the DEPT_NAME column is updated. The AFTER UPDATE OF DEPT_NAME clause in the CREATE TRIGGER statement in Step 6 only lets the trigger fire when the DEPT_NAME column is modified. Modifying other columns without the DEPT_NAME column will not fire the trigger. Figure 13.8 shows how the UPDATE statement causes the triggers to fire.

```
SQL> START CHP13_7
SQL> SET SERVEROUTPUT ON
SQL> INSERT INTO DEPT13
  2        VALUES (4, 'PURCHASING', 'BOSTON');
BEFORE INSERT TRIGGER FIRED
AFTER INSERT TRIGGER FIRED

1 row created.

SQL>
```

Figure 13.7 CHP13_7.SQL inserts a
record to fire both INSERT triggers.

```
SQL> START CHP13_8
SQL> SET SERVEROUTPUT ON
SQL> UPDATE DEPT13
  2      SET DEPT_NAME = 'BILLING';
AFTER UPDATE TRIGGER FIRED
AFTER UPDATE TRIGGER FIRED
AFTER UPDATE TRIGGER FIRED
AFTER UPDATE TRIGGER FIRED

4 rows updated.

SQL>
```

Figure 13.8 CHP13_8.SQL causes the
UPDATE trigger to fire.

Because four rows were updated by the statement, the AFTER UPDATE
trigger was fired four times. Had the FOR EACH ROW clause not been
specified in the CREATE TRIGGER statement, the trigger would have fired
only once. In the next step, all records will be deleted to show the
operation of the AFTER DELETE trigger presented in Step 8.

9. Execute a DELETE statement in CHP13_9.SQL to delete all the rows in
the table and then drop the table. Figure 13.9 shows the operation and the
output generated by the AFTER DELETE trigger.

Because the AFTER DELETE trigger does not contain the FOR EACH
ROW option, the trigger was only executed once by the DELETE
statement. All four underlying triggers created in this How-To are dropped
along with the table.

How It Works

The CREATE TRIGGER statement is used to create database triggers on a table.
Up to 12 triggers can be created on a single table. Table 13.1 shows the list of
triggers that can be created.

```
SQL> START CHP13_9
SQL> SET SERVEROUTPUT ON
SQL> DELETE FROM DEPT13;
AFTER DELETE TRIGGER FIRED

4 rows deleted.

SQL> DROP TABLE DEPT13;

Table dropped.

SQL>
```

Figure 13.9 CHP13_9.SQL causes the
DELETE trigger to fire.

Step 1 creates a sample table used throughout this How-To as the table for the new triggers. Step 2 creates a BEFORE INSERT trigger, which executes before a new row is inserted in the table. Step 3 creates an AFTER INSERT trigger, which includes the FOR EACH ROW clause and a WHEN clause. The WHEN clause can only be used on triggers containing the FOR EACH ROW clause and restricts firing the trigger to rows satisfying a Boolean condition. Step 4 creates an AFTER UPDATE trigger, which fires for each modified row but only when a particular column is updated. Step 5 creates an AFTER DELETE statement, which only fires once for each transaction. The absence of the FOR EACH ROW clause causes the trigger to fire only once per transaction.

The remaining steps demonstrate the execution of the database triggers by executing INSERT, UPDATE, and DELETE statements on the table. The table on which the row trigger is defined is called as a mutating table. An ORA-04091 error occurs if a row trigger (but not statement trigger) attempts to query or modify a mutating table that was in the middle of being modified by the statement that fired the trigger.

Comments

Use triggers when you need to guarantee that certain actions are performed when tables are modified. Avoid using triggers to perform operations that other Oracle features can execute. For example, referential integrity can be enforced using primary and foreign key constraints defined on the tables, but triggers come in handy if your needs are more complex, such as DELETE and UPDATE cascades. Oracle corporation recommends that trigger should be 60 lines or less, and if the trigger requires more than 60 lines of code, then it is better to pack the code in a separate stored procedure, and call the stored procedure from the trigger. Exception handling in triggers is the same as with stored procedures. Transaction control statements like COMMIT, ROLLBACK, and SAVEPOINT are not allowed in a trigger, but they can be issued inside a stored procedure called by the trigger. LONG and LONG RAW variables are not allowed in a trigger; AFTER row triggers are a bit more efficient than BEFORE row triggers.

To create a trigger on a table, the user account must either own the table or have the capability to create a trigger with the CREATE TRIGGER or CREATE ANY TRIGGER privilege; or must have the ALTER TABLE privilege for that table or have the ALTER ANY TABLE privilege. The trigger owner must also have direct privileges to schema objects referenced by the trigger.

COMPLEXITY
INTERMEDIATE

13.2 How do I...
Use column values within database triggers?

Problem

When I create database triggers, I need to use the values of the columns in the records being inserted, updated, or deleted. There are many times when I need to use both the values of columns before and after the operation. How do I use column values within database triggers?

Technique

The :NEW and :OLD pseudo-records are used to access new and old column values in a row trigger. You can access old column values of the record before the operation is performed by specifying the :OLD qualifier. The :NEW qualifier provides access to new column values of the record after the operation is performed. With an INSERT statement, the old column values are null, whereas with a DELETE statement, the new column values are null. The preceding colon is required when using the qualifiers in the trigger body. The colon is not allowed when using the qualifiers in the optional WHEN and REFERENCING clauses, as demonstrated in Step 3 of How-To 13.1. The REFERENCING option can be used to avoid name conflicts with qualifiers, if you have a table named as NEW or OLD or simply to increase code readability.

Steps

1. Run SQL*Plus and connect as the WAITE user account. Run CHP13_10.SQL, shown in Figure 13.10, which creates the sample table and data used in this How-To.

The sample table created by the script contains three columns and has database triggers created in the steps that follow. A sample record is created so the use of :OLD modifier can also be demonstrated with an existing record. Run the script to create the sample table and its sample record.

```
SQL> START CHP13_10
SQL> SET ECHO ON
SQL> CREATE TABLE DEPT13 (
  2        DEPT_NO      NUMBER(5),
  3        DEPT_NAME    VARCHAR2(30),
  4        LOCATION     VARCHAR2(20));

Table created.

SQL> INSERT INTO DEPT13
  2        VALUES (1, 'BILLING', 'CHICAGO');

1 row created.

SQL>
```

Figure 13.10 CHP13_10.SQL creates
the sample table and data used in
this How-To.

2. Run the CHP13_11.SQL file in SQL*Plus, as shown in Figure 13.11. The
CREATE TRIGGER statement contained in the file creates a BEFORE
UPDATE trigger referencing the new and old column values.

The :NEW and :OLD qualifiers are used to reference the columns in the
table. Line 1 presents the required keywords and specifies the name of the
trigger. Lines 2 and 3 specify the triggering statement and FOR EACH
ROW option. The trigger will fire any time a record in the table is
updated. Lines 5 through 10 use the :NEW and :OLD modifiers to display
the values of the columns before and after the operation. Lines 5 through
7 display the values of the columns before the operation. Lines 8 through
10 show the values of the record after the operation.

The next step will display the new and old values of the columns in the
existing record by executing an update statement on the table.

3. Run the CHP13_12.SQL file in SQL*Plus, as shown in Figure 13.12. The
SERVEROUTPUT SQL*Plus variable is set to ON, to display the results of

```
SQL> START CHP13_11
SQL> CREATE OR REPLACE TRIGGER DEPT_BUR_13
  2  BEFORE UPDATE ON DEPT13
  3  FOR EACH ROW
  4  BEGIN
  5      DBMS_OUTPUT.PUT_LINE('OLD DEPT_NO: '||TO_CHAR(:OLD.DEPT_NO));
  6      DBMS_OUTPUT.PUT_LINE('OLD DEPT_NAME: '||:OLD.DEPT_NAME);
  7      DBMS_OUTPUT.PUT_LINE('OLD LOCATION: '||:OLD.LOCATION);
  8      DBMS_OUTPUT.PUT_LINE('NEW DEPT_NO: '||TO_CHAR(:NEW.DEPT_NO));
  9      DBMS_OUTPUT.PUT_LINE('NEW DEPT_NAME: '||:NEW.DEPT_NAME);
 10      DBMS_OUTPUT.PUT_LINE('NEW LOCATION: '||:NEW.LOCATION);
 11  END;
 12  /

Trigger created.

SQL>
```

Figure 13.11 CHP13_11.SQL shows the use of :NEW
and :OLD.

```
SQL> START CHP13_12
SQL> SET SERVEROUTPUT ON
SQL> UPDATE DEPT13
  2     SET DEPT_NO = DEPT_NO + 1,
  3         DEPT_NAME = 'SALES';
OLD DEPT_NO: 1
OLD DEPT_NAME: BILLING
OLD LOCATION: CHICAGO
NEW DEPT_NO: 2
NEW DEPT_NAME: SALES
NEW LOCATION: CHICAGO

1 row updated.

SQL>
```

Figure 13.12 CHP13_12.SQL
causes the BEFORE UPDATE
trigger to fire.

the operation. The UPDATE statement contained in the file modifies the record in the sample table, firing the BEFORE UPDATE trigger. The UPDATE statement modifies two of the three columns in the table. The new value of the third column will still remain the same as its old value.

The output of the operation displays both the new and old values of the column. A new value was even available for the column not modified by the operation.

How It Works

The :NEW qualifier allows the trigger code to reference the new value of columns in the table. The :OLD qualifier provides access to the column values before the operation is performed. Step 1 creates a sample table and record used by the example trigger. Step 2 creates a BEFORE UPDATE trigger displaying the value of the columns in the table both before and after the update. Step 3 executes an UPDATE statement on the table, causing the trigger to fire.

Comments

The :NEW and :OLD qualifiers are necessary to reference column values in triggers. Make sure you use the right value in your trigger. If you use a new value when you should have used an old value, you may see invalid results. The :NEW and :OLD qualifiers cannot be used with LONG and LONG RAW columns. Triggers should not be created depending on the order in which rows will be processed.

13.3 How do I...
Fire triggers selectively using trigger predicates?

Problem

We have a lot of tables in the database. Instead of writing three different triggers for INSERT, UPDATE, and DELETE operations, I want to be write one trigger for each table in the system, and that trigger should handle any DML operations on that table. I need to know how to create such triggers and in the trigger body how do I recognize the type of DML operation that caused the trigger to fire. How do I fire triggers selectively using trigger predicates?

Technique

You can write a single trigger to handle multiple DML operations on a table. For instance, an INSERT, DELETE, or UPDATE statement can fire the same trigger with the use of the ON INSERT OR DELETE OR UPDATE OF clause while creating the trigger. The trigger body can use the conditional predicates INSERTING, DELETING, and UPDATING to execute specific blocks of code, depending upon the triggering statement.

Steps

1. Run SQL*Plus and connect as the WAITE user account. If you do not have the DEPT13 table in your schema, run CHP13_10.SQL from Step 1 of the previous How-To to create the table. In How-To 13.1, a separate trigger was created to handle an INSERT, UPDATE, and DELETE event. The steps presented in this How-To will create a trigger to handle a combination of these events.

2. Run the CHP13_13.SQL file in SQL*Plus, as shown in Figure 13.13. The CREATE TRIGGER statement in the file creates an all-in-one BEFORE INSERT, BEFORE UPDATE, and BEFORE DELETE trigger on the DEPT13 table.

Line 1 presents the keywords required to create the new trigger and names it as DEPT_ALL_13. Line 2 specifies that the trigger should be fired every time the DEPT13 table is manipulated by executing an INSERT, UPDATE, or DELETE statement. The FOR EACH ROW clause causes the trigger to

```
SQL> START CHP13_13
SQL> CREATE OR REPLACE TRIGGER DEPT_ALL_13
  2  .BEFORE INSERT OR UPDATE OR DELETE ON DEPT13
  3  FOR EACH ROW
  4  BEGIN
  5    IF INSERTING THEN
  6       DBMS_OUTPUT.PUT_LINE('BEFORE INSERT TRIGGER FIRED');
  7    ELSIF UPDATING THEN
  8       DBMS_OUTPUT.PUT_LINE('BEFORE UPDATE TRIGGER FIRED');
  9    ELSIF DELETING THEN
 10       DBMS_OUTPUT.PUT_LINE('BEFORE DELETE TRIGGER FIRED');
 11    END IF;
 12  END;
 13  /

Trigger created.

SQL>
```

Figure 13.13 CHP13_13.SQL makes use of trigger predicates.

be executed for each modified row. If it were not included in the statement, the trigger would only fire once for the statement, irrespective of the number of records updated or deleted. Line 5 uses the INSERTING trigger predicate to check if it is an INSERT statement being issued. Line 7 checks for an UPDATE operation and line 9 checks for a DELETE operation on the DEPT13 table.

Any modifications to the DEPT13 table will fire the trigger and the output displayed in SQL*Plus will correspond with the triggering statement.

3. Run the CHP13_14.SQL file is SQL*Plus, as shown in Figure 13.14. The INSERT statement contained in the file inserts a record in the DEPT13 table, causing the trigger to fire.

4. If you have not already created the DEPT_BUR_13 trigger in your schema by running the CHP13_11.SQL file from the previous How-To, you can run this file now to see the effects of multiple triggers on a table. Run the CHP13_15.SQL file is SQL*Plus (see Figure 13.15. The UPDATE statement contained in the file modifies both records in the DEPT13 table, causing the trigger to fire twice once for each row that is affected.

```
SQL> START CHP13_14
SQL> SET SERVEROUTPUT ON
SQL> INSERT INTO DEPT13
  2           VALUES (2, 'MARKETING', 'NEW YORK');
BEFORE INSERT TRIGGER FIRED

1 row created.

SQL>
```

Figure 13.14 CHP13_14.SQL inserts a record into the DEPT13 table.

```
SQL> START CHP13_15
SQL> SET SERVEROUTPUT ON
SQL> UPDATE DEPT13
  2     SET DEPT_NAME = 'ACCOUNTING';
BEFORE UPDATE TRIGGER FIRED
OLD DEPT_NO: 2
OLD DEPT_NAME: SALES
OLD LOCATION: CHICAGO
NEW DEPT_NO: 2
NEW DEPT_NAME: ACCOUNTING
NEW LOCATION: CHICAGO
BEFORE UPDATE TRIGGER FIRED
OLD DEPT_NO: 2
OLD DEPT_NAME: MARKETING
OLD LOCATION: NEW YORK
NEW DEPT_NO: 2
NEW DEPT_NAME: ACCOUNTING
NEW LOCATION: NEW YORK

2 rows updated.

SQL>
```

Figure 13.15 CHP13_15.SQL updates
both records in the DEPT13 table.

The output displayed shows the output from both triggers, the trigger
created in Step 2 and the trigger created by CHP13_11.SQL are fired for
each updated row of the DEPT13 table. When the trigger created in Step 2
is executed, the UPDATING predicate in the IF statement evaluates to
TRUE causing the corresponding message to be displayed in SQL*Plus.
Note that triggers of different types are fired in a specific order, but triggers
of the same type for the same triggering statement are not guaranteed to
fire in a specific order.

How It Works

Instead of creating a separate trigger for INSERT, UPDATE, and DELETE, you
can use trigger predicates in a trigger that will fire whenever a DML statement
operates on a table. Step 1 creates the sample table and data. Step 2 creates a
trigger that will fire before a row is manipulated in the DEPT13 table with an
INSERT, UPDATE, or DELETE statement. Note the use of **BEFORE INSERT OR
UPDATE OR DELETE ON DEPT13** as the triggering event clause. The trigger uses
the INSERTING, UPDATING, and DELETING conditional predicates in an IF
statement to determine the type of DML statement that caused the trigger to fire.
You can further refine the UPDATING predicate to include a column name, for
example, by specifying **IF UPDATING ('DEPT_NAME') THEN** would cause the
conditional predicate to evaluate to TRUE only if the DEPT_NAME column in
the DEPT13 table is updated. In Step 3, an INSERT statement is executed
causing the BEFORE INSERT trigger to fire. Step 4 updates the two records in
the DEPT13 table, causing the BEFORE UPDATE trigger to be fired twice. If a
DELETE statement was run the effects would be similar to the UPDATE
statement, here the BEFORE DELETE statement would be fired for each row
deleted from the table.

Comments

A trigger on a table that handles multiple DML operations can use conditional predicates INSERTING, UPDATING, and DELETING in the trigger body to determine the DML statement that fired the trigger. Separate actions can be taken in the trigger body depending on the type of DML operation that took place.

COMPLEXITY
INTERMEDIATE

13.4 How do I...

Perform cascading deletes with database triggers?

Problem

When my application deletes data in parent tables referenced by child tables, I want to ensure that data is deleted from the child tables to maintain proper referential integrity in the database. In order to ensure that the child records are deleted, I want to use database triggers. I know that when I use referential integrity constraints, I can make cascade deletes automatically. However, in some cases I do not want to use constraints, but still want the cascade delete operation. How do I perform cascading deletes using database triggers?

Technique

The BEFORE DELETE trigger can be used to delete child records referencing the record being deleted in the primary table. By placing DELETE statements in a BEFORE DELETE trigger, you can ensure that the child records are deleted. This technique cannot be used when referential integrity constraints exist, but can be used to perform more complex logic relating to the cascading deletes. The parent table is referred to as the constraining table when tables are related with referential integrity constraints. In this case, the trigger is not allowed to change values of the PRIMARY KEY, FOREIGN KEY, and UNIQUE key columns of the constraining table.

Steps

1. Run SQL*Plus and connect as the WAITE user account. CHP13_16.SQL, shown in Figure 13.16, creates the sample tables and data used in this How-To.

```
SET ECHO OFF
CREATE TABLE ORDER13 (
   ORDER_NO      NUMBER(10),
   CUST_NO       NUMBER(10));

CREATE TABLE CUST13 (
   CUST_NO       NUMBER(10),
   CUST_NAME     VARCHAR2(20),
   ADDRESS       VARCHAR2(20),
   CITY          VARCHAR2(10),
   STATE         VARCHAR2(2),
   ZIP           VARCHAR2(6));

INSERT INTO CUST13 VALUES
   (1, 'SMITH', '123 MAIN', 'CHICAGO', 'IL','60611');
INSERT INTO ORDER13 VALUES (1, 1);
INSERT INTO ORDER13 VALUES (2, 2);
INSERT INTO ORDER13 VALUES (3, 1);
```

Figure 13.16 CHP13_16.SQL creates the
sample table and data used in this
How-To.

The script creates two sample tables for demonstrating cascading deletes.
The CUST13 table contains detailed information about customers. The
ORDER13 table contains the orders placed by the customers. When a
customer is deleted from the CUST13 table, all associated records in the
ORDER13 table should also be deleted. Sample records are created in both
tables to demonstrate the process. Run the script to create the sample
tables and data.

SQL> START CHP13_16

Table created.

Table created.

1 row created.

1 row created.

1 row created.

Commit complete.

2. Run the CHP13_17.SQL file in SQL*Plus. The CREATE TRIGGER
statement contained in the file creates a BEFORE UPDATE trigger on the
CUST13 table to delete child records referencing a deleted record. Figure
13.17 displays the results of the operation.

Line 1 provides the required keywords to create or replace a trigger and
specifies the trigger name. Line 2 specifies the triggering event which
causes the trigger to fire, i.e. before a row is deleted from the CUST13
table. The FOR EACH ROW clause in line 3 ensures that the trigger is
fired once for each row being deleted. Lines 4 through 7 contain the
trigger body. The DELETE statement in lines 5 and 6 removes child

```
SQL> START CHP13_17
SQL> SET ECHO ON
SQL> CREATE OR REPLACE TRIGGER CUST_BDR_13
  2    BEFORE DELETE ON CUST13
  3    FOR EACH ROW
  4    BEGIN
  5      DELETE FROM ORDER13
  6      WHERE  CUST_NO = :OLD.CUST_NO;
  7    END;
  8    /

Trigger created.

SQL>
```

Figure 13.17 CHP13_17.SQL creates a
AFTER DELETE row trigger.

records from the ORDER13 table. The :OLD.CUST_NO column is used in
the WHERE clause of the DELETE statement to delete orders that belong
to the customer deleted from the CUST13 table.

When records are deleted from the CUST13 table, the trigger can delete
zero or more records from the ORDER13 table. In the next step, a record
is deleted from the CUST13 table to demonstrate the trigger operation.

3. Run the CHP13_18.SQL file in SQL*Plus, as shown in Figure 13.18. The
DELETE statement contained in the file deletes a row from the CUST13
table, causing the trigger to fire and the cascading delete to occur.

The WHERE clause in line 3 specifies that all customers with a value of 1
in the CUST_NO column should be deleted by the statement. The
BEFORE UPDATE trigger created in the previous step will also delete all
ORDER13 tables with a value of 1 in the CUST_NO column.

Although the message returned in SQL*Plus shows one row deleted, it
does not represent the records deleted by the BEFORE DELETE trigger.
The next step queries the ORDER13 table to show whether the records
were deleted.

4. Run the CHP13_19.SQL file in SQL*Plus. The query contained in the file
returns columns from the ORDER13 table. Figure 13.19 displays the
records returned by the query.

```
SQL> START CHP13_18
SQL> DELETE FROM
  2    CUST13
  3    WHERE CUST_NO = 1;

0 rows deleted.

SQL>
```

Figure 13.18 CHP13_18.SQL deletes
a record from the CUST13 table.

```
SQL> START CHP13_19
SQL> SELECT
  2       ORDER_NO,
  3       CUST_NO
  4  FROM
  5       ORDER13;

ORDER_NO    CUST_NO
---------- ----------
        2          2

SQL>
```

Figure 13.19 CHP13_19.SQL
queries the ORDER13 table.

The absence of a WHERE clause allows all records from the ORDER13 table to be returned by the query.

The records returned by the query do not include any records in which the CUST_NO column is 1. The BEFORE DELETE trigger removed the records when the DELETE statement was executed in Step 3.

How It Works

When referential integrity is not enforced through constraints, cascading deletes can be performed using BEFORE DELETE FOR EACH ROW triggers. Step 1 creates two sample tables. The CUST13 table contains the customer details and the ORDER13 table contains orders placed by the customers. When a customer is deleted from the database, it is important to remove all orders placed by that customer. Step 2 creates a BEFORE DELETE trigger on the CUST13 table, which deletes orders from the ORDER13 table for the customer being removed. Step 3 demonstrates the execution of the trigger by deleting a record from the CUST13 table. When the record is deleted, the BEFORE DELETE trigger removes all orders for that particular customer from the ORDER13_16 table. Step 4 queries the ORDER13 table to show that the order record has been removed.

Comments

Keep in mind that this technique does not work if referential integrity is enforced through constraints. If you are using constraints, you can have the constraints perform deletes automatically. Beware also of the effects of unintentional cascading of updates and deletes.

COMPLEXITY
INTERMEDIATE

13.5 How do I...
Disable and enable triggers?

Problem

When I perform batch processing and system management tasks on our database, I need to disable triggers from firing. Many of our triggers modify data in one or more tables. If I do not disable database triggers before performing these functions, they can fail. How do I disable and enable database triggers?

Technique

The ALTER TRIGGER statement is used to disable or enable a specific trigger. The DISABLE clause is used to disable a trigger, and the ENABLE clause is used to enable it. All triggers for a given table can be disabled or enabled together using the ALTER TABLE statement with the DISABLE ALL TRIGGERS or ENABLE ALL TRIGGERS clause.

Steps

1. Run SQL*Plus and connect as the WAITE user account. CHP13_20.SQL, shown in Figure 13.20, creates a sample table and triggers used in this How-To. Run the statement to create the objects.

```
SET ECHO OFF
DROP TABLE DEPT13;
CREATE TABLE DEPT13 (
    DEPT_NO      NUMBER(10),
    DEPT_NAME    VARCHAR2(30));

CREATE OR REPLACE TRIGGER DEPT_BI_13
BEFORE INSERT ON DEPT13
FOR EACH ROW
BEGIN
    DBMS_OUTPUT.PUT_LINE('DEPT_BI_13 HAS FIRED');
END;
/

CREATE OR REPLACE TRIGGER DEPT_AI_13
AFTER INSERT ON DEPT13
FOR EACH ROW
BEGIN
    DBMS_OUTPUT.PUT_LINE('DEPT_AI_13 HAS FIRED');
END;
/
```

Figure 13.20 CHP13_20.SQL creates the sample table and triggers used in this How-To.

The script first drops the DEPT13 table along with the triggers created in the previous How-To's. It then re-creates the DEPT13 table with two triggers that will be disabled and enabled in the examples. The BEFORE INSERT trigger—DEPT_BI_13—and an AFTER INSERT trigger—DEPT_AI_13—are created.

```
SQL>  START CHP13-20

Table created.

Trigger created.

Trigger created.
```

2. Run the CHP13_21.SQL in SQL*Plus. The file contains an ALTER TRIGGER statement to disable a specific trigger. Figure 13.21 displays the execution of the DDL statement.

Line 1 presents the ALTER TRIGGER statement. The ALTER TRIGGER statement can be used to disable a specific trigger. Line 2 provides the name of the trigger to be disabled and line 3 specifies the DISABLE clause to disable the trigger.

When a record is inserted into the table, the BEFORE INSERT trigger will not fire because it was disabled by the ALTER TRIGGER statement. When you are done performing your management tasks, the trigger should be enabled. The next step provides the technique to enable a specific trigger.

3. Run the CHP13_22.SQL file in SQL*Plus. The file contains an ALTER TRIGGER statement to re-enable the trigger disabled in the previous step. Figure 13.22 displays the results of the operation.

```
SQL> START CHP13_21
SQL> ALTER TRIGGER
  2      DEPT_BI_13
  3  DISABLE;

Trigger altered.

SQL>
```

Figure 13.21 CHP13_21.SQL
disables the DEPT_BI_13 trigger.

```
SQL> START CHP13_22
SQL> ALTER TRIGGER
  2      DEPT_BI_13
  3  ENABLE;

Trigger altered.

SQL>
```

Figure 13.22 CHP13_22.SQL
enables the DEPT_BI_13 trigger.

The format of the statement is the same as presented in Step 2. The only difference is that line 3 specifies the ENABLE clause, which causes the trigger to be enabled. Once the trigger is enabled, it will fire whenever the triggering event occurs.

4. It is often necessary to disable all of the triggers on a given table. Run the CHP13_23.SQL file in SQL*Plus. The file contains an ALTER TABLE statement, which disables all of the triggers on the sample table. Figure 13.23 shows the output in SQL*Plus.

Line 1 specifies the ALTER TABLE statement and Line 2 specifies the table to be altered. Line 3 presents the DISABLE ALL TRIGGERS clause, disabling all triggers on the specified table. Using this technique does not require that you know the names of the triggers on the table.

Once you have completed your management tasks with the table, the triggers should be enabled. The next step presents the statement used to enable all the triggers on the table.

5. All the triggers on a table can be enabled using the ALTER TABLE statement. Run the CHP13_24.SQL file in SQL*Plus. This file contains the statement to re-enable all the triggers disabled in the previous step. Figure 13.24 shows the output after running the statement.

The first two lines of the ALTER TABLE statement are identical to the statement provided in Step 6. Line 3 of the statement presents the ENABLE ALL TRIGGERS clause, enabling all triggers on the specified table.

```
SQL> START CHP13_23
SQL> ALTER TABLE
  2        DEPT13
  3  DISABLE ALL TRIGGERS;

Table altered.

SQL>
```

Figure 13.23 CHP13_23.SQL disables all triggers on the DEPT13 table.

```
SQL> START CHP13_24
SQL> ALTER TABLE
  2        DEPT13
  3  ENABLE ALL TRIGGERS;

Table altered.

SQL>
```

Figure 13.24 CHP13_24.SQL enables all triggers on the DEPT13 table.

How It Works

The ALTER TABLE and ALTER TRIGGER statements disable and enable triggers. The ALTER TRIGGER statement is used to disable or enable a specific trigger by name. The ALTER TABLE statement with the ENABLE ALL TRIGGERS or DISABLE ALL TRIGGERS clause is used to enable or disable all triggers on the specified table. Step 1 creates a sample table and the two triggers used throughout this How-To. Step 2 presents the ALTER TRIGGER statement using the DISABLE clause to disable one of the sample triggers. Step 3 presents the ENABLE clause, to enable the sample trigger. Step 4 uses the ALTER TABLE statement to disable all the triggers on the sample table. Step 5 uses the ALTER TABLE statement with the ENABLE ALL TRIGGERS clause, enabling all the triggers on the sample table.

Comments

Database triggers ensure that a specific operation is performed when a table is modified. There will be times when you need to modify the data in a table but do not want the triggers to fire. The ALTER TABLE statement is the easiest way to disable and enable all the triggers on a table. It does not require that you remember the names of the triggers on a table.

COMPLEXITY

BEGINNING

13.6 How do I...
List information about triggers?

Problem

I want to list information about the triggers in the database. I need to determine the trigger name, the table the trigger is on, and the status of the trigger. How do I list information about triggers?

Technique

Information about triggers is contained in the USER_TRIGGERS, ALL_TRIGGERS, or DBA_TRIGGERS data dictionary views. The columns of the USER_TRIGGERS view are described in Table 13.2. The TABLE_OWNER and TABLE_NAME columns identify the table containing the triggering event. The TRIGGER_NAME column specified returns the name of the trigger. The TRIGGER_TYPE column returns the type of trigger, such as BEFORE EACH ROW or BEFORE STATEMENT. The TRIGGERING_EVENT column returns the event, such as INSERT, UPDATE, or DELETE, that causes the trigger to file. The STATUS column tells whether the trigger is currently enabled or disabled.

Table 13.2 Columns of the USER_TRIGGERS view

COLUMN	DESCRIPTION
TRIGGER_NAME	Name of the trigger.
TRIGGER_TYPE	The type of trigger, such as BEFORE ROW, AFTER ROW, BEFORE STATEMENT, AFTER STATEMENT.
TRIGGERING_EVENT	Statement that fires the trigger: INSERT, UPDATE, DELETE.
TABLE_OWNER	Owner of the table on which the trigger is defined.
TABLE_NAME	Table on which the trigger is defined.
REFERENCING_NAMES	Names used to reference OLD and NEW.
WHEN_CLAUSE	WHEN clause for the trigger body to be executed on a condition.
STATUS	Trigger status: ENABLED or DISABLED.
DESCRIPTION	Trigger header.
TRIGGER_BODY	Trigger body.

Steps

1. Run SQL*Plus and connect as the WAITE user account. If you do not have the DEPT13 table and the triggers created on it in your schema, then run CHP13_20.SQL from Step 1 of the previous How-To. The DEPT13 table is created along with the two triggers, DEPT_BI_13 and DEPT_AI_13. The next step demonstrates how a query to the USER_TRIGGERS data dictionary view can provide you with valuable information about triggers.

2. Run the CHP13_25.SQL file in SQL*Plus. The query contained in the file queries the USER_TRIGGERS table to display information about the triggers on the specified table. Figure 13.25 displays the results of the query for the DEPT13 table.

```
SQL> START CHP13_25
SQL> COLUMN TRIGGER_NAME FORMAT A12
SQL> COLUMN TRIGGERING_EVENT FORMAT A16
SQL> COLUMN TRIGGER_TYPE FORMAT A25
SQL> COLUMN STATUS FORMAT A8
SQL> SELECT
  2     TRIGGER_NAME,
  3     TRIGGERING_EVENT,
  4     TRIGGER_TYPE,
  5     STATUS
  6  FROM
  7     USER_TRIGGERS
  8  WHERE
  9     TABLE_NAME = UPPER('&TABLE_NAME');
Enter value for table_name: DEPT13
old   9:    TABLE_NAME = UPPER('&TABLE_NAME')
new   9:    TABLE_NAME = UPPER('DEPT13')

TRIGGER_NAME TRIGGERING_EVENT TRIGGER_TYPE              STATUS
------------ ---------------- ------------------------- --------
DEPT_AI_13   INSERT           AFTER EACH ROW            ENABLED
DEPT_BI_13   INSERT           BEFORE EACH ROW           ENABLED

SQL>
```

Figure 13.25 CHP13_25.SQL queries the USER_TRIGGERS view.

The COLUMN commands format the columns before running the statement. After executing the statement, provide DEPT13_31 as the substitution variable. The query displays the two triggers created in Step 1. The columns returned by the query show you the name of the trigger, when it fires, and its status. Including the TRIGGER_BODY column would also show you the code executed when the trigger fires.

The TRIGGER_NAME column specified in line 2 returns the name of the trigger. The TRIGGERING_EVENT column specified in line 3 returns the type of event that causes the trigger to fire, such as INSERT, UPDATE, or DELETE. The TRIGGER_TYPE column specified in line 4 returns the type of trigger, such as BEFORE EACH ROW or BEFORE STATEMENT. Line 5 returns the STATUS column showing whether the trigger is ENABLED or DISABLED. Including the REFERENCING_NAMES column in the query will return the REFERENCING clause if it was specified while creating the trigger. The WHEN clause for the trigger, if one exists, can be queried from the WHEN_CLAUSE column of the USER_TRIGGERS view.

How It Works

The USER_TRIGGERS, ALL_TRIGGERS, and DBA_TRIGGERS data dictionary views contain information about the database triggers in the database. The TABLE_NAME column can be used in the WHERE clause of a query to either of the views for returning information about the views contained on a specific table. Step 1 creates the sample table and two sample triggers used to display the technique. Step 2 executes a query on the USER_ TRIGGERS data dictionary view to show information about the sample triggers.

Comments

A simple query to the USER_TRIGGERS data dictionary view will provide you with valuable information about the triggers on a table. If the triggers are not behaving the way you expect, query the data dictionary to verify that they are enabled, they fire when you want, and the code is valid for the operation.

Similar to stored procedures, triggers have dependencies. They can be invalidated if a referenced object has changed and recompiled when the trigger is invoked again. Refer to How-To 10.6, which explains how you can examine the USER_DEPENDENCIES view to detect trigger dependencies. Trigger compilation errors can be queried from the USER_ERRORS view, or by issuing the SHOW ERRORS command at the SQL*Plus prompt, which will display errors for the last trigger that was compiled in the session.

COMPLEXITY
ADVANCED

13.7 How do I...
Rebuild CREATE TRIGGER statements?

Problem

I need to re-create the statements used to create some of the triggers in the database. I either lost the original files or entered the trigger directly into SQL*Plus without saving the CREATE TRIGGER statements. I know that throughout the book we have used the data dictionary and SQL*Plus to rebuild statements. How do I rebuild CREATE TRIGGER statements?

Technique

There are data dictionary views containing information about triggers, which are USER_TRIGGERS, ALL_TRIGGERS, and DBA_TRIGGERS. When you rebuild the CREATE TRIGGER statement for a trigger, you can connect to the database as the owner of the trigger and use the USER_TRIGGERS or ALL_TRIGGERS data dictionary view. The DBA_TRIGGERS view contains all views in the database and requires privileges in the DBA role. The description of the USER_TRIGGERS view is shown in Figure 13.14. The TRIGGER_BODY column contains the text of the trigger. The datatype of the column is LONG, so it will be slightly harder to work with. The TRIGGER_NAME, TRIGGER_TYPE, and TRIGGERING_EVENT columns will be concatenated with the trigger body in order to rebuild the statement.

Steps

1. Run SQL*Plus and connect as the WAITE user account. If you do not have the DEPT13 table and the triggers created on it in your schema, then run CHP13_20.SQL from Step 1 of How-To 13.5. The DEPT13 table is created along with the two triggers, DEPT_BI_13 and DEPT_AI_13. The USER_TRIGGERS provides valuable information about triggers as examined in the previous How-To. In this How-To, the same view is used to rebuild the code that originally created the trigger.

2. Run the CHP13_26.SQL in SQL*Plus, as shown in Figure 13.26. The file contains a query of the USER_TRIGGERS data dictionary view displaying the header and body of the trigger.

```
SQL> START CHP13_26
SQL> SET ECHO ON
SQL> SELECT
  2      DESCRIPTION,
  3      TRIGGER_BODY
  4  FROM
  5      USER_TRIGGERS
  6  WHERE
  7      TRIGGER_NAME = 'DEPT_BI_13';

DESCRIPTION
----------------------------------------------------------------------
TRIGGER_BODY
----------------------------------------------------------------------
DEPT_BI_13
BEFORE INSERT ON DEPT13
FOR EACH ROW
BEGIN
    DBMS_OUTPUT.PUT_LINE('DEPT_BI_13 HAS FIRED');
END;


SQL>
```

Figure 13.26 CHP13_26.SQL chalks the skeleton of the rebuild statement.

The DESCRIPTION column in line 2 returns the trigger header. The TRIGGER_BODY column in line 3 returns the trigger body. Line 5 specifies the USER_TRIGGERS view as the source of the data and line 7 specifies the name of the trigger.

Because the TRIGGER_BODY column is of the LONG datatype, you may increase the value of the LONG SQL*Plus variable to 2000, if you have SQL*Plus complaints about the data being too long to display. Use the SET LONG 2000 command at the prompt and try running the query again. If a lot of columns are returned by a query, the ARRAYSIZE system variable can be decreased before running the query. For example, use the SET ARRAYSIZE 1 command at the prompt to reduce the value of SQL*Plus ARRAYSIZE variable.

LINESIZE is another SQL*Plus variable that you may occasionally need to adjust to fit the output of a column to a single line. For example, use the SET LINESIZE 132 command to set the SQL*Plus LINESIZE variable to 132.

With the DESCRIPTION and TRIGGER_BODY columns, the result of the query almost looks like a CREATE TRIGGER statement, except for the CREATE OR REPLACE TRIGGER keywords. The next step presents the query to actually rebuild the trigger code.

3. Load CHP13_27.SQL into the SQL buffer. The file contains a query that returns the actual trigger code to re-create the trigger. Figure 13.27 displays the results of the operation.

The HEADING SQL*Plus variable is set to OFF to suppress the column headings. Line 1 prefixes the CREATE OR REPLACE TRIGGER keywords

```
SQL> START CHP13_27
SQL> SET ECHO ON HEADING OFF
SQL> SELECT
  2      'CREATE OR REPLACE TRIGGER ' || DESCRIPTION,
  3      TRIGGER_BODY
  4  FROM
  5      USER_TRIGGERS
  6  WHERE
  7      TRIGGER_NAME = 'DEPT_BI_13';

CREATE OR REPLACE TRIGGER DEPT_BI_13
BEFORE INSERT ON DEPT13
FOR EACH ROW
BEGIN
    DBMS_OUTPUT.PUT_LINE('DEPT_BI_13 HAS FIRED');
END;


SQL>
```

Figure 13.27 CHP13_27.SQL rebuilds the trigger code.

and concatenates the trigger header to it. Line 3 retrieves the trigger body. When this query is executed, it returns the exact code that originally created the trigger. You can spool the output to a file using the SPOOL command and then run the spooled file to re-create the trigger.

With this query, you can only re-create triggers that belong to the current user account. A query to ALL_TRIGGERS or DBA_TRIGGERS enables you to create re-create all triggers in the system, provided you have DBA permissions.

How It Works

Throughout the book, we use dictionary views to create DDL statements. In this case, a CREATE TRIGGER statement is rebuilt. The ALL_TRIGGERS data dictionary view contains information about the triggers in the database.

Step 1 creates the sample table and trigger used throughout this How-To. Step 2 displays the DESCRIPTION and TRIGGER_BODY columns, returning the header and code section of the trigger. Step 2 also creates the trigger specification by prefixing the CREATE OR REPLACE TRIGGER keywords to the DESCRIPTION column value. The process is completed by concatenating the TRIGGER_BODY column value. The resulting output is the trigger code that originally created the trigger.

Comments

The process presented in this How-To can be used to rebuild CREATE TRIGGER statements when the original source code is no longer available. Rebuilding CREATE TRIGGER statements can be a necessary database management task. If you need to create all the triggers on a table or in the database, a simple modification to the WHERE clause of the query is all you need.

CHAPTER 14
SQL STATEMENT TUNING

14.

SQL STATEMENT TUNING

How do I...

Database tuning is not an exact science. Almost everyone agrees, however, that the first place to start tuning is at the application level. The most important part of this task is to review and tune the SQL statements that users or applications issue against the database. The tuning operations that will be outlined in Chapter 15 tune the database at a fairly low level, focusing on memory, disk load balancing, and the like. None of these measures are worthwhile, however, if Oracle8 is continually processing badly written SQL statements. This chapter presents techniques for identifying problematic SQL statements, examining their execution paths, and altering the statements or the database structure to improve application performance.

14.1 Identify Potentially Inefficient Queries with the V$SQLAREA View

Most databases process many queries and the first step towards tuning them is identifying the statements that may be responsible for performance problems. This How-To presents a method for identifying queries that have exceeded a user-defined threshold value of disk activity.

14.2 Use EXPLAIN PLAN to Analyze Query Execution Paths

The sequence of physical operations that Oracle8 performs to execute a particular statement is called the statement's *execution path*. One goal of application tuning is to maximize the proportion of operations that Oracle8 performs in memory versus those that the server performs on disk. Oracle8 can process most queries in more than one way. This How-To discusses the use of the EXPLAIN PLAN statement to reveal a SQL statement's execution path.

14.3 Use the AUTOTRACE System Variable to Analyze Query Performance

The AUTOTRACE system variable provides an alternative to EXPLAIN PLAN for SQL statement analysis. This How-To explains AUTOTRACE and compares this analysis method to EXPLAIN PLAN.

14.4 Determine Elapsed Execution Time

How long does it take? This is a common question you should ask about any new query or data management SQL statement. The first step to tuning a query is to identify performance problems. This How-To explores two methods for timing queries and presents examples of each method.

14.5 Analyze SQL Statements with SQL*Trace and the TKPROF Utility

SQL*Trace is similar to EXPLAIN PLAN in that it analyzes the performance of SQL statements when they are executed. It also generates physical execution statistics, however, such as rows returned, cpu time, elapsed time, and number of disk accesses.

Once a developer of DBA enables SQL*Trace, Oracle analyzes the execution of all of an application's SQL statements and writes this analysis to a trace file. The TKPROF utility converts the trace file to a readable form. This How-To presents the use of SQL*Trace and TKPROF to analyze SQL statements.

14.6 Set the Optimizer Mode

The optimizer mode setting indicates the method Oracle should use to determine the best access path to the data. Two optimizer modes are available in Oracle8 as well as three ways to tell Oracle which one to use. This How-To discusses optimizer modes and outlines techniques for setting them.

14.7 Pass Hints to the Optimizer

Skilled developers are sometimes able to make better decisions about statement execution paths than the optimizer. In these cases, users can employ optimizer hints to tell Oracle how to execute SQL statements. This How-To presents the method for passing hints to the optimizer.

14.8 Suppress Indexes in a Query

When a query returns more than five percent of the rows in a table developers should suppress an index. This is accomplished by using optimizer hints (explained in the previous How-To) or by modifying the WHERE clause of the query to change its syntax but not its effect. This How-To presents methods used to suppress an index during a query.

14.9 Structure Data Warehouses for Star Query Optimization

The star schema is common in data warehouses. It typically consists of multiple small *dimension* tables and one large table, called a *fact* table, storing data related to an ongoing enterprise business process. SQL statements typically target these tables during ad hoc, read-only queries. If the schema and the query are carefully structured, then special optimization techniques can result in dramatic performance gains. This How-To explains how to architect data warehouse structures for star query optimization.

14.10 Register Applications to Simplify Performance Tracking

With practice, DBAs and developers will be able to identify which SQL statements to tune and will know what SQL modifications are necessary to enhance application performance. What can remain elusive in a busy database, however, is the origin of SQL statements in need of tuning. In other words, you may not only know *what* to tune and *how* to tune it, but you may not know *where* it came from. Application registration can help and is the subject of this How-To.

14.1 How do I...
Identify potentially inefficient queries with the V$SQLAREA view?

Problem

My database serves many users and applications. I want to review the SQL that they issue against Oracle8, particularly those queries which are generating large amounts of I/O. How do I review the SQL statements that my database is processing?

Technique

The V$SQLAREA and V$SQLTEXT_WITH_NEWLINES dynamic performance views are the key to identifying the queries, if any, that are monopolizing database resources. The structures of these views appear in Tables 14.1 and 14.2.

Table 14.1 Part of the V$SQLAREA dynamic performance view

COLUMN	COLUMN DESCRIPTION
SQL_TEXT	First 80 characters of the SQL statement
DISK_READS	Number of disk reads generated by SQL_TEXT
BUFFER_GETS	Number of buffer gets generated by SQL_TEXT
ADDRESS	Address of the cursor for SQL_TEXT

Table 14.2 The structure of the V$SQLTEXT_WITH_NEWLINES dynamic performance table

COLUMN	COLUMN DESCRIPTION
ADDRESS	Cursor address
HASH_VALUE	Hash function value for a cached cursor
COMMAND_TYPE	Type of command (coded):
	insert = 2
	select = 3
	update = 6
	delete = 7
PIECE	Statement portion number (used to order SQL_TEXT pieces)
SQL_TEXT	Long version of the SQL statement containing line breaks

The V$SQLAREA view contains one row for every SQL statement that is ready for execution and residing in the shared pool. It is dynamic in the sense that any given SQL statement will appear and disappear from V$SQLAREA as the statement resides in and ages out of the shared pool. The V$SQLTEXT_WITH_NEWLINES lists a longer version of the SQL statement than the 80 character version residing in V$SQLAREA. The ADDRESS column in both views provides a way to join them.

It is not necessary to tune every SQL statement issued against a database; a horrific SQL statement that no user or application ever executes causes no real harm. No DBA or developer has time to examine execution paths for every SQL statement, anyway. The trick is to identify which SQL statements are both bad performers *and* generators of considerable database activity. The DISK_READS column in the V$SQLAREA table can help with this task.

Steps

1. Start an SQL*Plus session, log in as the WAITE user, and use the START command to load and execute the script CHP14_1.SQL.

2. The script is parameterized to include SQL statements generating more than some number of disk reads. The script asks you to supply this number. In Figure 14.1, showing script CHP14_1.SQL and its output, 250 is the disk read's cutoff for report inclusion.

```
SQL> start chp14_1
SQL>
SQL> SELECT vt.sql_text long_text,
  2         disk_reads, buffer_gets
  3  FROM v$sqlarea va, v$sqltext_with_newlines vt
  4  WHERE va.address = vt.address and
  5        disk_reads > &dreads
  6  ORDER BY va.disk_reads desc, va.buffer_gets, vt.piece;
Enter value for dreads: 250

LONG_TEXT                 DISK_READS  BUFFER_GETS
------------------------- ----------- ------------
select file#,                   391          408
block#, ts# from
seg$ where type# =
3

select f.file#,                 333         2135
f.block#, f.ts#,
f.length from fet$
f, ts$ t whe

re t.ts#=f.ts# and
t.dflextpct!=0


SQL> |
```

Figure 14.1 Running the script CHP14_1.SQL in SQL*Plus to identify expensive SQL statements.

The script uses a substitution variable in line 5 to prompt the user for the number of disk reads to serve as the cutoff criterion for inclusion in the report. In Figure 14.1, this criterion is 250 disk reads. The script uses an ORDER BY clause to present the offending SQL statements in descending order of generated disk reads. The SQL_TEXT column from the V$SQLTEXT_WITH_NEWLINES dynamic data dictionary view contains 64 byte pieces of SQL statements. So, one SQL statement can be broken across multiple rows in this view. The SQL_TEXT column in the V$SQLAREA clause has a 1-to-1 relationship with SQL statements, but statements in this view are truncated at 1,000 bytes. The PIECE column appears in the ORDER BY clause in the CHP14_1.SQL script to present the pieces of each SQL statement in the correct order.

How It Works

The script in Step 1 queries the V$SQLAREA and V$SQLTEST_WITH_NEWLINES dynamic performance views with a user-specified criterion for inclusion in the result set.

Comments

The results from the query in Step 1 provide a starting point for future tuning operations by helping you identify, out of the thousands of queries running against the database, which ones are generating the most work. For the purposes of this example, Step 1 returns all SQL statements responsible for 200 or more disk reads. For most production systems, the cut off for inclusion in the report should be at least 10,000 disk reads. In most environments, only two to three percent of the SQL statements issued against a database need additional tuning.

COMPLEXITY
INTERMEDIATE

14.2 How do I...
Use EXPLAIN PLAN to analyze query execution paths?

Problem

Some of the queries issued against my database do not seem to perform acceptably. I want to use the EXPLAIN PLAN statement to determine what physical operations Oracle8 is using to execute these queries. How do I analyze a query using EXPLAIN PLAN?

Technique

When DBAs and developers use the EXPLAIN PLAN statement with an SQL statement, Oracle8 reports the statement's execution path. This is the sequence of physical operations that Oracle8 uses to execute the statement.

The EXPLAIN. PLAN statement stores its results in a table called PLAN_TABLE. This table must exist prior to EXPLAIN PLAN execution and fortunately Oracle provides a script file to create this table. The script's name is system-dependent; under Windows NT, it resides in the \ORANT\RDBMS80\ADMIN subdirectory. After invocation of EXPLAIN PLAN, query the PLAN_TABLE to reveal the execution of a particular SQL statement.

Table 14.3 shows the structure of PLAN_TABLE. The most important output of EXPLAIN PLAN resides in PLAN_TABLE's OPERATION column, which reveals how Oracle has processed the statement on a physical level. The possible values of this attribute appear in Table 14.4.

Table 14.3 The structure of PLAN_TABLE

COLUMN	COLUMN DESCRIPTION
STATEMENT_ID	Statement ID (user-specified)
TIMESTAMP	Date and time of EXPLAIN PLAN execution
REMARKS	User-specified comments for EXPLAIN PLAN steps
OPERATION	Oracle-performed operation in this step
OPTIONS	More information on OPERATION
OBJECT_NODE	Database link name used to reference the object
OBJECT_OWNER	Username of schema owner containing the object
OBJECT_NAME	Table or index name
OBJECT_INSTANCE	Object's position
OBJECT_TYPE	Object descriptive information
OPTIMIZER	Optimizer mode in effect at execution time
SEARCH_COLUMNS	Not used
ID	Number of step in the execution plan
PARENT_ID	Number of the next step
POSITION	Processing order for each step with this PARENT_ID
OTHER	Other step-related information
OTHER_TAG	Further description of OTHER
PARTITION_START	Starting partition
PARTITION_STOP	Last partition accessed
PARTITION_ID	Number of step that computed PARTITION_START and PARTITION STOP
COST	If optimizer is in COST mode, this is the relative cost of the operation, and it is null if optimizer is in rule mode
CARDINALITY	Estimated number of rows accessed by OPERATION
BYTES	Estimated number of bytes accessed by OPERATION

Table 14.4 Possible values of the OPERATION column in PLAN_TABLE

OPERATION	OPTION	OPERATION DESCRIPTION
AND-EQUAL		Returns intersection of multiple ROWIDs without duplicates
CONNECT BY		Tree walk (hierarchical access)
CONCATENATION		UNION of multiple rows
COUNT		Row count
COUNT	STOPKEY	Row count limited by WHERE clause ROWNUM expression
FILTER		Row elimination based on a WHERE clause
FIRST ROW		Query that returns the first row only
FOR UPDATE		Row locking via the FOR UPDATE statement
INDEX*	UNIQUE SCAN	Index used to return one row
INDEX*	RANGE SCAN	Ascending index-based retrieval of multiple ROWIDs
INDEX*	RANGE SCAN DESC	Descending index-based retrieval of multiple ROWIDs
INTERSECTION		Accepts two sets of rows, returns intersection without duplicates
MERGE JOIN		Accepts and combines two sorted row sets and returns matching rows
MERGE JOIN	OUTER	MERGE-JOIN with outer join
MINUS		Accepts two row sets and returns rows in first set but not in second via MINUS operator
NESTED LOOPS		Accepts outer and inner rows sets and compares each outer row with each inner row
NESTED LOOPS	OUTER	NESTED LOOPS with outer join
PROJECTION		Returns subset of table columns
REMOTE		Use of database link
SEQUENCE		Access sequence values
SORT	AGGREGATE	Returns single row from group operation
SORT	UNIQUE	Returns set of rows, duplicates eliminated
SORT	GROUP BY	Accepts and groups set of rows for GROUP BY processing
SORT	JOIN	Accepts and sorts a row set in preparation for a merge-join operation.
SORT	ORDER BY	Accepts and sorts a row set in preparation for an ORDER BY operation.
TABLE ACCESS	FULL	Row retrieval via a full table scan
TABLE ACCESS	CLUSTER	Row retrieval via indexed cluster
TABLE ACCESS	HASH	Row retrieval via hash cluster
TABLE ACCESS	BY ROWID	Row retrieval based on ROWID
UNION		Accepts two sets of rows and returns union; eliminates duplicates.
VIEW		Performs view-based retrieval

Steps

1. Run SQL*Plus and connect as the WAITE user. Use the start command with a fully qualified path name describing the location of the UTLXPLAN script. The script creates a version of PLAN_TABLE in the schema of the invoking user. The invocation syntax under Windows NT appears below.

```
SQL> start \orant\rdbms80\admin\utlxplan.sql

Table created.
```

2. Use the START command to load and execute the script CHP14_2.SQL. The script and output appear in Listing 14.1.

Listing 14.1 Running the CHP14_2.SQL script in SQL*Plus to create some sample objects

```
SQL> start chp14_2
SQL>
SQL> CREATE TYPE emp_type14 AS OBJECT
  2  (empno     number(4),
  3   ename     varchar2(10)
  4  );

Type created.

SQL>
SQL> CREATE TYPE emp_table14 AS TABLE OF emp_type14;

Type created.

SQL>
SQL> CREATE TABLE dept14
  2  (
  3   deptno    number(2),
  4   dname     varchar2(14),
  5   emps      emp_table14
  6  )
  7  NESTED TABLE emps STORE AS store_dept_emps14;

Table created.

SQL>
SQL> CREATE INDEX idx_dept14
  2     ON dept14 (deptno);

Index created.

SQL>
```

continued on next page

continued from previous page

```
SQL> CREATE INDEX idx_emp_table14
  2    ON store_dept_emps14 (empno);

Index created.

SQL>
SQL> INSERT INTO dept14 VALUES
  2  (1, 'DATA MGMT', emp_table14(emp_type14(1,  'MARKIE'),
  3                                emp_type14(2,  'SARA'),
                                   emp_type14(3,  'DEBBIE'))
  4  );

1 row created.

SQL>
SQL> INSERT INTO dept14 VALUES
  2  (2, 'CHEMISTRY', emp_table14(emp_type14(4,  'STEVE'),
  3                                emp_type14(5,  'NANCY'))
  4  );
```

The CHP14_2.SQL script creates a table called DEPT14 containing the nested table EMPS (you'll read more about these in Chapter 16). EMPS is based on the EMP_TYPE14 object type that stores information about individual employees. The script creates two indexes. The first is a commonplace index on the DEPT14 table, but the second index is more interesting; it is on the column EMPNO of the nested table called EMP. To index a column of a nested table, use the storage clause in the CREATE INDEX statement.

3. Use the START command to load and execute the CHP14_3.SQL script. This issues the EXPLAIN PLAN statement for a query that selects data from the DEPT14 table and the EMPS nested table. The query and its output appear in Figure 14.2.

```
SQL> start chp14_3
SQL>
SQL> DELETE FROM plan_table WHERE statement_id = 'CHP14_3';

6 rows deleted.

SQL>
SQL> EXPLAIN PLAN
  2    SET STATEMENT_ID = 'CHP14_3'
  3    INTO plan_table FOR
  4      SELECT empno, ename
  5      FROM THE(SELECT emps
  6              FROM dept14
  7              WHERE deptno = 1)
  8      WHERE empno = 2;

Explained.

SQL>
```

Figure 14.2 Running the script CHP14_3.SQL in SQL*Plus to store the execution path in PLAN_TABLE.

The query appears in lines 4 through 8. The nuances of the syntax are not important for this discussion; they are explained more fully in Chapter 16. The output that EXPLAIN PLAN generates is labeled in the PLAN_TABLE by the value of the STATEMENT_ID column. The first statement in the script deletes any existing EXPLAIN PLAN output from PLAN_TABLE for statement ID CHP14_3. The next three lines invoke EXPLAIN PLAN, set the STATEMENT_ID, and tell Oracle to insert EXPLAIN PLAN output into PLAN_TABLE.

4. A straight SELECT from PLAN_TABLE is not particularly useful. Its output is too difficult to interpret. Use the START command to load and execute the script CHP14_4.SQL, which produces more useful output. Figure 14.3 shows the script and its output.

The script appears in the Oracle8 online documentation and is a tree walk through the PLAN_TABLE. One useful modification to the script is to have it prompt for the value of the STATEMENT_ID using a SQL*Plus substitution variable in lines 5 and 6. The double ampersands confine SQL*Plus to a single prompt for the value of STATID.

In Figure 14.4, the value of STATID is CHP14_3. Reading the output from the query is not intuitive; the general rule is to read PLAN_TABLE output from the inside out and from the top to the bottom. This only makes sense after a few practice attempts, but application of this rule to the output in Figure 14.3 reveals the following execution plan:

```
SQL> start chp14_4
SQL>
SQL> SELECT LPAD(' ',2*(LEVEL-1))||operation||' '||options
  2      ||' '||object_name
  3      ||' '||DECODE(id, 0, 'Cost = '||position) "Query Plan"
  4      FROM plan_table
  5      START WITH id = 0 AND statement_id = '&&statid'
  6      CONNECT BY PRIOR id = parent_id AND statement_id ='&&statid';
Enter value for statid: CHP14_3

Query Plan
---------------------------------------------------------------------------
SELECT STATEMENT     Cost =
  FILTER
    TABLE ACCESS BY INDEX ROWID STORE_DEPT_EMPS14
      INDEX RANGE SCAN IDX_EMP_TABLE14
    TABLE ACCESS BY INDEX ROWID DEPT14
      INDEX RANGE SCAN IDX_DEPT14

6 rows selected.

SQL>
SQL> Input truncated to 1 characters

SQL> |
```

Figure 14.3 Running the script CHP14_4.SQL in SQL*Plus to query the PLAN_TABLE.

✔ A range scan of the IDX_EMP_TABLE14 index

✔ A table access by ROWID of the STORE_DEPT_EMPS 14 nested table storage table

✔ A range scan of the IDX_DEPT14 index

✔ A table access by ROWID of the DEPT14 table

✔ An execution of a WHERE clause

How It Works

Create the plan table by running the UTLXPLAN script. When DBAs or developers invoke the EXPLAIN_PLAN command, it populates this table. Query the PLAN_TABLE using the script in Step 4 to illustrate the execution plan.

Comments

Every developer can write better SQL code through use of the EXPLAIN PLAN command, and there is no reason why a PLAN_TABLE cannot exist in every developer's schema to achieve this end. Oracle8 does not actually execute queries appearing in EXPLAIN PLAN; it only processes them enough to output the relevant execution plan. This is both an advantage and a drawback. The benefit is that if a developer knows a query performs poorly, then EXPLAIN PLAN provides a low resource analysis technique. On the other hand, looking at EXPLAIN PLAN output prior to actual query execution can lead users to incorrect conclusions about SQL statement performance. For this reason, most developers and DBAs confine EXPLAIN PLAN analysis to queries which are proven poor performers.

COMPLEXITY
INTERMEDIATE

14.3 How do I...
Use the AUTOTRACE system variable to analyze query execution paths?

Problem

I want to analyze query execution paths, but I also want to see query execution statistics. How do I use AUTOTRACE to generate this kind of information?

Technique

SQL*Plus automatically generates query execution path information and performance statistics when users set the AUTOTRACE system variable to a valid value other than OFF. Table 14.5 lists the AUTOTRACE values and their effects.

Table 14.5 Possible values for the AUTOTRACE system variable

AUTOTRACE VALUE	EFFECT
OFF	The default, SQL*Plus generates no report.
ON EXPLAIN	SQL*Plus generates query execution path.
ON STATISTICS	SQL*Plus generates query performance statistics.
ON	SQL*Plus generates execution path and performance statistics.

Steps

1. Run SQL*Plus and connect as the WAITE user. Use the START command to load and execute the CHP14_5.SQL script. The script, which creates and populates some sample tables, appears in Listing 14.2.

Listing 14.2 Running the CHP14_5.SQL script in SQL*Plus to create some sample objects

```
SQL> start chp14_5
SQL>
SQL> CREATE TABLE emp14_3
  2  ( empno   number(4),
  3    ename   varchar2(10),
  4    deptno number(2)
  5  );

Table created.

SQL>
SQL> CREATE INDEX idx_emp14_3
  2     ON emp14_3 (empno);

Index created.

SQL>
SQL> CREATE TABLE dept14_3
  2  ( deptno   number(2),
  3    dname    varchar2(14)
  4  );

Table created.

SQL>
```

continued on next page

continued from previous page

```
SQL> CREATE INDEX idx_dept14_3
  2      ON dept14_3 (deptno);

Index created.

SQL>
SQL> INSERT INTO dept14_3 VALUES
  2   (1, 'DATA MGMT');

1 row created.

SQL>
SQL> INSERT INTO dept14_3 VALUES
  2   (2, 'CHEMISTRY');

1 row created.

SQL>
SQL> INSERT INTO emp14_3 VALUES
  2   (1, 'MARKIE', 1);

1 row created.

SQL>
SQL> INSERT INTO emp14_3 VALUES
  2   (2, 'DEBBIE', 1);

1 row created.

SQL>
SQL> INSERT INTO emp14_3 VALUES
  2   (3, 'SARA', 1);

1 row created.

SQL>
SQL> INSERT INTO emp14_3 VALUES
  2   (4, 'STEVE', 2);

1 row created.

SQL>
SQL> INSERT INTO emp14_3 VALUES
  2   (5, 'NANCY', 2);

1 row created.

SQL>
```

2. Issue the SET AUTOTRACE ON command at the SQL*Plus prompt.

3. The script CHP14_6.SQL queries the tables created in Step 1 and includes a simple join. Since AUTOTRACE is on, SQL*Plus reports the query's execution plan and generates performance statistics. Use the START command to execute CHP14_6.SQL and produce the output shown in Listing 14.3.

Listing 14.3 Running the CHP14_6.SQL script in SQL*Plus to produce an AUTOTRACE report

```
SQL> start chp14_6
SQL>
SQL>    SELECT empno, ename
  2     FROM emp14_3 e, dept14_3 d
  3     WHERE e.deptno = d.deptno AND
  4         d.dname = 'CHEMISTRY' and e.empno = 4;

    EMPNO ENAME
--------- ----------
        4 STEVE


Execution Plan
----------------------------------------------------------
   0      SELECT STATEMENT Optimizer=CHOOSE
   1    0   NESTED LOOPS
   2    1     TABLE ACCESS (BY INDEX ROWID) OF 'EMP14_3'
   3    2       INDEX (RANGE SCAN) OF 'IDX_EMP14_3' (NON-UNIQUE)
   4    1     TABLE ACCESS (BY INDEX ROWID) OF 'DEPT14_3'
   5    4       INDEX (RANGE SCAN) OF 'IDX_DEPT14_3' (NON-UNIQUE)




Statistics
----------------------------------------------------------
        0   recursive calls
        0   db block gets
        5   consistent gets
        0   physical reads
        0   redo size
      271   bytes sent via SQL*Net to client
      339   bytes received via SQL*Net from client
        2   SQL*Net roundtrips to/from client
        0   sorts (memory)
        0   sorts (disk)
        1   rows processed
```

Reading the execution plan from the inside out and from the top to the bottom indicates that Oracle performed an index range scan and a table access by ROWID for table EMP14_3, did the same for table DEPT14_3, and submitted the results of these operations to a NESTED LOOPS join. The statistics section indicates, among other things, two SQL*Net round trips to execute the query.

How It Works

Step 1 creates some sample objects. Step 2 enables AUTOTRACE and instructs SQL*Plus to generate execution path and query performance data. Step 3 executes a simple query and generates an AUTOTRACE report.

Comments

The AUTOTRACE command frees users from some of the maintenance associated with the EXPLAIN PLAN command presented in the previous How-To. These tasks include clearing the contents of PLAN_TABLE, assigning statement identifiers, and modifying queries to include the EXPLAIN PLAN clause. The potential disadvantage of AUTOTRACE is that Oracle actually executes the target query. If the query requires protracted execution times, then this could make analysis tedious.

Any user granted the DBA role (like the WAITE user) can set AUTOTRACE in SQL*Plus. Users without this high level of privilege, however, do not have access to the requisite dynamic performance views (the V$ tables). Oracle provides a way to grant this access using the PLUSTRACE role. The name and location of the script to create this role is system-dependent, but under Windows NT the script is named PLUSTRCE.SQL and resides in the \ORANT\PLUS40 subdirectory. You must connect to Oracle as the SYS user to run this script successfully. Once the PLUSTRACE role is available any user with the DBA role can grant it to future AUTOTRACE users.

COMPLEXITY
BEGINNING

14.4 How do I...
Determine elapsed execution time in SQL*Plus?

Problem

How can I measure the SQL*Plus execution time of SQL statements I am writing or modifying?

Technique

Two methods can be used for timing the execution of SQL statements within SQL*Plus. Users can time the performance of a single query by setting the value of the TIMING system variable to ON. Alternatively, the SQL*Plus TIMING command enables you to set multiple timers and time groups of statements. This command allows you to give each timer a name and view timing information individually.

The command SET TIMING ON sets the SQL*Plus system variable ON so that SQL*Plus reports the duration of each SQL statement. This behavior will be in effect until the SET TIMING OFF command ends the timing of individual statements. The TIMING command has various keywords that control the use of the command. The syntax of the TIMING command is shown as follows:

```
TIMING START TIMERNAME
```

The command above creates a timer with the name specified on the command line.

NOTE

The SQL*Plus timer facility reports elapsed time in milliseconds. This is a real-time calculation; it does not account for system loads or CPU utilization levels in effect at the time of the query.

Steps

1. Start SQL*Plus, connect as the WAITE user and issue the SET TIMING ON command so that SQL*Plus starts timing individual SQL statements.

2. If you have not already done so for How-To's 14.2 and 14.3, run the scripts CHP14_2.SQL and CHP14_5.SQL. Both scripts create tables similar to the common EMP and DEPT tables residing in SCOTT's schema. The first script accomplishes this via an object enabled methodology and the second uses traditional purely relational tables. The output of CHP14_2.SQL appears in Listing 14.1 and the output of CHP14_5.SQL appears in Listing 14.2.

3. Use the START command to load and execute the script CHP14_7.SQL. This script contains two SQL statements to extract the employee numbers and names for all personnel in the chemistry department whose names contain the letter S. The script and its output appear in Figure 14.4.

```
SQL> start chp14_7
SQL>
SQL> SELECT empno, ename
  2  FROM THE(SELECT emps
  3              FROM dept14
  4              WHERE dname = 'CHEMISTRY')
  5  WHERE ename like '%S%';

    EMPNO ENAME
---------- -----------
        4 STEVE

 real: 21
SQL>
SQL> SELECT empno, ename
  2  FROM emp14_3 e, dept14_3 d
  3  WHERE e.deptno = d.deptno AND
  4        d.dname = 'CHEMISTRY' and e.ename like '%S%';

    EMPNO ENAME
---------- -----------
        4 STEVE

 real: 10
SQL> set timing on
SQL> |
```

Figure 14.4 Running the script CHP14_7.SQL in SQL*Plus to illustrate timing output.

The output indicates that the SELECT statement on the object embedded tables took 21 milliseconds while the functionally equivalent command on the purely relational tables required only 10 milliseconds.

4. Turn off the TIMING system variable by issuing the SET TIMING OFF command. The OFF keyword causes SQL*Plus to stop timing statements.

5. The TIMING system variable is useful should you need to time individual statements. You need the TIMING command, however, to generate the elapsed time for a script containing multiple SQL statements. It is possible to start multiple timers by starting another timer before stopping the first timer. The TIMING command does *not* exhibit elapsed time after Oracle8 processes each SQL statement. Instead, you must issue the TIMING SHOW or TIMING STOP command to review elapsed time since the beginning of the timing interval.

The CHP14_8.SQL script provides examples of the behavior of the TIMING command. Figure 14.5 shows the script and its output.

The first command in the script creates and starts a timer named MYTIMER. The next two commands select the name of the current user and the current date from the DUAL table. The next command shows the elapsed time since the script started the timer. The last command stops the timer and exhibits the final elapsed time value.

```
SQL> timing start mytimer;
SQL>
SQL> select user from dual;

USER
--------------------------------
WAITE

SQL>
SQL> select sysdate from dual;

SYSDATE
---------
18-SEP-97

SQL>
SQL> timing show mytimer;
timing for: mytimer
 real: 30
SQL> timing stop mytimer;
timing for: mytimer
 real: 40
SQL> |
```

Figure 14.5 CHP14_8.SQL uses the TIMING command in SQL*Plus.

How It Works

Step 1 shows how to set the TIMING system variable on, so that SQL*Plus will report timing information after processing each subsequent SQL statement. Step 2 implements some sample objects and tables to feed the queries in Step 3. Step 4 shows how to disable individual SQL statement execution timing. Step 5 explains the use of the TIMING command to time collections of SQL statements.

Comments

The TIMING STOP command shows the value of the timer when it is stopped. This value is the elapsed time since the timer started. Timers cannot indicate how much of the CPU or other resources the timed SQL statements used. You cannot reference a timer after you have stopped it; Oracle8 will generate a no timing elements to show message should you attempt to do so. The TIMING command should be used for timing an entire script or a set of statements. The usual timer invocation structure suggests that the first command of the script starts the timer and the last command stops it.

COMPLEXITY
INTERMEDIATE

14.5 How do I...
Analyze SQL statements with SQL*Trace and the TKPROF utility?

Problem

I want to use SQL*Trace to analyze the execution plan of SQL statements within my application. Because SQL*Trace can analyze all SQL statements executed by an application or by the entire instance, I can use it to analyze the entire application as it runs. How do I use SQL*Trace and TKPROF to analyze queries?

Technique

SQL*Trace writes a file containing performance statistics. The volume of SQL*Trace output can be huge and the utility can adversely affect database performance so DBAs and developers should use it with care. There are four initialization parameters you can set to control SQL*Trace's behavior; they appear in Table 14.6.

Table 14.6 Initialization parameters that control SQL*Trace

PARAMETER	SETTING	DESCRIPTION
MAX_DUMP_SIZE	Integer value	Specifies the largest physical size that a trace file can become
SQL_TRACE	TRUE	When set to TRUE, SQL*Trace is enabled for all database users. FALSE is the default. If TRUE, SQL*Trace is executed for ALL SQL statements on the database
TIMED_STATISITICS	TRUE	When set to TRUE, the database collects additional timing statistics that are important to SQL*Trace
USER_DUMP_DEST	Directory spec.	Specifies the location where the SQL*Trace will write the trace files

When the SQL_TRACE database parameter is TRUE, overall response time can degrade noticeably because a trace file is created for every statement executed. The trace files quickly become too large to use, so a more reasonable strategy is to enable SQL*Trace for individual sessions by issuing the ALTER SESSION SET SQL_TRACE=TRUE statement.

Within PL/SQL, the DBMS_SESSION.SET_SQL_TRACE procedure performs the same action and DBAs can also use this procedure to enable SQL*Trace for another user's session. The default format of the generated trace file is not legible, so the TKPROF utility reformats trace files to a more readable form. TKPROF runs from the operating system command line and the syntax of the statement is shown below. Table 14.7 summarizes the arguments TKPROF accepts. Table 14.8 lists valid values for the SORT parameter in the TKPROF command line.

```
TKPROF tracefile outputfile [SORT = parameters] [PRINT = number]
[INSERT = script filename] [SYS = yes/no] [TABLE = schema.tablename] \
[EXPLAIN = username/password] [RECORD = sql filename]
```

Table 14.7 Arguments to the TKPROF utility

ARGUMENT	DESCRIPTION
TRACEFILE	Name of input file produced by SQL*Trace
OUTPUTFILE	Name of output file produced by TKPROF
SORT	TKPROF presents output in order of parameters when this is specified (see Table 14.6).
PRINT	TKPROF only includes the number of SQL statements in its output file
INSERT	Creates a SQL script file named script filename to store trace statistics in a database table
SYS	If YES, the default, TKPROF includes recursive SQL calls from user SYS. If NO, TKPROF ignores recursive SQL
TABLE	Specifies which schema and tablename for TKPROF to explain plan output
EXPLAIN	TKPROF includes execution path information if the username and password of a database account is specified here
RECORD	TKPROF writes all analyzed statements to sql filename if this parameter is specified

Table 14.8 TKPROF sort parameters

PARAMETER	DESCRIPTION
EXECNT	Number of executes.
EXECPU	CPU time spent executing.
EXEELA	Elapsed time spent executing.
EXEDSK	Number of physical reads during execute.
EXEQRY	Number of consistent reads during execute.
EXECU	Number of current reads during execute.
EXEROW	Number of rows processed during execute.
EXEMIS	Number of library cache misses during execute.
FCHCNT	Number of fetches.
FCHCPU	CPU time spent fetching.
FCHELA	Elapsed time spent fetching.
FCHDSK	Number of physical reads during fetch.
FCHQRY	Number of consistent reads during fetch.
FCHCU	Number of current reads during fetch.
FCHROW	Number of rows fetched.
PRSCNT	Number of times parsed.
PRSCPU	CPU time spent parsing.
PRSELA	Elapsed time spent parsing.
PRSDSK	Number of physical reads during parse.
PRSMIS	Number of consistent reads during parse.
PRSCU	Number of current reads during parse.
PRSMIS	Number of library cache misses during parse.

Steps

1. Locate the INIT.ORA file for your database and open it using any text editor. Under Windows NT, the initialization file is in \ORANT\DATABASE and is named INIT<DATABASE INSTANCE ID>.ORA.

Edit or add the values for the MAX_DUMP_SIZE, TIMED_STATISTICS, and USER_DUMP_DEST parameters as shown in Figure 14.6. Shutdown and restart the database so that the new initialization parameters are active.

```
timed_statistics = true          # if you want timed statistics
max_dump_file_size = 5000000     # limit trace file size to 5 Meg each
user_dump_dest=%RDBMS80%\trace   # trace files destination
```

Figure 14.6 Initialization parameters necessary for SQL*Trace use.

NOTE

Do not set the SQL_TRACE parameter to TRUE unless you are the only user of the database and want to run the SQL*Trace facility on all statements. Running SQL*Trace on all SQL statements for an instance degrades performance and generates huge trace files.

2. The SQL script CHP14_9.SQL creates three sample tables similar to the familiar SCOTT schema objects. Start SQL*Plus, connect as the WAITE user, and use the START command to load and execute this script. The script appears in Figure 14.7.

3. Use the START command to load and execute the script CHP14_10.SQL. Figure 14.8 displays the script and its output.

The ALTER SESSION command enables the SQL*Trace facility to analyze all future SQL statements.

4. Use the START command to load and execute CHP14_11.SQL. Figure 14.9 features the query; the query's results, 100 rows of data from the three tables, is not shown to conserve space.

```
CREATE TABLE emp14_5
( empno   number(4),
  ename   varchar2(10),
  deptno number(3));
CREATE TABLE dept14_5
( deptno    number(3),
  dname     varchar2(14),
  locno     number(3));
CREATE TABLE loc14_5
( locno        number(3),
  loc_city   varchar2(15));
CREATE UNIQUE INDEX idx_loc14_5
  ON loc14_5 (locno);
BEGIN
    for i in 1..100
    LOOP
        INSERT INTO dept14_5 VALUES (i, 'IS' || to_char(i), 1);
        INSERT INTO emp14_5 VALUES (i, 'BILLIE' || to_char(i), 1);
        INSERT INTO loc14_5 VALUES (i, 'CITY'||to_char(i));
    END LOOP;
END;
```

Figure 14.7 CHP14_9.SQL creates three tables and populates them with sample data for use in How-To 14.5.

```
SQL> start chp14_10
SQL>
SQL> ALTER SESSION
  2    SET SQL_TRACE = true;

Session altered.

SQL> |
```

Figure 14.8 CHP14_10.SQL enables the
SQL*Trace facility for a user session in SQL*Plus.

```
SQL> @chp14_11
SQL>
SQL> SELECT 'chp14_11' FROM dual;

'CHP14_1
--------
chp14_11

SQL>
SQL> SELECT e.ename, d.dname, c.loc_city
  2  FROM emp14_5 e,
  3       dept14_5 d,
  4       loc14_5 c
  5  WHERE e.deptno = d.deptno and
  6        d.locno = c.locno
  7  ORDER BY e.ename;
```

Figure 14.9 CHP14_11.SQL issues a SQL statement.

The query extracts rows from the three tables created in Step 2, joins them
with a WHERE clause in lines 5 and 6, and finally presents them in
employee name order via an ORDER BY clause in line 7. Because Step 3
enabled the SQL*Trace facility, Oracle8 generates statistics in the trace file
when it executes this query.

5. Use the START command to load and execute the CHP14_12.SQL script
to disable the SQL*Trace utility (see Figure 14.10).

```
SQL> start chp14_12
SQL>
SQL> ALTER SESSION
  2    SET SQL_TRACE = FALSE;

Session altered.

SQL> |
```

Figure 14.10 CHP14_12.SQL disables the
SQL*Trace facility and Oracle will not analyze
subsequent SQL statements.

6. Get to an operating system prompt and locate the trace file that SQL*Trace created during Step 4. Enter the following command to execute the TKPROF utility and create a readable version of the trace file.

```
TKPROF ora00133.trc tkprof.out sys=no explain=waite/press
```

This command executes the raw trace file called ORA00133.TRC and creates a readable trace file called TKPROF.OUT. Replace the trace file name in the previous command with the name of the trace file you want to format. The SYS=NO option suppresses analysis of recursive (Oracle internal) SQL and the EXPLAIN option requests execution path analysis. The username and password is necessary because execution path analysis requires a database connection.

7. Use any ASCII text display facility, such as Windows Wordpad, to display the reformatted trace file. If the TKPROF command line included the EXPLAIN option, then the trace file will contain a statistics section and an execution path section for each analyzed SQL statement. The statistics section appears in Figure 14.11.

The PARSE row contains statistics for the parse steps the SQL statements generated. The EXECUTE row shows statistics for the execute steps of the statements. If the statement is a data manipulation statement, the number of rows processed are shown in this row. The FETCH row shows statistics for the fetch steps performed by the statement. The value of 100 shown in this row indicates that the SELECT statement processed 100 data rows. Table 14.9 shows the columns TKPROF includes in the statistics portion of its report.

```
SELECT e.ename, d.dname, c.loc_city
FROM emp14_5 e,
     dept14_5 d,
     loc14_5 c
WHERE e.deptno = d.deptno and
      d.locno = c.locno
ORDER BY e.ename

call     count      cpu    elapsed      disk      query    current    rows
-------  ------   ------  ---------  --------  ---------  ---------  ------
Parse        1     0.36       0.45         3          0          3       0
Execute      2     0.00       0.17         0          0          0       0
Fetch        8     0.19       1.65         5        105         14     100
-------  ------   ------  ---------  --------  ---------  ---------  ------
total       11     0.55       2.27         8        105         17     100

Misses in library cache during parse: 1
Optimizer goal: CHOOSE
Parsing user id: 18   (WAITE)
```

Figure 14.11 The statistics section of the SQL*Trace/TKPROF output file for the SQL statement issued in Step 4.

Table 14.9 Columns displayed in the statistics portion of the TKPROF report

COLUMN	DESCRIPTION
CALL	Type of call: parse, execute, or fetch
COUNT	Number of parses, executes, or fetches
CPU	Total CPU (in seconds) for this call type
ELAPSED	Total elapsed (real) time (in seconds) for this call type
DISK	Physical blocks retrieved from disk
QUERY	Consistent mode retrieves for this call type
CURRENT	Current mode retrieves for this call type
ROWS	Number of rows processed (not including subquery rows)

Figure 14.12 shows the execution path portion of the TKPROF output file. This section reports the execution path for the SQL statement and the number of rows processed in each step.

How It Works

Step 1 outlines the modifications to the initialization parameter file to enable SQL*Trace processing and Step 2 creates some sample objects for SQL*Trace analysis. The ALTER SESSION command enables the SQL*Trace utility in Step 3. The SQL statement in Step 4 results in a SQL*Trace statistics file, which Step 6 reformats via the TKPROF utility. Step 5 shows how to disable SQL statement analysis by turning the SQL*Trace utility off. Step 7 shows how to display and interpret SQL*Trace and TKPROF output using any ASCII text editor.

```
Misses in library cache during parse: 1
Optimizer goal: CHOOSE
Parsing user id: 18   (WAITE)

Rows      Execution Plan
-------   -------------------------------------------------------
      0   SELECT STATEMENT    GOAL: CHOOSE
    100    SORT (ORDER BY)
    100     MERGE JOIN
    100      SORT (JOIN)
    100       NESTED LOOPS
    100        TABLE ACCESS (FULL) OF 'DEPT14_5'
    100        TABLE ACCESS (BY INDEX ROWID) OF 'LOC14_5'
    100         INDEX (UNIQUE SCAN) OF 'IDX_LOC14_5' (UNIQUE)
    100      SORT (JOIN)
    100       TABLE ACCESS (FULL) OF 'EMP14_5'
```

Figure 14.12 The execution path section of the SQL*Trace/TKPROF output file for the SQL statement issued in Step 4.

Comments

SQL*Trace provides a good starting point for application tuning because it can analyze all SQL statements issued during any user session. The CHP14_10.SQL script highlights a useful minor technique to help developers find SQL*Trace output files for a database where many such files may exist. The inclusion of a statement like this one:

```
SELECT 'statement identifier' FROM DUAL;
```

will serve this purpose because the SELECT statement resides within the SQL*Trace output file as an aid in identification.

COMPLEXITY

INTERMEDIATE

14.6   How do I...
Set the optimizer mode?

Problem

I know that Oracle8 can optimize queries in more than one way and that DBAs and developers can help Oracle8 make the best choice among the available optimizer modes. How do I tell Oracle8 which optimizer mode to use?

Technique

Oracle8 users can instruct the optimizer to base its behavior on either the contents of the database or the syntax of SQL statements. The first way, in general, results in better performance, but it comes at a price. DBAs or developers, specifically, have to issue ANALYZE commands against database objects so that the Oracle8 data dictionary contains the information that the optimizer needs.

You can choose an optimizer mode in three ways: at the instance level via the OPTIMIZER_MODE initialization parameter, at the session level via the OPTIMIZER_GOAL option, or at the statement level via optimizer hints (these are covered in depth in How-To 14.7).

Steps

1. To set the optimizer goal at the instance level, use a text editor to edit the initialization parameter file. Under Windows NT, the default location for this file is the \ORANT\DATABASE subdirectory. The OPTIMIZER_GOAL parameter controls the optimizer's behavior and can assume any of the values summarized in Table 14.10. To activate a new OPTIMIZER_GOAL setting, shut down the database and restart it.

Table 14.10 Possible values for the OPTIMIZER_GOAL initialization parameter

VALUE	EFFECT
CHOOSE	Use cost-based optimization if table statistics exist. Otherwise, use rule-based optimization.
RULE	Use rule-based optimization regardless of the existence of statistics.
FIRST_ROWS	Use cost-based optimization with the objective of minimizing query response time.
ALL_ROWS	Use cost-based optimization with the objective of minimizing total resource consumption.

2. To modify the optimizer's behavior at the session level, use the ALTER SESSION SET OPTIMIZER_GOAL command. The possible values of OPTIMIZER_GOAL are the same as those listed in Table 14.8 for the OPTIMIZER_MODE initialization parameter. The script CHP14_13.SQL sets the optimizer mode at the session level. Figure 14.13 displays the script and its results.

3. To modify the optimizer's behavior at the statement level, use optimizer hints on individual SQL statements like this:

```
SELECT /*+ RULE */ ename FROM emp14_5 WHERE empno > 0;
```

The hint on this SQL statement forces Oracle8 to use rule-based optimization regardless of the presence or absence of ANALYZE statistics or the values of the OPTIMIZER_MODE initialization parameter or the OPTIMIZER_GOAL option. This is only one way to use optimizer hints; more methods of SQL statement tuning using optimizer hints are covered in How-To 14.7.

```
SQL> start chp14_13.sql
SQL>
SQL> ALTER SESSION
  2     SET OPTIMIZER_GOAL = ALL_ROWS;

Session altered.

SQL> |
```

Figure 14.13 The script CHP14_13.SQL sets the OPTIMIZER_GOAL option to ALL_ROWS in SQL*Plus.

How It Works

Step 1 shows how to modify the initialization parameter file to set the default optimizer mode for an entire instance. Step 2 shows how to set the optimizer mode at the session level using the ALTER SESSION command. Step 3 shows how to choose an optimizer mode at the statement level using an optimizer hint (continue to the next How-To for more information on optimizer hints).

Comments

Oracle7 supported two optimizer modes and Oracle8 continues to do so, but this is temporary. In some future release of the database, developers will cease to have a choice in this area. In fact, the Oracle8 documentation urges developers and DBAs to convert rule-based legacy applications to cost-based optimization as soon as possible. This entails implementing a schedule for database object analysis to support cost-based optimization decisions.

Optimizer settings at the session level override instance level settings. Settings at the statement level, indicated via statement hints, override all other optimizer directives.

COMPLEXITY
ADVANCED

14.7 How do I...
Pass hints to the optimizer?

Problem

I have used EXPLAIN PLAN, the AUTOTRACE option, or SQL*Trace—presented in How-To's 14.2, 14.3, and 14.5, respectively—to identify some poorly performing SQL statements. I think that the optimizer is making the wrong decision about how to execute some of these statements, degrading performance. How do I suggest an alternate execution path to the optimizer?

Technique

Optimizer hints reside in comment blocks; must follow the SELECT, UPDATE, INSERT, or DELETE keywords; and change the execution plan for the statement containing the hint. The syntax of an optimizer hint is /*+ hint */. Table 14.11 lists Oracle8 optimizer hints. Use the AUTOTRACE option, EXPLAIN PLAN, or SQL*Trace to determine how optimizer hints change the execution plan.

Table 14.11 Oracle8 optimizer hints

VALUE	EFFECT
ALL_ROWS	Optimize the statement for best total throughput.
AND_EQUAL	Use index merging on the specified table.
APPEND	Append data to a table, do not use existing free space.
CACHE	Look in the most recently used end of the buffer cache LRU list when performing a full table scan.
CHOOSE	Use cost-based optimization if ANALYZE statistics exist, otherwise use rule-based optimization.
FIRST_ROWS	Optimize the SQL statement for best response time.
CLUSTER	Use a cluster scan.
COST	Use cost-based optimization.
FULL	Use a full table scan on the specified table.
HASH	Use a hash search on the specified table.
HASH_AJ	Use a hash anti-join instead of NOT IN
INDEX	Use the specified index on the specified table.
INDEX_ASC	Use the specified index in ascending order.
INDEX_DESC	Use the specified index in descending order.
INDEX_COMBINE	Use a combination of bitmap indexes.
INDEX_FFS	Use a fast full index scan instead of a full table scan.
MERGE_AJ	Use a merge anti-join instead of a NOT IN subquery.
NO_APPEND	Do not append data to a table, use existing free space.
NO_CACHE	Look in the least recently used end of the buffer cache LRU list when performing a full table scan.
NO_MERGE	Join each table with a sort-merge join.
NO_PARALLEL	Do not scan the table in parallel.
ORDERED	Use the join sequence from the FROM clause.
PARALLEL	Specify the number of slave processes with which to accomplish the operation.
PARALLEL_INDEX	Parallelize fast full index scans.
PUSH_SUBQ	Evaluate non-merged subqueries as early in the execution plan as possible.
ROWID	Use the ROWID access method.
RULE	Use rule-based optimization.
STAR	Join the large table last with a nested loops join on an index.
USE_HASH	Join each specified table with a hash join.
USE_MERGE	Use sort-merge join techniques on the specified table.
USE_NL	Use nested-loop join techniques on the specified table.
USE_CONCAT	Use UNION ALL instead of the combined OR condition in the WHERE clause.

Steps

1. Run SQL*Plus and connect as the WAITE user. CHP14_14.SQL, shown in Figure 14.14, creates a sample table used in this How-To. Run this script using the START command.

The first SQL statement creates a table named EMP14_7. The second statement creates an index on the EMPNO column of the table, and the third statement block, an anonymous PL/SQL procedure, populates the table with 250 rows of sample data.

2. If you haven't already done so, follow the directions in the "Comments" section of How-To 14.3 to enable the AUTOTRACE option for the WAITE account.

3. In SQL*Plus, issue the SET AUTOTRACE ON command to reveal the execution paths of the following statements.

4. Use the START command to load and execute the CHP14_15.SQL script. The script and the AUTOTRACE output appear in Figure 14.15. The 250 rows returned by the script's query are not reproduced here to conserve space.

```
SQL> CREATE TABLE emp14_7
  2  (
  3   empno        NUMBER(4) NOT NULL,
  4   ename        VARCHAR2(10),
  5   job          VARCHAR2(9),
  6   mgr          NUMBER(4),
  7   hiredate     DATE,
  8   sal          NUMBER(7,2),
  9   comm         NUMBER(7,2),
 10   deptno       NUMBER(2)
 11  );

Table created.

SQL> CREATE INDEX idx_emp14_7
  2     ON emp14_7(empno);

Index created.

SQL> BEGIN
  2     for i in 1 .. 250 loop
  3        insert into emp14_7 (empno, ename) values (i, 'MARK'||to_char(i));
  4     end loop;
  5  END;
  6  /

PL/SQL procedure successfully completed.
```

Figure 14.14 The script CHP14_14.SQL creates and populates a sample table for use in How-To 14.7.

```
SQL> start chp14_15.sql
SQL>
SQL> SELECT /*+ INDEX(emp14_7 idx_emp14_7) */ empno
  2  FROM emp14_7;

Execution Plan
----------------------------------------------------------
   0      SELECT STATEMENT Optimizer=CHOOSE (Cost=26 Card=2000 Bytes=2
          6000)

   1    0   INDEX (FULL SCAN) OF 'IDX_EMP14_7' (NON-UNIQUE) (Cost=26 C
            ard=2000 Bytes=26000)

Statistics
----------------------------------------------------------
          0  recursive calls
          0  db block gets
         20  consistent gets
          0  physical reads
          0  redo size
       3665  bytes sent via SQL*Net to client
       1914  bytes received via SQL*Net from client
         18  SQL*Net roundtrips to/from client
          0  sorts (memory)
          0  sorts (disk)
        250  rows processed
```

Figure 14.15 The script CHP14_15.SQL tells the Oracle optimizer to use an index via an optimizer hint.

Assuming that no developer or DBA has applied the ANALYZE command to this table, the Oracle optimizer would normally use a full table scan for the query in the CHP14_15.SQL script. The index, however, contains all of the columns returned by the SELECT statement so an index scan would yield better performance. The hint in the SELECT statement forces the optimizer to perform a full index scan to complete the query.

5. Use the START command to load and execute the script CHP14_16.SQL. The script and its AUTOTRACE output appear in Figure 14.16.

Adding another optimizer hint can expedite this simple query even more. Through the INDEX_FFS hint, the CHP14_16.SQL script tells Oracle to perform a *fast* full index scan. This type of index scan offers a performance improvement over a normal full index scan because it can utilize multiblock reads. Comparison of the COST estimate in the AUTOTRACE output for this script and the script in the last step supports this assertion.

How It Works

Step 1 creates a sample table used throughout this How-To. Step 2 configures the WAITE account for AUTOTRACE analysis and Step 3 turns on the AUTOTRACE option. Step 4 passes a hint to the optimizer to enforce an index scan rather than a full table scan. Step 5 passes a similar hint forcing Oracle8 to perform a fast full index scan.

```
SQL> SQL> start chp14_16
SQL>
SQL> SELECT /*+ INDEX_FFS(emp14_7 idx_emp14_7) */ empno
  2  FROM emp14_7;

Execution Plan
----------------------------------------------------------
   0      SELECT STATEMENT Optimizer=CHOOSE (Cost=4 Card=2000 Bytes=26
          000)

   1    0   INDEX (FAST FULL SCAN) OF 'IDX_EMP14_7' (NON-UNIQUE) (Cost
          =4 Card=2000 Bytes=26000)


Statistics
----------------------------------------------------------
          8  recursive calls
          1  db block gets
         26  consistent gets
          0  physical reads
          0  redo size
       3665  bytes sent via SQL*Net to client
       1918  bytes received via SQL*Net from client
         18  SQL*Net roundtrips to/from client
```

Figure 14.16 The script CHP14_16.SQL tells the Oracle optimizer to perform a fast full index scan.

Comments

In the hands of skilled Oracle developers, optimizer hints can generate performance improvements. SQL statement writers should observe two features of hint usage, however. The first is that the optimizer will simply ignore hints that are syntactically or operationally incorrect. For example, the optimizer will pay no attention to a "use_nl" hint when the query involves only one table. Regardless of the reason, Oracle8 will issue no message when its optimizer ignores a hint. The second caveat is that Oracle's optimizer, particularly the cost-based optimizer, usually chooses the best execution plan. Developers should only override the Oracle optimizer with hints when armed with in-depth knowledge of the database's contents.

COMPLEXITY
ADVANCED

14.8 How do I...
Suppress indexes in a query?

Problem

I have used EXPLAIN PLAN, the AUTOTRACE option, or SQL*Trace to reveal the optimizer's execution plan for some queries. I have found that the optimizer occasionally uses an index when the query returns a significant number of table rows. In these cases, index suppression enhances performance. How do I tell the Oracle8 optimizer *not* to use an index?

Technique

Use EXPLAIN PLAN, the SQL*Trace utility, or the SQL*Plus autotrace option to reveal how SQL statements use indexes. Changes to the WHERE clause of a SQL statement that do not alter the clause's result can suppress index use. Specifically, if a SQL statement modifies an indexed column, then the optimizer will not use indexes based on that column.

Steps

1. Run SQL*Plus, connect as the WAITE user, and use the START command to load and execute the script CHP14_17.SQL as shown in Figure 14.17.

The script creates a partitioned version of the familiar EMP table traditionally found in SCOTT's schema. The partition key is column EMPNO. The script also creates a local prefixed index named IDX_EMP14_8. (You can read more about the three partitioned index types Oracle8 supports in How-To 5.8). Finally, the script uses an anonymous PL/SQL block to insert 500 rows into the EMP14_8 table.

> **NOTE**
>
> Partitioned tables are most useful in supporting very large databases. The small partitions featured in Figure 14.17 are not realistic and are intended for example purposes only.

```
SQL> start chp14_17
SQL>
SQL> CREATE TABLE emp14_8
  2  (  empno          NUMBER(4) NOT NULL,
  3     ename          VARCHAR2(10),
  4     job            VARCHAR2(9)
  5  )
  6  PARTITION BY RANGE (empno)
  7  (  PARTITION emp14_8p1 VALUES LESS THAN (251),
  8     PARTITION emp14_8p2 VALUES LESS THAN (MAXVALUE)
  9  );

Table created.

SQL> CREATE UNIQUE INDEX idx_emp14_8
  2     ON emp14_8(empno)
  3     LOCAL (PARTITION emp14_8p1,
  4            PARTITION emp14_8p2);

Index created.

SQL> BEGIN
  2     for i in 1 .. 500 loop
  3        insert into emp14_8 values (i, 'MARK'||to_char(i), 'PHYSICIST');
  4     end loop;
  5  END;
  6  /
```

Figure 14.17 The script CHP14_17.SQL creates a sample table for use in How-To 14.8.

2. If you haven't already done so, follow the directions in the "Comments" section of How-To 14.3 to enable the AUTOTRACE option for the WAITE account.

3. In SQL*Plus, issue the SET AUTOTRACE ON command to reveal the execution paths of the SQL statements in this How-To.

4. Use the START command to load and execute the script CHP14_18.SQL. The script and its result appear in Figure 14.18.

Because AUTOTRACE is on, SQL*Plus generates the execution plan for the SQL statement. The plan indicates use of the index on EMP14_8 even though the query returned 30% of the data residing in the table.

5. Load and execute the script CHP14_19.SQL with the START command as shown in Figure 14.19.

```
SQL> start chp14_18
SQL>
SQL> SELECT count(*)
  2  FROM emp14_8
  3  WHERE empno > 150 AND
  4        empno < 300;

  COUNT(*)
----------
       149


Execution Plan
----------------------------------------------------------
   0      SELECT STATEMENT Optimizer=CHOOSE (Cost=1 Card=1 Bytes=26)
   1    0   SORT (AGGREGATE)
   2    1    PARTITION (CONCATENATED)
   3    2     INDEX (RANGE SCAN) OF 'IDX_EMP14_8' (UNIQUE) (Cost=2 C
          ard=1 Bytes=26)
```

Figure 14.18 The script CHP14_18.SQL queries the partitioned table EMP14_8.

```
SQL> start chp14_19
SQL>
SQL> SELECT count(*)
  2  FROM emp14_8
  3  WHERE empno+0 < 150 AND
  4        empno+0 < 300;

  COUNT(*)
----------
       149


Execution Plan
----------------------------------------------------------
   0      SELECT STATEMENT Optimizer=CHOOSE (Cost=1 Card=1 Bytes=26)
   1    0   SORT (AGGREGATE)
   2    1    PARTITION (CONCATENATED)
   3    2     TABLE ACCESS (FULL) OF 'EMP14_8' (Cost=1 Card=1 Bytes=
          26)
```

Figure 14.19 The altered syntax of the query in CHP14_19.SQL forces the optimizer to perform a full table scan.

Lines 3 and 4 of the script change the WHERE clause syntax of the previous step by adding 0 to the value of EMPNO. This has no effect on the results of the WHERE clause but does prevent the optimizer from using the index on the EMPNO column. The execution plan results support this assertion by showing that the optimizer has performed a full table scan instead of utilizing the IDX_EMP14_8 index.

How It Works

Step 1 creates a sample partitioned table to illustrate the rest of this section. Steps 2 and 3 enable the AUTOTRACE facility so that SQL*Plus reveals SQL statement execution plans. Step 4 shows how the default behavior of a large volume query is to use an index. Step 5 shows how trivial changes to indexed columns in the WHERE clause can prevent Oracle8's optimizer from incorrectly using an index.

Comments

There is, of course, another way to suppress index use: hints! The script CHP14_20.SQL, shown in Figure 14.20, is just as effective at forcing a full table scan as the machinations in Step 5; it is also easier to read.

The method, and this How-To really presents a *trick* more than a *method*, has achieved some popularity among developers. It is included here for completeness and to enhance understanding of legacy code, but optimizer hints are the prescribed solution to this How-To's problem. Future changes in Oracle's optimizer may render obsolete the technique presented here.

```
SQL> start chp14_20
SQL>
SQL> SELECT /*+ FULL(emp14_8) */ count(*)
  2  FROM emp14_8
  3  WHERE empno > 150 AND
  4        empno < 300;

  COUNT(*)
----------
       149


Execution Plan
----------------------------------------------------------
   0      SELECT STATEMENT Optimizer=CHOOSE (Cost=1 Card=1 Bytes=26)
   1    0   SORT (AGGREGATE)
   2    1     PARTITION (CONCATENATED)
   3    2       TABLE ACCESS (FULL) OF 'EMP14_8' (Cost=1 Card=1 Bytes=
          26)
```

Figure 14.20 Using a hint to force a full table scan on the partitioned EMP14_8 table.

14.9 How do I...
Structure data warehouses for star query optimization?

Problem

My database contains some data warehouse structures, each featuring one large table and several smaller base tables. Some queries against this structure require extremely long processing times. How can I improve Oracle8's performance for queries against my data warehouse?

Technique

The classical data warehouse structure features one large table, called a *fact table*, where quantitative and categorical data for an ongoing business process resides. In most data warehouse implementations, this table is very large. Supplementing the fact table are several much smaller *dimension tables*, which store additional data about the grouping variables residing in the fact table. Entity relationship diagrams for a structure like this often surround the large fact table with the smaller dimension tables in a star pattern. The name "star schema" refers to this pattern.

Suppose, for the purposes of example, that computer help desk staff in a large company log requests for assistance in a database application. This application records the call duration, the software package that generated the question, and the caller's department. After years of use, the help desk database may come to contain hundreds of thousands of records. It is conceivable that the organization may choose to store this large volume in a data warehouse to provide a historical perspective of help desk activity. Ad hoc queries against the data warehouse may not perform well if developers let the Oracle optimizer choose an execution path. Some additional indexing on the schema, however, can provide some performance advantages.

Four factors influence the Oracle8's decision about star query optimization. They are the following:

✔ The index structure of the fact and dimension tables

✔ The setting of the STAR_QUERY_ENABLED initialization parameter

✔ The use of the STAR_TRANSFORMATION hint

✔ The use of the ANALYZE command to supply the data dictionary with fact and dimension table metadata

For this example, assume the following about these factors:

✔ At the start, the only indexes on the fact and dimension tables are those created by the CHP14_21.SQL script in Step 1.

✔ The initialization parameter STAR_QUERY_ENABLED is set to the default value FALSE.

✔ The STAR_TRANSFORMATION hint is not used.

✔ The fact and dimension tables are not analyzed.

Steps

1. Run SQL*Plus, connect as the WAITE user, and use the START command to load and execute the script CHP14_21.SQL. The script and its output appear in Listing 14.4.

Listing 14.4 Running the CHP14_21.SQL script in SQL*Plus to create a sample data warehouse schema

```
SQL> start chp14_21
SQL>
SQL> CREATE TABLE emp14_9
  2  (  emp_no      number(5),
  3     dept_name   varchar2(20),
  4  --
  5     CONSTRAINT emp14_9_pk PRIMARY KEY (emp_no)
  6  );

Table created.

SQL>
SQL> CREATE TABLE package14_9
  2  (  package_no    number(3),
  3     package_name  varchar2(20),
  4  --
  5     CONSTRAINT package14_9_pk PRIMARY KEY (package_no)
  6  );

Table created.

SQL>
SQL> CREATE TABLE priority14_9
  2  (  priority_no     number(2),
  3     priority_level  varchar2(20),
  4  --
  5     CONSTRAINT priority14_9_pk PRIMARY KEY (priority_no)
  6  );

Table created.
```

continued on next page

continued from previous page

```
SQL>
SQL> CREATE TABLE helpcall14_9
  2  ( package_no    number(3),
  3    emp_no        number(5),
  4    priority_no   number(2),
  5    call_duration number(3),
  6  --
  7    CONSTRAINT helpcall14_9_pk
  8      PRIMARY KEY (package_no, emp_no, priority_no),
  9    CONSTRAINT helpcall_package_fk
 10      FOREIGN KEY (package_no)
 11      REFERENCES package14_9(package_no),
 12    CONSTRAINT helpcall_emp_fk
 13      FOREIGN KEY (emp_no)
 14      REFERENCES emp14_9(emp_no),
 15    CONSTRAINT helpcall_priority_fk
 16      FOREIGN KEY (priority_no)
 17      REFERENCES priority14_9(priority_no)
 18  );

Table created.

SQL>
```

The script creates three dimension tables named PACKAGE14_9, EMP14_9, and PRIORITY14_9. It also creates a fact table named HELPCALL14_9. Each dimension table has one implicit primary key index. The fact table's primary key is the result of concatenating the primary keys of the dimension tables. The fact table also contains foreign key references on the grouping attributes that refer back to the dimension tables. Lines 9 through 17 of the CREATE TABLE statement for the fact table implement the foreign key constraints.

2. Enable the AUTOTRACE option for the SQL*Plus session by issuing the SET AUTOTRACE ON command at the SQL*Plus prompt.

3. Use the START command to load and execute the script CHP14_22.SQL. The script appears in Figure 14.21. There is no data in the star schema so the query returns no rows, but the AUTOTRACE option results in the execution path report appearing in Figure 14.22.

The execution path, read from inside out and from top to bottom, indicates that the optimizer's first step is an index scan followed by a table access by ROWID on the PRIORITY14_9 table. Oracle8 submits this output and the rows returned from a full table access on the HELPDESK14_9 fact table to a nested loops join. There is more to the execution path, but the damage has already been done. It is likely that the nested loops join will return enough rows to degrade the performance of the rest of the query.

```
SQL> start chp14_22
SQL>
SQL> SELECT
  2         he.call_duration,
  3         pa.package_name,
  4         em.dept_name,
  5         pr.priority_level
  6  FROM
  7         package14_9 pa,
  8         emp14_9 em,
  9         priority14_9 pr,
 10         helpcall14_9 he
 11  WHERE pa.package_name = 'WORD PROCESSOR' and
 12         pr.priority_level = 'HIGH' and
 13         em.dept_name = 'HUMAN RESOURCES' and
 14         he.package_no = pa.package_no and
 15         he.emp_no = em.emp_no and
 16         he.priority_no = pr.priority_no;

no rows selected
```

Figure 14.21 Querying the star schema by executing
CHP14_22.SQL in SQL*Plus.

```
Execution Plan
-------------------------------------------------------
   0      SELECT STATEMENT Optimizer=CHOOSE
   1   0    NESTED LOOPS
   2   1      NESTED LOOPS
   3   2        NESTED LOOPS
   4   3          TABLE ACCESS (FULL) OF 'HELPCALL14_9'
   5   3          TABLE ACCESS (BY INDEX ROWID) OF 'PRIORITY14_9'
   6   5            INDEX (UNIQUE SCAN) OF 'PRIORITY14_9_PK' (UNIQUE)
   7   2        TABLE ACCESS (BY INDEX ROWID) OF 'EMP14_9'
   8   7          INDEX (UNIQUE SCAN) OF 'EMP14_9_PK' (UNIQUE)
   9   1      TABLE ACCESS (BY INDEX ROWID) OF 'PACKAGE14_9'
  10   9        INDEX (UNIQUE SCAN) OF 'PACKAGE14_9_PK' (UNIQUE)
```

Figure 14.22 The traditional execution path the optimizer
chooses for the CHP14_22.SQL script.

4. Use the START command to load and execute the CHP14_23.SQL script.
The script creates indexes on the dimension table columns, which are
likely to appear in ad hoc queries against the HELPDESK14_9 fact table.
Figure 14.23 presents the script and its output.

```
SQL> start chp14_23
SQL>
SQL> CREATE INDEX idx_emp14_9 ON emp14_9(dept_name);

Index created.

SQL> CREATE INDEX idx_package14_9 ON package14_9(package_name);

Index created.

SQL> CREATE INDEX idx_priority14_9 ON priority14_9(priority_level);

Index created.

SQL> |
```

Figure 14.23 The CHP14_23.SQL script indexes some additional tables from the dimension tables.

5. Execute the CHP14_22.SQL script again using the START command. The execution path from the script appears in Figure 14.24.

This new execution plan is quite different from the one that Step 3 generated. The optimizer uses the indexes on the non-key columns of the dimension tables to perform range scans and nested loops joins. The large fact table HELPDESK14_9 is uninvolved in the query until the last step and even then table access is by ROWID (instead of the full table scan we saw in Step 2). This is often referred to as a star query execution path.

How It Works

Step 1 creates a set of tables consistent with a classical data warehouse star schema architecture. Step 2 enables the AUTOTRACE option so SQL*Plus reveals the execution plan for subsequent SQL statements. The script in Step 3 follows the traditional execution plan, Step 4 creates indexes on the non-key columns of the dimension tables, and Step 5 shows the new execution path.

Comments

Star query execution can result in huge performance benefits for traditional and data warehouse applications. The performance benefits intensify if the fact table is extremely large. Be advised, though, that if the fact table is not appreciably larger than the dimension tables then a traditional execution path may perform as well as, and perhaps better than, a star query.

The online documentation states that the rule-based optimizer does not recognize star queries and that developers must ANALYZE tables to realize star query execution paths. Under the 8.0.2.0.2 beta release of the Oracle8 server for Windows NT, this is not true; even the rule-based optimizer recognizes star queries in the presence of indexes on the non-key columns of the dimension tables.

```
Execution Plan
--------------------------------------------------------------------
   0          SELECT STATEMENT Optimizer=CHOOSE
   1      0    NESTED LOOPS
   2      1     NESTED LOOPS
   3      2      NESTED LOOPS
   4      3       TABLE ACCESS (BY INDEX ROWID) OF 'PRIORITY14_9'
   5      4         INDEX (RANGE SCAN) OF 'IDX_PRIORITY14_9' (NON-UNIQ
              UE)

   6      3       TABLE ACCESS (BY INDEX ROWID) OF 'EMP14_9'
   7      6         INDEX (RANGE SCAN) OF 'IDX_EMP14_9' (NON-UNIQUE)
   8      2      TABLE ACCESS (BY INDEX ROWID) OF 'PACKAGE14_9'
   9      8        INDEX (RANGE SCAN) OF 'IDX_PACKAGE14_9' (NON-UNIQUE)
  10      1     TABLE ACCESS (BY INDEX ROWID) OF 'HELPCALL14_9'
  11     10       INDEX (UNIQUE SCAN) OF 'HELPCALL14_9_PK' (UNIQUE)
```

Figure 14.24 The CHP14_22.SQL script's execution plan after indexing additional columns in the dimension tables.

Ordering the tables in the FROM clause of a potential star query in the order of their primary key columns in the fact table's primary key may induce the optimizer to use a star query. List the fact table last in the FROM clause and supply the ORDERED hint if the optimizer still ignores a star query execution path (see a full discussion of optimizer hints in How-To 14.7).

The bottom line is that the only way to tell that the optimizer has chosen a star query execution path is to review either SQL*Trace, EXPLAIN PLAN, or AUTOTRACE output. If the execution plan indicates the optimizer is using indexes other than the primary keys of the dimension tables then Oracle8 is executing a star query.

As always, pay close attention to elapsed time, query statistics, and the execution plan when bypassing the optimizer's default behavior. Otherwise, you may "tune" yourself right into a performance problem.

COMPLEXITY
INTERMEDIATE

14.10 How do I...
Register applications to simplify performance tracking?

Problem

I know how to use V$SQLAREA to identify poorly performing SQL statements and I know how to create, analyze, and improve optimizer execution paths. My database serves so many users and applications, however, that sometimes I am unable to determine what application issued the problematic SQL statement in the first place. How can I improve my ability to reveal the origin of SQL statements?

Technique

The DBMS_APPLICATION_INFO package, a built-in package that Oracle supplies, exists primarily to allow application developers to add more description to the dynamic performance view V$SQLAREA. Five procedures exist in this package, but the two most useful are SET_MODULE and SET_ACTION. The first updates the MODULE column in the V$SQLAREA view; the second sets the ACTION column in the view. Queries on the V$SQLAREA view can be much more instructive about application activity after DBMS_APPLICATION_INFO has enhanced the contents of V$SQLAREA.

Steps

1. Run SQL*Plus, connect as the WAITE user, and use the START command
to load and execute the CHP14_24.SQL script. The script's contents and
output appear in Listing 14.5.

Listing 14.5 Registering an application and generating database
activity with the CHP14_24.SQL script in SQL*Plus

```
 2   DECLARE
 3      i     integer;
 4      CURSOR dtc_c1 IS
 5      SELECT column_name
 6      FROM dba_tab_columns;
 7      CURSOR dv IS
 8      SELECT column_name
 9      FROM dba_ind_columns;
10   BEGIN
11   DBMS_APPLICATION_INFO.SET_MODULE
12   (   module_name => 'How-To 14-10',
13       action_name => user || ' reading dba_tab_columns'
14   );
15   for table_rec IN dtc_c1
16   LOOP
17      i := 0;
18   END LOOP;
19   DBMS_APPLICATION_INFO.SET_ACTION
20   (   action_name => user || ' reading dba_ind_columns');
21   for table_rec IN dv
22   LOOP
23      i := 0;
24   END LOOP;
25   DBMS_APPLICATION_INFO.SET_MODULE
26   (   module_name => null,
27       action_name => null
28   );
29*  END
```

The script sets the module name to How-To 14.10 and then uses the user
system variable to set the action name to WAITE reading
dba_tab_columns. In lines 15 through 17 the script generates some
database activity by selecting all of the rows from the
DBA_TAB_COLUMNS view and performing an assignment statement. In
lines 19 through 20, DBMS_APPLICATION_INFO resets the action name,

again with the user system variable, to WAITE reading dba_ind_ columns. The final loop in lines 21 through 24 selects every row from the DBA_IND_COLUMNS view and performs an assignment statement. The script sets the module and action names back to the null value in lines 25 through 28.

2. Query the V$SQLAREA dynamic performance view by using the SQL*Plus START command to load and execute the CHP14_25.SQL script, as shown in Figure 14.25.

This script is very similar to the CHP14_1.SQL script introduced in How-To 14.1. It prompts the user for a number of physical reads to serve as the cut off criteria for report inclusion. Unlike the CHP14_1.SQL script, however, it returns the ACTION and MODULE columns. The V$SQLAREA rows displayed in Figure 14.25 contain the values for ACTION and MODULE that Step 1 established using the DBMS_APPLICATION_INFO package.

How It Works

Step 1 uses the DBMS_APPLICATION_INFO package to register the script CHP14_24.SQL and proceeds to generate a non-trivial amount of database activity. Step 2 queries the V$SQLAREA dynamic performance view to reveal the most resource intensive SQL statements and the corresponding ACTION and MODULE columns.

```
SQL> start chp14_25.sql

SQL> SELECT vt.sql_text short_text, module, action,
  2          disk_reads
  3          FROM v$sqlarea va, v$sqltext_with_newlines vt
  4  WHERE va.address = vt.address and
  5          disk_reads > &dreads
  6  ORDER BY disk_reads desc;
Enter value for dreads: 500


SHORT_TEXT              MODULE        ACTION                                  DISK_READS
--------------------    ------------  ------------------------------------    -----------

SELECT COLUMN_NAME      How-To 14-10  WAITE reading dba_tab_columns                  829
FROM
DBA_TAB_COLUMNS

SELECT COLUMN_NAME      How-To 14-10  WAITE reading dba_ind_columns                  524
FROM
DBA_IND_COLUMNS
```

Figure 14.25 CHP14_25.SQL queries the V$SQLAREA dynamic performance view and includes the ACTION and MODULE columns.

Comments

The last call to the SET_MODULE procedure of the DBMS_APPLICATIION_INFO package is important. It sets the module and action names back to null at the culmination of the script. Without this clean-up process, Oracle will incorrectly attribute subsequent SQL statements to the How-To 14.10 module. This oversight would actually make application tracking more difficult! Do not forget to reset the module and action names at the culmination of an application.

If your database experiences heavy application traffic, it may be beneficial to educate developers in application registration so that the origins of problematic SQL statements are more apparent during tuning efforts.

CHAPTER 15

DATABASE TUNING

15

DATABASE TUNING

How do I...

Acceptable application performance begins with an optimized database design and with tuned component SQL statements. These measures are well documented and are certainly more science than art. Ensuring that an application operates at peak performance, though, requires review of the multitude of configurable parameters that Oracle8 offers and this is where tuning begins to be more art than science. This chapter addresses some of the most common tuning issues and provides general guidelines for healthy database operation. But this is not a tuning book and the treatment presented here is not exhaustive. After addressing database design and application SQL statements, most tuning methodologies focus on tuning memory, input/output, and contention. The How-To's in this chapter adhere to this time-tested approach. The files used in this chapter are found on the accompanying CD under the \SAMPLES\CHAP15 directory. Copy these files into your SQL*Plus working directory, or specify the complete path when executing the START command within SQL*Plus.

> **NOTE**
>
> All of the How-To's in this chapter are designated as "Advanced" in complexity. Database tuning requires DBA privilege levels, and only those users with an in-depth knowledge of database operation should attempt to implement the guidelines in this chapter.

The market provides many tools for Oracle performance monitoring; some of these, like the Performance Pack in Enterprise Manager, are offered by Oracle Corporation. The appearance of the command line interface shown in this chapter may not compare favorably to the graphical interfaces featured in other products but if you really want to understand Oracle performance issues, the data dictionary is the place to start. The graphical tools isolate users from a thorough understanding of the data dictionary. The irony is this: you should only use the graphical tools if you don't really need them. Otherwise, check out the dynamic performance tables and the statistics report to nurture an in-depth understanding of what's happening behind the scenes.

15.1 Run the UTLBSTAT and UTLESTAT Scripts

Oracle supplies two scripts, often referred to as the *statistics scripts*, which provide a fairly comprehensive overview of database performance. Experienced database tuners often start their analysis with these scripts. This How-To describes the scripts and their use, presents some tips for running them efficiently, and introduces the scripts' output. Many of the other How-To's in this chapter will refer to the report produced by the UTLESTAT script.

15.2 Identify Unbalanced I/O and I/O Contention

Most database servers can simultaneously access multiple disks and most database architects configure a database's physical files to reside on multiple disks. If one disk performs too much of the work while other disks are idle, then system performance is not maximized. This How-To covers the process for identifying I/O imbalance and mentions some guidelines for identifying I/O contention.

15.3 Stripe a Tablespace Across Multiple Devices

A tablespace can consist of multiple datafiles, which do not have to be located on the same device. If users and applications heavily access a tablespace, you may be able to improve performance by spreading (striping) the tablespace over multiple I/O devices to reduce contention. This How-To presents a method for creating a new tablespace spanning multiple devices and a method for modifying an existing tablespace by adding striped datafiles.

15.4 Determine Shared Pool Performance

The shared pool contains the data dictionary cache and the library (or SQL) cache. If the shared pool is too small, Oracle8 may need to go to the disk for information that should be in memory. Information about users, tables, indexes, privileges, and other data dictionary objects is part of the data dictionary cache. The most recently parsed and executed SQL statements are located in the library cache. Oracle8 needs much more time to read this information from disk than from memory and database performance can suffer greatly if the shared pool is not large enough. This How-To presents a method to determine the hit ratio for objects in the shared pool.

15.5 Identify the Database Buffer Cache Hit Ratio

The database buffer cache contains the database blocks most recently read. When a user or application requests data from the Oracle server, Oracle looks for the requested data block in the buffer cache. If Oracle is less than 70% successful when it tries to find data in the buffer cache, then you should consider increasing the size of the buffer cache if system memory permits. This How-To presents a method to determine the buffer cache hit ratio.

15.6 Assess the Impact of Adding Database Buffers

You have used the analysis in the preceding How-To and discovered that increasing the size of the database buffer cache is justified. In this case, it would be useful to know what kind of improvement in the buffer cache hit rate we could expect if we add some number of additional buffers to the cache. Oracle has provided a method to do just that and this How-To guides you through the process.

15.7 Record and Save Performance Statistics Over Time

It is fair to say that DBAs have a service contract with the users who depend on the database. One way to be sure that the terms of that contract are upheld is to refer to the historical performance of the database. Many tools, and indeed the techniques in this chapter so far, can summarize database performance *right now*, but do not provide a way of populating performance history. This How-To provides a method of tracking a few of the most important performance indicators, the cache hit rates, over time.

15.8 Identify Rollback Segment Contention

The Oracle8 server uses rollback segments primarily to allow users and applications to undo uncommitted database changes. Rollback segments also serve to provide a read-consistent view of the database in a multi-user environment. Oracle8 writes changed records to the rollback segments for all uncommitted transactions. If the database does not contain enough rollback segments for the system load, contention for rollback segments can reduce system performance. This How-To presents a method to identify and correct rollback segment contention within the database. This section also briefly considers some other common rollback segment problems.

15.9 Determine the Best Size for the Redo Log Buffer

Oracle redo log files are crucial to recovery operations. The redo log buffer is an area in the SGA where all Oracle redo data resides before the LGWR (Log Writer) process writes it to the physical redo log files. Insufficient space in the redo log buffer can degrade performance. This How-To discusses methods for determining if user processes are waiting for redo log buffer space.

15.10 Measure and Improve Checkpoint Performance

The Oracle server heavily utilizes memory as a temporary storage medium. Because memory is volatile, the Oracle background processes that comprise an Oracle instance copy data from memory to disk on a regular basis. Checkpoints are a particularly thorough example of this behavior and can degrade performance if ill-behaved. This How-To focuses on analyzing checkpoint performance and suggests ways to improve it.

15.11 Measure and Improve Overall Sort Performance

Sorting is a resource intensive database operation. The Oracle server provides many parameters that database users can change in an attempt to tune sorts, but the most important sort performance goal is to maximize the number of sorts Oracle performs in memory versus the sorts Oracle performs on disk. This How-To explains a method to compare memory sorts and disk sorts and provides some suggestions about improving this ratio if possible.

15.12 Detect Contention for the Database Buffer Cache

The best indicator of database buffer cache performance is the hit ratio discussed in How-To 15.5. It is possible, however, that contention for the database buffer cache could degrade database performance. This How-To focuses on determining the presence and cause of database buffer cache contention.

15.13 Detect and Resolve Lock Contention

Oracle provides safe data concurrency through locking mechanisms. There is no question that locks will cause contention; that is, after all, what they are designed to do. The kind of contention that DBAs and developers want to avoid is *unnecessary* lock contention. In almost all situations, Oracle's default locking mechanisms are satisfactory. When Oracle suffers from locking problems, it is often because a user or application has either requested an unnecessary lock or has failed to manage transactions properly. This How-To will not review all possible DML and DDL lock situations. It goes right to the bottom line and shows you how to determine who holds a lock that is blocking some other user and what you can do to resolve the situation.

COMPLEXITY
ADVANCED

15.1 How do I...
Run the UTLBSTAT and UTLESTAT scripts?

Problem

I want to run the UTLBSTAT and UTLESTAT scripts to get a general overview of my database's performance over a certain period of time. How and when should I do this?

Technique

Run the UTLBSTAT at database startup or, if you're interested in database activity during a particular time period, run it just prior to the beginning of that period. Run the UTLESTAT script at database shutdown or immediately after the period of database activity of interest. These scripts contain a CONNECT INTERNAL command so users cannot run them in their original form from the SQL*Plus environment; either Server Manager or the Oracle SQL Worksheet utility must be the calling environment for these scripts. This How-To shows how to call the statistics scripts from the SQL Worksheet utility and suggests modifications to these scripts to redirect their DDL activity away from the SYSTEM tablespace, which is the (unfortunate) default.

Steps

1. Run SQL Worksheet, connect as the WAITE user, and open the script called CHP15_1.SQL.

NOTE

Open scripts in SQL Worksheet by using the Open button on the left side of the window, or by using the Open command on the File drop-down menu.

Run the script by pressing the F5 key. The first action the script takes is to connect to the database as internal. This forces you to supply the password and the database service name again. The script and the last part of its output appear in Figure 15.1.

The first line of the CHP15_1.SQL script alters the user SYS so that SYS' default tablespace is USERS instead of SYSTEM. The second line calls the UTLBSTAT script and the third line sets SYS' default tablespace back to SYSTEM.

NOTE

The CHP15_1.SQL script assumes that your database has a tablespace called USERS as suggested in How-To 1.6. If this is not the case, then change the CHP15_1.SQL script so that it makes a valid change to user SYS' default tablespace.

---

2. Wait for the database activity of interest to occur. This can be a particular long-running batch job or it may just be standard business day database activity.

3. Run SQL Worksheet, connect as the WAITE user, and open the script called CHP15_2.SQL. Run the script by pressing the F5 key. The script and the last part of its output appears in Figure 15.2.

How It Works

UTLBSTAT creates tables and views containing cumulative database performance summary information at the time when the script runs. All the objects UTLBSTAT creates contain the word *begin*.

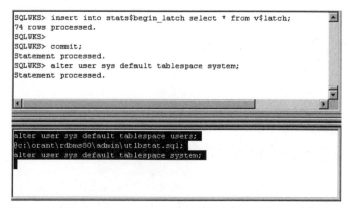

Figure 15.1 Running the script CHP15_1.SQL to call the Oracle-supplied UTLBSTAT script.

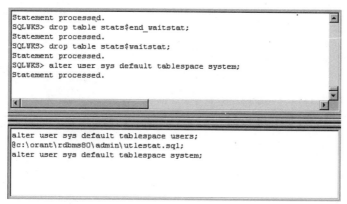

Figure 15.2 Running the script CHP15_2.SQL to call the Oracle-supplied UTLESTAT script.

UTLESTAT creates tables and views containing database objects containing cumulative database performance summary information at the time when its script runs. The names of the tables and views that UTLESTAT creates all contain the word *end*. UTLESTAT's most important function is to submit SQL statements summarizing performance information for the time period between UTLBSTAT and UTLBSTAT's submissions. UTLESTAT spools the results of these SQL statements to a file called REPORT.TXT, which resides in the directory that was current at the time of UTLESTAT's submission.

Comments

The UTLBSTAT and UTLESTAT scripts were developed by Oracle for Oracle kernel developers. Some of the information that UTLESTAT generates has little meaning even to experienced DBAs, but the report does contain valuable information if you know where to look.

This chapter takes a double-edged approach, and wherever possible, the How-To's refer to the relevant sections of the UTLESTAT report on the premise that no matter what Oracle installation readers call home, UTLBSTAT and UTLESTAT will be there. In order to provide a customizable approach, in addition, the chapter also contains scripts that query the data dictionary to reveal performance data.

The scripts CHP15_1.SQL and CHP15_2.SQL are nothing more than jackets for the UTLESTAT and UTLBSTAT scripts. Their sole purpose is to redirect the tables created by the statistics scripts to a tablespace other than SYSTEM. This is a worthwhile endeavor, because the statistics scripts create, populate, and drop a series of database objects, which is exactly the kind of activity that should *not* occur in the SYSTEM tablespace.

An alternative to the jacket scripts is to modify the UTLBSTAT and UTLESTAT scripts to use another tablespace. The only drawback to this strategy is the resulting need to create copies of the statistics scripts with each new release of the Oracle server.

COMPLEXITY
ADVANCED

15.2 How do I...
Identify unbalanced I/O and I/O contention?

Problem

I am trying to improve database performance. I want to detect unbalanced physical disk loading and disk I/O contention. How do I identify I/O contention and load imbalance?

Technique

The UTLESTAT report contains a section summarizing file statistics. This section appears in Listing 15.1. Table 15.1 summarizes each column in this section of the UTLESTAT report.

Listing 15.1 An excerpt from the FILE I/O section of the UTLESTAT report

```
SVRMGR> select table_space, file_name,
     2>        phys_reads reads, phys_blks_rd blks_read, phys_rd_time read_time,
     3>        phys_writes writes, phys_blks_wr blks_wrt, phys_wrt_tim write_time,
     4>        megabytes_size megabytes
     5> from stats$files order by table_space, file_name;

TABLE_SPACE  FILE_NAME      READS BLKS_READ READ_TIME WRITES BLKS_WRT WRITE_TIME
-----------  -------------  ----- --------- --------- ------ -------- ----------
AUTO09       C:\AUTO09.DAT      0         0         0      0        0          0
RBS          C:\RBS.DAT         8         8        10      8        8          8
SYSTEM       C:\SYSO8HT.ORA  1204      1632       517     86       86        146
TEMP         C:\TEMP.DAT        0         0         0      0        0          0
USERS        C:\USERS.DAT      13        13        21     28       28         24
```

Table 15.1 An explanation of the columns in the FILE I/O section of the UTLESTAT report

COLUMN	COLUMN DESCRIPTION
TABLE_SPACE	Name of the tablespace
FILE_NAME	Name of physical file name
READS	Number of physical reads completed
BLKS_READ	Number of blocks read

COLUMN	COLUMN DESCRIPTION
READ_TIME	Time in milliseconds for reads
WRITES	Number of physical writes completed
BLKS_WRT	Number of blocks written
WRITE_TIME	Time in milliseconds for writes
MEGABYTES (not shown)	Size of tablespace in megabytes

Steps

1. Make sure that the initialization parameter TIMED_STATISTICS is set to TRUE in the INIT.ORA file. If TIMED_STATISTICS is FALSE, then the read and write times in the UTLESTAT report are always 0.

To change the value of TIMED_STATISTICS, shutdown the database, change the INIT.ORA so that the parameter TIMED_STATISTICS is TRUE, and restart the database.

2. Repeat the steps in How-To 15.1 to create the statistics report. The section of this report that focuses on I/O performance appears in Listing 15.1. Alternatively, start SQL*Plus, connect as the WAITE user, and use the START command to load and execute the script CHP15_3.SQL. The script and its output appear in Figure 15.3.

3. Examine the section of the UTLESTAT report exhibited in Listing 15.1 or review the results of the CHP15_3.SQL script.

```
SQL> start chp15_3
SQL>
SQL> SELECT
  2        df.name,
  3        fs.phyrds reads,
  4        fs.phywrts writes,
  5        (fs.readtim / decode(fs.phyrds,0,-1,fs.phyrds)) readtime,
  6        (fs.writetim / decode(fs.phywrts,0,-1,phywrts)) writetime
  7   FROM
  8        v$datafile df,
  9        v$filestat fs
 10   WHERE
 11        df.file# = fs.file#
 12   ORDER BY
 13        df.name;

NAME                              READS    WRITES  READTIME  WRITETIME
--------------------------------- -------- ------- --------- ---------

D:\ORANT\DATABASE\RBS.DAT             27       175 3.1481481 1.6628571
D:\ORANT\DATABASE\SYSORCL.ORA       1951        73 .85853409 1.7260274
D:\ORANT\DATABASE\TEMP.DAT             0         0         0         0
D:\ORANT\DATABASE\USERS.DAT           28        98 9.7142857 2.2244898

SQL>
```

Figure 15.3 Running the script CHP15_3.SQL in SQL*Plus to report file I/O performance statistics.

How It Works

Step 1 ensures that timing information is part of the UTLESTAT report. Step 2 generates the report which is the subject of analysis in Step 3. The goal is to evenly distribute reads and writes across all of the I/O devices. If moving a data file furthers this aim, then take the tablespace containing the data file offline and use the ALTER TABLESPACE command with the RENAME DATAFILE option to move the datafile to an I/O device with lighter traffic.

If the physical disk load is balanced, then you can identify contention across I/O devices by examining the READ_TIME and WRITE_TIME columns in the section of the UTLESTAT report reproduced in Listing 15.1. If the I/O devices on a database server are of the same speed rating and there are significant differences between the read or write times for different devices, then contention is a problem. The only way to address this is to balance loads for all applications on the system, including non-Oracle applications, or to acquire more or faster I/O devices.

Comments

Remember that the UTLESTAT report can only indicate disk I/O generated by the Oracle8 server and that UTLESTAT will not reveal I/O from other applications. This is why, if possible, it is ideal to configure database servers so that Oracle and non-Oracle files exist on separate devices.

The exact causes of load imbalance depend on the focus of the database. In online transaction processing (OLTP) systems featuring heavy delete activity, one cause of load imbalance can be the placement of all the rollback segments in a single tablespace on a single device. In decision support systems (DSS) with significant sort activity caused by ORDER BY or GROUP BY operations, load imbalance can exist because there is only a single temporary storage area and every user needs it at the same time.

Load imbalance and contention may be alleviated by using tablespace striping, which is the subject of the next How-To. Another method is to utilize table and index partitioning to spread large and heavily-used tables across multiple I/O devices. Information on table partitioning can be referred to in Chapter 4.

COMPLEXITY
ADVANCED

15.3 How do I...
Stripe a tablespace across multiple devices?

Problem

Some heavily used tablespaces are causing contention on my database server's disk devices. It doesn't make sense to move the objects out of the tablespace and I want to stripe the tablespace across devices to reduce contention. Performance for simultaneous access of the tablespace will also be greatly improved if the tablespace spans multiple devices. How do I stripe a tablespace?

Technique

You can stripe a new tablespace at the database level when you initially create it by specifying multiple datafiles existing on more than one physical disk in the CREATE TABLESPACE statement. You can stripe an existing tablespace by using the ALTER TABLESPACE statement to create new, additional datafiles on other drives.

Steps

1. Run SQL*Plus and connect as the WAITE user account. Use the START command to load and execute the CHP15_4.SQL script. The script and its output appears in Listing 15.2. The file contains a CREATE TABLESPACE statement distributing a single tablespace over multiple devices. The format of this statement assumes that you have three disk drives with drive designations C:, D:, and E:. If you do not have these drives, or if your operating system environment features different physical path specifications, then change the statement in script CHP15_4.SQL to reference valid disk drives and physical files on your system.

Listing 15.2 Running script CHP15_4.SQL in SQL*Plus to create a striped tablespace

```
SQL>  START CHP15_4
  1   CREATE TABLESPACE WAITE_TBS
  2      DATAFILE 'C:\WAITE1.ORA' SIZE 1M,
  3               'D:\WAITE2.ORA' SIZE 1M,
  4               'E:\WAITE3.ORA' SIZE 1M
Tablespace created.
```

Line 1 identifies the statement with the CREATE TABLESPACE keyword and specifies the name of the tablespace as WAITE_TBS. Lines 2 through 4 specify the three datafiles making up the tablespace. The filename of the datafiles and the size are specified on each line.

2. Use the start command to load and execute CHP15_5.SQL into the SQL buffer. This script, which appears in Listing 15.3, adds an additional datafile to an existing tablespace. The goal is to add this new datafile to a disk other than the one housing the tablespace's original data files. In this case, the script adds the additional data file to the tablespace created in Step 1. This statement assumes that an F: drive exists on your system. If this is not a valid drive designation or physical filename for your system, change the drive and filename to comply with your operating system's conventions.

Listing 15.3 Running script CHP15_5.SQL in SQL*Plus to add a file on a different device to an existing tablespace

```
SQL>  START CHP15_5
  1   ALTER TABLESPACE WAITE_TBS
  2       ADD DATAFILE
  3       'F:\WAITE4.ORA' SIZE 1M
```

Line 1 identifies the statement as an ALTER TABLESPACE statement and specifies that the WAITE_TBS tablespace will be modified. Line 2 presents the keywords ADD DATAFILE to specify that a new datafile will be created. Line 3 specifies the datafile to be created and its size. The filename specification is operating system specific.

When a new datafile is created, the tablespace begins using it as space is needed. Adding a new datafile to a nearly empty tablespace does not ensure that the load will be balanced across the files, because no objects can reside in the new datafile until the first datafile no longer accommodates them.

How It Works

Step 1 creates a new tablespace using the CREATE TABLESPACE statement and distributes the tablespace over three datafiles, each located on a separate disk drive. Step 2 adds a datafile to the tablespace created in Step 1 using the ALTER TABLESPACE statement with an ADD DATAFILE clause. Striping a tablespace does not ensure that all the datafiles will be used equally; the Oracle8 server uses datafile blocks as needed.

Comments

The performance gains, which will be most dramatic on large database servers, only materialize if the datafiles created exist on separate physical devices. When you perform this How-To on your own computer, you may not have the disk drives specified in the statements. You can modify the statements to work on your computer. The method presented in this How-To is a less reliable performance enhancement than creating new tablespaces on separate drives and placing objects in them manually. Under this methodology users and DBAs can take advantage of their specific knowledge of database usage patterns to control precisely which objects exist on which physical drives.

Another way to stripe tablespaces is to use operating system striping if your database server supports this capability. UNIX and NT database servers, for example, support disk striping at the operating system level.

Indeed, if the SYSTEM tablespace is suffering from contention then this option may be the only viable choice. Operating system striping works best if the stripe size is a multiple of the batch size for full table scans. The initialization parameter DB_FILE_MULTIBLOCK_READ_COUNT determines the record batch size for full table scans.

Table and index partitioning is worth mentioning again here. These capabilities in conjunction with a DBA's intimate knowledge of data distributions afford Oracle8 users finer control over I/O balancing than operating system *or* database level striping.

COMPLEXITY
ADVANCED

15.4 How do I...
Determine shared pool performance?

Problem

As part of my performance tuning strategy, I want to make sure that the hit ratio in the shared pool is acceptable. Because the shared pool contains the dictionary cache and the library cache, performance can suffer greatly if it is not large enough. How do I determine the hit ratio in the shared pool?

Technique

The shared pool is one of the three main memory structures in the system global area (SGA). It is comprised of the data dictionary cache and the library cache. The data dictionary cache buffers in memory data dictionary objects that contain data about tables, indexes, users, and all the rest of the database's objects.

Every database action requires information from the data dictionary. If that information is not in the data dictionary cache section of memory, then Oracle8 must get it from disk. If this happens consistently, then database performance suffers.

The shared pool also contains the library or SQL cache. The library cache buffers previously executed queries, so they need not be reloaded and re-parsed if a user calls them again. If a SQL statement is executed repeatedly but cannot reside in the SQL cache because it is too small, performance improvements are possible.

The UTLESTAT report contains sections focusing on the library and dictionary caches. Listings 15.4 and 15.5 show excerpts from those sections of the report summarizing library and data dictionary cache performance, respectively.

Listing 15.4 The library cache performance section of the UTLESTAT report

```
SVRMGR> Rem Select Library cache statistics. The pin hit rate should be high.
SVRMGR> select namespace library,
    2>        gets,
    3>        round(decode(gethits,0,1,gethits)/decode(gets,0,1,gets),3)
    4>          gethitratio,
    5>        pins,
    6>        round(decode(pinhits,0,1,pinhits)/decode(pins,0,1,pins),3)
    7>          pinhitratio,
    8>        reloads, invalidations
    9>   from stats$lib;
```

LIBRARY	GETS	GETHITRATI	PINS	PINHITRATI	RELOADS	INVALIDATI
BODY	0	1	0	1	0	0
CLUSTER	36	1	16	1	0	0
INDEX	0	1	0	1	0	0
OBJECT	0	1	0	1	0	0
PIPE	0	1	0	1	0	0
SQL AREA	30	.767	81	.802	2	0
TABLE/PROCED	63	.968	57	.93	0	0
TRIGGER	0	1	0	1	0	0

In Listing 15.4, the column PINS represents the number of executions of SQL statements that reside, in parsed form, in the library cache. The column RELOADS indicates the number of attempts to execute items that existed at one time in the library cache but have been aged out of the cache to make room for other items. The general rule is that the ratio of RELOADS to PINS should not exceed .01 (or 1%).

Listing 15.5 The data dictionary cache performance section of the UTLESTAT report

```
SVRMGR> Rem get_miss and scan_miss should be very low compared to the requests.
SVRMGR> Rem cur_usage is the number of entries in the cache that are being used.
SVRMGR> select * from stats$dc
    2>  where get_reqs != 0 or scan_reqs != 0 or mod_reqs != 0;
```

NAME	GET_REQS	GET_MISS	SCAN_REQ	SCAN_MIS	MOD_REQS	COUNT	CUR_USAG

dc_tablespaces	5	0	0	0	0	10	4
dc_users	9	0	0	0	2	4	1
dc_objects	47	2	0	0	0	118	111
dc_usernames	24	0	0	0	0	20	1
dc_object_ids	36	2	0	0	0	84	83

In Listing 15.5, the values in the column GET_REQS are the number of times Oracle requested data dictionary information on the object categories in the NAME column. The column GET_MISS is the number of requests that the dictionary cache could not accommodate because the requested item had aged out of the cache. In these cases, Oracle8 had to go to disk to satisfy the request. A good rule of thumb is that the ratio of GET_MISS to GET_REQ should not exceed .15 (or 15%).

The V$LIBRARYCACHE view shown in Table 15.2 stores performance data for the library cache. The V$ROWCACHE view shown in Table 15.3 stores performance data for the data dictionary cache.

Table 15.2 Some of the columns comprising the V$LIBRARYCACHE view

COLUMN	COLUMN DESCRIPTION
NAMESPACE	Library cache namespace
GETS	The number of times a lock was requested for objects of this namespace
GETHITS	The number of times Oracle8 found an object's handle in memory
GETHITRATIO	The ratio of GETHITS to GETS
PINS	Number of executions of an item in this namespace
PINHITS	The number of times all the meta data pieces of the library object were found in memory
PINHITRATIO	The ratio of PINHITS to PINS
RELOADS	Number of times an item from this namespace must be reread from disk
INVALIDATIONS	The total number of times objects in this namespace were marked invalid because of a dependent object modification

Table 15.3 Some of the columns comprising the V$ROWCACHE view

COLUMN	COLUMN DESCRIPTION
CACHE#	Row cache ID number
COUNT	Total number of entries in the cache
GETS	Total number of requests for information of this cache#
GETMISSES	Number of unsatisfied requests

The library cache is working efficiently when the ratio of RELOADS to PINS is less than 1%. The data dictionary cache is optimized when the number of GETMISSES to GETS is less than 15%. If the cache performance does not satisfy these guidelines, then increase the value of the initialization parameter SHARED_POOL_SIZE.

Steps

1. Run SQL*Plus and connect as the WAITE user account. Use the START command to load and execute the CHP15_6.SQL script to query the V$LIBRARYCACHE view and report on library cache performance. The script and its output appear in Figure 15.4.

Lines 1 and 2 of the CHP15_6.SQL script compute the sums of all of the pins and reloads for all the object types maintained in the library cache. Line 3 calculates the miss ratio for the library cache. Remember that ideally this ratio will not exceed 1%.

2. While still connected as the WAITE user in SQL*Plus, use the START command to load and execute the CHP15_7.SQL script. The script and its output appears in Figure 15.5.

Line 1 of CHP15_7.SQL calculates the sum of all GETS and GETMISSES for the data dictionary cache. Line 2 computes the percentage of time the requested object did not reside in the cache. Ideally, this ratio will not exceed 15%.

```
SQL> start chp15_6
SQL>
SQL> SELECT sum(pins) pins,
  2          sum(reloads) reloads,
  3          round((sum(reloads) / sum(pins))*100,0) "LCache % Misses"
  4  FROM v$librarycache;

      PINS    RELOADS LCache % Misses
---------- ---------- ----------------
      3102          0                0

SQL> |
```

Figure 15.4 Running the script CHP15_6.SQL in SQL*Plus to report library cache performance statistics.

```
SQL> start chp15_7
SQL>
SQL> SELECT sum(gets), sum(getmisses),
  2          round(sum(getmisses)/sum(gets)*100,0) "DCache % Misses"
  3  FROM v$rowcache;

 SUM(GETS) SUM(GETMISSES) DCache % Misses
---------- -------------- ----------------
      1061            118               11

SQL> |
```

Figure 15.5 Running the script CHP15_7.SQL in SQL*Plus to report dictionary cache performance statistics.

How It Works

The miss percentages for the library cache and the data dictionary cache indicate the overall health of the shared pool. Step 1 highlights a SQL statement to determine the library cache miss ratio; Step 2 does the same for the data dictionary cache.

Comments

If the data dictionary cache miss percentage exceeds 15 percent, then you have no options for improvement except to increase the size of the shared pool by increasing the value of the SHARED_POOL_SIZE parameter in the initialization parameter file.

Other options to improve the performance of the library cache exist as well. Encourage users, for example, to share SQL statements whenever possible because even the subtlest difference in syntax, like a case change, can result in SQL statement reparsing. The use of packages, in addition, increases the library cache hit rate because whenever any user accesses any part of a package Oracle8 loads the entire package into the library cache.

Whether you use the UTLESTAT report or the queries from Steps 1 and 2 to assess the shared pool performance level, give the database sufficient time to calculate shared pool statistics. Otherwise, the numbers that either of these methods return may not be meaningful.

COMPLEXITY
ADVANCED

15.5 How do I...
Determine the buffer cache hit ratio?

Problem

I want to make sure that the database is reading from memory, rather than from disk, whenever possible. If the buffer cache hit ratio is too low, I could benefit by adding more database block buffers to the SGA. I don't want to add database block buffers without analyzing the hit ratio, however, because I may be unnecessarily committing memory that the operating system needs. How do I identify the database buffer cache hit ratio?

Technique

Whenever Oracle reads data from disk, it places that data into the database buffer cache so that it is available for future read requests generated by any database user. Data is "aged out" of the buffer cache using a least recently used

(LRU) algorithm. When users or applications request data, Oracle first looks in the buffer cache, starting at the most recently used (MRU) end of the LRU list. If the requested block does not exist in the buffer cache, either because it was never there or because it has aged out, then Oracle must search the disk-based data files that comprise the database.

On most production systems, Oracle should not have to resort to disk reads more than 20% of the time. Listing 15.6 shows an excerpt of the section of the UTLESTAT report that reveals the database buffer cache hit rate.

Listing 15.6 The data dictionary cache performance section of the UTLESTAT report

```
Statistic                    Total     Per Transact Per Logon   Per Second
--------------------------   ---------- ------------ ----------- -----------
consistent gets                 15100        15100        7550      188.75
db block gets                     110          110          55        1.38
physical reads                   1728         1728         864        21.6
```

To use this report to determine the buffer cache hit ratio, use this formula:

```
hit ratio = (consistent gets + db block gets)/( consistent gets +
db block gets + physical reads) * 100
```

Another method to determine the buffer cache hit rate is to query the V$SYSSTAT dynamic performance view. Table 15.4 contains a description of this view.

Table 15.4 The V$SYSSTAT dynamic performance view

COLUMN	COLUMN DESCRIPTION
STATISTIC#	Statistic number
NAME	Statistic name
CLASS	Statistic class:
	1 (User)
	2 (Redo)
	4 (Enqueue)
	8 (Cache)
	16 (OS)
	32 (Parallel Server)
	64 (SQL)
	128 (Debug)
VALUE	Statistic value

Steps

1. Start SQL*Plus and connect as the WAITE user. Use the start command to load and execute the script contained in the file called CHP15_8.SQL. This script and its output appear in Figure 15.6.

Lines 2 and 3 of this query calculate the total number of disk read operations that the buffer cache satisfied. Lines 5 through 7 of the query calculate the total number of read operations. The SUM operator in conjunction with the DECODE function forces the query to return a single row. This is preferable to joining the V$SYSSTAT table with itself three times to get the desired results.

How It Works

Step 1 queries the V$SYSSTAT dynamic performance view to calculate the hit ratio. The formula makes use of the SUM operator and the DECODE function to return a single calculation instead of multiple rows.

Comments

If the buffer cache hit value returned by Step 1 is less than 80 percent, you should consider increasing the size the database buffer cache in the SGA, which can be done by increasing the value for DB_BLOCK_BUFFER in the initialization parameter file. There is an economy to observe here, though. If you are too stingy with the DB_BLOCK_BUFFER parameter then the buffer cache hit rate will not improve, at least not by much. Increase DB_BLOCK_BUFFER too greatly, though, and the SGA will consume so much memory that general operating system performance will suffer. So if the database buffer cache hit rate *is* less than 80%, how many additional buffers do you need to bump this value up to 80%? The answer is the subject of the next section.

```
SQL> start chp15_8
SQL>
SQL> SELECT
  2      (sum(decode(name,'db block gets',value, 0)) +
  3      sum(decode(name, 'consistent gets', value, 0)))
  4      /
  5      (sum(decode(name,'db block gets',value, 0)) +
  6       sum(decode(name, 'consistent gets', value, 0)) +
  7       sum(decode(name, 'physical reads', value, 0))) * 100
  8      "DB Buffer Cache Hit %"
  9  FROM v$sysstat
 10  WHERE name IN ('physical reads', 'db block gets', 'consistent gets');

DB Buffer Cache Hit %
---------------------
          89.216821

SQL> |
```

Figure 15.6 Running the script CHP15_8.SQL in SQL*Plus to determine the database buffer cache hit rate.

15.6 How do I...
Assess the impact of adding database buffers?

Problem

I executed the steps in the preceding How-To and have discovered that I should increase the size of the database buffer cache. Is there some way of determining what sort of buffer cache hit rate improvement I can expect by devoting some number of additional buffers to the database buffer cache?

Technique

> **NOTE**
>
> The UTLESTAT report does not address this topic.

The database buffer cache is so important to the overall performance level of the Oracle server that a mechanism determines the improvements in the cache hit rate as a function of adding additional buffers to the buffer cache. Suppose, for example, that you know you can afford to devote 500 more buffers to the database buffer cache. (If the database block size is 2048 bytes, then these 500 additional buffers would consume 1 megabyte of memory). Oracle provides a way for you to assess the number of additional cache hits you will generate by increasing the buffer cache size by any amount between 1 and 500 database blocks.

Set the value of initialization parameter DB_BLOCK_LRU_EXTENDED_ STATISTICS to the number of database block buffers you are considering for addition to the database buffer cache. Query the table X$KCBRBH to determine the number of additional cache hits generated by each additional database buffer block. Use this number to determine the improvement in the buffer cache hit rate, and, finally, increase the size of the initialization parameter DB_BLOCK_BUFFERS accordingly.

The structure of the X$KCBRBH table appears in Table 15.5.

Table 15.5 Two helpful columns in the X$KCBRBH dynamic performance table

COLUMN	COLUMN DESCRIPTION
INDX	New buffer identifier
COUNT	How many additional cache hits will be generated by adding the buffer to the buffer cache

Steps

1. Check the value of the initialization parameter DB_BLOCK_LRU_EXTENDED_STATISTICS by manually reviewing the INIT.ORA file or by using the SHOW PARAMETER DB_BLOCK_LRU_EXTENDED_STATISTICS command in either the server manager or SQL Worksheet utilities.

2. If you want to change the value of this parameter, shut down the database, alter the INIT.ORA file by setting DB_BLOCK_LRU_EXTENDED_STATISTICS to the number of maximum number of buffers you wish to consider adding to the buffer cache, and restart the database.

3. Allow the database to run in normal mode during what is, for your installation, a typical period of database activity.

4. Start a SQL*Plus session and connect to the database as the SYS user; only SYS has access to the X$KCBRBH table we are about to use. Use the start command to load and execute the script in CHP15_9.SQL. This script queries the X$KCBRBH table as shown in Figure 15.7 and prompts the user for the number of additional buffers to consider.

Line 3 of the script contains a substitution variable for the number of additional buffers, the impact of which you want to assess. In Figure 15.7, the script reports that the addition of 25 buffers to the database buffer cache will result in 20 additional cache hits.

5. Use the start command to load and execute the script CHP15_10.SQL. This SQL statement in this script is a modification of a statement from the last How-To. The script prompts the user for the number of additional cache hits reported in the previous step. The script and its output appear in Figure 15.8.

```
SQL> start chp15_9 25
SQL>
SQL> SELECT sum(count) extra_cache_hits
  2  FROM x$kcbrbh
  3  WHERE indx < &1;
old    3: WHERE indx < &1
new    3: WHERE indx < 25

EXTRA_CACHE_HITS
----------------
              20

SQL>
```

Figure 15.7 Running the script CHP15_9.SQL in SQL*Plus to determine the number of additional cache hits resulting from adding buffers to the database buffer cache.

```
SQL> SELECT
  2    round (
  3     (sum(decode(name,'db block gets',value, 0)) +
  4      sum(decode(name, 'consistent gets', value, 0)))
  5     /
  6     (sum(decode(name,'db block gets',value, 0)) +
  7      sum(decode(name, 'consistent gets', value, 0)) +
  8      sum(decode(name, 'physical reads', value, 0))
  9       - &1) * 100,
 10     0) new_hit_rate
 11  FROM v$sysstat
 12  WHERE name IN ('physical reads', 'db block gets', 'consistent gets');
Enter value for 1: 20
old   9:     - &1) * 100,
new   9:     - 20) * 100,

NEW_HIT_RATE
------------
          91

SQL>
SQL>
SQL> |
```

Figure 15.8 Running the script CHP15_10.SQL in SQL*Plus
to determine the improvement in the buffer cache hit rate
generated by additional cache hits.

This script is a modification of CHP15_8.SQL. The change is in line 9, where the script reduces the number of physical disk reads by the number of additional cache hits generated in Step 4. The new cache hit rate, after the addition of 20 additional buffer blocks, will be 91%, an acceptable value.

How It Works

Oracle only populates the X$KCBRBH table if the DB_BLOCK_LRU_EXTENDED_STATISTICS parameter is set to a non-zero value in the initialization parameter file. Steps 1 and 2 describe how to reset this parameter. The scripts in Steps 4 and 5 report the number of additional cache hits and the improvement in the overall database buffer cache hit rate that will be generated by additional cache buffer blocks.

Comments

One PL/SQL procedure can contain the functionality of each of the scripts in Steps 4 and 5. The procedure BC_GROW (for "buffer cache grow") shows how; it appears in Listing 15.7.

Listing 15.7 The PL/SQL procedure BC_GROW created by CHP15_11.SQL and used to assess buffer cache hit improvements generated by additional buffer cache blocks

```
SQL> create or replace procedure bc_grow (buffers number)
  2  AS
  3      extra_cache_hits    number;
  4      new_hit_rate        number;
  5  BEGIN
  6
  6  SELECT SUM(t1.count) INTO extra_cache_hits
  7  FROM x$kcbrbh t1
  8  WHERE indx < buffers;
  9
  9  SELECT
 10     (sum(decode(name,'db block gets',value, 0)) +
 11      sum(decode(name, 'consistent gets', value, 0)))
 12      /
 13     (sum(decode(name,'db block gets',value, 0)) +
 14      sum(decode(name, 'consistent gets', value, 0)) +
 15      sum(decode(name, 'physical reads', value, 0))
 16      - extra_cache_hits) * 100
 17  INTO new_hit_rate
 18  FROM v$sysstat
 19  WHERE name IN ('physical reads', 'db block gets', 'consistent
gets');
 20
 20  dbms_output.put_line ('the number of additional cache hits is: '
 21     || to_char(extra_cache_hits));
 22
 22  dbms_output.put_line ('the new hit rate is: '
 23     || to_char(new_hit_rate));
 24
 24  END;
```

This procedure accepts one parameter as input, which contains the number of additional buffers whose impact you wish to assess. Lines 6 through 8 contain SQL that is functionally equivalent to script CHP15_9.SQL to generate the number of additional cache hits resulting from the extra buffers. Note that the use of the correlation column is necessary to avoid compilation errors. Without it, PL/SQL confuses the COUNT column name with the COUNT aggregation operator and complains about the absence of a GROUP BY clause. Lines 9 through 12 are functionally equivalent to the SQL contained in the CHP15_10.SQL and report the new buffer cache hit rate.

Run the **bc_grow** procedure using the EXECUTE command, as shown in Figure 15.9.

```
SQL> execute bc_grow(20);
the number of additional cache hits is: 21
the new hit rate is: 91

PL/SQL procedure successfully completed.

SQL> |
```

Figure 15.9 Running the bc_grow procedure to assess the impact of additional buffer cache memory.

It may be tempting to set the value of DB_BLOCK_LRU_EXTENDED_ STATISTICS and forget it. This way, you can query the X$KCBRBH table at will to determine the cost effectiveness of adding more buffers to the database cache. This may not be advisable, though, because Oracle incurs processing costs when DB_BLOCK_LRU_EXTENDED_STATISTICS is not 0.

COMPLEXITY

ADVANCED

15.7 How do I...
Record and save performance statistics over time?

Problem

I want to be able to refer to a history of performance statistics. This is important so that I can prove that the database is performing consistently, and also to help me recognize patterns in database performance. How can I save performance history data?

Technique

> **NOTE**
>
> The UTLESTAT report does not address this topic.

Create a table to hold performance history data. For the purposes of this How-To, the table will contain the hit rates for the library cache, the database buffer cache, and the dictionary cache. There are certainly other values of interest, but these will suffice as an example.

On a regular basis, run a script that determines the performance statistic values and stores them in the performance history table. The data definition language to create the performance history table is in CHP15_12.SQL and appears in Listing 15.8; Table 15.6 summarizes the table's structure.

Listing 15.8 The script CHP15_12.SQL creates the PERF_HIST table

```
SQL> create table perf_hist
  2  (
  3      insert_date       date,
  4      lc_miss_ratio     number(3,0),
  5      db_hit_ratio      number(3,0),
  6      dc_miss_ratio     number(3,0),
  7  constraint perf_hist_pk primary key (insert_date)
  8      using index pctfree 5 tablespace users
  9      storage(initial 100K
 10              next    10K
 11              pctincrease 0)
 12  )
 13  tablespace users
 14  storage
 15      (initial 200K
 16      next     20k
 17      pctincrease 0)
 18  pctfree 2 pctused 90;
```

Notice that the **pctused** parameter is quite large and that the **pctfree** parameter is quite small. These parameter values are justified for a table that will primarily be a target of *insert*, instead of *update*, activity.

Table 15.6 The structure of the PERF_HIST table

COLUMN	COLUMN DESCRIPTION
INSERT_DATE	Generation date of the performance statistic
LC_MISS_RATIO	Library cache miss ratio
DC_MISS_RATIO	Dictionary cache miss ratio
DB_HIT_RATIO	Database buffer cache hit ratio

Steps

1. Start SQL*Plus and connect as the WAITE user. Use the START command to load and execute the data definition language in CHP15_12.SQL. This script creates the PERF_HIST table in the USERS tablespace.

> **NOTE**
>
> The USERS tablespace will exist if you followed the suggestions in How-To 1.6. If your database does not include a USERS tablespace, then modify the CHP15_12.SQL script to place the PERF_HIST table in a valid tablespace.

2. Run the script in CHP15_13.SQL to populate the PERF_HIST table with the current values of the cache hit rates. The script appears in Listing 15.9.

Listing 15.9 The script CHP15_13.SQL in SQL*Plus populates the PERF_HIST table

```
SQL> insert into perf_hist (insert_date) values (sysdate);

1 row created.

SQL>
SQL> -- INSERT THE LIBRARY CACHE MISS RATIO
SQL> -- INTO THE PERFORMANCE HISTORY TABLE
SQL>
SQL> update perf_hist set lc_miss_ratio =
  2  (
  3   SELECT round((sum(reloads) / sum(pins))*100,0)
  4   FROM v$librarycache
  5  )
  6  where insert_date =
  7  (
  8   select max(insert_date) from perf_hist
  9  );

1 row updated.

SQL>
SQL>
SQL> -- INSERT THE DATABASE BUFFER CACHE HIT RATIO IN THE
SQL> -- PERFORMANCE HISTORY TABLE
SQL>
SQL> update perf_hist set db_hit_ratio =
  2  (
  3   SELECT
  4     (sum(decode(name,'db block gets',value, 0)) +
  5      sum(decode(name, 'consistent gets', value, 0)))
  6     /
  7     (sum(decode(name,'db block gets',value, 0)) +
  8      sum(decode(name, 'consistent gets', value, 0)) +
  9      sum(decode(name, 'physical reads', value, 0))) * 100
 10   FROM v$sysstat
 11   WHERE name IN ('physical reads', 'db block gets',
'consistent gets')
 12  )
 13  where insert_date =
 14  (
 15   select max(insert_date) from perf_hist
 16  );

1 row updated.

SQL>
SQL>
SQL> -- INSERT THE DICTIONARY CACHE MISS RATIO
SQL> -- IN THE PERFORMANCE HISTORY TABLE
SQL>
```

```
SQL> update perf_hist set dc_miss_ratio =
  2  (
  3    SELECT round(sum(getmisses)/sum(gets)*100,0) "DCache
% Misses"
  4    FROM v$rowcache
  5  )
  6  where insert_date =
  7  (
  8    select max(insert_date) from perf_hist
  9  );

1 row updated.
```

The first line of this script inserts the current date into the performance history table. The next three insert statements modify this newly inserted row. This technique results in a script that is easier to read than one featuring one large insert statement. The three update statements are slight variations on scripts appearing in previous sections in this chapter.

How It Works

The script in Step 1 creates the table to store the performance history data. The SQL statements in Step 2 update the table with cache performance data.

Comments

This section is not an exhaustive guideline for what performance statistics one should gather. Even a superficial consideration suggests that other statistics are just as worthy of preservation. The techniques in this section, though, will serve equally well for whatever statistics you wish to gather.

If your organization shuts down the database instance(s) on some regular schedule, then the shutdown script may be an a good place to run the performance statistic script (CHP15_13.SQL, shown previously). If your database must be available on a 24-by-7 basis, then CHP15_13.SQL, or some variation of it, could run as part of a scheduled job submitted with the DBMS_ JOB built-in package.

COMPLEXITY
ADVANCED

15.8 How do I...
Identify rollback segment contention?

Problem

I administer a database with significant amounts of update, delete, and insert activity. I know that rollback segment contention can degrade performance in a database environment like mine. How can I determine if my database is suffering from rollback segment contention?

Technique

Oracle8 uses rollback segments for all transactions that change the database and assigns every such transaction to one of the available rollback segments. Every rollback segment has a transaction table in its header and every write transaction, moreover, must periodically acquire update access to the transaction table of its rollback segment.

Contention becomes an issue when Oracle8 has assigned more than one transaction to any given rollback segment, and those transactions attempt to access the rollback segment's transaction table at the same time.

The UTLESTAT report contains a section on rollback segment statistics, which appears in Listing 15.10.

Listing 15.10 An excerpt from the rollback segment performance section of the UTLESTAT report

UNDO_SEGMENT	TRANS_TBL_GETS	TRANS_TBL_WAITS
0	7	0
1	412	42
2	652	57
3	1121	127
4	65	7
5	72	9

The column TRANS_TBL_GETS contains the number of number of times that Oracle accessed the header of the rollback segment specified (by rollback segment number, unfortunately) in the UNDO_SEGMENT column. The column TRANS_TBL_WAITS contains the number of these gets, which results in a temporary wait state because another transaction already accessed the rollback segment's header.

A school of thought maintains that any non-zero value in the TRANS_TBL_WAITS column should prompt the DBA to add rollback segments. This is too conservative for most production installations and a better guideline to follow is that whenever the ratio of TRANS_TBL_WAITS to TRANS_TBL_GETS is greater than 2 percent for any rollback segment, there is rollback segment contention.

Another way to detect rollback segment contention is to use the V$ROLLSTAT table. It appears in Table 15.7.

Table 15.7 The structure of the V$ROLLSTAT table

COLUMN	COLUMN DESCRIPTION
USN	Rollback segment number
EXTENTS	Number of rollback extents
RSSIZE	Rollback segment size in bytes
WRITES	Number of bytes written to rollback segment
XACTS	Number of currently active transactions
GETS	Number of header gets
WAITS	Number of header waits
OPTSIZE	Optimal size of rollback segment
HWMSIZE	High water mark of rollback segment size
SHRINKS	Number of times the size of a rollback segment decreases
WRAPS	Number of times rollback segment is wrapped
EXTENDS	Number of times rollback segment size is extended
AVESHRINK	Average shrink size
AVEACTIVE	Current size of active extents, averaged over time
STATUS	Rollback segment status
CUREXT	Current extent
CURBLK	Current block

Like the rollback performance section of the UTLESTAT report, the V$ROLLSTAT view uses the rollback segment number instead of the name to identify each rollback segment. The V$ROLLNAME table, appearing in Table 15.8, maps the rollback segment number to the rollback segment name.

Table 15.8 The structure of the V$ROLLNAME table

COLUMN	COLUMN DESCRIPTION
USN	Rollback segment number
NAME	Rollback segment name

Steps

1. Start SQL*Plus and connect as the WAITE user. Use the **START** command to load and execute the query in CHP15_14.SQL. The query and its result appear in Figure 15.10.

Line 4 of the script calculates the waits to gets ratio for each *online* rollback segment in the database.

```
SQL> start chp15_14
SQL>
SQL> SELECT  rn.name,
  2             rs.gets,
  3             rs.waits,
  4             round((rs.waits / rs.gets) * 100, 0) wg_ratio
  5  FROM
  6             v$rollstat rs,
  7             v$rollname rn
  8  WHERE
  9             rs.usn = rn.usn;

NAME         GETS        WAITS       WG_RATIO
------       --------    ---------   ---------
SYSTEM       229         0           0
RBS1         497         1           0
RBS2         215         0           0
RBS3         215         0           0
RBS4         215         0           0
RBS5         215         0           0

6 rows selected.

SQL>
```

Figure 15.10 Running the script CHP15_14.SQL
to detect rollback segment contention.

How It Works

The query in Step 1 joins the V$ROLLSTAT and V$ROLLNAME dynamic
performance tables to help detect rollback segment contention. If the value of
WG_RATIO consistently exceeds 2%, then adding more rollback segments may
help.

Comments

Oracle database literature often focuses on rollback segment contention and
sizing. Most discussions of rollback segment sizing begin with the expected size
of an "average" transaction. This number is difficult to come by in most
organizations. A better and much simpler strategy is to use the general rule of
thumb that there should be one rollback segment for every ten concurrent users
or one rollback segment for every four concurrent transactions.

Oracle indicates some common rollback segment errors with the messages
`failure to extend` and `snapshot too old`. The former error is easy to
understand: a large transaction has consumed all the rollback segment's extents
or all the available space in the rollback segment tablespace. The `snapshot too
old` message means that some transaction was using a rollback segment to
obtain a read consistent view of the database and the rollback segment was
overwritten with new rollback (or "undo") data. Either of these messages
indicates a need for larger rollback segments.

Most tuning literature currently suggests that rollback segments should be
composed of 20 equally sized extents. The OPTIMAL parameter of the

STORAGE clause for a rollback segment, as in script CHP1_4.SQL in Chapter 1, will request that Oracle8 attempt to maintain a particular rollback segment size. If the SHRINKS or EXTENDS columns in the V$ROLLSTAT table are significantly different than zero, then the DBA should reconsider rollback segment sizes.

It is often difficult to size rollback segments optimally for an Oracle instance if that instance is both a decision support system and an OLTP target. In the former case, users and applications probably will not be making significant use of the rollback segments because their database access is often of the read-only variety.

In the latter situation, even if the size of an average transaction is fairly clear and quite small, there will undoubtedly be a need for a large database batch job. Oracle developers realize this and Oracle features the SET TRANSACTION statement to enable users to specify a particular (and usually large) rollback segment.

COMPLEXITY
ADVANCED

15.9 How do I...
Determine the best size for the redo log buffer?

Problem

I accepted the default value for the LOG_BUFFER initialization parameter, which determines the size of the redo log buffer. How can I tell if the size of the redo log buffer is sufficient?

Technique

User processes that make database changes signal server processes to write redo entries into the redo log buffer. Oracle uses these entries during recovery operations to reconstruct database changes. Every time the Log Writer (LGWR) background process "wakes up," it writes the contents of the redo log buffer to the disk-based redo log files. Specifically, it writes every redo entry in the buffer that user processes have copied there since the last LGWR operation. This frees redo log buffers for subsequent writes from user processes. More than one event can trigger LGWR, but at the very least, LGWR writes every three seconds.

Usually, LGWR is fast enough to keep up with user processes' database changes. If it is not, then user processes may have to wait for free buffers in the redo log buffer, and this degrades performance.

The UTLESTAT report contains some statistics that can help you identify redo log buffer waits. Listing 15.11 contains the relevant section from the report.

Listing 15.11 An excerpt from the UTLESTAT report summarizing redo log buffer waits

```
Statistic                      Total     Per Transact Per Logon
----------------------------   --------- ----------- ---------
redo entries                      4686         16.33     60.08
redo log space requests              2           .01       .03
```

The value in the **Total** column for the statistic `redo log space requests` should be close to zero. If it is not, then try increasing the value of the initialization parameter LOG_BUFFER until the statistic is near zero, indicating few waits for redo log buffers.

Alternatively, use the dynamic performance table V$SYSSTAT which appeared previously in Table 15.4.

Steps

1. Start SQL*Plus and connect as the WAITE user. Use the START command to load and execute the query in CHP15_15.SQL. The query and its result appear in Figure 15.11.

How It Works

CHP15_11.SQL queries the V$SYSSTAT dynamic performance view. If the value of the `redo log space requests` statistic is significantly different from 0, then increase the size of the LOG_BUFFER initialization parameter.

Comments

Another alternative involves the V$SYSTEM_EVENT dynamic performance view which appears in Table 15.9.

```
SQL> start chp15_15
SQL>
SQL> SELECT name, value
  2  FROM v$sysstat
  3  WHERE name = 'redo log space requests';

NAME                            VALUE
------------------------------- ---------
redo log space requests             3

SQL> |
```

Figure 15.11 Running the script CHP15_15.SQL in SQL*Plus to detect redo log buffer waits.

Table 15.9 The structure of the V$SYSTEM_EVENT table

COLUMN	COLUMN DESCRIPTION
EVENT	Event name
TOTAL_WAITS	Total waits for EVENT
TOTAL_TIMEOUTS	Total timeouts for EVENT
TIME_WAITED	Time waited for EVENT (in hundredths of a second)
AVERAGE_WAIT	Average time waited for EVENT (in hundredths of a second)

One of the events in the V$SYSTEM_EVENT table is `log file space/switch`. If the value of TOTAL_WAITS is significantly and consistently different than zero, then consider increasing the value size of the redo log buffer. Figure 15.12 contains the result of the SQL script contained in CHP15_16.SQL.

NOTE

The statistics in V$SYSTEM_EVENT will not be meaningful unless the TIMED_STATISTICS initialization parameter is set to TRUE. Also, if there are no waits for a particular event, then that event will not appear in the V$SYSTEM_EVENT dynamic performance view.

The query includes the timing information from the TIME_WAITED and AVERAGE_WAIT columns to put this tuning effort into perspective. Unless response time is extremely precious at your installation, redo log buffer waits usually will not degrade performance noticeably.

```
SQL> start chp15_16
SQL>
SQL> SELECT event, total_waits, time_waited, average_wait
  2  FROM v$system_event
  3  WHERE event = 'log file space/switch';

EVENT                     TOTAL_WAITS TIME_WAITED AVERAGE_WAIT
------------------------- ----------- ----------- ------------
log file space/switch               9         326   36.2222222

SQL>
```

Figure 15.12 Running the script CHP15_16.SQL in SQL*Plus to detect redo log buffer waits via the V$SYSTEM_EVENT dynamic performance view.

15.10 How do I...
Measure and improve checkpoint performance?

Problem

I want to review my database's checkpoint performance. If it checkpoints too frequently, then performance will degrade, but if it does not checkpoint enough then recovery, if necessary, could be particularly time consuming. How do I analyze checkpoint performance and improve it if possible?

Technique

When a database checkpoints, the Log Writer (LGWR) and Database Writer (DBWR) background processes write all the dirty buffers in the database buffer cache and the redo log buffer to disk, respectively and in this order. Checkpoints occur in a variety of situations, but regardless of the values of all other database parameters, Oracle initiates a checkpoint at every log switch. Recall that LGWR writes to redo log files in a circular fashion, proceeding automatically to the next file (this is the log switch) when the current file is full.

The database can encounter two problems during a checkpoint. The first occurs when Oracle initiates a second checkpoint before a prior checkpoint is complete. This results in some unnecessary I/O but is not particularly detrimental to performance. The second problem is a bit more complex and requires some understanding of the redo log structure. Oracle cannot let LGWR overwrite any redo entries that might be necessary for instance recovery. Oracle cannot be sure that redo entries are unnecessary until the DBWR process has written the corresponding data from the database buffer cache to disk. So, if, during a checkpoint, LGWR tries to overwrite a redo log file before the DBWR process has written the corresponding database buffer cache buffers to disk, then Oracle forces LGWR to wait. If this happens often, then performance can degrade.

The UTLESTAT report helps you determine if your database is initiating a second checkpoint before Oracle has completed a prior one (the first problem). If this is a consistent problem, then the solution is to increase the size of the redo log files. The alert log indicates if LGWR is waiting for checkpoint completion during log switches (the second problem). As for problem 1, the solution here is also to increase redo log file size, but another possibility is to add more redo log groups.

Steps

1. Review the section of the UTLESTAT report indicated in Listing 15.12.

Listing 15.12 An excerpt from the UTLESTAT report summarizing checkpoint performance

Statistic	Total	Per Transact	Per Logon	Per Second
DBWR timeouts	8	8	4	.2
SQL*Net roundtrips to/from	28	28	14	.7
background checkpoints comp	2	4	2	.1
background checkpoints star	4	4	2	.1
background timeouts	38	38	19	.95

If the values in the total column for background checkpoints comp and background checkpoints star differ by more than one as they do in Listing 15.12, then Oracle does not have enough time between log switches to complete checkpoints. The only solution is to use larger redo log files.

2. Start a SQL*Plus session and connect as the WAITE user. Use the START command to load and execute the script CHP15_17.SQL. The script and its output appear in Figure 15.13.

This script is a subtle variation of the CHP1_5.SQL script from Chapter 1. The only difference is in line 3 where CHP15_17.SQL retrieves the size of each redo log member. This script reports that there are three redo log groups and that the size of each redo log member file is 200K.

3. The only way to change the size of redo log groups is to add new groups with redo log members of the desired size. Use the START command to load and execute the script CHP15_18.SQL. The script and its output appear in Figure 15.14.

```
SQL> start chp15_17
SQL>
SQL> SELECT vl.group#, members,
  2          vl.status groupstat,
  3          vf.member, vl.bytes
  4  FROM v$log vl, v$logfile vf
  5  WHERE vf.group# = vl.group#;

  GROUP#  MEMBERS GROUPSTAT MEMBER                                 BYTES
  ------- -------- --------- -------------------------------------- --------
       1        2 CURRENT   D:\ORANT\DATABASE\LOG1ORCL.ORA         204800
       1        2 CURRENT   D:\ORANT\DATABASE\LOG1ORCLM.ORA        204800
       2        2 INACTIVE  D:\ORANT\DATABASE\LOG2ORCL.ORA         204800
       2        2 INACTIVE  D:\ORANT\DATABASE\LOG2ORCLM.ORA        204800
       3        2 UNUSED    D:\ORANT\DATABASE\LOG3ORCL.ORA         204800
       3        2 UNUSED    D:\ORANT\DATABASE\LOG3ORCLM.ORA        204800

6 rows selected.
```

Figure 15.13 Running the script CHP15_17.SQL in SQL*Plus to determine the current redo log configuration.

```
SQL> start chp15_18
SQL>
SQL> ALTER DATABASE ADD LOGFILE
  2      ('d:\orant\database\log4orcl.ora',
  3       'd:\orant\database\log4orclm.ora')
  4  SIZE 500K;

Database altered.

SQL>
```

Figure 15.14 Running the script
CHP15_18.SQL in SQL*Plus to add a
new redo log group with larger
member files.

CHP15_18.SQL adds a fourth multiplexed redo log group where each
redo log member is of size 500K. Modify the script to create as many new
log groups as you need.

NOTE

Script CHP15_18 is operating system-specific because it contains
physical file names. Modify it to match your database's naming
conventions and your operating system's physical file names
before using it.

4. Use the START command to load and execute the script CHP15_19.SQL
to drop the log file groups whose members were too small. The script and
its output appear in Figure 15.15.

5. Oracle records important database events, like database startups and
shutdowns, in the alert log. The initialization parameter
BACKGROUND_DUMP_DEST points to the location of the alert log. The
alert log is a text file and its name usually contains the word *alert*. Review
the alert log for your database to determine if LGWR is waiting for
checkpoints to complete. Any messages resembling the one in Listing
15.13 indicate that LGWR is waiting for checkpoint completion.

```
SQL> start chp15_19
SQL>
SQL> ALTER DATABASE DROP LOGFILE GROUP 1;

Database altered.

SQL>
```

Figure 15.15 Running the script
CHP15_19.SQL in SQL*Plus to
drop redo log groups.

Listing 15.13 An excerpt from the alert log indicating that LGWR is waiting for a checkpoint to complete

```
Thread 1 cannot allocate new log, sequence 9905
Checkpoint not complete
```

6. If this message appears often in the alert log, then LGWR waits are probably adversely affecting database performance. The solution is to add more redo log groups or to increase the size of your redo log members. In either case, modify the scripts CHP15_18.SQL and CHP15_19.SQL to accomplish either of these tasks.

How It Works

Step 1 shows an excerpt from the UTLESTAT report indicating that Oracle does not have enough time between log switches to complete checkpoint processing. Step 2 highlights a script to report on the current redo log configuration. Steps 3 and 4 show how to add new redo log groups and drop existing groups respectively. Step 5 shows how the alert log can indicate contention between the checkpoint processing and the LGWR process.

Comments

If, in Step 4, you receive a message like this one:

```
ORA-01623: log 3 is current log for thread 1 - cannot drop
```

then the group you tried to drop is the current redo log group. Prior to re-attempting Step 4, force a log switch with this command:

```
alter system switch logfile;
```

The alert log is noteworthy. You should review it on a regular basis as part of proactive database monitoring. Oracle writes to this text file on a cumulative basis so it can grow very large. You may want to delete it or archive it to facilitate review.

Two initialization parameters affect checkpoint processing. The first is LOG_CHECKPOINT_TIMEOUT, which specifies the number of seconds between each checkpoint. Oracle ignores this parameter if its value is 0, the default. If this parameter has a non-zero value, then Oracle checkpoints at log switches and every X seconds, where X is the value of LOG_CHECKPOINT_TIMEOUT.

The second initialization parameter is LOG_CHECKPOINT_INTERVAL, which specifies the number of operating system blocks that Oracle writes to the redo log between each checkpoint. If you only want Oracle to checkpoint at log switches, make sure that the value of this parameter exceeds the size of the redo log members. Determining the operating system block size may not be straightforward; under NT or Windows 95, use the CHKDSK command on the drive where the redo log files reside. CHKDSK will report that some number of bytes exist in each allocation unit; this is the operating system block size. The default value of LOG_CHECKPOINT_INTERVAL under Windows NT is 10,000 operating system blocks.

The LOG_CHECKPOINT_INTERVAL and LOG_CHECKPOINT_TIMEOUT initialization parameters are useful if your installation features large redo log files and you want checkpoints to occur more frequently than at every log switch.

COMPLEXITY
ADVANCED

15.11 How do I...
Determine and improve overall sort performance?

Problem

I suspect that my database's sort performance is not optimal. I know that Oracle performs some sorts on disk and some sorts in memory and that memory-based sorts are faster than disk sorts. How can I tell if Oracle is performing too many disk-based sorts? If this is the case, how can I improve the situation?

Technique

When a user connects to the Oracle server and creates a session, Oracle creates an area in memory called the Process Global Area or Program Global Area (PGA). Part of this area is dedicated to user-requested sorts. Index creation, ORDER BY and DISTINCT clauses, and some joins all cause Oracle to undertake sorting operations.

If the sort area in the PGA is large enough then Oracle performs the sort in memory. Otherwise, Oracle splits the data to be sorted into smaller pieces, sorts them, writes them to temporary segments on disk, and finally reassembles them to complete the sort. This is one way that the Oracle server may use disk space, as opposed to memory, to complete a sort.

Oracle may also utilize disk for sorts, even when the entire sort could occur in memory. The sort could begin in memory, for example, but then Oracle may attempt to free some PGA memory to reference some data that is not part of the sort area. In this case, Oracle will write a temporary disk segment to contain some of the sorted data.

The UTLESTAT report contains a section summarizing sort performance; it appears in Listing 15.14.

Listing 15.14 An excerpt from the FILE I/O section of the UTLESTAT report

```
SVRMGR> Rem The total is the total value of the statistic between the time
SVRMGR> Rem bstat was run and the time estat was run. Note that the estat
SVRMGR> Rem script logs on as "internal" so the per_logon statistics will
SVRMGR> Rem always be based on at least one logon.
```

Statistic	Total	Per Transact	Per Logon	Per Second
sorts (disk)	40	3	1	.1
sorts (memory)	110	11	5.5	.2
sorts (rows)	653	653	326.5	12.09

The ratio given by sorts(disk)/sorts(memory)x100 should be less than five percent. If this is not the case, as shown in Listing 15.14, then you may wish to consider increasing the values of the initialization parameters SORT_AREA_SIZE or SORT_AREA_RETAINED_SIZE. SORT_AREA_SIZE is the initial size of the sort area in the PGA; its default under Windows NT is 65536 bytes. SORT_AREA_RETAINED_SIZE describes the minimum size to which Oracle can shrink the sort area during a sort. Its Windows NT default value is 0.

Another way to check the ratio of disk sorts to memory sorts is to query the dynamic performance view V$SYSSTAT. The structure of this view appeared earlier in this chapter in Table 15.4.

Steps

1. Run SQL*Plus, connect as the WAITE user, and use the start command to load and execute the script called CHP15_20.SQL. The script and its output appears in Figure 15.16.

The script joins the V$SYSSTAT dynamic performance view with itself in lines 3 through 5 to extract the values for disk sorts and memory sorts from the view.

```
SQL> start chp15_20
SQL>
SQL> SELECT sd.value disksorts, sm.value memsorts,
  2         round(sd.value/sm.value*100,0) "ratio(%)"
  3  FROM v$sysstat sd, v$sysstat sm
  4  WHERE sd.name = 'sorts (disk)' and
  5        sm.name = 'sorts (memory)';

DISKSORTS  MEMSORTS  ratio(%)
---------  --------  --------
        0      1613         0

SQL>
```

Figure 15.16 Running the script CHP15_20.SQL in SQL*Plus determines the ratio of disk sorts to memory sorts. The ratio should be less than 5%.

2. If the ratio reported by the CHP15_20 script or by the UTLESTAT report exceeds five percent, then increase the value of initialization parameter SORT_AREA_SIZE and/or SORT_AREA_RETAINED_SIZE by shutting down the database, modifying the values of these parameters in the INIT.ORA file, and restarting the database.

How It Works

Step 1 queries the V$SYSSTAT table to determine the ratio of memory sorts to disk sorts. If the ratio exceeds 5%, Step 2 increases the value of the appropriate initialization parameters.

Comments

Unless your Oracle installation is using the multithreaded server (MTS), increasing the value of initialization parameters SORT_AREA_SIZE and SORT_AREA_RETAINED_SIZE will not increase the size of the SGA. The sort area resides in the PGA in this case. If your installation is using the MTS, the sort area is part of the shared pool and in this case it could cause problems if it becomes too large.

The 5% guideline for the ratio of disk sorts to memory sorts is most realistic for an online transaction processing (OLTP) system. If your database is serving as a datamart or a decision support system (DSS), then the importance of response time will probably exceed any premium on the disk to memory sort ratio.

COMPLEXITY
ADVANCED

15.12 How do I...
Detect contention for the database buffer cache?

Problem

I have used the techniques from How-To's 15.5 and 15.6 to determine and tune the database buffer cache hit rate. I have heard that there can be contention for the database buffer cache. How do I detect database buffer cache contention and minimize or eliminate it?

Technique

There are two potential causes of database buffer cache contention. The first occurs when user processes have to skip an increasing number of dirty buffers to find a clean one. This situation generates waits. The second kind of contention is latch contention. A latch is a serialization mechanism that protects the structures residing in the SGA; Oracle uses many different types of latches.

User processes need a particular latch, the *cache buffer chains* latch, when they look for free buffers in the database buffer cache. A second user requesting this latch must wait for the current holder of the latch to release it. In this way, the cache buffer chains latch serializes requests on behalf of user processes that need to scan the database buffer cache.

The UTLESTAT report contains statistics that may help you identify both of these potential contention problems. Listings 15.15 and 15.16 show excerpts from the report, which highlights database buffer wait statistics and database buffer latch contention, respectively.

Listing 15.15 An excerpt from the UTLESTAT report showing buffer cache wait statistics

```
SQLDBA> Rem The total is the total value of the statistic between the time
SQLDBA> Rem bstat was run and the time estat was run. Note that the estat
SQLDBA> Rem script logs on as "internal" so the per_logon statistics will
SQLDBA> Rem always be based on at least one logon.

Statistic                      Total        Per Transact Per Logon
----------------------------   ----------   ------------ ---------
.
.
free buffer inspected              6             6          1
free buffer requested           3832          3832     638.67
.
.
```

Increasing values for the `free buffer inspected` statistic indicate an increasing number of database waits for the a clean buffer in the buffer cache. Increasing the size of the buffer cache can help.

Listing 15.16 An excerpt from the UTLESTAT report showing latch wait statistics

```
SQLDBA> Rem Sleeps should be low. The hit_ratio should be high.

LATCH_NAME          GETS       MISSES      HIT_RATIO   SLEEPS      SLEEPS/MISS
-----------------   ---------- ----------- ----------- ----------- -----------
.
.
cache buffer handl    50           0           1          0            0
cache buffers chai 66642          0           1          0            0
.
.
```

A hit ratio value, shown in the fourth column of Listing 15.16, of less than .95 may indicate a latch contention problem.

The statistics in the UTLESTAT report are also available in the dynamic performance views of the Oracle8 data dictionary. You can query the V$SYSSTAT dynamic performance view, shown previously in Table 15.4, to determine database buffer cache wait statistics. Query the V$LATCH dynamic performance views V$LATCH (it appears in Table 15.10) to show latch wait statistics.

Table 15.10 The structure of the V$LATCH dynamic performance view

COLUMN	COLUMN DESCRIPTION
ADDR	Address of latch
LATCH#	Latch number
LEVEL#	Latch level
NAME	Latch name
GETS	Satisfied latch requests
MISSES	Latch requests satisfied after one failure

Steps

1. Run SQL*Plus, connect as the WAITE user, and use the start command to load and execute the script CHP15_21.SQL. The script and its output appears in Figure 15.17.

2. Use the START command to load and execute the script CHP15_22.SQL (see Figure 15.18).

```
SQL> start chp15_21
SQL>
SQL> SELECT value FROM v$sysstat
  2  WHERE name = 'free buffer inspected';

    VALUE
----------
       20

SQL>
```

Figure 15.17 Running the script CHP15_21.SQL in SQL*Plus.

```
SQL> start chp15_22
SQL>
SQL> SELECT name, gets, misses,
  2         round((gets-misses)/gets, 1)*100 "HIT RATIO(%)"
  3  FROM v$latch
  4  WHERE latch# = 21;

NAME                        GETS    MISSES HIT RATIO(%)
------------------- ----------- ----------- ------------
cache buffers chains       13497           2          100

SQL> |
```

Figure 15.18 Running the script CHP15_22.SQL in SQL*Plus.

3. If the results of the scripts in the preceding steps suggest that buffer waits or latch contention is becoming problematic, shutdown the database, increase the value of initialization parameter DB_BLOCK_BUFFERS, and restart the database.

How It Works

Step 1 queries the V$SYSSTAT dynamic performance view to determine the number of buffers scanned by user processes looking for a free buffer. Step 2 queries the V$LATCH dynamic performance view to determine the hit rate for the cache buffers chains latch.

If Step 1 indicates a large number of buffers scanned or Step 2 reports that a cache buffers chains latch hit ratio is less than .98, then increasing the size of the database buffer cache, as shown in Step 3, may help.

Comments

In general, latch performance is easy to measure but difficult to improve. Often, the only way to do so is to increase the amount of resource governed by the latch, which in this case is the size of the database buffer cache. Increasing the number of latches may be useful in an SMP environment but will not improve latch performance on single processor platforms. Nor is there any general consensus on the effect of the SPIN_COUNT initialization parameter, which is alleged to change the behavior of all latches.

COMPLEXITY
ADVANCED

15.13 How do I...
Detect and resolve lock contention?

Problem

The users of my database are complaining about poor response times, but my database monitoring does not reveal any problems. I suspect that competing object locks may be the cause of the perceived performance problems. How can I determine if my database is suffering from locking problems and, if it is, how can I eliminate these difficulties?

Technique

Except for deadlocks, which this How-To briefly addresses in the comments section, lock wait requests in an Oracle database will *never* time out. Consequently, lock waits can make application performance look appalling to an end-user. The Oracle data dictionary captures more lock data than most people would ever want to know and in fact, so much locking information is in dynamic performance views, like V$SESSION and V$LOCK and in DBA_LOCKS, that it's difficult to know where to start. Stepping back for a moment though, it seems likely that DBAs and developers really want to answer one simple locking question when users are screaming that "the database is slow:" is anyone holding a lock that is delaying someone else?

Fortunately, Oracle provides a script, UTLLOCKT.SQL, that greatly simplifies the process of answering this question. In order to see it in action, suppose that the following events have occurred:

✔ User SCOTT has issued this DML statement:

```
SELECT * FROM emp FOR UPDATE;
```

✔ User WAITE has issued this DML statement:

```
UPDATE emp SET DEPTNO=30 WHERE username = 'MILLER';
```

In response to SCOTT's query, Oracle8 will issue a Row Share lock that involves an exclusive lock on all the rows (in this case, all the rows in the table) returned by SCOTT's query. WAITE's query needs a Row Exclusive DML lock on EMP also, but SCOTT is in the way. The important fact here is that SCOTT is blocking WAITE.

Steps

1. Run SQL*Plus, connect as the SYS user, and run the script CHP15_23.SQL. This script creates the database objects that the script in the next step requires. You need only run the CHP15_23.SQL script once.

2. Run the script CHP15_24.SQL. The script's output appears in Figure 15.19.

```
SQL> start chp15_24

WAITING_SID LOCK_TYPE                    MODE_REQUESTED MODE_HELD
----------- ---------------------------  -------------- --------------
9           None
    13      Transaction                  Exclusive      Exclusive


Table dropped.


USERNAME                              SID
---------------------------------- ----------
SCOTT                                  9
SYS                                   12
WAITE                                 13

SQL> |
```

Figure 15.19 Running the script CHP15_24.SQL in
SQL*Plus to determine monitor locking activity.

How It Works

The script in Step 1 creates a number of database objects needed by the
UTLLOCKT script. Step 2 runs a modified version of the UTLLOCKT script to
show locking contention. The first part of the output from the CHP15_24.SQL
script in Step 2 shows that session 13 is waiting for session 9. The second
section indicates that session 9 belongs to the user SCOTT and that session 13
belongs to the user WAITE.

Comments

What happened to the UTLLOCKT script, where did the script in Step 1 come
from, and what is its function?

The script in Step 1, CHP15_23.SQL, is a modification of the
CATBLOCK.SQL script that Oracle supplies with the Oracle8 release. It is
intended to configure the data dictionary for the use of the UTLLOCKT script.
Under Windows NT, CATBLOCK.SQL resides in the \ORANT\RDBMS80\
ADMIN subdirectory.

Unfortunately, in the Oracle8 beta release, an in-line comment on the last line
of the statement that creates the DBA_LOCK view prevents the script from
running correctly. Without this view, the UTLLOCKT script will not run either.
CHP15_23 is a corrected version of the original CATBLOCK.SQL script.

The script in Step 2, CHP15_24.SQL, is a modified version of the UTLLOCKT script that generates more legible output. Under Windows NT, the original version of the script resides in the\ORANT\RDBMS80\ADMIN subdirectory.

Once you have detected a locking problem, what should you do about it? There are essentially two options. The first is to find the user who holds the blocking lock, SCOTT in the example above, and ask him to rollback or commit his transaction. If SCOTT is unavailable, he may be very unpopular. You can restore some of his damaged reputation by issuing the `alter system kill session` command from server manager to rollback all of his transactions, release any locks that he holds, and terminate his connection to the database.

Deadlocks occur when two sessions are hung up waiting for each other. This is the only sort of lock that Oracle will resolve on its own. To do so, it will pick one session and rollback all of its transactions, releasing the locks that the session holds.

Oracle's locking mechanisms are usually fast and effective. Be careful if you choose to exceed Oracle's default locking levels in your applications.

CREATE AN OBJECT RELATIONAL DATABASE

16

CREATE AN OBJECT RELATIONAL DATABASE

How do I...

Oracle Corporation has chosen not to abandon its relational database roots with the release of Oracle8. Accordingly, this new version of the database is not purely object-oriented. It still supports all the relational technology that has

593

become an integral part of many organizations' database environments. Object extensions, however, comprise one of the most exciting enhancements to the Oracle database under Oracle8.

An *object relational* database is a fusion of relational and object-oriented technologies and enables users to gradually integrate object technology with existing relational applications. Developers can use objects in relational tables, create pure object tables, and define object views to allow object-oriented navigation of existing relational structures under the Oracle8 umbrella.

16.1 Create Object Types and Use Them in Relational Tables

The easiest way for relational database users to become familiar with object-oriented database technology is to draw parallels between database objects and standard relational database tables. In some ways, these entities are not that different. This How-To explains creation of object types and their inclusion in relational table definitions.

16.2 Use Constructor Methods to Populate Object Relational Tables

The SQL syntax for populating tables containing object columns is also new in Oracle8. This How-To introduces the concept of a method and shows how to use a particular type of method, called a *constructor* method, to insert data into object-enabled relational tables.

16.3 Create and Use Object Tables

How-To 16.1 showed how to integrate object types and relational table definitions. Object tables, the subject of this section, are one step closer to pure object-oriented constructions. This How-To defines object tables and discusses how to use them to enforce the foreign key relationships common to relational database designs.

16.4 Create and Use the VARRAY Collection Type

Collection types have played a major role in object-oriented languages for some time and Oracle8 offers an ordered collection type through the VARRAY datatype. Definition and use of VARRAYs are the subjects of this How-To.

16.5 Create and Use the Nested Table Collection Type

Nested tables are another collection type supported in Oracle8. Like VARRAYs, they can help model one-to-many relationships without the overhead associated with traditional joins. This How-To focuses on the definition and use of nested tables.

16.6 Create and Use Object Views

Object views provide a way to impose an object structure over a relational database design without disturbing legacy applications. They provide a low-risk migration path to object-oriented architectures. This How-To describes creating an object view of some familiar sample database tables.

16.7 Issue DML Commands on Object Views and Use INSTEAD OF Triggers

This How-To explains extracting and inserting data into underlying relational tables using object views. SELECT syntax is straightforward, but INSERT statements on object views featuring joins may require use of a new Oracle8 feature, the INSTEAD OF trigger.

This new capability also enhances the usefulness of a feature first found in Oracle 7.3: updatable join views. These database entities had some limitations arising from the inherent ambiguity of update operations on joined tables. INSTEAD OF triggers address these limitations for updatable join views and for updatable object views. This How-To discusses construction of an INSTEAD OF trigger to increase the update flexibility of the object view from the previous section.

16.8 Use MAP and ORDER Methods to Compare Objects

Many common database functions, including indexing, sorting, and joining require Oracle8 to compare database objects. The results of these comparisons are obvious when the values Oracle8 must compare are traditional scalar quantities. Users and developers need to instruct Oracle8, however, about how to compare database *objects*. This How-To introduces member methods and explains definition and use of MAP and ORDER methods in particular.

COMPLEXITY
BEGINNING

16.1 How do I...
Create object types and use them in relational tables?

Problem

I can see how database objects can closely model some of the business entities in my database. How do I create database objects and include these object types within traditional relational structures?

Technique

Most Oracle users are familiar with the tables in the schema SCOTT that contain data about a fictional company, its locations, and its employees. The structure of the DEPT table in SCOTT's schema appears in Table 16.1.

Table 16.1 The traditional structure of the DEPT table from the schema SCOTT

COLUMN	COLUMN DESCRIPTION
DEPTNO	Department Number
DNAME	Department Name
LOC	Department Location

This How-To will create an object type called DEPT_TYPE to model the structure of the DEPT table and use the new object type to define a new version of the EMP table. Table EMP's traditional structure appears in Table 16.2.

Table 16.2 The traditional structure of the EMP table from the schema SCOTT

COLUMN	COLUMN DESCRIPTION
EMPNO	Employee Number
ENAME	Employee Name
JOB	Employee Job Title
MGR	Number of Employee's Manager
HIREDATE	Employee's Hire Date
SAL	Employee's Salary
COMM	Employee's Commission
DEPTNO	Employee's Department Number

The Oracle8 data dictionary contains some new entities to accommodate object extensions. This How-To will query the DBA_TYPE_ATTRS view that appears in Table 16.3.

Table 16.3 The structure of the DBA_TYPE_ATTRS data dictionary view

COLUMN	COLUMN DESCRIPTION
OWNER	Type owner
TYPE_NAME	Type name
ATTR_NAME	Attribute name
ATTR_TYPE_MOD	Attribute's type modifier
ATTR_TYPE_OWNER	Attribute's type owner
ATTR_TYPE_NAME	Type attribute's name
LENGTH	Length of CHAR/VARCHAR attributes
PRECISION	Decimal precision of numeric attributes
SCALE	Scale of numeric attributes
CHARACTER_SET_NAME	Character set name

Steps

1. Start SQL*Plus, connect as the WAITE user, and use the START command to load and execute the script CHP16_1.SQL. The script and its output appear in Figure 16.1.

The script creates a new object type, called DEPT_TYPE16, with attributes matching the column definitions from the familiar DEPT table.

2. Use the START command to load and execute the script CHP16_2.SQL. The script and its output appear in Figure 16.2.

Note that the last line of the DESCRIBE statement's output lists the DEPT column with a datatype of NAMED TYPE.

```
SQL> start chp16_1
SQL>
SQL> CREATE TYPE dept_type16 (
  2       deptno      number(2),
  3       dname       varchar2(14),
  4       loc         varchar2(23)
  5  );

Type created.

SQL>
SQL>
```

Figure 16.1 Running the script CHP16_1.SQL in SQL*Plus to create the DEPT_TYPE16 object type.

```
SQL> start chp16_2
SQL>
SQL> CREATE TABLE emp16 (
  2     EMPNO     NUMBER(4),
  3     ENAME     VARCHAR2(10),
  4     JOB       VARCHAR2(9),
  5     MGR       NUMBER(4),
  6     HIREDATE DATE,
  7     SAL       NUMBER(7,2),
  8     COMM      NUMBER(7,2),
  9     DEPT      dept_type16
 10  );

Table created.

SQL> desc emp16
 Name                            Null?    Type
 ------------------------------- -------- ----
 EMPNO                                    NUMBER(4)
 ENAME                                    VARCHAR2(10)
 JOB                                      VARCHAR2(9)
 MGR                                      NUMBER(4)
 HIREDATE                                 DATE
 SAL                                      NUMBER(7,2)
 COMM                                     NUMBER(7,2)
 DEPT
```

Figure 16.2 Running the script CHP16_2.SQL in SQL*Plus to create the EMP16 table.

3. Use the START command to load and execute the script CHP16_3.SQL. This script queries the DBA_TYPE_ATTRS data dictionary view to confirm the structure of the DEPT_TYPE16 object type created in Step 1. The script and its output appears in Figure 16.3.

How It Works

Step 1 creates an object type that looks exactly like the traditional DEPT table, but the object type is just a template and Oracle8 devotes no physical storage to it. Another important feature of the DEPT_TYPE16 object type is that other DDL statements can use this object as necessary to implement business models. Step 2 creates a new version of the standard EMP table including a reference to the DEPT16 object type. Step 3 queries the DBA_TYPE_ATTRS table to confirm the creation and structure of the DEPT_TYPE16 object type.

Comments

The original version of the EMP table has a not null constraint on the DEPTNO column. Unfortunately, the beta version of Oracle8 under Windows NT will not allow constraint definitions in CREATE TYPE statements nor in ALTER TABLE statements. For example, this statement:

```
ALTER TABLE emp16 MODIFY (dept.deptno CONSTRAINT cst_deptno_nn NOT NULL) ;
```

is syntactically correct but is not legal under the current version of Oracle8. It will generate an ORA-01748 message stating that only simple column types are allowed in the statement.

The DBA_TYPE_ATTRS data dictionary view is similar to the DBA_TAB_COLUMNS view from previous versions of Oracle in that there are analogous user level views called USER_TYPE_ATTRS and ALL_TYPE_ATTRS.

Now there is a new "object" version of the EMP table. How do users and applications insert records into it, you may ask? Read on; How-To 16.2 contains the answer.

```
SQL> start chp16_3
SQL>
SQL> SELECT owner, type_name, attr_name, attr_type_name
  2  FROM dba_type_attrs
  3  WHERE type_name = 'DEPT_TYPE16';

OWNER    TYPE_NAME     ATTR_NAME                        ATTR_TYPE_NAME
-------- ------------- -------------------------------- --------------------
WAITE    DEPT_TYPE16   DEPTNO                           NUMBER
WAITE    DEPT_TYPE16   DNAME                            VARCHAR2
WAITE    DEPT_TYPE16   LOC                              VARCHAR2

SQL>
```

Figure 16.3 Running the script CHP16_3.SQL in SQL*Plus.

16.2 How do I...
Use constructor methods to populate object relational tables?

Problem

I have created some relational tables that contain object columns. The standard SQL INSERT statement fails when I issue it against this type of table. How do I populate relational tables that contain object data types?

Technique

A bit of terminology will enhance understanding of this How-To. A *method* in Oracle8 is a PL/SQL procedure or function that developers declare as part of the object type declaration. The method operates on the attributes of the object. Oracle8 creates at least one method for every object type even if the developer does not specify any methods as part of the object type declaration. This method is called a *constructor* method and always has the same name as the object.

When a user issues an object type declaration in Oracle8, as in Step 1 of the previous How-To, Oracle8 only creates a template for the object. An *instance* of the object does not exist until some user or application stores data in the object's attributes. When this happens, the object is *instantiated*.

So, when users want to instantiate an object, they can use a constructor method.

Steps

1. Start SQL*Plus, connect as the WAITE user, and use the START command to load and execute the script CHP16_4.SQL. The script and its output appears in Figure 16.4.

The CREATE TYPE statement creates an object type called ADDRESS_TYPE16 to act as a template for address data. The CREATE TABLE statement creates a table called PERSON16, which uses the ADDRESS_TYPE16 object type.

2. Use the START command to load and execute the script CHP16_5.SQL, which stores a single row in the PERSON16 table. Figure 16.5 contains the script and its output.

```
SQL> start chp16_4
SQL>
SQL> CREATE TYPE address_type16
  2  (  street     varchar2(30),
  3     city       varchar2(15),
  4     state      varchar2(2),
  5     zipcode    number(5)
  6  );

Type created.

SQL>
SQL> CREATE TABLE person16
  2  (  name       varchar2(20),
  3     address    address_type16
  4  Input truncated to 4 characters
);

Table created.

SQL>
```

Figure 16.4 Running the script CHP16_4.SQL in SQL*Plus.

```
SQL> start chp16_5
SQL>
SQL> INSERT INTO person16
  2  VALUES ('JULES',
  3          address_type16('2517 EZEKIEL STREET',
  4                          'ENGLEWOOD',
  5                          'CA', 27709)
  6          );

1 row created.

SQL>
```

Figure 16.5 Running the script CHP16_5.SQL in SQL*Plus.

In lines 3 through 5 the script invokes the constructor method for object type ADDRESS_TYPE16.

How It Works

Step 1 creates an object type and embeds it in a relational table. Step 2 populates the object relational table by using a standard INSERT statement with the constructor method for the object type created in Step 1.

Comments

Users cannot create their own constructor methods, nor can they create a method with the same name as the object type. Oracle8 reserves the name of the object type for the constructor method, which must be system defined.

16.3 How do I...
Create and use object tables?

Problem

I have created some relational tables containing column objects. If I reuse an object type definition as a column in other relational tables, then I will store the same data in more than one place. This seems inefficient and may adversely effect data integrity. How can I avoid these problems and still make use of Oracle8's object extensions?

Technique

How-To 16.1 introduced a relational table called EMP16 with an embedded object type called DEPT_TYPE16 to store three department attributes. Suppose that the organization of interest has some limited resource, say a set of graphics workstations, and management wants to maintain a record of which departments have received a share of this resource. In this case, it makes sense to enhance the corporate database to include a table containing workstation numbers and the departments where the graphics machines reside. The script in Listing 16.1 will do this.

Listing 16.1 A script to create a table called WORKSTN_LOC

```
SQL> CREATE TABLE workstn_loc16
  2 (    workstn_number     number(4),
  3       dept               dept_type16
  4 );
```

Now the table EMP16 and the table WORKSTN_LOC16 both contain the DEPT_TYPE16 object type as an embedded object. There must be a way to duplicate the functionality of foreign key constraints without introducing this redundancy, right?

Right. The place to start is with an object table. An object table is a table where each row is an instantiation of an object type. Other objects, like relational tables, can point to the rows of an object table through the Oracle8 REF operator. The single argument to this operator is a table alias of a row table; the operator returns the object ID of the requested row.

Steps

1. Start SQL*Plus, connect as the WAITE user, and use the START command to load and execute the script CHP16_6.SQL. This single line script and its output appear in Figure 16.6.

```
SQL> start chp16_6
SQL>
SQL> CREATE TABLE depts16 OF dept_type16;

Table created.

SQL> |
```

Figure 16.6 Running the script
CHP16_6.SQL in SQL*Plus.

The script creates an object table called DEPTS16.

2. Use the START command to load and execute the script CHP16_7.SQL. The script and its output appear in Figure 16.7.

This script creates a new version of the EMP16 table. This table differs from the earlier version of EMP16 only through the datatype of the DEPT column. Here, the DEPT column is a reference (or pointer) to an object of type DEPT_TYPE16.

NOTE

REF datatypes are more strongly typed than other datatypes in that they will only accept pointers to objects of one type.

3. Add a few rows to the DEPTS16 table by using the START command to load and execute the script CHP16_8.SQL. The script and its output appear in Figure 16.8.

```
SQL> DROP TABLE emp16;

Table dropped.

SQL>
SQL> CREATE TABLE emp16 (
  2      empno     number(4),
  3      ename     varchar2(10),
  4      job       varchar2(9),
  5      mgr       number(4),
  6      hiredate  date,
  7      sal       number(7,2),
  8      comm      number(7,2),
  9      dept      ref dept_type16 NOT NULL
 10  );

Table created.

SQL> |
```

Figure 16.7 Running the script
CHP16_7.SQL in SQL*Plus to create
a new version of the EMP16 table.

```
SQL> start chp16_8
SQL>
SQL> INSERT INTO depts16
  2  VALUES (1, 'IS', 'FLOOR 3');

1 row created.

SQL>
SQL> INSERT INTO depts16
  2  VALUES (dept_type16(2, 'TRAVEL', 'FLOOR 2'));

1 row created.

SQL> |
```

Figure 16.8 Running the script
CHP16_8.SQL in SQL*Plus to insert two
rows into the DEPTS16 table.

Notice that the first insert statement uses standard SQL syntax and that the
second statement uses the constructor method for the DEPT_TYPE16
object type.

4. Now add two employees to the EMP16 table by using the START
command to load and execute the script in CHP16_9.SQL; Figure 16.9
shows this script and its output.

The script uses two INSERT INTO…SELECT FROM… statements to
insert two rows into the EMP16 table, one for a programmer and a second
for his supervisor. The REF operator appears in line 4 in both statements
and takes the correlation variable for the DEPTS16 table as an argument.

5. To select rows from the EMP16 table, you will need to dereference the
pointer to the DEPTS16 table. The CHP16_10.SQL script shows you what

```
SQL> start chp16_9
SQL>
SQL> INSERT INTO emp16
  2  SELECT 1, 'Marcellus', 'IS Mgr', null, '1-JAN-74',
  3         55000, 0, ref(dx)
  4  FROM depts16 dx
  5       where dx.deptno = 1;

1 row created.

SQL>
SQL> INSERT INTO emp16
  2  SELECT 2, 'Vincent', 'Analyst', 1, '1-JAN-92',
  3         40000, 0, ref(dx)
  4  FROM depts16 dx
  5       where dx.deptno = 1;

1 row created.

SQL> |
```

Figure 16.9 Running the script
CHP16_9.SQL in SQL*Plus to insert two rows
into the EMP16 table.

output to expect if you do not dereference an object pointer. The script also shows how to use the DEREF operator or dot notation to dereference an object pointer. The script and its output appear in Figure 16.10.

The first SELECT statement does not dereference the object pointer to DEPT16 and the result is garbage. The second SELECT statement uses the DEREF operator and the third uses dot notation to dereference the object pointer.

How It Works

Step 1 creates an object table called DEPTS16 to store objects of the type DEPT_TYPE16. The second step creates the EMP16 table and references the object table DEPTS16 using the REF datatype. Steps 3 and 4 populate the DEPTS16 and EMP16 tables, respectively. Step 5 shows two ways to dereference the object pointers in the EMP16 table.

Comments

Although object pointers complicate the syntax for the INSERT statement slightly, they are a valuable object extension to the Oracle8 server. This is because dereferencing an object pointer is essentially a very fast join with almost no I/O overhead. In effect, Oracle8 enhances join performance considerably at the expense of slightly more complicated and frequent INSERTs. The trade off, however, is worthwhile.

```
SQL> start chp16_10
SQL>
SQL> SELECT empno, ename, dept FROM emp16 WHERE ename = 'Marcellus';

    EMPNO ENAME       DEPT
---------- ----------- --------------------------------------------------------
         1 Marcellus   00002202082226A708298911D1A751AE76BBAEA7413DE452DF
                       28B211D1A750E02FEBD3BE41

SQL>
SQL> SELECT empno, ename, deref(dept) deptinfo FROM emp16
  2 WHERE ename = 'Marcellus';

    EMPNO ENAME       DEPTINFO(DEPTNO, DNAME, LOC)
---------- ----------- ---------------------------------
         1 Marcellus   DEPT_TYPE16(1, 'IS', 'FLOOR 3')

SQL>
SQL> SELECT empno, ename, dept.dname from emp16 WHERE ename = 'Marcellus';

    EMPNO ENAME       DEPT.DNAME
---------- ----------- ----------------
         1 Marcellus   IS

SQL> |
```

Figure 16.10 Running the script CHP16_10.SQL in SQL*Plus to dereference and select rows from the EMP16 table.

COMPLEXITY
INTERMEDIATE

16.4 How do I...
Create and use the VARRAY collection type?

Problem

I have a one-to-many relationship involving a static number of elements on the "many" side. Unlike traditional relational designs, the order of these elements is significant. How do I use VARRAYs to model this type of relationship?

Technique

VARRAYs are perfect for modeling one-to-many relationships where the maximum number of elements on the "many" side of the relationship is known and where the order of these elements is important. In object-oriented parlance, these characteristics describe an *ordered collection*. Suppose that you track the monthly average database buffer cache hit rate for the Oracle8 instances comprising your enterprise. It's not difficult to model the relationship between the instance name and the monthly hit rate data using VARRAYs. There are also some limitations to consider when you use SQL DML statements to reference VARRAYs.

Steps

1. Start SQL*Plus, connect as the WAITE user, and use the START command to load and execute the script CHP16_11.SQL. The script and its output appears in Figure 16.11.

```
SQL> start chp16_11
SQL>
SQL> CREATE TYPE dbhit_type16 AS VARRAY(12) OF NUMBER(6,2);

Type created.

SQL>
SQL> CREATE TABLE dbhit_rate16
  2  (    instance_name    varchar2(20),
  3       monthly_rates    dbhit_type16
  4  );

Table created.

SQL> |
```

Figure 16.11 Running the script CHP16_11.SQL in SQL*Plus to create and use the VARRAY collection datatype.

The first statement creates a VARRAY type called DBHIT_TYPE16, which consists of 12 elements of datatype NUMBER(6,2). Each element stores the database buffer cache hit rate for one month. The second SQL statement creates a table called DBHIT_RATE16, which contains an embedded object called MONTHLY_RATES (see line 3) that is a VARRAY of type DBHIT_TYPE16.

2. Insert two rows into the DBHIT_RATE16 table by using the START command to load and execute the script CHP16_12.SQL as shown in Figure 16.12.

Notice that each insert statement uses the system-generated constructor for the VARRAY called DBHIT_TYPE16. Also, the first insert statement only inserts ten months of data; the second inserts 12 months, but two of the VARRAY elements are null.

3. Execute the anonymous PL/SQL procedure in CHP16_13.SQL to query the DBHIT_RATE16 table. The procedure appears in Listing 16.2.

Listing 16.2 A script to create a table called DBHIT_RATE16

```
SQL> DECLARE
  2     CURSOR dbhit_rate16_c1 IS
  3        SELECT instance_name, monthly_rates
  4        FROM dbhit_rate16;
  5  BEGIN
  6
  6  FOR hit_rec IN dbhit_rate16_c1
  7  LOOP
  8     dbms_output.put_line('instance_name: ' ||
hit_rec.instance_name);
  9     for i in 1 .. hit_rec.monthly_rates.count
 10     LOOP
 11        dbms_output.put_line(to_char(i) || ' ' ||
 12
to_char(hit_rec.monthly_rates(i)));
 13     END LOOP;
 14  END LOOP;
 15
 15  END;
```

The procedure uses a FOR loop in lines 6 through 14 to cycle through the DBHIT_RATE16 table. Line 8 contains code to print the instance name and lines 9 through 13 print the value of the database buffer cache hit rate from the VARRAY of type DBHIT_TYPE16. The FOR loop construct takes care of the record declaration and the loop exit criteria. The script addresses the individual elements of the VARRAY using a subscript in line 12. The output from this procedure appears in Figure 16.13.

```
SQL> start chp16_12
SQL>
SQL> INSERT INTO dbhit_rate16 VALUES
  2  (    'MIA',
  3        dbhit_type16(85.2, 86.1, 95.3, 91.2, 93.2, 89.7,
  4                     77.5, 82.7, 74.3, 91.5)
  5  );

1 row created.

SQL>
SQL> INSERT INTO dbhit_rate16 VALUES
  2  (    'BRAD',
  3        dbhit_type16(null, null, 85.3, 71.2, 83.5, 99.7,
  4                     87.0, 72.7, 94.1, 81.5, 94.8, 89.8)
  5  );

1 row created.

SQL>
```

Figure 16.12 Running the script CHP16_12.SQL in SQL*Plus to populate the DBHIT_RATE16 table.

```
instance_name: MIA
1    85.2
2    86.1
3    95.3
4    91.2
5    93.2
6    89.7
7    77.5
8    82.7
9    74.3
10   91.5
instance_name: BRAD
1
2
3    85.3
4    71.2
5    83.5
6    99.7
7    87
8    72.7
9    94.1
10   81.5
11   94.8
12   89.8

PL/SQL procedure successfully completed.
```

Figure 16.13 Running the script CHP16_13.SQL in SQL*Plus to query the DBHIT_RATE16 table.

How It Works

Steps 1 and 2 feature scripts to create a VARRAY collection type, embed an object of this type in a table, and finally populate the table. Step 3 exhibits some PL/SQL code to query the VARRAY.

Comments

Currently no alternative exists for the PL/SQL code in Step 3. Within standard SQL, you cannot query tables containing VARRAYs. Attempts to do so under Oracle8 version 8.02 beta for Windows NT generate the following error messages:

```
SQL*Plus internal error state 2231, context 0:0:0

Unsafe to proceed
```

There are obvious normalization questions here, too. It looks like VARRAYs contain repeating groups and so they violate first normal form. Oracle considers VARRAYs as atomic units, and thereby addresses the normalization concerns as well as explaining the lack of SELECT support.

The extra PL/SQL code aside, VARRAYs can eliminate some of the overhead associated with joining tables involved in one-to-many relationships. Unless the size of a VARRAY exceeds four kilobytes, VARRAYs are stored inline, meaning within the same segment containing data from the same table, so the overhead associated with querying and manipulating them is low. If SELECT capability or index support is a necessity, or if there can be no upper limit on the number of elements, then nested tables are a better choice. Nested tables are the subject of the next How-To.

COMPLEXITY
INTERMEDIATE

16.5 How do I...
Create and use the nested table collection type?

Problem

I want to model master-detail relationships within my database using collection objects, but for some of these relationships I don't know how many detail elements there will be, and for others there will be a large number of detail elements. I know that VARRAYs are not helpful in these situations. How do I implement nested tables in my database and do I insert and extract data from them?

Technique

Chapter 9 included a nested table definition to help explain unused segment space. This How-To revisits and more closely examines this definition. Nested table definitions start with an object table type definition and conclude by defining a relational table with an embedded object type (see How-To 16.3 for more information about object tables). Nested tables are similar to VARRAYs in that DML commands on them involve some modifications to traditional syntax; the THE keyword is an important new operator for manipulating data residing in nested tables.

Steps

1. The script CHP16_14.SQL contains DDL to define a nested table. Start SQL*Plus, connect as the WAITE user, and use the START command to load and execute this script. The script and its output appear in Figure 16.14.

The first CREATE statement in the script defines an object type, EMP_TYPE16_5, which acts as a template for the employee information the database must store. The second CREATE statement defines an object table type comprised of objects of the EMP_TYPE16_5 type. The final and most interesting CREATE command defines a relational table with an embedded column called EMPS to contain a nested table.

2. Load and execute the script CHP16_15.SQL to insert two rows into the DEPT16_5 table as shown in Figure 16.15.

The INSERT statements use nested constructor methods. As in earlier examples, Oracle8 defines these constructors for us. The outer constructor, EMP_TABLE16_5, instantiates an object of the nested table type. The inner constructor, EMP_TYPE16_5 instantiates an employee

```
SQL> start chp16_14
SQL>
SQL> CREATE TYPE emp_type16 AS OBJECT
  2  (empno      number(4),
  3   ename      varchar2(10)
  4  );

Type created.

SQL>
SQL> CREATE TYPE emp_table16 AS TABLE OF emp_type16;

Type created.

SQL>
SQL> CREATE TABLE dept16
  2  (
  3   deptno     number(2),
  4   dname          varchar2(14),
  5   emps           emp_table16
  6  )
  7  NESTED TABLE emps STORE AS store_dept_emps16;

Table created.

SQL>
```

Figure 16.14 Running the script CHP16_14.SQL in SQL*Plus to create the DEPT16_5 nested table.

```
SQL> start chp16_15
SQL>
SQL> INSERT INTO dept16 VALUES
  2  (1, 'JANITORIAL', emp_table16(emp_type16(1, 'CATHEY'),
  3                            emp_type16(2, 'JOANNE'))
  4  );

1 row created.

SQL>
SQL> INSERT INTO dept16 VALUES
  2  (2, 'STATISTICS', emp_table16(emp_type16(3, 'BARBARA'),
  3                            emp_type16(4, 'ROSALIE'))
  4  );

1 row created.

SQL>
```

Figure 16.15 Running the script CHP16_15.SQL in SQL*Plus to insert some data into the DEPT16_5 table.

object. In this case, the inner constructor is instantiating an employee object to store in the nested object table called EMPS.

3. Query the rows of the nested table EMPS by using the START command to load and execute the script CHP16_16.SQL. The script and its output appear in Figure 16.16.

The query in Figure 16.15 returns the employee numbers and names for the staff members in the janitorial department. The THE keyword prefixing the subquery beginning in line 2 indicates to Oracle that the subquery's result is a nested table and not a scalar value.

How It Works

The DDL statements in Step 1 set up the nested table structure by creating an employee object type and an object table type. The CREATE TABLE statement in

```
SQL> start chp16_16
SQL>
SQL> SELECT empno, ename
  2  FROM THE(SELECT emps
  3            FROM dept16
  4            WHERE dname = 'JANITORIAL');

    EMPNO ENAME
---------- ----------
        1 CATHEY
        2 JOANNE

SQL> |
```

Figure 16.16 Running the script CHP16_16.SQL in SQL*Plus to query the DEPT16_5 table.

Step 1 uses these definitions to create a relational table with a column containing a nested table reference. Step 2 uses constructors to populate the relational table and the nested table. Step 3 uses subquery syntax and the THE operator, new in Oracle8, to query the nested table.

Comments

Nested tables are stored in different data segments than the data from the main table (this is called out-of-line storage). Unlike VARRAYs, the amount of data that can reside in a nested table is limited only by available logical and physical space. Nested tables do accommodate SELECT statements in the form appearing in Step 3.

Subqueries prefaced by the THE keyword are sometimes called *flattened* subqueries to indicate that they return multiple rows from the nested table for a single row in the main table. Although Oracle8 selects this level of SELECT functionality, it is necessary to write a PL/SQL procedure to fashion a query returning columns from the main table and columns from the nested table or to create a subquery returning more than a single column value from the nested table.

Under Oracle8 version 8.02 beta for Windows NT, if you apply the familiar **SELECT** * construct to a table containing a nested table, you will generate a SQL*Plus internal error.

COMPLEXITY
ADVANCED

16.6 How do I...
Create and use object views?

Problem

My database contains some relational tables that are good candidates for object-oriented enhancement. Unfortunately, some existing applications use these tables and I don't have the development resources to rewrite these legacy applications. How can I use object-oriented design techniques to model these tables without invalidating my existing database structures and applications?

Technique

With *object views*, users can utilize object-oriented programming and modeling without making pervasive changes to existing database structures. Object retrievals, moreover, sometimes result in client/server performance enhancements because they allow multi-table retrievals with fewer network trips to the database server.

To create object views on existing relational tables, start by defining the necessary object types, then create the object view using a SELECT statement that extracts the appropriate columns from the relational tables.

Steps

1. Start SQL*Plus and use the START command to load and execute the script CHP16_17.SQL. This script creates the familiar EMP and DEPT tables that user SCOTT owns in the test database; the script's output appears in Figure 16.17.

Oracle8 uses the primary and foreign key structures in the EMP_TABLE16 and DEPT_TABLE16 tables to enforce the master-detail relationship between them.

2. Use the START command to load and execute the script CHP16_18.SQL as shown in Figure 16.18.

3. Load and execute the CHP16_19.SQL script using the start command as shown in Figure 16.19.

Notice that the DEPT_TYPE16 type looks exactly like the DEPT_TABLE16 table and that the EMP_TYPE16 object is almost identical to the EMP_TABLE16 table except that the last column is an embedded object of type DEPT_TYPE16 instead of a scalar attribute.

```
SQL>
SQL> CREATE TABLE dept_table16
  2  ( deptno        number(2),
  3    dname         varchar2(14),
  4    loc           varchar2(23),
  5    PRIMARY KEY (deptno)
  6  );

Table created.

SQL>
SQL> CREATE TABLE emp_table16
  2  (
  3    empno      number(4),
  4    ename      varchar2(10),
  5    job        varchar2(9),
  6    mgr        number(4),
  7    hiredate   date,
  8    sal        number(7,2),
  9    comm       number(7,2),
 10    deptno     number(2),
 11    PRIMARY KEY (empno),
 12    FOREIGN KEY (deptno) REFERENCES dept_table16(deptno)
 13  );

Table created.
```

Figure 16.17 Running the script CHP16_17.SQL in SQL*Plus to create the familiar relational tables EMP and DEPT.

```
SQL> start chp16_18
SQL>
SQL> insert into dept_table16
  2     values (1, 'IS', 'RALEIGH');

1 row created.

SQL>
SQL> insert into emp_table16
  2     values (1, 'FRANK', 'CEO', null,
  3              '25-OCT-97', 72500, 6, 1);

1 row created.

SQL> |
```

Figure 16.18 Running the script
CHP16_18.SQL in SQL*Plus to insert a
row into both the EMP_TABLE16 and
DEPT_TABLE16 relational tables.

```
SQL> start chp16_19
SQL>
SQL> CREATE TYPE dept_type16
  2  (  deptno     number(2),
  3     dname      varchar2(14),
  4     loc        varchar2(23)
  5  );

Type created.

SQL>
SQL> CREATE TYPE emp_type16
  2  (
  3     empno      number(4),
  4     ename      varchar2(10),
  5     job        varchar2(9),
  6     mgr        number(4),
  7     hiredate   date,
  8     sal        number(7,2),
  9     comm       number(7,2),
 10     dept       dept_type16
 11  );

Type created.

SQL>
```

Figure 16.19 Running the script
CHP16_19.SQL in SQL*Plus to
create object types that will be
used in the object view.

4. Load and execute the CHP16_20.SQL script to create the object view, as
shown in Figure 16.20.

```
SQL> start chp16_20
SQL>
SQL> CREATE OR REPLACE VIEW empdept16 OF emp_type16
  2  WITH OBJECT OID (empno)
  3  AS SELECT e.empno, e.ename, e.job, e.mgr, e.hiredate,
  4             e.sal, e.comm,
  5             dept_type16(d.deptno, d.dname, d.loc)
  6  FROM emp_table16 e, dept_table16 d
  7  WHERE e.deptno = d.deptno(+);

View created.

SQL> |
```

Figure 16.20 Running the script CHP16_20.SQL in SQL*Plus to create the EMPDEPT16 object view.

In line 3, the CREATE VIEW statement specifies that the primary key of the base table will be used as the object identifier for the view. In line 5, the statement uses the DEPT_TYPE16 constructor to instantiate the embedded DEPT object in each materialized row of the view. Notice that the outer join operator appears in line 7 of the script so that employee records with null values for the department items will still appear in the view.

How It Works

Start with some existing relational tables like those created and populated in Steps 1 and 2. Step 3 defined object types to model the relationships between the relational objects, and the script in Step 4 created an object view using these object types.

Comments

Object views come in two flavors; those with an object identifier and those without one. If the object view is based on a relational table then the WITH OBJECT OID clause is required so that Oracle8 can uniquely map each row in the materialized view with a row in the underlying relational table. The beta release documentation, which suggests it is possible to create an object view on an underlying relational table without the WITH OBJECT OID clause, is incorrect and generates a server error message as shown in Listing 16.3.

Listing 16.3 Attempting to generate a typed object view without the WITH OBJECT OID clause does not work

```
SQL> CREATE VIEW dept_oview16 OF dept_type16 AS
  2      SELECT deptno, dname, loc
  3      FROM dept_table16
  4      WHERE deptno <= 20;
CREATE VIEW dept_oview16 OF dept_type16 AS
                           *
ERROR at line 1:
ORA-22974: missing WITH OBJECT OID clause
```

COMPLEXITY
ADVANCED

16.7 How do I...
Issue DML commands on object views and use INSTEAD OF triggers?

Problem

I have created an object view to enable object operations on some existing relational tables. How do I insert, select, and update data in the relational tables using an object view?

Technique

The SELECT statement syntax used to extract data from an object view is not particularly noteworthy. INSERT and UPDATE statements are fairly straight-forward as well, unless the end result of the insert or update operation is to modify data residing in more than one base table. Oracle8 will not allow these operations by default; INSTEAD OF triggers provide a way for developers to overcome these limitations.

The name of this trigger type is indicative of its function. When an update state-ment fires an update INSTEAD OF trigger, for example, the trigger is executed instead of the originally issued update statement. INSTEAD OF triggers operate similarly for delete and insert operations. This type of trigger serves to resolve the ambiguity common to update operations on join views.

Steps

1. If you have not executed the scripts in the previous How-To, do so now by starting SQL*Plus, connecting as the WAITE user, and using the START command to load and execute the scripts CHP16_17.SQL, CHP16_18.SQL, CHP16_19.SQL, and CHP16_20.SQL. These scripts create two relational tables, two object types, and an object view. They are explained fully in the previous How-To.

2. Object views precipitate some changes to standard data manipulation language (DML). To see how, use the START command to load and execute the CHP16_21.SQL script. This script and its results appear in Listing 16.4.

Listing 16.4 A sample of DML statements issued against an object view

```
SQL> start chp16_21
SQL>
SQL> SELECT *                                        -- 1
  2  FROM empdept16;

      EMPNO ENAME        JOB       MGR       HIREDATE      SAL     COMM
---------- ---------- --------- ---------- ------------ ------- ----------
DEPT(DEPTNO, DNAME, LOC)
-----------------------------------------------------------------------
         1 FRANK        CEO                 25-OCT-97    72500   6
DEPT_TYPE16(1, 'IS', 'RALEIGH')


SQL>
SQL> SELECT empno, ename, dept.deptno, dept.dname   -- 2
  2  FROM empdept16
  3  WHERE dept.deptno = 1;

      EMPNO ENAME        DEPT.DEPTNO DEPT.DNAME
---------- ---------- ------------ ---------------
         1 FRANK                  1 IS

SQL>
SQL> UPDATE empdept16                                -- 3
  2  SET ename = 'BARBARA'
  3  WHERE ename = 'FRANK';

1 row updated.

SQL>
SQL> INSERT INTO empdept16 (empno, ename)           -- 4
  2  VALUES (2, 'JOE');

1 row created.

SQL>
SQL> INSERT INTO empdept16 (empno, ename, dept)     -- 5
   (THIS WON'T WORK!)
  2  VALUES (2, 'STEVE', dept_type16(1, null, null));
VALUES (2, 'STEVE', dept_type16(1, null, null))
                                              *
ERROR at line 2:
ORA-01776: cannot modify more than one base table through a
join view
```

The SQL statements are numbered in inline comments on the right side of the script. Statement 1 uses the familiar asterisk to select all columns from the object view. Statement 2 selectively extracts columns from the view, using dot notation where appropriate for the DEPT object.

Statements 3 and 4 insert and update data via the view, but note that they only modify one of the underlying base tables. Statement 5 fails because it attempts to modify more than one of the underlying relational base tables. The base tables comprise a master-detail relationship and Oracle8 needs to know how to resolve any ambiguity in the update statement.

3. Use the START command to load and execute the script CHP16_22.SQL. This script creates a trigger that fires whenever a user or application issues an INSERT statement against the EMPDEPT16 object view. The script appears in Listing 16.5.

Listing 16.5 Script CHP16_22.SQL creates an insert INSTEAD OF trigger on the EMPDEPT16 object view

```
SQL> start chp16_22
SQL>
SQL> CREATE OR REPLACE TRIGGER insert_empdept16
  2  INSTEAD OF INSERT ON empdept16
  3  FOR EACH ROW
  4  DECLARE
  5     thecount NUMBER(4);
  6  BEGIN
  7
  7  SELECT count(*) into thecount
  8     FROM dept_table16
  9     WHERE deptno = :new.dept.deptno;
 10
 10  if thecount = 0 then
 11     INSERT INTO dept_table16
 12        (deptno, dname, loc)
 13     VALUES
 14        (:new.dept.deptno,
 15         :new.dept.dname,
 16         :new.dept.loc);
 17  end if;
 18
 18  INSERT INTO emp_table16
 19     (empno, ename, job, mgr, hiredate, sal, comm, deptno)
 20  VALUES
 21     (:new.empno,
 22      :new.ename,
 23      :new.job,
 24      :new.mgr,
 25      :new.hiredate,
 26      :new.sal,
 27      :new.comm,
 28      :new.dept.deptno);
 29
 29  END;
 30  Input truncated to 1 characters
/

Trigger created.
```

All INSERT operations issued against the EMPDEPT16 object view will fire the trigger, and Oracle8 will execute the code in the trigger instead of the original INSERT statement. The SELECT statement in trigger lines 7 through 9 checks to see if the value of DEPTNO in the INSERT statement already exists in the DEPT_TABLE16 table. If it does, the trigger will not execute the INSERT statement in lines 11 through 16 (doing so would generate a constraint violation because DEPTNO is the primary key of the underlying relational table DEPT_TABLE16). The INSERT statement in lines 18 through 28 inserts the new row into the EMP_TABLE16 table.

4. Use the START command to load and execute the script CHP16_23.SQL. This script and its output appear in Figure 16.21.

Notice that the INSERT statement invokes the system-defined DEPT_TYPE16 constructor to instantiate an object of this type. The simple SELECT statement and its output indicate that the insert operation is successful.

How It Works

Step 1 creates the objects first used in How-To 16.6. Step 2 shows that some familiar DML statements are still valid against Oracle8 object views and that others, particularly INSERT statements that modify more than one underlying relational table, are not. The script in Step 3 generates an INSTEAD OF trigger for INSERT statements that users or applications issue against the EMPDEPT16 object view. The INSERT statement in Step 4 succeeds because the INSTEAD OF trigger resolves any ambiguity for the Oracle8 server.

```
SQL> start chp16_23
SQL>
SQL> INSERT INTO empdept16 (empno, ename, dept)
  2  VALUES (2, 'DAVE', dept_type16(3, 'HR', 'BANGKOK'));

1 row created.

SQL>
SQL> SELECT empno, ename, dept.deptno, dept.dname
  2  FROM empdept16;

   EMPNO ENAME      DEPT.DEPTNO DEPT.DNAME
---------- ---------- ------------ ---------------
       1 FRANK                1 IS
       2 DAVE                 3 HR

SQL> |
```

Figure 16.21 Running the script CHP16_23.SQL in SQL*Plus to insert a row into EMPDEPT16 and fire an INSTEAD OF trigger.

Comments

This is only a simple example. A production application would have additional INSTEAD OF triggers to accommodate UPDATE and DELETE operations against the EMPDEPT16 object view. The existence of Oracle7-style referential integrity checking mechanisms, as in the example, can complicate INSTEAD OF trigger creation because the trigger must operate in concert with these existing constraints.

COMPLEXITY
ADVANCED

16.8 How do I...
Use MAP and ORDER methods to compare objects?

Problem

Oracle8 is not able to sort or compare objects in my database. How do I configure objects so that the Oracle8 server knows how to compare them?

Technique

Previous How-To's have used constructor methods to instantiate objects. These methods are system defined; Oracle8 creates a constructor method whenever a user defines an object type. The Oracle8 object implementation also enables users to create methods of their own. The CREATE TYPE and CREATE TYPE BODY commands define member methods; these methods are actually PL/SQL functions and procedures that developers create at object type definition time.

Developers define MAP and ORDER methods to define rules for Oracle8 to use to compare object types. Without these rules, the only object comparisons that Oracle8 will accept are equality conditions, which is a serious limitation in an object relational database.

We will again make use of object analogs of some of the familiar database objects traditionally residing in SCOTT's schema. This How-To, however, will also make use of MAP and ORDER methods so that Oracle8 will accept requests to sort or compare objects.

Steps

1. Run SQL*Plus and connect as the WAITE user. Use the START command to load and execute the script CHP16_24.SQL as shown in Figure 16.22.

```
SQL> start chp16_24
SQL>
SQL> CREATE TYPE dept_typ16
  2  (   deptno                number(2),
  3        dname                varchar2(14),
  4        loc                  varchar2(23)
  5  );

Type created.

SQL> |
```

Figure 16.22 Running the script
CHP16_24.SQL in SQL*Plus to create
the DEPT_TYP16 object type.

The script creates a new object type with three attributes to describe any particular department.

2. Use the START command to load and execute the script CHP16_25.SQL. The script and its output appear in Listing 16.6.

Listing 16.6 Script CHP16_25.SQL creates and populates the EMP16 table

```
SQL> start chp16_25
SQL>
SQL> CREATE TABLE emp16
  2  (
  3      empno      number(4),
  4      ename      varchar2(10),
  5      job        varchar2(9),
  6      mgr        number(4),
  7      hiredate   date,
  8      sal        number(10,2),
  9      comm       number(7,2),
 10      dept       dept_typ16
 11  );

Table created.

SQL>
SQL>
SQL> INSERT INTO emp16
  2      VALUES (1, 'SAL', 'PHYSICIAN', 2, '17-SEP-55',
  3              115000, null,
  4              dept_typ16(1, 'PEDIATRICS', 'ROCHESTER'));

1 row created.

SQL>
SQL> INSERT INTO emp16
  2      VALUES (2, 'JOAN', 'NURSE', null, '17-SEP-76',
  3              300000, null,
  4              dept_typ16(2, 'ER', 'ROCHESTER'));

1 row created.
```

In line 10 of the of the CREATE TABLE command the script makes use of the object type created in Step 1. The INSERT statements use the system-defined constructor method to populate the EMP16 table.

3. Use the START command to load and execute the CHP16_26.SQL script. It appears with its result in Figure 16.23.

The script consists of two SELECT statements. The first attempts to select all rows from the EMP16 table where the value of the DEPT object is less than the value of a DEPT object in which the DEPTNO has a value of two, and the other two attributes are null. The second SELECT attempts to extract all the rows from the EMP16 table and present them in order of descending DEPTNO. Both of the statements fail with ORA-22950 errors because Oracle8 cannot compare the DEPT objects.

4. Drop the current definitions of the DEPT_TYP16 object type and the EMP16 table by using the START command to execute the script CHP16_27.SQL. The script and its output appear in Figure 16.24.

5. Use the START command to load and execute the script CHP16_28.SQL as pictured in Figure 16.25.

The CREATE TYPE command in Figure 16.25 is similar to the version in Step 1 except for line 5, which specifies that there will be a user-defined MAP function for this object type. The following CREATE TYPE BODY command creates a very basic MAP function. This function projects a DEPT_TYP16 object into a scalar quantity by returning the DEPTNO attribute. Oracle8 automatically uses this scalar value whenever a user or application asks Oracle8 to compare objects.

```
SQL> start chp16_26
SQL>
SQL> SELECT * FROM emp16
  2  WHERE dept < dept_typ16(2,null,null);
WHERE dept < dept_typ16(2,null,null)
      *
ERROR at line 2:
ORA-22950: cannot ORDER objects without MAP or ORDER method


SQL>
SQL> SELECT * FROM emp16
  2  ORDER BY dept DESC;
ORDER BY dept DESC
         *
ERROR at line 2:
ORA-22950: cannot ORDER objects without MAP or ORDER method

SQL> |
```

Figure 16.23 The CHP16_26.SQL script fails because Oracle8 does not know how to compare objects of type DEPT_TYP16.

```
SQL> start chp16_27
SQL>
SQL> DROP TABLE emp16;

Table dropped.

SQL> drop type dept_typ16;

Type dropped.

SQL> |
```

Figure 16.24 The CHP16_27.SQL
script dropping the DEPT_TYP16
type and the EMP16 table definitions in SQL*Plus.

```
SQL> start chp16_28
SQL>
SQL> CREATE TYPE dept_typ16
  2  (  deptno                number(2),
  3     dname                 varchar2(14),
  4     loc                   varchar2(23),
  5     MAP MEMBER FUNCTION    map_dept RETURN NUMBER
  6  );

Type created.

SQL>
SQL> CREATE TYPE BODY dept_typ16 AS
  2
  2  MAP MEMBER FUNCTION map_dept RETURN NUMBER IS
  3  BEGIN
  4     return deptno;
  5  END map_dept;
  6
  6  END;
  7  /

Type body created.

:
```

Figure 16.25 The CHP16_28.SQL script
creating a version of the DEPT_TYP16
script with a MAP member method.

6. Use the START command to execute the CHP16_25.SQL script again. This script creates and populates the EMP16 table and appears previously in Listing 16.6.

7. Use the START command to load and execute the CHP16_26.SQL script. This time it succeeds because Oracle8 knows how to compare objects of the DEPT_TYP16 type by using the MAP function created in Step 5.

How It Works

Steps 1 and 2 create an object type definition and embed it within a relational table. This is a common object construction for representing master-detail relationships. Step 3 shows how object comparisons fail in the absence of a MAP or ORDER method because Oracle8 does not know how to compare objects. Step 5 creates a new version of the DEPT_TYP16 object and defines a MAP method as part of the object definition. Step 6 embeds this map-enabled object type into a relational table and Step 7 shows how Oracle8 can compare objects of the DEPT_TYP16 type with help from the MAP method.

Comments

MAP methods are PL/SQL functions embedded within object type definitions. This type of method uses the attributes of its home object to calculate a scalar value. An ORDER method serves the same purpose for objects where projection to a scalar is difficult or impossible. Instead of the MAP method, Step 5 could have defined an order method within the DEPT_TYP16 declaration as shown in Listing 16.7.

> **NOTE**
>
> If you decide to run the CHP16_29.SQL script in Listing 16.7, execute CHP16_27.SQL first to drop the existing definitions of the DEPT_TYP16 object type and the EMP16 table.

Listing 16.7 Script CHP16_29.SQL creates the DEPT_TYP16 object with an ORDER member function

```
SQL> start chp16_29
SQL>
SQL> CREATE TYPE dept_typ16
  2  (   deptno              number(2),
  3      dname               varchar2(14),
  4      loc                 varchar2(23),
  5      ORDER MEMBER FUNCTION order_dept (d dept_typ16) RETURN NUMBER
  6  );

Type created.

SQL>
SQL> CREATE TYPE BODY dept_typ16 AS
  2
  2  ORDER MEMBER FUNCTION order_dept (d dept_typ16) RETURN NUMBER IS
  3      retval      number(2);
  4  BEGIN
  5      if self.deptno < d.deptno then
```

continued on next page

continued from previous page

```
 6          retval := -1;
 7      elsif self.deptno = d.deptno then
 8          retval := 0;
 9      else
10          retval := 1;
11      end if;
12      RETURN retval;
13  END order_dept;
14
14  END;
15  /
```

Type body created.

ORDER methods compare two instances of their home object type. Like all methods, ORDER methods accept an instance of their home types as their first parameter and refer to this object using the keyword SELF. In Listing 16.7, the SELF keyword appears in lines 5 and 7. Type body definitions can declare this parameter explicitly or implicitly (in Listing 16.7, the SELF parameter is implicitly declared). The method also accepts one explicit parameter containing the second object for the comparison. In the example in Listing 16.7, this passed parameter is named **D**. ORDER methods return -1, 0, or 1 to indicate that SELF is less than, equal to, or greater than the second parameter. Object type definitions can include one MAP method or one ORDER method but may not contain both.

CHAPTER 17
ORACLE WEB APPLICATION SERVER

17

ORACLE WEB APPLICATION SERVER

How do I...

17.1 Administer Database Access Descriptors (DADs) and Cartridges?

17.2 Return the results of a query to a web document?

17.3 Create an HTML form?

17.4 Use multi-valued form fields?

17.5 Use HTML tables in web documents?

17.6 Use JavaScript to handle events?

17.7 Access and use CGI environment variables?

17.8 Maintain persistent states with cookies?

The Oracle Web Application Server (OWAS) 3.0 supports the creation of HTML documents dynamically using stored procedures. The PL/SQL Web Toolkit is a set of stored packages that simplifies the creation of web documents by reducing the need to understand HTML programming. The Oracle Web Listener receives an URL from a web browser and determines whether the request requires the use of a Web Request Broker (WRB) Cartridge, or if the request is for a static HTML page that can be accessed from the file system.

For WRB requests, the WRB dispatcher dispatches the request to a WRB Cartridge. Cartridges for PL/SQL, Java, Perl, ODBC, LiveHTML, and Oracle Worlds are supported in OWAS 3.0. If a stored procedure is invoked from the URL, the PL/SQL Cartridge processes the request, and transmits the HTML documents back to the browser.

OWAS 3.0 also introduces a distributed transaction processing model, based on X/Open open standard. The examples presented in this chapter require that OWAS 3.0 be installed on your system. Before running examples in this Chapter, ensure that you have created the OWA_WAITE PL/SQL Agent and the WAITES Data Access Descriptor (DAD) as illustrated in How-To 17.1.

17.1 Administer Database Access Descriptors (DADs) and Cartridges

Database Access Descriptors (DADs) are required for database access. The PL/SQL Cartridge uses configurable PL/SQL Agents to execute stored procedures. After creating a DAD, it is also necessary to create a PL/SQL Agent and configure its WRB parameters. The virtual path for the application must be set up to map to the PL/SQL Agent. This How-To describes the steps necessary for administering DADs and Cartridges.

17.2 Return the Results of a Query to a Web Document

When developing business applications for the web, it is necessary to display the results of a query within a web page. Packages in the PL/SQL Web Toolkit are used to generate HTML formatted output to display query results. This How-To presents the technique used to display the results of a query within a web document.

17.3 Create an HTML Form

HTML forms allow passing parameters from the web browser to the web application, which in turn interfaces with the database. An HTML form enables the user to enter information in fields, which are then submitted to a stored procedure as parameters. This How-To presents the technique used to create HTML forms.

17.4 Use Multi-Valued Form Fields

There are several instances when you will have to submit a form variable that has multiple values. As each form variable is passed as a PL/SQL parameter, a PL/SQL table is required to handle a multi-valued form field. This How-To presents the technique for using multi-valued form fields.

17.5 Use HTML Tables in Web Documents

HTML tables can be used to organize data by rows and columns. When you query data from Oracle, you will probably want to format the data using HTML tables. Tables enable you to present a wide range of content and can include other HTML tags. This How-To presents the techniques used to create HTML tables using the PL/SQL Web Toolkit procedures.

17.6 Use JavaScript to Handle Events

JavaScript can be embedded in the generated HTML in order to control events triggered by changes to form fields. Using JavaScript becomes necessary especially if you are using frames in the generated web documents. In this How-To, you will learn some esoteric JavaScript techniques for event handling.

17.7 Access and Use CGI Environment Variables

Common Gateway Interface (CGI) environment variables provide valuable information that can be accessed and used in your web application by using the OWA_UTIL package. This How-To covers the process of retrieving CGI variables and using them in your web documents.

17.8 Maintain Persistent States with Cookies

Persistent variables in a session can be stored as cookies in the browser. Cookies are strings saved in the browser and maintain state information throughout the client session, or until the expiration date of the cookie if provided. This How-To demonstrates the use of the OWA_COOKIE package.

COMPLEXITY

INTERMEDIATE

17.1 How do I...

Administer Database Access Descriptors (DADs) and Cartridges?

Problem

I have installed Oracle Web Application Server 3.0 and now I want to configure it to access the database by setting up a Database Access Descriptor (DAD). I also need to create a PL/SQL Agent that the PL/SQL Cartridge will use to connect to the database and execute stored procedures. How do I administer DADs and Cartridges?

Technique

Database Access Descriptors (DADs) and PL/SQL Agents are not created automatically during installation, and DADs are required for database access. The PL/SQL Cartridge executes a PL/SQL procedure stored in an Oracle database in response to a web request. It also uses configurable PL/SQL Agents to execute stored procedures and an incoming request is mapped to an appropriate PL/SQL Agent. The DAD associated with PL/SQL Agent is then used to connect to the database. The PL/SQL Agent also contains the necessary information to invoke the database stored procedure. A PL/SQL Agent is a configuration description and not a program. You can use the web-based administration pages to configure and administer DADs and PL/SQL Agents. If you have only one DAD, all web applications connect using the same database account. Different web-based applications can be used to separate DADs in order to manage object privileges.

A new DAD and PL/SQL Agent are created by using the web administration URL. A new user account can be created before creating a DAD, or an existing user account can be assigned to the new DAD. After creating the DAD, a PL/SQL Agent must be created to use the DAD. The PL/SQL Web Toolkit packages can be installed in the user account's schema when the PL/SQL Agent is created or modified. Once a new PL/SQL Agent is created, the WRB parameters should be configured in order to make a virtual directory reference specifying the PL/SQL Agent and virtual path for the PL/SQL Cartridge. The default port for the administrative listener is port 8888.

Steps

1. By default, the installation procedure assigns 8888 as the port number for the administration Web Listener and port 80 for the default WWW Web Listener. The WRB processes and the administration Web Listener services must be started, which can be done by using either one of the following two procedures:

a) Select the Control Panel menu option from the Settings section of the Windows NT start menu. Enter the NT service manager by double-clicking Services. For each of the services—starting with OracleWWWListener30, OraMedia, OraWeb—if the status of the service is Stopped, then click the Start button to start the service. If the Startup column for the service indicates Manual and you want the service to start automatically whenever there is a request for that service, then double-click the line describing the service or single click the Startup button. Now click the radio button to the left of the word Automatic and click the OK button. Do not change the Web Listener's OracleListener30ADMIN and OracleListenerWWW to Automatic startup mode. Start the OracleListener30ADMIN and the OracleListenerWWW Web Listeners, if the status of the service is Stopped. Ensure that the Oracle SQL*NET services and the database have been started on the host. The Windows NT Service Manager is shown in Figure 17.1.

b) The owsctl utility can be used to start, stop, reload, and display the status of listeners and Cartridge processes. The owsstat utility is used to monitor the status of the Web Listener. The syntax for these commands is as follows:

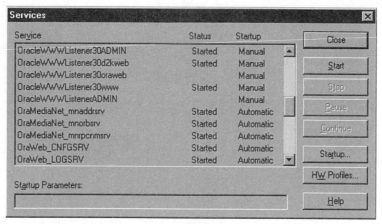

Figure 17.1 The Windows NT Service Manager screen.

```
owsctl { start ¦ stop ¦ reload ¦ status } <listener_name>

owsctl { start ¦ stop ¦ status } { [-e] wrb ¦ cartridge ¦ -p
<process_name> ¦ ncx }

owsctl { start ¦ stop ¦ status } -stat listener_name [ -p
<polling_period> ¦ -uri <uri> ¦ -timeout <timeout> ¦ -action
<trigger script> ]
```

In order to start the WRB processes and the Web Listener services, you need to open a DOS window and type three simple commands:

C:\ORANT\OWS\3.0\BIN>owsctl start wrb

C:\ORANT\OWS\3.0\BIN>owsctl start admin

C:\ORANT\OWS\3.0\BIN>owsctl start www

2. Run a web browser and open the http://localhost:8888/ URL, where localhost is the host name of the machine on which OWAS 3.0 is installed and 8888 is the default port number assigned to the administration Web Listener. You will be prompted for the web administration user name and password, which are case-sensitive. Follow the links to install a new DAD by clicking the Create New DAD link. Enter the values as shown in Figure 17.2.

The DAD name field specifies the name of the DAD to be created. The Database User field contains the name of the user account that will be used to connect to the database. If the user account does not exist, it can be created in this process.

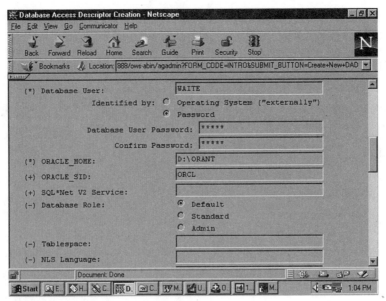

Figure 17.2 The DAD configuration screen.

The Identified by field specifies how the password is supplied while connecting to the database. The ORACLE_HOME field defaults to the current value of ORACLE_HOME for the default database. The ORACLE_SID field specifies the system identifier of the local database to which the user connects. If the Web Agent is not on the same computer as the database, use the SQL*NET V2 Service field instead. The checkbox for Store the User Name and Password in DAD should be checked. Click the Submit New DAD button to create the new DAD. Figure 17.3 shows the results of the operation.

3. Follow the links to install a new PL/SQL Agent: Click Cartridge Administration, PL/SQL Cartridge, and then Create New PL/SQL Agent. Enter the values as shown in Figure 17.4. The Name of PL/SQL Agent field specifies the name of the new PL/SQL Agent to be installed. In the select list for Name of DAD To Be Used, select the newly created WAITES DAD created in Step 2. The Protect PL/SQL Agent select list specifies whether or not you want to protect the PL/SQL Web Toolkit procedures and packages directly accessed from the URLs. The default is TRUE, to provide a secure application environment. The Authorized Ports field specifies the web listener ports the PL/SQL Agent will use. A Web Listener must be set to listen to the port specified. By default, port 80 is assigned to WWW Web Listener during the installation of OWAS 3.0. If you need to add, delete, start, and stop Web Listeners or to configure existing ones, the http://localhost:8888/ows-abin/wladmin URL can be used.

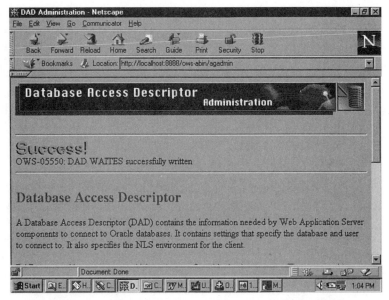

Figure 17.3 The success message after creating the DAD.

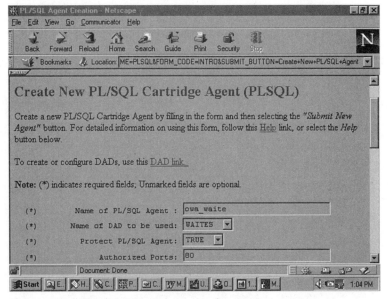

Figure 17.4 The PL/SQL Agent configuration screen.

The rest of the fields are optional. The HTML Error Page field is used to specify the pathname of an HTML file to be displayed when an error occurs. If you leave this field blank, the PL/SQL Cartridge returns a default error message. The Error Level field specifies the error level of reporting to use to display detailed error messages in the client browser from the Web Application Server and database server. This parameter takes values between 0 and 2; 0 masks all errors, 1 includes the time stamp from the error, and the name of the URL accessed. With 2, it displays all the information about the error in a HTML page. It includes the timestamp, the URL that called the PL/SQL procedure name, and parameters. The checkbox for Install Web Application Server Developer's Toolkit PL/SQL Packages should be checked in order to install the PL/SQL Toolkit packages into the schema of the user account specified in the DAD. If you have already installed the packages for the DAD, you do not need to re-install them. Press the Submit New Agent button to create the new PL/SQL Agent. Figure 17.5 shows the results of the operation.

4. To configure the WRB parameters for the PL/SQL Cartridge, follow the Configure Web Request Broker Parameters for PL/SQL link from the main PL/SQL Agent administration page. The Update Cartridge form appears. Move to the Virtual Paths section of the document by scrolling through the document. Add a new line here with /OWA_WAITE/PLSQL to the Virtual Path and %ORAWEB_HOME%\bin to the Physical Path. This causes any

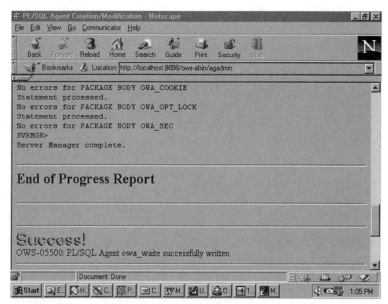

Figure 17.5 The success message after creating the PL/SQL Agent.

URL beginning with /OWA_WAITE/PLSQL to be handled by the PL/SQL Cartridge in the %ORAWEB_HOME%\BIN directory. Without this entry, the user will receive an **URL not found** error when attempting to use the new service. Click the Modify Cartridge button to apply the changes. Once the changes to the Cartridge are successfully made, it must be restarted for the changes to take effect.

5. Stop and start the Web Listener named WWW to make the changes effective. You can do this from the http://localhost:8888/ows-abin/wladmin document where you can click the Stop link to stop the port 80 listener.

After the listener has been stopped, click the Start link to restart the listener. Alternatively, you can use any of the two methods from Step 1. You also need to stop and restart the WRB processes for the WRB configuration changes to be effective. You can test samples from http://localhost:8888/samples.html and examples from this chapter to test whether the installation and configuration was done properly.

How It Works

A new DAD and PL/SQL Agent combination enables you to have applications to use separate user accounts for accessing the database. Agents are created and maintained through the Web Agent administration forms. The administration listener must be started before you can access these forms. Once an Agent is created, the WRB must be modified to include the virtual directories for referencing the Agent.

Step 1 shows how you can start and stop Web Listeners from the Control Panel or by using the **owsctl** utility. Step 2 creates a new DAD and Step 3 creates a new PL/SQL Agent. Step 4 configures the WRB parameters for the PL/SQL Cartridge to include the virtual directory for the new service. Step 5 restarts the Web Listener for the changes to take effect.

Comments

In previous versions, a separate Web Listener was required for applications using different user accounts. With OWAS 3.0, you can use the same Web Listener but simply create a new DAD and a PL/SQL Agent that makes use of the new DAD. If you want separate Web Listeners, then you can set that up as well by creating new Web Listeners and having the PL/SQL Agent accept requests from the ports serviced by one or more Web Listeners.

COMPLEXITY
INTERMEDIATE

17.2 How do I...
Return the results of a query to a web document?

Problem

I want to use Oracle web technology to display query results to users. By displaying the results of database queries within web documents, I can provide an easy way to generate reports and analysis information to our users. Many of the people who want this type of information do not need large applications and already have a web browser. How do I return the results of a query to a web page?

Technique

A web document can be generated dynamically by stored procedures you create. The results of functions, PL/SQL operations, and queries can be presented within web documents. The stored procedure is invoked through the PL/SQL Agent. The PL/SQL Agent executes the corresponding stored procedure and returns the resulting HTML to the browser. In the stored procedure, the results of the query executed is formatted into HTML by using functions and procedures in the HTP package to display the web document in the browser. The HTP package contains a set of procedures that print text and HTML tags to the browser. The HTF package contains functions that correspond to each of the HTP procedures. The functions return VARCHAR2 results that can be used within the PL/SQL code. The PL/SQL Web Toolkit makes it easy to display results of queries within web documents.

Steps

1. Run SQL*Plus and connect as the WAITE account. CHP17_1.SQL, shown in Figure 17.6, creates the sample table used in this How-To.

Run the file to create the sample table and data.

```
SQL> START CHP17_1

Table created.

1 row created.

1 row created.

1 row created.

1 row created.
```

```
SET ECHO OFF
CREATE TABLE DEPT17 (
       DEPT_NO      NUMBER(5) PRIMARY KEY,
       DEPT_NAME    VARCHAR2(30));

INSERT INTO DEPT17
       VALUES (1, 'MARKETING');

INSERT INTO DEPT17
       VALUES (2, 'SALES');

INSERT INTO DEPT17
       VALUES (3, 'ACCOUNTING');

INSERT INTO DEPT17
       VALUES (4, 'I/S');
```

Figure 17.6 CHP17_1.SQL creates the sample table and data.

2. Run the CHP17_2.SQL file in SQL*Plus, as shown in Figure 17.7. The procedure contained in the file queries the DEPT17 table created in Step 1 and displays the results of the query using the PL/SQL Web Toolkit packages.

Line 1 presents the keywords required to create a stored procedure and names the procedure. The cursor declared in lines 2 through 7 declares a cursor that is executed within the procedure body, which lines 8 through 21 contain. The HTP.HTMLOPEN procedure in line 9 and the HTP.HTMLCLOSE procedure in line 20 begin and end the document, respectively. Line 10 uses the HTP.HTITLE procedure to create the title tags, <TITLE> and </TITLE>, and heading tags, <H1> and </H1>,

```
File Edit Search Options Help
SQL> START CHP17_2
SQL> CREATE OR REPLACE PROCEDURE DEPT_LST17 AS
  2  CURSOR C1 IS
  3     SELECT
  4        DEPT_NO,
  5        DEPT_NAME
  6     FROM DEPT17
  7     ORDER BY DEPT_NO;
  8  BEGIN
  9     HTP.HTMLOPEN;
 10     HTP.HTITLE('Atul''s Internet Style Pizza from DC');
 11     HTP.PARAGRAPH;
 12     HTP.BOLD('Department Listing:');
 13     HTP.PARAGRAPH;
 14     HTP.ULISTOPEN;
 15     FOR I IN C1 LOOP
 16        HTP.PRINT(TO_CHAR(I.DEPT_NO)||' - '||I.DEPT_NAME);
 17        HTP.BR;
 18     END LOOP;
 19     HTP.ULISTCLOSE;
 20     HTP.HTMLCLOSE;
 21  END;
 22  /

Procedure created.

SQL>
```

Figure 17.7 CHP17_2.SQL generates dynamic HTML.

establishing a title and a heading for the document. The parameter passed to the procedure is used as both the title and the heading. Table 17.1 contains the HTP package procedures in the PL/SQL Web Toolkit used for formatting heading and structure related tags.

Table 17.1 Heading and structure related procedures

PROCEDURE	DESCRIPTION
htp.htmlOpen	Prints the <HTML> tag indicating the beginning of document.
htp.htmlClose	Prints the </HTML> tag indicating the end of document.
htp.headOpen	Prints the <HEAD> tag indicating the beginning of document head.
htp.headClose	Prints the </HEAD> tag indicating the end of document head.
htp.bodyOpen	Prints the <BODY> tag indicating the beginning of document body.
htp.bodyClose	Prints the </BODY> tag indicating the end of document body.
htp.title	Prints the title specified with the <TITLE> and </TITLE> tags.
htp.htitle	Creates both title tags and heading tags.
htp.base	Prints a tag that records the URL of the current document.
htp.meta	Prints a tag that embeds document meta-information.

Lines 14 and 17 begin and end an unordered list by using the HTP.ULISTOPEN and HTP.ULISTCLOSE procedures. Table 17.2 shows the procedures related to lists in the HTP package.

Table 17.2 List-related procedures

PROCEDURE	DESCRIPTION
htp.listHeader	Creates a header for any type of list.
htp.listItem	Generates a list item for an ordered or unordered list.
htp.ulistOpen	Opens an unordered list.
htp.ulistClose	Closes an unordered list.
htp.olistOpen	Opens an ordered list.
htp.olistClose	Closes an ordered list.
htp.dlistOpen	Opens a definition list.
htp.dlistClose	Closes a definition list.
htp.dlistDef	Creates a definition in a definition list.
htp.dlistTerm	Creates a term in a definition list.
htp.menulistOpen	Creates a list more compact than an unordered list.
htp.menulistClose	Closes the menu list.
htp.dirlistOpen	Creates a directory list.
htp.dirlistClose	Closes a directory list.

Rows fetched from the cursor are formatted and displayed within the document by the FOR loop in lines 15 through 18. Column values of each record returned by the query are printed to the document using the HTP.PRINT procedure. The print procedures in the HTP package needed to generate dynamic web content are listed in Table 17.3.

Table 17.3 Print procedures

PROCEDURE	DESCRIPTION
htp.print	Prints a text string to the browser.
htp.p	Same as HTP.PRINT.
htp.prn	Same as HTP.PRINT but does not put a new line at the end of the string.
htp.prints	Prints a text string to the browser and replaces all occurrences of <, >, ", and &.
	Characters with the corresponding entity are referenced so they can be displayed literally in the browser.
htp.ps	Same as HTP.PRINTS.

The HTP.PRINTS procedure must be used if data may contain the four special characters [<], [>], [&], and ["], which have a special meaning when HTML is interpreted. Thus, text containing these characters has to be displayed as entity references as shown in Table 17.4. Another function to filter data for special characters is called HTF.ESCAPE_SC, which is similar to the HTP.PRINTS procedure. Another important HTML entity reference is the non-breaking space represented by   used to align empty table cells.

Table 17.4 HTML text escaping

CHARACTER	ENTITY REFERENCE
<	&lt;
>	&gt;
&	&amp;
"	&quot;

3. In your browser, open the URL http://localhost/owa_waite/plsql/ dept_lst17 to display the document created in the previous step. Figure 17.8 shows the page in the Netscape Navigator.

The three records contained in the sample table created in Step 1 are displayed in the document. The header created by the HTP.HTITLE procedure is displayed as a top-level heading.

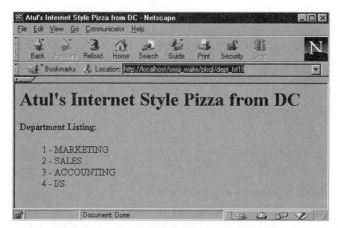

Figure 17.8 The results in Netscape Navigator.

4. Select View, Page Source from the Navigator menu to view the source of the document. This demonstrates how the Oracle procedures are translated to HTML tags and static text. Figure 17.9 shows the source created for the document.

The source code of the document is standard HTML code, as if it was read from a static file.

How It Works

A cursor within PL/SQL is used to execute a query and return its results to the PL/SQL code. The results of a query can be displayed within a web document by processing a cursor and displaying its contents using the HTP.PRINT procedure or other HTP procedures. Step 1 creates a sample table with data queried in the web document. Step 2 develops a stored procedure that creates and processes a cursor to display the results of a query within a web document. Step 3 executes

```
<HTML>
<TITLE>Atul's Internet Style Pizza from DC</TITLE><H1>Atul's Internet Style Pi
<P>
<B>Department Listing:</B>
<P>
<UL>
1 - MARKETING
<BR>
2 - SALES
<BR>
3 - ACCOUNTING
<BR>
4 - I/S
<BR>
</UL>
</HTML>
```

Figure 17.9 The source code of the document.

the procedure from within a browser to display the query results. Step 4 presents the HTML code generated from the results of the query.

Comments

The technique presented in this How-To is critical to developing business applications that use the Oracle database. Because web documents are created in stored procedures, you should refer to Chapter 10, "PL/SQL," for more information on creating stored procedures.

COMPLEXITY
INTERMEDIATE

17.3 How do I...
Create an HTML form?

Problem

In order to create sophisticated web applications, I need to include forms in my documents. I want to use the forms to insert new data into the database and pass information to the database to perform queries. How do I create an HTML form?

Technique

A complete set of procedures for creating HTML forms is provided by the PL/SQL Web Toolkit. When an HTML form is submitted to the Web Agent, a second stored procedure is called to process it. Each field in the form is passed to the second procedure as a parameter. Table 17.5 shows the form procedures within the HTP package.

Table 17.5 Form-related procedures

PROCEDURE	DESCRIPTION
htp.formOpen	Prints the tag that starts the form.
htp.formClose	Prints the tag that ends the form.
htp.formCheckbox	Inserts a checkbox into the form.
htp.formHidden	Sends the content of the field to the browser, although it is not visible to the user.
htp.formImage	Creates an image field that submits the form and returns the x and y coordinate of where the user clicked the image.
htp.formPassword	Creates a field where user's input is not readable as it is typed.
htp.formRadio	Creates a radio button in the form.
htp.formReset	Creates a reset button that clears all the fields of the form when clicked.
htp.formSubmit	Creates a submit button that submits the form when clicked.

continued on next page

continued from previous page

PROCEDURE	DESCRIPTION
htp.formText	Creates a field for a single line of text.
htp.formSelectOpen	Begins a select list that enables the user to select alternatives.
htp.formSelectOption	Represents one choice in a select list.
htp.formSelectClose	Ends a select list.
htp.formTextarea	Creates a text area that enables the user to create multiple lines of text.
htp.formTextareaOpen	Creates a text area that enables you to specify default values.
htp.formTextareaClose	Ends a text area field.

The HTP.FORMOPEN procedure is used to begin a new form. The name of the processing procedure must be passed to the procedure as a parameter. The HTP.FORMCLOSE procedure ends the definition of the form. Within the form definition, a variety of HTP procedures can be used to create text items, check boxes, radio buttons, text areas, and selection lists.

Steps

1. Run SQL*Plus and connect using the WAITE account. CHP17_3.SQL, shown in Figure 17.10, creates a sample table that receives the data entered into the form this How-To creates.

The EMP17 table created in the script will receive data entered into an HTML form. Run the script to create the sample file.

```
SQL>   START CHP17_3
```

Table created.

2. Run the CHP17_4.SQL file in SQL*Plus, as shown in Figure 17.11. The stored procedure contained in the file creates a form allowing data entry.

Line 1 specifies the keywords required to create a new procedure named FORM17. Lines 2 through 13 contain the procedure body. The HTP.HTITLE procedure in line 4 gives the HTML document a name by generating the <TITLE> and </TITLE> tags. The HTP.FORMOPEN procedure in line 5 begins the area of the HTML document containing the form and supplying the name of the processing procedure after the form

```
SET ECHO OFF
CREATE TABLE EMP17 (
  FIRST_NAME VARCHAR2(20),
  LAST_NAME  VARCHAR2(20));
```

Figure 17.10 CHP17_3.SQL creates the sample table used in How-To 17.2.

```
SQL> START CHP17_4
SQL> SET ECHO ON
SQL> CREATE OR REPLACE PROCEDURE FORM17 AS
  2  BEGIN
  3      HTP.HTMLOPEN;
  4      HTP.HTITLE('Employee input form');
  5      HTP.FORMOPEN('ACTION17');
  6      HTP.PREOPEN;
  7      HTP.P('LAST_NAME: '|| HTF.FORMTEXT('LAST_NAME'));
  8      HTP.P('FIRST_NAME: '|| HTF.FORMTEXT('FIRST_NAME'));
  9      HTP.PRECLOSE;
 10      HTP.PARAGRAPH;
 11      HTP.FORMSUBMIT;
 12      HTP.FORMCLOSE;
 13  END;
 14  /

Procedure created.

SQL>
```

Figure 17.11 CHP17_4.SQL generates a simple data entry form.

has been submitted. Line 6 uses the HTP.PREOPEN procedure and generates the <PRE> tag to begin a pre-formatted text area. Lines 7 and 8 use the HTP.P procedure to print to the document and the HTF.FORMTEXT function to create text fields, respectively. The names of the fields specified in the procedures are the parameters passed to the processing procedure. The HTP.PRECLOSE procedure in line 9 creates the </PRE> tag that ends the formatted text beginning on line 6. The HTP.PARAGRAPH procedure in line 10 begins a new paragraph in the document by generating the <P> tag. The HTP.FORMSUBMIT procedure in line 11 creates a Submit button that submits the form when clicked. The HTP.FORMCLOSE procedure in line 12 ends the declaration of the form.

The form can be displayed by opening the URL http://localhost/owa_waite/plsql/form17. Although the form can be displayed at this point, it cannot be submitted until the processing procedure is created, as shown in the following steps.

3. Run the CHP17_5.SQL file in SQL*Plus, as shown in Figure 17.12. The stored procedure contained in the file processes the form created in the previous steps.

Line 1 specifies the keywords for creating a stored procedure and gives it the name declared in the HTP.FORMOPEN procedure in the calling document. This ACTION17 procedure is executed when the Submit button is clicked. The two text fields from the calling document are specified as the procedure parameters. Lines 1 through 3 contain the procedure specification. All form fields must be provided as parameters to the processing procedure and must default to NULL. Lines 4 through 10 contain the procedure body. The INSERT statement on lines 5 and 6 creates a new record in the table using values in the form fields. Lines 8

```
SQL> START CHP17_5
SQL> CREATE OR REPLACE PROCEDURE ACTION17 (
  2           LAST_NAME  VARCHAR2 := NULL,
  3           FIRST_NAME VARCHAR2 := NULL) AS
  4  BEGIN
  5     INSERT INTO EMP17
  6           VALUES (LAST_NAME, FIRST_NAME);
  7     HTP.HTITLE('SUBMISSION COMPLETE');
  8     HTP.P('LAST NAME: ' || HTF.BOLD(LAST_NAME) || '<BR>');
  9     HTP.P('FIRST NAME: ' || HTF.BOLD(FIRST_NAME) || '<BR>');
 10  END;
 11  /

Procedure created.

SQL>
```

Figure 17.12 CHP17_5.SQL processes the form variables.

and 9 use the HTP.P procedure to display a submission message to the user when the record is created. Note the use of HTF.BOLD function to insert <B> and </B> tags for bold typeface. You can use the HTF package whenever you need a function equivalent of a procedure in the HTP package.

Although the procedure can be called directly as a URL, it will not perform any useful function unless called from the form created in Step 2. The next step demonstrates the form posting.

4. Start your browser and open the URL http://localhost/owa_waite/plsql/form17. Figure 17.13 shows the form within the Netscape Navigator browser.

Enter values into the two fields on the form and select the Submit button to process it. Figure 17.14 shows the results displayed after the fields are entered and the form submitted.

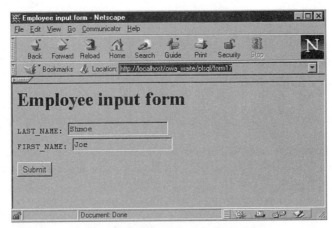

Figure 17.13 The form in Netscape Navigator.

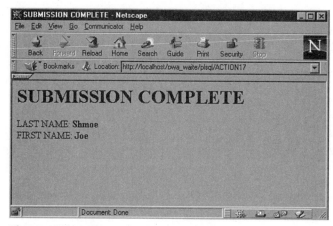

Figure 17.14 The submission message after posting the form.

In addition to displaying the information entered into the form, the values are inserted into the EMP17 table created in Step 1. The simple form created in the earlier steps does not display the numerous controls an HTML form can contain. The following steps create a more complex form using many of the available controls.

5. Run the CHP17_6.SQL file in SQL*Plus, as shown in Figure 17.15. The stored procedure contained in the file creates a complex form that includes text fields, radio buttons, a checkbox, and a select list.

```
SQL> START CHP17_6
SQL> CREATE OR REPLACE PROCEDURE EMP_FRM17 AS
  2   BEGIN
  3      HTP.HTMLOPEN;
  4      HTP.HTITLE('Employee Identification Form');
  5      HTP.LINE;
  6      HTP.FORMOPEN('EMP_ACTION17');
  7      HTP.PREOPEN;
  8      HTP.P('Last Name: '|| HTF.FORMTEXT('LAST_NAME')||' '||
  9              'First Name:'|| HTF.FORMTEXT('FIRST_NAME'));
 10      HTP.P('Sex: ');
 11      HTP.P('    Male:   '||HTF.FORMRADIO('SEX','M'));
 12      HTP.P('    Female: '||HTF.FORMRADIO('SEX','F'));
 13      HTP.FORMSELECTOPEN('Department', 'Department:');
 14      HTP.FORMSELECTOPTION('Marketing');
 15      HTP.FORMSELECTOPTION('Sales');
 16      HTP.FORMSELECTOPTION('I/S');
 17      HTP.FORMSELECTOPTION('Accounting');
 18      HTP.FORMSELECTCLOSE;
 19      HTP.P('Exempt: '||HTF.FORMCHECKBOX('Exempt'));
 20      HTP.PRECLOSE;
 21      HTP.PARAGRAPH;
 22      HTP.FORMSUBMIT;
 23      HTP.FORMRESET;
 24      HTP.FORMCLOSE;
 25      HTP.LINE;
 26      HTP.HTMLCLOSE;
 27   END;
```

Figure 17.15 CHP17_6.SQL generates a complex data entry form.

Line 1 specifies the keywords required to create the stored procedure and names it. Lines 2 through 27 contain the body of the stored procedure. Lines 3 and 26 begin and end the HTML document with the HTP, HTMLOPEN, and HTP.HTMLCLOSE procedures, respectively. Line 5 uses the HTP.LINE procedure to generate an <HR> tag for displaying a line. Line 6 begins a form with the HTP.FORMOPEN procedure. The parameter passed to the HTP.FORMOPEN procedure specifies the name of the procedure receiving the input form data when the form is submitted.

Line 7 uses the HTP.PREOPEN procedure to begin a section of pre-formatted text within the document. Lines 8 and 9 use the HTP.PRINT procedure containing the HTF.FORMTEXT function to create two text fields. Lines 11 and 12 create two radio buttons using the HTP.FORMRADIO procedure. By specifying the same name for the two radio buttons, the browser knows the buttons occupy the same radio group.

Lines 13 through 18 create a drop-down listbox containing the elements created by the HTP.FORMSELECTOPTION procedure. The selection list is created with the HTP.FORMSELECTOPEN procedure and ended with the HTP.FORMSELECTCLOSE procedure. The HTF.FORMCHECKBOX function contained in the HTP.PRINT procedure in line 19 creates a checkbox. The values generated by a checkbox are ON or OFF. The HTP.SUBMIT procedure in line 22 creates a Submit button that processes the form when selected. Line 23 uses the HTP.RESET procedure to create a reset button that clears the form when selected. The HTP.FORMCLOSE procedure in line 24 ends the form area.

Creating the procedure lets you call the /ows_waite/plsql/emp_frm17 page from any browser. The CHP17_6 procedure referenced by HTP.FORMOPEN must be created in order to process the form. The next step creates the stored procedure to process the form.

6. Run the CHP17_7.SQL file in SQL*Plus, as shown in Figure 17.16. The procedure within the file processes the form created in the previous step and displays the values entered into the items.

Lines 1 through 6 contain the specification for the stored procedure. The parameters to the stored procedure represent the form variables. As there is no guarantee that a value will be passed when the form is posted, a default value is included for each parameter. The order of the parameters is unimportant because the Web Agent reorders them at runtime.

```
SQL> START CHP17_7
SQL> CREATE OR REPLACE PROCEDURE EMP_ACTION17 (
  2          LAST_NAME  VARCHAR2 := NULL,
  3          FIRST_NAME VARCHAR2 := NULL,
  4          SEX VARCHAR2 := NULL,
  5          DEPARTMENT VARCHAR2 := NULL,
  6          EXEMPT VARCHAR2 := NULL) AS
  7  BEGIN
  8    HTP.HTMLOPEN;
  9    HTP.HTITLE('SUBMISSION COMPLETE');
 10    HTP.P('LAST NAME: ' || LAST_NAME || '<BR>');
 11    HTP.P('FIRST NAME: ' || FIRST_NAME || '<BR>');
 12    HTP.P('SEX : ' || SEX || '<BR>');
 13    HTP.P('DEPARTMENT: ' || DEPARTMENT || '<BR>');
 14    IF EXEMPT = 'on' THEN
 15       HTP.P('EXEMPT: EXEMPT<BR>');
 16    ELSE
 17       HTP.P('EXEMPT: NOT EXEMPT<BR>');
 18    END IF;
 19    HTP.HTMLCLOSE;
 20  END;
 21  /

Procedure created.

SQL>
```

Figure 17.16 CHP17_7.SQL processes the form variables.

Lines 7 through 16 contain the procedure body. Lines 8 and 19 begin and end the document by specifying the HTP.HTMLOPEN and HTP.HTMLCLOSE procedures, respectively. Line 9 uses the HTP.HTITLE procedure to generate the tags for the document's title and heading. Lines 10 through 13 use the HTP.P procedure to print the parameters passed from the calling document. The <B> tag is included in the parameter to print the values in boldfaced text. The <BR> tag is included to generate a linefeed. Notice that the value of the EXEMPT checkbox is either On or Off, and not TRUE or FALSE. The value for the EXEMPT checkbox is tested by the IF statement in line 14.

7. Run a browser and open the URL http://localhost/owa_waite/plsql/emp_frm17. Figure 17.17 shows the form displayed by the Netscape browser.

Enter a first and last name into the text fields, select a value from the radio buttons and listbox, and check the checkbox. If you want to clear information entered, you can select the Reset button. Submit the form by selecting the Submit button. Each of the values from the calling form are displayed by the processing form. Figure 17.18 shows the output in the Netscape Navigator window after the form is posted.

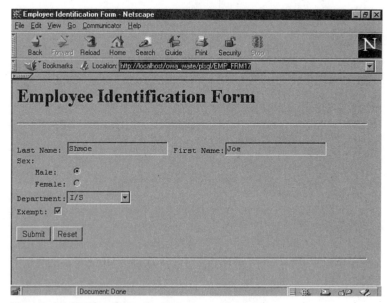

Figure 17.17 The form in Netscape Navigator.

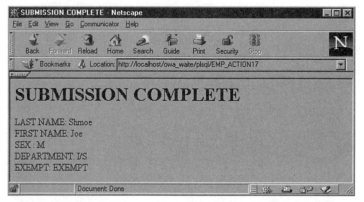

Figure 17.18 Netscape Navigator window after the form is posted.

How It Works

In order to create a form, two stored procedures are required. The first procedure lets the user enter values into the form, and the second procedure receives these values as parameters and processes the form.

A form begins with the <FORM METHOD="POST" ACTION="*processing procedure*"> tag and ends with the </FORM> tag. To use the GET method to post the form, use METHOD="GET" in the FORM tag. Between the tags, form elements and other HTML tags are defined. Text fields, selection lists, radio buttons, checkboxes, and text areas can all be defined within a form.

Step 1 creates a table that receives the data entered into a form. Step 2 creates a stored procedure that generates a simple form to enter a name. When the form is submitted, the procedure created in Step 3 inserts the data into the sample table and displays the values of the field in a document. Step 4 shows the operation of the simple form within a browser. Step 5 creates a stored procedure generating a form with many of the objects an HTML form uses. The form contains text boxes, radio buttons, a checkbox, and a selection list. The stored procedure created in Step 6 processes the data from the calling form by displaying the values within a document. Step 7 shows the posting of the complex form in a browser.

Comments

The PL/SQL Agent can receive parameters through a URL or from an HTML form when it is submitted. Forms enable you to generate sophisticated web applications, and you can choose between the GET and POST methods for posting a form. It is recommended that you use the POST method instead of the GET method whenever possible.

The GET method is used for links and non-form URLs, and is restricted by the operating system limit on the length of the QUERY_STRING CGI environment variable, which it uses while posting a form. On the other hand, CGI uses the standard input to read data sent by the POST method, and thus an unlimited number of parameters can be posted without worrying about the client or server truncating data.

The REQUEST_METHOD CGI environment variable is set to GET or POST depending on the method used to post the form. The order of parameters is unimportant, but providing a default value for parameters is a recommended practice if you cannot guarantee that a value will be passed from the browser for a particular parameter.

COMPLEXITY
INTERMEDIATE

17.4 How do I...
Use multi-valued form fields?

Problem

While designing forms in my web applications, I need to include multiple checkboxes or radio buttons that have the same name. When the form is posted, values of form fields are received as variables by a stored procedure. How do I use multi-valued form fields?

Technique

Irrespective of whether you use the GET or POST method to pass parameters from an HTML form, you do not need to be concerned how the PL/SQL Agent receives parameters unless you are using form fields that can be multi-valued. A multi-valued form field is a field that occurs several times in the form and has the same field name but different values.

You can also set fields of different types to be multi-valued if they bear the same field name. Typically, checkboxes and radio buttons are the multi-valued fields, but you can very well have other fields be multi-valued as well. For instance, a series of hidden form fields with the same name, or an HTML SELECT list with the SIZE parameter greater than 1, enables the user to select multiple values for the same form field by using the CTRL key while clicking multiple items in the SELECT list. Special care also has to be taken while passing multiple values for form fields as a parameter to the stored procedure that processes the submitted form. A PL/SQL table is used to create an array of values for the multi-valued form field when the form is submitted.

Steps

1. Run SQL*Plus and connect as the WAITE account. If you have not created the DEPT17 table from How-To 17.2, then run CHP17_1.SQL, shown in Figure 17.19, which creates the DEPT17 table used in this How-To.

```
SQL>  START CHP17_1

Table created.

1 row created.

1 row created.

1 row created.

1 row created.
```

```
SET ECHO OFF
CREATE TABLE DEPT17 (
        DEPT_NO      NUMBER(5) PRIMARY KEY,
        DEPT_NAME    VARCHAR2(30));

INSERT INTO DEPT17
        VALUES (1, 'MARKETING');

INSERT INTO DEPT17
        VALUES (2, 'SALES');

INSERT INTO DEPT17
        VALUES (3, 'ACCOUNTING');

INSERT INTO DEPT17
        VALUES (4, 'I/S');
```

Figure 17.19 CHP17_1.SQL creates the sample table and data.

2. Run the CHP17_8.SQL file in SQL*Plus, as shown in Figure 17.20. The procedure contained in the file queries the DEPT17 table created in Step 1 and displays the records as a multi-valued checkbox form field.

Line 1 specifies the keywords required to create the stored procedure and names it. Lines 2 through 4 define a cursor to fetch all records from the DEPT17 table. The HTP.HTITLE procedure in line 7 generates the header and title tags. Lines 6 and 19 begin and end the HTML document with the HTP.HTMLOPEN and HTP.HTMLCLOSE procedures, and lines 8 and 18 begin and end the body of the HTML document with the HTP.BODYOPEN and HTP.BODYCLOSE procedures. Line 9 begins a form with the HTP.FORMOPEN procedure. The parameter passed to the HTP.FORMOPEN procedure specifies the name of the procedure receiving the form data when the form is submitted.

Note the use of the HTP.FORMHIDDEN procedure in line 10 that creates a hidden form field named DEPTS with a value of DUMMY. Hidden form fields are usually used to pass state information from one form to another.

As we would be using a PL/SQL table to pass the values of the multi-valued form field to a stored procedure, and a PL/SQL table cannot default to NULL, it is necessary that we create the first element with a dummy value.

The FOR loop on lines 11 to 15 creates a checkbox for each department in the DEPT17 table. The HTP.FORMCHECKBOX procedure is used to create a checkbox. The value for the checkbox is the DEPT_NAME

```
SQL> START CHP17_8
SQL> SET ECHO ON
SQL> CREATE OR REPLACE PROCEDURE DEPT_FRM17 AS
  2      CURSOR DEPT_CURS IS
  3         SELECT DEPT_NO, DEPT_NAME
  4         FROM    DEPT17;
  5  BEGIN
  6      HTP.HTMLOPEN;
  7      HTP.HTITLE('Departments');
  8      HTP.BODYOPEN;
  9      HTP.FORMOPEN('DEPT_ACTION17');
 10      HTP.FORMHIDDEN('DEPTS', 'DUMMY');
 11      FOR DEPT_REC IN DEPT_CURS LOOP
 12          HTP.FORMCHECKBOX('DEPTS', DEPT_REC.DEPT_NAME);
 13          HTP.P(DEPT_REC.DEPT_NAME);
 14          HTP.NL;
 15      END LOOP;
 16      HTP.FORMSUBMIT;
 17      HTP.FORMCLOSE;
 18      HTP.BODYCLOSE;
 19      HTP.HTMLCLOSE;
 20  END;
 21  /

Procedure created.

SQL>
```

Figure 17.20 CHP17_8.SQL creates a form with a multi-valued form field.

column value. All checkboxes have the same DEPTS, each with a different value. The HTP.FORMSUBMIT procedure in line 16 creates a submit button that processes the form when selected. The HTP.FORMCLOSE procedure in line 17 ends the form. The next step creates the stored procedure to process the form.

3. Run the CHP17_9.SQL file in SQL*Plus, as shown in Figure 17.21. The procedure within the file processes the form created in the previous step and displays the departments for checked checkboxes.

In line 2, the only parameter to the procedure is of type OWA_UTIL.IDENT_ARR, which is defined as a PL/SQL table of VARCHAR2(30) in the OWA_UTIL package. The DEPTS parameter to the stored procedure represents the list of values for the multi-valued checkbox form field. As there is no guarantee that at least one checkbox will be checked when the form is submitted, a dummy string is included as the first value. Line 8 starts the counter at 2 because we had put in a dummy hidden field in the form. For PL/SQL tables, you can just loop through the values until the NO_DATA_FOUND exception is hit. This is exactly what is done in the loop in lines 9 through 13. The values for checkboxes that were checked are passed to the stored procedure using the PL/SQL table, and each value is printed to the web document in line 10. The NO_DATA_FOUND exception is raised when there are no more elements in the PL/SQL table. The exception handler in lines 15 to 17 handler merely prints the </BODY> and </HTML> tags to the web document before exiting.

```
SQL> START CHP17_9
SQL> CREATE OR REPLACE PROCEDURE
  2            DEPT_ACTION17 (DEPTS OWA_UTIL.IDENT_ARR) AS
  3    DEPT_CTR   INTEGER;
  4  BEGIN
  5     HTP.HTMLOPEN;
  6     HTP.HTITLE('Selected Departments');
  7     HTP.BODYOPEN;
  8     DEPT_CTR := 2;
  9     LOOP
 10       HTP.PRINT(DEPTS(DEPT_CTR));
 11       HTP.NL;
 12       DEPT_CTR := DEPT_CTR + 1;
 13     END LOOP;
 14  EXCEPTION
 15     WHEN NO_DATA_FOUND THEN
 16        HTP.BODYCLOSE;
 17        HTP.HTMLCLOSE;
 18  END;
 19  /

Procedure created.

SQL>
```

Figure 17.21 CHP17_9.SQL processes the multi-valued form field.

4. Run a browser and open the URL http://localhost/owa_waite/plsql/
dept_frm17. Figure 17.22 shows the form displayed by the Netscape
browser.

A checkbox is displayed before the name of each department. Check a few
checkboxes and press the Submit button. Each of the values for checked
checkboxes from the calling form are displayed. Figure 17.23 shows the
output in the Navigator window after the form is posted.

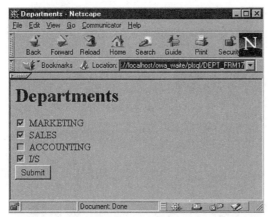

Figure 17.22 The form in Netscape Navigator.

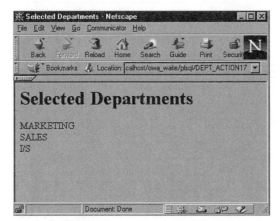

Figure 17.23 Netscape Navigator window
after the form is posted.

How It Works

PL/SQL tables are used to pass values of a multi-valued form field as an array of values to the processing stored procedure. The PL/SQL Agent can only pass parameters to PL/SQL tables, which have a base type of VARCHAR2. For other datatypes, the values can then be explicitly converted using conversion functions.

Step 1 creates a sample table and data. Step 2 creates a stored procedure that generates a form with a multi-valued checkbox form field with values from the sample table. When the form is submitted, the stored procedure created in Step 3 receives the values of checked checkboxes and prints those values to the browser. Step 4 shows the operation of the simple form within a browser.

Comments

A PL/SQL table is used as a parameter to the processing procedure to handle a multi-valued form field. Refer How-To 10.9 for more information on PL/SQL tables.

COMPLEXITY

INTERMEDIATE

17.5 How do I...
Use HTML tables in my web documents?

Problem

I want to use HTML tables to display information that should appear in row/column format. When I use a browser capable of displaying tables, I notice they greatly enhance the look of web documents. How do I use HTML tables in my page?

Technique

Tables are created within an HTML document by generating table-related tags in the document. The <TABLE> tag begins a table and can be generated by the HTP.TABLEOPEN procedure. Table 17.6 shows the PL/SQL Web Toolkit procedures related to the creation of tables.

Table 17.6 Table-related procedures

PROCEDURE	DESCRIPTION
htp.tableopen	Begins the creation of a table
htp.tableclose	Ends the table specification
htp.tablecaption	Creates a caption for the table
htp.tablerowopen	Starts the processing of row information
htp.tablerowclose	Ends the processing of row information
htp.tableheader	Creates column headers for the table
htp.tabledata	Creates a column data element
owa_util.cellsprint	Prints an HTML table from the output of a query
owa_util.tablePrint	Prints an Oracle table as a preformatted or an HTML table

Each row of the table is created beginning with the HTP.TABLEROWOPEN procedure, creating elements with the HTP.TABLEDATA procedure, and ending with the HTP.TABLEROWCLOSE procedure. A caption can be created for the table by using the HTP.TABLECAPTION procedure. Column headings can be created just like a row, or the HTP.TABLEHEADER procedure can be used. If the HTP.TABLEHEADER procedure is used, the column headings look slightly bolder.

Steps

1. Run SQL*Plus and connect as the WAITE user account. CHP17_10.SQL, shown in Figure 17.24, creates the sample table used in this How-To.

The SALES17 table contains regional sales information for a sample company. Four sample records to be queried into an HTML table in a later step are created. Run the file to create the sample table and its data.

```
SET ECHO OFF
CREATE TABLE SALES17 (
    CITY    VARCHAR2(30),
    JAN     NUMBER(5),
    FEB     NUMBER(5),
    MAR     NUMBER(5));

INSERT INTO SALES17 VALUES ('Chicago', 23, 45, 91);
INSERT INTO SALES17 VALUES ('New York', 11, 17, 13);
INSERT INTO SALES17 VALUES ('Seattle', 27, 41, 10);
INSERT INTO SALES17 VALUES ('Dallas', 28, 24, 53);
```

Figure 17.24 CHP17_10.SQL creates the sample table and data used in How-To 17.5.

```
SQL>    START CHP17_10

Table created.

1 row created.

1 row created.

1 row created.

1 row created.
```

2. Run the CHP17_11.SQL file in SQL*Plus, as shown in Figure 17.25. The procedure contained in the file queries the sample table created in Step 1 and creates an HTML table using the records fetched.

Line 1 specifies the keywords required to create the stored procedure and name it. Lines 2 through 5 create a cursor that queries the sample table created in Step 1. The cursor is executed within the procedure body and the rows displayed in a table.

Lines 6 through 26 contain the procedure body. Lines 7 and 25 use the HTP.HTMLOPEN and HTP.HTMLCLOSE procedures to begin and end the document, respectively. Line 8 begins the creation of the table using the HTP.TABLEOPEN procedure. The HTP.TABLECAPTION procedure is used to generate HTML tags for the table caption.

Lines 10 through 15 call the HTP.TABLEHEADER procedure to create a row containing column headings. Lines 16 through 23 use a FOR loop to

```
SQL> START CHP17_11
SQL> CREATE OR REPLACE PROCEDURE SALES_TBL17 AS
  2   CURSOR C1 IS
  3       SELECT CITY, JAN, FEB, MAR
  4       FROM   SALES17
  5       ORDER BY CITY;
  6   BEGIN
  7     HTP.HTMLOPEN;
  8     HTP.TABLEOPEN('BORDER');
  9     HTP.TABLECAPTION('Regional Sales','CENTER');
 10     HTP.TABLEROWOPEN;
 11     HTP.TABLEHEADER('City');
 12     HTP.TABLEHEADER('Jan');
 13     HTP.TABLEHEADER('Feb');
 14     HTP.TABLEHEADER('Mar');
 15     HTP.TABLEROWCLOSE;
 16     FOR I IN C1 LOOP
 17         HTP.TABLEROWOPEN;
 18         HTP.TABLEDATA(I.CITY);
 19         HTP.TABLEDATA(TO_CHAR(I.JAN),'CENTER');
 20         HTP.TABLEDATA(TO_CHAR(I.FEB),'CENTER');
 21         HTP.TABLEDATA(TO_CHAR(I.MAR),'CENTER');
 22         HTP.TABLEROWCLOSE;
 23     END LOOP;
 24     HTP.TABLECLOSE;
 25     HTP.HTMLCLOSE;
 26   END;
 27   /
```

Figure 17.25 CHP17_11.SQL generates an HTML table.

print each record returned by the query. A row is created for each record returned by the query by using the HTP.TABLEROWOPEN, HTP.TABLEDATA, and HTP.TABLEROWCLOSE procedures. The table is closed in line 24 with the HTP.TABLECLOSE procedure.

3. Open the http://localhost/owa_waite/plsql/sales_tbl17 URL in your browser. The URL invokes the stored procedure and the query is executed on the sample table to dynamically create an HTML table. The table is displayed in Figure 17.26 within Netscape Navigator.

When the table is generated in the document, it contains five rows and four columns. The first row contains the column headings, and the next four rows display data from the sample table.

4. Run the CHP17_12.SQL file in SQL*Plus, as shown in Figure 17.27. A much easier way to generate HTML tables from Oracle tables is by using the OWA_UTIL.TABLEPRINT function.

The OWA_UTIL.TABLEPRINT function returns a Boolean value TRUE or FALSE as to whether there are more rows available beyond the maximum rows requested, which is NULL by default if omitted in the call. As it is a function call, the IGNORE Boolean variable in line 2 simply serves as a placeholder for the value returned. HTML tags for the complete table are generated in a single call to the powerful OWA_UTIL.TABLEPRINT function as in lines 5 and 6. The only difference is the third parameter that specifies whether the table has to be generated as an HTML table or a pre-formatted table. By default, an HTML table is generated. Note that the first parameter is the name of the source Oracle table.

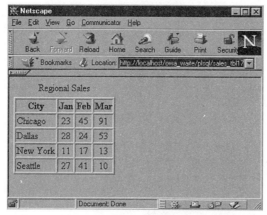

Figure 17.26 The table in Netscape Navigator.

```
SQL> START CHP17_12
SQL> CREATE OR REPLACE PROCEDURE SALES_EASY17 AS
  2    IGNORE BOOLEAN;
  3  BEGIN
  4    HTP.HTMLOPEN;
  5    IGNORE := OWA_UTIL.TABLEPRINT('SALES17', 'BORDER', OWA_UTIL.HTML_TABLE
  6    IGNORE := OWA_UTIL.TABLEPRINT('SALES17', 'BORDER', OWA_UTIL.PRE_TABLE)
  7    HTP.LINE;
  8    HTP.ADDRESS('(C)1797 Waite Group Press');
  9    HTP.HTMLCLOSE;
 10  END;
 11  /

Procedure created.

SQL>
```

Figure 17.27 CHP17_12.SQL demonstrates the use of the OWA_UTIL.TABLEPRINT function.

5. Open the URL http://localhost/owa_waite/plsql/sales_easy17 in your browser. The URL invokes the stored procedure created in the previous step. The two tables are displayed within Netscape Navigator as shown in Figure 17.28.

6. Run the CHP17_13.SQL file in SQL*Plus, as shown in Figure 17.29. A much easier way to paginate cells with column values from an Oracle view by using the OWA_UTIL.CELLSPRINT function.

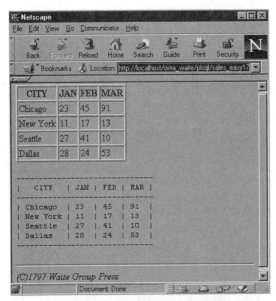

Figure 17.28 The HTML table and pre-formatted table in Netscape Navigator.

```
SQL> START CHP17_13
SQL> CREATE OR REPLACE PROCEDURE CELLS17 (ROW_START IN NUMBER DEFAULT 0) AS
  2        MORE_ROWS BOOLEAN DEFAULT FALSE;
  3  BEGIN
  4        HTP.HTMLOPEN;
  5        HTP.HTITLE('ALL OBJECTS');
  6        HTP.TABLEOPEN('BORDER');
  7        OWA_UTIL.CELLSPRINT('SELECT ROWNUM, ALL_OBJECTS.*
  8                           FROM ALL_OBJECTS',
  9                           10, 'YES', ROW_START, MORE_ROWS);
 10        HTP.TABLECLOSE;
 11        IF (ROW_START > 0) THEN
 12            HTP.FORMOPEN('CELLS17');
 13            HTP.FORMHIDDEN('ROW_START', ROW_START-10);
 14            HTP.FORMSUBMIT(CVALUE => 'PREVIOUS 10');
 15            HTP.FORMCLOSE;
 16        END IF;
 17        IF (MORE_ROWS) THEN
 18            HTP.FORMOPEN('CELLS17');
 19            HTP.FORMHIDDEN('ROW_START', ROW_START+10 );
 20            HTP.FORMSUBMIT(CVALUE => 'NEXT 10');
 21            HTP.FORMCLOSE;
 22        END IF;
 23        HTP.HTMLCLOSE;
 24  END;
 25  /

Procedure created.
```

Figure 17.29 CHP17_13.SQL demonstrates the use of the OWA_UTIL.CELLSPRINT function.

The OWA_UTIL.CELLSPRINT procedure generates an HTML table using the output of a SQL query on a data dictionary view as in lines 7 to 9. Each column value from a record fetched are mapped to cells of an HTML table. In lines 6 and 10, the HTML code for opening and closing the HTML table is specified explicitly. The first parameter to the procedure is the query, the second one is the maximum rows to display in a table, the third parameter specifies whether or not to format numbers, the fourth parameter specifies how many records to skip before fetching records to display in the table, and the last parameter is an out parameter indicating if there are more rows remaining in the table to be displayed. The last two parameters enable you to scroll through the result set. This is achieved by saving the last row seen in a hidden form field as in lines 13 and 17. Lines 14 and 20 create the corresponding buttons to scroll through the previous and next set of records.

7. Open the http://localhost/owa_waite/plsql/cells17 URL in your browser, which invokes the stored procedure created in the previous step. The scrolling operation is displayed within Netscape Navigator as shown in Figure 17.30.

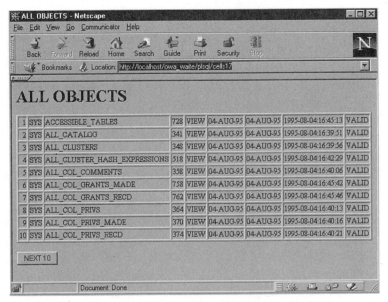

Figure 17.30 The first ten records in Netscape Navigator.

How It Works

HTML tables are created by the <TABLE> tag and terminated by the </TABLE> tag. Between the two tags, other tags create the format of the table. In order to put a border around the table and between the columns and rows, the BORDER attribute is supplied with the <TABLE> tag. The HTP.TABLEOPEN procedure generates the <TABLE> tag, and the HTP.TABLECLOSE procedure generates the </TABLE> tag. Within a table, the <TR> and </TR> tags enclose the rows contained in the table. They can be generated with the HTP.TABLEROWOPEN and HTP.TABLEROWCLOSE procedures. Table data is contained within the <TD> and </TD> tags. The HTP.TABLEDATA procedure generates both these tags containing a string. The <CAPTION> and </CAPTION> tags contain a caption for the table. These tags can be generated by the HTP.TABLECAPTION procedure. The OWA_UTIL.TABLEPRINT function provides a neat way of generating tags for HTML tables and pre-formatted tables. The OWA_UTIL.CELLSPRINT procedure works beautifully when you need to scroll through the result set of a query.

Step 1 creates a sample table, which is the source of data in a later step. Step 2 creates an HTML table that receives its data from a database query. The sample table created in Step 1 is queried by a cursor in the stored procedure. When the query is executed, each row of it is created as a row in the HTML table. Step 3 displays the table in a browser. Step 4 demonstrates the power of the OWA_UTIL.TABLEPRINT function to generate HTML tables. Step 5 displays the generated HTML and pre-formatted tables in a browser. Steps 6 and 7 demonstrate the use of the OWA_UTIL.CELLSPRINT procedure.

Comments

HTML tables are an appealing way to display row and column information. In your applications, you may find yourself often displaying the results of queries using HTML tables. HTML tables are a good method for presenting data from queries, because a query contains rows and columns.

COMPLEXITY
ADVANCED

17.6 How do I...
Use JavaScript to handle events?

Problem

Whenever there is a change to a form field, I want to trigger a JavaScript handler embedded in the generated HTML to handle that event. Since I need to use frames to create powerful web applications, I also need the ability to control the HTML in one frame by using JavaScript event handlers in another frame. How do I use JavaScript to handle events?

Technique

JavaScript is a scripting language developed by Netscape to enable web authors to design interactive sites. Although it shares many of the features and structures of the Java language, it was developed independently. JavaScript can interact with HTML source code to spice up sites with dynamic content. Note that JavaScript can be used if you are using Netscape Navigator browser. JScript is Microsoft's version of JavaScript, which is built into the Microsoft Internet Explorer (MSIE) browser. Microsoft supports only a subset of JavaScript, which it calls JScript. Unfortunately, Netscape's JavaScript and JScript are not entirely compatible. In order to use JavaScript for event handling, you must first understand how PL/SQL, JavaScript, and HTML interact:

- ✔ The application calls functions and procedures in the PL/SQL Web Toolkit to generate dynamic HTML.

- ✔ The application also embeds JavaScript code into the generated HTML.

- ✔ In the generated HTML, form fields have event handlers that invoke JavaScript functions embedded in HTML.

- ✔ PL/SQL variables can be passed to JavaScript directly or through the event handler.

- ✔ JavaScript has direct access to HTML form fields that can be referenced using objects.

✔ JavaScript can invoke a PL/SQL procedure using dynamic URLs, that can be targeted into the current window, new window, visible, or hidden frame.

✔ JavaScript functions and built-in methods can be used in HTML hyperlinks as `javascript:function_name()`.

✔ JavaScript can also be used to generate dynamic HTML.

Frames divide web pages into multiple, scrollable regions enabling information to be presented in a more flexible and useful fashion. Each region has a separate page, allowing the display of multiple web pages within one page. One frame can refer to another frame by using JavaScript, allowing one frame to be updated by clicking a link in another. Frames, when used properly, can improve navigability considerably. Currently, frames are well supported by Netscape Navigator 4 and MSIE 4. The procedures in the HTP package used to generate frame tags are listed in Table 17.7.

Table 17.7 Procedures for frame tags

PROCEDURE	DESCRIPTION
htp.framesetOpen	Prints an HTML tag to open a container of frames.
htp.framesetClose	Prints an HTML tag to close a container of frames.
htp.frame	Prints a tag that defines a single frame in the frameset.
htp.noframesOpen	Prints a tag to display text in a browser incapable of frames.
htp.noframesClose	Closing tag for a browser incapable of frames.

Steps

1. Run SQL*Plus and connect as the WAITE account. If you have not created the DEPT17 table from How-To 17.2, then run CHP17_1.SQL, shown in Figure 17.31, which creates the DEPT17 table used in this How-To.

```
SET ECHO OFF
CREATE TABLE DEPT17 (
        DEPT_NO      NUMBER(5) PRIMARY KEY,
        DEPT_NAME    VARCHAR2(30));

INSERT INTO DEPT17
        VALUES (1, 'MARKETING');

INSERT INTO DEPT17
        VALUES (2, 'SALES');

INSERT INTO DEPT17
        VALUES (3, 'ACCOUNTING');

INSERT INTO DEPT17
        VALUES (4, 'I/S');
```

Figure 17.31 CHP17_1.SQL creates the sample table and data.

```
SQL>   START CHP17_1

Table created.

1 row created.

1 row created.

1 row created.

1 row created.
```

2. Run the CHP17_14.SQL file in SQL*Plus, as shown in Figure 17.32. The procedure divides the web page into two frames and directs a separate URL to each frame.

A frameset is opened in line 5 by calling the HTP.FRAMESETOPEN procedure and closed in line 8 with the HTP.FRAMESETCLOSE procedure. Lines 6 and 7 use the HTP.FRAME procedure to create two frames within the frameset. The OWA_UTIL.GET_OWA_SERVICE_PATH function returns the partial URL containing the name of the PL/SQL Agent and the virtual path. The second parameter to HTP.FRAME gives a name to the frame created so that it can be referenced in JavaScript. The form is an example of using HTML frames to create a scrolling *select frame* on the right that has buttons to select items from a list to populate the non-scrolling *edit frame*. This technique allows for intelligent navigation.

Another use of frames is to have a table of contents that can remain fixed in one frame while the content frame is updated. Frames work well with JavaScript because they offer more control that can be used to update multiple frames with one click, and create sophisticated, interactive interfaces.

```
SQL> START CHP17_14
SQL> SET ECHO ON
SQL> CREATE OR REPLACE PROCEDURE FRAMES17 AS
  2  BEGIN
  3    HTP.HTMLOPEN;
  4    HTP.TITLE('Departments');
  5    HTP.FRAMESETOPEN(NULL, '50,50', 'FRAMEBORDER=1');
  6    HTP.FRAME(OWA_UTIL.GET_OWA_SERVICE_PATH || 'MENU17', 'editFrame');
  7    HTP.FRAME(OWA_UTIL.GET_OWA_SERVICE_PATH || 'QUERY17', 'selectFrame');
  8    HTP.FRAMESETCLOSE;
  9    HTP.NOFRAMESOPEN;
 10    HTP.PRINT('REQUIRES A BROWSER THAT SUPPORTS FRAMES.');
 11    HTP.NOFRAMESCLOSE;
 12    HTP.HTMLCLOSE;
 13  END FRAMES17;
 14  /

Procedure created.

SQL> |
```

Figure 17.32 CHP17_14.SQL creates two frames.

3. Run the CHP17_15.SQL file in SQL*Plus. The procedure is used to generate dynamic HTML for the first frame.

```
SQL> START CHP17_15
SQL> CREATE OR REPLACE PROCEDURE MENU17 AS
  2   BEGIN
  3     HTP.HTMLOPEN;
  4     HTP.SCRIPT('function checkNum(inObj)
  5                 {
  6                    inStr = inObj.value
  7                    for(var i = 0; i < inStr.length; i++) {
  8                       if (inStr.charAt(i) < "0" ¦¦
inStr.charAt(i) > "9") {
  9                          alert("Department No is a number, please
re-enter.")
 10                          inObj.value = ""
 11                          return
 12                       }
 13                    }
 14                 }', 'JavaScript');
 15     HTP.BODYOPEN;
 16     HTP.FORMOPEN('ACTION17', 'POST', '_top', CATTRIBUTES =>
'NAME = "editForm"');
 17     HTP.TABLEOPEN;
 18     HTP.TABLEROWOPEN('LEFT','TOP');
 17     HTP.TABLEHEADER('Department No:','RIGHT');
 20     HTP.TABLEDATA(HTF.FORMTEXT('deptNo', '5', '5', NULL,
'ONCHANGE="checkNum(this)"'));
 21     HTP.TABLEROWCLOSE;
 22     HTP.TABLEROWOPEN('LEFT','TOP');
 23     HTP.TABLEHEADER('Department Name:','RIGHT');
 24     HTP.TABLEDATA(HTF.FORMTEXT('deptName', '20', '20', NULL,
'ONCHANGE="this.value = this.value.toUpperCase()"'));
 25     HTP.TABLEROWCLOSE;
 26     HTP.TABLEROWOPEN('LEFT','TOP');
 27     HTP.TABLEDATA(HTF.FORMSUBMIT('addBtn','  Add  ', NULL),
'RIGHT');
 28     HTP.TABLEDATA(HTF.FORMRESET(' Clear ',
'ONCLICK="this.form.addBtn.value = ''  Add  ''"'));
 29     HTP.TABLEROWCLOSE;
 30     HTP.TABLECLOSE;
 31     HTP.FORMCLOSE;
 32     HTP.BODYCLOSE;
 33     HTP.HTMLCLOSE;
 34   END MENU17;
 35   /
```

JavaScript code is embedded within the generated HTML document. The HTP.SCRIPT procedure embodies the complete script. The second parameter specifies the language for the script. You can also use other scripting languages like JScript or VBScript as long your browser is capable of understanding the script.

checkNum() is a simple number validation function used to demonstrate how JavaScript can be fruitfully used to do petty validation checks at the client end, thus saving a trip to the server. In line 16, a form tag is specified. The name of procedure for processing the form when submitted is the first parameter. The second parameter is the REQUEST_METHOD CGI variable—GET or POST; we use POST for versatility. The third parameter specifies the target when the form is posted; the _top means that the any output generated by the action taking procedure will be targeted to the top container of the frame rather than the frame itself. You can specify the name of a frame as target, such as editFrame or selectFrame, if that is what you intend to do. The last parameter specifies a name for the form so that it can be referenced by name in JavaScript.

If a name is not specified for a frame or form, it can still be referred in JavaScript as frames[n] or forms[n], where n is the n occurrence of the frame within the frameset or the nth occurrence of the form within a frame, respectively.

Note the use of the Onchange event handler in line 20 to invoke the checkNum() JavaScript function that does simple numeric validation. In line 24, the built-in JavaScript function toUpperCase() is used to automatically change the text to uppercase upon data entry. Line 27 creates a submit button for posting the form and line 28 creates a reset button to clear field contents.

4. Run the CHP17_16.SQL file in SQL*Plus. The procedure is used to generate dynamic HTML for the second frame in the frameset.

```
SQL> START CHP17_16
SQL> CREATE OR REPLACE PROCEDURE QUERY17 AS
  2    CURSOR DEPT_CURS IS
  3      SELECT DEPT_NO, DEPT_NAME
  4      FROM DEPT17;
  5  BEGIN
  6    HTP.HTMLOPEN;
  7    HTP.SCRIPT('function pickItem(d_no, d_name)
  8               {
  9                    top.editFrame.document.editForm.deptNo.value =
d_no
 10                    top.editFrame.document.editForm.deptName.value
= d_name
 11                    top.editFrame.document.editForm.addBtn.value =
"Update"
 12               }', 'JavaScript');
 13    HTP.BODYOPEN;
 14    HTP.FORMOPEN('QUERY17', 'POST', 'selectFrame');
 15    HTP.TABLEOPEN('BORDER');
 16    HTP.TABLEROWOPEN('LEFT', 'TOP');
 17    HTP.TABLEHEADER('Sel', 'CENTER');
 18    HTP.TABLEHEADER('No:', 'CENTER');
 17    HTP.TABLEHEADER('Name:', 'CENTER');
 20    HTP.TABLEROWCLOSE;
```

```
21    FOR DEPT_REC IN DEPT_CURS LOOP
22        HTP.TABLEROWOPEN('LEFT', 'TOP');
23        HTP.TABLEDATA('<INPUT TYPE="button" VALUE=" < " ' ||
24                       'ONCLICK="pickItem(''' ||
25                        DEPT_REC.DEPT_NO || ''',''' ||
26                        DEPT_REC.DEPT_NAME || ''')">');
27        HTP.TABLEDATA(DEPT_REC.DEPT_NO, 'CENTER');
28        HTP.TABLEDATA(DEPT_REC.DEPT_NAME, 'LEFT');
29        HTP.TABLEROWCLOSE;
30    END LOOP;
31    HTP.TABLECLOSE;
32    HTP.FORMCLOSE;
33    HTP.BODYCLOSE;
34    HTP.HTMLCLOSE;
35 END QUERY17;
36 /
```

JavaScript is a scripting language with a horde of powerful features. The script provided in lines 7 through 12 in the body of the HTP.SCRIPT procedure dynamically changes the values of fields in the first frame when an item is selected from the second frame.

A form is opened in line 14 as we have a few buttons in this document. A common mistake is to not open a form before creating form elements. Although the form is never posted, note the recursive use of the same procedure name as the processing procedure when the form is posted. This can be useful in certain complex applications because the procedure is self-sufficient as it generates and processes the same form without the need for having two separate procedures.

Line 15 specifies the tag for a bordered HTML table. In lines 23 to 26, a button is created for each record in the DEPT17 table, and when clicked it causes the DEPT_NO and DEPT_NAME column values from that row to be sent to the form fields in the first frame. Note how PL/SQL variables are passed to a JavaScript function.

Passing JavaScript variables to PL/SQL gets a bit trickier, as you must use the GET method after creating dynamic URL to invoke a particular stored procedure. JavaScript poses the same difficulties as HTML with special characters.

Using JavaScript, URLs can by dynamically constructed, and using the GET method, targeted into a window or a frame for execution. This approach is powerful in having great control over the behavior of the application, but as mentioned earlier suffers a setback due to GET limitations.

While HTML uses entity references for escaping characters, JavaScript uses URL character encodings. Thus, any ISO Latin-1 character when escaped is represented by %hh where hh is the hex code corresponding to the character. URL character encoding is a superior escaping mechanism than entity references, but this leaves us with two different escaping schemes that have to be catered for separately depending on whether the data is embedded into HTML or handled by JavaScript. For instance, spaces have to be translated into plusses when doing a GET through HTML as in the FRAME tag, whereas spaces would be translated to 20 percent (20 is hex code for space) when using a dynamic URL to do a GET using JavaScript.

In JavaScript, a handy JavaScript function `escape()` does the escaping, while `unescape()` is used to restore original data. There are cases in which this escaping has to use PL/SQL, like when passing PL/SQL parameters to an embedded event handler JavaScript function. For this, a simple PL/SQL function needs to be used that replaces all special characters into the corresponding %*hh* code, where *hh* is the hex code corresponding to that character. Again, dynamic URLs to do a GET should be used only as a last resort, and care should be taken to ensure that the URL size does not exceed the operating system limit imposed on maximum size of environment variables.

When using GET, the URL is actually stored in a standard CGI environment variable called QUERY_STRING. For example, on Windows NT 4 the maximum size for environment variables is 1,024 bytes, and a URL longer than that will impose a bottleneck if data is such that the URL size exceeds the 1,024 byte limit.

5. Run the CHP17_17.SQL file in SQL*Plus, as shown in Figure 17.33. The procedure within the file processes the form is created in Step 1.

Lines 1 through 3 create a stored procedure with parameters corresponding with the fields contained in the form created in Step 1. Whenever the Add or Update button is clicked, this stored procedure is invoked to process the form.

```
SQL> START CHP17_17
SQL> CREATE OR REPLACE PROCEDURE ACTION17 (deptNo IN NUMBER,
  2                                        deptName IN VARCHAR2,
  3                                        addBtn IN VARCHAR2) AS
  4  BEGIN
  5    IF LTRIM(RTRIM(addBtn)) = 'Add' THEN
  6      INSERT INTO DEPT17 VALUES (deptNo, deptName);
  7    ELSE
  8      UPDATE DEPT17
  9      SET DEPT_NAME = deptName
 10      WHERE DEPT_NO = deptNo;
 11    END IF;
 12    FRAMES17;
 13  END ACTION17;
 14  /

Procedure created.

SQL>
```

Figure 17.33 CHP17_17.SQL processes the form.

The IF statement in line 5 checks if the Add button was clicked and inserts a record in the DEPT17 table using the form field values. The button name is changed to Update if a record was selected from the `selectFrame`. So if the name of the button is Update, the record is updated in lines 8 to 10. Because the target was specified to be _TOP in the form, the complete frameset is redrawn by calling FRAMES17 in line 12. If you specified the target to be `editFrame` then you would simply call MENU17 to redraw the first frame. The complete frameset is redrawn as we want the inserted or updated record to be appear in the `selectFrame`.

6. Open the http://localhost/owa_waite/plsql/frames17 URL in your browser. The two frames are displayed within Netscape Navigator. Enter a value for the form fields as shown in Figure 17.34 and press the Add button. The new screen is shown in Figure 17.35.

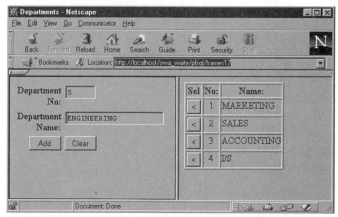

Figure 17.34 The two frames in Netscape Navigator.

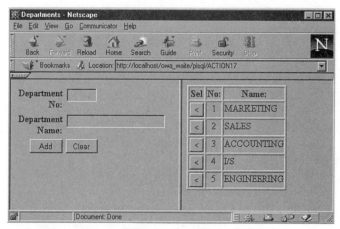

Figure 17.35 After adding a new record.

Select a record from the second frame. The Add button changes to Update. Change the values for the form fields as shown in Figure 17.36 and press the Update button. The new screen is shown in Figure 17.37.

How It Works

The HTP.SCRIPT procedure generates the <SCRIPT> and </SCRIPT> tags, which contain a script written in languages such as JavaScript, JScript, or VBScript. The text that makes up the script is provided as the first parameter and the language in which the script is written is provided as the second parameter. If this

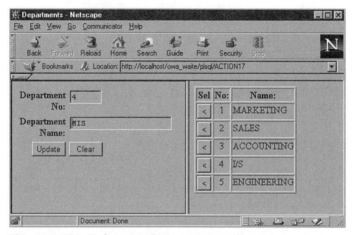

Figure 17.36 Before updating a record.

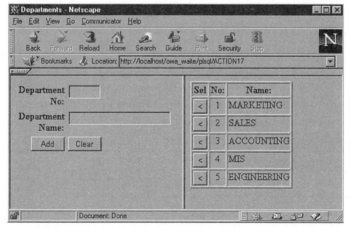

Figure 17.37 After updating a record.

parameter is omitted, the user's browser determines the scripting language. In this How-To, JavaScript is embedded in the generated HTML to handle events related to form fields. This enables you to create web pages that react directly to user interaction with form elements, and data to be preprocessed on the client before submission to the server.

Step 1 creates a sample table which is the source of data in a later step. Step 2 creates a frameset with two frames and directs an URL to each frame. In Step 3, a data entry form is created. The sample table created in Step 1 is queried by a cursor in the stored procedure created in Step 4 to display an HTML table in the second frame using the contents of the sample table. When the query is executed, a row is created along with a select button to transfer that record to the first frame. Step 5 creates a procedure to process form variables after the form is posted. Step 6 displays the two frames in a browser along with the add/update operation.

Comments

Although the procedures are created separately in this How-To, it would be a better idea to create a stored package to tie all procedures related to creation and processing of forms in a web document.

JavaScript allows for client-side scripting to take some of the processing load from the server, but bugs are waiting to be removed in the next versions of browsers. Indiscriminate use of JavaScript has pitfalls for the unwary. Currently, heavy use of JavaScript or Java leads to memory leaks, causing Netscape and MSIE on Windows 3.1 and Windows 95 to crash; on Windows NT the browser survives, but the buttons and other form elements stop working.

If you are planning to use Microsoft Internet Explorer and JScript, you also need to know how JavaScript and JScript relate. JScript remains a subset of JavaScript functions plus a few extensions. Netscape understands JavaScript functions that are not yet understood by MSIE, but few functions do exist in JScript that are not understood by Netscape. Some functions defined in both JavaScript and JScript may not work in one or the other browser, either due to a bug in the implementation of that function in a particular browser, or due to a browser-specific constraint on the way that function is expected to be called. Code written to be handled by JScript, and which is also standard JavaScript, will work in both browsers but should always be tested for both browsers.

JavaScript features that are lacking in JScript include the following:

✔ The capability of supporting dynamic image objects to change the source file of an image.

✔ External scripts that allow JavaScript code to be stored in an external file.

✔ Dynamic select objects, to add, delete, or change options in a select list on-the-fly.

✔ The `javaEnabled()`, `split()`, `scroll()`, and `reset()` methods.

JavaScript features that are modified in JScript include the following:

✔ The capability to create a new window and modify its properties; this works partially and frames have to referred as `frames[n]` instead of `framename`.

✔ `history.go()` accepts integers and not strings. JScript also needs casting of objects in `alert()`.

✔ `onAbort()` event handler is absent, and `onMouseMove()` and `onMouseOut()` work differently. The `onClick()` handler should also be followed by LANGUAGE="JavaScript".

✔ MAILTO: and ABOUT:BLANK protocols do not work; DOCUMENT.REFERER does not work; changing LOCATION.HREF and LINK.HREF does not work.

✔ JScript is case-insensitive, JavaScript is not.

✔ JScript has added new FOR and EVENT attributes to the SCRIPT tag.

Despite the fact that bugs remain in JavaScript and JScript, as long as those features are not used or are used with workarounds, scripting languages are very useful while developing interactive weblications. If you are using Designer/2000 1.3W, it automatically generates JavaScript code to do client side validation.

COMPLEXITY
ADVANCED

17.7 How do I...
Access and use CGI environment variables?

Problem

I need to retrieve and use CGI environment variables in my application. Information such as the IP address of the remote host making the request is necessary in developing sophisticated applications. How do I access and use CGI environment variables in my web applications?

Technique

All CGI environment variables that are part of the Common Gateway Interface specification are passed from the Oracle Web Listener to the PL/SQL Agent. All relevant environment variables are available through PL/SQL. The GET_CGI_ENV function from the OWA_UTIL package enables you to access

CGI environment variables. The procedures and functions provided by the OWA_UTIL package are shown in Table 17.8.

Table 17.8 OWA_UTIL package

PROCEDURE	DESCRIPTION
owa_util.get_cgi_env	Returns the value of the specified CGI variable.
owa_util.get_owa_service_path	Prints the currently active service path and its virtual path.
owa_util.print_cgi_env	Prints all CGI variables.
owa_util.signature	Enables the developer to create a signature line for the document.
owa_util.showpage	Allows the user to display the output from a procedure.
owa_util.showsource	Prints the source of the specified PL/SQL module.
owa_util.mime_header	Changes the default MIME header.
owa_util.http_header_close	Outputs two newlines to close the HTTP header.
owa_util.redirect_url	Redirects the browser to visit the specified URL.
owa_util.status_line	Enables the developer to send a standard HTTP status code to the browser.
owa_util.bind_variables	Prepares a SQL query by binding variables to it and stores the output in an opened cursor.
owa_util.who_called_me	Returns the name of the calling PL/SQL code unit.
owa_util.get_procedure	Returns the name of the current procedure.
owa_util.choose_date	Prints three HTML form elements to select the day, the month, and the year.
owa_util.to_date	Converts the owa_util.dateType datatype to the standard Oracle database DATE type.
owa_util.listprint	Prints an HTML select list from the output of a query.
owa_util.calendarprint	Prints a calendar in HTML.
owa_util.cellsprint	Prints an HTML table from the output of a query.
owa_util.tableprint	Prints an Oracle table as a pre-formatted HTML table.

The OWA_UTIL.GET_CGI_ENV function returns the value of the CGI variable that is passed in as a parameter.

Steps

1. Run SQL*Plus and connect as the WAITE user account. Run the CHP17_18.SQL in SQL*Plus. The stored procedure contained in the file displays the available CGI environment variables.

```
SQL> START CHP17_18
SQL> CREATE OR REPLACE PROCEDURE CGI_ENV17 AS
  2    X VARCHAR2(80);
  3  BEGIN
  4    HTP.PRINT('<TITLE>CGI_ENV17</TITLE>');
  5    HTP.PRINT('<H2>CGI Environment Variables</H2>');
  6    X := OWA_UTIL.GET_CGI_ENV('AUTH_TYPE');
  7    HTP.PRINT('AUTH_TYPE = '||X||'<br>');
```

```
 8    X := OWA_UTIL.GET_CGI_ENV('GATEWAY_INTERFACE');
 9    HTP.PRINT('GATEWAY_INTERFACE = '||X||'<br>');
10    X := OWA_UTIL.GET_CGI_ENV('HTTP_USER_AGENT');
11    HTP.PRINT('HTTP_USER_AGENT = '||X||'<br>');
12    X := OWA_UTIL.GET_CGI_ENV('PATH_INFO');
13    HTP.PRINT('PATH_INFO = '||X||'<br>');
14    X := OWA_UTIL.GET_CGI_ENV('PATH_TRANSLATED');
15    HTP.PRINT('PATH_TRANSLATED = '||X||'<br>');
16    X := OWA_UTIL.GET_CGI_ENV('REMOTE_HOST');
17    HTP.PRINT('REMOTE_HOST = '||X||'<br>');
18    X := OWA_UTIL.GET_CGI_ENV('REMOTE_ADDR');
17    HTP.PRINT('REMOTE_ADDR = '||X||'<br>');
20    X := OWA_UTIL.GET_CGI_ENV('REMOTE_USER');
21    HTP.PRINT('REMOTE_USER = '||X||'<br>');
22    X := OWA_UTIL.GET_CGI_ENV('REMOTE_IDENT');
23    HTP.PRINT('REMOTE_IDENT = '||X||'<br>');
24    X := OWA_UTIL.GET_CGI_ENV('SERVER_PROTOCOL');
25    HTP.PRINT('SERVER_PROTOCOL = '||X||'<br>');
26    X := OWA_UTIL.GET_CGI_ENV('SERVER_SOFTWARE');
27    HTP.PRINT('SERVER_SOFTWARE = '||X||'<br>');
28    X := OWA_UTIL.GET_CGI_ENV('SERVER_NAME');
29    HTP.PRINT('SERVER_NAME = '||X||'<br>');
30    X := OWA_UTIL.GET_CGI_ENV('SERVER_PORT');
31    HTP.PRINT('SERVER_PORT = '||X||'<br>');
32    X := OWA_UTIL.GET_CGI_ENV('SCRIPT_NAME');
33    HTP.PRINT('SCRIPT_NAME = '||X||'<br>');
34  END;
35  /
```

Procedure created.

Line 1 specifies the keywords required to create the stored procedure. Line 2 declares a variable used to hold the CGI variables as they are returned to the PL/SQL code. Lines 3 through 34 contain the procedure body. Line 6 is representative of most lines in the stored procedure. The OWA_UTIL. GET_CGI_ENV function is used to return the value of a CGI environment. The HTP.PRINT procedure is used to print a line to the browser.

When the page is displayed, the CGI variables are retrieved from the server by the OWA_UTIL procedures and displayed within the document.

2. Load your browser and browse the URL created by the stored procedure. Figure 17.38 shows the results of the operation.

How It Works

The GET_CGI_ENV function from the OWA_UTIL package returns the value of the specified CGI variable to the PL/SQL function. The PRINT procedure in the HTP package is used to print text or HTML commands to the browser. Step 1 creates a stored procedure using the OWA_UTIL.GET_CGI_ENV to retrieve the values of each available CGI environment variable. Step 2 displays the page within a browser.

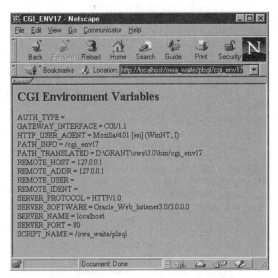

Figure 17.38 CGI environment variables.

Comments

CGI variables provide you with information required to create complex web documents and applications. The OWA_UTIL package gives you easy access to these variables for use within your applications. Other OWA_UTIL procedures enable you to control the environment and display debugging information.

COMPLEXITY
ADVANCED

17.8 How do I...
Maintain persistent states with cookies?

Problem

I know that I can use hidden fields in forms to maintain persistent variables in a session. If a lot of hidden fields are in a form, they have to travel back and forth from the client to the server, hurting performance. I want to use client cookies stored in the browser to maintain state information throughout the client session, or sometimes until the expiration date of the cookie. How do I maintain persistent state information with cookies?

Technique

Netscape introduced the concept of browser cookies also supported in Microsoft Internet Explorer. Cookies are strings that reside on the client that allow applications to maintain state. Once the cookie is set, it remains in memory throughout the client session or until it expires, which depends on the expiration time set with the cookie while creating it. If the browser is exited, it is saved in a file, and when the browser is restarted it is reloaded into memory if the cookie has not expired. You will need to use cookie variables of the OWA_COOKIE.COOKIE datatype defined as:

```
TYPE COOKIE IS RECORD (
    NAME        VARCHAR2(4096),
    VALS        VC_ARR,
    NUM_VALS    INTEGER);
```

The HTTP protocol allows cookie names to be overloaded; in other words, multiple values can be associated with the same cookie name. In the OWA_COOKIE.COOKIE datatype, VALS is a PL/SQL Index-By table of VARCHAR2 (4096) to hold all values associated with a given cookie name. The OWA_COOKIE package provides procedures and functions to send cookies to and get them from the browser, as shown in Table 17.9.

Table 17.9 Functions contained in the OWA_COOKIE package

FUNCTION/PROCEDURE	DESCRIPTION
owa_cookie.send	Transmits a cookie to the client.
owa_cookie.get	Returns values associated with a cookie name.
owa_cookie.get_all	Returns all cookie names and their values.
owa_cookie.remove	Forces a cookie to expire immediately.

Cookies use expiration dates defined in Greenwich Mean Time (GMT). If you are not on GMT and want to change the time zone used by cookies, the OWA_INIT package provides constants that you override to set the time zone used by cookies. The system date is calculated using the constants in the OWA_INIT package. You can change the value of the dbms_server_timezone or the dbms_server_gmtdiff to give the offset of your time zone from GMT and then reload the package.

Steps

1. Run SQL*Plus and connect as the WAITE account. Run the CHP17_19.SQL file in SQL*Plus, as shown in Figure 17.39. This example uses a cookie to store a counter in the browser, indicating how many times that page was visited by the user in last 24 hours.

```
SQL> START CHP17_19
SQL> CREATE OR REPLACE PROCEDURE COOKIE17 IS
  2      COOKIE OWA_COOKIE.COOKIE;
  3  BEGIN
  4      COOKIE := OWA_COOKIE.GET('COUNTER');
  5          OWA_UTIL.MIME_HEADER('TEXT/HTML', FALSE);
  6      IF (COOKIE.NUM_VALS > 0) THEN
  7          OWA_COOKIE.SEND('COUNTER', COOKIE.VALS(1) + 1, SYSDATE +
  8       ELSE
  9          OWA_COOKIE.SEND('COUNTER', 1, SYSDATE + 1);
 10      END IF;
 11      OWA_UTIL.HTTP_HEADER_CLOSE;
 12      HTP.HTMLOPEN;
 13      HTP.HTITLE('Cookie Counter');
 14      IF (COOKIE.NUM_VALS > 0) THEN
 15          HTP.BOLD('You have visited this page '
 16           || HTF.STRONG(COOKIE.VALS(1) + 1) || ' times in the last
 17       ELSE
 18          HTP.BOLD('First time you have visited this page in the l
 19      END IF;
 20      HTP.LINE;
 21      HTP.ITALIC('Each time you visit the page, the counter will
 22      HTP.ANCHOR('http://home.netscape.com/newsref/std/cookie_spe
 23      HTP.HTMLCLOSE;
 24  END;
 25  /

Procedure created.
```

Figure 17.39 CHP17_19.SQL demonstrates a cookie counter.

Line 2 declares a variable for the cookie of the OWA_COOKIE.COOKIE datatype. Line 4 calls the OWA_COOKIE.GET function to retrieve the cookie from the browser. In line 5, the OWA_UTIL.MIME_HEADER procedure is used to change the default MIME header before sending the cookie using the OWA_COOKIE.SEND procedure, which sends a Set-Cookie header to the browser, as in lines 7 and 9.

Line 11 closes the MIME header. The NUM_VALS variable in the cookie indicates the number of values in the cookie for a given cookie name. When the procedure is invoked for the first time, the cookie does not exist in the browser and NUM_VALS is 0. A cookie named COUNTER is set to 1 on the first visit. The value in the cookie is simply incremented by 1 on subsequent visits to the same page. As only one value is set for the cookie, the value is retrieved from the array of values in the cookie as COOKIE.VALS(1).

The OWA_COOKIE.REMOVE procedure is not used in the example as the expiration time was set as 24 hours by using the SYSDATE + 1 in the OWA_COOKIE.SEND call. If you are not using an expiration time with cookies, then it is recommended that cookies be explicitly removed whenever they are no longer in use.

Note that the OWA_UTIL.MIME_HEADER must be called before any other calls to procedures in the HTP package. If the default MIME header is opened by any other call, two newline characters are sent and the header is closed; all this is transparent to the user. Note that in line 5, the second parameter is set to FALSE so that only one newline is sent, and the HTTP header is still open until it is closed explicitly in line 11 using the OWA_UTIL.HTTP_HEADER_CLOSE procedure. If you are calling any other procedure from the OWA_UTIL package that manipulates with the HTTP header sent to the browser, such as the OWA_UTIL.REDIRECT_URL, make sure that you use the technique described in this step.

2. Open the URL for the cookie example in your browser. Figure 17.40 shows the document in the browser.

Exit the browser and restart it again. Open the URL for the cookie example in your browser again. Figure 17.41 shows the results in the browser on the second visit to the page.

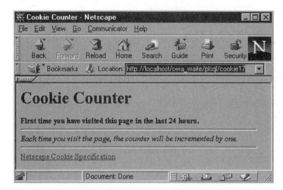

Figure 17.40 The page on the first visit.

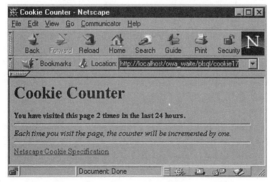

Figure 17.41 The page on the second visit.

How It Works

The OWA_COOKIE.SEND procedure and OWA_COOKIE.GET function provide a means to send and receive cookies to and from the browser. An HTTP header must be opened by calling OWA_UTIL.MIME_HEADER before sending the cookie to the browser. The HTTP header is closed by calling the OWA_UTIL.HTTP_HEADER_CLOSE.

Step 1 creates a stored procedure that generates an HTML document which maintains a counter cookie in the browser. Within the document, the cookie is sent to the browser by using the OWA_COOKIE.SEND procedure and retrieved from the browser using the OWA_COOKIE.GET function. Step 2 demonstrates the operation in Netscape Navigator. Click the Netscape Cookie Specification link if you want to find out more about cookies.

Comments

With Netscape Navigator, cookie size cannot exceed 4 KB and only 20 cookies are allowed per domain, which is far less than what would be required when building robust business applications. A fairly simple technique to achieve persistence on the server side is to store state information in the database itself. Cookies can be saved in the database itself to provide server-side cookie support. For more complex applications, it would be beneficial to exploit the Transaction Service in OWAS 3.0 to overcome HTTP statelessness.

With Microsoft Internet Explorer, cookies work differently. Only one cookie per domain is allowed as compared to Netscape's 20. Also, cookies only from a server with a network domain are accepted.

INDEX

Symbols

A

J-K

MACMILLAN COMPUTER PUBLISHING USA

A VIACOM COMPANY

Technical ---- Support:

If you need assistance with a particular situation in the book, please feel free to check out the Knowledge Base on our Web site at **http://www.superlibrary.com/general/support**. We have answers to our most Frequently Asked Questions listed there. If you do not find your specific question answered, please contact Macmillan Technical Support at **(317) 581-3833**. We can also be reached by email at **support@mcp.com**.

SATISFACTION REPORT CARD

Please fill out this card if you wish to know of future updates to
Oracle8 How-To, or to receive our catalog.

First Name: _____ Last Name: _____

Street Address: _____

City: _____ State: _____ Zip: _____

Email Address: _____

Daytime Telephone: (____) _____

Date product was acquired: Month _____ Day _____ Year _____ Your Occupation: _____

Overall, how would you rate *Oracle8 How-To*?

☐ Excellent   ☐ Very Good   ☐ Good
☐ Fair   ☐ Below Average ☐ Poor

What did you like MOST about this book? _____

_____

_____

What did you like LEAST about this book? _____

_____

_____

**Please describe any problems you may have encountered with
installing or using the disc:** _____

_____

How did you use this book (problem-solver, tutorial, reference...)?

_____

What is your level of computer expertise?

☐ New   ☐ Dabbler   ☐ Hacker
☐ Power User   ☐ Programmer   ☐ Experienced Professional

What computer languages are you familiar with? _____

_____

Please describe your computer hardware:

Computer _____ Hard disk _____

5.25" disk drives _____ 3.5" disk drives _____

Video card _____ Monitor _____

Printer _____ Peripherals _____

Sound Board _____ CD-ROM_____

Where did you buy this book?

☐ Bookstore (name): _____
☐ Discount store (name): _____
☐ Computer store (name): _____
☐ Catalog (name): _____
☐ Direct from WGP   ☐ Other _____

What price did you pay for this book? _____

What influenced your purchase of this book?

☐ Recommendation   ☐ Advertisement
☐ Magazine review   ☐ Store display
☐ Mailing   ☐ Book's format
☐ Reputation of Waite Group Press   ☐ Other

How many computer books do you buy each year?_____

How many other Waite Group books do you own?_____

What is your favorite Waite Group book?_____

_____

**Is there any program or subject you would like to see Waite
Group Press cover in a similar approach?**_____

_____

Additional comments?_____

_____

_____

Please send to: **Waite Group Press**
                        200 Tamal Plaza
                        Corte Madera, CA 94925

☐ **Check here for a free Waite Group catalog**

Be sure to visit the
Oracle8 How-To
Companion Web site
at `www.mcp.com/info`,
where you'll find:

- Source code from the book
- Links to

    Oracle resources

    Author Web pages

    Updated information
- And more!